Collins
Primary
Thesaurus

Collins

Collins Primary Thesaurus

First published 2004
This edition published 2005
© HarperCollinsPublishers Ltd 2005

10 9 8 7 6

ISBN-13:978-0-00-720392-5
ISBN-10:0-00-720392-6

A catalogue record for this book is available from the British Library.

Published by Collins
A division of HarperCollinsPublishers Ltd
77–85 Fulham Palace Road
Hammersmith
London W6 8JB
www.collins.co.uk

Browse the complete Collins catalogue at
www.collinseducation.com

Compiler	John McIlwain
Literacy consultants	Kay Hiatt, Rosemary Boys
Cover designer	Nicola Croft
Design	Neil Adams
Editor	Jo Kemp
Indexer	Eleanor Holme
Project Editors	Lee Newman, Shannon Park
Proofreaders	Ian Brooke, Kay Cullen

Acknowledgements

The publishers would like to thanks all the teachers,
staff and pupils who contributed to this book:

Teacher advisors

Jill Burton
Ruth Grainger
Krys Hill
Lawrence Keel

Sarah McKissock
Maggie McLaren
Amanda Sullivan

Schools

Hobbayne Primary School
Lena Gardens Primary School
Old Oak Primary School
Standens Barn Primary School
St Gregory's RC Primary School
Vicar's Green Primary School

Printed in Malaysia by Imago.

Contents

Using this thesaurus   iv

Using the index   vi

The thesaurus   1

Index   349

Using this thesaurus

Collins Primary Thesaurus helps you to improve your writing by avoiding overused words such as **good**, **bad** or **go**.

How to find a word

You want to find a different word or phrase for the noun **thoughtful**, meaning **kind**. Use the **alphabet line** at the side of the page to find the letter **t**.

You will probably find that there are several words that start with the same letter as **thoughtful**, so you will have to look at the second or third letter to help you find the right word.

You are looking for a word beginning with **th**. Use the **guide word** at the top of the page. The guide word at the top left tells you the *first word* on that page. The guide word at the top right tells you the *last word* on that page. The guide word for this page is **thought**, so you have found the right page. Now look at the blue words, or **headwords**, to find **thoughtful**. Once you have found it you can choose the synonym.

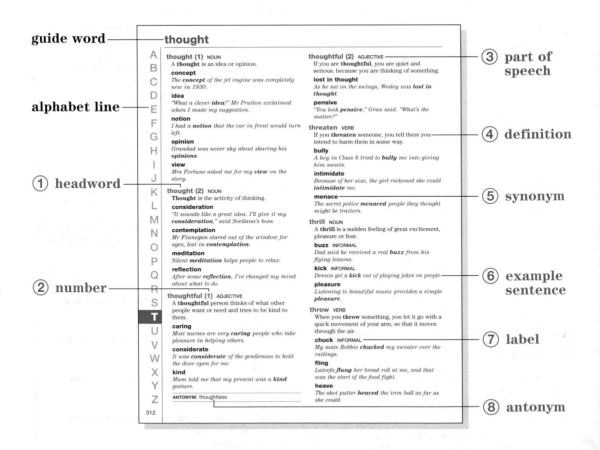

guide word

thought

A B C D E F G H I J K L M N O P Q R S **T** U V W X Y Z
312

alphabet line

① **headword**

② **number**

thought (1) NOUN
A **thought** is an idea or opinion.
concept
The concept of the jet engine was completely new in 1930.
idea
"What a clever idea!" Mr Prutton exclaimed when I made my suggestion.
notion
I had a notion that the car in front would turn left.
opinion
Grandad was never shy about sharing his opinions.
view
Mrs Fortune asked me for my view on the story.

thought (2) NOUN
Thought is the activity of thinking.
consideration
"It sounds like a great idea. I'll give it my consideration," said Svetlana's boss.
contemplation
Mr Finnegan stared out of the window for ages, lost in contemplation.
meditation
Silent meditation helps people to relax.
reflection
After some reflection, I've changed my mind about what to do.

thoughtful (1) ADJECTIVE
A **thoughtful** person thinks of what other people want or need and tries to be kind to them.
caring
Most nurses are very caring people who take pleasure in helping others.
considerate
It was considerate of the gentleman to hold the door open for me.
kind
Mum told me that my present was a kind gesture.

ANTONYM: thoughtless

thoughtful (2) ADJECTIVE
If you are **thoughtful**, you are quiet and serious, because you are thinking of something.
lost in thought
As he sat on the swings, Wesley was lost in thought.
pensive
"You look pensive," Gran said. "What's the matter?"

threaten VERB
If you **threaten** someone, you tell them you intend to harm them in some way.
bully
A boy in Class 6 tried to bully me into giving him sweets.
intimidate
Because of her size, the girl reckoned she could intimidate me.
menace
The secret police menaced people they thought might be traitors.

thrill NOUN
A **thrill** is a sudden feeling of great excitement, pleasure or fear.
buzz INFORMAL
Dad said he received a real buzz from his flying lessons.
kick INFORMAL
Dennis got a kick out of playing jokes on people.
pleasure
Listening to beautiful music provides a simple pleasure.

throw VERB
When you **throw** something, you let it go with a quick movement of your arm, so that it moves through the air.
chuck INFORMAL
My mate Robbie chucked my sweater over the railings.
fling
Lateefa flung her bread roll at me, and that was the start of the food fight.
heave
The shot putter heaved the iron ball as far as she could.

③ **part of speech**

④ **definition**

⑤ **synonym**

⑥ **example sentence**

⑦ **label**

⑧ **antonym**

Choosing the right synonym

(1) The **headword** is the word that you want to find a synonym for.

(2) On the same line as the headword, you may see a **number** in brackets. This tells you that the headword can have different meanings.

(3) Next you will see the **part of speech**, such as noun, verb, adjective, adverb or pronoun. If the word you want to find is a verb, make sure the headword you look at is also a verb.

(4) Underneath the headword you will find the **definition**. The definition tells you what the headword means.

(5) The **synonyms** are listed below the definition of each headword. Find the synonym which best matches the word you need to replace.

(6) An **example sentence** is given for every synonym in *Collins Primary Thesaurus*. This shows you how the word might be used in speech or writing.

(7) You may see a **label** next to the headword or synonym, such as FORMAL, INFORMAL or OLD-FASHIONED. This gives you extra information about the word or how it is used.

(8) An **antonym** is a word that means the opposite of another. When a headword has an antonym, the antonym is shown at the end of the entry.

Other useful features of this thesaurus

- Some entries include a **pronunciation guide** to help you learn how to pronounce the headword.

> **wind (2)** RHYMES WITH "**MIND**" VERB
> If something **winds**, it twists and turns.

- A tick ✔ indicates a **usage tip**, which provides extra information about the headword.

> **great (5)** ADJECTIVE
> Something that is **great** is very large in amount or degree.
> **considerable**
> *It takes **considerable** skill to walk a tightrope.*
> **extreme**
> *Hermione showed **extreme** courage in facing the hungry lioness.*
> ✔ Don't confuse **great** with the homophone **grate**.

- Some entries provide a list of **useful words** connected to the headword, within a blue panel.

> **space (2)** NOUN
> **Space** is the area beyond the earth's atmosphere surrounding the stars and planets.
>
> | Words related to space: | |
> |---|---|
> | astronaut | meteorite |
> | asteroid | moon |
> | black hole | orbit |
> | blast off | planet |
> | capsule | rocket |
> | comet | satellite |
> | control centre | space shuttle |
> | flightpath | space station |

- Some definitions tell you where you can find **more information** under another headword.

> **junk** NOUN
> **Junk** is old, unwanted or worthless things that are sold cheaply or thrown away.
> **clutter**
> *"Some day I will clear that **clutter** from our loft," Dad promised.*
> **jumble**
> *We bagged up the **jumble** and took it to the charity shop.*
> **scrap**
> *The millionaire had made his fortune as a **scrap** metal merchant.*
> *See **rubbish***

Using the index

The index lists all the synonyms in *Collins Primary Thesaurus* in alphabetical order. You can use it as a quick way to find synonyms, or to find synonyms for words which are not headwords.

How to find a synonym

You want to find a different way of saying **amusement**, which is a synonym in the thesaurus.

First, find the word **amusement** in the index. What letter does it begin with? Flick through the index until you reach the section beginning with **Aa**.

Think about the second and third letters of the word. All the synonyms in the index are in alphabetical order. Run your finger down the list. You will find more than one word beginning with **amu**.

Keep looking until you find the word **amusement**.

Looking up the synonym in the thesaurus

① Find the **synonym**. This is the word or phrase in the first column.

② Then find the **headword**. This is in the column next to the synonym.

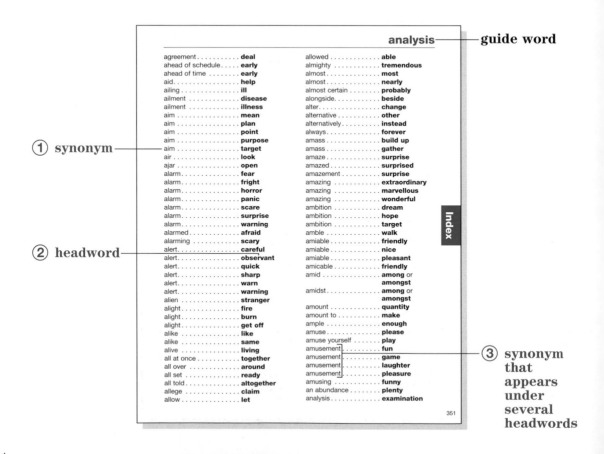

analysis —————— guide word

agreement	deal
ahead of schedule	early
ahead of time	early
aid	help
ailing	ill
ailment	disease
ailment	illness
aim	mean
aim	plan
aim	point
aim	purpose

① **synonym** — aim | target

air	look
ajar	open
alarm	fear
alarm	fright
alarm	horror
alarm	panic
alarm	scare
alarm	surprise
alarm	warning
alarmed	afraid
alarming	scary

② **headword** — alert | careful

alert	observant
alert	quick
alert	sharp
alert	warn
alert	warning
alien	stranger
alight	fire
alight	burn
alight	get off
alike	like
alike	same
alive	living
all at once	together
all over	around
all set	ready
all told	altogether
allege	claim
allow	let

allowed	able
almighty	tremendous
almost	most
almost	nearly
almost certain	probably
alongside	beside
alter	change
alternative	other
alternatively	instead
always	forever
amass	build up
amass	gather
amaze	surprise
amazed	surprised
amazement	surprise
amazing	extraordinary
amazing	marvellous
amazing	wonderful
ambition	dream
ambition	hope
ambition	target
amble	walk
amiable	friendly
amiable	nice
amiable	pleasant
amicable	friendly
amid	among or amongst
amidst	among or amongst
amount	quantity
amount to	make
ample	enough
amuse	please
amuse yourself	play
amusement	fun
amusement	game
amusement	laughter
amusement	pleasure
amusing	funny
an abundance	plenty
analysis	examination

③ **synonym that appears under several headwords**

Index

351

vi

③ Sometimes the **synonym appears under several headwords**, for example, **amusement** appears under **fun**, **game**, **laughter** and **pleasure**. If you are sure which meaning you want to use, choose the right headword. If you are not sure, look up each headword and check its definition. In this case, you choose the headword **game**.

④ There may be more than one headword for the word you have chosen. This is indicated by a **number** in brackets. Read the definition for each headword and choose the one that matches your writing.

Choosing the right synonym

- Use the **alphabet line** and **guide word** to find the page your synonym appears on.

- Find the **headword** you selected in the index.

- Look for the **synonym** that suits your writing.

- Use the **example sentences** to understand how each synonym can be used.

- There may also be a label, usage tip, or a panel of words related to the headword.

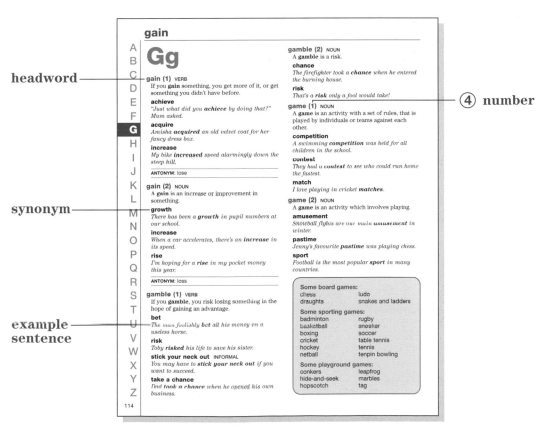

headword

synonym

example sentence

④ **number**

gain

Gg

gain (1) VERB
If you **gain** something, you get more of it, or get something you didn't have before.

achieve
"Just what did you achieve by doing that?" Mum asked.

acquire
Amisha acquired an old velvet coat for her fancy dress box.

increase
My bike increased speed alarmingly down the steep hill.

ANTONYM: lose

gain (2) NOUN
A **gain** is an increase or improvement in something.

growth
There has been a growth in pupil numbers at our school.

increase
When a car accelerates, there's an increase in its speed.

rise
I'm hoping for a rise in my pocket money this year.

ANTONYM: loss

gamble (1) VERB
If you **gamble**, you risk losing something in the hope of gaining an advantage.

bet
The man foolishly bet all his money on a useless horse.

risk
Toby risked his life to save his sister.

stick your neck out INFORMAL
You may have to stick your neck out if you want to succeed.

take a chance
Dad took a chance when he opened his own business.

gamble (2) NOUN
A **gamble** is a risk.

chance
The firefighter took a chance when he entered the burning house.

risk
That's a risk only a fool would take!

game (1) NOUN
A **game** is an activity with a set of rules, that is played by individuals or teams against each other.

competition
A swimming competition was held for all children in the school.

contest
They had a contest to see who could run home the fastest.

match
I love playing in cricket matches.

game (2) NOUN
A **game** is an activity which involves playing.

amusement
Snowball fights are our main amusement in winter.

pastime
Jenny's favourite pastime was playing chess.

sport
Football is the most popular sport in many countries.

Some board games:
chess   ludo
draughts   snakes and ladders

Some sporting games:
badminton   rugby
basketball   snooker
boxing   soccer
cricket   table tennis
hockey   tennis
netball   tenpin bowling

Some playground games:
conkers   leapfrog
hide-and-seek marbles
hopscotch   tag

114

Aa

ability NOUN
If you have **ability**, you have the intelligence and skill to do things.

competence
*Sunita showed **competence** in most school subjects, particularly science.*

gift
*Jack had a **gift** for remembering long and complicated equations.*

skill
*Brackford United played with enthusiasm but little **skill** in Saturday's match.*

talent
*Seamus has a **talent** for cooking delicious seafood dishes.*

ANTONYM: inability

able ADJECTIVE
If you are **able** to do something, you can do it.

allowed
*"I'm **allowed** to play for half an hour, but then I have to go home," Ron complained.*

available
*Rhys said he was **available** to swim for the team on Saturday.*

capable
*Mrs Diss said that my twin brother was a **capable** pupil, but rather lazy.*

free
*My big sister is **free** to take me bowling now.*

ANTONYM: unable

Other adjectives related to able:

able...
... to be dissolved	– **soluble**
... to be easily fooled	– **gullible**
... to be eaten safely	– **edible**
... to be heard	– **audible**
... to be seen	– **visible, noticeable**
... to catch fire	– **flammable**

---

about (1) PREPOSITION
If you talk or write **about** a particular thing, you say things that are to do with that subject.

concerning
*The police interviewed the bank manager **concerning** the robbery.*

regarding
*Parents were sent a letter **regarding** half term.*

to do with
*Mum had a long phone conversation **to do with** our holiday plans.*

about (2) ADVERB
You say **about** in front of a number to show it is not exact.

approximately
*The theatre held **approximately** 800 people.*

around
Around 50 000 people attended the big game.

in the region of
*The bike cost **in the region of** £100.*

more or less
*Each jar holds **more or less** five litres.*

roughly
*We had to wait for **roughly** three hours.*

about (3) ADVERB
About can mean in different directions.

around
*"Stop dancing **around** while I'm talking to you," Mum said irritably.*

here and there
*My sister's clothes were scattered **here and there** in her room.*

hither and thither OLD-FASHIONED
*The bee flew **hither and thither** collecting pollen from the flowers.*

about to PREPOSITION
If you are **about to** do something, you are just going to do it.

on the point of
*I was **on the point of** closing the front door, when the phone rang.*

ready to
*The pilot was **ready to** turn back, when he saw the missing boat.*

above (1) PREPOSITION
If one thing is **above** another, it is directly over or higher than it.

on top of
Ali balanced the bag of flour on top of the door, so that it would fall on Craig when he came in.

over
A cloud of smoke hung ominously over the grumbling volcano.

ANTONYM: below

above (2) PREPOSITION
Above can mean greater than something in level or amount.

beyond
The dancer's skill was beyond anything we could have imagined.

greater than
The number of visitors to the museum this year is greater than last year.

higher than
The cost of the repairs was higher than Mum had expected.

ANTONYM: below

absolutely ADVERB
If you are **absolutely** sure about something, you are completely sure of it.

completely
Anoop was completely satisfied with his new computer.

thoroughly
"I am thoroughly fed up of washing dishes," moaned Cinderella.

totally
We sat totally enthralled by the magician's amazing tricks.

utterly
The instructions to the board game left me utterly confused.

abuse (1) SAID "AB-**YOOSS**" NOUN
Abuse is the cruel treatment of someone.

cruelty
Sadly, many animals are injured through cruelty or neglect.

harm
Fortunately, the two lost children were found with no harm done to them.

ill-treatment
Oliver Twist suffered much ill-treatment in the workhouse.

abuse (2) SAID "AB-**YOOSS**" NOUN
Abuse is rude and unkind remarks.

insults
The two boys exchanged insults, which led to a fight.

obscenities
The vandals had written obscenities all over the wall.

swear words
Many people are offended by swear words.

abuse (3) SAID "AB-**YOOZ**" VERB
To **abuse** someone is to treat them cruelly.

harm
Now the dog was at the rescue kennels, no one could harm it any more.

ill-treat
People who ill-treat their animals should face heavy fines.

mistreat
Cinderella was constantly mistreated by her two ugly sisters.

misuse
The dictator misused his power by giving jobs to his relatives.

abuse (4) SAID "AB-**YOOZ**" VERB
If you **abuse** someone, you speak to them in a rude and insulting way.

be rude to
Maya was rude to me when I accidentally trod on her toe.

curse
Long John Silver cursed the pirates who had found the treasure before him.

insult
"Did you mean to insult me with that remark?" asked Emma.

swear at
It is not polite to swear at people.

accident NOUN

An **accident** is something that happens suddenly or unexpectedly, causing people to be hurt or killed.

collision
*Eight vehicles were involved in a **collision** during the heavy rain.*

crash
*The police advised that the airport should be closed because of the plane **crash**.*

mishap
*Falling off my bike was a minor **mishap**, but luckily I wasn't hurt.*

*See **disaster***

accidental ADJECTIVE

Something that is **accidental** has not been planned.

unexpected
*The sail's tearing in the wind was a totally **unexpected** problem.*

unintentional
*"I didn't mean to stand on the flowers. It was quite **unintentional**," I apologized.*

unplanned
*Although our beach volleyball tournament was **unplanned**, it was a great success.*

ANTONYM: deliberate

accurate ADJECTIVE

If something is **accurate**, it is absolutely correct.

exact
*In order to set my watch, I need to know the **exact** time.*

factual
*Non-fiction books are **factual** accounts of real people and events.*

faithful
*The French version of the book is a **faithful** translation of the English original.*

precise
*Tightrope walkers must be very **precise** in their movements.*

spot-on INFORMAL
*Your guess about the train's arrival time was **spot-on**.*

true
*"Is this statement a **true** record of where you were?" queried the police officer.*

ANTONYM: inaccurate

ache VERB

If a part of your body **aches**, you feel a continuous, dull pain there.

be sore
*Jane's leg muscles **were sore** after aerobics.*

hurt
*"Ouch!" said Devendra as the nurse cleaned his cut knee. "That **hurts**!"*

throb
*My knee really **throbbed** after I fell over on the uneven pavement.*

action (1) NOUN

An **action** is something you do for a particular purpose.

act
*Rescuing the baby from the burning house was an **act** of great courage.*

deed
*Theseus's bravest **deed** was the slaying of the dreaded Minotaur.*

exploit
*The explorer, Sir Archie Pounder, told the school of his **exploits** in the jungle.*

feat
*To build Stonehenge without modern equipment was a great **feat**.*

move
*I think resting after dinner is a sensible **move**.*

action (2) NOUN

An **action** is a physical movement, such as jumping.

activity
*Our classroom was a hive of **activity** as we got ready for the concert.*

motion
*The up-and-down **motion** of the boat made me feel queasy.*

movement
*The **movements** of the conductor's baton guided the orchestra.*

actual ADJECTIVE

Actual can mean something is real, rather than imaginary or guessed at.

genuine
"This table is a genuine antique," said Gran.

real
The film is based on a real story.

true
"Is this a true record of what you said?" the judge demanded to know.

very
The guide told us Ann Boleyn was beheaded on the very spot where we stood.

add (1) VERB

If you **add** something to a number of things, you put it with those things.

combine
Orange juice combined with lemonade makes a refreshing drink.

include
"Don't forget to include a sentence about what your friends think," Mr Bishop reminded us.

✔ Remember that you add something **to** something else, but combine something **with** something else.

add (2) VERB

If you **add** numbers together, or **add** them up, you work out the total.

count up
I counted up the spoons, and found there were three missing.

total
Miss Dobson told us to total the figures at the bottom of each column.

tot up INFORMAL
It took me ages to tot up how many hours I had worked that week.

ANTONYM: subtract

adjust VERB

If you **adjust** something, you change its position or alter it in some other way.

change
I changed the time on my new watch so that it was correct.

correct
Fortunately, the pilot corrected the plane's course before it hit the storm clouds.

modify
The racing car's tyres had been specially modified for wet weather.

tune
Dad tuned the radio to a different station.

tweak INFORMAL
Mrs Tordoff asked me to tweak my story to include more dialogue.

admit VERB

If you **admit** something, you agree that it is true.

acknowledge
Good drivers acknowledge when they have made a mistake.

confess
The prisoner confessed that she had lied.

grant
"I grant that it's not a great meal," my brother said, "but at least I cooked it myself."

own up
The head teacher asked whoever had broken the window to own up to it.

adult ADJECTIVE

An **adult** is a mature and fully developed person.

grown-up
Dad asked another grown-up for directions.

man
Jim is now a man of 42.

woman
A woman was seen leaving the building.

adventure NOUN

An **adventure** is something that is exciting, and perhaps even dangerous.

escapade
Entering the Sheriff of Nottingham's chamber was perhaps Robin Hood's boldest escapade.

exploit
Several films have been made of the brave exploits of the Three Musketeers.

feat
To abseil down a skyscraper would certainly be a daring feat.

venture
The expedition proved a dangerous venture.

advice NOUN
Advice is a suggestion from someone about what you should do.

guidance
Larissa needed guidance from her teachers about which college to apply for.

recommendation
Mum followed the doctor's recommendation, and gave up smoking.

suggestion
My friend's suggestion was to do our work first and play later.

tip INFORMAL
A good tip is to test the water with your toe before you jump in.

advise VERB
If you **advise** someone to do something, you tell them you think they should do it.

recommend
Mrs Singh recommended that I should sit nearer the front of the classroom.

suggest
"I suggest we go home," said Mum.

urge
In his speech, the MP urged people to vote for him in the election.

affect VERB
If something **affects** someone or something else, it influences or changes them.

concern
The issue of global warming concerns everybody on the planet.

have an effect on
The moon's gravity has an effect on the oceans, creating high and low tides.

influence
The judge's sentence was influenced by the prisoner's previous good behaviour.

involve
The accident happened nearby, but fortunately our car was not involved.

✔ Be careful not to confuse the verb **affect** with the noun **effect**.

afraid ADJECTIVE
If you are **afraid**, you are frightened.

alarmed
"Don't be alarmed," Mum said calmly. "It's only the wind rattling the windows."

anxious
As I had not revised my spellings, I was anxious about the test the next morning.

fearful
Faiza is fearful of the dark.

frightened
"Don't be frightened," said the giant. "I won't hurt you."

nervous
Alim was nervous before his driving test.

petrified
My brother is petrified of going to the dentist.

scared
I told my brother there was nothing to be scared of.

terrified
I used to be terrified of injections, but now that I've had one I'm not scared any more.

timid
I was quite timid on my first day at school.

✔ To be afraid of something is to **fear** or **dread** it.

ANTONYM: unafraid

after (1) ADVERB
After can mean later than a particular time, date or event.

afterwards
We had our lunch and afterwards went out to the school field.

following
Following the professor's talk on birds, we had the chance to ask her questions.

later than
It was later than six o'clock when we finally finished shopping.

subsequently
The injured driver was taken to hospital, but was allowed to go home subsequently.

ANTONYM: before

A
B
C
D
E
F
G
H
I
J
K
L
M
N
O
P
Q
R
S
T
U
V
W
X
Y
Z

after (2) PREPOSITION
If you come **after** someone or something, you are behind them and following them.

behind
Behind the royal procession came the jester, prancing about and waving some sort of wand.

following
Off went the removal van, with Dad following.

again ADVERB
Again can mean happening one more time.

afresh
The couple moved abroad to start life afresh.

a second time
The traveller waited before knocking at the door a second time.

once more
Once more Dad tried to put up the deckchair, and once more it collapsed.

against PREPOSITION
Something that is **against** something else is in opposition to it.

anti INFORMAL
Our entire family is anti hunting. We think it's cruel.

opposed to
I was opposed to the idea of moving house.

versus
In our playground game, it was Rachel and me versus the rest of the class.

✔ If something is against the law, it is **illegal**.

aim (1) VERB
If you **aim** to do something, you are planning to do it.

intend
One day, I intend to own a chocolate factory.

mean
The player meant to hit the ball down the line, but it flew into the crowd.

plan
Dad had planned to work abroad, but then he was offered a job in Britain.

propose
Mr Potter proposes to put on a school play this year.

set your sights on
Louis had set his sights on becoming an artist, but became a photographer instead.

aim (2) NOUN
Your **aim** is what you intend to achieve.

goal
Cassandra's goal is to make a million dollars before she is 25.

object
The object of the game is to throw the ball in your opponents' basket.

objective
"Men," barked the Major, "our objective is to cross that river before the enemy sees us."

purpose
The purpose of the meeting was to decide what our class would do for the school concert.

target
The target for this year's bring-and-buy sale is to raise a thousand pounds.

aircraft NOUN
An **aircraft** is any vehicle that can fly.

Types of aircraft:

aeroplane	helicopter
glider	hot-air balloon
hang-glider	microlite

alike ADJECTIVE
Things that are **alike** are very similar in some way.

comparable
The two boys had had comparable experiences at primary school.

identical
The twins were identical except for the way they styled their hair.

indistinguishable
The forgery and the original painting were indistinguishable.

similar
Phoebe's house is like ours, and Justin's is similar too.

ANTONYM: different or unlike

all right (1) ADJECTIVE

If something is **all right**, it is satisfactory, but not especially good.

acceptable
*Your work is **acceptable**, Watts, but by no means outstanding.*

adequate
*The nurse thought her temporary bandage would be **adequate** to stop the bleeding.*

average
*"My exam marks were **average**, but I'm sure I can do better," said Ron.*

fair
*Leo made a **fair** attempt at the test, considering he had felt so ill earlier.*

satisfactory
*The car was in a **satisfactory** condition to pass the safety test.*

all right (2) ADJECTIVE

If someone is **all right**, they are safe and not harmed.

safe
*"You'll be quite **safe** provided that you wait here," the police officer said.*

unharmed
*After getting lost in the hills, the boys were returned **unharmed** to their parents.*

unhurt
*The stunt rider escaped **unhurt** after his bike cartwheeled into the air.*

uninjured
*I was shaken but **uninjured** after falling during the race.*

almost ADVERB

Almost can mean very nearly.

just about
*We were **just about** ready to go, when Mum's phone bleeped.*

nearly
*It was **nearly** five years since Hanif had seen his aunt and uncle.*

not quite
*I had **not quite** finished the test when Mr Halliday said the time was up.*

practically
***Practically** all the sandwiches had been eaten.*

virtually
*Despite having **virtually** no time to practise, Darius played the piano piece perfectly.*

alone (1) ADJECTIVE

Someone or something that is **alone** is not with other people or things.

detached
*The elephant was **detached** from the herd.*

isolated
*The old man lived in a cottage on the cliff top. He felt quite **isolated**.*

solitary
*Robinson Crusoe was **solitary** on his desert island home.*

alone (2) ADVERB

Something that happens **alone**, happens without other people or things.

independently
*Sian did her homework **independently**.*

separately
*The teachers came with us on the bus, except for the head who came later, **separately**.*

solo INFORMAL
*The pilot now flew **solo** for the first time.*

also ADVERB

Also can mean in addition to something that has just been mentioned.

as well
*Mum had just bought the lettuce when she remembered to get some tomatoes **as well**.*

besides
*The competition winner received a sports bag, and a signed bat to go in it **besides**.*

furthermore FORMAL
*"You've worked well," the teacher said, "and **furthermore** you've worked quietly."*

in addition
*My prize was free tickets to the show. **In addition**, it included a meal afterwards.*

moreover FORMAL
*It was cold, and **moreover** it was getting dark.*

too
*William is nine, and Rina is **too**.*

a
b
c
d
e
f
g
h
i
j
k
l
m
n
o
p
q
r
s
t
u
v
w
x
y
z

although CONJUNCTION

Although can mean in spite of the fact that.

even though

*Jessica managed to win the marathon, **even though** she'd had flu earlier that week.*

while

While the work on an oil rig is tough, the pay is good.

altogether ADVERB

Altogether can mean in total and is used when talking about amounts.

all told

*There were over two thousand people at the show, **all told**.*

everything included

***Everything included**, the fête raised enough money for the new equipment.*

in total

***In total**, the auction raised well over five thousand pounds.*

always (1) ADVERB

Always can mean all the time.

consistently

*Andy is **consistently** the best player on our hockey team.*

constantly

*We are **constantly** receiving junk e-mails.*

continually

*My mum is **continually** nagging me to keep my room tidy.*

continuously

*The generator chugged away **continuously** throughout the night.*

invariably

*Aissa is **invariably** late for school.*

regularly

*Stars are **regularly** asked for their autographs.*

repeatedly

*"I'm **repeatedly** telling you not to speak with your mouth full!" Dad said crossly.*

time after time

***Time after time**, my little brother asked me to play with him.*

ANTONYM: never

always (2) ADVERB

Always can mean forever.

endlessly

*I shall be **endlessly** grateful to the woman who saved my life.*

forever

*"Madam, I am **forever** in your debt," the musketeer said as he swept from the room.*

perpetually

*The Olympic flame burns **perpetually**.*

ANTONYM: never

amazing ADJECTIVE

If something is **amazing**, it is very surprising.

astonishing

*It is **astonishing** that we breathe, on average, 500 million times in our lives.*

astounding

*The marathon runner kept up an **astounding** pace for the whole 26 miles.*

breathtaking

*Seeing Niagara Falls was a **breathtaking** experience.*

sensational

*The show was **sensational**, with superb music and dancing.*

staggering

*It is **staggering** to realize that 60 per cent of our body is water.*

among or amongst PREPOSITION

Among or **amongst** can mean surrounded by.

amid

*Workers searched **amid** the wreckage for any sign of survivors.*

amidst

***Amidst** all the weeds, a single rose bloomed.*

in the middle of

***In the middle of** the herd of cows was a newborn calf.*

surrounded by

*Mum and I found ourselves **surrounded by** inquisitive sheep.*

✔ If there are more than two things, you should use **among(st)**. If there are only two things, you should use **between**.

amount NOUN
An **amount** is how much there is of something.

mass
There was a great mass of tadpoles in our garden pond.

quantity
"For sale: a quantity of unused garden tools," read the advert.

sum
The house was sold for an undisclosed sum of money.

total
Our little sideshow raised quite a total at our school fête.

volume
A huge volume of water cascades over the waterfall every minute.

anger NOUN
Anger is the strong feeling you get about something unfair or cruel.

annoyance
You could see the annoyance on the little boy's face when he couldn't have any sweets.

fury
Her face purple with fury, the duchess stormed from the room.

indignation
Our dog, Jim, stared in indignation as I ate the last biscuit.

irritation
Sissy stormed out in irritation.

rage
The wizard flew into a rage and instantly turned the king and queen into toads.

temper
In a fit of temper, I flung my sister's hairbrush into the garden.

wrath SAID "ROTH"
The player incurred the wrath of the referee for committing a foul.

angry ADJECTIVE
Someone who is **angry** is very annoyed.

annoyed
Mr Danesh was annoyed that Anna hadn't handed in her homework.

apoplectic
The team manager was apoplectic, dancing with rage when the referee disallowed the goal.

beside yourself with anger
The head teacher was beside herself with anger when the money was stolen.

cross
You could tell Mum was cross. Her forehead had turned red and wrinkly.

displeased
"Smithers, I'm displeased with the poor spelling in this report," Sir Hector boomed.

enraged
The bull, enraged, came charging, head down, towards the matador.

fuming
Mrs Stevenson was fuming when she realized Peter was absent yet again.

furious
Furious at such a messy piece of work, Mr Ross flung my book back on my desk.

hot under the collar INFORMAL
Many motorists were getting hot under the collar as the traffic jam built up.

indignant
You could see by her face that our terrier, Tess, was indignant that we had left her behind.

infuriated
The stressed commuter was infuriated to find that the train had left seconds earlier.

irate
It made Mrs Mawdsley irate to find the staffroom key missing.

irritated
I was irritated to find that Alex had borrowed my pencil.

livid
Father was livid that I had broken his favourite fishing rod.

outraged
Many townsfolk were outraged that the lovely old cinema was to be torn down.

seething
I knew from his gritted teeth that the boss was seething.

animal NOUN
An **animal** is any living being that is not a plant.

beast
*The thoroughbred horse was a beautiful but temperamental **beast**.*

creature
*The platypus is a strange-looking **creature**.*

✔ General names for animals are **fauna** and **wildlife**.

annoy VERB
If someone or something **annoys** you, they make you angry or impatient.

aggravate
*My gran is often **aggravated** by noisy motorbikes late at night.*

bother
*"Please don't **bother** me now. I'm really very busy," said Dad.*

drive someone up the wall INFORMAL
*"Some of these stupid TV adverts **drive me up the wall**!" said Grandad.*

get on someone's nerves INFORMAL
*Mitchi's whiny voice really **gets on my nerves**.*

harass
*Many famous people are **harassed** by reporters and photographers.*

irritate
*My mum was **irritated** by the constant dripping of the tap in the night.*

needle INFORMAL
*The soccer player tried to **needle** his opponent by muttering insults.*

provoke
*My sister **provoked** me into an argument by saying I was no good at singing.*

answer (1) VERB
If you **answer** someone, you reply to them in speech or writing.

answer back
*When spoken to by the judge, the defendant was foolish enough to **answer back** rudely.*

reply
*If you receive an invitation, it's polite to **reply** promptly.*

respond
*The captain asked for volunteers, and two crewmen **responded**.*

retort
*"I'd love to go to the ball," said Cinderella. "No chance!" **retorted** her ugly sister.*

return
*"Yes, I'd love to come to the theatre," Genevieve **returned**.*

answer (2) NOUN
An **answer** is the reply you give when you answer someone.

acknowledgement
*The palace sent a brief letter as an **acknowledgement** to my request.*

reaction
*The mayor received an angry **reaction** to his scheme to sell off the sports field.*

reply
*The salesman rang the door bell, but there was no **reply**.*

response
*There was a terrific **response** to the famine appeal.*

retort
*"Ouch, that hurt!" I said. "Serves you right!" came the **retort**.*

appear VERB
When something **appears**, it moves from somewhere you could not see it to somewhere you can see it.

come into sight
*A woolly mammoth **came into sight**, lumbering from behind the rock.*

come into view
*A triceratops **came into view**, its serrated back appearing over the ridge.*

emerge
***Emerging** from his bedroom, my lazy brother rubbed his eyes.*

loom
*The gigantic airship blotted out the sun as it **loomed** nearer.*

See **arrive**

area (1) NOUN
An **area** is a particular part of a place, country or the world.

community
*We live in a friendly **community**, with lots going on.*

district
*It was a poor **district**, where litter and street crime were a problem.*

neighbourhood
*In our **neighbourhood**, everybody helps one another.*

region
*This **region** of Italy is famous for its pizzas.*

zone
*That **zone** is open only to airport staff.*

area (2) NOUN
Area can mean the measurement of a flat surface.

extent
*From the top of the tower, Jamie could see the **extent** of the city.*

size
*"What **size** of paper shall I use?" Dani asked.*

area (3) NOUN
The **area** of a piece of ground or surface is the amount of space it covers.

expanse
*When Noah looked from his ark, all he saw was a huge **expanse** of water.*

patch INFORMAL
*The police officer said he would miss the people in his **patch** when he retired.*

plot
*My parents bought a **plot** of land, hoping to build a house there.*

stretch
*You can see otters on this **stretch** of the river.*

argue (1) VERB
If you **argue** with someone about something, you disagree with them about it, sometimes in an angry way.

bicker
*My sisters are always **bickering** at the table.*

disagree
*Simon and Sanjiv **disagreed** passionately about which team would win.*

fall out
*Hazel and I **fell out** when she broke her promise to keep my secret.*

have a difference of opinion
*The two neighbours **had a difference of opinion** over who owned the fence.*

have an argument
*Dad and Mum **had an argument** about whose turn it was to get up and see to the baby.*

quarrel
*Jack and Wilbur **quarrelled** over land, and their two families have not spoken since.*

row SOUNDS LIKE "COW"
*The couple next door were always **rowing**. Now they've gone we'll get some peace!*

squabble
*"Stop **squabbling**, you two!" Mum said, exasperated. "You'll both get a turn."*

argue (2) VERB
If you **argue** that something is true, you give reasons why you think that it is.

assert
*The prisoner continues to **assert** his innocence.*

claim
*Mervyn **claimed** he was the lost King of Albania, but nobody believed him.*

debate
*"I think we'll be **debating** this issue forever!" joked Mrs Evans.*

hold
*Before 1492, many people **held** that the earth was flat.*

maintain
*Columbus always **maintained** that the earth was round, and proceeded to prove it.*

put the case
*In the debate, Scarlet **put the case** for hunting and I opposed it.*

reason
*Mum tried to **reason** with my little brother, but it was a waste of time.*

a
b
c
d
e
f
g
h
i
j
k
l
m
n
o
p
q
r
s
t
u
v
w
x
y
z

argument (1) NOUN

An **argument** is a talk between people who do not agree.

barney INFORMAL
*Kayla and I had a bit of a **barney**, but we soon made up.*

difference of opinion
*Panna and Liz had a **difference of opinion** over which team would win.*

disagreement
*The tennis players had a **disagreement** about whether the service was in or out.*

dispute
*The long-running **dispute** between the two neighbours ended in a court case.*

feud
*Occasionally, the **feud** between the Campbell clan and the MacDonald clan erupted into violence.*

fight
*Two girls in our class got into a **fight** over a missing purse.*

quarrel
*The **quarrel** started when Colin was left out of the team in favour of Barry.*

row SOUNDS LIKE "COW"
*I was upstairs in my room when the **row** between Dad and Grandad started.*

squabble
*It was a silly **squabble** over who would sleep in the top bunk.*

✔ A formal talk between people who do not agree is a **debate**.

argument (2) NOUN

An **argument** is a point or set of reasons you use to convince people about something.

case
*The barrister set out the **case** for the prosecution.*

grounds
*The judge decided there were no **grounds** on which to find the defendant guilty.*

reason
*Guy Fawkes was asked to give his **reasons** for wishing to blow up Parliament.*

army NOUN

An **army** is a large group of soldiers who are trained to fight on land.

✔ **Military** means "connected with an army".

> **Here are some more words associated with the military, or armed forces:**
>
> | | |
> |---|---|
> | air force | marine |
> | battalion | navy |
> | brigade | paratrooper |
> | cavalry | platoon |
> | commando | regiment |
> | company | reinforcements |
> | garrison | squad |
> | legion | squadron |

around (1) PREPOSITION

You can use **around** when something is surrounding or encircling a place or object.

on all sides of
On all sides of the camp, a barbed-wire fence rose menacingly towards grim watchtowers.

on every side of
*The word "Fragile" was written **on every side of** the box.*

around (2) PREPOSITION

Around can mean at approximately the time or place mentioned.

about
*"I'll meet you at **about** three o'clock," Kamilah whispered.*

approximately
*"The train will be **approximately** five minutes late," said the announcer.*

in the region of
*The government spent **in the region of** 30 billion pounds on new roads.*

roughly
*The new garage will be **roughly** ten metres in length.*

around (3) PREPOSITION

You say **around** when things are in various places.

all over
*Papers were scattered **all over** Mum's office.*

everywhere
In the wind, fallen leaves flew everywhere.

here and there
"I always find the odd bargain here and there," said Gran cheerfully.

arrange (1) VERB
If you **arrange** to do something, or arrange something for someone, you make plans for it or make it possible.

fix
Mr Pearson fixed our soccer game for next Tuesday afternoon.

organize
Mum said she would organize a trip to the zoo during the holidays.

plan
Dad planned a secret birthday surprise for Mum.

prepare
Most good chefs prepare their menu well in advance.

settle
The old lady settled her affairs before she left town.

arrange (2) VERB
If you **arrange** objects, you set them out in a particular way.

group
For the photograph, all the wedding guests were grouped in front of the hall door.

organize
For the tournament, players were organized into teams of five.

place
The artist carefully placed the objects she was going to paint.

position
Guards were positioned outside the palace.

arrest VERB
If the police **arrest** someone, they take them to a police station because they believe they may have committed a crime.

capture
A search party captured the escaped prisoner in an isolated shack.

nick INFORMAL
The bloke next door got nicked for burglary the other day.

take someone into custody
Police officers cautioned the suspect and took her into custody.

arrive VERB
When you **arrive** at a place, you reach it at the end of your journey.

appear
The film star finally appeared, an hour late.

show up INFORMAL
Jeremy showed up just in time.

turn up INFORMAL
"If you turn up late, the coach will have gone," warned the driver.

ANTONYM: depart

artist NOUN
An **artist** is a person who draws or paints, or produces other works of art such as novels or music.

Types of artist:

artist	playwright
film director	poet
musician	potter
novelist	sculptor
painter	writer

ashamed ADJECTIVE
If you are **ashamed**, you feel embarrassed or guilty.

embarrassed
Karen was embarrassed to find that the rain had streaked her make-up.

guilty
I hadn't done anything, but I still felt guilty about the missing money.

humiliated
Jade felt humiliated after the coach had publicly blamed her for losing the game.

sorry
Misha was sorry that his stupid comment had caused so much upset.

A
B
C
D
E
F
G
H
I
J
K
L
M
N
O
P
Q
R
S
T
U
V
W
X
Y
Z

ask (1) VERB

If you **ask** someone something, you put a question to them.

enquire or inquire

*"If you want more information, **enquire** at the desk over there," the woman said.*

interrogate

*Secret police **interrogated** the spy about his mission, but he told them nothing.*

query

*Mr Blake **queried** the bill, saying he'd been overcharged.*

question

*The suspicious-looking stranger was stopped and **questioned** about what she was doing.*

quiz

*My mum **quizzed** me about where I was going, and who with.*

ask (2) VERB

If you **ask** for something, you say you would like to have it.

appeal

*Our church **appealed** for money to help repair the roof.*

apply

*If you are travelling abroad, you must **apply** for a passport.*

beg

*I **begged** Mum to let me go to the party, but she said no.*

beseech

*"Have mercy on me, I **beseech** you!" the frog prince cried to the princess.*

demand

*The angry diner **demanded** to know what a beetle was doing in his pudding.*

implore

*"I **implore** you to think twice before running away," said Emma.*

plead

*The princess **pleaded** to be set free by the wicked witch.*

request

*The soccer player **requested** a transfer to another club.*

ask (3) verb

If you **ask** someone to come or go somewhere, you invite them there.

ask someone round

*The vicar **asked us round** for a cup of tea.*

bid OLD-FASHIONED

*His lordship **bade** me enter and enquired if I would drink wine with him.*

invite

*Whoopee! Della has **invited** me to her party.*

summon

*King Arthur **summoned** his knights to an assembly at the Round Table.*

asleep ADJECTIVE

If you are **asleep**, your eyes are closed and your whole body is resting.

dead to the world INFORMAL

*Dad was **dead to the world** in the armchair.*

fast asleep

*Jim, our dog, was **fast asleep** with his legs in the air.*

sound asleep

*I was so **sound asleep** that my little brother had to sit on me to wake me up.*

✔ Animals that **hibernate** spend the winter in a state like a deep sleep.

ANTONYM: awake

See **sleep**

attack (1) VERB

If a person or an animal **attacks** another person or animal, they use violence in order to hurt or kill them.

assault

*The muggers **assaulted** the man, then tried to steal his wallet.*

charge

*The Light Brigade **charged** the enemy's guns at full tilt.*

mug

*Unfortunately, some people are **mugged** on dark city streets.*

raid

*Police **raided** the house where the escaped criminal was living.*

storm

*Troops **stormed** the cliffs and succeeded in silencing the machine guns above.*

✔ In sport, to attack is to **move forward**.

ANTONYM: defend

attack (2) NOUN

An **attack** is a violent, physical action against someone or something.

assault

*"This was a serious **assault**, for which you must pay," said the judge grimly.*

charge

*The Light Brigade's **charge** was brave but doomed.*

invasion

*The 1944 D-Day landings in France formed the biggest **invasion** in world history.*

raid

*The air **raids** continued night after night.*

strike

*The missile **strike** destroyed the buildings.*

ANTONYM: defence

automatic ADJECTIVE

An **automatic** machine is programmed to do a task without needing a person to operate it.

automated

*The new **automated** answering service kept Dad waiting for half an hour.*

computerized

*Most photocopiers are **computerized** these days.*

robotic

*In car factories, **robotic** arms put most of the parts together.*

self-propelling

*My **self-propelling** model glider worked by twisting an elastic band.*

avoid (1) VERB

If you **avoid** someone or something, you keep away from them.

dodge

*We **dodged** our nosy neighbour by hiding behind a tree as she went past.*

elude

*By going out of the back door, the celebrity **eluded** the photographers.*

evade

*The criminal managed to **evade** the police for several days, but was eventually caught.*

shun

*The shy film star **shunned** publicity, preferring a quiet family life.*

steer clear of INFORMAL

*"If I were you I'd **steer clear of** that quarry," my dad said sternly.*

avoid (2) VERB

If you **avoid** doing something, you make an effort not to do it.

dodge INFORMAL

*My lazy brother tried to **dodge** cleaning the car, but Dad made him do it.*

duck out of INFORMAL

*I tried to **duck out of** unpacking the dishwasher, with no success.*

escape

*The prisoner tried to **escape**, but the police officer stopped him.*

get out of

*"It's no use trying to **get out of** it. You'll have to mow the lawn," said Dad.*

shirk

*The farmer tried to **shirk** responsibility for the pollution in the river.*

away ADVERB

If you are **away** from somewhere, you are not in that place.

absent

*With such a high temperature, Edward was forced to be **absent** from school.*

elsewhere

*I searched the house for my gran, but she was obviously **elsewhere**.*

on holiday

*Our family is going **on holiday** to Florida this summer.*

✔ To be away from school when you should be there is to **play truant**.

A
B
C
D
E
F
G
H
I
J
K
L
M
N
O
P
Q
R
S
T
U
V
W
X
Y
Z

awful ADJECTIVE

Something **awful** is very unpleasant or very bad.

appalling

*The karaoke singer's voice was **appalling** – he sounded like a dog howling!*

dreadful

*We had a **dreadful** time in Venice. All the streets were flooded.*

fearful INFORMAL

*Mr Bellamy had a **fearful** cold and sneezed all the way to London.*

frightful

*The house was in a **frightful** state after it had been burgled.*

ghastly INFORMAL

*Mum made a **ghastly** mistake, and put salt in the cake mixture instead of sugar.*

gruesome

*The room where the murder had taken place was a **gruesome** sight.*

harrowing

*The film was **harrowing** to watch.*

hideous

*The monster's head was truly **hideous**: bloated, scarred and covered in scales.*

horrendous

*It was a **horrendous** meal, with half of the food burnt and the other half undercooked.*

horrible

*For one **horrible** moment, I thought my wallet had been stolen.*

horrid

*"William, that was a perfectly **horrid** thing to say," said Mrs Brown.*

horrific

*"Unless this fog goes, I'm afraid there'll be a **horrific** accident," the police officer said.*

shocking

*"I think it's **shocking**," put in Dad, "that those refugees should be left without shelter."*

terrible

*The sun rose on the scene of the earthquake, a **terrible** sight to behold.*

unpleasant

*Shingles is a very **unpleasant** disease to have.*

ANTONYM: lovely

awkward (1) ADJECTIVE

If a situation is **awkward**, it is difficult to deal with.

delicate

*It was a **delicate** situation: to ask Julie about her exams or not to mention the subject.*

embarrassing

*It was very **embarrassing** to be stuck outside in my pyjamas in the pouring rain!*

tricky

*"Now this bit could be **tricky**," muttered Bond coolly. "Which wire should I cut?"*

uncomfortable

*The spy had an **uncomfortable** moment when the guards stared in through the car window.*

awkward (2) ADJECTIVE

If a person or animal is **awkward**, they are difficult to deal with.

hard to handle

*Donkeys have a reputation for being **hard to handle**.*

stubborn

*My brother can be very **stubborn** when it comes to helping me wash up.*

troublesome

*On the journey to Scotland, the car proved **troublesome**, but eventually we got there.*

uncooperative

*The lady at the enquiries desk was **uncooperative** and didn't help at all.*

Bb

baby NOUN

A **baby** is a child in the first year or two of its life.

infant

*The shepherds found the **infant** in a stable, lying in a manger.*

newborn child

*The mother proudly gazed at her tiny **newborn child**.*

toddler

*Waddling on bandy legs, the **toddler** was off round the corner in a flash.*

tot INFORMAL

*'Don't tease your brother," said Mum. "He's only a **tot**."*

✔ The babies of animals and humans are their **offspring**. Together, the babies of an animal are sometimes called a **litter**.

back NOUN

The **back** of something is the part behind the front.

end

*At the **end** of the queue, people were setting up tents for the night.*

rear

*I could see smoke coming from the **rear** of the vehicle in front.*

reverse

*Genevieve wrote her answers on the **reverse** of the worksheet.*

✔ The back part of an animal is its **rear**, **rump** or **hindquarters**.
The back end of a ship is the **stern**.

ANTONYM: front

bad (1) ADJECTIVE

Bad things are harmful or upsetting.

appalling

*The weather for our sports day was **appalling**.*

damaging

*The fumes emitted by jet aircraft can be highly **damaging** to the environment.*

dangerous

*Building sites are **dangerous** places which should be avoided.*

distressing

*Melinda found it **distressing** to see pictures of starving children.*

dreadful

*It was a **dreadful** shame: all Barak's hard work disappeared as the blaze took hold.*

grave

*A spokesperson announced the **grave** news that the king was dying.*

serious

*The artist's illness was too **serious** for him to continue painting.*

terrible

*Our goalkeeper was **terrible** today. She let in four easy shots!*

ANTONYM: good

bad (2) ADJECTIVE

A **bad** person is naughty or unkind.

corrupt

*The **corrupt** politician had taken money from all sorts of people.*

cruel

*I can't stand people being **cruel** to children or animals.*

disobedient

*The **disobedient** boy ignored the warning notice and fell into the quarry.*

evil

*The **evil** villain plotted how to ensnare the handsome knight.*

mischievous

*Tying Kerry's shoelaces together was a **mischievous** prank.*

naughty

*"You're a **naughty** girl, Cassandra," said her mother angrily.*

wicked

*The **wicked** witch lived alone.*

✔ Names for bad people include **rogue**, **villain** and **scoundrel**.

ANTONYM: good

A
B
C
D
E
F
G
H
I
J
K
L
M
N
O
P
Q
R
S
T
U
V
W
X
Y
Z

bad (3) ADJECTIVE
Bad can also mean of poor quality.

abysmal
*"Such **abysmal** work will have to be redone,"
said Mr Malone severely.*

atrocious
*The reporter admitted that his spelling was
atrocious.*

decaying
*The **decaying** fruit was starting to go soft.*

faulty
*Engineers soon fixed the **faulty** telephone line.*

inferior
*The paint Dad bought was of **inferior** quality
– it was hard to use and didn't last long.*

rotten
***Rotten** meat smells very bad.*

shoddy
*Owing to **shoddy** workmanship, the house had
to be redecorated.*

unsatisfactory
*The head teacher wrote that my school report
was **unsatisfactory**.*

ANTONYM: excellent

bad-mannered ADJECTIVE
Bad-mannered people are rude and
thoughtless.

disrespectful
*It is **disrespectful** to interrupt people when
they are speaking.*

inconsiderate
*It was **inconsiderate** of Meg to take a second
helping when others had not had their first.*

rude
*We decided not to leave a tip for the
rude waiter.*

bad-tempered ADJECTIVE
Bad-tempered people often lose their temper.

grumpy
*Dad is always cheerful in the mornings. It's
me that is **grumpy**.*

irritable
*Some people get **irritable** when you read over
their shoulder.*

moody
*When people are **moody**, you never quite know
how they will greet you.*

quarrelsome
*The two **quarrelsome** brothers were always
looking for a fight.*

sulky
*"If you're going to be **sulky**, miss, you can go
to your room," Dad replied.*

sullen
*The **sullen** waiter snatched my plate and
stalked off to the kitchen.*

bag NOUN
A **bag** is a container for carrying things in.

Some types of bag:	
backpack	rucksack
briefcase	sack
carrier bag	satchel
duffel bag	shopping bag
handbag	shoulder bag
holdall	suitcase

ban VERB
If you **ban** something, you forbid it to be done.

make illegal
*The government proposes to **make illegal** the
sale of imitation guns.*

prohibit
*Using all sorts of barricades, the landowner
prohibited walkers from crossing his land.*

bang (1) NOUN
A **bang** is a hard, painful bump against
something.

blow
*Kirstin suffered a **blow** to her head when the
door opened suddenly.*

knock
*When I slipped on the stairs, I got a sharp
knock on my funny bone.*

bang (2) NOUN
A **bang** is a sudden, short, loud noise.

blast
*The **blast** echoed round the quarry.*

thud
*With a **thud**, the encyclopedia hit the floor.*

bare (1) ADJECTIVE
If your body is **bare**, it is not covered by any clothing.

in your birthday suit INFORMAL
I dreamt I was walking down the high street in my birthday suit.

naked
*Lady Godiva rode **naked** on a horse through the middle of town.*

nude
*For many centuries, the **nude** body has been a popular subject for artists.*

undressed
*The nurse asked me to get **undressed**, ready for the medical examination.*

without a stitch on INFORMAL
*"And there I was, **without a stitch on**," Mrs Lee, our neighbour, told me.*

bare (2) ADJECTIVE
If something is **bare**, it is not covered with anything.

barren
*The Grand Canyon, although magnificent, is a **barren** wilderness.*

bleak
*The Brontë sisters lived on the edge of a **bleak**, windswept moor.*

desolate
*The abandoned town was **desolate**.*

See **empty (1)**

barrier NOUN
A **barrier** is a fence or wall that prevents people or animals getting from one area to another.

barricade
*The protesters erected a **barricade** across the main street.*

obstacle
*There are lots of **obstacles** to get over and under in an obstacle race.*

obstruction
*The roadworks were an **obstruction** and drivers had to be diverted around them.*

base (1) NOUN
The **base** is the lowest part of something.

bottom
*The lost cat mewed at the **bottom** of the well.*

foot
*"Please would you stand on the **foot** of my ladder to stop it slipping?" Dad asked.*

foundation
*The **foundations** of New York's skyscrapers rest on solid rock.*

base (2) NOUN
A **base** is the headquarters of an organization.

centre
*A humble office in a run-down district was the unlikely **centre** of a huge corporation.*

headquarters
*We arranged to meet at our scout **headquarters** at four o'clock.*

HQ ABBREVIATION
*"**HQ** calling Tank 5," the colonel snapped.*

bat NOUN
A **bat** is a specially shaped piece of wood with a handle, used for hitting a ball in some games.

> You play with ...
> a **bat** in baseball, cricket, rounders, softball and table tennis.
> a **club** in golf.
> a **cue** in pool and snooker.
> a **racket** in badminton, squash and tennis.
> a **stick** in hockey.

battle NOUN
A **battle** is a fight between armed forces, or a struggle between two people or groups with different aims.

action
*It was the first time that the young soldier had seen **action**.*

conflict
*There was a **conflict** of opinions: the red party on one side, the greens on the other.*

struggle
*The **struggle** for power between the king and the government was a long one.*

a
b
c
d
e
f
g
h
i
j
k
l
m
n
o
p
q
r
s
t
u
v
w
x
y
z

beach

beach NOUN

The **beach** is an area of sand or pebbles beside the sea.

sands
*The lifeguards sprinted down the **sands** and plunged into the waves.*

seashore
*After the tanker disaster, much of the **seashore** was coated in an oily sludge.*

seaside
*Aaron much preferred **seaside** holidays to ones spent in the country.*

shore
*We walked along the **shore**, looking for attractive shells.*

water's edge
*The **water's edge** was a seething mass of turtles.*

beat (1) VERB

If someone or something **beats** someone or something else, they hit them hard and repeatedly.

batter
*The burglar had **battered** down the door.*

flog
*In Nelson's day, sailors who stole would be **flogged** with a whip called a cat-o'nine-tails.*

pound
*Waves **pounded** the shore as the wind rose to screaming pitch.*

thrash
*The bully threatened, "Tom Brown, I shall **thrash** the living daylights out of you."*

beat (2) VERB

If you **beat** someone in a race or game, you defeat them or do better than them.

conquer
*William, Duke of Normandy, **conquered** England in 1066.*

lick INFORMAL
*Abdel really **licked** me in the 100 metres sprint race.*

run rings round INFORMAL
*Our speedy attackers **ran rings round** their lumbering defenders.*

thrash INFORMAL
*"It's a safe bet that we'll get **thrashed** when we play you," said Tim.*

wipe the floor with INFORMAL
*Our school team **wiped the floor with** kids much bigger than they were.*

beautiful ADJECTIVE

You say someone or something is **beautiful** if they are very pleasing to look at.

attractive
*People say my sister is **attractive**.*

delightful
*Mr Pobjoy said that they had a **delightful** evening at the ballet.*

gorgeous
*I overheard Dad telling Mum she looked **gorgeous**.*

lovely
*The photograph, I had to admit, even made my aunt look **lovely**.*

pretty
*Even some garden weeds can look **pretty** at certain times.*

stunning INFORMAL
*The sunset over the mountains was nothing less than **stunning**.*

ANTONYM: ugly or unattractive

beauty (1) NOUN

If a person has **beauty**, they have the quality of being beautiful.

elegance
*Every movement the duchess made had an **elegance** about it.*

good looks
*The actor possessed rugged **good looks**.*

loveliness
*The opera singer's **loveliness** was not matched by her selfish behaviour.*

beauty (2) NOUN

If a place has **beauty**, it has the quality of being beautiful.

charm
*This country cottage has tremendous **charm** and character.*

loveliness
*I think the **loveliness** of Athens is somewhat spoilt by the pollution.*

splendour
*Rome is famous for the **splendour** of its ancient buildings.*

ANTONYM: ugliness

because CONJUNCTION
Because is used with other words to give a reason for something.

as
As you've been so helpful, I'll treat you to an ice cream.

owing to
Owing to work on the track this Sunday, trains will be delayed.

since
"Since Fred is here, why don't we build a tree house?" my sister suggested.

thanks to
I got no pocket money, thanks to my brother telling tales on me.

bed NOUN
A **bed** is a piece of furniture that you lie on when you sleep.

Some types of bed:
bunk beds	hammock
double bed	inflatable bed
cot	single bed
cradle	sofa bed
futon	water bed

Some things that are put on a bed:
bedspread	pillow
blanket	pillowcase
duvet	quilt
eiderdown	sheet
mattress	sleeping bag

before ADVERB
If something happens **before**, it happens earlier than something else.

formerly
Formerly, Mrs Patterson was a teacher at my dad's old school.

previously
Previously, Mr Cruickshank had always let us off homework, but not today.

sooner than
*Each year spring seems to arrive **sooner than** it did the previous year.*

✔ Something that goes before something else **precedes** it.

begin VERB
If you **begin** something, you start it.

commence
*The king shouted "Let battle **commence**!" and the two knights thundered towards each other.*

embark on
*As soon as we'd **embarked on** our journey to the park, it started to rain.*

set about
*We **set about** digging the vegetable garden.*

start
*Dad told me to **start** my homework soon.*

ANTONYM: end

beginner NOUN
A **beginner** is someone who has just started to learn something.

learner
*Swimmers use the big pool, while **learners** use the shallower pool.*

novice
*Although a complete **novice**, Britney showed a flair for ski jumping.*

ANTONYM: veteran

beginning NOUN
The **beginning** of something is when or where it starts.

introduction
*In the **introduction**, the author explains how she came to write the book.*

opening
*The band played at the **opening** of the fête.*

origin
*The **origin** of the universe is still a mystery.*

ANTONYM: end

behave

behave VERB

If you **behave** in a particular way, you act that way.

act

*Emir is **acting** like a spoilt child.*

function

*"The girls are finally **functioning** as a team!" exclaimed the coach.*

operate

*Sally **operates** in a certain way to get what she wants.*

work

*Anoup **worked** methodically in order to get the work done.*

believe (1) VERB

If you **believe** someone, you accept that they are telling the truth.

accept

*It took some people a long time to **accept** that the world was round.*

be certain of

*"We have to **be certain of** your story before we can take action," warned the sergeant.*

have faith in

*It is important to **have faith in** your own ability, Grandad says.*

trust

*I **trust** my sister, even if she is rotten to me sometimes.*

✔ Something that you cannot believe is **unbelievable** or **incredible**.

ANTONYM: disbelieve or doubt

believe (2) VERB

If you **believe** that something is true, you think that it is true.

feel

*"How do you **feel** the match will go?" asked the interviewer.*

presume

*Mr Jackson said, "I **presume** you will all be handing in your homework tomorrow."*

suppose

*I **suppose** that the school sports day will be in July as usual.*

bell NOUN

A **bell** is a cup-shaped metal object with a piece inside it called a clapper that hits the side and makes a ringing sound.

Verbs that express the sound of bells:		
chime	peal	strike
clang	ring	tinkle
jingle	sound	toll

belongings NOUN

Your **belongings** are all the things that you own.

possessions

*Almost all their **possessions** were destroyed in the fire.*

property

*"Make sure your **property** is labelled," insisted Miss Carter.*

stuff INFORMAL

*The firefighters grabbed their **stuff** and jumped in the cab.*

below PREPOSITION OR ADVERB

If something is **below** something else, it is in a lower position.

beneath

***Beneath** the trees, bluebells were waving in the breeze.*

under

*With the help of a torch, I could read secretly **under** my duvet.*

underneath

***Underneath** the streets are hundreds of miles of sewers.*

ANTONYM: above

bend (1) VERB

When something **bends**, it becomes curved or crooked.

buckle

*The car **buckled** when the elephant sat on it.*

curve

*After the village, the road **curves** to the left.*

twist

*The ornament was made of glass **twisted** into patterns.*

22

warp
*My DVD **warped** when I left it in the sun.*

ANTONYM: straighten

bend (2) VERB
When you **bend**, you move your head and shoulders forwards and downwards.

crouch
*Lyra **crouched** behind the bushes, waiting for the policeman to turn away.*

duck
***Duck**, or you'll hit your head on the beam!*

stoop
*Farouk **stooped** to pick up a coin from the path.*

beside PREPOSITION
If one thing is **beside** another, it is next to it.

adjacent to
***Adjacent to** the station was an old signal box.*

alongside
*The lifeboat rowed up **alongside** the stricken yacht, and the crew jumped across.*

next to
*The boy sitting **next to** me kept prodding me with a ruler.*

besides PREPOSITION
Besides can mean in addition to.

apart from
***Apart from** some shorts and a T-shirt, I'm taking very little with me.*

other than
***Other than** our family, there was hardly anybody on the beach.*

best ADJECTIVE
Best is the superlative of good and well.

finest
*Wuffles is the **finest** dog food money can buy.*

foremost
*"This is the **foremost** house in the area," the agent began.*

leading
*The operation will be performed by the world's **leading** surgeon.*

outstanding
*Our birthday presents from Grandma are always **outstanding**.*

supreme
*The judges thought that our dog Crumpet was the **supreme** entrant in the competition.*

ANTONYM: worst

better (1) ADJECTIVE
Better is the comparative of good and well.

higher quality
*Steak is usually **higher quality** than other cuts of meat.*

more suitable
*The lightweight tent proved **more suitable** for the expedition.*

preferable
*Of the two designs, I think the red is **preferable**.*

superior
*Usually, **superior** products cost more than inferior ones.*

ANTONYM: worse

better (2) ADJECTIVE
If you are **better** after an illness, you are no longer ill.

healed
*The doctor told Sheila that her broken leg was completely **healed**.*

improved
*Gran was much **improved** after her operation.*

recovered
*Ali is now **recovered** after a bout of flu.*

beware VERB
If you tell someone to **beware** of something, you are warning them that it might be dangerous or harmful.

be careful
*"**Be careful**, child, for there are wolves in the forest!" said Red Riding Hood's mother.*

guard against
*With exams, it's important to **guard against** being over-confident.*

look out
***Look out!** Here comes another avalanche.*

watch out
***Watch out**, or that sail will hit you when the boat turns!*

a
b
c
d
e
f
g
h
i
j
k
l
m
n
o
p
q
r
s
t
u
v
w
x
y
z

A
B
C
D
E
F
G
H
I
J
K
L
M
N
O
P
Q
R
S
T
U
V
W
X
Y
Z

big (1) ADJECTIVE
Something or someone **big** is large.

colossal
To an ant, an elephant must seem colossal.

enormous
Why do singers always get presented with enormous bunches of flowers?

extensive
View our extensive range of furniture today!

giant
Get the new giant pack of Whizzo miracle washing liquid.

gigantic
The section of bridge required a gigantic crane to lift it.

huge
Gran gave me a huge hug.

immense
The floods had covered an immense area of the county.

infinite
Outer space is infinite, with no known limits.

mammoth
Barnum and Bailey's mammoth circus had two separate rings.

massive
"Astronomers believe a massive asteroid is heading for earth," said the newsreader.

mighty
Mighty Tarzan flexed his muscles, then swung off through the trees.

mountainous
The lady wrestler was truly mountainous and towered over her puny opponent.

roomy
"You'll find this is a roomy loft," the estate agent said.

sizable
Our house has a sizable garden.

spacious
The living room is spacious, but the kitchen is cramped.

vast
The Sahara Desert is a vast area of rolling sand dunes.

big (2) ADJECTIVE
Something **big** is important.

important
It was an important day in Sophie's life – her first at her new school.

momentous
The Prime Minister made the momentous decision – the country was going to war.

serious
A serious accident had blocked the road.

significant
Having an injured soldier to carry made a significant difference to their progress.

bit (1) NOUN
A **bit** of something is a small amount of it.

chunk
Sam broke off a chunk of chocolate and gobbled it up.

fraction
I arrived a fraction of a moment too late. The bus was just leaving.

fragment
Fragments of the wrecked aircraft were found all over the field.

morsel
"Kind sir, please spare me a morsel of food," begged Oliver.

part
A part of me wanted to stay and yet I was also desperate to leave.

piece
Marina cut the cake into pieces and took the largest one for herself.

scrap
My dad writes reminders to himself on scraps of paper.

bite VERB
If you **bite** something, you use your teeth to hold, cut or tear it.

champ
The horse champed at the bit as it waited impatiently for the race to begin.

chomp
Dad says that I chomp my food like a waste-disposal unit.

gnaw
*Mice had **gnawed** through the electric wires.*

nibble
*Some creature had **nibbled** at the chair leg.*

bitter ADJECTIVE
A **bitter** taste is sharp and unpleasant.

sour
*If you leave milk in the sun, it turns **sour**.*

tart
*The lemon cake was slightly **tart**.*

blame VERB
If someone **blames** a person for something bad that has happened, they believe that person caused it to happen.

accuse
*The woman was **accused** of kidnapping the young child.*

charge
*Police **charged** the man with being drunk and disorderly.*

hold responsible
*At the enquiry, the bus company was **held responsible** for the accident.*

block (1) VERB
If someone or something **blocks** a road or channel, they put something across it so that nothing can get through.

bar
*Access to the back road was **barred** by a police checkpoint.*

bung up INFORMAL
*I could hardly breathe, my nose was so **bunged up**.*

choke
*The traffic jam **choked** the road into town for many hours.*

clog up
*Don't pour liquid fat down the sink as it **clogs up** the drains when it sets.*

dam
*Beavers **dam** streams with logs to create a pool which will not freeze solid in winter.*

obstruct
*Uncle Pete tried to **obstruct** the door as I went through, but I ducked under his arm!*

block (2) VERB
If someone tries to **block** something, they try to stop it happening.

hinder
*Our dog, Jim, **hinders** Mum by attacking the vacuum cleaner.*

impede
*The walkers' progress was **impeded** by an angry goat on the path.*

obstruct
*The protesters were arrested for **obstructing** the police.*

prevent
*Residents **prevented** a nightclub from being built near their houses.*

thwart
*The wicked baron was **thwarted** in his evil plans by a quick-thinking boy.*

block (3) NOUN
A **block** is something put across a road or channel so that nothing can get through.

barrier
*For the parade, **barriers** were erected to keep the crowds back.*

blockage
*"There's a **blockage** in the drain under the sink," the plumber said.*

obstacle
*Alpa had to overcome many **obstacles** on his road to success.*

obstruction
*If you swallow chewing gum, it may cause an **obstruction** in your stomach.*

block (4) NOUN
A **block** is a large, rectangular, three-dimensional piece of something.

bar
*The robbers put the gold **bars** in the back of the getaway van.*

chunk
*A **chunk** of metal fell off the back of the truck as it left the scrap yard.*

lump
*With the help of a wheel, the potter formed the shapeless **lump** of clay into a vase.*

boast VERB

If you **boast**, you talk proudly about what you have or what you can do.

brag
*Alison couldn't resist **bragging** about her new DVD player.*

blow your own trumpet
*I prefer modest people to those who **blow their own trumpet**.*

crow
*Paulo was so busy **crowing** about his marks, that he didn't see Mrs Walker behind him.*

show off
*Brian is always **showing off** about the amount of pocket money he gets.*

boat NOUN

A **boat** is a floating vehicle for travelling across water.

craft
*At that distance, it was hard for the coastguard to identify the **craft**.*

ship
*Sir Francis Drake sailed in a **ship** he named the Golden Hind.*

vessel
*The tiny tug was nevertheless a sturdy **vessel**, capable of pulling much larger boats.*

Leisure boats:

canoe	raft
catamaran	rowing boat
dinghy	sailing boat
kayak	speedboat
powerboat	yacht

Working boats:

barge	liner
ferry	steamboat
galleon OLD-FASHIONED	tanker
hovercraft	trawler
hydrofoil	tug

Boats used in war:

aircraft carrier	frigate
cruiser	galleon OLD-FASHIONED
destroyer	submarine

body (1) NOUN

Your **body** is all of you, from your head to your feet.

build
*Although flyweight boxers only have a slight **build**, they are powerful for their size.*

figure
*My sister maintains her **figure** by practising yoga regularly.*

form
*A shadowy **form** hovered at the end of Nikki's bed, but it was only her mum, tucking her in!*

physique
*Most sportspeople lift weights in the gym to improve their **physique**.*

✔ The upper body is the **trunk** or **torso**.

body (2) NOUN

A **body** is a dead person.

cadaver AMERICAN
*"Let's get this **cadaver** to the morgue, sergeant," drawled the detective.*

corpse
*The doctor said quietly, "I think this **corpse** ought to go to the mortuary."*

remains
*The saint's **remains** lie in a stone tomb beneath the shrine.*

✔ A dead animal body is a **carcass**.

Some parts of the body:

ankle	foot	neck
arm	genitals	shin
calf	head	shoulder
chest	hip	teeth
elbow	knee	thigh
eye	leg	toe
eyelash	lips	tongue
finger	mouth	wrist

bog NOUN

A **bog** is an area of land that is always wet and spongy.

marsh
*The **marsh** is full of wild flowers at this time of year.*

morass
After the agricultural show had finished, the field was a morass.

quagmire
Thanks to the pouring rain, the fairground became a quagmire.

swamp
"Be careful of that swamp," Holmes warned.

boil VERB
When a liquid **boils**, or when you **boil** it, it starts to bubble and give off steam.

bubble
The witch cackled as she stirred the potion bubbling in the cauldron.

steam
The geyser steamed for an hour before erupting violently.

book NOUN
A **book** is a number of pages held together inside a cover.

✔ A word for all books is **literature**.

> **Some other words for a book:**
>
> | edition | publication |
> | hardback | volume |
> | paperback | work |
>
> **Some types of book:**
>
> | address book | exercise book |
> | album | guidebook |
> | annual | hymnbook |
> | anthology | jotter |
> | atlas | manual |
> | brochure | notebook |
> | catalogue | novel |
> | cookbook | reference book |
> | diary | scrapbook |
> | dictionary | storybook |
> | directory | textbook |
> | encyclopedia | thesaurus |

boring ADJECTIVE
Something **boring** is dull and uninteresting.

dreary
"That's a dreary picture," said Dad. "Who painted it?"

monotonous
The professor's monotonous voice droned on through the hot afternoon.

tedious
Waiting in traffic jams is a tedious business.

ANTONYM: interesting

boss NOUN
Someone's **boss** is the person in charge of the place where they work.

employer
My Dad's employer is an American.

head
The shop assistant worked so hard, she soon became head of her department.

leader
The party leader hoped one day to be elected Prime Minister.

manager
Dad is manager of a supermarket. Mum is manager of a shoe shop.

supervisor
Carol's supervisor let her have the afternoon off work to go to the doctor.

bossy ADJECTIVE
If you are **bossy**, you like to order other people around.

arrogant
The arrogant boss had a rather unfriendly management style.

domineering
The timid husband had a domineering wife.

overbearing
My Uncle Ted can be overbearing.

bother (1) NOUN
A **bother** is a trouble, fuss or difficulty.

inconvenience
We apologize for any inconvenience our repair work may cause you.

nuisance
"Toddlers can be a real nuisance – always getting in the way!" said Nurse Adams.

trouble
Miss Pollard apologized on arrival. "I don't want to be any trouble to you," she said.

bother (2) VERB

If something **bothers** you, you are worried about it.

annoy

*Mum said irritably, "Turn that music down please. It's really **annoying** me!"*

concern

*The pilot was clearly **concerned** about the poor weather.*

disturb

*The Kemps were **disturbed** by the disappearance of their dog.*

fluster

*My sister is easily **flustered**, especially if she's in a hurry.*

trouble

*"Please don't **trouble** to give me a lift. I'll get the bus," my gran offered.*

worry

*"Don't **worry**, you won't forget your lines," said Ajay.*

bottom (1) NOUN

The **bottom** of something is the lowest part of it.

base

*The **base** of the iceberg is hidden beneath the surface of the water.*

foot

*The chest of gold lay at the **foot** of a long, winding flight of stairs.*

ANTONYM: top

bottom (2) NOUN

The **bottom** is the lowest part of an ocean, sea or river.

bed

*To his utter delight, the prospector saw gold nuggets glinting on the river **bed**.*

depths

*The **depths** of the ocean are darker than we can imagine.*

floor

*The Titanic lay unseen and undisturbed on the sea **floor** for 70 years.*

ANTONYM: surface

bottom (3) NOUN

Your **bottom** is the part of your body that you sit on.

backside

*"Ashraf, get off your **backside** and give me a hand!" Dad said.*

behind

*My **behind** ached for days after the injection.*

buttocks

*Horse riding develops the muscles in one's **buttocks** and thighs.*

posterior

*The toddler fell on his **posterior**.*

rear end

*"Get lost, Alfie!" said Olly, and aimed a tennis ball at Alfie's **rear end**.*

bounce VERB

When an object **bounces**, it springs back from something after hitting it.

bob

*The White Rabbit **bobbed** up from nowhere.*

bound

*The ball **bounded** off the post, straight into the goalkeeper's hands.*

ricochet SAID "RIK-OSH-AY"

*During the gun battle, bullets **ricocheted** off the walls in a terrifying fashion.*

box NOUN

A **box** is a container with a firm base and sides, and usually a lid.

✔ A box in which a dead body is buried or cremated is a **coffin**.

> **Types of box:**
> | | | |
> |---|---|---|
> | carton | chest | package |
> | case | container | packet |
> | casket | crate | trunk |

brainy ADJECTIVE INFORMAL

Someone who is **brainy** is clever and good at learning things.

bright

*"We're looking for someone **bright** for the job," the interviewer said.*

brilliant
*You could tell Narinder was **brilliant** from the start. He could read fluently at the age of two.*

intelligent
*Air-traffic controllers have to be **intelligent** and alert.*

smart
*"As you're so **smart**, Rumpold, I'm promoting you!" the manager said.*

brave ADJECTIVE
A **brave** person is willing to do dangerous things and does not show any fear.

bold
*It was a **bold** move of the sisters to start their own dance studio.*

courageous
*Many ordinary situations demand **courageous** behaviour.*

daring
*The **daring** stuntwoman jumped across ten cars on her motorbike.*

fearless
*The **fearless** St George rode straight towards the dragon.*

intrepid
*The **intrepid** explorer risked death to reach the Pole.*

break (1) VERB
When an object **breaks**, or when it is **broken**, it becomes damaged or separates into pieces.

crack
*The giant egg **cracked**, and a pink beak pushed its way out.*

fracture
*"You have **fractured** your leg in three places," said the doctor.*

shatter
*The windscreen **shattered** as the car careered into the barrier.*

smash
*At the fête, there's a chance to **smash** plates by throwing balls at them.*

snap
*Sanjiv **snapped** the bar of chocolate in half and gave some to Kelly.*

splinter
*The boat's hull **splintered** as the novice yachtsman rammed the pier.*

break (2) NOUN
A **break** is a short period during which you rest or do something different.

breather INFORMAL
*"Let's stop for a **breather**," suggested Josie.*

interval
*Between the two acts of the play there will be an **interval** of 15 minutes.*

pause
*There was a **pause** of several seconds before the audience started to applaud.*

rest
*"What you need is a long **rest**," said the head teacher to the exhausted teacher.*

break down VERB
When a machine or a vehicle **breaks down**, it stops working.

conk out INFORMAL
*The motorcyclist looked helpless. "Give us a push please, mate. My bike's **conked out**."*

fail
*When the steam train **failed**, a diesel had to tow it back to the depot.*

go wrong
*"I just knew that fancy vacuum cleaner would **go wrong**," Mum sighed.*

seize up
*Our lawn mower **seized up** when a twig got jammed in the blades.*

✔ If someone's car has a **breakdown**, it stops working during a journey.

break up VERB
If something **breaks up**, it comes apart.

disintegrate
*Because of the explosion, the plane **disintegrated** in midair.*

fall apart
*My wonderful go-kart **fell apart** during its maiden trip.*

✔ When a married couple break up, they **separate** or get a **divorce**.

A B C D E F G H I J K L M N O P Q R S T U V W X Y Z

breakable ADJECTIVE
Something that is **breakable** is easy to break.

brittle
*Dry earth is **brittle** and crumbles easily.*

delicate
*"Handle that antique vase gently. It's **delicate**," the auctioneer shouted.*

easily broken
*Pottery is **easily broken**.*

flimsy
*In traditional Japanese houses the interior walls are often **flimsy**, almost see-through.*

fragile
*The label on the box read "**Fragile**", but the camera within was damaged beyond repair.*

breathless ADJECTIVE
If you are **breathless**, you are breathing very fast or with difficulty.

gasping
*By the time we reached the ridge of the hill, we were **gasping**.*

out of breath
*My gran gets **out of breath** even when she bends down.*

puffed out INFORMAL
*After running for the train I was **puffed out**.*

puffing and panting INFORMAL
*By the end of the fathers' race Dad was **puffing and panting**.*

wheezing
*The poor asthmatic girl was still **wheezing** even after using her inhaler.*

bright (1) ADJECTIVE
Bright colours or things are strong and startling.

brilliant
*The **brilliant** diamond glittered in the light.*

dazzling
*We stepped out into **dazzling** sunshine.*

gleaming
*I polished Dad's car until it was **gleaming**.*

glistening
*The **glistening** dewdrop sat like a jewel on the leaf.*

glittering
*For the show, Mum made me a **glittering** dress with sequins all over.*

glowing
*The **glowing** fire lit the old cottage kitchen far into the night.*

shimmering
*The sun rose as the ship sailed out onto the **shimmering** sea.*

shining
*The **shining** stars lit up the night.*

twinkling
*From the opposite shore we could see the **twinkling** lights of the town.*

vivid
*The parrot's feathers were **vivid** shades of red, green and blue.*

ANTONYM: dim or dull

bright (2) ADJECTIVE
Someone who is **bright** is clever.

clever
*My aunt is **clever**. At antique fairs, she never misses a bargain.*

intelligent
*Collies are **intelligent** dogs and can understand many commands.*

quick-witted
*Reginald's **quick-witted** action saved his house from burning down.*

smart
*People say I'm **smart** because I'm as quick as lightning at identifying pop songs.*

bright (3) ADJECTIVE
Someone who is **bright** is cheerful and brisk.

brisk
*With a **brisk** "Good morning, class," Mr Moor strode into the room.*

cheerful
*A **cheerful** manner is important if you are dealing with the public.*

jolly
*My grandpa is a **jolly** man who always seems to be smiling.*

light-hearted
*In our class, discussions are always **light-hearted**, never too serious.*

lively
*Mrs Fenkle is a **lively** teacher, who always makes lessons interesting.*

brilliant (1) ADJECTIVE
A **brilliant** colour or light is extremely bright.

bright
*The dentist shone a **bright** light into my mouth so he could see my teeth clearly.*

dazzling
*The magnificent ruby was a **dazzling** red.*

sparkling
*As the plane came in to land, we could see the **sparkling** city lights below.*

brilliant (2) ADJECTIVE
Someone who is **brilliant** is extremely clever or skilful.

exceptional
*Parvinder is an **exceptional** pupil and is certain to go to university.*

gifted
*The Russian was a **gifted** pianist before he became a conductor.*

talented
*Nicole is a **talented** actress who would like to go to stage school.*

bring VERB
If you **bring** something with you when you go to a place, you take it with you.

carry
*A hotel porter's job is to **carry** people's luggage to their rooms.*

convey
*The minibus **conveyed** people out to the waiting aircraft.*

transport
*Cable cars **transport** sightseers to the top of the mountain.*

bubbles PLURAL NOUN
Bubbles are balls of gas in a liquid.

fizz
*"My cola has lost its **fizz**," Wayne complained.*

foam
*As the tap kept running, the **foam** spilt over the sides of the bath.*

froth
*As we added the lemonade to the orange juice, **froth** started to appear on top.*

suds
*The washing-up bowl was full of **suds**.*

bug NOUN INFORMAL
A **bug** is an infection or virus that makes you ill.

disease
*The **disease** spread rapidly, and soon thousands were infected.*

germ
*Lydia must have caught some sort of **germ**, because she's very poorly.*

infection
*Hospitals have to fight a constant battle against **infection**.*

virus
*Antibiotics are not effective in curing a **virus**.*

build VERB
If you **build** something, you make it from all its parts.

assemble
*"**Assembling** a bookcase from a kit is easy," Dad said. Ours collapsed two days later.*

construct
*Grandad helped me **construct** a tree house in our back garden.*

erect
*The monument was **erected** within a week.*

ANTONYM: demolish

build up VERB
If something **builds up**, it becomes greater.

accumulate
*Snow **accumulated** on the snowball as it rolled downhill.*

amass
*Old Mr Godber **amassed** a fortune through dealing in scrap metal.*

collect
*A layer of dust and dead flies had **collected** on top of my wardrobe.*

building

building NOUN

A **building** is a structure with walls and a roof.

construction

The huge **construction** on the edge of town is going to be the new sports centre.

structure

The Eiffel Tower in Paris is perhaps the world's best-known **structure**.

Buildings to live in:

bungalow	maisonette
cabin	mansion
castle	palace
cottage	semidetached house
flat	terraced house
house	tower block

Buildings to work in or visit:

barn	police station
college	post office
factory	power station
fire station	restaurant
gallery	school
garage	shop
hospital	skyscraper
laboratory	store
library	supermarket
lighthouse	theatre
museum	warehouse
office block	windmill

Buildings to worship in:

cathedral	mosque
chapel	synagogue
church	temple

---

bully VERB

If someone **bullies** you into doing something, they make you do it by using force or threats.

frighten

The boys who **frightened** me by calling me names got into trouble.

intimidate

"Don't try to **intimidate** me," the old lady called. "I'm not afraid of you!"

terrorize

Some fanatics try to **terrorize** others by setting off bombs.

threaten

When the bully **threatened** me, I used my judo skills to stop him in his tracks.

bump (1) VERB

If you **bump** into something, you knock into it accidentally.

collide with

My bike **collided with** a tree at top speed.

knock

Julian **knocked** his knee against the table leg.

strike

Allegra fell downstairs, **striking** her head on the banister.

✔ To **bump into someone** is to meet them by chance.

bump (2) NOUN

A **bump** is a sound like something knocking into something else.

thud

I heard a **thud** from upstairs – my sister had fallen out of bed.

thump

The apple landed with a **thump** on the ground beneath the tree.

bump (3) NOUN

A **bump** is a raised, uneven part of a surface.

bulge

The **bulge** under the shoplifter's coat proved to be a clock radio.

lump

I couldn't sleep last night because of a **lump** in my mattress.

swelling

When I banged my head I got a **swelling** over my eye, but it soon went down.

bumpy ADJECTIVE

Something that is **bumpy** has a rough, uneven surface.

rough

The pirate's chin was **rough**, as though he had shaved with a knife and fork.

uneven

Our soccer pitch is **uneven**, which makes the ball's bounce unpredictable.

bunch (1) NOUN
A **bunch** is a group of things together.

bundle
*The servant gathered a **bundle** of twigs.*

cluster
***Clusters** of grapes hung from the vine.*

✔ A bunch of flowers is a **bouquet**, **posy** or **spray**.
A bunch of flowers for a funeral is a **wreath**.

bunch (2) NOUN
A **bunch** is a group of people.

crowd
*The **crowd** grew restless as the floodlights stayed off.*

gang
*In the old days, **gangs** of sailors would use force to persuade men to join the navy.*

party
*A **party** of people from each school turned up for the tug-of-war.*

burglar NOUN
A **burglar** is someone who breaks into buildings and steals things.

intruder
*Dad woke up and realized that there was an **intruder** downstairs.*

robber
*The traveller was set upon by **robbers**, who stole his money.*

thief
***Thieves** broke into the warehouse and stole 100 televisions.*

burn (1) VERB
If something is **burning**, it is on fire.

be alight
*The stove **was** still **alight** when we came down in the morning.*

blaze
*A fire **blazed** merrily in Mole's sitting room.*

flame
*The barbecue **flamed** up around the burgers.*

flicker
*The fire **flickered** and crackled.*

✔ Something burning is said to be **ablaze**.

burn (2) VERB
To **burn** something can mean to damage or destroy it with fire.

char
*The barbecue was too hot and **charred** the sausages.*

scorch
*The baking sun had **scorched** the dry grass on the prairies.*

shrivel
*The heat of the desert had **shrivelled** even the toughest of the plants.*

singe
*I leaned too close to the bonfire and **singed** my hair.*

burst VERB
When something **bursts**, or you **burst** it, it splits open suddenly.

break
*The coffin **broke** open and the zombie's hands grasped the fractured lid.*

explode
*Shells were **exploding** just behind the enemy trenches.*

rupture
*A water pipe had **ruptured**.*

split
*With the force of the player's shot, the leather ball had **split**.*

bury VERB
If something is **buried** under something, it is covered by it.

conceal
*The secret door was **concealed** behind the bookshelves in the library.*

cover
*I couldn't find my homework as I had accidentally **covered** it with my dirty socks!*

hide
*Sometimes Dad **hides** a bone in the garden so that our dog Sadie can find it and dig it up.*

secrete
*The thief **secreted** the stolen jewels in a box under the floorboards.*

*See **hide** (2)*

a
b
c
d
e
f
g
h
i
j
k
l
m
n
o
p
q
r
s
t
u
v
w
x
y
z

business

business (1) NOUN
A **business** is an organization that produces or sells goods, or provides a service.

company
*My mum runs her own **company**.*

corporation
*Whizzo Fireworks is part of a big **corporation** making flares and explosives for quarries.*

firm
*My uncle's **firm** deals in electrical supplies.*

organization
*"Grappo Inc," boasted the president, "is a big **organization** full of high achievers."*

business (2) NOUN
Business is work relating to buying and selling goods and services.

industry
*The steel **industry** requires plenty of water for cooling the metal.*

trade
*The clothing business is sometimes called the rag **trade**.*

business (3) NOUN
Business is a general word for any event, situation or activity.

affair
*"That Baskerville murder was a strange **affair**," said Sherlock Holmes.*

issue
*Who owned the buried treasure? It was a complex **issue**!*

matter
*"Stop waffling and stick to the **matter** in hand," the chairman cut in.*

busy (1) ADJECTIVE
If you are **busy**, you are doing something.

employed
*Amal would clearly be **employed** for the next half hour, dealing with a difficult customer.*

hard at work
*My brother was **hard at work** revising when his friends came round.*

occupied
*I was **occupied** looking after my baby brother.*

working
*I was **working** on my school project when I was interrupted by the phone ringing.*

ANTONYM: idle or unoccupied

---

busy (2) ADJECTIVE
A **busy** place is full of people doing things or moving about.

bustling
*Trafalgar Square is the **bustling** heart of London.*

hectic
*All our family lead **hectic** lives.*

lively
*There is a **lively** market in the town centre every Saturday.*

but CONJUNCTION
But is used to introduce an idea that is opposite to what has gone before.

however
*The games were about to start. **However**, I felt poorly and sat in the corner.*

nevertheless
*In my opinion, Sunita had the best fancy dress. **Nevertheless**, Emma got the prize.*

on the other hand
*My sister said she'd had a good time. **On the other hand**, she always says things like that.*

yet
*Back home, Mum ordered us to bed, **yet** I wasn't really tired.*

buy VERB
If you **buy** something, you get it by paying money for it.

acquire
*The school **acquired** a piece of land to extend the playing field.*

obtain
*Dad **obtained** tickets for the match.*

pay for
*We saved up our pocket money and used it to **pay for** a new CD player.*

purchase
*"My good man, where in your emporium can I **purchase** a handbag?" sniffed Lady Bracknell.*

Cc

café NOUN

A **café** is a place where you can buy light meals and drinks.

coffee shop
*My sister took me into her favourite **coffee shop** for a treat.*

snack bar
*Dad remembers when that expensive restaurant was a simple **snack bar**.*

teashop
*On holiday, we had tea and scones in an old-fashioned **teashop**.*

call (1) VERB

If you **call** someone or something a particular name, that is their name.

christen
*My mum has **christened** her little soft-top car William.*

name
*My parents wanted to **name** me Humphrey, but changed their minds.*

call (2) VERB

If you **call** someone, you telephone them.

phone
*"Dad just **phoned** to say he'll be home shortly," I told Mum.*

ring
*Lisa **rang** the hospital to see how her brother was doing.*

telephone
*"If you **telephone** between twelve and one o'clock, you'll catch me," the salesman said.*

call off VERB

If something is **called off**, it is cancelled.

abandon
*When the heavy rain turned to snow, the referee decided that the match should be **abandoned**.*

cancel
*Owing to lack of support, the dance had to be **cancelled**.*

postpone
*Because of building repairs, we had to **postpone** our bowling until Tuesday.*

calm (1) ADJECTIVE

Someone who is **calm** is quiet and does not show any worry or excitement.

composed
*Mrs Yamamoto is a very **composed**, businesslike woman.*

level-headed
*Sanjay is a **level-headed** individual who would never panic in a crisis.*

relaxed
*Cameron was so **relaxed** about his exam, he fell asleep on the first page.*

unflappable INFORMAL
*The lifeboat crew were selected for being **unflappable** as well as skilled sailors.*

ANTONYM: excitable

calm (2) ADJECTIVE

If the sea is **calm**, the water is not moving very much.

peaceful
*The sea was **peaceful** as we walked along the beach in the early morning.*

quiet
*After the storm the sea became **quiet** again.*

still
*The lake was absolutely **still**, reflecting the mountains behind.*

tranquil
*It was a hot, sunny day and the children enjoyed swimming in the **tranquil** bay.*

ANTONYM: rough

calm down VERB

If you **calm** someone **down**, you help make them less upset or excited.

quieten
*A lollipop helped to **quieten** the squealing toddler.*

soothe
*Some farmers turn on the radio to **soothe** pigs in their pens.*

a
b
c
d
e
f
g
h
i
j
k
l
m
n
o
p
q
r
s
t
u
v
w
x
y
z

cancel VERB

If you **cancel** something that has been arranged, you stop it from happening.

abandon
*The match was **abandoned** at half-time when the floodlights failed.*

abort
*Mission Control decided to **abort** the mission and bring the shuttle back.*

call off
*When I caught chickenpox, Mum and Dad **called off** the party.*

scrap INFORMAL
*"Let's **scrap** the idea of Paris, and go to Rome instead," Dad suggested.*

capable ADJECTIVE

Someone who is **capable** is able to do something well.

able
*My dad is an **able** businessman.*

accomplished
*Rajesh is an **accomplished** violinist.*

competent
*Sir Winston Churchill was a surprisingly **competent** artist.*

efficient
*Mrs Kemp was very **efficient**; everything was done to a tight schedule.*

skilful
*My sister is a **skilful** horsewoman, with several medals to her name.*

ANTONYM: incompetent

captain NOUN

A **captain** is the officer in charge of a ship or aeroplane.

commander
*Uncertain what to do, Lieutenant Zarg called the spacecraft **commander** to the bridge.*

master
*The **master** of the oil tanker reluctantly gave the order to abandon ship.*

pilot
*"It looks as if we're in for some turbulence," the **pilot** announced.*

skipper
*Trawler **skippers** and their crews have to endure awful weather conditions.*

capture VERB

If someone **captures** someone or something, they take them prisoner.

arrest
*Police **arrested** the woman on suspicion of blackmail.*

kidnap
*The villains **kidnapped** the wealthy businessman's son and held him hostage.*

nab INFORMAL
*Sergeant Philpot **nabbed** the burglar as he tried to make his escape.*

take captive
*After being **taken captive**, the explorer was imprisoned in a hut.*

ANTONYM: release

car NOUN

A **car** is a four-wheeled road vehicle with an engine and room to carry a few passengers.

automobile
*"This motorcar," boasted Mr Toad, "is the finest **automobile** ever built."*

banger INFORMAL
*Our new teacher drives a real old **banger**.*

motorcar
*The sign read, "This road is unsuitable for **motorcars**".*

✔ The word **vehicle** can be used for a car, but also for other forms of transport, especially those with wheels.

Some kinds of car:	
4x4 (four by four or four-wheel drive)	Mini™
	off-road vehicle
convertible	people carrier
coupé	racing car
estate car	saloon
hatchback	sedan
Jeep™	soft top
Land Rover™	sports car
limousine	vintage car

care (1) VERB

If you **care** about something or someone, you are concerned about them and interested in them.

be concerned

*Yolanda didn't seem to **be concerned** about next week's test.*

bother

*"If you don't care about the state of your room, why should I **bother**?" my mother snapped.*

mind

*Graham didn't **mind** if Sanjiv borrowed some of his pens.*

care (2) NOUN

A **care** is a worry or trouble.

anxiety

*The twins hadn't returned, and Dad was showing signs of **anxiety**.*

concern

*Our **concern** is that Midori will miss too much school while she's off with mumps.*

trouble

*"Please don't go to any **trouble**. I'm happy to walk home," I said.*

worry

*One **worry** for the head teacher was what to do if several teachers were ill at once.*

care (3) NOUN

If you do something with **care**, you concentrate very hard on it so that you don't make any mistakes.

attention

***Attention** to detail is an important aspect of an architect's work.*

caution

*You must always exercise **caution** when you cross a road.*

ANTONYM: carelessness

care for VERB

If you **care for** a person or animal, you look after them.

look after

*Connor and I **looked after** Mum when she was ill.*

nurse

*Mrs Nelson **nursed** her sick husband for some months before he recovered.*

tend

*We take it in turns to **tend** the three class guinea pigs.*

ANTONYM: neglect

careful (1) ADJECTIVE

If someone is **careful**, they act sensibly and with care.

alert

*"Be **alert** at all times," the major warned. "You don't know who's out there!"*

attentive

*The nurse was very **attentive** when she stitched up Paul's cut forehead.*

cautious

*I have learnt always to be **cautious** about so-called "free" offers.*

sensible

*My gran is very **sensible** and always takes a coat if the weather looks doubtful.*

wary

*The barons were right to be **wary** of King John's cunning schemes.*

careful (2) ADJECTIVE

Something that is **careful** shows a concern for detail.

accurate

*If you work in a shop, it's important to be **accurate** in giving change.*

meticulous

*Alyssa produces **meticulous** work. She gets very upset if the slightest detail is criticized.*

painstaking

*I admired Nicholas for his **painstaking** work. His painting took weeks to finish.*

precise

*"Be very **precise** in your workings," said Mr Matthews, our maths teacher.*

thorough

*Mrs Chan is very **thorough**; she always cleans behind her furniture.*

ANTONYM: careless

careful (3) ADJECTIVE

If you are **careful** in what you say, you think before you speak.

discreet

*Jamila was **discreet** in not mentioning the party, in case Tanya hadn't been invited.*

tactful

*Shopkeepers have to be **tactful**, for some customers are easily offended.*

ANTONYM: careless

careless ADJECTIVE

If you are **careless**, you do not pay enough attention to what you are doing.

inaccurate

*The clerk's **inaccurate** adding up cost the company thousands of pounds.*

slapdash

*"This is **slapdash** work, Rachel," snapped Miss Greer. "Do it again slowly!"*

slipshod

***Slipshod** tiling by the builders caused our roof to leak.*

sloppy INFORMAL

*Mr Ismail told me off for my **sloppy** handwriting.*

ANTONYM: careful

carry VERB

When you **carry** something, you hold it and take it somewhere.

convey

*The robot arm **conveyed** the large nut to the bolt, and screwed them together.*

lug

*It was hard work **lugging** the case upstairs.*

transport

*Mrs Bartlett **transported** the table to her home by car.*

carry on VERB

If you **carry on** with something, you continue doing it.

continue

*"Please **continue** with what you were doing," the head teacher said when she came in.*

persevere

*It pays off, in the end, to **persevere** with a job.*

persist

*"If you **persist** in talking, you'll lose your playtime," Mrs Rasheed warned.*

proceed

*Grandad took a sip of his tea and then **proceeded** with his story.*

castle NOUN

A **castle** is a large building with walls or ditches round it to protect it from attack.

fort

*The cavalry rode out from their **fort**, trumpets blaring and guns blazing.*

fortress

*On the very peak of the mountain stood the enemy **fortress**.*

stronghold

*King Edward I built **strongholds** in Wales.*

catch (1) VERB

If you **catch** a person or animal, you capture them.

arrest

*Navy police **arrested** the drunken sailor.*

capture

*By luck, the cowboys managed to **capture** the runaway horse.*

ensnare

*The unfortunate trespasser found herself **ensnared** in barbed wire.*

trap

*In the forests of Russia, hunters **trap** animals for their skins.*

catch (2) NOUN

A **catch** is a hidden difficulty.

disadvantage

*One of the **disadvantages** of having long hair is that it can get very tangled.*

drawback

*There is a **drawback** to eating too much chocolate. It can make you feel sick!*

snag

*When putting the shelves up we came across a **snag** – we didn't have enough screws.*

cause (1) VERB

If someone or something **causes** something, they make it happen.

bring about
*The curse of the Baskervilles **brought about** the family's doom.*

create
*Last night some lads **created** a disturbance in our street.*

lead to
*More policemen on the beat **led to** a drop in the crime rate.*

produce
*Who would have thought that a small baby would **produce** so much noise?*

cause (2) NOUN

The **cause** of something is the thing that makes it happen.

origin
*The **origin** of the tradition was a mystery.*

source
*Gambling was the **source** of all the earl's troubles.*

cautious ADJECTIVE

Someone who is **cautious** acts carefully to avoid possible danger or disappointment.

careful
*Ashley was **careful** about handling the precious eggs.*

wary
*The sparrows were **wary** of the nearby cat.*

ANTONYM: reckless

celebration NOUN

A **celebration** is an occasion to mark a happy day or event.

Types of celebration:

anniversary party	fête
banquet	gala
birthday party	jubilee
carnival	party
feast	reunion
festival	wedding

centre NOUN

The **centre** of an object or area is the middle of it.

core
*The earth's **core** consists of molten rock.*

focus
*"Maths is going to be the **focus** of our work today," Mrs Watson said.*

heart
*In the **heart** of the city, a musician played on a street corner.*

hub
*At the **hub** of operations was my brother, with his walkie-talkie set.*

middle
*The bull's-eye is in the **middle** of a dartboard.*

certain (1) ADJECTIVE

If you are **certain** about something, you are sure it is true.

confident
*Shula was **confident** that the rumour she had heard was true.*

convinced
*Al was **convinced** that he would pass his exam.*

positive
*"Are you **positive** that's what you want for your birthday?" Mum asked.*

sure
*"I'm **sure** I put my homework in my bag, but I can't find it," I said.*

ANTONYM: uncertain

certain (2) ADJECTIVE

If something is **certain** to happen, it is likely to happen.

inevitable
*It was **inevitable** that the bully would meet his match before long.*

likely
*According to the weather forecast, it's **likely** to be a sunny afternoon.*

unavoidable
*When its brakes failed, the lorry faced an **unavoidable** collision.*

ANTONYM: unlikely

certainly ADVERB

Certainly can mean without any doubt.

definitely

*"Put me down for a ticket," Dad said. "I'm **definitely** going to the game."*

undoubtedly

*The horse was **undoubtedly** the fastest that Jo had ridden.*

without doubt

***Without doubt**, geography was John's favourite subject.*

chair NOUN

A **chair** is a seat for one person to sit on, with a back and legs.

> Types of chair:
> armchair   highchair
> deckchair   office chair
> dining chair   rocking chair

chance (1) NOUN

If there is a **chance** that something will happen, it might happen.

danger

*At oil refineries, there is always a **danger** of fire breaking out.*

likelihood

*With those clouds, there was a **likelihood** of rain before long.*

possibility

*"Is there any **possibility** of a lift, please?" Hamal asked.*

probability

*It is a **probability** that humans will one day walk on Mars.*

chance (2) NOUN

Something that happens by **chance** happens unexpectedly, without being planned.

accident

*It was totally by **accident** that Mum bumped into her old friend.*

coincidence

*"What a **coincidence**!" Grandad gasped. "I went to that school too!"*

fortune

*By good **fortune**, a passer-by heard the calls of the stricken climber.*

luck

*The tennis player's injury was just bad **luck**.*

stroke of luck

*By a **stroke of luck**, the massive doors were unguarded.*

change (1) VERB

When something **changes**, or you **change** it, it becomes different.

alter

*Gavin has really **altered** since he won the "Be a Pop Star" competition.*

convert

*Dad **converted** the old shed into a play hut.*

mutate

*Before Kirk's eyes, the handsome crewman **mutated** into a fanged, drooling monster.*

transform

*Bond's car **transformed** into a boat.*

change (2) VERB

If you **change** something, you swap or replace it.

exchange

*We had to take my new shoes back and **exchange** them for a larger size.*

replace

*Today Mr Woo **replaced** his old banger with a smooth sports car.*

substitute

*"What happens if you **substitute** milk for water?" the teacher asked.*

swap

*Dylan **swapped** his cards for Salman's.*

trade

*Mum joked that she wanted to **trade** my dad for a newer model!*

change (3) NOUN

A **change** is a difference or alteration in something.

difference

*Mum and I noticed the **difference** in Gran after her illness.*

A
B
C
D
E
F
G
H
I
J
K
L
M
N
O
P
Q
R
S
T
U
V
W
X
Y
Z

metamorphosis
Caterpillars undergo an amazing **metamorphosis** *into butterflies.*

transformation
When Mum emerged from the hairdresser's, what a **transformation**!

character NOUN
Someone's **character** is all the qualities which combine to form their personality.

nature
It was not in Abigail's **nature** *to be rude.*

personality
Gran had a bubbly **personality**, *and was always making friends.*

temperament
A dog's **temperament** *depends largely on how it is treated.*

charge VERB
If something or someone **charges**, they rush forward.

attack
The infantry **attacked** *the fortress at dawn.*

rampage
Boadicea's angry tribesmen **rampaged** *through the streets, yelling and whooping.*

run wild
Leaving their longships, the Viking marauders **ran wild** *in the Saxon village.*

rush
When the bell went, Boris **rushed** *for the door, only to be hauled back.*

storm
On D-Day 1944, Allied troops **stormed** *the beaches and cliffs of Normandy.*

chase VERB
If you **chase** someone, you run after them or follow them in order to catch them.

follow
Fans **followed** *the pop idol wherever he went.*

hound
Reporters **hounded** *the star until she gave them an interview.*

hunt
Lions **hunt** *antelope as their prey.*

pursue
Detectives **pursued** *the gangster to South America.*

track
Sniffer dogs **tracked** *the thief to a disused dockside warehouse.*

cheap ADJECTIVE
Something that is **cheap** costs very little money.

bargain
My **bargain** *laptop computer cost half of what most people pay.*

economical
My old car is very **economical** *on fuel, but costs more in repairs.*

inexpensive
The jacket was **inexpensive** *but looked very smart.*

reasonable
Mum thought that it was a **reasonable** *price for a second-hand mountain bike.*

cheat (1) VERB
If someone **cheats**, they lie or do unfair things to win or get what they want.

con INFORMAL
The thief **conned** *his way into the old woman's house by asking if he could use her phone for an emergency.*

deceive
"It's no good trying to **deceive** *me," Mum said. "I know you're up to something!"*

double-cross INFORMAL
The thief **double-crossed** *his accomplice and took all the cash.*

dupe
The stamp collectors were **duped** *into buying some very convincing fakes.*

rip off INFORMAL
"We were **ripped off** *there!" snorted my brother disgustedly, as we left the burger bar.*

swindle
The cashier had systematically **swindled** *the bank for years before she was caught.*

trick
Trying to **trick** *his pursuers, the getaway driver doubled back.*

A
B
C
D
E
F
G
H
I
J
K
L
M
N
O
P
Q
R
S
T
U
V
W
X
Y
Z

cheat (2) NOUN

A **cheat** is a person who lies or does unfair things to win or get what they want.

con man INFORMAL
*The **con man** pretended to be from the electricity company.*

double-crosser
*The gangster snarled "You dirty **double-crosser!**" and pulled the trigger.*

swindler
*The **swindler** sold villas to his clients which did not really exist.*

check (1) VERB

If you **check** something, you examine it to make sure that everything is all right.

assess
*Miss Connolly **assessed** our term's work before writing her report.*

examine
*Sherlock Holmes picked up the knife and **examined** it.*

inspect
*The council team **inspected** the food cupboards carefully.*

test
*To **test** our multiplication tables, Mr Murphy fires questions at us.*

check (2) NOUN

A **check** is an inspection to make sure that everything is all right.

assessment
*Every soldier has to do his PFA, or Physical Fitness **Assessment**.*

check-up
*After his fall, Grandad had to visit the doctor's for a **check-up**.*

examination
*Detectives carried out a minute **examination** of the crime scene.*

inspection
*Even the best schools are subject to regular **inspections**.*

test
*Older vehicles have to go through a safety **test** to ensure that they are roadworthy.*

cheeky ADJECTIVE

Someone who is **cheeky** is rude and disrespectful, often in an amusing way.

disrespectful
*It's a mistake to be **disrespectful** to teachers.*

impertinent
*What an **impertinent** thing to say to someone who has helped you!*

impudent
*The **impudent** waiter said the cheekiest things to his customers.*

rude
*"Try not to be **rude** to people, even if they are unpleasant to you," said Mum.*

ANTONYM: respectful or polite

cheerful ADJECTIVE

A **cheerful** person is happy.

bright
*I'm quite **bright** in the morning.*

cheery
*The postman gave us a **cheery** wave.*

chirpy INFORMAL
*Despite her aches, Gran is always **chirpy**.*

jolly
*The **jolly** poacher chuckled as he popped another salmon in his bag.*

light-hearted
*After Scrooge changed his character, he was **light-hearted** at Christmas.*

merry
*Mum and her friend had a **merry** time looking at old school photos.*

chew VERB

When you **chew** something, you use your teeth to break it up in your mouth before swallowing it.

chomp
*The horse **chomped** its way through a field of lettuces.*

crunch
*Some people **crunch** their lollipops. Others suck them.*

gnaw
*Beavers had **gnawed** away the bark of the tree.*

munch
*I hate it when people **munch** their lunch with their mouth open.*

child NOUN
A **child** is a young person who is not yet an adult.

juvenile
*In the eyes of the law, anyone under 18 is a **juvenile**.*

kid INFORMAL
*Mum takes several **kids** to school, not just us.*

nipper INFORMAL
*"When I was a **nipper**," Grandad said, "I used to climb that oak tree."*

youngster
*The **youngster** ran out into the road without even looking.*

✔ A child whose parents are dead is an **orphan**.

See **baby**

childish ADJECTIVE
If someone is **childish**, they are not acting in an adult way.

immature
*To lark around like that was **immature** for a man of his age.*

infantile
*Jafar's temper tantrum was very **infantile**.*

juvenile
*"Such **juvenile** behaviour must be punished," the head teacher said grimly.*

choice (1) NOUN
A **choice** is a range of different things that are available to choose from.

selection
*What a **selection** of chocolates greeted my eyes when I opened the box!*

variety
*There was a **variety** of films to choose from on the plane.*

choice (2) NOUN
A **choice** is something that you choose.

option
*We had no **option** but to accept a refund when our flights were cancelled.*

preference
*My **preference** is action movies rather than romances.*

selection
*To her disgust, the judges' **selection** did not include Mrs Whipple's fairy cakes.*

✔ If you have a choice whether or not to do something, it is **optional**.

choose VERB
If you **choose** something, you decide to have it or do it.

opt for
*Mum and Dad couldn't decide which holiday to **opt for**: Florida or France.*

pick
*My mean sister always **picks** the chocolates that I want.*

select
*The archer **selected** an arrow.*

single out
*The dog show judge **singled out** Wuffles as being especially intelligent.*

circle VERB
If someone or something **circles** an object, they move around it in a circle.

lap
*The cyclist **lapped** the track for the final time.*

orbit
*The earth takes around 365 days, or one year, to **orbit** the sun.*

✔ To sail round the world is to **circumnavigate** it.

See **go round (1)**

circumstances NOUN
The **circumstances** of a situation or event are the conditions that affect what happens.

background
*Our history teacher explained the **background** of the American Civil War.*

context
*The police had to consider the **context** of the accident.*

situation
*The **situation** was difficult for everyone.*

A
B
C
D
E
F
G
H
I
J
K
L
M
N
O
P
Q
R
S
T
U
V
W
X
Y
Z

claim VERB

If you **claim** that something is the case, you say that it is so.

allege
*The witness **alleged** that Jones had threatened several people.*

argue
*The boss **argued** that it was fair to sack someone who worked slowly.*

declare
*The smuggler **declared** that he had nothing illegal in his case.*

insist
*The arrested woman **insisted** that the officer had made a mistake.*

maintain
*Hal **maintained** that only Leroy was better than him at basketball.*

class (1) NOUN

A **class** is a group of pupils or students who are taught together.

group
*Mum's quilting **group** meets on Tuesday.*

set
*My clever sister is in the top maths **set**.*

stream
*At the grammar school, children were put in **streams** according to their ability.*

tutor group
*Jennifer is in Mrs Burton's **tutor group**.*

class (2) NOUN

A **class** of people or things is a group of them that are alike in some way.

category
*Nitesh entered the junior **category** of the poetry competition.*

kind
*Beavenutti is the best restaurant of its **kind** in the area.*

sort
*"What is your favourite **sort** of music?" Carly asked Hannah.*

type
*The market stall sold lots of different **types** of vegetables and fruits.*

clean (1) ADJECTIVE

If something is **clean**, it is free from dirt or unwanted marks.

immaculate
*The car was **immaculate** when Dad bought it, but filthy two days later.*

spotless
*"I want this cabin **spotless**," rasped the captain, "or you're for the high jump!"*

ANTONYM: dirty

clean (2) VERB

If you **clean** something, you remove dirt from it.

Different ways to clean:		
bathe	mop	sponge
brush	polish	sweep
dry-clean	rinse	swill
dust	scour	vacuum
hoover	scrub	wash
launder	shampoo	wipe

clear (1) ADJECTIVE

If something is **clear**, it is easy to understand, see or hear.

apparent
*It was **apparent** we were going to lose, right from the start of the match.*

definite
*There were **definite** indications that the swallows were nesting in the eaves.*

distinct
*We could hear the **distinct** sound of church bells in the distance.*

evident
*It was **evident** from the wet roads that it had been raining.*

obvious
*The man showed **obvious** signs of having been in a fight.*

plain
*"It's **plain** to see that you have learnt very little," the head teacher said.*

ANTONYM: unclear

clear (2) ADJECTIVE

A **clear** sky has no clouds in it.

bright

*A very **bright** morning can mean rain later.*

cloudless

*Skylarks sang high in the **cloudless** sky.*

moonlit

*The UFO slid silently across the **moonlit** sky.*

starlit

*On that **starlit** night, I could have stayed for hours by the shore.*

ANTONYM: cloudy

clear (3) ADJECTIVE

If something is **clear**, it is easy to see through.

see-through

*My mum has a **see-through** plastic coat.*

translucent

*The dragonfly's **translucent** wings beat against the sky.*

transparent

*Scott covered his book with **transparent** sticky-backed plastic.*

ANTONYM: murky or opaque

clever ADJECTIVE

Someone who is **clever** is intelligent and quick to understand things.

brainy

*My **brainy** brother came top of his class.*

bright

*Jim was **bright**. Even as a puppy, he knew the names of all his toys.*

intelligent

*"It's no good just being **intelligent**. You have to work hard too," said my English teacher.*

smart

*In one **smart** move, the backstop caught the ball and threw it to first base.*

ANTONYM: unintelligent

climb VERB

When you **climb**, you move upwards.

ascend

*Alice **ascended** the stairs, carrying a candle.*

clamber up

*Having locked himself out, Dad had to **clamber up** the drainpipe to an open window.*

scale

*The daring climber had to **scale** the overhanging rockface.*

clock NOUN

A **clock** is an instrument that measures and shows the time.

Other instruments that measure the time:

alarm clock	stopwatch
digital clock	sundial
egg timer	timer
grandfather clock	watch
hourglass	wristwatch

close (1) SAID "KLOHZ" VERB

If you **close** something, you move it so that it is no longer open.

seal

*The crewman **sealed** the hatch and the submarine was ready to dive.*

secure

*"Make sure you **secure** all the bolts on that cage," the zookeeper warned.*

shut

*"**Shut** the door behind you, but first check you've got your key," said Mum.*

ANTONYM: open

close (2) SAID "KLOHSS" ADJECTIVE

If something is **close** to something else, it is near to it.

adjacent

*The amusement arcade was **adjacent** to the holiday camp.*

handy

*Our chalet was **handy** for the camp shop.*

nearby

*Grabbing a towel that was **nearby**, Jacinth soaked it and threw it over the flaming pan.*

neighbouring

*The **neighbouring** woods are full of bluebells.*

ANTONYM: far

cloth NOUN
Cloth is fabric made by a process such as weaving.

fabric
"This **fabric** will make lovely curtains for the spare room," said Gran.

material
The tailor used only the best **material** for the suits he made.

textiles
Natural **textiles** such as wool are warmer than man-made ones.

clothes PLURAL NOUN
Clothes are the things people wear on their bodies.

clothing
"My son is in the **clothing** trade," Manny told everyone proudly.

costume
At the open-air museum, the guides wore period **costume**.

dress
"Shorts and trainers are hardly suitable **dress** for a wedding," Lady Etherington said.

garments
The notice read: "To try **garments** on, please use the changing room".

gear INFORMAL
As the forecast was poor, Kayla took her wet weather **gear** with her.

cloudy (1) ADJECTIVE
If the sky is **cloudy**, it is full of clouds.

dull
The weather was **dull**, but there was some sunshine forecast for later.

gloomy
It was a **gloomy** day for the start of our holiday.

overcast
The sky was **overcast** when the plane took off.

cloudy (2) ADJECTIVE
Cloudy can mean difficult to see through.

muddy
The scuba divers could not find the shipwreck in the **muddy** water.

murky
The travellers could see a faint light shining through the **murky** evening – shelter at last!

opaque
The bottle was made of **opaque** glass, so we could not see clearly what was in it.

club (1) NOUN
A **club** is an organization of people with a particular interest, who meet regularly.

association
Grandad belongs to an ex-servicemen's **association**.

group
Mr Fanshaw runs a local pottery **group**.

society
Dad is a member of a **society** for the protection of wildlife.

club (2) NOUN
A **club** is a thick, heavy stick used as a weapon.

baton
Police carry **batons** in case they need to defend themselves.

truncheon
In Grandad's day, all police officers were issued with **truncheons**.

clumsy ADJECTIVE
Someone who is **clumsy** moves awkwardly and carelessly.

accident-prone
Matt is **accident-prone**; he's always hurting himself somehow.

awkward
There's something **awkward** about the way Indira holds her cutlery.

blundering
The **blundering** chef clattered about in the kitchen.

butterfingered INFORMAL
Butterfingered people should not work in china shops!

lumbering
Giant Grumbleweed was a **lumbering** hulk with a knack for breaking things.

uncoordinated
My Dad is a very **uncoordinated** dancer.

coat (1) NOUN

An animal's **coat** is the fur or hair on its body.

fleece

*In a blur of movement, the shearer had the sheep's **fleece** off in seconds.*

fur

*Stephanie sobbed into her dog Cassie's **fur**.*

hide

*The **hide** of cows is treated to make leather.*

✔ The fur from certain dead animals is called a **pelt**.

coat (2) NOUN

A **coat** is a piece of clothing with long sleeves, that you wear over other clothes.

✔ A **waistcoat** is a sleeveless piece of clothing, often worn under a suit or jacket, which buttons up at the front.

Types of coat:	
anorak	kagoul
blazer	mackintosh
bomber jacket	overcoat
duffel coat	raincoat
jacket	waterproof

cold ADJECTIVE

If something is **cold**, it has a very low temperature.

Words for cold weather:	
arctic	harsh
biting	icy
bitter	nippy
bleak	perishing
chilly	raw
freezing	snowy
frosty	wintry

Words for feeling cold:	
chilled to the bone	numb
freezing	perished
frozen	quaking
frozen to the marrow	shivering

ANTONYM: hot or warm

collapse (1) VERB

If something such as a building **collapses**, it falls down suddenly.

cave in

*The miners were trapped when the roof of the passage **caved in**.*

crumple

*As the charges exploded, the walls **crumpled** to the ground.*

give way

*In 1879, the poorly built Tay Bridge in Scotland **gave way** in a storm.*

collapse (2) VERB

If a person **collapses**, they fall down suddenly because they are ill.

faint

*I nearly **fainted** when I saw our angry neighbour brandishing my ball.*

pass out

*The parade ground was so hot that several soldiers **passed out**.*

collect VERB

If you **collect** things, you gather them together for a special reason.

assemble

*For the exhibition, the gallery **assembled** paintings from all over the world.*

cluster

*Interested buyers **clustered** around the beautiful bronze statue.*

compile

*The editor **compiled** an anthology of poems.*

gather

*"**Gather** your tools up before you run off," Dad reminded me.*

collection NOUN

A **collection** is a group of things brought together over a period of time.

array

*The shelf held a dazzling **array** of trophies.*

compilation

*The book is a **compilation** of short stories by famous writers.*

✔ A collection of poems is an **anthology**.

a
b
c
d
e
f
g
h
i
j
k
l
m
n
o
p
q
r
s
t
u
v
w
x
y
z

come VERB

If you **come** to a place, you move there or arrive there.

arrive

As soon as we **arrived**, my auntie started hugging people.

materialize

In no time at all, thanks to Ratty, a splendid tea had **materialized**.

show up INFORMAL

Josh **showed up** at the very last minute, just when we had started to panic.

turn up INFORMAL

Sarah and I weren't expecting Faith to **turn up**, but she did.

come about VERB

If something **comes about**, it happens.

happen

Mr Abiola was walking past the shop when the robbery **happened**.

occur

The incident **occurred** at the swimming pool.

take place

The party will **take place** from three to five o'clock on Saturday afternoon.

comfortable (1) ADJECTIVE

Something that is **comfortable** makes you feel relaxed.

comfy INFORMAL

Our sofa is **comfy** – at least our dog Wuffles thinks so!

cosy

The hobbit was extremely reluctant to leave his **cosy** home.

relaxing

On holiday, Mum loves a **relaxing** sauna.

restful

The seaside resort had a **restful** atmosphere.

comfortable (2) ADJECTIVE

If you are **comfortable**, you are at ease and relaxed.

at ease

Sir George was the sort of person to make you feel **at ease** straight away.

contented

Gran was **contented** in her little flat.

relaxed

After a week of her holiday, Mrs Archer felt completely **relaxed**.

ANTONYM: uncomfortable

common ADJECTIVE

Something that is **common** exists in large numbers or happens often.

average

The **average** person doesn't know much about nuclear physics.

everyday

In a quarry, explosions are an **everyday** occurrence.

normal

It was **normal** for Harry to take his granny up a morning cup of tea.

ordinary

In my opinion, my parents and I are just **ordinary** people.

standard

"A **standard**-class ticket, please," I said to the train guard.

usual

The **usual** lunch on Friday is fish.

ANTONYM: uncommon

company NOUN

A **company** is a business that sells goods or provides a service.

business

My father runs an electrical **business**.

corporation

Mrs Fletcher's tiny company belongs to a huge global **corporation**.

firm

Mum's **firm** is paying for her to go on a management course.

competition NOUN

A **competition** is an event in which people take part to find out who is the best at something.

championship

Wimbledon is a famous tennis **championship**.

contest
*The two villages faced each other in a tug-of-war **contest**.*

event
*The Olympic Games is the world's leading sporting **event**.*

tournament
*Our school entered two teams in the Under-11 netball **tournament**.*

complain VERB
If you **complain**, you say that you are not happy about something.

bleat
*Sam kept **bleating** that he had lost his pen.*

fuss
*The customer was **fussing** over a minute mark on the desk.*

grouse
*"It's no good **grousing** now. You had your chance and didn't take it," said Gran.*

grumble
*Mum always **grumbles** about the dreadful state of my room.*

moan
*All my big sister ever does is **moan**!*

whinge
*The millionaire rock star was always **whingeing** about how unfair life is.*

complete (1) ADJECTIVE
If something is **complete**, none of it is missing.

entire
*At the end, the **entire** cast took a bow.*

full
*"Pay me the **full** amount now," the greedy landlord insisted.*

whole
*"I swear to tell the **whole** truth," the witness declared to the court.*

complete (2) ADJECTIVE
Complete can mean to the greatest degree possible.

absolute
*"You're talking **absolute** rubbish," the major replied to the private.*

sheer
*The winning jockey leapt off his horse in **sheer** joy.*

thorough
*The disobedient little girl made a **thorough** nuisance of herself.*

utter
*Chander felt an **utter** fool dressed as a clown.*

complete (3) VERB
If you **complete** something, you finish it.

conclude
*Professor Boffin **concluded** his talk and then asked if there were any questions.*

end
*The crowd was in tears as he **ended** his speech.*

finalize
*The airline staff **finalized** arrangements for the plane to take off.*

finish
*When Gran had **finished** her tea she turned on the radio.*

round off
*We **rounded off** our day out with a delicious meal in a steakhouse.*

wrap up INFORMAL
*"OK, darlings, we'll **wrap** it **up** for today," the film director announced.*

ANTONYM: begin

completely ADVERB
Completely can mean totally, absolutely and utterly.

absolutely
*By the end of the sponsored swim, Kalil was **absolutely** exhausted.*

entirely
*"I **entirely** agree with you," put in Kaylee.*

fully
*The new manager said he was **fully** committed to the club and the team.*

totally
*Fire **totally** destroyed the pier buildings.*

utterly
*You could see by the expression on her face that Isha was **utterly** fed up.*

a
b
c
d
e
f
g
h
i
j
k
l
m
n
o
p
q
r
s
t
u
v
w
x
y
z

complicated ADJECTIVE

Something that is **complicated** has so many parts or aspects that it is difficult to understand or deal with.

complex

*It was a **complex** engine, which my brother struggled to understand.*

elaborate

*Blofeld had spent years on an **elaborate** plan for world domination.*

intricate

*Clock mechanisms are too **intricate** for you or me to tamper with.*

ANTONYM: simple or straightforward

concentrate VERB

If you **concentrate** on something, you give it all your attention.

apply yourself to

*Previously lazy, Watkins now **applied himself to** his work and did well in the exam.*

be engrossed in

*My sister **was** so **engrossed in** some telly programme, she failed to see me sneaking up.*

focus

*"Today, we are going to **focus** on fractions," Mrs Abrahams said, to a chorus of groans.*

pay attention to

*"**Pay attention to** what I'm saying, Jamie," said Dani. "It's important."*

condition NOUN

The **condition** of someone or something is the state they are in.

fitness

*Army doctors examine the **fitness** of soldiers each year.*

order

*The television was in good working **order** when we sold it.*

shape

*My grandad is in pretty good **shape** for a man of 75 – he still goes for a run every morning.*

state

*"Just look at the **state** of your trousers!" my stepmum sighed.*

confess VERB

If you **confess** to something, you admit that you did it.

admit

*After questioning, the suspect **admitted** she had stolen the bag.*

come clean INFORMAL

*"Now **come clean**, David," Auntie Julie said. "I know you've been at the chocolates."*

own up

*The head teacher demanded that the person responsible for the damage should **own up**.*

confused ADJECTIVE

If you are **confused**, you are uncertain about what is happening or what to do.

baffled

*Lyra was **baffled**. What on earth was the significance of the dust?*

bewildered

***Bewildered** by his sudden fame, Robbie went completely off the rails.*

muddled

*The useless new parking scheme was a prime example of **muddled** thinking.*

perplexed

*Frank stood at the crossroads, totally **perplexed** by the map he'd been given.*

puzzled

*"Then I'm **puzzled**," Mum said. "How did the biscuit tin fly to your room?"*

confusing ADJECTIVE

If something is **confusing**, it makes you uncertain about what is happening or what to do.

baffling

*No body. No weapon. No witnesses. The whole thing was **baffling**.*

bewildering

*There was a **bewildering** choice of stereos.*

perplexing

*The mystery got more **perplexing**. Where on earth had the shoe gone?*

puzzling

*Sergeant Assad found it **puzzling** that everyone had volunteered for the job.*

connect (1) VERB

If you **connect** two things, you join them together.

attach
When Mum receives nice postcards, she attaches them to the fridge with magnets.

couple
The man in the overalls dropped from the platform to couple the engine to the coaches.

fasten
Phil fastened the papers together with a clip.

join
Siamese twins are joined at birth, and often have to be separated to survive.

link
"This deal," said the chairman, "will link two fine companies."

unite
On their wedding day, the couple were united in marriage.

connect (2) VERB

If one thing or person is **connected** with another, there is a link between them.

associate
"I am proud," the mayor boomed, "to be associated with such a deserving charity."

relate
In good non-fiction writing, each sentence should relate to the one before.

connection NOUN

A **connection** is a link or relationship between two things.

association
Dad has always had a close association with the school. He attended as a pupil when he was a boy and is now a governor.

bond
There was a bond between the two brothers that could not be broken.

link
There are strong historical links between Britain and India.

relationship
Luis' relationship with his stepfather was not always an easy one.

contact VERB

If you **contact** someone, you telephone them or write to them.

communicate with
Television reporters often communicate with the studio by satellite phone.

get in touch with
Message for Mr Sample: please urgently get in touch with your son.

make contact
Joe wants me to make contact when I arrive in New York.

> **Different ways to make contact:**
> card   postcard
> e-mail   telegram
> fax   telephone
> letter   text message

contain VERB

The things that something **contains** are the things in it.

accommodate
The narrowboat could accommodate up to nine people.

comprise
Our cottage comprises six rooms: three upstairs and three down.

consist of
Pancake mix mainly consists of flour, eggs and milk.

hold
An average household bucket will hold ten litres of liquid.

include
The holiday package includes all flights, accommodation and meals.

container NOUN

A **container** is something that you keep things in, such as a box or a jar.

receptacle
"What we need," said Mr Vanstone, "is some sort of receptacle for these tadpoles."

vessel
A pitcher is a vessel for carrying liquids.

a
b
c
d
e
f
g
h
i
j
k
l
m
n
o
p
q
r
s
t
u
v
w
x
y
z

A B C D E F G H I J K L M N O P Q R S T U V W X Y Z

contest NOUN

A **contest** is a competition or game.

battle

The Cup Final was a **battle** between a giant club and one of the league's minnows.

bout

The wrestling announcer began, "This is a **bout** of eight rounds of three minutes each."

competition

Mum is a fanatic for entering **competitions**. She's always thinking up catchy slogans.

head-to-head INFORMAL

The finish of the sack race was a close-run **head-to-head** between Mrs Robinson and Miss Penn.

match

The **match** against Holcombe was played in pouring rain.

tournament

The chess **tournament** featured players from all over the country.

continue VERB

If you **continue** to do something, you keep doing it.

carry on

"If you **carry on** prodding me, I'll prod you back," I said to Barry.

keep on

"If you **keep on** forgetting your homework, you'll get detention," I told Anita.

persevere

Although she was tired, Jamilah **persevered** with her drawing.

persist

Although I hate it, Dad **persists** in calling me by my nickname.

continuous ADJECTIVE

Something that is **continuous** goes on without stopping.

ceaseless

The **ceaseless** noise of drilling was driving me mad.

constant

Bill and Ben were **constant** companions. You never saw them apart.

incessant

After a few minutes, Mrs Snell's **incessant** chatter became annoying.

nonstop

The disco played **nonstop** music throughout the evening.

uninterrupted

Good weather meant **uninterrupted** play at Wimbledon for the whole fortnight.

See **endless**

control (1) VERB

To **control** something is to have power over it.

be in charge of

Our dad **is in charge of** our local Under-11s soccer team.

command

Captain Hardy **commanded** HMS Victory, the flagship of Admiral Lord Nelson.

direct

The fire chief **directed** operations from a mobile control centre.

manage

Mum's sister **manages** a supermarket down the road.

control (2) NOUN

Control is the power over something.

authority

The mayor had **authority** over the city's transport system.

command

The conductor was in complete **command** of the orchestra.

direction

The team is playing well under the **direction** of the new manager.

power

"The Wizard of Oz has the **power** to give you courage, Lion," said Dorothy.

convenient (1) ADJECTIVE

If a time to do a particular thing is **convenient**, it is suitable for those concerned.

agreeable

"Is three o'clock **agreeable** to you, Mrs Williams?" the receptionist enquired.

appropriate

*Max felt it was an **appropriate** moment to ask the question.*

suitable

*"Eight o'clock would be a **suitable** time for me to pick you up," my stepdad said.*

ANTONYM: inconvenient

convenient (2) ADJECTIVE

If something is **convenient**, it is easy to use, do or go to.

handy

*The store is really **handy** for Grandma to pop down to.*

helpful

*Mrs Hakim handed out a **helpful** fact sheet at the end of the lesson.*

useful

*Tin-openers are a **useful** invention which we couldn't do without!*

ANTONYM: inconvenient

conversation NOUN

When people have a **conversation**, they talk to each other.

chat

*Auntie Doris often pops in for a **chat** on her way home from work.*

dialogue

*The opening scene of Macbeth consists of a **dialogue** between three witches.*

discussion

*Our **discussion** centred on whether to play indoors or outdoors.*

cook VERB

When you **cook** food, you prepare it for eating by boiling, baking or frying it.

Some ways to cook food:		
bake	fry	simmer
barbecue	grill	steam
blanch	microwave	stew
boil	poach	stir-fry
braise	roast	toast

cool (1) ADJECTIVE

Something **cool** has a low temperature but is not cold.

chilly

*It was **chilly** outside, so we stayed by the fire.*

fresh

*A **fresh** breeze blew off the estuary, flapping the flag on the church tower.*

nippy

*"It's rather **nippy**," Mum said. "I'd take a pullover if I were you."*

refreshing

*In summer there's nothing to beat **refreshing** orange juice.*

ANTONYM: warm

See **cold**

cool (2) ADJECTIVE

If you are **cool** in a difficult situation, you stay calm.

calm

*"Now everybody keep **calm**," the captain said. "There is no need for panic."*

laid back INFORMAL

*My friend Chris was totally **laid back** about the exam. "If I fail, I fail," he said.*

relaxed

*Despite the tension in those around him, the sub's commander looked **relaxed**.*

ANTONYM: nervous

cope VERB

If you **cope** with a task or problem, you deal with it successfully.

carry on

*Despite the rain, the team **carried on** and eventually won the game.*

get by

*Although money was tight, Mum **got by** doing all sorts of odd jobs for people.*

manage

*"That piano's heavy. Can you **manage**?" a kind passer-by enquired.*

survive

*During the exams, Liam **survived** by drinking cups of coffee and going to bed early.*

cope with VERB

If you have to **cope with** a difficult situation, you have to deal with it.

contend with

Apart from blizzards, Captain Scott had to ***contend with*** *a growing shortage of food.*

deal with

I don't know how teachers ***deal with*** *30 kids like my little brother.*

copy (1) NOUN

A **copy** is something made to look like something else.

duplicate

As the new car came with only one key, Dad had a ***duplicate*** *made.*

forgery

The banknotes were such good ***forgeries*** *that only an expert could tell they weren't the real thing.*

imitation

"If that diamond is an ***imitation****, it's very like the real thing," I thought.*

replica

The miniature locomotive was an exact ***replica*** *of the real train.*

reproduction

As the real painting is worth millions, our family was quite happy with a ***reproduction****.*

ANTONYM: original

copy (2) VERB

If you **copy** what someone does, you do the same thing.

follow

If you set a good example, others may ***follow****.*

imitate

Jordan sits behind me, ***imitating*** *Mr Heaney's funny voice.*

impersonate

To gain access to the jewels, the thief ***impersonated*** *the head porter.*

copy (3) VERB

If you **copy** something, you make a copy of it.

counterfeit

The criminals tried to ***counterfeit*** *passports with false names.*

duplicate

Before you mail the completed form, ***duplicate*** *it so we have a copy for the files.*

forge

The sly couple ***forged*** *tickets and then tried to sell them outside the stadium.*

replicate

The artist ***replicated*** *paintings and passed them off as originals.*

cost NOUN

The **cost** is the amount of money needed to buy, do or make something.

charge

"You know, sir, there'll be a ***charge*** *for any phone calls," the hotel clerk said smoothly.*

expense

My father didn't want the ***expense*** *of a new roof, but the leaks changed his mind.*

price

The money I made from errands was just about the ***price*** *of the model I wanted.*

✔ The cost of travelling on transport is the **fare**.

cosy ADJECTIVE

Somewhere **cosy** is warm and comfortable.

comfortable

Gramps finds his new reclining armchair very ***comfortable****.*

comfy INFORMAL

I was very ***comfy*** *in my little room right up in the loft.*

snug

The two dogs were ***snug*** *in their baskets when Peter foolishly mentioned "walkies".*

ANTONYM: uncomfortable

count (1) VERB

If you **count**, or count up, all the things in a group, you add them up to see how many there are.

add up

Irina ***added up*** *the number of times Mr Reid clapped his hands.*

calculate

The salesman ***calculated*** *the money he would make that week.*

reckon up
If you reckon up the rainy days we've had recently, you'll get a surprise.

tot up INFORMAL
My friend Ainsley and I totted up the number of cakes our dads had eaten.

count (2) VERB
If something **counts** in a situation, it is important or valuable.

carry weight
The politician assured people that their opinions did carry weight.

make a difference
The crook's previous crimes certainly made a difference to the length of his jail sentence.

matter
The goals you scored before don't matter. It's the ones you get now that are important.

count (3) VERB
If you can **count** on someone or something, you can rely on them.

bank
We were banking on good weather for the school fête.

depend
"I'm depending on you, Smithers. Don't let me down," the lieutenant said.

rely
"Can I rely on you to check that all doors are locked?" my mother asked.

country (1) NOUN
A **country** is one of the political areas the world is divided into.

kingdom
Beyond the barren plains of Kremmen lay the kingdom of the Wargs.

land
"We're very proud of our land," said the large Welshman.

nation
Napoleon once said that England was a nation of shopkeepers.

state
After the war a new state was created which united the people.

country (2) NOUN
The **country** is land away from towns and cities.

bush NEW ZEALAND, AUSTRALIA AND AFRICA
The Pritchards' farm is right out in the bush.

countryside
The countryside was a patchwork of fields.

outback AUSTRALIA AND NEW ZEALAND
A lot of the outback in Australia is really very wild.

wilds
The gamekeeper lived out in the wilds in a small cottage.

✔ The adjective used to describe things in the country is **rural**.

courage NOUN
Courage is the quality shown by people who do things that they know are dangerous or difficult.

bravery
His bravery in saving the child brought him letters from all over the world.

daring
The daring of King Arthur's knights is recorded in legend.

guts INFORMAL
The timid girl showed real guts when she went down the rope slide.

heroism
For her heroism in an enemy country, the undercover agent received a secret award.

ANTONYM: cowardice

course NOUN
A **course** is the route something such as an aircraft, river or ship takes.

path
The plane's flight path brought it close to the enemy coast.

route
Our quickest route to the Far East is, surprisingly, over the North Pole.

trajectory
The stone's trajectory was a graceful arc from my catapult to our greenhouse.

way
"Which way do you go home?" I asked Sunil.

a
b
c
d
e
f
g
h
i
j
k
l
m
n
o
p
q
r
s
t
u
v
w
x
y
z

of course PHRASE
If you say **of course**, you are showing that you are absolutely sure about something.

certainly
*School meals are **certainly** tastier than they used to be.*

definitely
*"I'm **definitely** coming to camp," Vadim confirmed.*

undoubtedly
*I bragged that my team was **undoubtedly** the best in the world.*

crack NOUN
A **crack** is a narrow gap.

cranny
*In a tiny **cranny** in the cupboard lay the key that they sought.*

crevice
*Climbers use **crevices** in the rock to hold the pieces of equipment that support them.*

crafty ADJECTIVE
Someone who is **crafty** gets what they want by tricking people in a clever way.

cunning
*Bond's **cunning** trick was to hide above the door.*

sly
*The **sly** fox hid behind the henhouse.*

wily
*The **wily** coyote was no match for the even cleverer roadrunner.*

crash (1) NOUN
A **crash** is an accident in which a moving vehicle hits something and is damaged.

accident
*Queues built up, as the **accident** had blocked both sides of the road.*

collision
*The **collision** took place at a busy road intersection.*

pile-up
***Pile-ups** often occur during fog, when vehicles collide with one another.*

smash
*It was a bad **smash**, with two people injured.*

crash (2) VERB
If a vehicle **crashes**, it hits something and is badly damaged.

bump
*The motorbike **bumped** into the back of the car.*

collide
*My dad's car **collided** with a quarry truck on a narrow bend.*

plough into
*The runaway lorry **ploughed into** the wall.*

crazy (1) ADJECTIVE INFORMAL
Someone or something **crazy** is very strange or foolish.

insane
*I reckon that bungee jumping is an **insane** thing to do.*

strange
*The cowboy had a **strange** look in his eye.*

crazy (2) ADJECTIVE INFORMAL
Something **crazy** is very strange or foolish.

absurd
*How **absurd** that you should think that baked beans grow on trees!*

bizarre
*To see my brother on a bike dressed as a teddy bear was a **bizarre** experience.*

outrageous
*Uncle Will is aways doing **outrageous** things.*

ridiculous
*Dad thought the idea was **ridiculous**.*

creep VERB
If you **creep** somewhere, you move there quietly and slowly.

edge
*I **edged** towards the door, hoping that no one would notice me leave.*

slink
*"Don't try to **slink** off. I haven't finished yet!" snapped the irritable countess.*

sneak
*The cat **sneaked** up the fire escape and crept in through the back door.*

tiptoe
*I heard my big brother **tiptoe** past my room.*

creepy ADJECTIVE

Someone or something **creepy** is strange and frightening.

eerie

Eerie noises floated down from the moor.

mysterious

*The **mysterious** stranger disappeared into the mist with a flourish of his cloak.*

sinister

*With his eyepatch and wooden leg, Long John looked a truly **sinister** character.*

spooky INFORMAL

*The film was so **spooky** Hailey had to cover her eyes.*

criminal NOUN

A **criminal** is someone who has committed a crime.

crook INFORMAL

*Two **crooks** called at our door pretending to be from the water company.*

offender

*As a young **offender**, the 15-year-old was not sent to prison.*

villain

*"Have nothing to do with him. He's a total **villain**," Mum warned.*

Types of criminal:	
assassin	murderer
bandit	pickpocket
blackmailer	pirate
burglar	robber
gangster	shoplifter
highwayman	smuggler
hijacker	terrorist
kidnapper	thief
mugger	vandal

Types of crime committed by criminals:	
abduction	murder
assassination	robbery
blackmail	shoplifting
burglary	smuggling
hijacking	terrorism
kidnapping	theft
mugging	vandalism

crisp ADJECTIVE

Food that is **crisp** is pleasantly fresh and firm.

crispy

*To really be enjoyed, lettuce needs to be fresh and **crispy**.*

crunchy

*The apples were **crunchy** and juicy.*

ANTONYM: soft

criticize VERB

If you **criticize** someone or something, you say what you think is wrong with them.

disapprove of

*My parents **disapprove of** expensive fast food which is full of chemicals.*

find fault with

*The duchess managed to **find fault with** everyone in the room.*

crooked (1) SAID "**KROO**-KID" ADJECTIVE

Something that is **crooked** is bent or twisted.

deformed

*Gran's hands are **deformed** with arthritis.*

distorted

*The **distorted** shape of the trees was caused by the onshore wind.*

twisted

*The wreckage of the car was **twisted** beyond all recognition.*

ANTONYM: straight

crooked (2) SAID "**KROO**-KID" ADJECTIVE

A **crooked** person is dishonest.

corrupt

*The **corrupt** police officer accepted bribes.*

criminal

*"You have committed a **criminal** offence," intoned the judge.*

dishonest

*Something made me suspect that the salesman was **dishonest**.*

shady INFORMAL

*"He looks a **shady** customer" said Carlos, nodding towards a surly man across the street.*

ANTONYM: law-abiding or honest

a
b
c
d
e
f
g
h
i
j
k
l
m
n
o
p
q
r
s
t
u
v
w
x
y
z

cross ADJECTIVE

Someone who is **cross** is rather angry.

angry
*My friend Anna was rather **angry** when I lost her favourite CD.*

annoyed
*Dad was **annoyed** that I hadn't washed up as I'd promised.*

cantankerous
*The **cantankerous** old farmer used to shout at anyone who walked past his farm.*

crotchety
*Gran sometimes gets **crotchety** when her arthritis is painful.*

grumpy
*My brother is always **grumpy** when it comes to having a bath.*

irritable
*Mum was rather **irritable** because she had a bad headache.*

snappy
*"There's no need to get **snappy**," Lynn retorted. "Here's your wretched comb."*

crouch VERB

If you **crouch**, you lower your body with your knees bent.

squat
*In games, Mrs Ince makes us **squat** on the floor so we can see and hear her.*

stoop
*The tall man had to **stoop** to get through the cottage doorway.*

crowd (1) NOUN

A **crowd** is a large group of people gathered together.

mass
*The whole square was a seething **mass** of red, white and blue flags.*

mob
*Enraged, the **mob** surged through the streets like a human tide.*

multitude
*The prophet spoke to the **multitude**, foretelling the great events to come.*

swarm
*A **swarm** of demonstrators headed for the parliament building.*

crowd (2) NOUN

A **crowd** is a large number of people watching an event.

audience
*The concert **audience** clapped when the conductor took the stage.*

gate
*Fifty thousand were there – the biggest **gate** that United had had all season.*

spectators
*In the past, the **spectators** cheered as people were publicly executed.*

cruel ADJECTIVE

Cruel people deliberately cause pain or distress to other people or to animals.

callous
*The **callous** emperor made his slaves work their fingers to the bone.*

hard-hearted
***Hard-hearted** Scrooge begrudged giving Cratchit a day off at Christmas.*

heartless
*The **heartless** landlord threw the poor widow into the street.*

merciless
*The **merciless** sniper picked off his victims one by one with precision.*

ruthless
*Anyone who disagreed with the **ruthless** dictator disappeared.*

vicious
*The **vicious** crocodile clamped its jaws on the unfortunate swimmer.*

crumble VERB

When something **crumbles**, or you **crumble** it, it breaks into small pieces.

collapse
*Weak foundations caused the apartment block to **collapse**.*

decay
*The beam had **decayed**, bringing the floor above it crashing down.*

decompose
Plants, animals and humans begin to ***decompose*** *when they die.*

disintegrate
The agent ***disintegrated*** *as Morpheus fired his phaser weapon.*

cry (1) VERB
When you **cry**, tears come from your eyes because you are unhappy or hurt.

bawl
The moment the baby's bottle was put in its mouth it stopped ***bawling***.

blubber
After being refused an ice cream, the toddler ***blubbered*** *for the next half hour.*

shed tears
Dad's advice is not to ***shed tears*** *over something that is in the past.*

snivel
"Stop ***snivelling*** *and you might get a lolly," the girl's mother snapped.*

sob
Milly ***sobbed*** *her heart out to think that her dog was dead.*

weep
After her sisters had left for the ball, Cinderella ***wept*** *silently as she swept.*

cry (2) VERB
If you **cry** something, you shout it or say it loudly.

bawl
Everyone came running when the camp cook ***bawled*** *"Dinner's ready!"*

bellow
"Time to go to school," Dad ***bellowed*** *up the stairs to us.*

boom
"Attention!" ***boomed*** *the sergeant major to the new recruits.*

call
When I saw my friend on the other side of the street I ***called*** *out her name.*

shout
Ben ***shouted*** *for help when he saw the child fall into the pond.*

yell
"Watch out!" ***yelled*** *Yanni as he saw the cricket ball flying in Aidan's direction.*

cry (3) NOUN
A **cry** is a shout or other sound made with your voice.

bellow
A loud ***bellow*** *came from the bull at the end of the field.*

howl
The wolf let out a ***howl*** *as he prowled through the moonlit night.*

shout
The crowd gave a ***shout*** *of joy as another goal hit the back of the net.*

shriek
My silly brother gave a ***shriek*** *when he saw the spider in the bath.*

yell
With a ***yell***, *Aidan jumped out of the way of the speeding cricket ball.*

cupboard NOUN
A **cupboard** is a piece of furniture with doors and shelves.

Some types of cupboard:

cabinet	safe
larder	sideboard
locker	wardrobe

cure NOUN
A **cure** is something that heals or helps someone to get better.

antidote
There is no known ***antidote*** *to the bite of that particular snake.*

medicine
Dad took some ***medicine*** *for his stomach ache.*

remedy
The ***remedy*** *for boredom is simple. You need to get out more!*

treatment
Fortunately, the ***treatment*** *helped and my ankle soon felt better.*

A
B
C
D
E
F
G
H
I
J
K
L
M
N
O
P
Q
R
S
T
U
V
W
X
Y
Z

curious ADJECTIVE

Someone who is **curious** wants to know more about something.

inquiring

"Dad, it said on my report that I've an inquiring mind. What does that mean?"

inquisitive

Inquisitive about anything mechanical, Fiona dismantled the cuckoo clock.

interested

If it's anything about trains, then my brother is interested.

nosy

Our nosy neighbour was anxious to hear any gossip she could.

curl VERB

If something **curls**, it moves in a curve or spiral.

coil

The boa constrictor coiled its body slowly round the hapless victim.

entwine

Climbing clematis plants entwined themselves with the telephone wire.

spiral

Smoke spiralled up from the cottage chimney.

twist

The string from the kite twisted as it came tumbling down.

wind

The country road wound round in a series of bends.

curly ADJECTIVE

Curly hair has many curls in it.

curled

My sister's hair was all curled when she came out of the hairdresser's.

frizzy

In the Afro look of the 1970s, people had a mop of bushy, frizzy hair.

kinky

If your hair is naturally straight, you can make it kinky by having it permed.

wavy

I would love to have wavy hair, but mine's dead straight.

cut (1) NOUN

A **cut** is a mark made with a knife or other sharp tool.

gash

The nasty gash in Billy's knee needed to have several stitches.

groove

Uncle Ken chiselled a groove in the shelf for plates to stand up in.

nick

I was clumsy with the knife and made a nick in the desk.

slit

To make the pocket, Mum cut a slit in the fabric.

cut (2) VERB

If you **cut** something, you use a pair of scissors, a knife or another sharp tool to mark it or remove parts of it.

cut a little:
chip

When she fell, Vanessa chipped her tooth.

chisel

I tried to chisel out a hole for the lock, but I split the wood.

clip

Ross clipped the hedge for his auntie.

prune

When you prune roses in winter, you cut them right back near the base.

shave

Kay shaved a little off the shelf to make it fit.

snip

For a practical joke, I snipped a bit off Dad's tie, but he didn't find it funny.

trim

Grandad has his hair trimmed each month – what's left of it, that is.

cut hard at something:
chop

The karate expert chopped the brick in half with a single blow.

hack

Hacking her way through the jungle, the botanist searched for the rare plant.

slash

*Bluebeard **slashed** downward with his cutlass, through the rope.*

cut something down:

chop

*Dad had to **chop** the old tree down after it was damaged in the storm.*

fell

*The stupid lumberjack proceeded to **fell** the wrong tree.*

mow

*It's useless to **mow** the lawn in wet weather.*

cut something in two:

bisect

*With one swing of the axe the man **bisected** the thick log.*

divide

*Using a sharp knife, Mum **divided** the last piece of pie for my brother and me.*

halve

*"If I **halve** this apple, will you share it with me?" I asked Helen.*

Tools you can use to cut things:

axe	mower
carving knife	razor
chisel	saw
cleaver	scalpel
clippers	scissors
guillotine	secateurs
knife	shears

a
b
c
d
e
f
g
h
i
j
k
l
m
n
o
p
q
r
s
t
u
v
w
x
y
z

Dd

damage (1) VERB

If you **damage** something, you harm or spoil it.

deface

The teacher turned purple when she saw Craig had defaced his language book.

harm

Fortunately, no one was harmed in the crash.

spoil

My painting was spoilt when I spilt water on it.

vandalize

It's very sad when people vandalize buildings.

✔ Someone who damages something useful or beautiful on purpose and for no good reason is a **vandal**.

See **destroy**

damage (2) NOUN

Damage is injury or harm done to something.

destruction

"The destruction of rainforests should worry everyone on earth," said my sister.

harm

The stolen painting was returned with no harm done to it.

vandalism

Owing to vandalism, the public lavatory had to be closed.

damp ADJECTIVE

Something that is **damp** is slightly wet.

clammy

Beneath her jungle gear, the explorer's skin felt clammy.

drizzly

All day the weather had been dull and drizzly.

humid

In tropical places, the weather is hot and humid.

moist

As its soil was still moist, Sophie didn't water the plant.

muggy

We all expected thunder as the air was muggy.

dance (1) VERB

When you **dance**, you move around in time to music.

caper

The clown capered about to the music.

cavort

The party guests cavorted to the loud music on the dance floor.

dance (2) NOUN

A **dance** is a series of rhythmic movements that you do in time to music.

Types of dance:	
ballet	jive
ballroom dancing	line dancing
belly dancing	mambo
break-dancing	salsa
disco dancing	tap dancing

danger NOUN

Danger is the possibility that someone may be harmed or killed.

hazard

That raised paving stone is a hazard. Someone might trip over it.

menace

Pollution from farm fertilizers is a menace to fish in the rivers.

peril

Ivan put himself in peril by walking near the cliff edge.

risk

Despite the risks, the medic crawled out to help the wounded soldier.

threat

The prime minister tried to avert the threat of war by having meetings with other leaders.

ANTONYM: safety

dangerous ADJECTIVE

If something is **dangerous**, it is likely to cause hurt or harm.

hazardous

Road tankers have signs to show if their liquid cargo is hazardous.

perilous
*Captain Scott set out on his **perilous** trek to the South Pole.*

risky
*Jenny knew that climbing the cliff was **risky**, but she had to escape the waves.*

treacherous
*"Keep away from those mud flats. They're **treacherous**," warned the boatman.*

unsafe
*The derelict buildings were **unsafe**, and about to be demolished.*

ANTONYM: safe or harmless

dare (1) VERB
If you **dare** to do something, you have the courage to do it.

brave
*Ray decided to **brave** a visit to the dentist's.*

have the courage
*The airman **had the courage** to go back to the burning plane.*

risk
*The athlete was not willing to **risk** getting an injury.*

venture
*Dad **ventured** to ask his boss for a pay rise.*

dare (2) VERB
If you **dare** someone to do something, you challenge them to do it.

challenge
*Yoshi **challenged** Tim to climb the wall.*

defy
*I **defied** my sister to race me.*

daring ADJECTIVE
A **daring** person is bold and willing to take risks.

adventurous
*"Rihana is the **adventurous** type," her dad said. "She's always getting into scrapes."*

brave
*It was a **brave** and unexpected move by the submarine captain.*

fearless
*Even as a young midshipman, Nelson displayed a **fearless** character.*

dark (1) ADJECTIVE
If it is **dark**, there is not enough light to see properly.

dim
*In the **dim** light of the cave, Crusoe could make out a heap of bones.*

dingy
*With the shutters closed, the villa was **dingy** after the bright sunlight outside.*

gloomy
*On every **gloomy** landing, paintings of the baron's ancestors stared out from the walls.*

murky
*The divers could not see anything in the **murky** depths of the lake.*

shadowy
*A sinister figure appeared from a **shadowy** side street.*

ANTONYM: light

dark (2) NOUN
The **dark** is the lack of light in a place.

dusk
*Street lights began to twinkle in the **dusk**.*

gloom
*In the **gloom** of the attic, Nathan made out two staring eyes.*

murk
*Zora wished she was on the beach, not in the **murk** of a Manchester night.*

ANTONYM: light

dawn NOUN
Dawn is the time in the morning when light first appears in the sky.

break of day
*A chorus of hungry birds started up at the **break of day**.*

daybreak
*The search for the missing girl resumed at **daybreak**.*

sunrise
*By **sunrise**, the diver and his team were already at the pier.*

ANTONYM: dusk

a
b
c
d
e
f
g
h
i
j
k
l
m
n
o
p
q
r
s
t
u
v
w
x
y
z

dazed ADJECTIVE

If you are **dazed**, you are confused and bewildered.

bewildered
*Mum was **bewildered** by the huge range of mobile phones on offer.*

confused
*Granny sometimes gets **confused** and says odd things.*

light-headed
*The paint smell was so strong that I began to feel **light-headed**.*

shocked
*After the bomb, **shocked**, dusty people wandered hopelessly around.*

stunned
*I felt **stunned** by the unexpected news about James's accident.*

dead ADJECTIVE

A person, animal or plant that is **dead** is no longer alive.

deceased
*It was thought that the **deceased** man came originally from Ireland.*

extinct
*The **extinct** moa of New Zealand was a flightless bird like an ostrich.*

late
*Many people paid tribute to Mrs Suleiman's **late** husband.*

✔ A dead body is called a **corpse** or the **remains**.
A person who has recently died is often referred to as the **deceased**.

ANTONYM: alive

deadly ADJECTIVE

Something **deadly** is likely or able to cause death.

lethal
*The machine guns dispensed a **lethal** curtain of fire across the muddy wilderness.*

mortal
*Frodo suddenly came face to face with his **mortal** enemy.*

deal NOUN

A **deal** is an agreement or arrangement, especially in business.

agreement
*The countries formed an **agreement** about imports and exports.*

arrangement
*Dad made an **arrangement** to pick the car up on Tuesday.*

contract
*The player's **contract** with his club will expire in a year's time.*

deal with VERB

If you **deal with** something, you do what is necessary to sort it out.

attend to
*The receptionist has promised to **attend to** me in a moment.*

handle
*Mum **handled** all the holiday arrangements.*

see to
*"Please would you **see to** that customer," the manager said to the sales assistant.*

sort out
*Thank heavens Mrs Ito was there to **sort out** the problem.*

take care of
*"I'll **take care of** the flowers if you buy the chocolates," my sister said on Mother's Day.*

See **cope with**

dear (1) ADJECTIVE

Something or someone **dear** is much loved.

beloved
*The card read, "To my **beloved** wife".*

cherished
*Grandad has **cherished** memories of his time in Italy.*

treasured
*His gran's rocking chair was a **treasured** possession.*

dear (2) ADJECTIVE

Something that is **dear** is very expensive.

costly
*The furniture was **costly** but superbly made.*

pricey INFORMAL
*"That computer game's a bit **pricey**," my
friend Sean muttered.*

ANTONYM: cheap

decay VERB

When things **decay**, they rot or go bad.

biodegrade
*Most plastic does not **biodegrade**, which is a
problem for the environment.*

decompose
*I had a sinking feeling that my sandwiches
were **decomposing** in my locker.*

perish
*The hot-water bottle leaked, as its rubber
stopper had **perished**.*

rot
*Most softwood will **rot** if it is not painted.*

decide VERB

If you **decide** to do something, you choose to do
it, usually after thinking about it carefully.

commit yourself
*In signing up for the course, my brother
committed himself to do a year's study.*

make a decision
*The hobbit **made a decision** to cross the river
before camping.*

make up your mind
*"Ted, will you **make up your mind**!" Dad
demanded impatiently.*

reach a decision
*My parents **reached a decision**: we were
going to move house.*

decision NOUN

A **decision** is a choice or judgment that is made
about something.

choice
*Daniel faced a **choice** – to continue and risk
getting lost, or to go back the way he had come.*

conclusion
*I came to the **conclusion** that I hadn't been
working hard enough.*

judgment
*The panel's **judgment** was that Mrs Flaherty
had been fairly treated.*

verdict
*The courtroom fell silent as the jury's **verdict**
was announced.*

decorate VERB

If you **decorate** something, you make it more
attractive by adding things to it.

adorn
*For the wedding, the gate to the churchyard
was **adorned** with flowers.*

festoon
*The whole of Wall Street was **festooned** with
tickertape streamers.*

trim
*The Christmas tree was **trimmed** with tinsel.*

decrease VERB

If something **decreases**, or if you **decrease** it, it
becomes less.

decline
*Bird-lovers are worried that the number of
house sparrows is **declining**.*

diminish
*The glow from the fire **diminished** as the dogs
slumbered on.*

dwindle
*Once the mines closed, the valley population
began to **dwindle**.*

lessen
*The driver decided to **lessen** his speed, as the
engine was overheating.*

reduce
***Reducing** your salt intake will help you to
stay healthy.*

ANTONYM: increase

deep (1) ADJECTIVE

If something is **deep**, it goes a long way down
from the surface.

bottomless
*"The way you spend, you must think I've got
bottomless pockets!" Dad grumbled.*

yawning
*The earth shook violently, and a **yawning** hole
opened up in the street.*

ANTONYM: shallow

a
b
c
d
e
f
g
h
i
j
k
l
m
n
o
p
q
r
s
t
u
v
w
x
y
z

deep (2) ADJECTIVE

Deep can mean great or intense.

intense
*Van Gogh painted vibrant pictures with **intense** colour.*

profound
*The discovery of penicillin had a **profound** effect on medicine.*

strong
*A **strong** wind blew the sailing boat safely back on course.*

deep (3) ADJECTIVE

A **deep** sound is a low one.

bass
*The **bass** sound of the foghorn echoed through the mist.*

low
*Mrs Quail's voice is so **low** that she is sometimes mistaken for a man on the telephone.*

ANTONYM: high

---

defeat (1) VERB

If you **defeat** someone or something, you win a victory over them, or cause them to fail.

beat
*"I hope my team **beats** yours," Pete said cheekily to Smithy.*

conquer
*To **conquer** Wales was King Edward's lifelong wish.*

overcome
*The girl **overcame** her disability to become a great champion.*

overpower
*Legions of screeching auks **overpowered** the tiny band of travellers.*

rout
*The forces of evil in Narnia were **routed** in the last battle.*

defeat (2) NOUN

A **defeat** is the state of being beaten or of failing.

beating
*Class 3a crowed that the team from 3b had taken a **beating**.*

conquest
*The **conquest** of England by the Normans in 1066 was a turning point in history.*

downfall
*The dictator's **downfall** was sudden and spectacular.*

pasting INFORMAL
*Mighty Hawk took a severe **pasting** from the new wrestler.*

trouncing INFORMAL
*"What a **trouncing**," Mitch moaned.*

ANTONYM: victory

---

defence NOUN

Defence is the action that is taken to protect someone or something against attack.

immunity
*The nurse assured me that the vaccination would give **immunity** from measles.*

protection
*"Our paint offers ten-year **protection** from the rain," the advert boasted.*

resistance
*"**Resistance** is useless. Come out with your hands up!" bawled the loudspeaker.*

safeguard
*Taking out insurance acts as a **safeguard** against misfortune.*

✔ A country's defences are its armed forces and its weapons.

defend VERB

If you **defend** someone or something, you protect them from harm or danger.

fortify
*The manor house was **fortified** by the addition of a large wall around it.*

guard
*Brushing your teeth helps **guard** against decay and keeps your breath fresh.*

protect
*King Edward **protected** the castle with no fewer than six main gates!*

safeguard
*The sentries **safeguarded** the palace.*

See **shelter (1)**

defend (2) VERB

If you **defend** a person or their ideas, you argue in support of them.

justify

The woman justified the killing by pleading that it was in self-defence.

speak up for

Amal spoke up for his friend, despite the bully's threats.

stick up for

"Thank you for sticking up for me," said Lisa gratefully.

support

Dad supported me when our neighbour complained about the noise.

definite ADJECTIVE

Something that is **definite** is clear and unlikely to be changed.

certain

"It is certain that I will be having a birthday party," Molly told us.

guaranteed

My uncle secured us guaranteed seats for the big game.

positive

The contestant gave a very positive answer. Sadly, it was the wrong one.

sure

Being sulky is a sure way to lose friends.

ANTONYM: uncertain

definitely ADVERB OR INTERJECTION

Definitely can mean certainly and without doubt.

absolutely

"Are you able to play?" I asked. "Absolutely!" came Deepak's reply.

beyond any doubt

Beyond any doubt, the German was the best racing driver in the world.

certainly

The coach admitted, "We've certainly got a good team this year."

plainly

The witness was plainly going to say nothing.

unquestionably

The banquet was unquestionably the largest meal he had ever eaten.

delay (1) NOUN

If there is a **delay**, something does not happen until later than planned or expected.

hold-up

At the last minute, there was a hold-up in the live TV broadcast.

pause

After a pause, the mayor continued his speech.

postponement

Owing to the storms, there was a 24-hour postponement in the rocket launch.

setback

There were a few minor setbacks before the house was built.

wait

We had a slight wait before being ushered in to meet the prince.

delay (2) VERB

If something **delays** you, it makes you late or slows you down.

hinder

My baby brother did his best to hinder Mum's vacuum cleaning.

hold up

Traffic was held up by a burst water main.

slow down

Our progress was slowed down by a crawling tractor in front.

deliberate ADJECTIVE

If you do something that is **deliberate**, you do it on purpose.

calculated

The head teacher took a calculated risk and told staff to put the stalls outdoors.

conscious

"I want you to make a conscious effort to get to school on time," Mrs Lenster said.

intentional

The referee decided that the dangerous tackle was intentional, and sent the player off.

ANTONYM: unintentional

a b c **d** e f g h i j k l m n o p q r s t u v w x y z

A B C **D** E F G H I J K L M N O P Q R S T U V W X Y Z

delicious ADJECTIVE

Delicious food or drink tastes very nice.

appetizing
The waiter brought round all sorts of ***appetizing*** *titbits.*

delectable
"Thank you, that was a ***delectable*** *meal, Mrs Kean," Marie said politely.*

scrumptious INFORMAL
I think meringues are ***scrumptious****. My sister hates them.*

tasty
Some cheese is ***tasty****. Some tastes like rubber.*

ANTONYM: horrible

depend (1) VERB

If you **depend** on someone or something, you trust them and rely on them.

bank on
Mr Marshall said he was ***banking on*** *me to score a few goals.*

count on
I was ***counting on*** *Dennis to give me some good passes.*

rely on
Lyra knew she could ***rely on*** *the huge bear to come to her aid.*

trust
The owners ***trusted*** *you to put the correct money in the box.*

depend (2) VERB

If one thing **depends** on another, it is influenced by it.

be based on
"Our firm's success ***is based on*** *the hard work of the staff," the boss stated.*

hinge on
The battle ***hinged on*** *whether the cavalry could break through the enemy line.*

describe VERB

If you **describe** someone or something, you say what they are like.

define
The supply teacher asked me to ***define*** *what a hexagon is.*

explain
Beatrice ***explained*** *what she had done and her reasons for doing it.*

relate
My pal Vadim was bursting to ***relate*** *what had happened on the way to school.*

report
On Monday, I was expected to ***report*** *on our weekend camping trip.*

description NOUN

A **description** is an account or picture of something in words.

account
The witness gave his ***account*** *of the incident.*

profile
Police assembled a ***profile*** *of the burglar, making him easy to identify.*

report
Class 6 gave a ***report*** *on all the activities they had taken part in.*

deserve VERB

If you **deserve** something, you earn it or have a right to it.

be worthy of
The girl's bravery ***was worthy of*** *the highest possible honour.*

earn
The president's forgiveness of his kidnappers ***earned*** *him the respect of the world.*

justify
The boy's terrific courage ***justified*** *his award.*

merit
"Tidings of our great victory ***merit*** *a celebration," said the duke.*

despair NOUN

Despair is a total loss of hope.

desperation
In ***desperation****, the pilot ejected.*

gloom
The team had been relegated and ***gloom*** *filled the dressing room.*

hopelessness
The ***hopelessness*** *of the starving people made the reporter weep.*

desperate ADJECTIVE
A **desperate** situation is extremely dangerous or serious.

critical
*The sick woman's condition was **critical**.*

drastic
*Sealing the city was a **drastic** action, but it stopped the spread of the plague.*

grave
*"We are in a **grave** predicament," said the king, "we must fight for our lives."*

hopeless
*The situation of the soldiers seemed **hopeless**.*

despite PREPOSITION
If you do something **despite** some difficulty, you manage to do it anyway.

in spite of
***In spite of** her age, Granny is very fit.*

regardless of
***Regardless of** the danger, the medic carried the injured man to safety.*

destroy VERB
If you **destroy** something, you damage it so much that it is completely ruined.

annihilate
*Scientists think that changes in the climate may have **annihilated** the dinosaurs.*

demolish
*Workmen **demolished** the disused factory.*

devastate
*In 1945, two Japanese cities were utterly **devastated** by atom bombs.*

ruin
*"They've **ruined** that park by chopping those trees down," Grandad grumbled.*

wreck
*A lifetime playing loud music **wrecked** the guitarist's hearing.*

determination NOUN
Determination is a great strength and will to do something.

dedication
*The nurse's **dedication** earned her the thanks of all the soldiers.*

drive
*To get to the top, businesspeople need **drive** and imagination.*

perseverance
*The tortoise's **perseverance** helped him beat the foolish hare in the race.*

will
*Matthew's **will** to win saw him achieve Olympic gold.*

determined ADJECTIVE
If you are **determined** to do something, you will not let anything stop you from doing it.

intent
*She was so **intent** on doing well, she made herself ill with worry.*

persistent
*The salesman was so **persistent** that Mum shut the door on him.*

single-minded
*Sometimes you have to be **single-minded** to do a job properly.*

die (1) VERB
When a person, animal or plant **dies**, they stop living.

expire
*Tragically, the old man **expired** from the effort of the hill climb.*

pass away
*In memory of John Silver, who **passed away** this day in 1792.*

perish
*Around 700 seamen **perished** when the Mary Rose went down.*

die (2) VERB
When something **dies**, **dies away** or **dies down**, it becomes less intense and disappears.

dwindle
*Support for the team **dwindled** when they were relegated.*

fade
*As the fire brigade approached, the desperate hammering **faded** to a faint knocking.*

peter out
*Just before the finish line, the old car's engine **petered out**.*

difference NOUN

The **difference** between two things is the way in which they are unlike each other.

contrast

Although they look similar, there is a big ***contrast*** *in the characters of the twins.*

distinction

Colour-blind people often cannot see a ***distinction*** *between red and green.*

variation

We noticed a terrific ***variation*** *in price between one shop and another.*

ANTONYM: similarity

different (1) ADJECTIVE

If one thing is **different** from another, it is not like it.

contrasting

In the story, honest Cinderella is a ***contrasting*** *character to her scheming stepsisters.*

distinct

The taste of blue cheese is quite ***distinct*** *from ordinary cheese.*

opposed

The couple's viewpoints were ***opposed***.

✔ One thing is **different from** another thing. Some people think that **different to** is wrong. **Different than** is used in American English.

ANTONYM: similar or identical

different (2) ADJECTIVE

If several things are **different** from each other, they are not the same.

assorted

My pockets contained ***assorted*** *coins, mice, sweet wrappers, paperclips and fluff.*

varied

The plants were of ***varied*** *colours, including some lovely reds and purples.*

✔ If something is different from everything else in the world, it is **unique**.

ANTONYM: similar or identical

difficult (1) ADJECTIVE

Difficult things are not easy to do, understand or solve.

difficult to work out or deal with:
awkward

The tap was in an ***awkward*** *place for the plumber to get at.*

challenging

"It's the most ***challenging*** *operation I've ever tackled," the surgeon admitted.*

demanding

Dad had a ***demanding*** *week at work.*

formidable

Rescuing thousands from the earthquake rubble was a ***formidable*** *task.*

knotty

It was a ***knotty*** *problem: to cross the deep river without a bridge!*

puzzling

Zara is ***puzzling***. *One minute she's pleasant, the next she's horrid.*

tricky

The climbers were in a ***tricky*** *situation, stuck on the ledge as night drew in.*

physically difficult:
backbreaking

Digging the canals by hand was a ***backbreaking*** *job for the navvies.*

laborious

Archeology is ***laborious*** *work, digging slowly and sifting carefully.*

strenuous

Marathon running is a ***strenuous*** *business.*

difficult (2) ADJECTIVE

Someone who is **difficult** behaves in an unreasonable way.

awkward

"That horse is ***awkward***," *said the cowboy, "but I'll ride him eventually."*

troublesome

The ***troublesome*** *twins made their teacher's life a hard one.*

trying

Mrs Kray had a ***trying*** *time with Class 6 and their spellings.*

uncooperative

Uncooperative *people never work well in a team.*

difficulty NOUN

A **difficulty** is a problem.

complication

*The biggest **complication** for Brunel was that his tunnel kept flooding.*

dilemma

*Karen faced a **dilemma**. Should she play with her friends or help her mum?*

hitch

*After a **hitch** with the curtains, the play began five minutes late.*

obstacle

*The star encountered many **obstacles** on the road to fame.*

plight

*"Your **plight** is indeed a sorry one," said the knight to the damsel in the tower.*

snag

*Progress on the house was smooth, until they hit a **snag** when they found a hole in the roof.*

dig VERB

If you **dig**, you make a hole in earth or sand, especially with a spade or shovel.

burrow

*Rabbits create warrens by **burrowing** into hillsides.*

delve

*The diggers **delved** deeper, looking for a glimmer of gold.*

excavate

*Rescue workers **excavated** the rubble to free the trapped people.*

hollow out

*We **hollowed out** a dip in the sand in which to build our camp fire.*

scoop out

*The squirrel **scooped out** a hole in the early snow to reach the acorns beneath.*

dim ADJECTIVE

Something that is **dim** is lacking in brightness and badly lit.

faint

*As they neared Mordor, **faint** lights shone in the hills beyond.*

gloomy

*The **gloomy** passages of the castle were lit by flaming torches on the walls.*

shadowy

*I had trouble finding my way across the **shadowy** room to reach the light switch.*

vague

*Ben Nevis was just a **vague** outline seen through the morning mist.*

ANTONYM: bright

dirt NOUN

Dirt is any unclean substance such as dust, mud or stains.

filth

*Below the sink, the shelf was caked with **filth**.*

grime

***Grime** from a thousand mill chimneys had blackened the local buildings.*

muck

*It took me hours to clean the **muck** from the wheels of my bike.*

dirty (1) ADJECTIVE

Something that is **dirty** is marked or covered with dirt.

filthy

*"Get rid of that **filthy** rag," my dad ordered.*

grimy

*The windows were so **grimy** we could barely see out of them.*

grubby

*Mum suggested my little brother wash his **grubby** hands.*

mucky

*My father enjoys **mucky** jobs like gardening.*

mud-caked

*Everywhere in the wood, **mud-caked** motorcyclists roared like angry wasps.*

soiled

*The sign said, "Please place **soiled** nappies in the bin provided".*

stained

*The penny was badly **stained**, but came up shining after it was polished.*

ANTONYM: clean

dirty (2) ADJECTIVE

Water that is **dirty** is made unclean by poisonous substances.

contaminated
*The **contaminated** stream was an ominous red colour.*

polluted
***Polluted** lakes and waterways cannot support any wildlife.*

dirty (3) ADJECTIVE

Dirty language is unpleasant and offensive.

crude
*"That joke is very **crude** and not funny at all," the girl snapped.*

foul
*The player was sent off for using **foul** language.*

rude
***Rude** words offend many people.*

vulgar
*"There's no need to be **vulgar**," Mum told my big sister.*

disadvantage NOUN

A **disadvantage** is something that makes things difficult.

drawback
*The **drawback** of being late for school was that I missed out on Nicky's birthday cake.*

handicap
*My brother's broken leg was a **handicap** to him for a couple of months.*

inconvenience
*Mum doesn't find walking to work an **inconvenience**. It helps keep her slim.*

snag
*The only **snag** with the hotel was that it was a long way from the beach.*

ANTONYM: advantage

disagree (1) VERB

If you **disagree** with someone, you have a different opinion or view from them.

argue with
*"If you **argue with** me," Mum said stiffly, "you will go to your room!"*

differ
*Dad and Mum **differed** in their attitude to bedtimes.*

disagree (2) VERB

If you **disagree** with an action or proposal, you believe it is wrong.

dispute
*The player **disputed** the umpire's decision and was disqualified.*

object to
*Fran **objected to** what I'd said about her.*

oppose
*The mayor **opposed** the government's policy on city traffic.*

disappear VERB

If someone or something **disappears**, they go where they cannot be seen or found.

drop out of sight
*The toddler had **dropped out of sight** before his mother realized he was not at her side.*

evaporate
*The wizard uttered his spell and **evaporated** into thin air.*

fade
*The flight of geese **faded** into the twilight.*

melt away
*The crowd **melted away**, taking their memories of the music with them.*

vanish
*Without a second thought, Hermione made herself **vanish** in an instant.*

ANTONYM: appear or reappear

disaster NOUN

A **disaster** is a very bad accident, such as an earthquake or a plane crash.

calamity
*Mr and Mrs Hassan suffered a **calamity** when they lost all their savings.*

catastrophe
*The earthquake killed 1500 people – a **catastrophe** on a huge scale.*

tragedy
*The fire in the old couple's home was a **tragedy** for them.*

discuss VERB

When people **discuss** something, they talk about it in detail.

chat about
*Lisa and I **chatted about** our favourite movie.*

debate
*"I'm not willing to **debate** the matter. Go to bed!" said my big sister.*

exchange views on
*The two presidents **exchanged views on** a possible agreement.*

disease NOUN

A **disease** is an illness that affects human beings, other animals or plants.

ailment
*Grandma was feeling ill, but the doctor wasn't sure what **ailment** she was suffering from.*

complaint
*We have to put cream on our dog, Sadie, every day because she has an itchy skin **complaint**.*

illness
*Grandad had suffered from various **illnesses** in the last two years.*

sickness
*Passengers fell victim to a strange **sickness**.*

disgrace NOUN

Disgrace is the state you are in when other people disapprove of what you have done.

embarrassment
*My dad suffered the **embarrassment** of coming last in the fathers' race.*

humiliation
*The king's **humiliation** was complete when he had to crawl on all fours before his people.*

shame
*The politician suffered the **shame** of being sent to prison.*

disgusting ADJECTIVE

Something **disgusting** is very unpleasant and makes people feel a strong sense of dislike.

foul
*A **foul** smell emanated from the drain.*

loathsome
*Gollum was a **loathsome**, slimy creature.*

obnoxious
*That **obnoxious** woman is always causing trouble in the village.*

revolting
*I made a chocolate cake for Mum's birthday, but it tasted **revolting**.*

sickening
*It was **sickening** to read of children being used as cheap labour.*

vile
*"The whole **vile** trade in fur ought to be stopped," my aunt declared.*

dishonest ADJECTIVE

If someone is **dishonest**, they are not truthful and not to be trusted.

corrupt
*There will be an investigation to discover if the businessman is **corrupt**.*

crooked
*The **crooked** bank clerk embezzled thousands of pounds before she was caught.*

deceitful
*"You **deceitful** girl!" Mrs Flemming exploded. "How dare you tell me lies!"*

ANTONYM: honest

dislike VERB

If you **dislike** something or someone, you think they are unpleasant.

detest
*Mum **detests** people who promise lots but do very little.*

disapprove of
*My gran **disapproves of** any modern music.*

have no time for
*"I **have no time for** people who boast," Mr MacCuish said, looking at me.*

loathe
*The prisoner was **loathed** by the public.*

not be able to bear
*Mrs Arbuthnot **couldn't bear** anybody who didn't like hunting.*

ANTONYM: like

See **hate**

a
b
c
d
e
f
g
h
i
j
k
l
m
n
o
p
q
r
s
t
u
v
w
x
y
z

disobedient ADJECTIVE

If someone is **disobedient**, they refuse deliberately to do what they are told.

mutinous

*Captain Bligh saw that the ship's mate had a **mutinous** look in his eye.*

rebellious

***Rebellious** troops in the west rose up against the king.*

ANTONYM: obedient

display (1) NOUN

A **display** is an arrangement of things designed to attract people's attention.

demonstration

*Mrs Paulin gave a **demonstration** with her falcon, Kraa.*

exhibition

*An **exhibition** of Mum's paintings was very successful.*

parade

*The fancy-dress **parade** was bright and lively.*

presentation

*In assembly, we did a **presentation** on what our class had been studying during the term.*

display (2) VERB

If you **display** something, you show it to people.

demonstrate

*Dad **demonstrated** how to start the new lawn mower.*

exhibit

*Our dog **exhibited** signs of some sort of rash.*

parade

*That bighead Nazim **paraded** his new motorbike outside our house.*

put on show

*The winning entries were **put on show** in the school hall.*

district NOUN

A **district** is an area of a town or country.

area

*This **area** is dotted with farms and villages.*

locality

*"We're building in your **locality** soon," the salesman announced.*

neighbourhood

*Our **neighbourhood** is busy by day, but very quiet at night.*

region

*The Champagne **region** of France is famous for its sparkling wine.*

disturb (1) VERB

If you **disturb** someone, you interrupt their peace or privacy.

bother

*"I'm sorry to **bother** you," our neighbour said, "but have you seen Tibbles?"*

interrupt

*My baby brother kept **interrupting** me while I was trying to read.*

intrude on

*Mrs Mosely said she didn't want to **intrude on** us, but that's just what she was doing.*

disturb (2) VERB

If something **disturbs** you, it makes you feel upset or worried.

concern

*I was **concerned** that the toddler was playing very near the busy road.*

trouble

*You could tell that my parents were **troubled** by the anxious look they both wore.*

unsettle

*Thunder and lightning always **unsettle** our parrot Percival.*

worry

*"We'll be quite safe. You mustn't let it **worry** you," I reassured Sara.*

disused ADJECTIVE

Something **disused** is neglected or no longer used.

abandoned

*Although dangerous to explore, the **abandoned** mine was an exciting find nevertheless.*

derelict

*The tramp slept in the **derelict** warehouse.*

deserted

*The old air base was **deserted** except for some horses kept in a hangar.*

dive VERB

To **dive** is to move suddenly and quickly, often downwards.

plummet
*The rocket soared upwards, only to **plummet** back down seconds later.*

plunge
*Holden **plunged** into the cool water of the mountain stream.*

pounce
*From behind the acacia tree, the cheetah suddenly **pounced** on its prey.*

swoop
*The kestrel hovered above, then **swooped** on the unsuspecting vole.*

divide VERB

When you **divide** something, or when it **divides**, it is separated into two or more parts.

segregate
*In South Africa's past, different races were **segregated**.*

separate
*It took courage on the part of the police officer to **separate** the fighting dogs.*

split
*The thieves had just **split** the banknotes when there was an almighty knock on the door and the police came charging in.*

ANTONYM: unite

dizzy ADJECTIVE

If you feel **dizzy**, you feel that you are losing your balance and are about to fall.

dazed
*The dog was **dazed** after the collision and wandered about, whining.*

faint
*Gran said she felt **faint**, so we sat her down and brought her some water.*

giddy
*Looking down from the skyscraper roof made me feel **giddy**.*

light-headed
*With all the excitement of the party, I felt quite **light-headed**.*

do VERB

Do has many meanings, some of which are listed below.

To do a job can mean to carry out a task
carry out
*After the fire, Dad asked the builders to **carry out** repairs.*

perform
*The children **performed** miracles in transforming the derelict shed into a den.*

tackle
*"How would you like to **tackle** a bigger slope?" the instructor asked.*

To do something can mean to complete it
accomplish
*The hobbits **accomplished** things that stronger people could not.*

achieve
***Achieving** what you set out to do is always satisfying.*

complete
*My friend Ali **completed** the tables test in three minutes!*

finish
*It took me about ten minutes to **finish** the washing up.*

If something will do, it is enough
be adequate
*"Ten pounds ought to **be adequate** reward," said Dad.*

be enough
*"That will **be enough**, thank you," I said to Mrs Lampard, as she ladled out the soup.*

be sufficient
*"Will that bread **be sufficient** for all those in camp?" the head teacher enquired.*

If you can do something such as a puzzle, you can work it out
figure out
*In the maths test, it took me a while to **figure out** the answers.*

solve
*Gran is good at **solving** crossword puzzles.*

work out
*Mrs Faisal **worked out** our schedule for the coming week.*

dodge VERB

If you **dodge** something, you move suddenly to avoid being seen, hit or caught.

avoid

*The driver **avoided** the pedestrian by only a few inches.*

evade

*Trying to **evade** capture, the criminal climbed up the fire escape.*

sidestep

***Sidestepping** one defender, the forward ran smack into the next.*

swerve round

*The roadrunner **swerved round** the coyote and scooted off into the distance.*

doubt (1) NOUN

A **doubt** is a feeling of uncertainty as to whether something is true or possible.

distrust

*As he handed the ransom over, you could see the **distrust** in his eyes.*

suspicion

*Lyra had a **suspicion** that Mrs Coulter was not all she seemed to be.*

uncertainty

*As he waited for news of the battle, Will found the **uncertainty** hard to bear.*

doubt (2) VERB

If you **doubt** something, you think that it is probably not true or possible.

distrust

*You could see that the Roho brothers **distrusted**, even feared, the tall stranger who rode into town.*

query

*"Are you **querying** my authority?" the general snorted arrogantly.*

question

*"No, but I am **questioning** your judgment!" the major replied.*

suspect

*Holmes knew the murderer had given others no reason to **suspect** him.*

ANTONYM: trust

doubtful (1) ADJECTIVE

If you are **doubtful** about something, you are not sure about it.

distrustful

*Zoe was immediately **distrustful** of the slimy salesman.*

hesitant

*Despite her cruel father, Jayni was **hesitant** about leaving home.*

in two minds INFORMAL

*Legolas was **in two minds** whether to press on or to camp for the night.*

sceptical

*I was confident about United's chances in the final, whereas Dad was **sceptical**.*

suspicious

*The police were **suspicious** of the woman's alibi for the time of the crime.*

uncertain

*When the shop had to close, Mum faced an **uncertain** future.*

unsure

*The ruler of the bears was **unsure** whether to fight or not.*

ANTONYM: sure

doubtful (2) ADJECTIVE

If something is **doubtful**, it is uncertain or unlikely.

debatable

*My sister told Mum and Dad that it was **debatable** whether I would pass the test, but I was determined to prove her wrong.*

dubious

*The e-mail contained a **dubious** story about a man who was desperate for money.*

questionable

*The judge warned the jury that the witness's honesty was **questionable**.*

drag VERB

If you **drag** a heavy object somewhere, you pull it there slowly and with difficulty.

haul

*The lifeboat crew **hauled** the last of the injured seamen aboard.*

heave
*When the cox gave the word, the eight rowers **heaved** on their oars together.*

lug
*We had to **lug** our heavy suitcases up three flights of stairs at the hotel.*

draw VERB
When you **draw** something, you use a pen or pencil to make a picture of it.

doodle
*Mrs Wilson caught me **doodling** during her history lesson.*

sketch
*Artists usually **sketch** the outlines of a picture before they paint it.*

trace
*I like **tracing** pictures from my storybook.*

drawing NOUN
A **drawing** is a picture made with a pencil, pen or crayon.

Types of drawing:

cartoon	illustration	plan
diagram	landscape	portrait
doodle	map	sketch

dreadful ADJECTIVE
Something that is **dreadful** is very bad or unpleasant.

atrocious
*For our entire holiday, the weather was absolutely **atrocious**.*

awful
*India felt **awful** after speaking to her father like that.*

frightful
*"Darling, the whole thing was a **frightful** mess," the actress said, very loudly.*

ghastly
*"I couldn't agree more, my dear. The play was **ghastly**!" brayed her friend.*

shocking
*The drunken driver's **shocking** conduct could have cost lives.*

terrible
*Faith knew instantly that she had made a **terrible** mistake.*

dream (1) NOUN
Your **dream** is a hope or ambition that you often think about because you would very much like it to happen.

ambition
*It was Will's **ambition** to find the truth about his father.*

fantasy
*Madaleine's **fantasy** was to meet her favourite pop group.*

dream (2) VERB
When you **dream**, you see events in your mind, often while you are asleep.

daydream
*During Maths I **daydreamed** of far-off mountains topped by lonely castles.*

imagine
*Kesia was staring out of the window, **imagining** what it would be like to be famous.*

drill NOUN
A **drill** is a routine exercise or routine training.

exercise
*The commando unit built a dummy village for their **exercises**.*

procedure
*In case of fire, it's important to follow the correct **procedure**.*

drink (1) NOUN
A **drink** is an amount of liquid for drinking.

Cold drinks:

cola	orangeade
fizzy drinks	smoothie
fruit juice	soya milk
lemonade	sparkling water
milk	squash
milk shake	still water

Hot drinks:

cocoa	hot milk
coffee	malted milk
hot chocolate	tea

a
b
c
d
e
f
g
h
i
j
k
l
m
n
o
p
q
r
s
t
u
v
w
x
y
z

drink

drink (2) VERB
When you **drink** a liquid, you take it into your mouth and swallow it.

gulp
*Camels **gulp** a lot of water and then store it in their humps.*

guzzle
*I didn't notice that my brother was **guzzling** all the lemonade.*

sip
***Sipping** her tea, the countess gazed through the window.*

swig
*The outlaw drew the cork out with his teeth and **swigged** from the bottle.*

✔ When animals drink using their tongue, they **lap**.

drip VERB
When liquid **drips**, it falls in small drops.

dribble
*Water from the hose **dribbled** into the soil.*

plop
*I could hear the steady **plopping** of raindrops.*

splash
*The clumsy artist accidentally **splashed** paint on her canvas. It sold for lots of money.*

trickle
*In the baking depths of the canyon, the river **trickled** where it had previously gushed.*

drive VERB
If someone **drives** a vehicle, they operate it and control its movements.

control
*Raoul **controlled** his go-kart well, cornering at high speed.*

handle
*"Ah, but could you **handle** a Formula One racing car?" the instructor asked.*

droop VERB
If something **droops**, it hangs or sags downwards with no strength or firmness.

flop
*Gavin's hair always **flops** into his eyes.*

sag
*The guesthouse bed **sagged** unpleasantly in the middle.*

wilt
*If you put bluebells in a vase, they **wilt** after a few hours.*

drop (1) VERB
If something **drops**, it falls straight down.

descend
*To her alarm, the parachute jumper **descended** faster than she expected.*

plummet
*The stricken Spitfire **plummeted** into the sea.*

plunge
*I watched my brother fasten his harness, then **plunge** towards the river below.*

drop (2) NOUN
A **drop** is a very small quantity of liquid.

bead
*After the race the athlete had **beads** of sweat on her forehead.*

dash
*"Just a **dash** of vinegar, please," I said to the man serving the chips.*

drip
***Drips** of water continued to fall from the trees after the rain had stopped.*

droplet
*As the rain fell, **droplets** of water did ski jumps off my nose.*

dry ADJECTIVE
If ground is **dry**, it is not wet and contains no water.

arid
*That desert is an **arid** but beautiful region of rolling sand hills.*

barren
*Wind blew uninterrupted across the **barren**, treeless landscape.*

parched
*The river bed was **parched** and cracked where once torrents of water had flowed.*

✔ If your throat is dry, you may be **dehydrated** and need to drink fluid.

duck VERB

If you **duck**, you move your head quickly downwards in order to avoid being hit by something.

bob down

*Dad had to keep **bobbing down** to avoid the beams in the old cottage.*

crouch

*To avoid the gunfire, the soldier **crouched** behind the fence.*

stoop

*Tom had to **stoop** to get through the door.*

dull (1) ADJECTIVE

If the weather is **dull**, the sky is not bright.

cloudy

*The clear sky became more and more **cloudy**.*

dismal

*The weather was **dismal** and the birds, for once, were silent.*

overcast

*Despite the **overcast** sky, the rain held off until the match was over.*

ANTONYM: bright

dull (2) ADJECTIVE

If something is **dull**, it has no bright colours.

drab

*It was a **drab** room, without picture or ornament.*

dreary

*Heathcliff gazed through the raindrops at the **dreary** landscape beyond.*

gloomy

*There were **gloomy** paintings of the earl's ancestors hanging on many of the castle walls.*

ANTONYM: bright

dull (3) ADJECTIVE

Someone or something that is **dull** is not interesting.

boring

*Don't write **boring** stories. Fill them with life!*

tedious

*"I do find long speeches **tedious**," my uncle whispered.*

uninteresting

*Somehow, my photos always manage to look **uninteresting**.*

ANTONYM: interesting

dull (4) ADJECTIVE

A **dull** sound is low-pitched and difficult to hear.

indistinct

*Although the sound was **indistinct**, the rescue team definitely heard something.*

muffled

*A **muffled** explosion came from deep within the mine.*

ANTONYM: clear

dumb ADJECTIVE INFORMAL

Dumb can mean stupid.

dim

*Although Tim was rather **dim**, his heart was made of gold.*

slow

*The cat ran playfully around the **slow** dog.*

unintelligent

*"That was a pretty **unintelligent** thing to say," said my brother.*

dummy NOUN

A **dummy** is an imitation or model of something which is used for display.

imitation

*I couldn't believe that the cake in the shop was an **imitation**. It looked so delicious!*

model

*In St Paul's Cathedral, London, you can see the architect's original **model**.*

dump VERB

If something is **dumped** somewhere, it is put there because it is no longer wanted.

dispose of

*Because of the gases inside them, fridges are not always easy to **dispose of**.*

jettison

*To maintain height, the balloon pilot **jettisoned** everything he could spare.*

throw away

*We had to **throw away** some of the fruit as it had gone bad.*

Ee

early (1) ADJECTIVE OR ADVERB

If something happens **early**, it happens before the arranged or expected time.

ahead of schedule
*Contractors completed the bridge three months **ahead of schedule**.*

ahead of time
*"As we're **ahead of time**," Mum said as she drove, "let's stop for a coffee."*

in advance
*The builder needed some money **in advance** to buy sand, cement and bricks.*

in good time
*Our coach arrived **in good time** to catch the cross-Channel ferry.*

ANTONYM: late

early (2) ADJECTIVE

Early relates to something that happened in a period far back in time.

ancient
***Ancient** man was a hunter gatherer: hunting animals and gathering fruits and nuts.*

first
*The **first** type of bicycle, known as a "penny-farthing", had a huge front wheel.*

primitive
***Primitive** tribes all have their own creation story, as we do.*

ANTONYM: modern or recent

earth (1) NOUN

The **earth** is the planet we live on.

globe
*In 1961, Yuri Gagarin became the first astronaut to orbit the **globe**.*

planet
*The water in the seas and oceans makes up the majority of the **planet**.*

world
*My big sister took a year off to travel around the **world**.*

earth (2) NOUN

Earth is another word for soil.

ground
*The **ground** arrived much sooner than the parachute jumper expected it.*

land
*"The **land** here is good for animals but poor for crops," Farmer Gabriel said.*

soil
*Between my sister and me, we moved three tonnes of **soil**.*

easily ADVERB

If you do something **easily**, you do it without difficulty.

comfortably
*Iain was **comfortably** the winner in the 100 metres race.*

effortlessly
*The superhero's jet-powered car cruised **effortlessly** at 300 miles per hour.*

simply
*Border collie dogs are **simply** trained because they are intelligent and keen to work.*

with ease
*My brother bragged that he would pass his driving test **with ease**. How wrong he was!*

without difficulty
*The expedition reached 27 000 feet **without difficulty**, but then the storms came.*

ANTONYM: with difficulty

easy (1) ADJECTIVE

If something is **easy**, you can do it without difficulty.

a piece of cake INFORMAL
*"Anyone could do that!" my brother crowed. "It's **a piece of cake**!"*

effortless
*With her loping stride, the athlete made marathon running look **effortless**.*

no trouble
*Despite their size, it was **no trouble** for the dwarves to move the giant gates.*

simple
*For once, our maths homework was **simple**.*

straightforward

*The route is fairly **straightforward**, so we shouldn't need a map.*

ANTONYM: difficult

easy (2) ADJECTIVE

An **easy** life is comfortable and without problems.

carefree

*The two dogs lived a **carefree** life, eating, sleeping and going for walks.*

comfortable

*Flying first class is **comfortable** but boy, is it expensive!*

leisurely

*I spotted Mum and Dad taking a **leisurely** stroll on the seafront.*

relaxed

*Felicity spent a **relaxed** morning reading in the sun lounge.*

ANTONYM: hard

eat VERB

When you **eat** food, you chew it and swallow it.

eat normally:

consume

*To save them from disease, Nelson's sailors were made to **consume** fruit.*

dine

*After the theatre, the baroness **dined** at a smart restaurant.*

feed

*The newborn lamb still wasn't **feeding** properly, so Dad took it to the vet.*

eat greedily:

devour

*Bunter **devoured** his food greedily.*

gobble

*"Don't **gobble** your food – you'll get hiccups," my mother warned.*

gulp

*Zina **gulped** down her lunch and ran to catch the bus.*

scoff INFORMAL

*"Oy! You've **scoffed** my ice cream!" my brother yelled as I sprinted out of the door.*

eat a lot:

banquet

*Henry the Eighth's court **banqueted** on pheasant, quail and swan.*

feast

*While the nobles were **feasting**, minstrels played in the gallery.*

eat too much:

gorge

*Verrucca **gorged** herself on chocolate, to the point where she felt ill.*

overeat

*Grandad clutched his stomach and complained of having **overeaten**.*

eat in small amounts:

nibble

*Still feeling poorly, Hakim could only **nibble** at his cheese and biscuits.*

peck

*There was so much to choose from on the buffet that I **pecked** at lots of different things.*

taste

*The competition judges merely **tasted** the food rather than tucking in.*

> **Different places to eat:**
> | | |
> |---|---|
> | café | dining room |
> | canteen | refectory |
> | coffee shop | restaurant |
> | diner | snack bar |

edge NOUN

The **edge** is the part along the side or end of something.

> **Other nouns related to edge:**
> The edge of
> | | |
> |---|---|
> | ...a circle | – **circumference** |
> | ...a city | – **outskirts**, **suburb** |
> | ...a country | – **border**, **coast** |
> | ...a pavement | – **kerb** |
> | ...a picture | – **frame** |
> | ...a piece of land | – **boundary**, **perimeter** |
> | ...a piece of paper | – **border**, **margin** |
> | ...a shape | – **perimeter** |

effect (1) NOUN

An **effect** is something that happens as a result of something else.

consequence
*The day after the storm the **consequences** could be seen everywhere.*

outcome
*The **outcome** of Dad stopping for petrol was that I was late for school!*

result
*David worked hard for his exam, and was promoted as a **result**.*

effect (2) NOUN

An **effect** is the impression something makes.

impact
*Winning the lottery had a big **impact** on our neighbours' life.*

impression
*Hearing a real orchestra play made a huge **impression** on Carla.*

influence
*Under the **influence** of the anaesthetic, Craig had some strange dreams.*

✔ Do not confuse the noun **effect** with the verb **affect**.

emphasize VERB

If you **emphasize** something, you make it look or sound more important than the things around it.

focus on
*The newspaper article **focused on** where to look for antiques.*

highlight
*In his speech, the minister **highlighted** the need for a good railway network.*

stress
*In the word "telephone", you should **stress** the first syllable.*

empty (1) ADJECTIVE

Something that is **empty** has no people or things in it.

bare
*Wandering round the **bare** rooms, I said goodbye to the house I had always lived in and still loved.*

deserted
*From within the **deserted** warehouse came a muffled bark.*

unfurnished
*My big sister rented an **unfurnished** flat, so our parents lent her lots of household stuff.*

uninhabited
*The film star's mansion looked **uninhabited**.*

unoccupied
*As they were due to be demolished, the houses were left **unoccupied** for some weeks.*

vacant
*Luckily, the hotel had several **vacant** rooms that night.*

✔ The antonym **full** is used to describe things and the antonym **occupied** is used to describe places.

ANTONYM: full or occupied

empty (2) VERB

If you **empty** something, you remove the contents.

drain
***Drain** the boiling water from the pan before you serve the vegetables.*

pour out
*I **poured out** the cold tea from my cup.*

unload
*It was Tariq's job to **unload** the truck.*

ANTONYM: fill

empty (3) VERB

If a building is **emptied**, everybody in it has to go outside.

clear
*The bomb squad **cleared** the building.*

evacuate
*For our fire practice, the teachers had to **evacuate** the school.*

encourage (1) VERB

If you **encourage** someone, you give them the confidence to do something.

inspire
***Inspired** by the example of Shackleton, Rupert resolved to become a polar explorer.*

motivate

*The instructor **motivated** us to have a go at the abseil.*

urge

*"Ladies and gentlemen, I **urge** you to vote for me!" the politician shouted.*

encourage (2) VERB

If you **encourage** someone, you support them.

boost

*Winning the cup **boosted** the team's confidence.*

foster

*Mrs Ali's sense of humour **fostered** a terrific relationship with her pupils.*

further

*The new library was added to **further** children's interest in reading.*

promote

*Adverts were no longer allowed to **promote** cigarette smoking.*

support

*Dad **supported** my idea about joining the hockey team.*

end (1) NOUN

The **end** of an event is the last part of it.

close

*At the **close** of play today, Australia had scored 452 runs.*

conclusion

*In the **conclusion** of her speech, Mrs Abrahams said how much she would miss us.*

ending

*Every story needs an interesting **ending**.*

finale

*For the show's **finale**, all the dancers came on stage in a spectacular jazz number.*

finish

*At the **finish**, three horses were neck and neck.*

ANTONYM: beginning or start

end (2) NOUN

The **end** of something is the furthest point of it.

boundary

*In cricket, if the ball goes over the **boundary**, four runs are scored.*

edge

*When I got to the **edge** of the diving board, I was shaking with nerves.*

limit

*At the **limit** of her ropes, the abseiler was still several metres above the ground.*

end (3) VERB

When something **ends**, it finishes.

conclude

*The evening **concluded** with a vote of thanks to the school choir.*

culminate

*The fireworks display **culminated** in a huge explosion of colour and noise.*

terminate

*For his bad behaviour, the club **terminated** the player's contract.*

ending NOUN

The **ending** of something is when it finishes.

climax

*For the **climax**, the lion tamer put her head inside the great beast's mouth.*

culmination

*As a **culmination** to the week's events, Saturday's grand parade took some beating.*

finale

*Our grand **finale** involved the whole school.*

ANTONYM: beginning or start

endless ADJECTIVE

Something that is **endless** has, or seems to have, no end.

continual

*Our **continual** arguing was driving Mum mad.*

continuous

*Day and night, the **continuous** throb of the generator echoed through the woods.*

everlasting

*The couple knew their love was **everlasting**.*

perpetual

*"That **perpetual** din is driving me crackers!" I heard Dad bawling from downstairs.*

✔ The word **continual** describes things which happen again and again, but not constantly. **Continuous** actions happen without ceasing.

A
B
C
D
E
F
G
H
I
J
K
L
M
N
O
P
Q
R
S
T
U
V
W
X
Y
Z

endure VERB
If you **endure** someone or something unpleasant, you put up with them.

bear
*For the swordsman, mortally wounded, the pain was hard to **bear**.*

brave
*Grace **braved** the wind and the waves to rescue her drowning brother.*

cope with
*Sometimes my mum finds Gran and Grandad difficult to **cope with**.*

experience
*The refugees **experienced** great hardship on their trek to freedom.*

stand
*I don't know how the people who live near the sewage works **stand** the smell.*

suffer
*Malik has **suffered** years of pain from arthritis.*

undergo
*Dad had to **undergo** surgery on his knee.*

enemy NOUN
Your **enemy** is someone who is very much against you and may wish to harm you.

adversary
*Finally, King Harold faced his **adversary**, William of Normandy.*

foe
*At Agincourt, the French **foe** were defeated by English archers.*

opponent
*Early on, the **opponents** had the upper hand, but our team had more stamina.*

rival
*The evil sheriff was Robin Hood's **rival** for the hand of Maid Marion.*

ANTONYM: friend or ally

energetic ADJECTIVE
Someone who is **energetic** is full of energy.

active
*Even though he is in his 70s, Grandpa is still very **active**, especially in his garden.*

lively
*My **lively** grandparents love to go dancing.*

vigorous
*Apparently, **vigorous** exercise is the best way to stay healthy.*

ANTONYM: lethargic

energy NOUN
Energy is the physical strength you need to do active things.

drive
*My big brother's **drive** and ambition earned him the top sales award.*

get-up-and-go INFORMAL
*My mum has more **get-up-and-go** than I do! She's always busy.*

stamina
*To survive a marathon run, you need **stamina** more than speed.*

vigour
*We laughed at the **vigour** with which our head teacher strutted up and down.*

vitality
*Uncle Archie is full of **vitality**; he plays squash, hockey and golf.*

enormous ADJECTIVE
Something that is **enormous** is very large in size or amount.

colossal
*My greedy brother grabbed a **colossal** helping of pudding.*

gargantuan
*After a sea trip, the fisherman's appetite was **gargantuan**.*

gigantic
*The tidal wave formed a **gigantic** wall, visible for miles out to sea.*

huge
*It was a **huge** relief to pass my exams.*

massive
*In one **massive** surge, the surfer was swept towards the shore at 80 miles an hour.*

vast
*The Sahara desert covers a **vast** area of northern Africa.*

enough ADJECTIVE

Enough can mean as much or as many as is necessary.

adequate
I wasn't sure if my knowledge was adequate to pass the test.

ample
Mum offered us more meat, but I had eaten ample already.

sufficient
"Have you all got sufficient wet weather gear?" Miss Perkins asked.

enthusiasm NOUN

If you show **enthusiasm** for something, you show much interest and excitement.

excitement
You could feel the excitement in the school as Christmas approached.

interest
Grandad has always had an interest in trains.

passion
Olga's passion for horses rules her life.

zeal
My mum plays tennis with zeal.

enthusiastic ADJECTIVE

If you are **enthusiastic** about something, you show great excitement, eagerness and approval for something.

ardent
As an ardent Reds fan, my friend wore as much red clothing as he could find.

eager
Janet was so eager to get to the food, she tripped and fell headfirst into the trifle.

keen
When it comes to fishing, Mr Hayles is as keen as anyone.

passionate
Jill is a passionate believer in green issues and often goes on protest marches.

wholehearted
Crudsea Town Council gave its wholehearted support to our club's plan.

ANTONYM: unenthusiastic

envious ADJECTIVE

If you are **envious**, you wish you could have what someone else has.

green with envy
The wicked witch was green with envy that her good sister was liked by everybody.

jealous
Our dog, Tess, gets jealous if the cat gets more attention than she does.

resentful
The bear Lofur was resentful of humans and the powers that they had.

envy VERB

If you **envy** someone, you wish you had what they have.

begrudge
Scrooge begrudged every penny that he paid his poor clerk.

be jealous
Several of the others were jealous of Lyra's skill and intelligence.

covet
You could tell from his envious glances that my brother coveted my bike.

resent
Because she was unsuccessful herself, the artist resented the success of other painters.

equal (1) ADJECTIVE

If two things are **equal**, they are the same in size, number or amount.

balanced
Our attack and defence were balanced in size and ability.

equivalent
A hundred centimetres are equivalent to one metre.

equal (2) VERB

If something **equals** something else, it is equivalent to it.

be equal to
In soccer, two yellow cards are equal to one red card, and the player is sent off.

match
Caroline's skill at multiplication matched my skill at spelling.

A
B
C
D
E
F
G
H
I
J
K
L
M
N
O
P
Q
R
S
T
U
V
W
X
Y
Z

equipment NOUN

Equipment is all the things that are needed or used for a particular job or activity.

apparatus
*I love gymnastics, especially when we use all of the **apparatus**.*

gear
*Dave the mechanic has all the **gear** for welding metal.*

paraphernalia
*Granny would insist on taking all her **paraphernalia** with her on holiday.*

tackle
*Mum makes Dad keep all his fishing **tackle** in the garage.*

tools
*My brother keeps his plumbing **tools** in a huge expanding box.*

escape VERB

If you **escape** from someone or something, you succeed in getting away from them.

break free
*Frightened by the storm, the horse **broke free** from its stable.*

break out
*Prisoners planned to **break out** with the aid of a helicopter.*

flee
*When they heard the police siren, the vandals tried to **flee** the scene.*

make a getaway
*The robbers **made a getaway** in a stolen van.*

make your escape
*After an hour of boredom, the twins **made their escape** through a back door.*

especially ADVERB

You say **especially** to show that something applies more to one thing, person or situation than to others.

in particular
*Krim, the alien, liked all earthlings, but Sean **in particular**.*

particularly
*"I **particularly** fancy that lampshade," Mum said thoughtfully.*

specifically
*Dad said any colour of front door would do, while Mum **specifically** wanted blue.*

essential ADJECTIVE

Something that is **essential** is absolutely necessary.

crucial
*Food and other supplies are **crucial** to any expedition's success.*

indispensable
*Florence and her nursing team proved **indispensable** to the hospital's doctors.*

key
*"Listen up. This is **key** to the whole operation!" the general barked.*

vital
*Before exams, it's **vital** to be well rested.*

ANTONYM: unnecessary

even (1) ADJECTIVE

An **even** surface is level, smooth and flat.

flat
*For a land speed record, the surface must be perfectly **flat**.*

level
*Builders always make sure that each layer of bricks is **level**.*

smooth
*After a bumpy journey, the aircraft made a **smooth** landing.*

ANTONYM: uneven

even (2) ADJECTIVE

An **even** measurement or rate stays at about the same level.

constant
*My Uncle Jim went on about the **constant** beat of his motorbike engine.*

regular
*Outside my window, the trees kept up a **regular** tapping in the wind.*

steady
*Viking longships were rowed to the **steady** beat of a drum.*

ANTONYM: irregular

even (3) ADJECTIVE

Something that is **even** is equally balanced between two sides.

balanced

*The jury was **balanced** between "guilty" and "not guilty".*

equal

*Both players had an **equal** chance of winning the tennis match.*

level

*The two athletes were **level** as they came to the last hurdle.*

tied

*At full time, the scores were **tied**, so we took penalties to decide the winner.*

well-matched

*Our team and my sister's were **well-matched**, and we just scraped a win.*

ANTONYM: uneven

evening NOUN

The **evening** is the part of the day between the end of the afternoon and the time you go to bed.

dusk

*As the **dusk** gathered, street lights flickered on.*

nightfall

*By **nightfall**, most creatures were asleep and the wood was silent.*

sunset

***Sunset** over the sea is a magical sight.*

twilight

*Angela started telling stupid stories about ghosts and zombies coming alive at **twilight**.*

event (1) NOUN

An **event** is something that happens, especially when it is unusual or important.

episode

*"The **episode** where my bicycle brakes failed is not one I want to repeat," Dad said.*

incident

*Police were called to an **incident** outside a bar. A woman was arrested.*

occurrence

*After the house shook, Gran remembered a similar **occurrence** over 20 years before.*

event (2) NOUN

An **event** is an organized activity, such as a sports match or a concert.

ceremony

*The wedding **ceremony** took place at the registry office.*

competition

*The first **competition** of the afternoon was the long jump.*

function

*Last night there was a very noisy **function** in the town hall.*

occasion

*"This christening is an **occasion** to remember!" announced Uncle George.*

evil (1) ADJECTIVE

Something or someone **evil** is very bad and causes harm to people.

nasty

*"I couldn't believe the **nasty** things she came out with," my mum said in dismay.*

vicious

*It was a **vicious** attack, causing the victim severe injuries.*

vile

*Von Hugo was a **vile** man who fully deserved his prison sentence.*

villainous

*The **villainous** Cruella plotted to capture the Dalmatian puppies.*

wicked

*The witch's **wicked** plans were thwarted by the good fairy.*

evil (2) NOUN

Evil is used to refer to all the wicked or bad things that happen in the world.

corruption

*"Where **corruption** exists, bribes are taken. Money, not honesty, is king," said Grandpa.*

wickedness

*The baron was the soul of **wickedness**, enjoying the misery he inflicted.*

wrongdoing

*Towards the end of his life, the once wicked count repented of his lifetime of **wrongdoing**.*

a
b
c
d
e
f
g
h
i
j
k
l
m
n
o
p
q
r
s
t
u
v
w
x
y
z

exact ADJECTIVE
If something is **exact**, it is accurately measured or made.

accurate
"Here's an **accurate** time check. Synchronize your watches," the colonel called.

detailed
Bonnie wrote down **detailed** notes of what she had witnessed.

precise
It's difficult to give a **precise** date for the painting.

specific
"Be **specific** about what equipment you need," said our science teacher.

true
The excellent new portrait was a **true** likeness of the earl.

ANTONYM: inaccurate

exaggerate VERB
If you **exaggerate**, you make something seem better, worse, bigger or more important than it really is.

lay it on thick INFORMAL
The chap was telling us of his exploits and **laying it on thick**.

overdo
That bit about wrestling the polar bear was **overdoing** it, I thought.

overemphasize
"I can't **overemphasize**," the skipper said, "the importance of life jackets."

overstate
In her concern for the children, Mrs Lucas had **overstated** the actual danger.

examination (1) NOUN
If you take an **examination**, you take a test to find out how much you know about a subject.

assessment
Many workers have to have a yearly **assessment** of their performance.

exam
"My next **exam** is on Wednesday," remarked my cousin gloomily.

test
Mr Ricketts' weekly Latin **test** was always a real killer.

examination (2) NOUN
An **examination** is a close inspection of something.

analysis
An **analysis** of what the dead man had eaten revealed no poison.

checkup
Uncle Steve had to go to the local hospital for a **checkup**.

inspection
Dad asked his friend to do an **inspection** of the second-hand car he wanted to buy.

investigation
Detectives conducted an **investigation** into the missing jewels.

study
A **study** of the ancient axe proved it was of Viking origin.

survey
Our class conducted a **survey** on children's heroes and heroines.

examine VERB
If you **examine** something, you inspect it carefully.

analyse
"When you **analyse** what went wrong, the causes are plain," the scientist said.

check
Mrs Knox tells us to **check** our work, then check it again.

inspect
Scientists in radiation suits **inspected** the shattered reactor.

investigate
Our dog, Jim, **investigates** every interesting smell along the road.

scrutinize
An official **scrutinized** the trials results to make sure every rider had been fairly treated.

study
For some time, my parents **studied** the menu on the restaurant window.

example NOUN
An **example** is something that is typical of a particular group of things.

illustration
*"This is an **illustration** of the kind of work I'd like to see," said Mrs Clarke.*

instance
*"In this **instance** you should contact your doctor," advised the leaflet.*

sample
*Mum brought home a **sample** of the carpet, to check for colour.*

specimen
*To give the pupil a guide, some books have **specimen** answers to exam questions.*

excellent ADJECTIVE
Something that is **excellent** is very good indeed.

first-class
*I thought the acting was **first-class**, even if the singing was not as good.*

first-rate
*Becky gave a **first-rate** talk about her trip to Australia.*

outstanding
*Mrs Burton is an **outstanding** head teacher.*

superb
*"That was a **superb** meal, thank you," said Natalie, rubbing her tummy.*

ANTONYM: terrible

except PREPOSITION
Except can mean apart from or not including.

apart from
***Apart from** London, which other European cities have royal palaces?*

besides
***Besides** Ashley, everyone was going to the school camp.*

excluding
*The whole team got a medal, **excluding** poor Eric, who missed the final.*

with the exception of
***With the exception of** my brother, the whole family went to the beach.*

excited ADJECTIVE
If you are **excited** about something, it makes you feel very happy and enthusiastic.

enthusiastic
*Greg was very **enthusiastic** about anything to do with tennis.*

thrilled
*All the class were **thrilled** to take part in the television quiz.*

ANTONYM: unexcited

exciting ADJECTIVE
Something **exciting** makes you feel very happy and enthusiastic.

dramatic
*It was a **dramatic** scene, with ambulances and police cars all over the place.*

enthralling
*To watch such a spectacular show was an **enthralling** experience.*

inspiring
*Seeing those children and what they could do was absolutely **inspiring**.*

stirring
*The **stirring** sound of the bagpipes caused many Scots' hearts to quicken.*

thrilling
*The marathon race was **thrilling**, with the two athletes neck and neck for the last two miles.*

ANTONYM: unexciting

excitement NOUN
Excitement is the feeling of being excited.

eagerness
*The kids were all full of **eagerness** to be off on the school trip.*

enthusiasm
*I love the bubbly **enthusiasm** which my sister puts into her dancing lessons.*

passion
*My dad has a **passion** for fishing, but I think it's boring.*

thrill
*Lots of people love the **thrill** of horse racing, especially my Uncle Rupert.*

a
b
c
d
e
f
g
h
i
j
k
l
m
n
o
p
q
r
s
t
u
v
w
x
y
z

excuse

A B C D E F G H I J K L M N O P Q R S T U V W X Y Z

excuse NOUN

An **excuse** is a reason you give to explain why something has been done, has not been done, or will not be done.

explanation
Serena came out with all sorts of **explanations** *for her missing homework, but none of them were true.*

justification
The judge declared that there could be no **justification** *for such a wicked crime.*

reason
"What possible **reason** *can you have for borrowing my wetsuit?" Dad exploded.*

exercise (1) NOUN

Exercise is any activity that you do in order to improve at something, or to get fit and stay healthy.

activity
One **activity** *we did was to run up and down bouncing the ball.*

exertion
Hassan was tired after the **exertion** *of football practice.*

training
For any type of sport, **training** *is essential if you want to do well.*

exercise (2) VERB

When you **exercise**, you do activities that help you to get fit and stay healthy.

keep fit
The prisoner **kept fit** *by doing yoga regularly in her cell.*

train
Every Wednesday, we had to **train** *for Saturday's soccer match.*

expect (1) VERB

If you **expect** something to happen, you believe that it will happen.

anticipate
For some months, Crusoe **anticipated** *rescue, but eventually ceased to think about it.*

believe
Gita **believed** *that she would fulfil her ambition to be a dancer.*

predict
As Mum's teachers had all **predicted***, she did very well in her exams.*

expect (2) VERB

If you **expect** something, you believe that you ought to get or have it.

bank on
"I was **banking on** *you to remind me to do my homework," complained my sister.*

count on
The injured climber was **counting on** *his friend to get help.*

rely on
"Can I **rely on** *you to feed the dogs?" my brother asked, staring at me hard.*

expedition NOUN

An **expedition** is an organized journey made for a special purpose, often to explore.

mission
Perhaps the most dangerous space **mission** *will be to land on an outer planet of the galaxy.*

trek
Shackleton's men were faced with an exhausting **trek** *to the whaling station.*

expensive ADJECTIVE

If something is **expensive**, it costs a lot of money.

costly
"Jewels that are **costly** *are only for the rich," I agreed.*

exorbitant
"But that's **exorbitant***!" my father burst out. "We can't afford that!"*

overpriced
"It's my view that perfumes are grossly **overpriced***," said my grandmother.*

ANTONYM: inexpensive or cheap

---

experience (1) NOUN

Experience is knowledge or skill in a particular job or activity, which you have gained from doing that job or activity.

expertise
The expedition leader's medical **expertise** *made the difference between life and death.*

know-how INFORMAL
It was good of Mrs Flaherty to share her **know-how** *on cookery with me.*

knowledge
I was amazed by Gran's wide **knowledge** *of computers.*

practice
The old gardener had had many years' **practice** *at growing plants from cuttings.*

understanding
Gus's **understanding** *of the area was useful on our treasure hunt.*

experience (2) NOUN

An **experience** is something that you do or something that happens to you, especially something new or unusual.

adventure
For many children, a train trip is a real **adventure***.*

incident
"I'll never forget the **incident** *when your grandma lost her passport!" Grandpa told me.*

ordeal
The hostage's **ordeal** *was one that she never wanted to experience again.*

experienced ADJECTIVE

An **experienced** person has been doing a particular job or activity for a long time, and knows a lot about it.

accomplished
My dad, an **accomplished** *pianist, plays the organ in church.*

expert
D'Artagnan was an **expert** *swordsman and a reasonable shot with a pistol.*

practised
The con man was a **practised** *liar.*

skilful
Already a **skilful** *ice skater, Philip took to skiing like a veteran.*

ANTONYM: inexperienced or novice

expert (1) NOUN

An **expert** is a person who is very skilled at something, or who knows a lot about a particular subject.

authority
My dad is an **authority** *on mice, and gives lectures on them.*

professional
We saw our neighbour, a **professional** *pianist, playing on TV the other day.*

specialist
As the mechanic is a **specialist** *in old cars, Grandad took his jalopy to him.*

wizard INFORMAL
One of my brothers is a computer **wizard***. He's like lightning!*

expert (2) ADJECTIVE

If someone is **expert** at something, they are very skilled at it, or know a lot about it.

experienced
My gran is an **experienced** *cook who makes brilliant chocolate cake.*

knowledgeable
Our teacher, Mrs Crowther, is very **knowledgeable** *about local history.*

proficient
Mrs Fiddis, our French teacher, is **proficient** *in several languages.*

skilled
The **skilled** *photographer took some great photographs of the wedding.*

explain VERB

If you **explain** something, you give information about it or reasons for it so that it can be understood.

clarify
I asked Mr Ledbetter to **clarify** *what he meant by the word "hypothetical".*

give an explanation of
"Now Sian," Miss Cooke said, "give us **an explanation of** *the water cycle."*

interpret
"Can you **interpret** *these instructions for me?" Dad asked Mum.*

make clear
The instructions in the recipe book did not **make clear** *what I should do next.*

See **describe**

explanation (1) NOUN

An **explanation** is something that helps people understand something.

clarification

*The minister requested **clarification** about certain parts of the proposed treaty.*

interpretation

*The astrologer's **interpretation** of my stars didn't match what actually happened.*

explanation (2) NOUN

An **explanation** is something that explains why something happens.

excuse

*There was no **excuse** for the new system of parking machines being worse than the old.*

reason

*Robert's **reason** for being late was that the dog overslept and didn't wake him up.*

explore VERB

If you **explore** a place, you travel around it to discover what it is like.

reconnoitre

*The captain sent two men to **reconnoitre** the machine-gun post.*

scout

*Graham **scouted** ahead to make sure no one was around, before he and Carl crept out.*

search

*"We **searched**, sir, but there's no sign of the enemy," Trooper Smith said.*

survey

*My brother and I **surveyed** the holiday camp eagerly.*

take a look around INFORMAL

*Tamara and Craig **took a look around** the garden of their new house.*

explosion NOUN

An **explosion** is a sudden violent burst of energy, for example one caused by a bomb.

blast

*The **blast** from the quarry echoed round the surrounding hillside.*

detonation

*When a car engine runs, a repeating series of small **detonations** takes place.*

expression NOUN

Your **expression** is the look on your face that shows what you are thinking or feeling.

Some expressions of the face:	
serious	– frown, glare, grimace, poker-face, pout, scowl, sneer
happy	– beam, grin, smile, smirk
in pain	– wince
menacing	– glower, leer

extra ADJECTIVE

You use **extra** to mean more than is usual, necessary or expected.

additional

*"I'll need **additional** time for this job," the writer said wearily.*

further

*The refugees received **further** aid in the form of tents and cooking equipment.*

supplementary

*Some people believe in taking **supplementary** vitamins, besides their normal diet.*

See **spare**

extraordinary ADJECTIVE

Someone or something that is **extraordinary** is very unusual or surprising.

amazing

*A volcano erupting is an **amazing** sight.*

remarkable

*"What a **remarkable** coincidence," exclaimed the old lady. "That's my name too!"*

surprising

*I found it **surprising** that no one besides me had heard of the explorer.*

unheard-of

*Everybody gasped. It was **unheard-of** for Martin to say more than a single word!*

unique

*The beautiful antique vase was **unique**.*

unusual

*It was **unusual** for my sister to wash up, but there she was at the sink!*

ANTONYM: ordinary

Ff

fabulous ADJECTIVE
Someone or something **fabulous** is wonderful
or very impressive.

astounding
The new drug for asthma sufferers achieved
***astounding** results.*

marvellous
*"It's **marvellous** news that Colin is going on
the school skiing trip!" Mrs Finch exclaimed.*

phenomenal
To score that many home runs was a
***phenomenal** achievement.*

superb
*The weather was **superb** and the picnic was
quite delicious.*

wonderful
*We had a **wonderful** holiday in Cyprus.*

face NOUN
Your **face** is the front part of your head, from
your chin to your forehead.

countenance
*Scrooge's **countenance** betrayed no emotion.*

features
*The film star's rugged **features** appeared in
magazines throughout the world.*

fact NOUN
If something is a matter of **fact**, it is true.

certainty
*"Looking at this traffic jam, it is a **certainty**
that we will miss the train," said Dad.*

reality
*Callum dreamt of being a superhero, although
in **reality** he was just an everyday boy.*

truth
*The **truth** was that the climber was in danger.*

fail VERB
If someone or something **fails**, they do not
succeed.

be unsuccessful
*At their first attempt to launch, the balloonists
were **unsuccessful**.*

come to grief
The sailing ship Hesperus ***came to grief** on
the rocks at Norman's Woe.*

fall through
*Our plans for a new hall **fell through** owing
to lack of money.*

flop INFORMAL
*The Broadway show **flopped**, closing after
only three nights.*

ANTONYM: succeed

failure NOUN
A **failure** is a lack of success in doing
something.

breakdown
*There was a **breakdown** in communications
between us, and Finn didn't turn up.*

defeat
*The Blues suffered a bad **defeat** to the Reds.*

disaster
*Our caravan holiday was a total **disaster**.
Just about everything went wrong!*

lack of success
*My brother's **lack of success** in finding a job
could be because he's very lazy.*

washout INFORMAL
*Sadly, because of the awful weather, the
country show was a **washout**.*

ANTONYM: success

faint (1) ADJECTIVE
A **faint** sound is not loud and cannot be
heard easily.

distant
*To her delight, Anastasia heard the **distant**
tinkle of sleigh bells.*

dull
*There was a **dull** thud from upstairs. My sister
had fallen out of bed.*

indistinct
*Throughout the wood was the **indistinct**
murmur of a thousand animal voices.*

muffled
*From within the mine came a **muffled** cry.*

ANTONYM: loud

A B C D E F G H I J K L M N O P Q R S T U V W X Y Z

faint (2) ADJECTIVE

A **faint** light or colour is not strong or intense.

dim
*In the **dim** light of the evening, it was difficult to find the path off the hill.*

hazy
*A **hazy** sun shone through the skeletal branches of the trees.*

pale
*From the moorland cottage, the **pale** glow of a lamp shone into the night.*

subdued
*The lighting in the restaurant was **subdued**.*

ANTONYM: strong

faint (3) ADJECTIVE

If you feel **faint**, you feel dizzy and unsteady.

dizzy
*Gran felt **dizzy** and had to sit down.*

giddy
*Emily was almost **giddy** with excitement. A new pony!*

light-headed
*After hours writing sentences on the computer, John felt quite **light-headed**.*

unsteady
*The old man, a little **unsteady** at first, stood up and brushed the crumbs off his suit.*

*See **weak (1)***

fair (1) ADJECTIVE

Something that is **fair** seems reasonable to most people.

impartial
*It's important that umpires are **impartial**.*

just
*The judge's verdict was a **just** one, although the prisoner didn't see it that way.*

right
*Ami felt it only **right** that she should be paid for the hard work she did.*

unbiased
*We asked an outsider to give us her **unbiased** opinion on the argument.*

ANTONYM: unfair

fair (2) NOUN

A **fair** is a form of entertainment that takes place outside, with stalls, games and rides.

Some things you might find at a fair:	
big wheel	merry-go-round
bumper cars	roller coaster
coconut shy	roundabout
fortune-teller	shooting gallery
ghost train	stalls
helter-skelter	swingboat

fairly ADVERB

Fairly can mean quite or rather.

moderately
*Mum was **moderately** pleased with her painting, but felt she could do better.*

quite
*Marcel was **quite** happy to watch the game, rather than join in.*

rather
***Rather** worried by the black clouds, Dad brought the washing in.*

reasonably
*We were **reasonably** sure that this was the place we'd started from.*

somewhat
*"I was **somewhat** surprised, Potter," the principal said, "to find you missing."*

faithful ADJECTIVE

If you are **faithful** to someone or something, you are loyal and continue to support them.

dependable
*The **dependable** farm horse would plod up and down all day long.*

devoted
*The card with the flowers read, "To a **devoted** wife and mother".*

loyal
*Despite his low wages, the servant stayed **loyal** to his employers.*

staunch
*My pal Sanjay is a **staunch** City supporter.*

ANTONYM: unfaithful

fake (1) NOUN

A **fake** is an imitation of something, made to trick people into thinking that it is genuine.

copy
*The painting was clearly not an original, but merely a poor **copy**.*

forgery
*I handed over the banknote, not realizing it was a **forgery**.*

imitation
*The diamonds were only **imitation**, but they fooled the thief.*

reproduction
*The gallery displayed a **reproduction** of the painting because the original was damaged.*

fake (2) ADJECTIVE

Something that is **fake** is an imitation and not genuine.

artificial
*There were **artificial** flowers in all the vases at the restaurant.*

bogus INFORMAL
*Beware of **bogus** callers who pretend to be from the electricity company.*

counterfeit
*The shop assistant accidentally accepted a **counterfeit** note from the forger.*

false
*The spy had a **false** passport to travel with.*

forged
*The cashier immediately spotted the **forged** signature on the cheque.*

imitation
*The wallpaper had an **imitation** brick design.*

phoney INFORMAL
*The count didn't fool anybody with his **phoney** French accent.*

ANTONYM: genuine

fake (3) VERB

If you **fake** a feeling, you pretend that you are experiencing it.

feign
*Avinash **feigned** happiness at being visited by his grandparents.*

pretend
*I thought at first that my brother was angry, but he was only **pretending**.*

simulate
*To help the first-aiders practise for their test, some people **simulated** being ill.*

✔ A person who fakes the identity of another person is an **impostor**.

fall (1) VERB

When someone or something **falls**, or **falls over**, or **falls down**, they drop towards the ground.

collapse
*Exhausted, Della **collapsed** into a chair.*

keel over
*Several soldiers in the parade **keeled over** in the sweltering heat.*

topple
*As the angry crowd pulled and pushed, the dictator's statue **toppled** to the ground.*

tumble
*The toddler **tumbled** awkwardly, but soon picked herself up.*

fall (2) VERB

If something **falls**, it becomes less or lower.

decrease
*The number of people unemployed **decreased** this year.*

drop
*The cost of foreign holidays has **dropped** over the past five years.*

tumble
*House prices **tumbled** last year.*

ANTONYM: rise

fall (3) NOUN

If there is a **fall** in the amount of something, it gets smaller.

decrease
*Bosses say that a **decrease** in orders is going to lead to a loss of jobs.*

reduction
*All over the store there was a 20 per cent **reduction** of prices.*

ANTONYM: rise

a b c d e f g h i j k l m n o p q r s t u v w x y z

A
B
C
D
E
F
G
H
I
J
K
L
M
N
O
P
Q
R
S
T
U
V
W
X
Y
Z

fall out VERB

If you **fall out** with someone, you disagree and quarrel with them.

quarrel

*Marsha and I **quarrelled** because she wouldn't let me have my turn.*

squabble

*I could hear my sister and brother **squabbling** over a game.*

false (1) ADJECTIVE

Something that is **false** is not real or genuine, but intended to seem real.

artificial

*Douglas Bader, a famous World War Two pilot, had **artificial** legs and still managed to fly.*

bogus

*The count made a **bogus** claim to the throne.*

fake

*The **fake** painting fooled most people.*

forged

*Customs officers took one look at the **forged** passport and arrested its owner.*

false (2) ADJECTIVE

If something you say is **false**, it is untrue or incorrect.

deceptive

*The politician's answer was **deceptive**, as it only told half the truth.*

fictitious

*Sherlock Holmes's **fictitious** address was 221b Baker Street, London.*

untrue

*"It's quite **untrue** to say that money brings happiness," sighed the miserable millionaire.*

wrong

*Carruthers had the **wrong** idea, and was wasting his time.*

ANTONYM: true

famous ADJECTIVE

Someone or something **famous** is very well-known.

acclaimed

*Roald Dahl was the **acclaimed** author of many popular children's books.*

celebrated

*The programme was presented by the **celebrated** Italian chef, Alfonso Fatti.*

renowned

*Luigi's restaurant was **renowned** for its pasta.*

well-known

*My mum is **well-known** for her paintings.*

✔ A person who is well-known for being bad or evil is **infamous**.

ANTONYM: unknown

fan NOUN

If you are a **fan** of something or someone famous, you like them very much.

enthusiast

*My Grandad, being an ex-railwayman, was a great rail **enthusiast**.*

fiend INFORMAL

*Omar is a real go-kart **fiend**. He may well become a champion some day.*

supporter

*After the match, the team jogged round the pitch, waving to their **supporters**.*

fancy ADJECTIVE

Something that is **fancy** is highly decorated and special.

decorative

*Fiona added **decorative** sequins to her dress.*

elaborate

*The cathedral had **elaborate** carved wood choir stalls.*

ornate

*Around the ancient manor stretched **ornate** gardens with fountains.*

ANTONYM: plain

fantastic ADJECTIVE

Something **fantastic** is wonderful and very pleasing.

excellent

*At the zoo, you have an **excellent** underwater view of penguins swimming.*

out-of-this-world INFORMAL

*The dress the film star wore to the premiere was **out-of-this-world**.*

sensational

*Mum's chocolate cakes are always **sensational**.*

superb

*It was a **superb** day out: great weather and a beautiful beach.*

far (1) ADVERB

Far can mean a long distance away.

a great distance

*The elves travelled **a great distance** from their homeland to help others.*

a long way

*We had to travel **a long way** before we found somewhere to spend the night.*

miles

*"You don't want to cycle there, it's **miles** away!" my friend scoffed.*

ANTONYM: near or close

far (2) ADVERB

You can use **far** to mean very much or to a great extent.

considerably

*The game cost **considerably** more than Dad had anticipated.*

decidedly

*Mum's cooking is **decidedly** more tasty than school dinners.*

much

*Mrs Cornelius said my handwriting was **much** neater than it was last year.*

far (3) ADJECTIVE

A **far** place is one that is very distant, or the more distant of two things.

distant

*Across the meadows, a **distant** bell tolled.*

faraway

*Isla dreamed of lying on a **faraway** beach by a clear turquoise sea.*

far-flung

*Dad's job took him to **far-flung** places.*

remote

*The **remote** villages of the rainforest are hundreds of miles from the nearest town.*

ANTONYM: near or close

farm NOUN

A **farm** is an area of land and buildings used for growing crops or raising animals.

✔ **Agriculture** is a formal word for farming. A person who runs a farm is called a **farmer**.

Types of farm:
arable farm	mixed farm
cattle farm	pig farm
dairy farm	poultry farm
fish farm	smallholding
fruit farm	stud farm

fashion NOUN

A **fashion** is a style of dress or way of behaving that is popular at a particular time.

craze

*There seems to be a new **craze** for toys based on television characters.*

fad

*Mum's latest **fad** was for pasta dishes. Pasta was all we got for a month!*

style

*My sister's jeans were the latest **style**.*

trend

*Gran says she can't keep up with all the new **trends**.*

fast (1) ADJECTIVE

If something is **fast**, it is quick.

breakneck

*At **breakneck** speed, the ski jumper hurtled down the launch ramp.*

rapid

*With **rapid** thrusts of his sword, Athos tore his opponent's coat to ribbons.*

speedy

*After I'd finished my homework, I made a **speedy** exit and headed for the playground.*

swift

*With a few **swift** strokes of his brush, the artist had painted a beautiful yet simple picture.*

✔ Something that goes faster than the speed of sound is **supersonic**.

ANTONYM: slow

a b c d e f g h i j k l m n o p q r s t u v w x y z

fast (2) ADVERB

Something that moves **fast**, moves quickly or with great speed.

in a flash INFORMAL

*The rocket took off and, **in a flash**, was roaring away into the blue, many miles up.*

like a shot INFORMAL

***Like a shot**, the greyhounds were off round the track after the rabbit.*

quickly

*"If you don't come **quickly** we'll miss the bus," my sister shouted up the stairs.*

rapidly

*The magician **rapidly** slipped out of the handcuffs and dropped through the trapdoor.*

speedily

*Max **speedily** popped the sweet into his mouth before anyone could see.*

swiftly

*The stuntman rode **swiftly** towards the burning lorry.*

ANTONYM: slowly

fasten VERB

If you **fasten** something, you close it or attach it firmly to something else.

attach

*"Make sure you **attach** the label firmly to your luggage," advised Mum.*

connect

*To restore the power, the electrician had to **connect** the two cables.*

fix

*Dad **fixed** the shelf to the wall.*

join

*The Siamese twins were **joined** at the hip.*

fasten a door closed:
bolt

*Dancer's groom **bolted** the stable door and said goodnight to her horse.*

lock

*Make sure you **lock** the door when you leave.*

padlock

*As his tractor was in the field, Farmer Palfrey **padlocked** the gate.*

secure

*It's wise to **secure** all doors and windows before going away.*

fasten two surfaces together:
nail

*It was John's foolish idea to **nail** shut the door of the grandfather clock.*

screw

*The picture was firmly **screwed** to the wall.*

fasten metal together:
rivet

*The hulls of ships are made by **riveting** plates of steel together.*

solder

*Using a soldering iron, Don **soldered** the wires to their terminals.*

weld

*The process of **welding** melts and blends the edges of metal surfaces.*

fasten clothes or fabric:
button

*"**Button** your shirt," Mum ordered. "We can't have you looking scruffy."*

tie

*"**Tie** your shoelaces before you trip up!" Mrs Akhbar said.*

zip

*The front of the tent **zipped** up to keep out the wind and rain.*

fasten paper:
clip

*The papers were **clipped** together in the correct order.*

pin

*Several notices had been **pinned** on the board.*

staple

*Miss Jeffers **staples** our best work onto a display board.*

fasten shoes:
buckle

*Gulliver **buckled** his shoes and crept away.*

lace

*The game stopped while a player **laced** his boots which had come undone.*

ANTONYM: unfasten

fat ADJECTIVE

Someone or something that is **fat** has a lot of flesh on their body.

chubby

*The pop star had become quite **chubby** since he stopped doing live shows.*

overweight

***Overweight** and unfit, the jockey knew he had work to do in the gym.*

plump

*Gran got quite thin when she was ill, but now she's pleasantly **plump** again.*

podgy

*"If you eat too much pudding, you'll get **podgy**!" my horrible brother called out.*

rotund

*The **rotund** old gentleman got up with difficulty and waddled to the bar.*

stout

*The **stout** gentleman had trouble fitting comfortably into the aeroplane seat.*

ANTONYM: slim or thin

fault NOUN

A **fault** is a mistake or something wrong with the way something is made.

defect

*A **defect** in the aerial cable meant that our television picture was fuzzy.*

flaw

*The crash was ultimately caused by a slight **flaw** in the metal of the wing.*

glitch INFORMAL

*A mystery **glitch** in the signalling system delayed several trains.*

problem

*Our boiler had a **problem**, so Mum sent for the engineer.*

favourite ADJECTIVE

Your **favourite** person or thing is the one you like best.

best-loved

*Gran had a CD called "Your Hundred **Best-Loved** Tunes". They certainly weren't my favourite tunes!*

favoured

*The big-headed prince was clearly the king's **favoured** son.*

preferred

*When you vote, you put a cross against your **preferred** candidate.*

fear NOUN

Fear is the feeling of worry you have when you think you are in danger or that something bad might happen.

alarm

*As the tide rose around her, Caitlin was filled with **alarm**.*

dread

*My sister has a **dread** of spiders.*

panic

*As the first bomb fell, the crowd began to flee in **panic**.*

terror

***Terror** was written all over the faces of the hostages.*

✔ A fear of a specific thing is a **phobia**.

> Some common phobias:
> A **fear** of…
> …enclosed spaces – **claustrophobia**
> …flying – **aerophobia**
> …ghosts – **phasmophobia**
> …going out – **agoraphobia**
> …spiders – **arachnophobia**
> …thunder – **brontophobia**
> …water – **hydrophobia**

feel (1) VERB

If you **feel** something, you touch it.

feel with your hands:

finger

*In the dark, I **fingered** the light switch and finally switched it on.*

handle

*Mum doesn't like buying vegetables that have been **handled** by others.*

touch

*"If you **touch** that paint, you're in trouble," Dad warned.*

feel

A
B
C
D
E
F
G
H
I
J
K
L
M
N
O
P
Q
R
S
T
U
V
W
X
Y
Z

feel in a loving way:

caress
*The mother **caressed** her newborn baby.*

fondle
*Tyrone made me laugh, the way he kept **fondling** his new watch.*

stroke
*Wuffles enjoys being **stroked**, especially on his tummy.*

feel roughly:

maul
*One man picked up a cabbage to inspect it and, having **mauled** it, put it back.*

paw
*I reckon that girl **pawed** every sweet in the pick 'n' mix.*

feel your way around in the dark:

fumble
*Mum **fumbled** for her car keys in her bag.*

grope
*Through the smoke, Rajesh managed to **grope** his way to the door.*

feel (2) VERB
If you **feel** an emotion or sensation, you experience it.

feel pain or pleasure:

experience
*After his accident, Dad **experienced** headaches for several weeks.*

have a sensation of
*When you get an electric shock, you **have a sensation of** lightning going through you.*

feel or be aware:

be aware
*In the dark, I **was aware** that something hairy was in the room. It was the dog!*

feel in your bones
*A storm was brewing – I could **feel it in my bones**.*

have a hunch
*I **had a hunch** that it was you on the phone!*

sense
***Sensing** she was cold, I gave her my jacket.*

suspect
*I would never have **suspected** that a dog could be so frightening.*

feeling (1) NOUN
If you have a **feeling** about something, you have thoughts about it without being certain.

idea
*Going shopping was Indira's **idea**.*

suspicion
*Emilia had a **suspicion** that the man loitering round the shop was a thief.*

feeling (2) NOUN
A **feeling** is an emotion.

emotion
*Strong **emotions** were expressed by several people at the meeting.*

passion
*Mrs Kalim had a real **passion** for games, especially tennis.*

✔ A feeling of liking someone is **affection** or **fondness**.
A feeling of worry is **anxiety** or **concern**.

fetch VERB
If you **fetch** something, you go to where it is and bring it back.

collect
*Mum sent me to **collect** a parcel that had been delivered next door.*

retrieve
*Our dog Snuffler is brilliant at **retrieving** a ball when you throw it for her.*

transport
*Dad was asked to **transport** some furniture for a school disco.*

few ADJECTIVE
Few can mean not many or a small number of things.

hardly any
***Hardly any** people returned the questionnaire I sent out.*

infrequent
*Ships made only **infrequent** visits to the remote Pacific islands.*

rare
*Visits to the studio were **rare**, and Monica jumped at the chance.*

ANTONYM: many

fiddle (1) VERB

If you **fiddle** with something, you keep touching it and playing with it in a restless way.

fidget

"Stop *fidgeting* with your pencil!" Mrs O'Keefe ordered Christopher.

twiddle

Even after I had **twiddled** with all the knobs, the radio sounded no better, so then I fiddled with the aerial.

fiddle (2) VERB INFORMAL

To **fiddle** can mean to swindle, or change something dishonestly for your own profit.

cheat

The con man **cheated** an old couple out of their life savings.

swindle

A shop assistant was sacked for trying to **swindle** his employers.

fidget VERB

If you **fidget**, you keep changing your position or making small restless movements because you are nervous or bored.

squirm

Angela **squirmed** in her seat as she waited to go into the dentist's surgery.

twitch

Miss Westwood told Craig to stop **twitching** or go outside.

wriggle

Mum told me to stop **wriggling**, but speech day was lasting ages!

field NOUN

A **field** is an area of land where crops are grown or animals are kept.

meadow

Across the **meadows** lay the village and, beyond that, the sea.

paddock

The racehorses were kept in several large, fenced **paddocks**.

pasture

The land by the river was perfect **pasture** for cattle and sheep.

✔ A general word for fields is **grassland**.

fierce (1) ADJECTIVE

A person or animal who is **fierce** is very aggressive.

dangerous

Although the monster looked **dangerous**, it was really a big softy.

ferocious

The **ferocious** tiger sprang from the branch onto the hapless antelope.

savage

Many dogs are only **savage** because they have been mistreated.

fierce (2) ADJECTIVE

Someone or something that is **fierce** is very intense.

keen

"There is always **keen** competition between these two athletes," said the commentator.

relentless

After my mum's **relentless** nagging, I finally tidied my room.

strong

I've always had a **strong** dislike of any food with mushrooms in.

fight (1) VERB

When people **fight**, they take part in a battle, a boxing match, or in some other attempt to hurt or kill someone.

battle

In Roman times, gladiators **battled** with each other to entertain the crowds.

come to blows

The two women **came to blows** over a purse.

exchange blows

When Mr Rae arrived on the scene, the two boys were **exchanging blows**.

scrap INFORMAL

"I will not have anyone **scrapping** in this school," the head teacher thundered.

struggle

Pete and I **struggled** for a minute or two, then started laughing.

wrestle

The two athletes **wrestling** in the ring were both talented, but only one could win.

a b c d e f g h i j k l m n o p q r s t u v w x y z

fight (2) NOUN

A **fight** is a situation in which people hit or try to hurt each other.

battle
*The famous **battle** was fought not at Hastings, but several miles away.*

brawl
*When Lee insulted Jesse, a **brawl** began.*

conflict
*The **conflict** was ended by lack of food, diseases and bitter cold.*

scuffle
*Several protestors were involved in a **scuffle** outside parliament.*

skirmish
*Two platoons met in a **skirmish** on the edge of the woods.*

tussle
*In summer, playtimes, we have **tussles** on the grass. It's great!*

war
*The American Civil **War** lasted four years.*

Other nouns related to fight:
General fighting is called **combat** and **warfare**.
A long-running fight between two groups is a **feud**.
A fight between two people with pistols or swords is a **duel**.
A boxing or wrestling match is a **bout** or **contest**.

---

fill VERB

If you **fill** something, or if it **fills** up, it becomes full.

load
*We all helped **load** the car, then set off on our summer holidays.*

pack
*My brother foolishly **packed** his rucksack with the camera right at the bottom.*

replenish
*Mum sent me to **replenish** the water barrel at the campsite tap.*

stuff
*I **stuffed** my suitcase with presents for everyone back home.*

top up
*"Please would you **top up** my radiator water," Dad asked the attendant.*

fill in (1) VERB

If you **fill in** a form, you write information in the spaces on it.

complete
*Please **complete** the slip below and send it to us at this address.*

fill out
*I **filled out** the internet questionnaire, but the wretched thing wouldn't upload to the website.*

fill in (2) VERB

If you **fill in** for somebody, you take their place temporarily.

deputize
*I usually sort out the PE equipment. My assistant **deputizes** for me if I am away.*

replace
*As Mrs Kirkpatrick was off sick, another teacher **replaced** her.*

stand in
*Mum sometimes **stands in** for her friend who drives people to hospital.*

substitute
*I had to **substitute** the team captain when she was poorly.*

find VERB

If you **find** someone or something, you see them or discover where they are.

come across
*In the loft we **came across** an old painting.*

discover
*I **discovered** my old diary under my bed.*

stumble upon
*Dad **stumbled upon** his old record collection.*

track down
*The police promised to **track down** whoever had left the box there.*

unearth
*After interviewing the criminal, the police **unearthed** the truth about the robbery.*

find out VERB

If you **find out** something, you learn or discover it.

become aware

*As I gazed at the stars, I **became aware** that one of them was moving.*

discover

*After a long search, Paula **discovered** where she had left her wallet.*

realize

*We were so busy we didn't **realize** the time.*

fine (1) ADJECTIVE

If something is **fine** it is satisfactory or suitable.

acceptable

*"Your homework is **acceptable**," Mr Hill said.*

satisfactory

*The fit of the shoes was **satisfactory**, so Mum bought them.*

suitable

*"Come round this afternoon, if that's **suitable**," Indira said.*

ANTONYM: unsatisfactory or unacceptable

fine (2) ADJECTIVE

Fine material is thin and delicate.

delicate

*The bride's veil was made of a **delicate** gauze.*

flimsy

*The **flimsy** fishing line snapped.*

light

*In summer people tend to wear **light** clothing.*

✔ Fine sand or powder is made up of very small particles.

ANTONYM: thick or heavy

finish (1) VERB

When you **finish** something, you do the last part of it and complete it.

bring to a close

*A sudden thunderstorm **brought** the fête **to a close** rather early.*

complete

*Both my parents **completed** the marathon.*

ANTONYM: begin or start

finish (2) NOUN

The **finish** of something is the last part of it.

completion

*The **completion** of the tunnel was delayed because of flooding.*

end

*A fight on stage meant the **end** for the band.*

termination

*The **termination** of the player's contract occurred when he was sent to jail.*

ANTONYM: beginning or start

fire (1) NOUN

Fire is the flames produced when something burns.

blaze

*Firefighters put out the **blaze** in the heather.*

flames

*In the burning tower block, several people were trapped by the **flames**.*

inferno

*A helicopter airlifted them from amid the blazing **inferno**.*

on fire PHRASE

If something is **on fire**, it is burning.

ablaze

*By the time firefighters arrived, the house was **ablaze** from end to end.*

alight

*Although our campfire was **alight**, there was little heat coming from it.*

in flames

*After the air raid, the town was **in flames**.*

set on fire PHRASE

If something is **set on fire**, it starts burning.

ignite

*An accidental spark **ignited** the gunpowder.*

kindle

*We **kindle** our fire with rolled-up paper and small sticks.*

light

*Dad **lit** the firework and stood well back.*

set ablaze

*Sparks from the steam train **set ablaze** the grass by the line.*

fire (2) VERB

If someone **fires** a gun, they shoot a bullet.

pull the trigger

*When the Ringo Kid made a move, the sheriff **pulled the trigger**.*

shoot

*The burglar was unable to escape because he had accidentally **shot** himself.*

fire (3) VERB INFORMAL

If an employer **fires** someone, that person loses their job.

dismiss

*"Smithers, I'm **dismissing** you for your persistent late arrival," the manager said sternly.*

give someone their marching orders INFORMAL

*My brother's boss **gave him his marching orders** for being late too often.*

sack

*It's unfair! Lily was **sacked** just because she overslept one day.*

show someone the door INFORMAL

*The manager **showed Dad the door** when he asked for a pay rise.*

firm (1) ADJECTIVE

Something that is **firm** is fairly hard and does not move or change shape very much when it is pressed.

rigid

*"Make sure that tent pole is **rigid** before you crawl inside," said Dad.*

solid

*The plaster quickly set **solid** around Tristan's broken wrist.*

ANTONYM: soft

firm (2) ADJECTIVE

Something that is **firm** is fastened securely and is not movable.

fixed

*Once the concrete had set, the post was **fixed**.*

secure

*We thought the door was **secure**, but then the hurricane started and it came off its hinges.*

stable

*Ships have special fixtures underwater to help keep them **stable** in rough weather.*

ANTONYM: insecure or unsteady

firm (3) NOUN

A **firm** is a business that sells or produces something.

business

*Fujita's parents run an electronics **business**.*

company

*The **company** which Dad works for is building a new factory.*

first ADJECTIVE

The **first** of something happened, came or was done before all others.

earliest

*The **earliest** motorcars had to observe an eight miles per hour speed limit.*

oldest

*Remains of the **oldest** known humans are reputed to have been found in East Africa.*

original

*This picture is a print. The **original** painting hangs in a New York gallery.*

✔ A person who was the first to discover or do something is called a **discoverer**, **founder**, **inventor**, **originator** or **pioneer**.

fit (1) VERB

If something **fits**, it is the right shape or size.

correspond

*One side of a reflection **corresponds** exactly with the other.*

match

*Leah **matched** the pegs with the holes.*

suit

*"Those jeans really **suit** you," my aunt said admiringly.*

fit (2) ADJECTIVE

Someone who is **fit** is healthy and physically strong.

healthy

*It is hard to stay **healthy** if you eat junk food.*

in good condition

*Our dog Jim is **in good condition**.*

in good shape

*The boxer looked **in good shape** for his forthcoming title fight.*

ANTONYM: unfit

fit (3) ADJECTIVE

If you say someone or something is **fit** to do something, you mean they are suitable.

appropriate

*The mayor said my mum was a very **appropriate** person to be a councillor.*

suitable

*When Jade moved, her parents did not think her new school was **suitable**.*

worthy

*The mystery knight was a **worthy** opponent for Sir Bedivere.*

fix (1) VERB

If you **fix** something somewhere, you attach it there securely.

attach

*Mrs Archer **attached** an extra page to my school report.*

connect

*When the heating man **connected** the boiler to the gas pipes, it blew up.*

fasten

*Uncle Michael **fastened** the shelf to the living room wall.*

secure

*Gaby **secured** the mirror firmly above the hand basin with two strong nails.*

> **Ways of fixing something:**
> | | | |
> |---|---|---|
> | bolt | nail | staple |
> | glue | screw | weld |

fix (2) VERB

If you **fix** something that is broken, you repair it.

mend

*Dad managed to **mend** the car without taking it to the garage.*

repair

*My grandad likes to **repair** things that are broken, rather than buy new ones.*

fizzy ADJECTIVE

A **fizzy** drink has a gas called carbon dioxide in it to make it bubbly.

bubbly

*Champagne is so **bubbly** it explodes out of the bottle if shaken up.*

effervescent

*The **effervescent** tablets fizzed as they dissolved in the water.*

foaming

*I watched in horror as my drink tipped over and lay **foaming** on my homework.*

frothy

*Carla put her straw through the **frothy** bit and sucked the milk shake beneath.*

sparkling

*I don't like **sparkling** water in bottles – it gives me hiccups.*

ANTONYM: flat or still

flap VERB

Something that **flaps** moves quickly up and down or from side to side.

flail

*The sailor's arms **flailed** about helplessly as he tried to stay afloat.*

flutter

*In the marina, the pennants on the boats **fluttered** in the sea breeze.*

wave

*The flags on the marquee **waved** in the gusty wind.*

flat ADJECTIVE

Something that is **flat** is level and smooth.

even

*For outdoor bowling, the grass needs to be **even** and well cut.*

horizontal

*Dad's wall looked vaguely **horizontal**, but his spirit level told a different story.*

level

*Despite the mountains around, the land in the valley was dead **level**.*

smooth

*Painters use sandpaper to make sure every coat of paint they put on is **smooth**.*

ABCDEFGHIJKLMNOPQRSTUVWXYZ

float VERB

Something that **floats** is supported by liquid or hangs in the air.

bob
*After the liner passed, the moored boats started **bobbing** up and down.*

drift
*The pilot of the rescue plane sighted a raft, **drifting** but empty.*

hover
*Dragonflies **hovered** above the pond.*

ANTONYM: sink

flood (1) VERB

If water **floods** an area that is usually dry, or if the area floods, it becomes covered with water.

inundate
*When the bath upstairs overflowed, the ceiling came down and our kitchen was **inundated**.*

submerge
*The holed tanker was **submerged** as the weight of water took it down.*

swamp
*Massive waves **swamped** the promenade.*

flood (2) NOUN

A **flood** of something is a large amount of it occurring suddenly.

deluge
*A sudden **deluge** of rain put a swift end to the school fête.*

torrent
*The dam burst, and a **torrent** of water swept down the narrow valley.*

flop VERB

If something or someone **flops**, they bend or fall loosely and heavily.

collapse
*The runners **collapsed** onto the grass at the end of the marathon.*

droop
*Left unwatered, flowers will soon **droop** in hot, dry weather.*

sag
*The elderly peasant **sagged** under the weight of his burden.*

slump
*Disappointed with her game, the tennis player **slumped** in a corner of the dressing room.*

flow (1) VERB

If something **flows** somewhere, it moves there in a steady and continuous manner.

pour
*Water **poured** over the waterfall into the pool.*

ripple
*The **rippling** stream sparkled in the sunshine.*

stream
*Tears of relief **streamed** down my dad's face, as he saw Mum was safe.*

surge
*The torrent **surged** down the hillside, taking boulders with it.*

sweep
*As the river broke its banks, water **swept** into nearby streets.*

flow (2) NOUN

A **flow** of something is a steady, continuous movement of it.

current
*A **current** of water flowed round the rocks.*

stream
*The northern lights are caused by a **stream** of electrical particles from the sun.*

tide
*A **tide** of people made its way to the stadium.*

fly VERB

When a bird, insect or aircraft **flies**, it moves through the air.

flit
*In summer, bees **flit** from flower to flower.*

glide
*Against the sky, gannets **glided** effortlessly, their wings hardly moving.*

soar
*With a deafening roar, the spy plane **soared** almost vertically into the air.*

fog NOUN

Fog is a thick mist caused by tiny drops of water in the air.

mist
*A cotton-wool **mist** rolled in the valleys.*

murk
*Through the **murk**, the car headlights picked out a shadowy figure.*

foggy ADJECTIVE
If the weather is **foggy**, there is fog in the air.

hazy
Hazy winter sunshine shone through the trees.

misty
*I love the cool of **misty** summer mornings.*

murky
*The afternoon was **murky** and the street lights were haloed in fog.*

follow (1) VERB
If you **follow** someone or something, you move along behind them.

pursue
***Pursued** by the hounds, the fox sought shelter in a barn.*

shadow
*Unknown to the suspect, police were **shadowing** her every move.*

stalk
*Some celebrities are continually **stalked** by newspaper photographers.*

tail
*Looking in his mirror, the police officer saw a car **tailing** him.*

track
*Sniffer dogs **tracked** the missing man to a hut in the woods.*

follow (2) VERB
If you **follow** instructions or advice, you do what you are told.

comply
*If you don't **comply** with the rules, you will be disqualified.*

conform
*Pupils are expected to **conform** to the rules about uniform.*

obey
*The police officer signalled Mum to pull over, and she **obeyed**.*

observe
*In any country, it's important to **observe** the code about driving behaviour.*

follow (3) VERB
If you **follow** an explanation or the plot of a story, you understand each stage of it.

grasp
*Julian at last **grasped** the plot of the film.*

understand
*"Do you **understand** what you have to do?" Mr Peabody enquired, scanning the room.*

fond ADJECTIVE
If someone treats you in a **fond** way, they show that they like you.

affectionate
*Gran gave Mum an **affectionate** hug.*

loving
*The gravestone read, "In **loving** memory of a dear father".*

tender
*Most children are not keen on receiving **tender** kisses from adoring aunties.*

food NOUN
Food is what people and other animals eat.

diet
*It's important that your **diet** includes fresh fruit and vegetables.*

nourishment
*Babies need plenty of **nourishment** to grow.*

nutrition
*In the prison camp, **nutrition** levels were far too low for the backbreaking work.*

Some fruits that can be food:

apple	orange
apricot	papaya
banana	peach
grapes	pear
guava	strawberries
mango	raspberries

Some types of meat that can be food:

bacon	fish
beef	ham
chicken	pork
duck	turkey

*See **vegetable***

fool

fool (1) VERB

If you **fool** someone, you deceive or trick them.

bamboozle INFORMAL
*My pals **bamboozled** me into believing their story about the aliens.*

deceive
*We were all **deceived** by Mike. He seemed so honest, yet he stole our money.*

hoodwink
*The crooks were **hoodwinked** into attending the party, which in fact was a trap.*

take in
*"You really **took** me **in** with that disguise!" Jessie gasped.*

trick
*They **tricked** me into phoning the zoo and asking for Mr C. Lyon.*

fool (2) NOUN

A **fool** is someone who is silly and is not sensible.

dimwit
*What a **dimwit**! I forgot my lunch money.*

idiot
*"You blithering **idiot**," the boss snapped.*

moron
*I felt a complete **moron**, wandering round in a penguin costume.*

foolish ADJECTIVE

A **foolish** idea is not sensible and shows poor judgment.

half-baked INFORMAL
*"Whose **half-baked** plan was this?" Aunt Vera demanded.*

hare-brained INFORMAL
*Building a canal on porous rock was a **hare-brained** scheme.*

ridiculous
*"What a **ridiculous** suggestion!" Dad laughed.*

silly
*It was a **silly** thing to say, and Keara was really upset.*

unwise
*Riding three on a bike was an **unwise** idea.*

ANTONYM: sensible

foot NOUN

Your **foot** is the part of your body at the end of your leg.

The name for the foot of a	
...bird	– claw
...bird of prey (e.g. eagle)	– **talon**
...cat	– **paw**
...crab	– **claw**
...deer	– **hoof**
...dog	– **paw**
...horse	– **hoof**
...lobster	– **claw**
...penguin	– **webbed foot**
...pig	– **trotter**
...sheep	– **hoof**

forbid VERB

If someone **forbids** you to do something, they order you not to do it.

ban
*Chewing gum is **banned** at our school.*

outlaw
*Advertising cigarettes has been **outlawed** in some countries.*

prohibit
*Smoking is **prohibited** throughout the train.*

veto
*Dictators tend to **veto** anybody's decisions they do not like.*

ANTONYM: permit

force (1) VERB

If you **force** someone to do something, you make them do it.

compel
*All of my brother's classmates were **compelled** to do woodwork or metalwork.*

drive
*They are **driving** the engineering company into bankruptcy.*

order
*The sergeant **ordered** his troops to do another circuit of the parade ground.*

force (2) NOUN
Force can mean violence or great strength.

impact
*The **impact** of a meteorite is shown by the area of the crater.*

power
*All over the world, the **power** of water, wind and sun is being harnessed.*

strength
*With unbelievable **strength**, the monster tossed the car into the hedge.*

forever ADVERB
Forever means eternally.

always
*I think I'll **always** like dogs.*

eternally
*The damsel vowed that she was **eternally** grateful to the knight who had saved her.*

forget VERB
If you **forget** something, you do not remember it.

omit
*I was so nervous that I **omitted** a whole section of the test!*

overlook
*Cassandra was so busy talking, she **overlooked** the time.*

✔ If you forget to do something, you can say that it **slipped your mind**.

forgive VERB
If you **forgive** someone who has done something wrong, you stop being angry with them.

excuse
*As Nori's tooth was so painful, we **excused** her for being rather snappy.*

pardon
*The wise emperor **pardoned** the apologetic thief for his crime.*

✔ A phrase for forgiving someone is to **let bygones be bygones**.

foul (1) ADJECTIVE
If something is **foul**, it is extremely unpleasant.

disgusting
*"What a **disgusting** mess!" was all my Mum could say about my room.*

filthy
*Mice ran all over the place and every nook and cranny was **filthy**.*

offensive
*There was an **offensive** smell coming from the fields where the farmer had spread manure.*

repulsive
*"Don't be **repulsive**," my sister said. "It's rude to pick your nose."*

revolting
*The corned beef hash that Dad made when we were camping tasted **revolting**.*

unpleasant
*Clearing drains is one of life's more **unpleasant** experiences.*

foul (2) ADJECTIVE
Foul language is very unpleasant.

coarse
*Mrs Giles did not approve of old Mr Giles's **coarse** vocabulary.*

obscene
*The player was sent off for making an **obscene** gesture at the crowd.*

rude
*If you use **rude** language at school you will get into trouble.*

vulgar
*"Don't be so **vulgar**!" Mum said, after I had been rude to my sister.*

fragile ADJECTIVE
Something that is **fragile** is easily broken or damaged.

breakable
*The poisonous chemicals had been stored carelessly in **breakable** flasks.*

brittle
*As we grow older, our bones become more **brittle** and can break easily.*

delicate
*Flora was a **delicate** child who regularly had to go into hospital.*

flimsy
*The box was **flimsy**, and Mum's groceries crashed to the ground.*

A
B
C
D
E
F
G
H
I
J
K
L
M
N
O
P
Q
R
S
T
U
V
W
X
Y
Z

free (1) ADJECTIVE

If something is **free**, you can have it without paying for it.

complimentary
*Through Mum's work, we received **complimentary** tickets to the exhibition.*

free of charge
*My little brother, being under five, was allowed into the match **free of charge**.*

on the house
*"Drinks are **on the house**!" called the bar owner, having heard of his lottery win.*

free (2) ADJECTIVE

Someone who is **free** is no longer a prisoner.

at large
*The escaped prisoner was still **at large** after three days.*

liberated
*The dictator fled and the country was **liberated**.*

released
*The **released** hostages were taken to hospital.*

free (3) VERB

If you **free** someone or something that is trapped, you release them.

liberate
*In 1944, the Allies **liberated** France from enemy occupation.*

release
*"**Release** those number balls!" the lottery announcer cried excitedly.*

set free
*The hostages were **set free** in a daring rescue.*

turn loose
*Spring had come, and the cattle were **turned loose** in the fields.*

freezing ADJECTIVE INFORMAL

If someone or something is **freezing**, they are very cold indeed.

arctic
*The wind was almost **arctic**, and our breath froze in the air.*

biting
*A **biting** chill gnawed at Cratchit's bones as he worked in the gloom.*

bitter
***Bitter** February was followed by windy March.*

chilled to the bone INFORMAL
*After two hours in the carnival parade, Coco the clown was **chilled to the bone**.*

frozen
*The reporters were **frozen**, having waited for the star for three hours.*

icy
*On an **icy** bend, the car skidded off the road.*

perishing
*Despite it being summer, the weather on our holiday was **perishing**.*

ANTONYM: hot

friend NOUN

A **friend** is someone you know well and like, but who is not related to you.

buddy
*Padma and I have been **buddies** since we were at nursery school.*

mate
*Dominic and Hyram are best **mates**.*

pal
*My dog Sadie is a real **pal**.*

✔ An **acquaintance** is someone you know but who is not a full friend.

friendly ADJECTIVE

A **friendly** person is kind and pleasant to others.

amiable
*The woman gave me an **amiable** smile.*

amicable
*Dad came to an **amicable** agreement with our neighbour about sharing a lawn mower.*

good-natured
*Although Grandad is basically a **good-natured** soul, he gets angry about politics.*

kind
*Everyone was very **kind** to Marie on her first day at school.*

welcoming
*When the carol singers called on her, Mrs Moss was very **welcoming**.*

ANTONYM: unfriendly

fright NOUN

Fright is a sudden feeling of fear.

alarm

*The air-raid siren's eerie wailing filled householders with **alarm**.*

dismay

*To Sissy's utter **dismay**, the train pulled out of the station without her.*

horror

*The pilot was filled with **horror** when his plane began to judder and jolt.*

panic

Panic set in, and people fled in all directions.

terror

*You could see the **terror** in the eyes of the people watching the scary movie.*

frighten VERB

If something or someone **frightens** you, they make you afraid.

alarm

*The barking dog **alarmed** the kitten.*

petrify

*To say the hobbit was **petrified** of the dragon was an understatement.*

scare

*"You can't **scare** me!" I called into the darkness, my knees knocking with fear.*

terrify

*Some people are simply **terrified** of spiders.*

terrorize

*Until they were jailed, the three brothers had **terrorized** their neighbourhood.*

frightening ADJECTIVE

If something or someone is **frightening**, they make you afraid.

fearsome

*The **fearsome** monster roared ferociously.*

hair-raising

*That new theme-park ride is an absolutely **hair-raising** experience.*

menacing

*The music stopped as the **menacing** stranger thrust open the doors of the saloon.*

terrifying

*The car crash was a **terrifying** ordeal.*

front NOUN

The **front** is the part of something that is furthest forward.

head

*Davina went straight to the **head** of the queue.*

lead

*In the **lead** was a runner from East Africa.*

✔ The front end of a ship or boat is the **bow**. The front end of an ancient ship (e.g. a Viking longboat) is the **prow**.

ANTONYM: rear

full (1) ADJECTIVE

Something that is **full** contains as much as it is possible to hold.

brimming

*I had left the tap on and the bath was **brimming** when I got back.*

chock-a-block

*When we reached the cinema, the foyer was **chock-a-block** with people.*

crammed

*The underground train was **crammed** with people, like a tin of sardines.*

loaded

Loaded with presents, the sleigh absolutely refused to budge.

packed

*Our class newspaper was **packed** with useful information.*

ANTONYM: empty

full (2) ADJECTIVE

The **full** amount of something is the complete or whole amount.

complete

*In a three-CD package, the author read the **complete** novel, unabridged.*

comprehensive

*To view the **comprehensive** range of our products, go to our website.*

entire

*Mr Fox had spent his **entire** life living in the same cottage.*

whole

*Mandy told me the **whole** story.*

fun NOUN
Fun is a pleasant, enjoyable and light-hearted activity.

amusement
*I got stuck in the mud, which caused the others some **amusement**.*

enjoyment
*We all had terrific **enjoyment** out of our battered old-style surfboards.*

entertainment
*Listening to my uncle crack jokes was torture, not **entertainment**!*

pleasure
*It was with great **pleasure** that the soldier received his bravery award.*

make fun of PHRASE
If you **make fun of** someone or something, you tease them or make jokes about them.

mock
*At school, we secretly **mock** Mrs Caywood, imitating her warbly voice.*

poke fun at
*Bullies enjoy **poking fun at** weaker people.*

ridicule
*Jamal's sisters **ridiculed** him because of his new haircut.*

tease
*If you ignore people who **tease** you, they soon give up.*

funny (1) ADJECTIVE
Funny people or things cause amusement or laughter.

amusing
*Grandma read out an **amusing** article.*

comical
*Mr Mahler thought he was **comical**; we thought otherwise.*

hilarious
*For once my brother told a **hilarious** story.*

humorous
*Grandpa used to write **humorous** poems.*

witty
*Everyone laughed at my **witty** reply to Mrs Skinner's question – except Mrs Skinner.*

funny (2) ADJECTIVE
Funny people or things are strange or puzzling.

curious
*Holmes found it **curious** that the window was open when we arrived.*

mysterious
*We shadowed the **mysterious** stranger around the town.*

odd
*"That's **odd**," Will thought. "Lyra was here just a second ago."*

peculiar
*Mr Agnelli has a **peculiar** sense of humour.*

puzzling
*How **puzzling** to find a ship abandoned, with the crew's table set for a meal.*

weird
*It's **weird** to think how much change Gran must have seen in her lifetime.*

furious ADJECTIVE
Someone who is **furious** is extremely angry.

beside yourself
*The colonel was **beside himself** at the prospect of a ban on hunting.*

enraged
*The bull, **enraged** by the matador's taunting, charged towards him.*

infuriated
*My big sister was **infuriated** that her boyfriend had forgotten her birthday.*

livid
*You could see the shopkeeper was **livid** from her red face and glaring eyes.*

up in arms
*The whole town was **up in arms** about the planned new superstore.*

fuss NOUN
A **fuss** is unnecessarily anxious or excited behaviour.

agitation
*The new rule caused **agitation** among the parents at the school gate.*

bother
*"What's all the **bother** about?" demanded Mrs Edwards sternly.*

commotion

*The escaped circus elephant caused something of a **commotion** in town.*

fussy ADJECTIVE

If you are **fussy**, you worry too much about unnecessary details.

choosy

*Our dog Jim is so **choosy**, he refuses to eat cheap dog food.*

hard to please

*In the store, the loud tourist was proving **hard to please**.*

particular

*My sister is so **particular** about her food, Mum threatens to give her nothing.*

future ADJECTIVE

Future things relate to or occur at a time after the present.

eventual

*The **eventual** outcome of global warming is still unknown.*

forthcoming

*There is a great spy film among the **forthcoming** cinema releases.*

impending

*My sister was rather worried about her **impending** operation.*

subsequent

*Stan scored three goals on his debut, but his **subsequent** appearances were disappointing.*

ANTONYM: past or previous

Gg

gain (1) VERB

If you **gain** something, you get more of it, or get something you didn't have before.

achieve
*"Just what did you **achieve** by doing that?"
Mum asked.*

acquire
*Amisha **acquired** an old velvet coat for her
fancy-dress box.*

increase
*My bike **increased** in speed alarmingly down
the steep hill.*

ANTONYM: lose

gain (2) NOUN

A **gain** is an increase or improvement in
something.

growth
*There has been a **growth** in pupil numbers at
our school.*

increase
*When a car accelerates, there's an **increase** in
its speed.*

rise
*I'm hoping for a **rise** in my pocket money
this year.*

ANTONYM: loss

gamble (1) VERB

If you **gamble**, you risk losing something in the
hope of gaining an advantage.

bet
*The man foolishly **bet** all his money on a
useless horse.*

risk
*Toby **risked** his life to save his sister.*

stick your neck out INFORMAL
*You may have to **stick your neck out** if you
want to succeed.*

take a chance
*Dad **took a chance** when he started his own
business.*

gamble (2) NOUN

A **gamble** is a risk.

chance
*The firefighter took a **chance** when he entered
the burning house.*

risk
*That's a **risk** only a fool would take!*

game (1) NOUN

A **game** is an activity with a set of rules that is
played by individuals or teams against each
other.

competition
*A swimming **competition** was held for all
children in the school.*

contest
*They had a **contest** to see who could run home
the fastest.*

match
*I love playing in cricket **matches**.*

game (2) NOUN

A **game** is an activity that involves playing.

amusement
*Snowball fights are our main **amusement** in
winter.*

pastime
*Jenny's favourite **pastime** was playing chess.*

sport
*Football is the most popular **sport** in many
countries.*

Some board games:

chess	ludo
draughts	snakes and ladders

Some sporting games:

badminton	rugby
basketball	snooker
boxing	soccer
cricket	table tennis
hockey	tennis
netball	tenpin bowling

Some playground games:

conkers	leapfrog
hide-and-seek	marbles
hopscotch	tag

gang NOUN

A **gang** is a group of people who join together for some purpose.

band

A **band** of robbers attacked the stagecoach.

crowd

Wayne went round with a **crowd** that I didn't like much.

group

The pop star was mobbed by a **group** of screaming fans.

gap NOUN

A **gap** is a space between two things or a hole in something solid.

break

The sun shone through a **break** in the clouds.

chink

There was a tiny **chink** in the cell door.

opening

The miners saw an **opening** in the tunnel ahead of them.

space

Dad managed to find a **space** in which to park the car.

gate NOUN

A **gate** is a barrier which is used at the entrance to a garden or field.

barrier

A **barrier** prevented cars from driving into the park.

entrance

Soldiers **guarded** the entrance to the palace.

gateway

The bride and groom paused at the **gateway** to the churchyard.

gather (1) VERB

To **gather** is to bring things together in one place.

accumulate

As it rolled down the hill, the snowball **accumulated** more and more snow.

amass

Over the years, Gran had **amassed** a huge pottery collection.

collect

The waiter went round **collecting** up the dirty dishes.

hoard

The miser **hoarded** gold coins.

gather (2) VERB

When people **gather**, they come together in a group.

assemble

When the fire alarm sounds, **assemble** in the playground.

collect

Protesters **collected** in the park before starting their march.

come together

Every Monday, the whole school **came together** for assembly.

congregate

We **congregated** in the hall, waiting for instructions.

ANTONYM: disperse

general (1) ADJECTIVE

Something that is **general** is true in most cases, or applies to most people or things.

broad

This is a film with **broad** appeal to people of all ages.

common

Putting apostrophes into plurals is a **common** mistake which people make.

universal

There are **universal** rules for soccer.

widespread

Famine is a **widespread** problem in that country.

general (2) ADJECTIVE

Something that is **general** includes or involves a range of different things.

broad

The winner of the quiz had a **broad** general knowledge.

comprehensive

Shannon's guidebook to the city was **comprehensive**.

a b c d e f **g** h i j k l m n o p q r s t u v w x y z

generous

A
B
C
D
E
F
G
H
I
J
K
L
M
N
O
P
Q
R
S
T
U
V
W
X
Y
Z

generous ADJECTIVE

Someone who is **generous** gives or shares what they have, especially time or money.

benevolent

*The millionaire author was **benevolent** to many charities.*

big-hearted

*The **big-hearted** star was always ready to help new musicians.*

charitable

*Mrs Sood is always **charitable** when I ask her for sponsorship.*

unselfish

*An **unselfish** boy gave up his seat for the pregnant lady.*

ANTONYM: selfish

gentle ADJECTIVE

Someone or something that is **gentle** is mild and calm.

calm

*My mum's voice always remained **calm**, no matter how flustered other people were.*

mild

*The doctor's **mild** manner relaxed her nervous patients.*

peace-loving

*Being a **peace-loving** man, Dad hated fights.*

tender

*The princess gave the frog a **tender** kiss.*

genuine ADJECTIVE

Something that is **genuine** is real and exactly what it appears to be.

authentic

*Is this autograph of Elvis Presley **authentic**?*

original

*This is an **original** painting by Van Gogh, not a print.*

sincere

*You could tell by Allana's face that her apology was **sincere**.*

true

*Is this a **true** likeness of the man you saw?*

ANTONYM: fake

get (1) VERB

Get can mean to change from one thing to another.

become

*The sky **became** darker as the moon crossed in front of the sun.*

grow

*Each day the weather **grew** warmer as spring finally arrived.*

turn

*The rooms suddenly **turned** cold when the ghost appeared.*

get (2) VERB

If you **get** something, you fetch it or receive it.

collect

*We spent hours **collecting** different shells for our sand castle.*

fetch

*I asked Simeon to **fetch** some paper for me.*

retrieve

*Spot **retrieved** the stick from the river.*

get (3) VERB

If you **get** a joke or the point of something, you understand it.

comprehend

*It was hard to **comprehend** the instructions the first time Maria explained them.*

follow

*"Did you **follow** what I said?" asked the science professor.*

grasp

*Everyone laughed when they **grasped** the joke.*

understand

*The French lady **understood** what I meant, when I spoke slowly.*

get off VERB

To **get off** can mean to leave a certain kind of transport.

alight

*We **alighted** from the school bus at the stop close to our house.*

disembark

*Because the plane had a fault, we were forced to **disembark**.*

dismount

*The mountain-bike rider **dismounted** and trudged off miserably.*

get on (1) VERB

If you **get on** with a task, you start or continue doing it.

continue

*Abdul **continued** with his piano practice even though he was tired.*

keep on

*Although I had a sore knee, I **kept on** with the sponsored walk.*

persevere

*Even when it started raining, the rock band **persevered** with the concert.*

get on (2) VERB

If you are **getting on** well, you are making good progress.

cope

*I **coped** well in the test, even though I felt quite nervous.*

fare

*"How did you **fare** in your exam?" asked Dad.*

manage

*"Can you **manage** all right carrying those heavy bags?" the man asked Gran.*

get on (3) VERB

To **get on** can mean to board a particular kind of transport.

board

*We **boarded** the bus for the campsite.*

embark

*The passengers **embarked** on the cruise liner.*

mount

*The highwayman **mounted** his horse and was gone in seconds.*

get out of VERB

If you **get out of** something, you avoid doing it.

avoid

*The lazy girls **avoided** school PE by pretending to be ill.*

dodge INFORMAL

*Keith tried to **dodge** doing the washing-up by creeping upstairs.*

escape

*Gertrude made a weak excuse to try and **escape** her piano practice.*

ghost NOUN

A **ghost** is the spirit of a dead person that appears to someone who is still alive.

phantom

*The **phantom** of the opera walked the stage at the dead of night.*

spectre

*Scrooge quaked before the **spectre** of his former friend.*

spirit

*The old inn was haunted by some form of evil **spirit** who made noises in the night.*

giant (1) NOUN

A **giant** is a huge person in a myth or legend.

colossus

*In Greek mythology, Atlas was a **colossus** of the ancient gods.*

monster

*A **monster** was guarding the entrance to the cave where the treasure was kept.*

ogre

*The **ogre** took another thunderous step towards the beanstalk.*

giant (2) ADJECTIVE

Something **giant** is much larger than other similar things.

colossal

*The sequel was a **colossal** success – even better than the original film.*

enormous

*The dinosaur's body was **enormous** compared with its brain.*

gigantic

*A **gigantic** wave swept towards the shore.*

huge

*The **huge** castle loomed out of the darkness in front of the elves.*

massive

*The **massive** bulldozer dwarfed everything around it.*

ANTONYM: tiny

a
b
c
d
e
f
g
h
i
j
k
l
m
n
o
p
q
r
s
t
u
v
w
x
y
z

A B C D E F **G** H I J K L M N O P Q R S T U V W X Y Z

give (1) VERB

If you **give** something to someone, you hand it to them, or provide it for them.

hand
*Nassir **handed** me the hammer.*

pass
*"**Pass** me the salt, please," I requested.*

present
*Our teacher **presented** the trophy to Keisha.*

supply
*A network of spies **supplied** secrets to the enemy government.*

give (2) VERB

If you **give** something, you grant, present or donate it.

award
*The girl was **awarded** a medal for her bravery during the flood.*

contribute
*Mum **contributed** money to Mrs Jones's farewell present.*

donate
*Tara's father **donated** one of his kidneys to save her life.*

present
*He **presented** a cheque to the charity.*

✔ A person who gives blood is a **blood donor**.

give in VERB

If you **give in**, you admit that you are defeated.

concede
*Chess players have to **concede** when their king is in checkmate.*

submit
*The intense pain in his back forced the wrestler to **submit**.*

surrender
*The troops **surrendered** after they were surrounded by the enemy.*

give out VERB

If you **give** things **out**, you hand out or distribute them to people.

distribute
*The aid workers **distributed** food to the starving people.*

issue
*"Please **issue** these uniforms to the sailors," said the captain.*

supply
*The organizers **supplied** vests to all the marathon runners.*

give up VERB

If you **give up**, you stop doing something.

abandon
*Another fire forced the crew to **abandon** their efforts to save the ship.*

quit
*The DJ threatened to **quit** the show if he didn't get his way.*

resign from
*She had to **resign from** her work because of a serious illness.*

surrender
*The marines **surrendered** after their ship was attacked.*

glad ADJECTIVE

If someone is **glad**, they are happy or pleased.

contented
*Gran led a **contented** life in her little bungalow.*

delighted
*Seamus was **delighted** when he heard that he had won a prize.*

happy
*Mum was **happy** to have my cousin to stay.*

pleased
*Dad was **pleased** that we had offered to help.*

ANTONYM: displeased

glitter VERB

If something **glitters**, it shines in a sparkling way.

glint
*The farmer spotted something **glinting** in the soil – a gold coin!*

glisten
*Snowy treetops **glistened** in the sunshine.*

shimmer
*The lake **shimmered** in the golden light of the setting sun.*

go (1) VERB
If you **go** somewhere, you walk, move or travel there.

advance
Troops advanced over the enemy lines.

depart
No sooner had we departed than Dad realized he'd forgotten his wallet.

journey
Marco Polo journeyed to eastern lands.

set off
Some of the group set off in the wrong direction.

travel
The car was travelling far too fast.

go (2) VERB
If something **goes** somewhere, it leads or passes through there.

lead to
This street leads to the Roman city walls.

pass through
We need to pass through that town in order to get home.

reach
The rocky road reaches out onto the peninsula, beside the lighthouse.

go (3) VERB
Go can mean to become.

become
At the sight of the pop star, Millie became weak at the knees.

turn
Mike turns green at the thought of what they put in some beefburgers.

go (4) VERB
If something **goes**, it works properly.

function
The old car refused to function.

operate
Water sprinklers operate when the smoke alarm starts ringing.

work
The stereo wouldn't work after I spilt my drink on it.

go (5) NOUN
A **go** is an attempt or a turn at doing something.

attempt
It was the weightlifter's second attempt at 100 kilograms.

shot
I didn't win any prizes with my first shot at the hoop game.

stab
Luckily, Jacob's first stab at guessing the answer was correct!

try
Lucinda had a try at horse riding, but kept falling off.

go back VERB
If you **go back**, you return to a place you have been before.

retrace your steps
Lost in the jungle, our only hope was to retrace our steps.

retreat
Faced with foul weather, we retreated to the cosy café.

return
As he began his descent, the climber promised he would return to his injured friend.

go off VERB
If something such as a bomb **goes off**, it explodes.

detonate
The beach was cleared quickly, before the bomb could detonate.

explode
Land mines are dangerous because they explode when you step on them.

go on VERB
If something is **going on**, it is happening.

happen
What happened while we were away?

occur
The incident occurred at the swimming pool on a hot summer day.

take place
Sanjay's party will take place in the village hall at three o'clock.

A
B
C
D
E
F
G
H
I
J
K
L
M
N
O
P
Q
R
S
T
U
V
W
X
Y
Z

go round (1) VERB
Something that **goes round** moves in a circular motion.

circle
*The plane **circled** the airport several times before landing.*

revolve
*The hotel porter told me that doors which **revolve** prevent draughts.*

rotate
*When the pilot turned on the helicopter engine, the rotor blade started to **rotate**.*

go round (2) VERB
If you **go round** something, you avoid it by moving around it.

avoid
*My mum, riding her bike, **avoided** the dog but hit the lamppost.*

dodge
*We **dodged** the crowds by walking through backstreets.*

go through VERB
If something **goes through** another thing, it pierces it.

penetrate
*No bullet could **penetrate** the robot's thick body armour.*

pierce
*The nail **pierced** the skin of my foot when I trod on it.*

puncture
*Broken glass in the road **punctured** the tyre on my new bike.*

gobble VERB
To **gobble** can mean to eat food or drink very quickly.

bolt
*Harvey **bolted** his meal and rushed off to play rugby.*

devour
*The hungry leopard **devoured** the remains of the antelope.*

gulp
*Charlene **gulped** down her tea and fled upstairs to phone her friends.*

guzzle INFORMAL
*I **guzzled** down a bottle of water when I finished the race.*

wolf
*Our dog Wuffles always **wolfs** down his breakfast.*

good (1) ADJECTIVE
Something **good** is pleasant or enjoyable.

delightful
*"What a **delightful** visit it's been!" said the bishop in his speech.*

enjoyable
*We had an **enjoyable** time at the zoo.*

pleasant
*The weather was **pleasant** for our walk.*

ANTONYM: bad

good (2) ADJECTIVE
Something **good** is of a high quality.

excellent
*"This is **excellent** writing," Mrs Watts said.*

splendid
*Mr Kaye said we had made a **splendid** effort.*

thorough
*I gave my room a **thorough** clean.*

useful
*Our guidebook proved very **useful** on holiday.*

ANTONYM: poor

good (3) ADJECTIVE
If you are **good**, you are kind and thoughtful.

considerate
*Kamal is a **considerate** boy.*

decent
*They were a **decent** family who would never do anything dishonest.*

generous
*It was **generous** of you to spend so much time helping me.*

merciful
*The **merciful** king spared the life of the peasant.*

thoughtful
*It was **thoughtful** of them to send flowers.*

ANTONYM: unkind or thoughtless

good (4) ADJECTIVE

If you are **good** at something, you are competent or talented at it.

capable
*Elliot was a **capable** writer but he was poor at history.*

competent
*I am a **competent** enough speller, but my writing is poor.*

expert
*Chris was an **expert** mechanic when it came to mending vintage cars.*

skilful
*Aseem proved to be a **skilful** tennis player.*

goodbye INTERJECTION

You say **goodbye** when you are leaving someone or ending a telephone conversation.

farewell OLD-FASHIONED
*The captain said **farewell** to his crew and disembarked for the last time.*

so long AMERICAN
*"**So long**, partner!" cried the sheriff as he rode away from the ranch.*

> **Words from other languages that mean goodbye:**
> **adieu; auf wiedersehen** (German)
> **adieu; au revoir** (French)
> **adios** (Spanish)
> **arrivederci; ciao** (Italian)
> **e noho rā; haere rā** (Māori – New Zealand)
> **sayonara** (Japanese)
> **tot siens** (Afrikaans)

grab VERB

If you **grab** something, you take or pick it up roughly.

pluck
*In the nick of time, the helicopter winchman **plucked** the girl from the raging river.*

seize
*The weightlifter **seized** the bar and thrust it above his head.*

snatch
*Muggers **snatched** the bag and ran off with it.*

gradually ADVERB

Gradually means happening slowly over a long period of time.

little by little
***Little by little**, the climber inched his way up the rock face.*

slowly
*The classroom alterations are being done far too **slowly** for my liking.*

step by step
*I'm learning to play the piano **step by step**.*

ANTONYM: suddenly

grateful ADJECTIVE

If you are **grateful** for something, you feel thankful for it.

appreciative
*The old lady was very **appreciative** of my help in crossing the road.*

thankful
*After hours in the blizzard, we were **thankful** for a warm fire.*

ANTONYM: ungrateful

graveyard NOUN

A **graveyard** is a place where dead people are buried.

burial ground
*The **burial ground** overlooked the beach where the sailors had perished.*

cemetery
*My gran was buried in the town **cemetery**.*

great (1) ADJECTIVE

Something that is **great** is very large in size.

colossal
*The tidal wave was **colossal**.*

enormous
*Until you actually see them, you don't realize just how **enormous** space rockets are.*

gigantic
*A **gigantic** boom echoed round the hillsides.*

vast
*The Sahara desert covers a **vast** area of land.*

ANTONYM: small

a b c d e f **g** h i j k l m n o p q r s t u v w x y z

great (2) ADJECTIVE
Something that is **great** is very good.

excellent
*"That was an **excellent** meal, thank you," said my cousin.*

superb
*The gymnast gave a **superb** display of floor exercises.*

wonderful
*"It's **wonderful** to see you," gushed the queen to the nobleman.*

great (3) ADJECTIVE
A **great** person is very important and highly respected.

eminent
*The **eminent** scientist has won the Nobel Prize two years in a row.*

important
*Picasso had made an **important** contribution to art.*

outstanding
*Muhammad Ali was the **outstanding** boxer of his generation.*

ANTONYM: unknown or insignificant

great (4) ADJECTIVE
A **great** event is very important.

grand
*The coronation was a **grand** occasion.*

magnificent
*The invention of the steam engine was a **magnificent** achievement.*

spectacular
*The millionaire's party ended in a **spectacular** firework display.*

great (5) ADJECTIVE
Something that is **great** is very large in amount or degree.

considerable
*It takes **considerable** skill to walk a tightrope.*

extreme
*Hermione showed **extreme** courage in facing the hungry lioness.*

✔ Don't confuse **great** with the homophone **grate**.

greedy ADJECTIVE
Someone who is **greedy** wants more of something than is necessary or fair.

gluttonous
*Augustus was a **gluttonous** child who never seemed to stop eating.*

piggish INFORMAL
*"Well, I think it's **piggish** to have eight roast potatoes!" exclaimed George.*

selfish
*The **selfish** lottery winner kept all his winnings for himself.*

voracious
*Charlie had a **voracious** appetite, especially for chocolate.*

groan VERB
If you **groan**, you make a long, low sound of pain, unhappiness or disappointment.

cry out
*The wretched queen **cried out** as she was dragged to the scaffold.*

moan
*At night, the wind **moans** through the trees near my bedroom window.*

sigh
*When he heard my corny joke, Jim **sighed** and walked away.*

ground (1) NOUN
Ground is the surface of the land.

earth
*The meteorite made a vast crater in the **earth** when it landed.*

land
*Mr Palfrey farms the **land** next to our house.*

soil
*The **soil** in our garden is good for growing vegetables.*

ground (2) NOUN
Ground is an area of land, especially land that is used for a particular purpose.

pitch
*That baseball **pitch** gets very muddy in winter.*

stadium
*You could see the lights of the sports **stadium** from miles around.*

group NOUN

A **group** is a number of things or people that are linked in some way.

category
There were five nominations in the "Best Actor" category.

class
Fifi won a rosette in the "Senior Poodle" class at the dog show.

set
To her dismay, Mum won a matching set of screwdrivers in the raffle.

Different groups

A group of things:

batch	→	a **batch** of doughnuts
clump	→	a **clump** of trees
cluster	→	a **cluster** of jewels
collection	→	a **collection** of stamps

A group of people:

band	→	a **band** of pilgrims
crowd	→	a **crowd** of protesters
gathering	→	a **gathering** of leaders
party	→	a **party** of tourists

A group that has members:

association	→	The Automobile **Association**
club	→	an after-school **club**
society	→	The **Society** for the Preservation of Ancient Buildings

A group of animals:

brood	→	a **brood** of chickens
flock	→	a **flock** of birds; a **flock** of sheep
gaggle	→	a **gaggle** of geese
herd	→	a **herd** of cattle
kindle	→	a **kindle** of kittens
litter	→	a **litter** of puppies
murder	→	a **murder** of crows
pack	→	a **pack** of wolves
school	→	a **school** of whales
shoal	→	a **shoal** of fish
swarm	→	a **swarm** of insects
troop	→	a **troop** of monkeys

grow (1) VERB

When someone or something **grows**, it gets bigger.

develop
In their teenage years, children develop into adults.

expand
That city has expanded into the countryside.

spread
The bush's branches spread all over the place.

swell
Each bud swells until it bursts open as a leaf.

ANTONYM: shrink

grow (2) VERB

When plants **grow**, they increase in size or develop.

flourish
While we were on holiday, weeds had flourished everywhere.

germinate
The flower seeds germinated in the warmth of the greenhouse.

sprout
The magic tree suddenly sprouted legs, and ran off, chuckling.

grow up VERB

Grow up can mean to become an adult.

develop
Calves soon develop into cows.

mature
Nadia has matured into a kind and sensitive person.

grown-up ADJECTIVE

Someone who is **grown-up** is adult in age or behaviour.

adult
His adult behaviour made him seem older than he was.

fully-grown
At 14 hands high, the horse was considered to be fully-grown.

mature
Mr Jessop said he expected us to behave in a mature way.

a
b
c
d
e
f
g
h
i
j
k
l
m
n
o
p
q
r
s
t
u
v
w
x
y
z

A B C D E F **G** H I J K L M N O P Q R S T U V W X Y Z

grumble VERB

If you **grumble**, you complain in a bad-tempered way.

moan
*My mum is always **moaning** about the state of my bedroom.*

whine
*After he lost his sweets, my little brother wouldn't stop **whining**.*

whinge
*"It's no good **whingeing**," said Dad. "You said you wanted piano lessons."*

grumpy ADJECTIVE

Someone who is **grumpy** is bad-tempered and fed up.

bad-tempered
*"Just because your team lost, there's no need to be **bad-tempered**," said Victoria.*

cross
*I was **cross** when my mum wouldn't let me play outside.*

crotchety
*Babies often get **crotchety** when they are teething.*

irritable
*I tend to get **irritable** when I'm hungry, but I soon cheer up once I've eaten.*

sulky
*My big sister gets very **sulky** if her boyfriend doesn't phone her.*

See **angry**

guard (1) VERB

When you **guard** someone or something, you watch them carefully to protect them.

keep watch
*While the other bandits slept, the Ringo Kid **kept watch** by the campfire.*

protect
*Twenty soldiers **protected** the queen's palace.*

shield
*The police **shielded** the prisoner from the protesters.*

tend
*It was the shepherd's job to **tend** the sheep and goats in the rocky mountains.*

guard (2) NOUN

A **guard** is a person whose job is to watch over a person, object or place.

lookout
*Robin Hood posted **lookouts** on all roads into the forest.*

sentry
***Sentries** stood to attention as the royal car swept through the palace gates.*

warden
*The jail was staffed by 200 **wardens** who worked in shifts.*

guess (1) VERB

If you **guess** something, you form an opinion about it without knowing all the relevant facts.

estimate
*At the fête, we had to **estimate** how many sweets were in the jar.*

reckon
*I **reckon** the Blues are a certainty to win the league this year.*

suppose
*"With all this rain, I **suppose** the race will be cancelled," pondered Faraji.*

suspect
*Roberto **suspected** that someone was following him home.*

guess (2) NOUN

A **guess** is an opinion formed without knowing all the facts.

estimate
*Harry's **estimate** was that the spell would last for half an hour.*

hunch
*Nancy's **hunch** was that her friend was in danger.*

guide VERB

If you **guide** someone somewhere, you lead or show them the way there.

conduct
*The historian **conducted** the party round the ancient manor house.*

direct
*"Can you **direct** me to the city centre, please?" asked Berta.*

lead
The delicious smell of bread led us straight to the bakery.

steer
With my hands on his shoulders, I steered the blindfolded boy towards his target.

guilty (1) ADJECTIVE
If you are **guilty** of doing something wrong, you did it.

at fault
After the collision, the lorry driver admitted he was at fault.

responsible
When we saw the mess after the party, everyone felt responsible.

to blame
As for the chewed furniture, we couldn't tell which of the puppies was to blame.

ANTONYM: innocent

guilty (2) ADJECTIVE
If you feel **guilty**, you are unhappy because you think you have done something wrong.

ashamed
I felt ashamed that I had eaten all of Ashley's sweets.

repentant
The repentant thief resolved to return what he had stolen.

sorry
Mai-Lin felt sorry about the lies she had told.

gullible ADJECTIVE
If someone is **gullible**, they are easily tricked.

innocent
The innocent children thought that all the magician's tricks were real.

naive
Only a very naive person would believe the statements made by the fraudster.

trusting
My aunt has an open, trusting nature, so she falls for all my jokes.

unsuspecting
A crowd of unsuspecting tourists was taken to lots of souvenir shops.

ANTONYM: suspicious

gun NOUN
A **gun** is a weapon that fires bullets or shells.

✔ The general name for lighter guns is **firearms**.
The general name for heavy guns is **artillery**.
A group of heavy guns is a **battery**.

Some types of hand guns:
automatic
pistol
revolver

Some types of longer hand-held guns:
air gun
blunderbuss OLD-FASHIONED
musket OLD-FASHIONED
rifle
shotgun

Some other types of guns:
bazooka
cannon
machine gun
mortar

---

guts PLURAL NOUN INFORMAL
Guts is courage.

bravery
Jassem demonstrated great bravery in facing the bullies.

courage
I hadn't the courage to own up about the broken window.

nerve
Eliza showed nerve in tackling the burglar.

a
b
c
d
e
f
g
h
i
j
k
l
m
n
o
p
q
r
s
t
u
v
w
x
y
z

Hh

habit NOUN

A **habit** is something that you do often or regularly.

custom
*There's an old Greek **custom** of smashing plates for good luck.*

routine
*It was Wallis's **routine** to brush his teeth twice a day, morning and evening.*

hair NOUN

Hair is the fine threads that grow on the heads and bodies of people and animals.

✔ Hair on animals can be called their **fur** or **coat**. The long hair on the necks of horses and lions is called their **mane**.

Some types of hairstyle:

Afro	dreadlocks
bob	pigtail
braids	plaits
bunches	ponytail
crew cut	ringlets

Hair colours:

auburn	fair
black	ginger
blond (male)	grey
blonde (female)	mousy
brown	red

---

handsome ADJECTIVE

A **handsome** person is very attractive in appearance.

attractive
*Melanie has a very **attractive** smile.*

good-looking
*The film star is **good-looking** and skilful.*

ANTONYM: ugly

handy (1) ADJECTIVE

If something is **handy**, it is conveniently near.

accessible
*The hotel is **accessible** by rail and road.*

convenient
*Our school's location is quite **convenient** – we can walk there in ten minutes.*

nearby
*We also have a post office **nearby**, which is behind the supermarket.*

ANTONYM: inconvenient

handy (2) ADJECTIVE

If something is **handy**, it is useful.

convenient
*Credit cards are a **convenient** way of paying for things over the phone.*

helpful
*The instructions that came with the game are very **helpful**.*

practical
*Dad had given me very **practical** advice on mending a puncture.*

user-friendly
*The instruction book was **user-friendly** – short, very clear and with helpful diagrams.*

hang VERB

If something **hangs** from a hook, nail or line, it is attached so that it does not touch the ground.

be suspended
*The sides of beef **were suspended** from hooks in the cold room.*

dangle
*The climber fell off the rock face and **dangled** on her rope.*

droop
*The flag **drooped** on the pole in the still air.*

swing
*The inn sign **swung** creakily in the wind.*

hang about or **hang around** VERB
INFORMAL

If you **hang about** or **hang around** somewhere, you stay or wait there.

dawdle
*"Will you stop **dawdling** and get a move on!" Mum shouted irritably.*

linger
*Moira **lingered** by the bakery window. Those cakes looked so tempting!*

loiter
*The spy **loitered** in the shadows, hoping that no one would see her.*

remain
*We **remained** in our seats for some time after the match was over.*

happen VERB
When something **happens**, it occurs or takes place.

arise
*The secret to being organized is to deal with problems as they **arise**.*

crop up
*"A meeting has **cropped up**, so I'll have to see you next week instead," apologized Daniel.*

occur
*When I was three, a strange event **occurred** in our family.*

take place
*The concert will **take place** next Tuesday.*

✔ Something that happens before something else **precedes** it.
Something that happens after something else **follows** it.
Something that happens again **recurs** or **reoccurs**.

happiness NOUN
Happiness is a feeling of great contentment or pleasure.

cheerfulness
*Her **cheerfulness** despite her problems was a lesson to us all.*

contentment
*The couple lived a life of great **contentment**.*

delight
*Zara opened her presents with great **delight**.*

ecstasy
*Luke was in **ecstasy** – at last he'd got the puppy he'd always wanted.*

joy
*The missing sailor's parents were filled with **joy** when they knew he was safe.*

jubilation
*There were scenes of **jubilation** in the winning team's changing room.*

pleasure
*"It gives me great **pleasure** to open this library," announced the chairwoman.*

satisfaction
*Gran got **satisfaction** from the blankets she made for charity.*

ANTONYM: sadness

happy ADJECTIVE
If you are **happy**, you feel full of contentment or joy.

cheerful
*The popular boy greeted everyone with a **cheerful** smile.*

content
*I could have scored more, but I was **content** with two goals.*

delighted
*Mum and Dad were **delighted** with the book I bought them.*

ecstatic
*My big sister was **ecstatic**. Her boyfriend was coming round!*

glad
*"I'll be **glad** when the holidays are over," said Mum gloomily.*

jolly
*Reginald was a **jolly** old man with a cheery word for everyone.*

joyful
*The bells rang out in **joyful** thanksgiving as the bride and groom left the church.*

jubilant
*We were **jubilant** that all the team's hard training had paid off.*

merry
*The Cratchit family had a **merry** time, thanks to the reformed Scrooge's generosity.*

pleased
*Victoria was **pleased** that people noticed her new hairstyle.*

satisfied
*Whatever the result, I was **satisfied** that I had tried my hardest.*

ANTONYM: sad

a b c d e f g **h** i j k l m n o p q r s t u v w x y z

harbour NOUN

A **harbour** is a protected area of deep water where boats can be moored.

> **Places in a harbour where ships can dock or shelter:**
> | | | |
> |---|---|---|
> | dock | marina | quay |
> | jetty | pier | wharf |

hard (1) ADJECTIVE

An object that is **hard** is not easy to bend or break.

firm
*The snow had been packed **firm** by dozens of sledges sliding over it.*

rigid
*We left the washing hanging out overnight and the frost had turned it **rigid**.*

solid
*There is no land at the North Pole – just metres of thick, **solid** ice.*

stiff
*Dad's best shirt was so full of starch, it was too **stiff** to wear.*

tough
*Castles needed walls **tough** enough to survive an attack.*

ANTONYM: soft

hard (2) ADJECTIVE

If something is **hard** to do, it requires a lot of effort.

arduous
*Women and children did **arduous** work in Victorian mills.*

backbreaking
*Shifting the rocks was a **backbreaking** task.*

exhausting
*The walk up the hill was **exhausting**.*

strenuous
*The more **strenuous** the exercise, the more calories you burn up.*

tiring
*Garden work can be **tiring**, especially if the weather is hot.*

tough
*It was a **tough** job keeping the lawn clear of fallen leaves.*

ANTONYM: easy

hard (3) ADJECTIVE

Something that is **hard** is difficult to understand.

complicated
*The problem was far too **complicated** for me to understand.*

difficult
*"Work's **difficult** enough without kids interrupting me," Dad said tetchily.*

perplexing
*It was a **perplexing** decision: one tunnel led to freedom, the other to a trap, but which was which?*

puzzling
*I found my Maths homework quite **puzzling**. I should have listened harder in the lesson.*

ANTONYM: easy or simple

hard (4) ADVERB

If you do something **hard**, you do it with a lot of force.

sharply
*The magician pulled the cloth **sharply** and the plates stayed on the table!*

vigorously
*Grandad shook my hand so **vigorously** I thought it would come off.*

with all your might
*"Now, make a wish **with all your might**," the fairy godmother said.*

ANTONYM: gently

hard (5) ADVERB

If you work **hard**, you give a lot of time and effort to the work.

doggedly
*Aksana didn't find it easy, but studied **doggedly** and passed the test.*

industriously
*For days, the divers worked **industriously** to salvage the treasure.*

harden VERB
If something **hardens**, it sets or stops being soft.

set
"Wait for that concrete to **set** before you walk on it," Dad ordered.

solidify
The paint had **solidified** in the tin.

stiffen
The fluffy egg whites **stiffened** into meringues as they were cooked.

ANTONYM: soften

hard-working ADJECTIVE
A **hard-working** person works hard.

conscientious
Craig was very **conscientious**, feeding the hamsters every day without fail.

diligent
Mr Hassan said I was a **diligent** worker.

industrious
Mum and I had been very **industrious**, with lots of jam to prove it.

ANTONYM: lazy

hardly ADVERB
If you can **hardly** do something, you can only just do it.

barely
The fog was so thick, I could **barely** see the tree in the back yard.

only just
Because of the heavy traffic, we **only just** caught the train.

scarcely
A Roman coin in our garden! Dad could **scarcely** believe his luck.

harmful ADJECTIVE
Something **harmful** has a bad effect on something.

damaging
Chemicals are **damaging** to the ozone layer.

dangerous
"That quarry is **dangerous**. Stay away," warned my uncle.

destructive
Locusts are hugely **destructive** to crops, eating everything in minutes.

detrimental
Late nights had a **detrimental** effect on Keisha's school work.

ANTONYM: harmless

hat NOUN
A **hat** is a covering for the head.

Some types of hat:

baseball cap	hardhat
beret	helmet
boater	stetson
bonnet	sun hat
bowler hat	top hat
cork hat	trilby
cowboy hat	turban
crash helmet	woollen hat
fez	yarmulke

hate VERB
If you **hate** someone or something, you dislike them very much.

abhor
Pauline **abhors** cheese.

despise
If there's one thing I **despise**, it's people who tell lies.

detest
My brother **detests** me tweaking his ears.

loathe
My dad **loathes** getting up early on Saturday mornings.

ANTONYM: love

have (1) VERB
If you **have** something, it belongs to you or you possess it.

own
The millionaire **owned** far more houses and cars than he needed.

possess
My report read, "Abby **possesses** a good sense of humour".

have

A B C D E F G **H** I J K L M N O P Q R S T U V W X Y Z

have (2) VERB
If you **have** something such as a cold or an accident, you feel or experience it.

endure
*The climbers **endured** three days of blizzards.*

experience
*Going on holiday, we **experienced** a few delays, but nothing too dreadful.*

undergo
*Captain Craddock **underwent** an operation on his injured knee.*

have to VERB
If you **have to do** something, you must do it.

be compelled to
*When Grandad was in the army, the soldiers **were compelled to** have cold showers.*

be forced to
*Because her injury proved too painful, the runner **was forced to** drop out of the race.*

must
*We **must** drink plenty of water each day in order to stay healthy.*

should
*"You really **should** see that film. It's terrific!" Kelly told me.*

healthy (1) ADJECTIVE
Someone who is **healthy** is fit and well, and is not suffering from any illness.

in good condition
*Our dog Tess is **in good condition**, considering her age.*

in good shape
*The champion felt **in good shape** for his bout with Basher Muggs.*

physically fit
*For their job, soldiers, sailors and air crew need to be **physically fit**.*

ANTONYM: sick

healthy (2) ADJECTIVE
Something that is **healthy** is good for you.

beneficial
*A glass of orange juice a day can be **beneficial** to your immune system.*

nutritious
***Nutritious** food is full of vitamins.*

wholesome
*A **wholesome** diet does not include junk food.*

ANTONYM: unhealthy

heap NOUN
A **heap** is an untidy pile of things.

mound
*Mum despaired at the **mound** of washing that greeted her.*

mountain
*A **mountain** of comics stands in my bedroom cupboard.*

pile
*A **pile** of unopened letters lay on the doormat.*

stack
*Unfortunately, in the kitchen there was a **stack** of dirty dishes.*

hear (1) VERB
When you **hear** sounds, you are aware of them because they reach your ears.

catch
*"I didn't quite **catch** what you said, dear," Gran confided.*

overhear
*I **overheard** Mum and Dad planning a day at the seaside for the family.*

✔ To hear someone else's conversation by accident is to **overhear**.
To listen to someone else's conversation deliberately is to **eavesdrop**.

*See **listen***

hear (2) VERB
If you **hear** about something, you get to know about it.

discover
*Myles **discovered** that his friend had been telling lies.*

learn
*My mum **learnt** by phone last night that Grandpa was seriously ill.*

receive the news
*The king **received** the news of his army's defeat in dignified silence.*

130

heavy (1) ADJECTIVE
Something that is **heavy** weighs a lot.

bulky
*A delivery man brought us a **bulky** parcel.*

hefty
*Mum said the rock was too **hefty** for my dad to try lifting on his own.*

weighty
*With PE kit and books in it, my school bag was fairly **weighty**.*

ANTONYM: light

*See **big (1)***

heavy (2) ADJECTIVE
Heavy rain falls hard and in great quantities.

pouring
***Pouring** rain ruined the witch's spell by putting her fire out.*

torrential
*The downpour was **torrential**, flooding roads.*

ANTONYM: light

hello INTERJECTION
You say **hello** when you meet someone or answer the telephone.

> **Words from other languages that mean hello:**
> **bonjour** (French)
> **ciao** (Italian)
> **dag** (Afrikaans)
> **guten tag** (German)
> **hola** (Spanish)
> **kia ora** (Mâori – New Zealand)
> **konnichiwa** (Japanese)

help (1) VERB
If you **help** someone, you make something easier or better for them.

aid
*I think that it is a rich country's duty to **aid** poorer countries.*

assist
*The off-duty nurse rushed to **assist** the man lying at the roadside.*

cooperate with
*The companies **cooperated with** one another to develop the new medicine.*

lend a hand
*Most people are happy to **lend a hand** to their neighbours.*

*See **support (2)***

help (2) NOUN
If you get **help** from someone, they give you assistance.

a helping hand
*Most mums appreciate **a helping hand** every now and then.*

aid
*When I sprained my ankle, I needed my friend's **aid** to walk.*

assistance
*Dad offered his pal our **assistance** in moving house.*

cooperation
*The police thanked the public for their **cooperation** with the investigation.*

helpful (1) ADJECTIVE
If you are **helpful**, you cooperate with others and support them.

cooperative
*It's important to be **cooperative** with others if you're part of a team.*

obliging
*The shop assistant was very **obliging**, taking Gran's shopping to her car.*

supportive
*When Grandad died, Gran's friends were very **supportive**.*

helpful (2) ADJECTIVE
If something is **helpful**, it helps you in some way.

beneficial
*That bit of extra homework was **beneficial** to Khalid's maths.*

useful
*My old tracksuit is **useful** when I have to help in the garden.*

ANTONYM: useless or of no help

helpless

helpless ADJECTIVE
If you are **helpless**, you are unable to protect yourself or do anything useful.

defenceless
*The refugees were **defenceless** as the fighters swooped in.*

powerless
*The Australian family were **powerless** as the bush fire roared towards their home.*

unprotected
*The orphaned child wandered the streets, **unprotected** in the blizzard.*

vulnerable
*The evil orcs realized that the castle was **vulnerable** to attack from the air.*

weak
*When they were born, the puppies were small and **weak**, but they soon grew strong.*

hesitate VERB
If you **hesitate**, you pause or show uncertainty.

dither
*"Stop **dithering** and dive forwards!" Huh! It was all right for the bungee jumper to talk.*

falter
*The little plane's engine **faltered**, died, then roared into life again.*

pause
*The group **paused** at the monument to think of the brave people who had died in the war.*

hidden ADJECTIVE
If something is **hidden**, you cannot see it.

buried
*The painting lay **buried** beneath old furniture in the loft.*

concealed
*My big sister's spot was **concealed** beneath a ton of make-up.*

out of sight
*Mum found the empty biscuit tin, but my brother and I were safely **out of sight**.*

secreted
*The money was **secreted** in a box beneath the floorboards.*

ANTONYM: visible

hide (1) VERB
If you **hide**, you go somewhere where you cannot be seen or found easily.

go into hiding
*The pop star **went into hiding** when news of her wedding got out.*

lie low
*The train robbers hoped to **lie low** at the farm for a while.*

stow away
*The refugee **stowed away** in the ship's hold.*

take cover
*"**Take cover** everyone!" the sheriff ordered as the Clancy Gang rode into town.*

hide (2) VERB
If you **hide** something, you put it where it cannot be seen, or prevent it from being discovered.

conceal
*The singer managed to **conceal** her grief, but burst into tears when the show was over.*

mask
*Skilful use of make-up **masked** the scars Adhira had from the accident.*

secrete
*The hijacker tried to **secrete** the knife in his left sock.*

ANTONYM: reveal

high (1) ADJECTIVE
If something is **high**, it reaches a long way above the ground.

lofty
*From the **lofty** ceiling of the castle's main hall hung a beautiful chandelier.*

soaring
*The **soaring** columns of the temple filled me with wonder.*

tall
*In the top of a **tall** fir tree, the vulture awaited its chance.*

towering
*We were surrounded by **towering** volcanic peaks.*

ANTONYM: low

high (2) ADJECTIVE

Something that is **high** is great in degree, quantity or intensity.

exceptional
*The head teacher did not often give such **exceptional** praise.*

excessive
*She wrapped up the delicate ornaments with **excessive** care.*

extreme
*Electronic work requires an **extreme** degree of concentration.*

ANTONYM: low

high (3) ADJECTIVE

A **high** voice is pitched high in tone.

high-pitched
*I was immediately aware of the toddler's **high-pitched** cries.*

piercing
*A **piercing** scream cut like a rapier through the tranquillity of the wood.*

piping
*The **piping** voices of children at play drifted over the village roof tops.*

shrill
*With a **shrill** whistle, the steam locomotive began to depart.*

ANTONYM: deep

hinder VERB

If you **hinder** someone or something, you get in their way and make it difficult for them to do what they want to do.

hamper
*Returning down the mountain, Celine was **hampered** by her twisted ankle.*

hold back
*"Don't let us **hold** you **back**," Mum said. "You go on ahead."*

obstruct
*The major did all he could to **obstruct** the building work.*

prevent
*The protests delayed the new bypass, but could not **prevent** it.*

hit VERB

If you **hit** someone or something, you strike or knock them with force.

bash INFORMAL
*"Sir, Syd **bashed** me on the nose," the bully whined.*

batter
*Police **battered** on the door, but no one answered.*

clout INFORMAL
*Grandad told me that when he was a boy he would often be **clouted** for being late.*

pound
*I watched the TV chef **pound** the steak to make it tender before he cooked it.*

punch
*The two heavyweights **punched** each other to a standstill.*

slap
*I saw my big sister **slap** her boyfriend's face!*

smack
*At school we had a debate about whether parents should **smack** children.*

thump
*The ball **thumped** me in the stomach and I doubled up.*

wallop INFORMAL
*Dennis the Menace is often getting **walloped** with his Dad's slipper.*

whack
*I **whacked** the ball with the bat.*

hoarse ADJECTIVE

A **hoarse** voice sounds rough and unclear.

croaky
*With her sore throat, all Karen could manage was a **croaky** hello.*

husky
*The singer's deep, **husky** voice is her trademark.*

rasping
*Mr Quelch's **rasping** voice gave Bunter the creeps.*

throaty
*The large motorbike gave a **throaty** roar as it surged away.*

hold

hold (1) VERB

When you **hold** something, you keep it in your hands or arms.

clasp

The eagle **clasped** the crag with its strong, crooked claws.

cling to

As the Titanic sank, people **clung to** wreckage in the icy water.

clutch

The panic-stricken driver **clutched** the wheel in terror.

get hold of

To remove the wheel, undo the nuts, **get hold of** the tyre and pull hard.

grip

Lyra **gripped** Iorek's furry paw in fear.

hold (2) VERB

If something **holds** a certain amount of something, it can contain or carry that amount.

bear

The old bridge will not **bear** too much weight.

contain

Mrs Abernathy asked, "How much liquid does this cup **contain**?"

support

A pyramid of gymnasts **supported** the triumphant girl.

✔ The number of people a theatre stadium holds is the number of people it **seats**.

hold out VERB

If you **hold out** something to someone, you offer it to them.

extend

The captain **extended** his hand, expecting his opponent to shake it.

offer

With a slight bow, the waiter **offered** us black pepper for our pizza.

hold up VERB

If something **holds** you **up**, it delays you.

delay

The unfortunate accident **delayed** the procession by half an hour.

detain

"You mustn't let me **detain** you," the injured explorer begged his colleagues.

hinder

Rebellious workers did their best to **hinder** the introduction of the new system.

hole NOUN

A **hole** is an opening or hollow space in something.

gap

Through a **gap** in the curtains, Mrs White saw the colonel with a dagger.

opening

In an instant, the Pied Piper had created an **opening** in the rock before him.

a small hole:
cavity

"Hmm! Plenty of **cavities** there," said the dentist disapprovingly.

perforation

The tiny **perforations** in tea bags allow the water to get to the tea leaves.

puncture

Mum's tyre had a **puncture** and went flat.

split

The **split** in the acorn widened. An oak tree was beginning to grow.

tear

The x-ray showed I had a **tear** in a leg muscle.

a hole in the ground:
crater

The meteorite left a massive **crater** in the desert landscape.

excavation

The archeologists dug a huge **excavation**.

hollow

The squirrel stared at Vicky from a **hollow** at the foot of the tree.

pit

There were too many **pits** in the road for a bicycle to travel safely.

a deep hole in the ground:
abyss

Beneath the gaze of Legolas, a yawning **abyss** descended to infinite depths.

chasm
Smoke signals could be seen from the far side of the enormous chasm.

pothole
From the top of the pothole, I could hear the gush of an underground river.

shaft
The lift cage full of miners descended the shaft to the coalface.

home NOUN
Your **home** is the building or place in which you live.

dwelling
"Welcome to my humble dwelling," said Rat.

residence
The ambassador's residence was an impressive villa among palm trees.

Some homes made by animals:			
ant	– **hill**	hare	– **form**
badger	– **sett** or **set**,	mole	– **fortress**
	earth	otter	– **holt**
bear	– **den, lair**	rabbit	– **burrow,**
bee	– **hive**		**warren**
bird	– **nest**	snake	– **nest**
fox	– **earth, lair**	squirrel	– **drey**

See **house**

honest ADJECTIVE
If you are **honest**, you can be trusted to tell the truth.

frank
"Now," Bhoomi's dad asked, "I want you to be frank with me. Is anything the matter?"

sincere
Mrs Fletcher felt that Susan had made a sincere effort to behave well.

trustworthy
My gran often said, "If you're not trustworthy, you're nothing!"

truthful
As the girl was normally truthful, her version of events was accepted.

ANTONYM: dishonest

hooligan NOUN
A **hooligan** is a destructive and violent young person.

delinquent
Mum said she would like to get hold of the delinquents who wrecked the scout hut.

lout
"You looking for trouble?" the lout said, his face two centimetres from mine.

vandal
Vandals had broken the windows.

yob INFORMAL
Some yobs came into the youth club, but Mr Trainer sent them packing.

hope (1) VERB
If you **hope** that something will happen, you want or expect it to happen.

anticipate
Krishnan anticipated that his mum would bake him a cake on his birthday.

count on
"You mustn't count on me," my friend Wendy warned. "I might not be there."

dream
Vicky dreamt that one day she would be on that stage.

look forward to
Mrs Phillips was looking forward to going to the cinema when her car broke down.

trust
"I trust you all had a good holiday," said the head teacher at first assembly.

hope (2) NOUN
A **hope** is the wish or expectation that things will go well in the future.

ambition
It was Jasmine's ambition to be a professional ice skater one day.

anticipation
The sailor's proud parents put up decorations in anticipation of his homecoming.

dream
Napoleon's dream was to conquer Europe.

ANTONYM: desperation or hopelessness

hopeful

hopeful (1) ADJECTIVE
If you are **hopeful** about something, you hope it will turn out well.

confident
*Our team were **confident** that we could win the trophy.*

optimistic
*My **optimistic** uncle is always looking on the bright side.*

ANTONYM: doubtful

hopeful (2) ADJECTIVE
If a situation is **hopeful**, it looks as if it will turn out well.

encouraging
*"An **encouraging** report" was all that the head teacher had written.*

promising
*The conductor told my mum that I was a **promising** violinist.*

ANTONYM: hopeless

hopeless (1) ADJECTIVE
You say something is **hopeless** when it is very bad and you do not feel it can get any better.

futile
*The dog made **futile** attempts to run away, but its lead was firmly tied to the railings.*

pointless
*"It's **pointless** asking me," my sister protested. "I don't know anything."*

vain
*The commuter puffed up the platform in a **vain** attempt to catch the train.*

ANTONYM: promising

*See **impossible***

hopeless (2) ADJECTIVE
Someone who is **hopeless** is unable to do something well.

incompetent
*Yet again, the **incompetent** stuntman hobbled to the waiting ambulance.*

pathetic INFORMAL
*"I've never seen such a **pathetic** effort," Miss Marsden ranted.*

useless
*David was a **useless** salesman. Even his mother wouldn't buy from him.*

ANTONYM: able or competent

horrible ADJECTIVE
Someone or something that is **horrible** is disagreeable and unpleasant.

abominable
*"That was an **abominable** thing to do," said the police officer.*

appalling
*There was an **appalling** smell coming from the drains.*

awful
*My new haircut is **awful**.*

dreadful
*My grandma made me a **dreadful** sweater for Christmas, but I had to pretend I liked it.*

hideous
*Into view came a beast so **hideous** that none could behold it.*

horrid
*Having one's property stolen is a **horrid** thing to happen.*

nasty
*"Investigating murders must be a **nasty** business," Dad remarked.*

terrible
*The monster uttered a **terrible** roar.*

horror NOUN
Horror is a strong feeling of alarm caused by something very unpleasant.

alarm
*Filled with **alarm**, the mother rushed to stop her baby falling in the pool.*

disgust
*Katrina's **disgust** at such a mean trick showed in her face.*

dismay
*To the shy man's **dismay**, the spotlight suddenly turned onto him.*

dread
*My mum has a **dread** of heights.*

fear

*There was a look of **fear** on Miss Muffet's face when she saw the spider.*

terror

***Terror** turned to anger when Latisha found out I had put a worm in her lunchbox.*

*See **fright** and **panic** (2)*

hot ADJECTIVE

Something that is **hot** has a high temperature.

> **Hot weather:**
> baking   burning   sweltering
> blistering   scorching   tropical
> boiling   sultry
>
> **Hot water:**
> boiling   heated   scalding
> burning   piping hot   steaming
>
> **Hot-flavoured food:**
> fiery   piquant
> peppery   spicy

house NOUN

A **house** is a building where people live.

dwelling

*Badger's **dwelling** lay deep in the heart of the Wild Wood.*

home

*House martins made their **home** under the eaves of the cottage.*

property

*The house agent said that the **property** had been empty for some time.*

residence

*Immaculate lawns ran from the ambassador's **residence** down to the river.*

> **Types of houses:**
> bungalow   manor
> castle   mansion
> cottage   ranch
> detached house   semidetached house
> flat   terraced house
> maisonette   villa

hug VERB

If you **hug** someone, you put your arms round them and hold them close to you, usually to comfort them or to show affection.

cuddle

*A nurse **cuddled** the poorly child in her arms to comfort him.*

embrace

*The man and his elderly father **embraced** each other after years apart.*

squeeze

*I thought Auntie Flo was going to **squeeze** me to death. Ugh!*

huge ADJECTIVE

Something that is **huge** is extremely large in amount, size or degree.

colossal

*Unexpectedly, the school show turned out to be a **colossal** success.*

enormous

*Towed behind six horses came a truly **enormous** carriage.*

gigantic

*There was a **gigantic** cake at the film star's birthday party.*

immense

*It was an **immense** favour to ask, but what else could I do?*

massive

*When the filling fell out, the crater in my tooth was **massive**.*

vast

*The Sahara desert covers a **vast** area of land in North Africa.*

ANTONYM: tiny

hunch NOUN

If you have a **hunch** about something, you have a feeling or suspicion about it that is not based on facts or evidence.

idea

*"I've an **idea** that you may be just the girl for the job!" the manager said.*

inkling

*Mrs Lindsey had an **inkling** the class was planning a surprise for her.*

hungry

hungry ADJECTIVE
If you are **hungry**, you need or want food.

empty
"Please hurry up with that food, Mum, I'm **empty**!" Lisa called from upstairs.

famished
Our rations had run out, and we sat in the rain, soaked and **famished**.

ravenous
After helping with the harvest all day, Hugh was **ravenous**.

starving
While we waste food, millions of children in the developing world are **starving**.

hunt (1) VERB
When people **hunt**, they chase and kill wild animals for food or sport.

pursue
The hunters **pursued** the elephants.

stalk
The gamekeeper silently **stalked** the red deer as it grazed.

hunt (2) VERB
If you **hunt** for something, you search for it.

ferret about INFORMAL
For some reason, my sister was **ferreting about** in the loft above my room.

look high and low
"There it is!" Mum said. "I've **looked high and low** for that remote control."

scour
The neighbours helped us **scour** the area for our missing cat.

search
Although Ron **searched** for the book, there was no trace of it.

hurry (1) VERB
If you **hurry** somewhere, you go there quickly.

dash
Dad had to **dash** down to the shop to buy a lottery ticket before it was too late.

hasten
Brown **hastened** to Flashman's study for fear of being punished for lateness.

rush
Anxious to see the end of the golf match, the crowd **rushed** towards the final green.

scurry
When Whiskers appeared, mice **scurried** to all parts of the garden.

step on it INFORMAL
"**Step on it**, old bean, we're late," Wooster said to his chauffeur.

hurry (2) NOUN
If you are in a **hurry** to do something, you want to do it quickly.

haste
In her **haste**, Mrs Pepperpot left her umbrella behind.

rush
"What's the **rush**?" Dad asked. "We'll get there two hours early."

hurt (1) VERB
If you **hurt** yourself or someone else, you injure or cause physical pain to yourself or someone else.

bruise
The hockey ball **bruised** Jamie's leg when Craig cracked it towards goal.

harm
I managed to get the butterfly out of the window without **harming** it.

injure
Dozens of people were **injured** in the pile-up.

wound
The ricocheting bullet **wounded** the old sheriff in the arm.

hurt (2) VERB
If you **hurt** someone, or hurt their feelings, you upset them by being unkind towards them.

distress
It **distressed** my dad to think that Sean wasn't going to join the navy.

upset
We could tell that Miss Kielty was **upset** by the news she had received.

wound
Devesh was **wounded** to think that a friend would believe such lies about him.

hurt (3) ADJECTIVE

If you are **hurt**, you are injured.

harmed

Although the ceiling collapsed, no one was harmed.

injured

A nurse bandaged my injured wrist.

wounded

Wounded troops were evacuated from the beach by the landing craft.

hurt (4) ADJECTIVE

If you feel **hurt**, you are upset because of someone's unkindness towards you.

offended

Scarlet felt offended that her friend had not invited her.

upset

My mum was visibly upset when she saw how poorly Gramps looked, but the nurse assured her he was on the road to recovery.

hut NOUN

A **hut** is a small house or shelter.

cabin

The old Canadian trapper lived in a log cabin in the woods.

shack

A few tumbledown shacks was all that remained of the gold miners' village.

shed

On Grandad's allotment is a shed where he keeps his tools.

a
b
c
d
e
f
g
h
i
j
k
l
m
n
o
p
q
r
s
t
u
v
w
x
y
z

icy ADJECTIVE
Something that is **icy** has ice on it, or is very cold.

arctic
Without a fire, conditions in our front room were nearly arctic.

bitter
A bitter wind was blowing off the sea as we walked along the promenade.

freezing
When we arrived in Canada for our holiday, it was the middle of winter and the weather was freezing.

frozen
With the sub-zero temperatures, all the lakes were frozen to some depth.

raw
A raw wind penetrated Shackleton's inadequate polar clothing.

idea (1) NOUN
An **idea** is a plan or possible course of action.

brainwave
Someone had the brainwave to use old tyres in making road surfaces.

proposal
The proposal to build an electric dishwasher was made as early as 1912.

suggestion
"That's a spiffing suggestion, Jeeves," replied Bertie Wooster.

idea (2) NOUN
If you have an **idea** of something, you have a general but not a detailed knowledge of it.

inkling
We had an inkling that something odd was going on.

notion
Leonardo da Vinci first had the notion of humans flying.

suspicion
I had a strong suspicion that Letitia was lying to me.

have an idea VERB
If you **have an idea**, you think something up.

conceive
Sir Frank Whittle first conceived the jet engine in 1930.

devise
People are trying to devise new television game shows all the time.

dream up
"Who on earth could have dreamt up that strange-looking car?" Dad remarked.

suggest
Darren suggested we should go bowling and then for a pizza.

idiot NOUN
An **idiot** is someone who is stupid or foolish.

fool
"Don't touch those wires, you fool!" the electrician shouted.

imbecile
"Get out of my sight, you clumsy imbecile!" bellowed Clouseau's boss.

nincompoop INFORMAL
What a nincompoop I was to get up for school on Saturday!

twit
What a twit my little sister is – she believed me when I told her that I could fly.

idiotic ADJECTIVE
Someone or something that is **idiotic** is very stupid.

crazy
I must have been crazy to let my friend talk me into bungee jumping.

foolish
It was foolish to think that I could carry all those plates at once.

hare-brained
"Whoever thought of this hare-brained new scheme?" moaned the head teacher.

senseless
The way we damage the atmosphere by burning fuels is senseless.

ANTONYM: sensible

ill ADJECTIVE
Someone who is **ill** is unhealthy or sick.

ailing
*The old man was **ailing**, but then he recovered and lived for many more years.*

laid up INFORMAL
*I went upstairs to see Dad, who was **laid up** with flu.*

poorly
*The nurse saw at once that the lady was very **poorly** and needed an ambulance.*

sick
*Moira was off **sick** last week, but she's back at school this week.*

unwell
*The visitor complained of feeling **unwell**, and asked to sit down.*

ANTONYM: healthy

illness NOUN
An **illness** is a particular disease.

ailment
*The explorer came back from the tropics with a mystery **ailment**.*

complaint
*Mum took me to the doctor's because I had a stomach **complaint**.*

disease
*Tuberculosis was once a common **disease**.*

sickness
*Many children suffer from travel **sickness**.*

imaginary ADJECTIVE
Something that is **imaginary** exists only in your mind, not in real life.

fictitious
*My favourite **fictitious** characters are The Twits, from Roald Dahl's book of that name.*

mythological
*The Minotaur was a **mythological** creature, said to have lived in the catacombs of Crete.*

unreal
*The incredible beauty of the Himalayan mountains seemed almost **unreal**.*

ANTONYM: real or actual

imagine VERB
If you **imagine** something or someone, you create a picture of them in your mind.

dream
*Rebecca **dreamed** she was back at the home where she had once lived.*

envisage
*Dillon **envisaged** what his bedroom in their new house would be like.*

fantasize
*As I trudged through the snow I **fantasized** about being at home in front of the fire.*

picture
*"Before you write, just **picture** yourself in a boat on a river," Mr Lennon said.*

visualize
*I tried to **visualize** what would happen if all cars grew legs.*

imitate VERB
If you **imitate** someone or something, you copy them.

do an impression of
*Sally made me laugh by **doing an impression of** our teacher.*

impersonate
*My brother is very good at **impersonating** my dad in a bad mood.*

mimic
*The clown walked behind the circus master, **mimicking** him perfectly.*

immediate ADJECTIVE
If something is **immediate**, it happens or is done without delay.

instant
*To make **instant** coffee, just add boiling water to the granules.*

instantaneous
*The huge flash of lightning was followed by an **instantaneous** peal of thunder.*

prompt
*Kamal's **prompt** action in phoning an ambulance saved the girl's life.*

urgent
*The message needed an **urgent** answer.*

a
b
c
d
e
f
g
h
i
j
k
l
m
n
o
p
q
r
s
t
u
v
w
x
y
z

immediately ADVERB

If something happens **immediately**, it happens at once.

directly

*The phrase: "Go **directly** to jail. Do not pass 'Go'." can be found on a Monopoly board.*

instantly

*Michaela recognized the film star **instantly** when she saw him in the street.*

promptly

*My annoying brother borrowed my watch and **promptly** broke it.*

right away

*I told Auntie Maureen I would run the errand **right away**.*

straight away

Straight away, Lyra resolved to find out what the dust was all about.

important (1) ADJECTIVE

Something that is **important** is very valuable, necessary or significant.

crucial

*It was absolutely **crucial** that supplies reached the famine zone soon.*

serious

*"The school is in a **serious** position," the head teacher said. "We need more staff."*

urgent

*The matter was **urgent**, and needed a quick response.*

vital

*"If you want to do well as an adult, it's **vital** that you work hard now," my father advised.*

ANTONYM: unimportant

important (2) ADJECTIVE

An **important** person has a lot of influence or power.

distinguished

*Many **distinguished** guests attended the banquet.*

eminent

*My Uncle Armand is an **eminent** scientist.*

influential

*When it comes to government policy, Sir Brian is an extremely **influential** man.*

powerful

*The Canadian was a **powerful** man, owning a global business empire.*

ANTONYM: unimportant

impossible ADJECTIVE

Something that is **impossible** cannot happen or cannot be done.

hopeless

*The situation seemed **hopeless**, but the rescuers found another survivor.*

out of the question

*"A holiday abroad is not **out of the question**," Mum said. "We'll have to wait and see."*

unworkable

*The government's plan proved **unworkable**, and schools reverted to the old system.*

✔ If a place is impossible to reach, it is **inaccessible**.

If someone's story is impossible to believe, it is **incredible**.

ANTONYM: possible

improve VERB

If something **improves**, or if you **improve** it, it gets better.

advance

*Medical technology has **advanced** a great deal since my grandparents were children.*

develop

*Thomas's batting has **developed** this year.*

make progress

*My report said that I was **making progress** in most subjects.*

upgrade

*"Why should I **upgrade** my computer, when this one works perfectly?" John protested.*

include VERB

If one thing **includes** another, the second thing is part of the first thing.

comprise

*Mathematics **comprises** three main parts: arithmetic, geometry and algebra.*

contain

*A lot of food today **contains** chemicals.*

a
b
c
d
e
f
g
h
i
j
k
l
m
n
o
p
q
r
s
t
u
v
w
x
y
z

incorporate

*The package holiday **incorporates** excursions and a flight over the Grand Canyon.*

involve

*"Will Mum's new job **involve** a lot of time away?" I asked.*

ANTONYM: exclude

increase (1) VERB

If something **increases**, or if you **increase** it, it becomes larger in number, level or amount.

add to

*Hywell **added to** his reputation by scoring three goals.*

boost

*The **boost** in the number of goals meant that the team would be in the semifinals.*

build up

*"I want you to **build up** your exercise slowly," the doctor advised after I sprained my ankle.*

enhance

*My brother hoped a smart suit would **enhance** his chances of getting the job.*

enlarge

*The photograph was **enlarged**, and is now pinned on my wall.*

extend

*To reach the gutters, Dad had to **extend** his ladder by two metres.*

ANTONYM: decrease

increase (2) NOUN

An **increase** is a rise in the number, level or amount of something.

development

*There has been a **development** in organic farming over the past few years.*

growth

*Rapid population **growth** is a problem that affects many countries.*

rise

*There has been a **rise** in pupil numbers.*

ANTONYM: decrease

incredible ADJECTIVE

Something that is **incredible** is totally amazing or impossible to believe.

astonishing

*The Roman coins were an **astonishing** discovery.*

astounding

*To put a man on the moon was an **astounding** achievement.*

beyond belief

*It is **beyond belief** to think that a woman could row across the Atlantic on her own.*

extraordinary

*"How **extraordinary**! That's the third time I've seen Mrs Grimes today," Mum observed.*

marvellous

*The choirboy had a **marvellous** voice for one so young.*

sensational

*A **sensational** performance by the captain helped the team to victory.*

unbelievable

*We had **unbelievable** luck in catching the ferry after so many delays.*

infect VERB

To **infect** is to cause disease in someone or something.

affect

*Our school was closed for two days to stop more people being **affected** by the virus.*

contaminate

*A chemical leak **contaminated** the pond near our house.*

infection NOUN

An **infection** is an illness caused by germs.

bug INFORMAL

*The sick people were put in quarantine to prevent the **bug** spreading.*

disease

*Measles is a highly contagious **disease** that causes red spots on the skin.*

virus

*Amanda missed three weeks of school because she had a throat **virus**.*

inhabitant (1) NOUN

If you are an **inhabitant** of a place, you live there.

citizen

Although born in Great Britain, Steve became a citizen of New Zealand.

native

A native of New York, Christina moved with her family to California at the age of 10.

resident

My aunt and uncle are residents of Denton, a suburb close to where we live.

✔ The general name for all the inhabitants of a town or area is its **population**.

inhabitant (2) NOUN

If you are an **inhabitant** of a building, you live there.

occupier

We weren't sure who was the occupier of the flat on the top floor.

resident

Mrs O'Connell is a resident of the old people's home near us.

tenant

The landlord rented out several flats, and had all kinds of tenants.

injure VERB

If you **injure** someone, you hurt or harm them in some way.

damage

The accident damaged Iain's shoulder.

harm

Electricity has great power to harm people, if used carelessly.

wound

My great grandad was wounded by shrapnel in the Second World War.

innocent ADJECTIVE

Someone who is **innocent** is not guilty of a crime or of doing something wrong.

blameless

The Roman governor thought the prisoner was blameless, and wanted to release him.

guiltless

Tammy stood there with a guiltless expression on her face.

not guilty

The jury found that the accused was not guilty of the robbery charge.

ANTONYM: guilty

inside (1) ADJECTIVE

Inside refers to the inner part of something.

inner

The monastery's inner courtyard was where monks worked and taught.

interior

A car's interior lights come on when you open the door.

internal

The stomach, liver, kidneys and lungs are all internal organs of the body.

✔ **Inside out** means with the inside part facing outwards.

ANTONYM: external or outside

inside (2) ADVERB

Inside can mean in something.

indoors

It was raining heavily, so we had to play indoors.

within OLD-FASHIONED

"Who dwells within this castle?" the knight enquired of the guard.

ANTONYM: outside

instant ADJECTIVE

Something **instant** happens immediately and without delay.

fast

Fast food tends to be quickly available, but lacking in nutrition.

immediate

New Whizzo cleaner gets immediate results on stubborn stains!

on-the-spot

With scratchcards, if you're lucky, you get an on-the-spot win.

prompt

The café impressed us by the prompt service we received on arrival.

instead ADVERB

If you choose one thing **instead** of another, you choose it as an alternative to the other.

alternatively
*I thought to myself, "Shall I have a cup of tea or, **alternatively**, a soft drink?"*

in place
In place of a forward, the coach brought on another defender.

interest (1) NOUN

If you have an **interest** in something, you want to know more about it.

concern
*Mitchell had always had an avid **concern** for wildlife.*

curiosity
*Nell's **curiosity** took her towards an ancient antique shop.*

involvement
*For some years, my parents have had an **involvement** with our local tennis club.*

interest (2) NOUN

An **interest** is something you enjoy doing.

activity
*My baby sister's favourite **activity** is shaking her rattle.*

hobby
*The **hobby** Nimesh most fancied was dinghy sailing.*

pastime
*Jigsaws are a very popular **pastime** with all ages.*

pursuit
*Angling is one of the most common leisure **pursuits** in the world.*

interest (3) VERB

If something **interests** you, you want to know more about it.

attract
*Supposedly, anything shiny **attracts** jackdaws.*

fascinate
*The birds which perched on her pram **fascinated** young Cinderella.*

intrigue
*It **intrigued** Will to find out how you could move between worlds so easily.*

interesting ADJECTIVE

If something is **interesting**, you enjoy it or want to know more about it.

absorbing
*Mum and Dad had a very **absorbing** conversation over dinner.*

appealing
*"I think the patterned dress is more **appealing** than the plain one," I said to Lisa.*

captivating
*The audience found the show **captivating**.*

enthralling
*"I found the model dinosaurs **enthralling**," Jodie told her dad excitedly.*

fascinating
*Bob thought the magic show was **fascinating**.*

gripping
*The story that Dad read to us was so **gripping** that I couldn't stop thinking about it.*

riveting
*We followed the **riveting** news story of the missing actor with interest.*

spellbinding
*It was quite **spellbinding** to watch the glass maker blowing and spinning the glass.*

ANTONYM: uninteresting

interfere VERB

If you **interfere** in a situation, you try to influence it, although it does not concern you.

meddle
*My aunt's problem was that she would always **meddle** in other people's business.*

poke your nose in INFORMAL
*"Don't you **poke your nose in** what doesn't concern you," Gran said.*

pry
*"I hope I'm not **prying**, but I'd love to know your cake recipe," Mum said to the baker.*

tamper
*The accident was caused because someone had **tampered** with my bike wheel.*

a
b
c
d
e
f
g
h
i
j
k
l
m
n
o
p
q
r
s
t
u
v
w
x
y
z

A B C D E F G H I J K L M N O P Q R S T U V W X Y Z

international ADJECTIVE
Something that is **international** involves different countries.

global
*These days, **global** communications are achieved via satellites.*

intercontinental
***Intercontinental** flights leave from Terminal 3, domestic flights from Terminal 4.*

universal
*Many Hollywood actors and actresses have become **universal** superstars.*

worldwide
*The singer was hoping for **worldwide** success with his latest release.*

interrupt (1) VERB
If you **interrupt** someone, you start talking while they are talking.

barge in
*Mum and I were chatting when my brother **barged in**, asking for sweets.*

butt in
*Dad **butted in** to say that my uncle had left his car lights on.*

chip in
*Mrs Ellis was pleased that Priya had **chipped in** with her comments.*

intrude
*"I don't want to **intrude**," the man panted, "but I've an urgent message for you."*

interrupt (2) VERB
If you **interrupt** a process or activity, you stop it for a time.

disrupt
*The match was **disrupted** by some people invading the pitch.*

halt
*Rain **halted** play at Wimbledon for a second day yesterday.*

hold up
*Our journey was **held up** by a few minutes, when some cows got loose ahead.*

invade VERB
If an army **invades** a country, it enters it by force.

attack
*Boadicea's wild hordes **attacked** the Roman township.*

occupy
*Soldiers **occupied** the town within a few minutes.*

seize
*In a daring raid, the outlaws **seized** the Sheriff's castle.*

invasion NOUN
An **invasion** is the entering or attacking of a place.

assault
*Air strikes paved the way for an **assault** on the beaches.*

attack
*The **attack** was timed for 06:30 hours.*

offensive
*A huge enemy **offensive** was planned, involving 12 armoured divisions.*

raid
*In a lightning **raid**, Drake's crews burnt several enemy ships.*

ANTONYM: withdrawal

invent VERB
If you **invent** something, you are the first person to think of it or make it.

come up with
*My friend's dad **came up with** a gadget to relieve hay fever.*

conceive
*Laszlo Biro **conceived** the idea of a pen with a small ball at its tip.*

create
*It takes many people to **create** a film.*

design
*A light vacuum cleaner was **designed** by Mr Spangler, but marketed by Mr Hoover.*

devise
*Sir Isaac Newton built the first telescope, using an idea **devised** by Galileo.*

dream up
*People **dream up** all sorts of ideas about what life in the future will be like.*

invention NOUN

An **invention** is something that is a completely new idea.

brainchild
*The bicycle was the **brainchild** of a Scottish blacksmith, Kirkpatrick Macmillan.*

creation
*The telephone was the **creation** of Alexander Graham Bell.*

inventor NOUN

An **inventor** is a person who invents something.

creator
*He was the **creator** of many popular children's television programmes.*

designer
*A man called Levi Strauss was the **designer** of the first jeans, around 1850.*

originator
*The **originator** of the printing press was a 15th-century German called Gutenberg.*

pioneer
*The Wright brothers of the USA were **pioneers** of aeroplane flight.*

investigate VERB

If someone **investigates** something, they try to find out all the facts about it.

explore
*Mum gave us permission to **explore** the cave in the cliff.*

make enquiries
*After the murder, police **made enquiries** at all the houses on the estate.*

probe
*The lander's mission was to **probe** the surface of Mars for evidence of life.*

research
*Scientists are constantly **researching** the causes of cancer.*

snoop INFORMAL
*"What are you doing **snooping** round here?" the doorman asked the private investigator.*

See **examine**

invisible ADJECTIVE

If something is **invisible**, you cannot see it.

hidden
*The hill-top monument was **hidden** in the clouds.*

out of sight
*As soon as Mrs Frost was **out of sight**, some of us started a pillow fight.*

unseen
*Guided by an **unseen** hand, the candle moved upwards towards the ceiling.*

ANTONYM: visible

involve VERB

If a situation or activity **involves** something, that thing is a necessary part of it.

entail
*This mission will **entail** long hours and great bravery.*

mean
*Taking on a business **meant** a lot of hard work for my parents.*

necessitate
*The making of concrete **necessitates** mixing cement, sand, gravel and water.*

require
*Driving a car **requires** concentration, skill and common sense.*

a b c d e f g h **i** j k l m n o p q r s t u v w x y z

A
B
C
D
E
F
G
H
I
J
K
L
M
N
O
P
Q
R
S
T
U
V
W
X
Y
Z

Jj

jail (1) NOUN
A **jail** is a building where criminals are locked up.

nick BRITISH, AUSTRALIAN AND NEW ZEALAND SLANG
*He spent seven years in the **nick**.*

penitentiary AMERICAN
*"The state **penitentiary** is where the bad guys go," the American guide told us.*

prison
*Despite attempts to improve them, most old **prisons** are grim-looking places.*

jail (2) VERB
To **jail** someone can mean to lock them up in a jail.

detain
*Police **detained** the suspect until he was due in court.*

imprison
*For her outburst in court, the woman was **imprisoned** for a further three months.*

jam (1) NOUN
A **jam** is a situation where there are so many people or things that it is difficult to move.

bottleneck
*Those traffic lights are a notorious **bottleneck**, with queues every day.*

hold-up
*Minor roadworks caused a major **hold-up**.*

queue
*"Expect long **queues** at Junction 5," my radio warned.*

tailback
*Fortunately, Dad saw the long **tailback** ahead, and managed to turn off.*

jam (2) NOUN INFORMAL
If you are in a **jam,** you are in a difficult situation.

dilemma
*The family faced a **dilemma** in the floods: to stand on the roof or to swim.*

quandary
*I was in a **quandary** when I lost my purse.*

tight spot
*When the other plane opened fire from behind, Officer Kite knew he was in a **tight spot**.*

jam (3) VERB
If you **jam** something into a place, you squeeze it in.

cram
*At rush hour in the city, people **cram** themselves into trains and buses.*

force
*Guards **forced** the gates shut as the enemy battered the other side.*

pack
*The school hall was **packed** for our end-of-term concert.*

ram
*Mum always **rams** salad into her help-yourself tub until it's overflowing.*

stuff
*Milos **stuffed** his PE kit into his bag and ran for the bus.*

wedge
*My brother **wedged** a book under the leg of his desk to stop it rocking.*

jam (4) VERB
If something **jams**, it becomes stuck or is unable to work properly.

block
*The ball **blocked** the drain and water flooded the back yard.*

clog
*Never put candle holders in a dishwasher, or the wax will **clog** the pipes when it sets.*

jealous ADJECTIVE
If you feel **jealous**, you feel envious of others, wanting to have what they have or wanting to be like them.

envious
*Clark was **envious** of his brother's new bike.*

green with envy
Green with envy, the wicked witch plotted revenge on her beautiful sister.

resentful
*It is not worth being **resentful**, as there will always be people richer than you.*

job (1) NOUN
A **job** is the work that someone does to earn money.

career
*Fiona decided she was going to make a **career** in industry.*

occupation
*Being a teacher is not an easy **occupation**.*

profession
*My brother is studying to go into the nursing **profession**.*

trade
*Dad's **trade** is plumbing and heating.*

Some jobs that people do:

accountant	midwife
architect	milkman
artist	miner
astronaut	model
barber	musician
barmaid or barman	nurse
barrister	optician
bricklayer	paramedic
builder	pharmacist
butcher	photographer
caretaker	physiotherapist
carpenter	pilot
cashier	plumber
chauffeur	police officer
chef	politician
cleaner	porter
conductor	postman
courier	receptionist
curator	reporter
decorator	sailor
dentist	secretary
doctor	security guard
dustman	shopkeeper
electrician	social worker
firefighter	soldier
gardener	solicitor
hairdresser	surgeon
joiner	teacher
journalist	traffic warden
lawyer	typist
librarian	vet
mechanic	waiter or waitress

---

job (2) NOUN
A **job** is a particular task that has to be done.

assignment
*Ethan's **assignment** was to get the case from the vault – by dangling from the ceiling.*

chore
*On Saturdays, all of us have to help with the household **chores**.*

errand
*Mum asked me to do an **errand** for our next-door neighbour.*

mission
*The astronauts' **mission** was to repair the satellite telescope.*

task
*Moving the whole vegetable patch was a huge **task** for Mum.*

job (3) NOUN
A **job** is a duty or responsibility.

duty
*A doorman's **duty** is to check that no one unsuitable comes in.*

function
*The generator's **function** was as a back-up if the electricity failed.*

responsibility
*"Felicity, it's your **responsibility** to put out the games equipment," Mrs Beerbohm said.*

role
*A head teacher's **role** is to manage the school effectively.*

join (1) VERB
To **join** can mean to fasten or connect things.

attach
*The dry-cleaners **attached** the label to the garment with a safety pin.*

connect
*"Once the pipes are **connected**, the sink will be finished," the plumber announced.*

couple
*The man in overalls jumped down to **couple** the carriages together.*

link
*For the TV programme, they built tree houses in the jungle **linked** by rope bridges.*

join (2) VERB

When two things **join**, or when one thing **joins** another, they come together

combine
*Our school **combined** with St Mary's for the Christmas carol service.*

merge
*The two companies **merged** to form a giant corporation.*

unite
*Several tribes **united** to form one vast Zulu army.*

ANTONYM: separate

join (3) VERB

If you **join** a club or organization, you become a member of it.

enlist
*In the First World War, men who did not **enlist** in the army were handed a white feather.*

enrol
*My sister has **enrolled** in an acting class at our local college.*

sign up for
*Several children **signed up for** the after-school gym club.*

joke (1) NOUN

A **joke** is something that you say to make people laugh.

gag INFORMAL
*The comedian's **gags** were too rude for Mum.*

pun
*My favourite **pun** is: It was a sad wedding. Even the cake was in tiers!*

wisecrack INFORMAL
*Uncle Ted can never be serious; he's always coming out with **wisecracks**.*

joke (2) VERB

If you are **joking**, you are teasing someone.

jest
*Callum said he was **jesting**, but Morag was in tears nevertheless.*

kid INFORMAL
*Dad tried to **kid** me that he had sold my bike, but I knew he wouldn't be that mean.*

tease
*I knew Jazlyn was **teasing**, but my mate took her seriously.*

journey NOUN

A **journey** is the act of travelling from one place to another.

drive
*My parents made the long **drive** from Paris to the south of France.*

expedition
*Mr Malone told us we were going on an **expedition** through the mountains.*

trek
*The long **trek** ended at a youth hostel.*

voyage
*Columbus's four **voyages** took him to North and Central America.*

judge VERB

If you **judge** someone or something, you decide what they are like.

assess
*It was the inspector's job to **assess** how clean the kitchen was.*

determine
*Mum had a job **determining** whether the fish was fully cooked.*

estimate
*The tour guide **estimated** we would arrive in an hour's time.*

evaluate
*At the end of the debate, Mrs Fitch **evaluates** how we have done.*

weigh up
*Paula **weighed up** whether to take the jumps slowly or to go full tilt.*

jumble (1) NOUN

A **jumble** is an untidy muddle of things.

chaos
*My sister's room was a scene of utter **chaos**.*

clutter
*You could have filled ten sacks with the **clutter** in my sister's room.*

muddle
*The wind reduced Mrs Jackson's record sheets to a complete **muddle**.*

jumble (2) VERB

If you **jumble** things, you mix them up untidily.

muddle

*Mum is always **muddling** her papers then losing them.*

shuffle

*With an expert flourish, the gambler **shuffled** the cards and dealt.*

tangle

*The angler **tangled** his lines up and consequently lost the fish.*

jump VERB

When you **jump**, you spring off the ground using the muscles in your legs.

bound

*The greyhound **bounded** up to our dog, who let out a huge growl.*

hurdle

*All the runners managed to **hurdle** the fence, except Kyle, who fell on his face.*

leap

*Chased by the guards, the escaped prisoner tried to **leap** across the ditch.*

pounce

*Our cat waits near the shed to **pounce** on unsuspecting mice.*

spring

*When she heard the word "chocolate", my sister **sprang** out of bed.*

vault

*In the cross-country race, we had to **vault** a gate.*

junk NOUN

Junk is old, unwanted or worthless things that are sold cheaply or thrown away.

clutter

*"Some day I will clear that **clutter** from our loft," Dad promised.*

jumble

*We bagged up the **jumble** and took it to the charity shop.*

scrap

*The millionaire had made his fortune as a **scrap** metal merchant.*

See **rubbish (1)**

a
b
c
d
e
f
g
h
i
j
k
l
m
n
o
p
q
r
s
t
u
v
w
x
y
z

Kk

keen ADJECTIVE

If you are **keen** to do something, or for something to happen, you want very much to do it or for it to happen.

eager
*Nazirah was **eager** to help set up the school sports day.*

enthusiastic
*My report said, rather puzzlingly, "John is an **enthusiastic** worker."*

willing
*Our neighbour was very **willing** for us to borrow his lawn mower.*

keep (1) VERB

If you **keep** something somewhere, you store it there.

collect
*My brother **collected** swap cards in a secret tin.*

deposit
*We **deposited** our money in the hotel safe.*

hold
*"Our stock is **held** in the warehouse," explained the manager.*

retain
*At the theatre, the ushers tear off half your ticket, and you **retain** the other half.*

stock
*"I'm sorry, madam, we don't **stock** that brand," the shopkeeper said.*

store
*You can **store** apples for several months if you do it properly.*

keep (2) VERB

If you **keep** doing something, you do it again and again.

carry on
*"**Carry on** working. Don't let me interrupt," interrupted the head teacher.*

continue
*Despite the pouring rain, we **continued** kicking our ball around.*

persist
*"If you **persist** in talking," Miss Hassan said, "there's going to be big trouble."*

keep (3) VERB

If you **keep** a promise, you do what you say you will do.

carry out
*The council **carried out** its promise to restore the crumbling church.*

fulfil
*The knight **fulfilled** his oath to the princess and slew the dragon.*

honour
*Dad **honoured** his promise to take us all bowling.*

kidnap VERB

If someone **kidnaps** someone else, they take them away by force and demand something in exchange for returning them.

abduct
*While travelling, the millionaire's son was **abducted** by bandits.*

hold to ransom
*The pirates **held** the boy **to ransom** for a million dollars.*

seize
*Having **seized** the hostage, the guerrillas didn't know what to do with her.*

snatch INFORMAL
*The message came through to HQ: "The boss's wife has been **snatched**!"*

✔ Money that is demanded to free someone who has been kidnapped is a **ransom**.

kill VERB

If someone **kills** a person, animal or plant, they make them die.

bump off INFORMAL
*"Send Legs to **bump off** Fat Antonio," drawled Luigi, the Mafia boss.*

dispatch
*The assassin coldly **dispatched** his target with a single bullet.*

do away with
*The evil duke planned to **do away with** all his enemies.*

A B C D E F G H I J **K** L M N O P Q R S T U V W X Y Z

murder
*Luigi went on trial for **murdering** a man and was imprisoned for life.*

slay OLD-FASHIONED
*The book of legends contains a picture of St George **slaying** the dragon.*

take someone's life
*At the command of the king, the four knights **took the archbishop's life**.*

kill as a punishment:
execute
*King Henry VIII had two of his wives **executed**.*

put to death
*Ann Boleyn, his second wife, was **put to death** at the Tower of London.*

kill many people or animals:
annihilate
*The terrible disease caused whole herds of cattle to be **annihilated**.*

exterminate
*The council sent someone to **exterminate** the cockroaches that had invaded our flat.*

massacre
*The army was **massacred** by rebel forces.*

kill people or animals brutally:
butcher
*Anyone who disagreed with the leader was **butchered** by his henchmen.*

slaughter
*Hundreds of people were **slaughtered** in this way.*

kill animals humanely:
cull
*Because of foot-and-mouth disease, many cattle had to be **culled**.*

put down
*Mark's dog Kiwi had to be **put down** yesterday.*

slaughter
*Many animals are **slaughtered** for human consumption.*

✔ If someone kills themselves, they **commit suicide** or **take their own life**.
To kill someone famous or important is to **assassinate** them.

kind (1) NOUN
A **kind** of thing is a particular thing of the same type as other things.

brand
*The interviewer asked Mum which **brand** of soap she used.*

breed
*Our favourite **breed** of dog is the Staffordshire bull terrier.*

class
*Dad admitted that his friend played a better **class** of tennis altogether.*

species
*The finch is the **species** of bird that helped Darwin form his theory of evolution.*

type
*A baguette is my favourite **type** of sandwich.*

variety
*It is amazing how many **varieties** of rose there are.*

kind (2) ADJECTIVE
Someone who is **kind** behaves in a caring and helpful way towards other people.

caring
*Mum was very **caring** when it came to looking after Gran in her old age.*

humane
*Our cat was old and ill; it was only **humane** to have her put down.*

kindly
*"What a **kindly** gesture," my aunt said, when I gave her the flowers.*

sympathetic
*I wish my sister had been more **sympathetic** when I fell off my bike.*

thoughtful
*It was **thoughtful** of Dad to buy Mum her favourite wine on Mother's Day.*

understanding
*Nurses have to be **understanding** when dealing with distressed patients.*

warm-hearted
*Mrs Thomas will be remembered as a **warm-hearted**, generous lady.*

ANTONYM: unkind or cruel

kindness NOUN

Kindness is the act of being kind.

goodness
*The monk's **goodness** showed in his gentle manners and understanding nature.*

humanity
*Despite his fame and success, the rock star showed **humanity** and concern for all he met.*

sympathy
*Many townsfolk offered their **sympathy** to the man whose wife had died.*

understanding
*It takes **understanding** to deal with people who are ill.*

king NOUN

A **king** is a man who is the head of state in a country, and who inherited his position from his parents.

emperor
*The **Emperor** of Japan sat serenely on his gilded throne.*

monarch
*After almost 40 years as **monarch**, the king handed over to his son, the crown prince.*

sovereign
*In mythology, Neptune was the **sovereign** of the seas.*

✔ The wife of a king is a **queen**. The son of a king and queen is a **prince** and their daughter is a **princess**.

kit NOUN

A **kit** is a collection of equipment and clothing that you use for a sport or other activity.

gear
*"Stow your **gear** in the back of the car," Dad said to the hitchhiker.*

tools
*Nicholas was under strict instructions not to touch the **tools** in the shed.*

knock VERB

If you **knock** on something, you hit it hard with your hand to make a noise.

pound
*In rage, the angry diner **pounded** on the table.*

rap
*The messenger **rapped** smartly on the door.*

tap
*A sound awoke Karl. It was someone **tapping** gently on the window.*

know (1) VERB

If you **know** something, you have it in your mind and you do not need to learn it.

be aware of
*Sunil **was aware of** the rules of the competition.*

understand
***Understanding** how dangerous some crooks can be, the detective reached for the revolver.*

know (2) VERB

If you **know** a person, place or thing, you are familiar with them.

be acquainted with
*"Are you **acquainted with** the school rules?" Mr Holdsworthy asked, sarcastically.*

be familiar with
*"Then perhaps you **are familiar with** the rule about eating in class?" he added.*

knowledge NOUN

Knowledge is all the facts and information that you know.

education
*He was a man with little **education** but a kind heart.*

learning
*After a lifetime of quiet study, the old man was full of wisdom and **learning**.*

scholarship
*My grandma enjoyed a lifetime of **scholarship**, completing her third degree when she was 70.*

understanding
*At last Jacintha felt she had an **understanding** of algebra.*

wisdom
*The old man was a source of great **wisdom**.*

ANTONYM: ignorance

A B C D E F G H I J **K** L M N O P Q R S T U V W X Y Z

Ll

lag VERB
If a person or a thing **lags** behind, they make slower progress than other people or other things and do not keep up.

dawdle
*"Stop **dawdling** at the back," Miss Finch called out, as we walked to the playing field.*

linger
*Two fans **lingered** outside the grounds after the rest of the crowd had left.*

straggle
*The sheepdog dashed off to round up the sheep that were **straggling** at the back.*

trail
*Marcie and Grace **trailed** behind the rest of the class on the walk up the steep hill.*

lame ADJECTIVE
Someone who is **lame** has an injured leg and cannot walk easily.

crippled
*They stretchered the **crippled** athlete off the field with a thigh injury.*

disabled
*The ex-soldier had been made **disabled** by a bullet wound to the leg.*

hobbling
*The **hobbling** player signalled that he needed to come off the pitch.*

limping
*The sheriff had a **limping** deputy.*

land (1) NOUN
Land is the parts of the earth's surface that are not covered by water.

dry land
*When the boat reached **dry land**, the pirates leapt out silently.*

earth
*A plough slices downwards and beneath the surface, turning the **earth** over.*

ground
*A supermarket is being built on waste **ground** behind our house.*

land (2) NOUN
Land is an area of ground.

estate
*The millionaire's **estate** was surrounded by an electric fence.*

grounds
*"Guests are welcome to wander around the **grounds**," the hotel brochure told us.*

property
*I had no idea that I was trespassing on someone's **property**.*

land (3) NOUN
A **land** is a country.

country
*Switzerland had borders with four other **countries**.*

nation
*Churchill told the **nation** that the war would be a long, hard struggle.*

land (4) VERB
When you **land** somewhere on a plane or a ship, you arrive there.

berth
*Coming in on the high tide, the cruise liner **berthed** at Southampton.*

dock
*"What time will we **dock**, skipper?" the deckhand asked.*

touch down
*Despite the aeroplane's burst tyre, the pilot managed to **touch down** safely.*

language (1) NOUN
A **language** is a system of words used by a particular group of people to communicate with each other.

dialect
*Some people find Shona's Scottish **dialect** difficult to understand.*

jargon
*The report was full of scientific **jargon** that I couldn't understand.*

tongue
*French was his mother **tongue**, but Cyril spoke three other languages fluently.*

a
b
c
d
e
f
g
h
i
j
k
l
m
n
o
p
q
r
s
t
u
v
w
x
y
z

language (2) NOUN

Language is the style in which you speak or write.

phrasing
*The angry driver's meaning was clear, even if the **phrasing** was rather basic.*

style
*"Sandra's **style** of speaking is very grown-up," commented Mum.*

wording
*Mrs Cahill suggested changing the **wording** to add punch to the sentence.*

large ADJECTIVE

Someone or something **large** is bigger than usual.

big
*Joe wasn't a **big** man, but he could certainly hit a ball hard!*

colossal
*Our uncle in New York says that the Empire State building is a **colossal** building.*

enormous
*At over two metres tall, the man looked **enormous** in the model village.*

giant
*King Kong picked up the helpless Miss Darrow in one **giant** paw.*

gigantic
*My favourite football team has got a **gigantic** new stadium.*

great
*A **great** swathe of golden corn covered the rolling hillside.*

huge
*There is a **huge** medieval cathedral in the city's main square.*

immense
*Our town's sports centre has an **immense** swimming pool.*

massive
*The Colossus at Rhodes was a **massive** statue straddling the harbour entrance.*

vast
*The majority of Mongolia is a **vast** desert.*

ANTONYM: small

last (1) ADJECTIVE

The **last** part of something happens after all the others.

closing
*The head teacher's **closing** remarks were aimed at the parents.*

concluding
*In the **concluding** chapter, Lyra and Will are parted.*

final
*"As a **final** word, I want to thank all of you for coming," the mayor said.*

ANTONYM: opening

at last PHRASE

At last can mean after a long time.

eventually
Eventually, the lost hikers saw the lights of a distant farmhouse.*

finally
*After ten hours, the train **finally** reached the capital.*

last (2) ADJECTIVE

The **last** thing or event is the most recent one.

latest
*"Have you heard the **latest** news?" my sister asked excitedly.*

most recent
*The **most recent** report from the hospital says that Gran is doing well.*

last (3) VERB

If something **lasts**, it continues to exist or happen.

continue
*"We hope," said the mayor, "that the friendship between our towns **continues** for years."*

endure
*Gran's marriage to Gramps had **endured** through all life's ups and downs.*

hold out
*"Let's hope that wing **holds out** till we land," muttered the pilot.*

remain
*On its hill top, the monument **remained** as a memorial to the great general.*

survive
*The Oxford–Cambridge boat race **survives** today after over 170 years.*

late ADJECTIVE
If you are **late** arriving somewhere, you get there after the time that was arranged or expected.

delayed
*The plane was **delayed** because of fog.*

last-minute
*The delay in our departure meant we had a **last-minute** dash to catch the train.*

overdue
*As we were **overdue**, Mum began to worry.*

ANTONYM: punctual

laugh (1) VERB
When you **laugh**, you make a noise that shows that you are amused or happy.

be in stitches
*The audience **was in stitches** when the clown came on.*

chortle
*The White Rabbit **chortled** to himself.*

chuckle
*Jojo **chuckled** at the thought of her brother covered in mud.*

crease up
*Mum **creased up** when she first saw Dad in his long shorts.*

giggle
*As usual, the twins were **giggling** at the back of the class.*

guffaw
*The colonel **guffawed** loudly at the regiment's annual show.*

snigger
*I couldn't help **sniggering** when I saw my brother trip up in front of the girl he liked.*

split your sides
*I usually **split my sides** at Homer Simpson's antics.*

titter
*Miss Kahn **tittered** weakly at the joke we thought was hilarious.*

laugh (2) NOUN
A **laugh** is the sound you make when you laugh.

chuckle
*Seif and I could hardly suppress our **chuckles**.*

giggle
*My sister has a really infectious **giggle** – if you hear it you will soon be giggling too.*

guffaw
*The major let out a **guffaw** when the private came on dressed as a woman.*

roar of laughter
*You could hear the **roar of laughter** from outside the theatre.*

shriek of laughter
*When the comedian mentioned sausages, there was a **shriek of laughter** from the kids.*

snigger
*Karim was having a quiet **snigger** at the back of the class when Mrs Rackman spotted him.*

titter
*The girl gave a **titter** of embarrassment when I bumped into her.*

laughter NOUN
Laughter is the action of laughing or the sound of people laughing.

amusement
*"I cannot see any cause for **amusement**," Mr Jones said stonily.*

hilarity
*During the pantomime there was much **hilarity** in the audience.*

layer (1) NOUN
A **layer** is a single thickness of something that lies underneath or above something else.

blanket
*A **blanket** of snow lay on the ground.*

coating
*The pond was covered in a **coating** of ice.*

film
*A **film** of wax protected the new car.*

seam
*The miners found a **seam** of gold in the rock.*

sheet
*The car skidded on a **sheet** of black ice.*

a
b
c
d
e
f
g
h
i
j
k
l
m
n
o
p
q
r
s
t
u
v
w
x
y
z

lazy ADJECTIVE

If you are **lazy**, you are idle and are unwilling to work.

idle

*"You have no chance of success, if you're **idle**," Mrs Krishnan warned.*

slack

*Mum warned me that I would be in trouble if I was **slack** about my homework.*

ANTONYM: hard-working

lead (1) SAID **"LEED"** VERB

If you **lead** someone somewhere, you go in front of them to show them the way.

conduct

*A talkative guide **conducted** us round the mansion.*

escort

*The prisoner was **escorted** to the van by two armed guards.*

guide

*We were **guided** to our seats by a member of the cabin crew.*

steer

*Mum **steered** the little boy through the crowd to where his mother was looking for him.*

lead (2) SAID **"LEED"** VERB

Someone who **leads** a group of people is in charge of them.

command

*The colonel **commanded** a regiment in Cyprus.*

govern

*The king **governed** the country firmly but fairly for many years.*

head

*Professor Saharawi **headed** a team of research scientists.*

manage

*Ron Knee **manages** our local soccer team.*

rule

*Republics are **ruled** by presidents, monarchies by kings and queens.*

supervise

*My mum **supervises** a team of sales people.*

leader NOUN

If you are the **leader** of a group, you are in charge of it.

boss

*A good **boss** cares for his or her workforce.*

captain

*Camilla is the **captain** of our netball team.*

chief

*Native American **chiefs** once wore elaborate headdresses of feathers.*

commander

*During the assault, the **commander** of the troops was severely wounded.*

director

*"Meet the **director** of studies, Mr Rivett," our young guide said.*

head

*Auntie Diane is **head** of the history department at a secondary school.*

ringleader

*"This damage is serious, and I want to know who the **ringleader** is!" snapped Mr Matheson.*

✔ The leader of a country is the **ruler**, **president** or **prime minister**.

learn (1) VERB

When you **learn** something, you gain knowledge or a skill by practice or by being taught.

acquire the ability

*After many hours of practice, Amy **acquired the ability** to juggle.*

grasp

*Equations were hard to **grasp**, but Alex eventually did so.*

master

*Matilda **mastered** the art of coaxing more pocket money from her parents.*

pick up

*As her mother was Spanish, little Anna soon **picked up** the language.*

learn (2) VERB

When you **learn** something, you get to know it off by heart.

commit to memory

*For the school play, Tariq had to **commit** many lines **to memory**.*

memorize
*"It is important to **memorize** your tables,"
said Miss Graham, our maths teacher.*

learn (3) VERB
If you **learn** of something, you get to know
about it.

discover
*Selima was shocked to **discover** what her
friend had done.*

find out
*I hoped Mum wouldn't **find out** that I'd broken
her favourite mug before I replaced it.*

gather
*"I **gather** from the expression on your face
that you haven't done your homework," Mr
Jason said.*

hear about
*"I was sorry to **hear about** your illness," said
Miss Copperfield.*

understand
*"I **understand** that you're moving away," our
neighbour said to Mum.*

least ADJECTIVE
The **least** of something is the smallest possible
amount of it.

lowest
*The winning golfer is the one who takes the
lowest number of strokes.*

minimum
*The **minimum** requirement for the job is a
degree in French.*

✔ **Least** and **fewest** are often confused. **Least**
applies to singular nouns (e.g. least butter,
least money), while **fewest** applies to plurals
(e.g. fewest errors, fewest marks).

ANTONYM: most

leave (1) VERB
When you **leave** a place, you go away from it.

depart
*The train **departed** on time, leaving my dad
behind because he was running late.*

exit
*When I mentioned what she owed me, Aislinn
exited hurriedly.*

withdraw
*Unable to hold the city, King Charles
withdrew with his forces to a nearby hill top.*

ANTONYM: arrive

See **disappear**

leave (2) VERB
When you **leave** a person, you go away from
them, often when they do not want you to go.

abandon
*The explorers were forced to **abandon** their
injured colleague at base camp.*

desert
*My brother **deserted** me just as our parents
were coming in to find the mess we'd made.*

leave (3) VERB
If you **leave** something somewhere, you let it
stay there or put it there before you go away.

deposit
*We **deposited** our bags in a left-luggage locker
and went off to explore the city.*

place
*The technician **placed** the test tube in the rack.*

ANTONYM: take

leave (4) VERB
If you **leave** a job or a school, you stop being a
part of it.

give up
*Matthew **gave up** his job to go travelling
round the world for a year.*

quit
*My big brother **quit** school as soon as he
finished his exams.*

✔ The noun **leave** is a period of holiday or
absence from a job.

leave (5) VERB
If someone **leaves** money or property to you,
you will receive it after they die.

bequeath
*My grandad **bequeathed** me the telescope
from his naval days.*

✔ A **will** is a legal document in which you say
what you want to happen to your money and
property when you die.

a
b
c
d
e
f
g
h
i
j
k
l
m
n
o
p
q
r
s
t
u
v
w
x
y
z

length

length (1) NOUN
The **length** of something is the distance from one end to the other.

distance
*The carpet fitters had to measure the **distance** from one end of the corridor to the other.*

extent
*Even the full **extent** of the wire wouldn't reach the plug.*

span
*The **span** of suspension bridges is amazing, considering that they don't have any support beneath them.*

✔ The **length** of something from one side to the other is its width.

length (2) NOUN
The **length** of an event or activity is the amount of time it continues.

duration
*The three-hour **duration** of the film made me fidgety.*

term
*The judges suggested a short **term** of imprisonment followed by community service.*

let VERB
If you **let** someone do something, you allow them to do it.

allow
*"Will you **allow** Sumehra to come as well?" I implored.*

authorize
*The government **authorized** James Bond to take any action necessary.*

give permission
*I asked Gran to **give permission** for my friends to sleep over.*

permit
*"I cannot **permit** you to enter this area," said the police officer.*

let down VERB
If you **let** someone **down**, you don't do what they expected you to do for them.

disappoint
*Arkan **disappointed** me when he didn't back up what I said.*

fail
*"You fools have **failed** me," roared Dr Evil. "You will be punished!"*

leave in the lurch
*Marie **left** me **in the lurch**, just when I needed her help.*

let off (1) VERB
If someone **lets** you **off**, they do not punish you for something you have done wrong.

forgive
*As I apologized, Dad **forgave** me for breaking the spade.*

pardon
*Lord Asriel **pardoned** the intruders.*

reprieve
*After a year expecting to be beheaded, Sir Walter Raleigh was **reprieved**.*

let off (2) VERB
If you **let off** a firework, you make it explode.

detonate
*After making sure everyone was at a safe distance, Mum **detonated** the firework.*

ignite
*Rockets are **ignited** by lighting the touchpaper.*

let out VERB
If you **let** someone **out** of somewhere, you release them.

free
*Lucy hoped the wicked witch would **free** her.*

liberate
*I sometimes wish I could **liberate** all the poor chickens kept in sheds.*

release
*The lions were **released** into the wild.*

✔ If you **let the cat out of the bag**, you tell someone something that is a secret.

level (1) ADJECTIVE
A surface that is **level** is flat and even.

even
*Pool tables must have an **even** surface to be played on properly.*

horizontal
*Builders always have to check that rows of bricks and blocks are **horizontal**.*

smooth

*For once, the sea was **smooth** and the sky was clear.*

ANTONYM: rough or uneven

level (2) NOUN

A **level** is a standard or grade of achievement.

grade

*Hanan achieved a good **grade** in her piano exam.*

standard

*Even Mrs Jennings was forced to admit that the **standard** of our work was high.*

lie (1) VERB

If someone or something **lies** somewhere, they rest there in a flat position.

lounge

*My big sister spends most of the weekend **lounging** around.*

recline

*Our dog, Jim, likes to **recline** in front of the fire in the evening.*

sprawl

*When Dad sleeps in a chair, he **sprawls** with his arms and legs out.*

lie (2) VERB

If you **lie**, you say something that you know is not true.

bluff

*Caught leaving the store, the shoplifter tried to **bluff** her way out of the situation.*

fib INFORMAL

*To avoid hurting Eddie's feelings, I **fibbed** that I liked his haircut.*

ANTONYM: tell the truth

lie (3) NOUN

A **lie** is something you say that you know is not true.

deceit

*My mate tried to say he was from America, but the lady saw through the **deceit**.*

falsehood

*When the police looked at the man's statement, it was full of **falsehoods**.*

fib INFORMAL

*"Now, no **fibs**," said my mum. "Where did that chocolate come from?"*

whopper INFORMAL

*I don't know how Dennis tells such **whoppers** to his parents and gets away with it.*

life (1) NOUN

Your **life** is the way you live.

existence

*Melanie lived an ideal **existence**, full of happiness and wealth.*

lifestyle

*The **lifestyle** of people in developing countries is hugely different from our own.*

way of life

*Tired of the commuter **way of life**, they decided to move to the country.*

life (2) NOUN

If you say someone is full of **life**, you mean they are lively and enthusiastic.

energy

*Despite his age, Grandad has loads of **energy**.*

get-up-and-go INFORMAL

*Arthur came down to breakfast full of **get-up-and-go**.*

spirit

*The team showed real **spirit** in coming back from three goals down.*

vitality

*All our class like Miss Sherwood. She's so full of **vitality** and jokes.*

lift VERB

If you **lift** something, you move it to a higher position.

elevate

*Over the altar, the priest ceremonially **elevated** the golden dish.*

hoist

*Medieval builders used a human treadwheel to **hoist** stones to the roof of buildings.*

raise

***Raising** his glass, my uncle proposed a toast to the bride and groom.*

ANTONYM: lower

a
b
c
d
e
f
g
h
i
j
k
l
m
n
o
p
q
r
s
t
u
v
w
x
y
z

light (1) NOUN

Light is the brightness from the sun, moon, fire or lamps, that lets you see things.

brightness
*For a second, the driver was dazzled by the **brightness** of the headlights.*

brilliance
*The **brilliance** of the moon as it rose over the horizon took our breath away.*

glow
*At night, the **glow** of the forest fires could be seen many miles away.*

radiance
*The sun rose majestically, spreading its **radiance** over the sea.*

Some types of natural light:

daylight	starlight
moonlight	sunlight

Some types of man-made light:

candle	light bulb
flare	neon light
floodlight	searchlight
fluorescent tube	spotlight
lantern	torch

ANTONYM: darkness or dark

light (2) VERB

If you **light** a fire, you make it start burning.

ignite
*The burning paper **ignited** the sticks above.*

kindle
*There's no doubt that firelighters help **kindle** a barbecue fire.*

set light to
*Dad used matches to **set light to** the camp fire.*

ANTONYM: extinguish

light (3) VERB

If the sun, moon, a fire or lamps **light** a room, they make it brighter.

brighten
*The rising sun **brightened** Bonnie's normally dingy room.*

illuminate
*Neon gas is used to **illuminate** city advertisements.*

ANTONYM: darken

like (1) VERB

If you **like** someone or something, you find them pleasing.

admire
*Vega **admired** the way her mum coped after her dad died.*

appreciate
*Gran really **appreciated** the flowers I picked for her.*

be fond of
*Cake is one of the things I **am** most **fond of**.*

be keen on
*My big brother **is keen on** a girl in his class.*

be partial to
*"I **am partial to** a slice of cake now and again," Dad admitted.*

enjoy
*All our family **enjoys** holidays by the seaside.*

love
*Our dog Wuffles **loves** going for walks.*

ANTONYM: dislike

like (2) ADJECTIVE

If one thing is **like** another, it is similar to it.

alike
*The twins were so **alike**, only their family could tell them apart.*

comparable with
*The Dutch language is in many ways **comparable with** Afrikaans.*

identical to
*The countess turned purple when she realized the woman's dress was **identical to** hers.*

similar to
*Your dad's car is **similar to** ours.*

✔ If one thing is like another, you can say that it **resembles** it.

ANTONYM: unlike

*See **same (1)***

likely ADJECTIVE

If something is **likely**, it will probably happen or is probably true.

expected
*It was **expected** that the old man would recover before long.*

liable
*"Be careful," warned the farmer. "This road is **liable** to flood without much warning."*

probable
*It was **probable** that the elves would reach their destination safely.*

ANTONYM: unlikely

limp VERB

If you **limp**, you walk in an uneven way because you have hurt your leg or foot.

hobble
*After twisting her ankle, the tennis player **hobbled** off the court.*

hop
*When I trod on a drawing pin I had to **hop** over to a chair to sit down.*

shuffle
*For a month after her stroke, Gran could only **shuffle** along.*

line (1) NOUN

A **line** of people or things is a number of them in a row.

chain
*Firefighters formed a **chain** to pass buckets of water along.*

column
*A huge **column** of people waited to pay their respects to the dead president.*

file
*We walked in single **file** to the playing fields.*

queue
*When we arrived at the cinema, the **queue** stretched round the block.*

rank
***Ranks** of police stood in full riot gear, waiting for the brawl to erupt.*

row SOUNDS LIKE "SNOW"
*The **row** of old shops was demolished.*

line (2) NOUN

A **line** is a long, thin mark.

A line on paper:

dash	rule
margin	stripe
mark	stroke

A line cut into the surface of something:

furrow	score
groove	scratch

A line on skin:

crease	wrinkle

A line marking the edge of something:

border	frontier
boundary	margin

link (1) VERB

If someone or something **links** people, places or things, they join them together.

attach
*Amber **attached** the competition slip to her drawing with a paperclip.*

connect
*The telephone operator **connected** me with Grandad in America.*

couple
*Dad **coupled** the car and the caravan together.*

fasten
*Safety pins are useful for **fastening** babies' nappies.*

join
*On a vehicle, the axle **joins** a pair of wheels together.*

link (2) NOUN

The **link** between two things is the relationship or connection between them.

association
*The two families had a close **association**.*

connection
*There's a strong **connection** between a mother and her child.*

relationship
*One **relationship** between five and ten is that five is half of ten.*

A
B
C
D
E
F
G
H
I
J
K
L
M
N
O
P
Q
R
S
T
U
V
W
X
Y
Z

liquid NOUN
A **liquid** is a substance such as water, which is neither a solid nor a gas, and which can be poured.

fluid
*Blood and water are the two main **fluids** in the body.*

solution
*Dr Jekyll drank the **solution** in one gulp, and soon he was Mr Hyde.*

list (1) NOUN
A **list** is a set of words or items written after the other.

catalogue
*I picked up a **catalogue** of toys to choose one I would like.*

register
*Schools are obliged by law to keep a **register** of pupils.*

series
*I sat down to memorize a **series** of spellings before the test.*

list (2) VERB
If you **list** a number of things, you write them or say them one after another.

catalogue
*My Mum's job was to **catalogue** all the paintings in the gallery.*

itemize
*Dad says it's a good job the phone company **itemizes** every call on our phone bill so that he can keep track of them.*

record
*The names of the dead were **recorded** in stone on the war memorial.*

listen VERB
If you **listen** to something, you pay attention to its sound.

be all ears
*Ben **was all ears** when he heard his name mentioned.*

eavesdrop
*Sneakily, Emily decided to **eavesdrop** on her friend's phone call.*

*See **hear (1)***

litter NOUN
Litter is rubbish in the street and other public places.

debris
*After the bomb attack, it took months to clear the **debris**.*

refuse
*The county aims to recycle as much **refuse** as it can.*

rubbish
*"Why can't people put their **rubbish** in the bin, instead of littering the streets?" I wondered.*

waste
*Not too long ago, **waste** was just dumped into the sea.*

little (1) ADJECTIVE
Little can mean small in size or amount.

compact
*"This **compact** music centre can be yours for next to nothing!" the advertisement read.*

diminutive
*Chihuahuas are **diminutive** dogs.*

mini
*A **mini** hurricane struck the island, but fortunately it didn't do too much damage.*

miniature
*My Auntie Joan brought me a **miniature** Eiffel Tower back from her holiday in Paris.*

minute SAID "MY-NYOOT"
*Carly's writing is so **minute** that I can hardly read it.*

tiny
*My sister is quite **tiny**, and would pass for someone much younger.*

ANTONYM: big or large

little (2) ADJECTIVE
Little can mean young in age.

infant
Infant children often go to nursery school.

young
*The trouble with my **young** sister is that she always wants me to play silly games with her.*

ANTONYM: grown-up or mature

little (3) NOUN

A **little** of something is a small amount or degree of it.

> **A little of something is:**
> ...a **bit** of attention
> ...a **bite** of lunch
> ...a **dab** of paint
> ...a **dash** of romance
> ...a **drop** of milk
> ...a **hint** of garlic
> ...a **pinch** of salt
> ...a **sip** of tea
> ...a **spot** of gardening
> ...a **taste** of soup
> ...a **touch** of frost

live (1) RHYMES WITH "GIVE" VERB

If someone or something **lives**, they are alive.

exist
*Dinosaurs **existed** long before humans lived on the earth.*

survive
*Fortunately, all the passengers in the bus **survived** the crash.*

ANTONYM: die

live (2) RHYMES WITH "GIVE" VERB

If you **live** in a place, that is where your home is.

inhabit
*Stig, once a cave dweller, now **inhabited** a rubbish dump.*

occupy
*Last summer, several swallows **occupied** our garage.*

reside
*The old duchess expressed a wish to **reside** in a house by the sea.*

lively (1) ADJECTIVE

Someone who is **lively** is full of energy and enthusiasm.

active
*Despite her age, our dog Tess is very **active**.*

energetic
*"I don't know how you can be so **energetic**," Mum said from the depths of her armchair.*

fit
*It pays to stay **fit**. Good health is important.*

sprightly
*Grandad is a **sprightly** old gent of 76, who enjoys going for walks.*

vigorous
*After a **vigorous** game of squash, Dad looked shattered.*

ANTONYM: listless

lively (2) ADJECTIVE

If someone has a **lively** personality, they are enthusiastic and full of energy.

bubbly
*The checkout lady with the **bubbly** personality always said a cheery "hello".*

high-spirited
***High-spirited** lambs were jumping about the field together.*

ANTONYM: dull

lively (3) ADJECTIVE

If you say a place is **lively**, it is busy, noisy and full of people.

bustling
*The city centre is always a **bustling** place on a Saturday afternoon.*

buzzing
*As the rocket launch approached, the control room was **buzzing** with activity.*

ANTONYM: quiet

living ADJECTIVE

If someone or something is **living**, they are alive.

alive
*Sniffer dogs found someone **alive** under the rubble of the earthquake.*

existing
*The **existing** species on earth are very different from the animals they evolved from.*

surviving
*Kiara's only **surviving** great grandparent lives in Australia.*

ANTONYM: dead or extinct

a b c d e f g h i j k l m n o p q r s t u v w x y z

load (1) NOUN

A **load** is something large or heavy that is being carried.

burden

*The elderly peasant was stooped from a lifetime of carrying heavy **burdens**.*

weight

*To lift a heavy **weight** safely, bend your knees and keep your back straight.*

load (2) NOUN

A **load** is a large quantity of goods that is being transported.

cargo

*Customs officers inspected the ship's **cargo**.*

consignment

*In this container is a **consignment** of televisions from Japan.*

lock VERB

If you **lock** something, you fasten it with a key.

bolt

*I heard Mum **bolt** the door and come upstairs to bed.*

fasten

*"Please would you **fasten** the gate, Grant?" I asked.*

latch

*Gran said to **latch** the door when we came in from the garden.*

padlock

*The yard was securely **padlocked** to keep the Alsatian dogs in and thieves out.*

secure

*Police recommend **securing** all doors and windows before going out.*

ANTONYM: unlock

lonely (1) ADJECTIVE

If you are **lonely**, you are unhappy because you are alone.

forlorn

*The tiny terrier looked **forlorn** on its own in the show ring.*

friendless

*The wealthy widow died in a seaside hotel, **friendless** and alone.*

solitary

*Old Wes was a **solitary** person, but quite happy with his own company.*

lonely (2) ADJECTIVE

A **lonely** place is one which very few people visit.

isolated

*The house was **isolated** in a field, quite apart from the rest of the village.*

remote

*A huge sea bird population colonized the **remote** Scottish island.*

secluded

*In a **secluded** corner of the beach, Summer sat and had her picnic.*

long (1) ADJECTIVE

Something that is **long** is great in length or distance.

extended

*To avoid roadworks, we had an **extended** journey to reach Glasgow.*

extensive

*The newly built country mansion had an **extensive** drive.*

lengthy

*We had to drive down a **lengthy** track before we reached the farm.*

ANTONYM: short

long (2) ADJECTIVE

Something that is **long** continues for a great amount of time.

drawn-out

*Dad looked shattered after his **drawn-out** meeting.*

interminable

*Our wait at the dentist's seemed **interminable**.*

lengthy

*We had a **lengthy** wait before the level crossing gates lifted.*

prolonged

*We had a **prolonged** discussion about where to go on our class outing.*

ANTONYM: brief

look (1) VERB

If you **look** at something, you turn your eyes towards it so that you can see it.

look briefly:
glance
*The driver **glanced** right, then turned into the main road.*

glimpse
*The lookout **glimpsed** smoke on the horizon as the warning beacons were lit.*

peep
*To his horror, the butler realized that someone was **peeping** through the keyhole.*

look for a long time:
feast your eyes on
*I **feasted my eyes on** the vast array of cakes.*

gaze
*Rupert **gazed** lovingly at his new bike.*

view
*For some time, the prince **viewed** the paintings in the gallery.*

look hard at something:
stare
*"Never **stare** at a gorilla. They don't like it," Dad warned.*

peer
*Without his specs, Harry was forced to **peer** at the odd notice.*

look in surprise:
gape
*Mum said she **gaped** when she saw the size of the Grand Canyon.*

goggle
*I **goggled** at the huge present before me. I could barely believe my eyes.*

look around:
scan
*"Every 10 seconds, that radar dish **scans** the horizon," explained the guide.*

survey
*The farmer smiled as he **surveyed** his fields of swaying corn.*

look carefully at something:
examine
*"**Examine** this," said Mr Parnevik, making way for his colleague at the microscope.*

observe
*The police officers **observed** the house from their unmarked car, keeping a note of who came and went.*

scrutinize
*Independent experts **scrutinized** the election process to ensure it was fair.*

study
*Javier spent some time **studying** the game's instruction booklet.*

look for something:
hunt
*Liam **hunted** high and low for the missing ticket.*

search
*Although we **searched** for several hours, we couldn't find the missing keys.*

seek
*"The treasure ye **seek** be found up the creek," the ancient parchment read.*

look (2) NOUN

If you have a **look** at something, you look at it.

gaze
*Nothing could deflect her steady **gaze**.*

glance
*"Can I have a **glance** at the TV guide?" my brother asked.*

glimpse
*We caught a **glimpse** of the sea through the gap in the hedge.*

peek
*"You can come and have a **peek** at the puppies," Farmer Threlwell told us.*

look (3) NOUN

The **look** on your face is the expression on it.

air
*My brother wore an **air** of innocence when Mum asked who had spilt their juice on the new carpet.*

appearance
*I tried to give the **appearance** of being confident, but really I was rather nervous.*

expression
*Gran's **expression** of delight when she saw the cake we'd baked made the effort worthwhile.*

look after VERB

If you **look after** someone or something, you take care of them.

care for

Bradley cared for the bird with the broken wing until it could fly again.

protect

It is everyone's responsibility to help to protect wildlife.

tend

My grandad tends his garden with loving care so that it always looks pretty.

See guard (1)

loose (1) SAID "**LOOSS**" ADJECTIVE

Something that is **loose** is not firmly held or fixed in place.

slack

The dog's collar was slack, and he slipped out of it to chase the cat.

unsecured

The load of hay was unsecured, and had tumbled off the trailer.

wobbly

Angelica's tooth was wobbly, and she knew it would soon fall out.

ANTONYM: firm

loose (2) SAID "**LOOSS**" ADJECTIVE

If clothing is **loose**, it does not fit tightly.

baggy

Baggy trousers are comfortable clothes for travelling in.

sloppy

Jo loves wearing sloppy jumpers.

✔ The adjective and adverb **loose** is spelt with two *o*s. Do not confuse it with the verb **lose**.

ANTONYM: tight

lose (1) SAID "**LOOZ**" VERB

If you **lose** something, you cannot find it, or you no longer have it because it has been taken away from you.

mislay

"Can you see my purse? I've mislaid it," Fiona said desperately.

misplace

Scott had misplaced the ticket and now it was time to leave for the show!

ANTONYM: find

lose (2) SAID "**LOOZ**" VERB

If you **lose** an argument or a game, you are beaten.

be beaten

"I'll admit it. We were beaten by a better team," said Gamal.

be defeated

In a debate today, the government was defeated by a small majority.

suffer defeat

United suffered defeat in three matches in succession.

ANTONYM: win

lost ADJECTIVE

If something is **lost**, you cannot find it.

mislaid

We were late because Dad's keys were mislaid yet again!

misplaced

Faizah finally found her misplaced glasses in the laundry basket!

missing

Mrs Howe was delighted that her missing cat had been found.

ANTONYM: found

lot NOUN

A **lot** of something is a large amount of it.

a great deal

A great deal of time and effort has gone into this thesaurus.

a large quantity

For our patio, Dad required a large quantity of paving slabs.

a vast number

From the helicopter we could see a vast number of antelope.

heaps INFORMAL

"I've had heaps of replies to my party invitations," Daisy said excitedly.

masses INFORMAL

*Pop stars receive **masses** of fan mail.*

stacks INFORMAL

*"You should see Lucy's CD collection. She's got **stacks** of them!" Atifa exclaimed.*

loud ADJECTIVE

A **loud** noise produces a lot of sound.

booming

*The **booming** bass note of the foghorn echoed along the misty decks.*

deafening

*At the air show, our dog Molly sat calmly through the **deafening** fly-past.*

ear-splitting

*According to our neighbour, my sister's music was an **ear-splitting** racket.*

noisy

*Mum's samba band are really **noisy** when they get going.*

piercing

*Suddenly, a **piercing** scream cut through the peaceful night.*

ANTONYM: quiet

love (1) VERB

If you **love** someone or something, you have strong feelings of affection for them.

adore

*My baby sister **adores** her teddy bear, Scruff.*

dote on

*I **dote on** my Grandma and Grandpa.*

idolize

*Mum and Dad **idolize** one or two of the old heavy metal rock groups.*

ANTONYM: hate

love (2) VERB

If you **love** doing something, you like doing it very much.

delight in

*I'm told that my great grandmother **delighted in** skating on frozen canals.*

enjoy

*"**Enjoy** your honeymoon!" everyone shouted, as the newlyweds drove off.*

relish

*The Roman emperor **relished** watching the gladiators in the ring.*

ANTONYM: hate or loathe

love (3) NOUN

Love is a strong feeling of affection for someone or something.

adoration

*The pop star basked in the **adoration** of his devoted fans.*

fondness

*My uncle was ruined by having too great a **fondness** for gambling.*

ANTONYM: hatred

lovely ADJECTIVE

Someone or something **lovely** is very beautiful, attractive or pleasant.

adorable

*"Isn't that baby just **adorable**?" the lady in the pink hat cooed.*

attractive

*Simone has an **attractive** personality and is always smiling.*

beautiful

*Even I had to admit my sister looked **beautiful** in her new dress.*

delightful

*A **delightful** scene met our eyes as we came round the bend in the road: a river, willow trees and swans.*

enchanting

*The desert sky at night was **enchanting**, with stars everywhere.*

gorgeous

*"Wow, he's **gorgeous**!" my big sister said as the pop star came on television.*

pleasant

*All in all, we had a very **pleasant** afternoon on the lake.*

pretty

*Both bridesmaids looked **pretty** in their matching outfits.*

ANTONYM: unattractive or unpleasant

low ADJECTIVE

A **low** noise is low in tone and not always easy to hear.

muffled

Muffled voices could be heard coming from within the hut.

muted

The muted sound of music travelled across the bay.

quiet

The quiet lapping of the waves against the shore was very soothing.

soft

Lyra spoke in a soft whisper.

subdued

From behind the heavy door came the subdued sounds of conversation.

ANTONYM: high

luck NOUN

Luck can mean something that happens by chance.

chance

It was only chance that brought Mum and Dad together.

destiny

Some people think that destiny brings people together who will be friends.

fate

By a simple twist of fate we both went to the same school.

fortune

By amazing fortune, the hostel was empty when the fire started.

good luck NOUN

Good luck is anything good that happens to you which is not a result of your own efforts.

blessing

It was a blessing when the rain started after the long drought.

godsend

"Auntie's money was a real godsend when we were so hard-up," my mum said.

good fortune

At the air show, I had the good fortune to see a very rare Second World War plane.

lucky break INFORMAL

The young tenor's lucky break came when another singer fell ill.

a stroke of luck

"Finding that Roman coin was a stroke of luck!" Travis said.

ANTONYM: good luck

bad luck NOUN

Bad luck is anything bad that happens to you which is not a result of your own efforts.

hard luck

The sudden storm was hard luck on the organizers of the barbecue.

misfortune

Was the Titanic's sinking a case of misfortune or mismanagement?

stroke of bad luck

It was a stroke of bad luck for Dad when he broke his leg playing soccer.

ANTONYM: bad luck

lucky ADJECTIVE

Something that is **lucky** has good effects or consequences.

fortuitous

It was fortuitous that someone handed in my money when I lost it.

fortunate

It was fortunate that just after Mum's car had broken down, Dad happened to be driving past.

ANTONYM: unlucky

luggage NOUN

Your **luggage** is the bags and suitcases that you take with you when you travel.

baggage

Our baggage arrived two days after us!

belongings

"We'll look after your belongings while you shop," said the shop assistant at the airport.

lump (1) NOUN

A **lump** is a solid piece of something.

cake

Neil stamped his feet and cakes of snow fell off the soles of his boots.

chunk
*The explosion sent **chunks** of metal flying everywhere.*

clod
*The clumsy golfer sliced a great **clod** of earth from the fairway.*

hunk
*All I wanted was a **hunk** of cheese and a few chunky slices of bread.*

nugget
*At the sight of the gold **nugget**, the prospector began to dance with glee.*

slab
*Great **slabs** of rock slid down the hillside during the earthquake.*

lump (2) NOUN

A **lump** is a small, hard piece of flesh on someone's body.

bump
*After her fall, Sîan developed a large **bump** on the head.*

hump
*In the story, the man who lived in Notre Dame cathedral had a **hump** on his back.*

swelling
*Our dog had a **swelling** on her right leg.*

luxury (1) NOUN

Luxury is a great comfort, especially among expensive and beautiful surroundings.

comfort
*The five-star hotel oozed **comfort** from every plush corner.*

richness
*Scores of people queued to view the famous **richness** of the palace decorations.*

splendour
*The **splendour** of the water gardens really impressed us.*

luxury (2) NOUN

A **luxury** is something that you would like to have but do not need, and is usually expensive.

extra
*Because I have a Saturday job, I can afford a few **extras**.*

indulgence
*The expensive chocolates were sheer **indulgence**, but we loved them!*

treat
*For a special **treat**, Dad took us all to the cinema and then bowling.*

ANTONYM: necessity

a b c d e f g h i j k l m n o p q r s t u v w x y z

171

Mm

machine NOUN

A **machine** is a piece of equipment designed to do a particular job. It is usually powered by an engine or electricity.

apparatus

*Firefighters use breathing **apparatus** to enter smoke-filled buildings.*

appliance

*For some reason, most kitchen **appliances** seem to be white.*

contraption INFORMAL

*"What on earth's that **contraption**?" Dad asked when he saw my DIY go-kart.*

mad (1) ADJECTIVE

Someone who is **mad** has a mental illness that causes them to behave in strange ways.

crazy

*The princess was driven **crazy** by love for the prince she could not marry.*

insane

*Neighbours claimed they were being driven **insane** by the loud music.*

out of your mind

*"I think I'm going **out of my mind**," said Mum. "I've lost my keys again!"*

ANTONYM: sane

mad (2) ADJECTIVE

Someone who is **mad** is angry.

berserk

*The bull went **berserk** when the matador waved his cape in front of it.*

crazy

*My brother went **crazy** when he found out I'd broken his guitar.*

furious

*What started as a reasonable discussion developed into a **furious** argument.*

incensed

*Gran became **incensed** when she realized the burglar had stolen her wedding ring.*

irate

*Mum was really **irate** when I dismantled the cuckoo clock.*

livid

*Mrs Vine was **livid** when she heard about the bad behaviour on the school trip.*

See **angry**

mad (3) ADJECTIVE

If you describe an idea as **mad**, you mean that it very foolish or silly.

absurd

*It is **absurd** to believe the earth is flat, but that is what people used to think.*

crazy

*It was **crazy** to think we'd win the lottery, but we couldn't help hoping.*

daft

*Jade had the **daft** idea of riding on my bicycle handlebars.*

ludicrous

*"That's a **ludicrous** suggestion," said Dad. "Of course you can't stay out until midnight!"*

preposterous

*It was **preposterous** to bring a snake to school, but that's what Carly did for "show and tell"!*

ridiculous

*"A mongrel? Don't be **ridiculous**. It's a pedigree poodle!" the lady said snootily.*

mad (4) ADJECTIVE

If you are **mad** about someone or something, you like them very much.

enthusiastic

*People in some countries are very **enthusiastic** about playing cricket.*

fanatical

*Many Americans are **fanatical** about baseball.*

passionate

*Uncle Tim is **passionate** about travel, and tries to get abroad at least three times a year.*

magic (1) NOUN

In fairy stories, **magic** is a special power that can make impossible things happen.

sorcery

*Merlin was famed for his spells and **sorcery**.*

witchcraft
*Dorothy was thwarted by **witchcraft** on her journey to the Emerald City.*

wizardry
*People from the past would think modern technology is some form of **wizardry**.*

✔ A magician in fairy stories is a **sorcerer**, **witch** or **wizard**.

magic (2) NOUN
Magic is the art of performing tricks to entertain people.

conjuring
*The magician's **conjuring** tricks went down well at the party.*

✔ A magician who entertains people is a **conjuror**.

magnificent ADJECTIVE
Something that is **magnificent** is extremely beautiful or impressive.

glorious
*The packed stadium in the sunshine made a **glorious** setting for the final.*

grand
*Venice has many **grand** buildings and the Grand Canal.*

impressive
*There are few sights more **impressive** than the pyramids of Egypt.*

splendid
*King Charles was rowed down the Thames in a **splendid** barge.*

ANTONYM: unimpressive

main ADJECTIVE
If something is the **main** thing, it is the most important or largest.

chief
*The boss's **chief** reason for holding the meeting was to announce his retirement.*

foremost
*Italy is the **foremost** producer of pasta in the world.*

major
*Language skills form a **major** part of primary education.*

principal
*Brasilia is the capital of Brazil, but Rio is the **principal** city.*

ANTONYM: least important

mainly ADVERB
Mainly can mean mostly, chiefly or usually.

chiefly
*"This morning," said Mrs Lucas, "we'll **chiefly** be doing maths."*

generally
*Mum said that **generally** she was pleased with the way I had tidied my bedroom.*

largely
*The Congo is **largely** covered by rainforest.*

mostly
*Although he was tired, Will's weakness was **mostly** due to his illness.*

on the whole
***On the whole**, I think our city is a great place to live.*

usually
*We **usually** go to Cornwall for our holidays, but this year we are going to Spain.*

make (1) VERB
If you **make** something, you create or produce it.

assemble
*It was very funny watching Dad trying to **assemble** the wardrobe.*

build
*"I'm hoping to **build** my own den in that oak tree," Morgan told Ron.*

construct
*Mrs Jones asked us to **construct** different shapes with the same area.*

create
*As well as inventions, Leonardo da Vinci **created** the Mona Lisa and other paintings.*

manufacture
*At my mum's work, they **manufacture** brakes for cars.*

produce
*My brother and his friend **produced** their own film. It was awful!*

a b c d e f g h i j k l **m** n o p q r s t u v w x y z

make

make (2) VERB

If you **make** someone do something, you force them to do it.

compel
*An injury **compelled** the athlete to retire.*

force
*The giant bear **forced** his arrogant rival to fight him.*

oblige
*All of the pupils at our school are **obliged** to wear school uniform.*

order
*The colonel **ordered** the enemy troops to surrender.*

make (3) VERB

If you **make** something happen, you cause it.

bring about
*The revolution **brought about** many changes in the country.*

cause
*James **caused** a fire by letting the frying pan overheat.*

provoke
*My sister is always **provoking** arguments, especially with me.*

make (4) VERB

Two amounts added together **make** a sum.

add up to
*Six and six **add up to** twelve.*

amount to
*My pocket money and yours **amount to** enough for a game of tennis.*

total
*Our school's fundraising **totalled** the amount needed to build the new sports hall.*

make (5) NOUN

A **make** is the name of a product of a particular manufacturer.

brand
*"Which **brand** of washing-up liquid do you use?" asked the man conducting the survey.*

model
*Our neighbour always has to have the latest **model** of car.*

variety
*"This **variety** of jewellery is well known for its quality," said the sales assistant.*

make up VERB

If you **make** something **up**, you invent it.

concoct
*To explain his absence, my friend **concocted** an amazing story about being kidnapped.*

create
*Mum is great at **creating** tasty meals out of very few ingredients.*

devise
*Over the years, the production team had **devised** many game shows.*

dream up
*"What plans have you **dreamt up** for your future?" my uncle asked.*

invent
*My grandad once **invented** a new type of rollerskate.*

man (1) NOUN

A **man** is an adult, male human being.

bloke INFORMAL
*"A **bloke** in the street tried to sell me a watch," Dad said.*

chap INFORMAL
*My uncle was a nice **chap**, always willing to help.*

fellow
*The **fellow** being interviewed looked more like a farmer than a professor.*

gentleman
*"Ladies and **gentlemen**, a toast to the bride and groom!" said the best man.*

guy INFORMAL
*"You're a great **guy**," the tourist said. "Thanks for your help."*

✔ An unmarried man is a **bachelor**.
A man who is engaged is a woman's **fiancé**.
A man on his wedding day is a **bridegroom**.
A married man is a **husband**.
A man whose wife has died is a **widower**.
A man who has children is a **father**.

ANTONYM: woman

man (2) NOUN

Human beings, both male and female, are sometimes referred to as **man**.

mankind

Mankind has existed for only a tiny fraction of the life of the earth.

the human race

The human race has evolved over thousands of years.

manage (1) VERB

If someone **manages** an organization or business, they are responsible for controlling it.

be in charge of

Joseph was in charge of preparing for the great famine.

control

The Australian controlled a vast television and publishing empire.

direct

My mum directed a play for the local drama group.

run

Granny and Grandad run a car parts business.

manage (2) VERB

If you **manage** to do something, you succeed in doing it even if it is difficult.

be successful in

Dad was successful in getting the job he had applied for.

bring off

Despite the awful weather, the helicopter crew brought off the rescue.

succeed in

The crew of the rescue boat succeeded in winching aboard five shipwrecked fishermen.

manage (3) VERB

If you **manage** in difficult circumstances, you carry on successfully.

cope

After the airline lost our cases, we had to cope for three days without our things.

get by

When the car broke down, the family got by using the bus.

manners PLURAL NOUN

Your **manners** are the way you behave.

behaviour

Mr O'Leary complimented us on our behaviour at camp.

conduct

The coach driver complained about the conduct of Class 3B on the school outing.

etiquette

The duchess considered etiquette to be very important in a young woman.

many ADJECTIVE

If there are **many** people or things, there are a large number of them.

abundant

Thanks to irrigation, abundant crops grow in some parts of the desert.

countless

There are parts of the world where countless people do not have enough food.

numerous

Dad showed me numerous ways to do the same sum.

several

We have several newts in our garden pond.

umpteen INFORMAL

"I've asked you umpteen times to make your bed," my mother said.

ANTONYM: few

mark (1) NOUN

A **mark** is a small stain or damaged area on a surface.

blemish

Because of a slight blemish, the shop assistant reduced the price of the jacket.

blotch

Siobhan's biro made blotches on every word she wrote.

smudge

A massive smudge of ink had somehow made its way on to my exercise book.

spot

Mum was livid because of the spot on her best blouse.

mark (2) VERB

If something **marks** a surface, it stains or damages it in some way.

blemish
*All my careful work was **blemished** by an ink blot on the page.*

smear
*Greasy thumbprints were **smeared** all over the new window.*

smudge
*My little sister's face was **smudged** with dirt when she came in from the garden.*

mark (3) VERB

When a teacher **marks** a student's work, they decide how good it is and give it a mark.

assess
*Teachers from another school had to **assess** my brother's coursework.*

correct
*We hand in our maths for Mrs Abiola to **correct**.*

marvellous ADJECTIVE

Something that is **marvellous** is wonderful or excellent.

amazing
*The Niagara Falls is an **amazing** sight to behold.*

incredible
*From the cliff top there was an **incredible** view over the bay below.*

miraculous
*Our dog made a **miraculous** recovery after being run over.*

phenomenal
*In my opinion, anyone who runs a marathon has **phenomenal** strength and stamina.*

terrific
*"Thanks very much. We've had a **terrific** day out," I said to Della's mum.*

massive ADJECTIVE

Someone or something that is **massive** is extremely large in size and weight.

colossal
*Some of the skyscrapers in New York are **colossal** buildings.*

enormous
*Some cranes can extend to an **enormous** height.*

gargantuan
*Many dinosaurs were **gargantuan** compared to today's creatures.*

great
*The **great** stone rolled back to reveal a hidden passageway beneath the mountain.*

huge
*Putting his head through the cloud at the top of the beanstalk, Jack spied a **huge** man.*

immense
*We gasped as we saw the **immense** banquet in front of us.*

vast
*I was very excited to see the **vast** array of flavours the ice-cream parlour had.*

whopping INFORMAL
*"Buy a ticket and you could win a **whopping** prize!" read the sign.*

ANTONYM: tiny

match (1) NOUN

A **match** is an organized game of football, cricket or some other sport.

bout
*It was an evenly fought **bout** between the two wrestlers.*

competition
*Our chess **competition** was a great success.*

contest
*Lucy and I held a chocolate-eating **contest**.*

head-to-head
*A tennis singles final is a **head-to-head** between the two unbeaten players.*

match (2) VERB

If one thing **matches** another, it is similar to it.

correspond
*What we see in a mirror **corresponds** with what we are really like.*

go with
*Charlotte's shoes **went with** her dress.*

ANTONYM: clash

mathematics NOUN

Mathematics is the study of numbers, quantities and shapes.

maths INFORMAL
*Many adults are scared of **maths**, but it's straightforward really.*

numeracy
*We have a **numeracy** lesson most mornings.*

✔ The main branches of mathematics in schools are **arithmetic**, **geometry** and **algebra**. The main processes of arithmetic are **addition**, **subtraction**, **multiplication** and **division**. A person who studies mathematics is a **mathematician**.

matter (1) NOUN

A **matter** is a task or situation that you have to attend to.

affair
*I kept putting off the **affair** of tidying my messy room.*

business
*The **business** of moving house upset Gran.*

issue
*Mum and Dad couldn't agree on the **issue** of where to go for the day.*

situation
*The **situation** in the Middle East causes a lot of discussion.*

subject
*Mr Carew asked us to talk on any **subject** we were keen on.*

topic
*In the playground, the only **topic** of conversation was the school trip.*

matter (2) VERB

If something **matters**, it is important.

be significant
*Sherlock Holmes realized that the man's red hair **was significant** in the case.*

count
*Small details can **count** just as much as big issues when it comes to making decisions.*

make a difference
*Every penny you can give to charity **makes a difference**.*

maybe ADVERB

If you think there is a possibility that something will happen, but you are not sure, you use **maybe**.

perhaps
***Perhaps** you'll catch a fish; perhaps not.*

possibly
***Possibly** Mrs Jenkins, our science teacher, will take us to the power station.*

meal (1) NOUN

A **meal** is an occasion when people eat, and the food people eat at meal times.

> **Meals of the day:**
> | breakfast | lunch |
> |---|---|
> | dinner | supper |
> | elevenses | tea |
>
> **Other types of meal:**
> **Brunch** is a combination of breakfast and lunch, and is eaten in the late morning.
> A small meal is a **bite** or a **snack**.
> A large meal is a **feast**.
> A large, formal meal is a **banquet**.
> An outdoor meal is a **barbecue** or **picnic**.
> A meal where you help yourself to food is a **buffet**.
> A ready-cooked hot meal is a **takeaway**.

mean (1) ADJECTIVE

Someone who is **mean** is unwilling to share with others.

miserly
*The **miserly** old woman turned the carol singers away.*

penny-pinching
***Penny-pinching** people are reluctant to part with their money.*

stingy
*My **stingy** sister wouldn't give me a bite of her ice cream.*

tightfisted
*"Don't be so **tightfisted**," I exclaimed when my brother wouldn't share his sweets.*

ANTONYM: generous

mean (2) ADJECTIVE

Someone who is **mean** is unkind.

horrible

*I can't believe how **horrible** my sister sometimes is to me.*

malicious

*The neighbour delighted in spreading **malicious** gossip.*

nasty

*The **nasty** witch gave a cruel laugh.*

spiteful

*Because he was **spiteful**, Malfoy looked for any chance of revenge.*

ANTONYM: nice

mean (3) VERB

If you ask someone what something **means**, you want them to explain it to you.

denote

*The squiggle at the bottom of the letter **denoted** that Gran had signed the card.*

indicate

*Polly's red face **indicated** that she was embarrassed.*

signify

*"What does this red dot **signify**?" I asked, pointing at the diagram.*

mean (4) VERB

If you **mean** to do something, you intend to do it.

aim

*"We **aim** to raise plenty of money for charity from the fête," announced Mrs Partridge.*

intend

*I hadn't **intended** to be home late, but I lost track of time.*

plan

*"What do you **plan** to do over the summer?" Malika asked.*

meaning NOUN

The **meaning** of a word, expression or gesture is what it refers to or expresses.

definition

*Dictionaries contain the **definitions** of words.*

explanation

*The **explanation** for Paul's late arrival was that he had got lost.*

gist

*Although I couldn't understand everything, I got the **gist** of the French conversation.*

sense

*There are several different **senses** to the word "bright".*

significance

*At last, Lyra understood the **significance** of the dust.*

measure VERB

If you **measure** something, you find out the size or amount of it.

assess

*The firefighters tried to **assess** how far the fire had spread.*

calculate

*In maths we had to **calculate** the area of a triangle.*

gauge

*The skipper found the wind direction difficult to **gauge**.*

survey

*Map makers need to **survey** an area in order to map it.*

measurement NOUN

A **measurement** is the result you obtain when you measure something.

dimensions

*"We need to measure the **dimensions** of the cupboard before we buy it," said Dad.*

extent

*It was difficult to assess the **extent** of the forest fires from the ground.*

size

*Scientists were amazed at the **size** of the crater left by the meteorite.*

✔ The measurement of the space in a flat (two-dimensional) surface is **area**.
The measurement of the space within a three-dimensional shape is **volume**.
The measurement of how much a container will hold is **capacity**.

meet VERB

If you **meet** someone, you happen to be in the same place as them.

bump into INFORMAL
*"Guess who I **bumped into** today?" said Mum when she got home.*

come across
*At the show, we **came across** our next door neighbour.*

encounter
*The troops **encountered** more troublemakers than they expected.*

meeting (1) NOUN

A **meeting** is an occasion when you meet someone by arrangement.

appointment
*I groaned when Dad told me I had an **appointment** with the dentist.*

rendezvous
*Daniel arranged a secret **rendezvous** with his ex-wife.*

meeting (2) NOUN

A **meeting** is an event at which people discuss things or make decisions.

assembly
*At an **assembly**, we showed the school the work we had done.*

conference
*Mrs Guptah said she was off to a teachers' **conference**.*

get-together INFORMAL
*Mum has a **get-together** with the book club every fortnight.*

melt VERB

When something **melts**, or when you **melt** it, it changes from a solid to a liquid because it has been heated.

defrost
*The ice cream had to be slightly **defrosted** before we could scoop it out of the tub.*

thaw
*As the snow and ice **thawed**, the witch's power over Narnia waned.*

ANTONYM: freeze

mend VERB

If you **mend** something that is broken, you repair or fix it.

fix
*"Can you **fix** the fridge, or do we need a new one?" Mum asked the repair man.*

patch
*My brother was in the garden helping Dad **patch** the broken fence.*

renovate
*Our sofa has been completely **renovated** and is now as good as new.*

repair
*Dad lay on his back trying to **repair** the van's exhaust.*

✔ If you mend a sock with a hole in, you **darn** it.

mention VERB

If you **mention** something, you speak or write briefly about it.

bring up
*"I'm glad you **brought** that **up**," the mayor said. "I wanted to thank you."*

comment on
*Grandma **commented on** how lovely the weather was.*

point out
*Mum **pointed out** that I had forgotten my school bag.*

refer to
*In her speech, the head teacher **referred to** the parents' support.*

mess (1) NOUN

A **mess** is something dirty or untidy.

chaos
*After the explosion, the whole area was in complete **chaos**.*

clutter
*"Get rid of all this **clutter**, Max," Mum ordered.*

pigsty INFORMAL
*The twins' bedroom was an absolute **pigsty** until their mum told them to tidy it.*

shambles
*When my parents took it over, the hotel was a total **shambles**.*

a b c d e f g h i j k l **m** n o p q r s t u v w x y z

A
B
C
D
E
F
G
H
I
J
K
L
M
N
O
P
Q
R
S
T
U
V
W
X
Y
Z

mess (2) NOUN

A **mess** is a situation full of problems.

dilemma
*My parents were in a **dilemma**: should they sell the business and move to Spain?*

predicament
*I was in a **predicament** about which party to go to, as they were both on the same day.*

mess (3) VERB

If you **mess** with something, you play around with it.

meddle
*"Don't **meddle** with that box. It's your father's," Mum warned.*

tamper
*Someone had been **tampering** with the padlock.*

tinker
*Dad and I enjoy **tinkering** with car engines.*

mess about or mess around VERB

If you **mess about** or **mess around**, you spend time doing silly or casual things.

fool around
*Amy and I were **fooling around** when she fell and hurt herself.*

muck about INFORMAL
*It's great to **muck about** in the snow with sledges.*

play around
***Playing around** on the railway is a very foolish thing to do.*

mess up (1) VERB

If you **mess up** something, you make it untidy.

dirty
*The wretched dog had **dirtied** the bed with his muddy paws.*

jumble
*Our dog, Wuffles, had totally **jumbled** all Dad's papers.*

muddle
*"You have to be careful not to **muddle** the wires," Dad explained as he changed the plug.*

spoil
*Jess **spoilt** her work by doodling around the edges.*

mess up (2) VERB

If you **mess up** something, you do it badly.

botch
*The cowboy builders had really **botched** the roof repair.*

bungle
*We had **bungled** the arrangements, and now confusion reigned.*

make a hash of
*Carrie can **make a hash of** any situation.*

muck up
*By turning up late, Izzy **mucked up** her chance to be in the first team.*

ANTONYM: fix or sort out

message NOUN

A **message** is a piece of information or a request from one person to another.

> **Types of message:**
> call   fax   note
> communication   letter   text message
> e-mail   memo

messy ADJECTIVE

Something **messy** is dirty, untidy or confused.

chaotic
*Carter's bedroom was **chaotic**, with clothes and shoes everywhere.*

mucky
*There were lots of **mucky** pots and pans to clear up when we had finished baking.*

muddled
*Miss Harrison told me off for producing a **muddled** piece of writing.*

untidy
***Untidy** work is something Mr Illes won't tolerate.*

ANTONYM: neat

method NOUN

A **method** is a particular way of doing something.

approach
*Iorek's **approach** to battle was simple: hit them, and hit them hard.*

procedure
*"As part of the **procedure**, you have to fill out this form," the clerk said.*

technique
*In sport, try to learn **techniques** that will help you perform better.*

way
*My sister has a special **way** of revising for her exams.*

middle (1) NOUN
The **middle** of something is the part furthest from the edges, ends or surface.

centre
*In the **centre** of the field was a crop circle.*

core
*At the **core** of the earth, temperatures are extremely high.*

heart
*At night, you may find foxes even in the **heart** of the city.*

hub
*The control room was the **hub** of all the emergency services.*

ANTONYM: edge or end or surface

middle (2) ADJECTIVE
The **middle** thing in a series is the one with an equal number of things on each side.

central
*Only the **central** bowling pin remained standing.*

inner
*The castle had a protected **inner** courtyard.*

ANTONYM: outer

mind (1) VERB
If you **mind** when something happens to you, you are annoyed or bothered by it.

be bothered
*"I **am bothered** that so many of you have turned in your homework late," Mr Juffar said.*

be offended
*I **was** quite **offended** when I wasn't invited to the party.*

disapprove
*Granny **disapproves** if we arrive late.*

object
*Mum really **objects** when people smoke in the kitchen.*

resent
*We **resented** being woken up by our neighbour's noisy guests.*

mind (2) VERB
If you **mind** something for someone, you look after it for a while.

keep an eye on
*At the airport, a lady asked us to **keep an eye on** her luggage.*

look after
*"Please **look after** this bear," read Paddington Bear's label.*

take care of
*Megan and I **took care of** little Bethany while her mum bathed the baby.*

minimum ADJECTIVE
The **minimum** amount of something is the smallest amount that is possible, allowed or needed.

least
*Trust me to get the **least** amount of roast potatoes at lunch!*

lowest
*The **lowest** mark we needed to pass the test was 50 per cent.*

smallest
*Ten euros was the **smallest** amount with which you could open a bank account.*

ANTONYM: maximum

minute SAID "MY-NYOOT" ADJECTIVE
Something that is **minute** is extremely small.

microscopic
*It was **microscopic** bacteria, not weapons, that brought the alien invaders to their knees.*

minuscule
*You should have seen the **minuscule** amount of food they gave us at camp!*

tiny
*A **tiny** glitch can cause a computer to crash.*

ANTONYM: gigantic or huge or massive

miserable ADJECTIVE

If you are **miserable**, you are very unhappy.

brokenhearted

Brokenhearted, the knight said a farewell to his faithful horse.

dejected

After being turned down for college, my sister was dejected for days.

depressed

We were all quite depressed when the holiday was cancelled.

melancholy

I couldn't understand why Suzannah looked so melancholy.

wretched

I felt wretched after I'd been mean to George, my little brother.

ANTONYM: cheerful

miss (1) VERB

If you **miss** something that nearly hits you, it does not hit you.

avoid

Dad just managed to avoid a cyclist who had no lights on her bike.

dodge

When he was a soldier, Grandad once dodged a bullet from an enemy rifle.

evade

The pop stars evaded the waiting fans by escaping in a meat van.

ANTONYM: hit

miss (2) VERB

If you **miss** someone or something, you feel sad because they are no longer with you.

grieve for

All our family grieved for our cat, Barnaby, when he died.

mourn for

For many years, Queen Victoria mourned for her late husband, Albert.

pine for

Daniel pined for his children, and decided then and there to see them next weekend at all costs.

mistake NOUN

If you make a **mistake**, you do something wrong without intending to.

blunder

It was a bit of a blunder to let the dog off its lead in a field full of sheep.

error

A simple error led to the loss of all the computer data.

slip

One slip of the pen meant writing the whole page again.

mix VERB

If you **mix** things, you combine them.

blend

Instant coffee is blended from several types of coffee bean.

combine

This dish combines the flavour of beef with the tang of horseradish.

mingle

Security guards mingled with the crowd, watching like hawks.

ANTONYM: separate

mixed ADJECTIVE

If a quantity of something is **mixed**, it combines two or more different types.

assorted

I bought a box of assorted Christmas cards.

miscellaneous

Miss Mason brought in miscellaneous stamps from her collection.

various

It was great when we went out for tea – we could choose from various types of cake.

mixture NOUN

A **mixture** is two or more things mixed together.

assortment

Grandma brought us a big box of chocolates containing an assortment of flavours.

blend

We used a blend of paints to get the colour we wanted for the bathroom.

combination

*A **combination** of drugs helped bring Grandad's pain under control.*

compound

*The scientist used a **compound** of several chemicals to perfect his formula.*

fusion

*The meal was a **fusion** of Caribbean- and British-style cooking.*

jumble

*Mrs Harris gave us a **jumble** of word cards that we had to sort into verbs and nouns.*

mix up VERB

If you **mix up** things, you get confused.

confuse

*Grandad **confused** his washing with ours.*

muddle

*In maths my sister still **muddles** multiplication and division.*

moan (1) VERB

If you **moan**, you make a low, miserable sound because you are in pain or unhappy.

groan

*I couldn't help **groaning** when Elijah accidentally trod on my sore toe.*

sigh

*Mr Gupta **sighed** when he saw what a mess my tray was in.*

moan (2) VERB

If you **moan** about something, you complain about it.

complain

*My sister is always **complaining** about one thing or another.*

grumble

*Our upstairs neighbour **grumbled** about the state of the building.*

whine

*Jerry wouldn't stop **whining** about the fact that I'd forgotten his birthday, even though I'd got him a present eventually.*

whinge INFORMAL

*"Stop **whingeing**!" Dad said. "You're not having an ice cream."*

model NOUN

A **model** is a copy of something that shows what it looks like or how it works in real life.

dummy

*Shop window **dummies** don't usually look at all like real people.*

imitation

*Although the jewels were **imitations**, they looked real to me.*

replica

*My aunt has a business marketing **replicas** of Roman coins.*

modern ADJECTIVE

Something **modern** is new and involves the latest ideas or equipment.

advanced

***Advanced** technology means that you can plan your journey by satellite navigation.*

newfangled

*Grandad doesn't want to get involved with **newfangled** things like computers.*

state-of-the-art

*Dad spends a fortune on all the **state-of-the-art** camera equipment.*

the latest

*"Our health suite contains all **the latest** exercise equipment", read the gym notice.*

up-to-date

*It's an expensive business having **up-to-date** computers at school.*

*See **recent***

ANTONYM: old-fashioned

moment NOUN

A **moment** is a very short period of time.

instant

*The **instant** Mum had gone, I hid her present in the cupboard.*

second

*"Just wait. I won't be a **second**," Dad said as I headed out of the door.*

split second

*I was a **split second** too late. The bus was already leaving.*

moment

in a moment PHRASE
If something happens **in a moment**, it happens very quickly.

in a flash
In a flash, *the greyhounds had left the traps.*

in a jiffy INFORMAL
*"Don't worry, I'll have your car fixed **in a jiffy**," the cheery mechanic announced.*

in a trice
In a trice, *the kettle was on and Badger was getting cups ready.*

in an instant
*The thief was out of the door **in an instant**.*

in no time at all
*We were very late, but **in no time at all**, Mrs Abrahams had made us a meal.*

money (1) NOUN
Money is the coins and banknotes that you use to buy things.

cash
*When I asked for my pocket money, Dad pretended he was short of **cash**.*

currency
*After the holiday, we had some foreign **currency** left over.*

dosh INFORMAL
*"Do you have any **dosh** I could borrow?" my brother asked.*

dough INFORMAL
*"I've made loads of **dough** washing cars," Gupta told us.*

monster NOUN
A **monster** is a large, imaginary creature that looks very frightening.

beast
*The **beast** had cruel eyes and sharp teeth.*

brute
*With an upward thrust of his sword, St George felt the **brute** stiffen and then go limp.*

fiend
*What foul **fiend** could have inflicted such terrible havoc?*

giant
*Lumbering across the cloud, the **giant** stared at the top of the beanstalk.*

ogre
*Jack could hear the **ogre** crashing moodily about in his castle.*

mood NOUN
Your **mood** is the way you are feeling at a particular time.

frame of mind
*To win at games, you have to be in a positive **frame of mind**.*

temper
*It pays to try to keep an even **temper**.*

moody (1) ADJECTIVE
Moody people change their mood often and very quickly, seemingly for no reason.

changeable
*I find **changeable** people difficult to handle.*

temperamental
*The **temperamental** tennis player banged his racket on the ground.*

unpredictable
*Fiery and **unpredictable**, the artist was always sacking her assistants.*

moody (2) ADJECTIVE
If you are **moody**, you feel miserable and bad-tempered.

down in the mouth INFORMAL
*"You're looking **down in the mouth**. What's the matter?" Phillipa asked.*

in a huff
*Just because I had borrowed her brush, my sister got **in a huff**.*

irritable
*Trouble at work was making Dad **irritable** in the evenings.*

sulky
*I hate it when my best friend is **sulky**.*

sullen
*Sharon gave her mum a **sullen** look.*

more ADJECTIVE
More of something is an additional thing or amount of something.

added
Added salt can make many snacks very bad for you.

additional
*The club needed **additional** money to finish the project.*

extra
*Wesley asked for **extra** ice cream, as there was some spare.*

further
*"One **further** thing," the bear said. "We shall need to surprise them."*

ANTONYM: less

most ADJECTIVE
Most of a group of things or people means nearly all of them.

almost all
Almost all my friends are around the same age as I am.

the majority of
The majority of the class walked to school.

mountain NOUN
A **mountain** is a very high piece of land with steep sides.

mount
Mount Olympus is where the Olympic flame starts its journey to the Games.

peak
*A **peak** overlooks the wonderful sight of Hong Kong harbour.*

✔ The top of a mountain is its **peak** or **summit**.
A long stretch of mountains is a **range**.
A narrow, high stretch of a mountain is a **ridge**.
A high valley between two mountains is a **pass**.

move (1) VERB
If you **move** something, or when it **moves**, its position changes.

budge INFORMAL
*We couldn't **budge** the tree trunk that was blocking the path.*

shift
*It was clear from the crack that the earth beneath the house had **shifted**.*

move slightly or slowly:
crawl
*Traffic **crawled** down the busy high street in the rush hour.*

creep
*Every day, the stark frame of the skyscraper **crept** upwards.*

edge
*Hardly daring to breathe, we **edged** past the unexploded bomb.*

inch
*The giant crane **inched** its way into position.*

nose
*With its bow doors opening, the ferry **nosed** towards the docking ramp.*

stir
*The house was dark and silent. Nothing **stirred** within.*

move fast:
hurtle
*I stood in amazement as the lorry **hurtled** past me, down the hill.*

race
*Monica **raced** into the room, grabbed a comic and **raced** out again.*

shoot
*As soon as it saw us, the red squirrel **shot** up the tree.*

speed
*Soon the fire engine was **speeding** towards the scene of the accident.*

zoom
*My brother **zoomed** past me on his way out of the house.*

move forward or closer to:
advance
*The invading army had **advanced** several miles inland.*

approach
Approaching the house, we could see a shadow moving in the front room.

near
*As the plane **neared** its destination, we had to fasten our seat belts.*

proceed
Proceeding towards the summit, the climbers turned on their oxygen.

progress
*Building had **progressed** swiftly since Dad had last been to check.*

move

A
B
C
D
E
F
G
H
I
J
K
L
M
N
O
P
Q
R
S
T
U
V
W
X
Y
Z

move backwards:

back

*Some drivers have awful difficulty **backing** into parking spaces properly.*

retreat

*As the rain began to teem down, the golfers **retreated** to a hut.*

reverse

***Reversing** a canal boat is always a tricky operation.*

withdraw

*The colonel decided to **withdraw** rather than risk his troops being wiped out.*

move upwards:

ascend

*With a deafening racket, the hovercraft **ascended** on its cushion of air.*

climb

*The desert temperature **climbed** as the lost explorers staggered onward.*

soar

*High above, a golden eagle swooped and **soared** in the sunlight.*

move downwards:

descend

*Holmes cautiously **descended** the stairs, aware that the killer might still be below.*

dive

*Hearing the ominous whistle of a falling bomb, they **dived** under the table.*

fall

*When they were ripe, the apples **fell** to the ground beneath the tree.*

swoop

*The hawk hovered above the roadside, ready to **swoop** at any second.*

move smoothly:

float

*In a total dream, Carly **floated** past wearing a long dress.*

glide

*Modern trains **glide** along with remarkably little noise.*

skate

*Totally out of control, the car **skated** across the icy surface.*

move clumsily:

lumber

*The bulky lorry **lumbered** up the steep mountain pass.*

trundle

*Bouncing and clattering, the cart **trundled** along the bumpy road.*

move suddenly:

dart

*A kingfisher **darted** from the bank and flashed away down the canal.*

lunge

*The Sheriff **lunged** for the dagger, but Robin Hood was too quick for him.*

lurch

*Dev **lurched** forward when he tripped on the uneven paving stones.*

move quietly:

prowl

*Cats **prowl** at night, looking for small mammals to kill.*

slink

*The spy **slunk** through the bushes, dressed in black to blend with the night.*

steal

*The attack party **stole** past the sleeping guards at the gate.*

move (2) VERB

If you **move** things, you take them from one place to another.

convey

*Containers are used for **conveying** goods by ship.*

transfer

*I was upset when my favourite player **transferred** to another club.*

transport

*Fragile items are more difficult to **transport** than robust ones.*

See **carry**

move (3) VERB

If you **move**, you go to live in a different place.

move house

*People who serve in the armed forces tend to **move house** quite often.*

relocate
*Rob's parents were keen to **relocate** to the country.*

✔ When you move from one country to another, you **emigrate**.
When animals move in a particular season, usually to breed or find food, they **migrate**.

mud NOUN
Mud is wet, sticky earth.

muck
*Poor old Wuffles, our dog, was up to his tummy in **muck**.*

slime
*After the rain, **slime** oozed from the pig pens.*

sludge
*"Put your wellies on," Mum shouted. "The rain has turned the path to **sludge**."*

muddle (1) NOUN
If there is a **muddle**, things get confused.

confusion
*There was a **confusion** over dates, and only three people turned up.*

misunderstanding
*The firm apologized for the **misunderstanding**, and offered Mum a free holiday.*

mix-up
*What a **mix-up**! Dad was in Australia and his luggage was in Singapore.*

muddle (2) NOUN
A **muddle** is a state of disorder or untidiness.

jumble
*Our loft is a **jumble** of unwanted items that we can't bring ourselves to throw out.*

mess
*The **mess** in my sister's bedroom looked like the aftermath of a riot.*

tangle
*Amid the **tangle** of wires, I managed to find the plug I was looking for.*

muddle (3) VERB
If things **muddle** you, they confuse you.

bewilder
*Computers may be clever things, but they **bewilder** some people.*

perplex
*We stood at the crossroads, unable to find it on the map and totally **perplexed** about which way to go.*

muddle (4) VERB
If you **muddle** things, you mix them up.

jumble
*My friend Adhira managed to **jumble** the letters she had to deliver.*

mess up
*Over the years, Grandad's papers had become totally **messed up**.*

murder (1) VERB
To **murder** someone means to kill them deliberately.

assassinate
*Police uncovered a plot to **assassinate** the king and queen.*

bump off INFORMAL
*The gangster **bumped off** those people who annoyed him.*

slaughter
*In the First World War, machine guns **slaughtered** men in their thousands.*

slay OLD-FASHIONED
*Legend has it that St George **slew** a dragon with his mighty sword.*

✔ Someone who kills another person is a **killer** or **murderer**.

murder (2) NOUN
Murder is the deliberate killing of a person.

assassination
*The **assassination** of President Kennedy took place in 1963.*

homicide AMERICAN
*We often hear the term **homicide** in American films and television programmes.*

killing
*No one knew how many **killings** the dictator had ordered.*

slaughter
*Chicago gangsters of the 1920s used to go in for wholesale **slaughter** of rivals.*

✔ The killing of someone without intending to do so is **manslaughter**.

music NOUN

Music is the pattern of sounds performed by people singing or playing instruments.

Some kinds of music:

blues	jazz
big band	opera
classical	pop
country	punk
disco	rap
garage	rhythm and blues
gospel	rock
heavy metal	salsa
hip-hop	soul
indie	

Some kinds of musical instruments:

accordion	lute
bagpipes	lyre
banjo	maracas
bass guitar	oboe
bassoon	organ
bongos	piano
bugle	piccolo
castanets	recorder
cello	saxophone
clarinet	sitar
cymbals	synthesizer
double bass	tambourine
drums	triangle
flute	trombone
glockenspiel	trumpet
guitar	tuba
harmonica	ukulele
harp	viola
horn	violin
keyboard	xylophone
kettledrum	zither

---

mutiny NOUN

A **mutiny** is a rebellion against someone in authority.

rebellion

The **rebellion** began because the regiment was being underfed.

revolt

Deck hands staged a **revolt** at the unfair treatment of one of their mates.

revolution

Many people were killed in the French **Revolution**.

uprising

An **uprising** in the North was brutally put down by the king's men.

mutter VERB

If you **mutter**, or if you mutter something, you speak very quietly so that it is difficult for people to hear you.

mumble

As Farmer Gabriel **mumbled**, we often had to ask him to repeat things.

murmur

In the wood, Frodo heard the **murmur** of a thousand tiny creatures.

mysterious ADJECTIVE

Something **mysterious** is strange and puzzling.

baffling

Even more **baffling**: why was the light on in the attic?

curious

"This Baskerville case is a **curious** business," Holmes said.

eerie

Eerie howlings had been heard, coming from the moor.

inexplicable

It was **inexplicable**. Why should anyone wish to go out on a stormy night?

mystifying

What was behind the **mystifying** message written on the wall?

mystery NOUN

A **mystery** is something that is not understood or known about.

conundrum

Mr Powers had to figure out Dr Evil's little **conundrum**, or die.

puzzle

It was a real **puzzle**: how on earth could she have escaped?

riddle

The meaning of the ancient signs was a **riddle** that took years to solve.

Nn

nag VERB

If you **nag** someone, you keep complaining to them or pestering them about something.

badger

*My little brother kept **badgering** me to take him to the park.*

hassle INFORMAL

*If you're famous, you can expect to be **hassled** by all sorts of people.*

pester

*"Stop **pestering** me, Mum!" Jasmine said. "I'll tidy my room very soon."*

name NOUN

A **name** is a word that you use to identify a person, animal, place or thing.

term

*The **term** for a doing word is a verb, for example "run" and "say".*

title

*On forms, when it asks for your **title**, you have to write Mr, Mrs, Miss, Ms, Lord or Lady.*

> Your first names can be called **forenames** or **Christian names**.
> In most European languages, your last name is your **family name** (also called a **surname** in English).
> In languages such as Chinese and Urdu, your first name is your family name.
> A false name for someone trying to hide or escape is an **alias**.
> A writer's false name is a **pen name** or **pseudonym**.
> An actor or musician's false name is their **stage name**.

name VERB

If you **name** someone or something, you give them a name.

baptize

*My friend's little brother is going to be **baptized** on Sunday as George.*

call

*We **called** our new kitten Paws, as she has a black body and white paws.*

christen

*My Mum was **christened** Patricia, but everyone calls her Pat.*

narrow ADJECTIVE

Something that is **narrow** measures a small distance from one side to the other.

slender

*The tall, **slender** poplar tree swayed gently in the breeze.*

slim

*Cinderella's **slim** foot fitted perfectly into the glass slipper.*

thin

*The black cat slipped easily through the **thin** gap in the fence.*

ANTONYM: wide

nasty (1) ADJECTIVE

Nasty behaviour is very unpleasant.

disgusting

*"Don't speak with your mouth full. It's **disgusting**!" complained my sister.*

foul

*When the joiner hit his thumb, he came out with some **foul** language.*

horrible

*"Mya, that was a **horrible** thing to say!" protested Alex.*

offensive

*The behaviour of the football hooligans was most **offensive**.*

rude

*"It's **rude** to interrupt," said Grandma when I tried to get a word in edgeways.*

sickening

*It was **sickening** to see the way the journalist tried to flatter the pop star.*

unpleasant

*My brother is sometimes **unpleasant** to me, but we always make up.*

vile

*Blackmail is a **vile** crime.*

nasty (2) ADJECTIVE
Nasty comments are very unpleasant.

cruel
*I don't like it when the other children say **cruel** things to new children.*

malicious
*In the **malicious** letter, the writer threatened to kidnap the businessman's son.*

mean
*My brother made some **mean** remarks about my haircut, but his isn't so smart!*

spiteful
*Her **spiteful** comments lost Jocelyn her best friend.*

unkind
*"You mustn't say **unkind** things like that," Mum warned me.*

natural (1) ADJECTIVE
Something **natural** is normal and to be expected.

common
*It was a **common** occurrence for us to pass the pop star on his daily jog.*

normal
*The doctor reassured Givon that his spots were **normal**, and would go.*

ordinary
*To the world, the spy seemed just an **ordinary**, everyday sort of person.*

*See **regular** and **usual***

natural (2) ADJECTIVE
Something **natural** exists or happens in nature, rather than being caused or made by people.

organic
*Our local shop sells **organic** food that is free from pesticides and has grown naturally.*

plain
*I loved the **plain** wood finish of the panels in the old manor.*

wholesome
*Mum's meals were always made of good, **wholesome** ingredients.*

ANTONYM: artificial

natural (3) ADJECTIVE
If you have a **natural** ability, you are born with it.

inherent
*Gymnasts need an **inherent** sense of balance to succeed.*

innate
*Henry had an **innate** ability to get on well with people.*

instinctive
*It was only the racing driver's **instinctive** reaction that saved his life.*

ANTONYM: unnatural

naughty ADJECTIVE
A child who is **naughty** behaves badly.

badly-behaved
*The girl was suspended from school for being persistently **badly-behaved**.*

disobedient
*My brother isn't usually **disobedient**, but does what he's told.*

mischievous
*While the family were out, the **mischievous** goblin rearranged the house.*

troublesome
*Mum says I was quite **troublesome** when I was little, but I'm much better behaved now.*

ANTONYM: well-behaved or obedient

near (1) PREPOSITION, ADJECTIVE AND ADVERB
If something is **near** a particular place, it is a short distance from it.

adjacent
***Adjacent** to the old pigsty was a room for storing horse harnesses.*

close
*When we go swimming we can walk to the pool, as it is so **close** to home.*

nearby
*Mrs Irons told us to wait while she asked the way in a **nearby** shop.*

neighbouring
*Bilal and I built a den beneath a tree in **neighbouring** woods.*

within easy reach
*Our house is **within easy reach** of the station.*

near (2) PREPOSITION, ADJECTIVE AND ADVERB
If an event is **near**, it will happen soon.

approaching
*Anish was excited at the thought of the **approaching** concert.*

close at hand
*The midnight hour was **close at hand**, as the coffin lids creaked open.*

forthcoming
*The local newspaper has details of **forthcoming** events.*

imminent
*We knew from the countdown that the rocket launch was **imminent**.*

nigh OLD-FASHIONED
*"As night is **nigh**, prithee stay with us, kind sir," said the innkeeper.*

nearly ADVERB
Something which is **nearly** done is not completely finished, but almost.

almost
*I'd **almost** finished my homework when Alan called round.*

practically
*Our supplies were **practically** exhausted, and water was short too.*

virtually
*Building was **virtually** completed when fire destroyed the house.*

See **roughly**

neat (1) ADJECTIVE
Something that is **neat** is tidy and smart.

orderly
*Mr Khan told us to form an **orderly** queue as we waited to get on the bus.*

shipshape
*Gramps praised me for leaving my room **shipshape**.*

smart
*Mum likes me to look **smart** when we visit my aunt and uncle.*

spick-and-span
*The holiday apartment was **spick-and-span** when we arrived.*

tidy
*Skylar was always **tidy** in her school work.*

ANTONYM: messy

neat (2) ADJECTIVE
If someone makes a **neat** move, they do it skilfully.

clever
*The way that my mum worded the birthday card was really **clever**.*

nifty INFORMAL
*With a **nifty** sidestep, the forward was through to the goal.*

skilful
*Alastair admired the **skilful** way the magician handled the cards.*

necessary ADJECTIVE
Something that is **necessary** is needed or must be done.

essential
*Napoleon insisted that good food was **essential** for his troops.*

imperative
*"It is **imperative** that this message gets through," the sergeant urged the rider.*

required
*To become a teacher, a good education is **required**.*

vital
*At the end of an exam, it's **vital** to check what you've written.*

ANTONYM: unnecessary

need VERB
If you **need** something, you cannot achieve what you want without having it or doing it.

demand
*Being a good nurse **demands** stamina, intelligence and a caring attitude.*

require
*The advert read, "**Required**: honest boy or girl for newspaper deliveries."*

A
B
C
D
E
F
G
H
I
J
K
L
M
N
O
P
Q
R
S
T
U
V
W
X
Y
Z

neighbourhood NOUN
Your **neighbourhood** is the area where you live.

area
*There are many tower blocks in our **area**.*

community
*Each Wednesday, there's a luncheon club for old people in the **community**.*

district
*Our school is the best in the **district**.*

locality
*Our **locality** does not have very many facilities for young people.*

vicinity
*"Police warn that a thief is operating in the **vicinity**," announced the newsreader.*

nervous ADJECTIVE
If someone is **nervous**, they are easily worried and agitated.

anxious
*As midnight approached, Cinderella was becoming **anxious**.*

apprehensive
*I always feel a little **apprehensive** before I go to the dentist.*

edgy
*As the day of his test approached, Karl became increasingly **edgy**.*

jittery INFORMAL
*Many actors and actresses get **jittery** before they go on stage.*

jumpy INFORMAL
*The swarthy man was so **jumpy** that I knew he was up to no good.*

worried
*When Mum was in hospital, we could tell Dad was **worried**.*

ANTONYM: calm

never ADVERB
Something that has **never** happened, has happened at no time in the past, and will not happen at any time in the present or future.

at no time
*"**At no time** did I leave the room, sir," the witness insisted.*

on no account
*"**On no account** must you touch those wires," my mother warned.*

under no circumstances
*Mr Osman said that **under no circumstances** would he let us off our homework.*

new (1) ADJECTIVE
Something **new** is recently made.

fresh
*I love the smell of **fresh** bread.*

unused
*The car was advertised as being in **unused** condition.*

✔ A new, unused coin or stamp is in **mint condition**.

new (2) ADJECTIVE
Something **new** is recently created or discovered.

current
*"You can bet that **current** trends will be tomorrow's old news," said the reporter.*

latest
*"For my birthday I got the **latest** version of my favourite computer game," said Gamal.*

modern
*Our school is a **modern** building near the town centre.*

recent
*My mum's car is the most **recent** model.*

up-to-date
*My brother insists on buying all the **up-to-date** computer gadgets.*

ANTONYM: old

next (1) ADJECTIVE
The **next** thing, person or event is the one that comes immediately after the present one.

following
*We went to the seaside one day, and the **following** day to the hills.*

subsequent
*On Tuesday I planned my story, and wrote it the **subsequent** day.*

ANTONYM: previous

next (2) ADJECTIVE

The **next** place or person is the one nearest to you.

adjacent
*My friends Ivan and Isabella live in the flat **adjacent** to ours.*

neighbouring
*The ball hit the headpin, which then knocked all the **neighbouring** pins down.*

next (3) ADVERB

You use **next** to refer to an action that follows immediately after the present one.

afterwards
*Shane and I had a swim and **afterwards** sat by the pool.*

subsequently
*The man was injured in the accident but **subsequently** made a full recovery.*

ANTONYM: previous

nice (1) ADJECTIVE

A **nice** person is pleasant and kind.

amiable
*My parents find our teacher **amiable**, but she's not always amiable with us.*

charming
*Scoresby, the balloonist, turned out to be a **charming** fellow.*

delightful
*When we were at the jumble sale a **delightful** old lady offered us a cup of tea.*

entertaining
*My dad can be very **entertaining**, telling us all sorts of stories.*

kind
*It was very **kind** of Alexia to invite me over to her house for tea.*

likeable
*Crystal was a **likeable** character who had lots of friends.*

pleasant
*The interviewer was **pleasant**, with a kind smile and a nice voice.*

ANTONYM: awful or rude

nice (2) ADJECTIVE

A **nice** event is pleasant and enjoyable.

delightful
*"This has been a **delightful** evening," I heard Dad say to our host.*

enjoyable
*Ellie and Magda spent an **enjoyable** half-hour chatting on the phone.*

pleasant
*The sun shone and the whole barbecue was a **pleasant** event.*

satisfying
*It was **satisfying** to have helped the old lady with her garden.*

ANTONYM: unpleasant

nice (3) ADJECTIVE

A **nice** view is pleasant to look at.

pleasing
*The hotel balcony had a **pleasing** outlook over the estuary.*

scenic
*Switzerland's mountains are very **scenic**.*

stunning
*The mist cleared, revealing a **stunning** view to the mountain peak.*

nice (4) ADJECTIVE

A **nice** meal is tasty.

appetizing
*An **appetizing** smell wafted from the bakery.*

delicious
*Strawberry jam, cream and scones make a **delicious** combination.*

scrumptious
*"That was a **scrumptious** supper," Omar said to my mum.*

nice (5) ADJECTIVE

Nice weather is warm and pleasant.

fine
*The day was **fine** and a gentle breeze stirred the flags.*

lovely
*It was a **lovely** autumn day, with a blue sky.*

ANTONYM: unpleasant

a
b
c
d
e
f
g
h
i
j
k
l
m
n
o
p
q
r
s
t
u
v
w
x
y
z

nice (6) ADJECTIVE
Nice clothes are stylish and smart.

beautiful
*The dress in the window was **beautiful** but very expensive.*

elegant
*I thought Mum and Dad looked wonderful in their **elegant** evening clothes.*

nip VERB
If you **nip** somewhere, you go there quickly.

dart
*The squirrel **darted** across the garden.*

dash
*As the rain bucketed down, we **dashed** from the car to the doorway.*

hurry
***Hurrying** past, our next-door neighbour didn't notice me.*

rush
*Jade banged the door, threw her bag on the chair and **rushed** upstairs.*

no INTERJECTION
You say **no** when you do not want something or do not agree.

✔ To say no to someone's request is to **deny** it, **refuse** it or **turn** it **down**.
To say no when asked if you have done something is to **deny** it.

noise (1) NOUN
A **noise** can be a loud or unpleasant sound.

cacophony
*There was a **cacophony** from the orchestra as the musicians warmed up.*

commotion
*There was a **commotion** at the back, and someone burst forward, shouting.*

din
*In the **din** of the cotton mill, it was impossible to hear yourself speak.*

hubbub
*Gran doesn't like the **hubbub** of the city.*

hullabaloo INFORMAL
*"What's all this **hullabaloo** about?" the sergeant enquired.*

racket
*My brother's music makes quite a **racket**.*

row SOUNDS LIKE "COW"
*Mum asked us not to make too much of a **row** out in the garden.*

uproar
*When the pop star finally came on stage there was **uproar** in the crowd.*

noise (2) NOUN
The **noise** of people talking is what they sound like as they speak.

babble
*The head teacher raised a hand, and the **babble** of voices subsided.*

chatter
*A ceaseless **chatter** comes from my sister's room when her friend Hope comes round.*

hubbub
*There is usually quite a **hubbub** in the school dining hall at dinner time.*

noisy (1) ADJECTIVE
When something is **noisy**, it makes a lot of noise.

deafening
*The sound of the waterfall was **deafening**.*

ear-splitting
*With an **ear-splitting** crash, the building was demolished.*

loud
*From windows throughout the neighbourhood, **loud** music boomed into the summer streets.*

piercing
*The **piercing** screech of the parrot echoed through the house.*

thunderous
*The **thunderous** boom of artillery fire can be heard many miles away.*

ANTONYM: quiet

noisy (2) ADJECTIVE
When someone is **noisy**, they make a lot of noise.

boisterous
*The **boisterous** children were obviously enjoying the party.*

rowdy
*The crowds in the street were **rowdy** but friendly.*

ANTONYM: quiet

nonsense NOUN
Nonsense is foolish or meaningless words or behaviour.

drivel
*My dad reckons that modern radio DJs mostly talk **drivel**.*

rot
*"Bunter, you do talk **rot**!" the fourth-former snapped.*

rubbish
*"I think a lot of television programmes are utter **rubbish**," I told my best friend, Keisha.*

twaddle
*What she was saying was **twaddle**, and everyone there knew it.*

normal (1) ADJECTIVE
If people or things are **normal**, they are usual and ordinary.

average
*The **average** person doesn't go to the opera very often.*

common
*Mrs Parham was very special – certainly not the **common** type of teacher.*

conventional
*Vanya never likes to wear **conventional** clothes – always something a bit different.*

typical
*The weather was **typical** for this time of year.*

ANTONYM: different

normal (2) ADJECTIVE
If someone's behaviour is **normal**, it is usual for them to behave this way.

habitual
*Gran's **habitual** routine is to sit down with a cup of coffee at eleven o'clock each morning.*

regular
*They looked like a **regular** pair of shoes, but they actually had magic powers.*

usual
*Mum said she'd pick me up from school at the **usual** time.*

nosy or nosey ADJECTIVE
Nosy people always want to know about other people's business, and like to interfere where they are not wanted.

curious
***Curious** to discover more, we followed the sound of the voices.*

inquisitive
*Mum's quite **inquisitive** and loves to hear all the gossip from the neighbours.*

meddlesome
*"Go away, you **meddlesome** children!" shouted the caretaker.*

nothing NOUN
Nothing means not a single thing, or not a single part of something.

none
*When I asked my brother to pass the roast potatoes, there were **none** left.*

nought
*I was quite ashamed when I got **nought** out of ten in the test.*

zero
*My sister checked her bank balance and was horrified to see that it was **zero**.*

✔ In tennis, no points is called **love**.
In sports such as rugby or soccer, no points is called **nil**.

notice (1) VERB
If you **notice** something, you become aware of it.

detect
*The sniffer dog **detected** the stolen jewels in the woman's luggage.*

observe
*I **observed** that, unusually, no trains had passed for an hour.*

perceive
*"I **perceive** more in you than you realize," Gandalf the wizard told the hobbit.*

spot
*Mum **spotted** a mark on my shirt.*

a b c d e f g h i j k l m **n** o p q r s t u v w x y z

notice (2) NOUN

A **notice** is a written announcement.

advertisement

*Dad placed an **advertisement** for the bike in the local paper.*

poster

*For our garage sale, we put **posters** all round the neighbourhood.*

now (1) ADVERB

If someone asks you to do something **now**, they want it done straight away.

at once

*"You must flee **at once**," the wizard said urgently.*

immediately

*"Do it **immediately**, or there'll be trouble," Mum ordered.*

straight away

*"We need an ambulance, **straight away**, please," the caller said.*

now (2) ADVERB

Now can mean at the present time or moment.

at the moment

*Because of the fog, no planes are taking off **at the moment**.*

nowadays

Nowadays, *we can travel abroad much more easily than in the past.*

these days

*"**These days** I can't run around like I did," my grandad said.*

nuisance NOUN

A **nuisance** is someone or something that is annoying or causing problems.

annoyance

*Our neighbour found my brother's loud music a great **annoyance**.*

bother

*"Let me help you with those bags. It's no **bother**," I said as I took my gran's shopping into the house.*

hassle INFORMAL

*"If you come shopping, I want no **hassle**," warned my mother.*

inconvenience

*The company apologized for the **inconvenience** caused by their roadworks.*

See **problem**

number (1) NOUN

A **number** is a word or symbol used for counting or calculating.

digit

*The number one million (1 000 000) has seven **digits** in it.*

figure

*"Think of a number with three **figures**," the magician commanded.*

numeral

*The **numerals** we use come from the Arab countries of the Middle East.*

number (2) NOUN

A **number** of things or people is several of them.

collection

*For the TV series, a **collection** of old vehicles was needed.*

crowd

*A large **crowd** of supporters gathered to cheer the team as they left.*

host OLD-FASHIONED

*Seeing a **host** of golden daffodils beside the lake, the poet sat down to write.*

quantity

*"What **quantity** of bricks do you need?" the builder's merchant enquired.*

Oo

obey VERB

If you **obey** a person or an order, you do what you are told to do.

abide by
*Games are much more fun when people **abide by** the rules.*

follow
*Building models from kits is easier if you **follow** the instructions.*

ANTONYM: disobey

object VERB

If you **object** to something, you dislike it, disagree with it or disapprove of it.

disagree
*Shania **disagreed** with Wayne's choice of DVD, but she watched it anyway.*

disapprove
*Gran **disapproves** of us playing our music too loudly.*

oppose
*Many local people **opposed** the new road.*

protest
*Thousands of people turned out to **protest** against the missiles.*

ANTONYM: approve or support

See **argue**

observant ADJECTIVE

An **observant** person notices things that are not usually noticed.

alert
*Fortunately Dad was **alert** enough to avoid the deer that ran out in front of the car.*

eagle-eyed
*Thanks to the **eagle-eyed** lookout, the tanker avoided the sailing dinghy.*

perceptive
*Mrs Bower said how **perceptive** Jack was to notice her new shoes.*

ANTONYM: unobservant

obvious ADJECTIVE

Something that is **obvious** is easy to see or understand.

apparent
*As soon as she spoke, it was **apparent** that Lyndsay came from the USA.*

blatant
*Tripping the player up was a **blatant** foul by the opposition's team captain.*

clear
*It was **clear** that the climber was totally stuck and would need some help.*

evident
*"It's **evident**, Yoshi," said Mr Leonard, "that you have learned nothing."*

plain
*From her wonderful performance, it was **plain** that Alana had been practising hard.*

ANTONYM: unclear

occasionally ADVERB

If something happens **occasionally**, it happens sometimes, but not often.

from time to time
***From time to time** Granny and Grandad come to visit us.*

now and then
*Mum takes us to the seaside **now and then**.*

once in a while
***Once in a while**, my computer will do strange things.*

periodically
*My father has to go abroad **periodically**, but not very often.*

ANTONYM: often or regularly

odd (1) ADJECTIVE

If something is **odd**, it is strange or unusual.

curious
*It was **curious** how tame the baby birds were.*

peculiar
*How **peculiar**! A talking goldfish!*

queer
*The king noticed there was something **queer** about the woods beyond the castle.*

a
b
c
d
e
f
g
h
i
j
k
l
m
n
o
p
q
r
s
t
u
v
w
x
y
z

odd (2) ADJECTIVE

If someone is **odd**, they do not behave in a normal way.

eccentric
My Aunty Rose is rather **eccentric**. She's 70, but wears trendy clothes and rides a bicycle.

unconventional
Deena has always been **unconventional**. Now she rides a unicycle to school.

zany
I love the old silent films, especially ones with that **zany** chap with his eyes crossed.

ANTONYM: conventional

off ADJECTIVE

If an event is **off**, it is cancelled or postponed.

cancelled
Because of cattle disease, the agricultural show was **cancelled**.

postponed
United's game with City was **postponed** owing to the fog.

ANTONYM: on

often ADVERB

Something that happens **often**, happens many times or a lot of the time.

frequently
My father **frequently** takes us to the beach in the summer.

regularly
Regularly in July, old Mr Lowry went to stay at the seaside.

repeatedly
"I've told you **repeatedly**," Mum snapped, "don't wipe your mouth on your sleeve!"

time after time
"You forget your kit **time after time**," Mrs Quincy sighed.

ANTONYM: occasionally

okay or OK (1) ADJECTIVE INFORMAL

If you say something is **okay**, it is all right.

acceptable
Miss Chowdri said it was **acceptable** for me to miss PE, as I'd hurt my ankle.

in order
"Is it **in order** for me to have Tuesday off?" the clerk asked.

satisfactory
"That will be perfectly **satisfactory**," replied the manager.

okay or OK (2) ADJECTIVE INFORMAL

If something is **okay**, it is moderately good.

adequate
The expedition's supplies were **adequate** for their needs.

fair
According to the head teacher, my report was **fair**, but nothing more.

passable
"This lasagne is **passable**, but not as good as I usually make," remarked Dad.

satisfactory
Mrs Freeman said my work was **satisfactory**.

old (1) ADJECTIVE

If a person is **old**, they have lived for a long time.

aged
The **aged** actor received a "Lifetime Achievement" award.

elderly
Each week, my gran meets three other **elderly** ladies for lunch.

getting on INFORMAL
Grandad is **getting on**, and finds climbing stairs a problem.

past their prime
The tennis players were **past their prime**, but they were still entertaining to watch.

ANTONYM: young or youthful

old (2) ADJECTIVE

If something is **old**, it has existed for a long time.

ancient
Europe has many **ancient** cathedrals and my dad intends to visit them all.

antique
The **antique** chairs were worth a great deal of money.

archaic
*"Shakespeare uses some **archaic** language,"*
explained Mrs Tordoff.

original
*Our cottage still has some of its **original**
features from the 19th century.*

primitive
*The **primitive** way of moving heavy stones
was to roll them along on logs.*

veteran
*Some **veteran** radio broadcasters keep going
until they are 80 or more.*

vintage
*Our neighbour has a lovely **vintage** car.*

✔ Something **prehistoric** is from the time
before written records were kept.

old (3)   ADJECTIVE
An **old** tradition has existed for a long time.

long-established
*The school has the **long-established** tradition
of a feast in April.*

long-standing
*"Our firm has a **long-standing** reputation for
fine meat," the butcher said proudly.*

traditional
*The harbour town has a **traditional** street
parade in May.*

ANTONYM: new

old (4)   ADJECTIVE
You use **old** to talk about something that
is no longer used or has been replaced by
something else.

ex-
*We still get Christmas cards from my sister's
ex-boyfriend.*

former
*Because she was a **former** ballerina, Mrs
Fountain still looked very slim and fit.*

one-time
*The **one-time** player is now a coach.*

previous
*My mum's **previous** car was a real old banger.*

ANTONYM: current

old-fashioned   ADJECTIVE
Something **old-fashioned** is out of date and no
longer fashionable.

antiquated
*My dad's shed is rather **antiquated**, but he
likes working there.*

dated
*With their black-and-white pictures, some of
our school textbooks look very **dated**.*

obsolete
*The school is changing some of its **obsolete**
computers for more up-to-date ones.*

outdated
*The factory manager aimed to get rid of the
outdated machinery.*

traditional
*Lumley's **traditional** oatcakes have been made
here since 1758.*

unfashionable
*These clothes were once very trendy, but are
now **unfashionable**.*

ANTONYM: up-to-date or modern

once   ADVERB
If something was **once** true, it was true in the
past, but is no longer true.

at one time
***At one time**, Mrs Schwarz used to read us a
story every day.*

formerly
*Bilbo was **formerly** a comfortable and
unadventurous hobbit.*

in the past
***In the past**, Dad used to be able to carry me
upstairs to bed.*

at once (1)   PHRASE
If several things happen **at once**, they all
happen at the same time.

at the same time
*"If you all talk **at the same time**, no one can
hear," said Miss Bell.*

simultaneously
*On the night of the golden jubilee, celebratory
bonfires were lit **simultaneously** all over
the country.*

A
B
C
D
E
F
G
H
I
J
K
L
M
N
O
P
Q
R
S
T
U
V
W
X
Y
Z

at once (2) PHRASE

If you do something **at once**, you do it immediately.

immediately
*The bell rang for break time, and **immediately** children streamed out of their classrooms.*

instantly
*At the wave of a wand, the prince was **instantly** transformed into a frog.*

right away
*I promised to do the errand **right away**.*

this minute
*"If you don't come down here **this minute**, your supper will get cold!" Mum yelled.*

without hesitation
***Without hesitation**, the fireman raced into the burning house to save the woman.*

only (1) ADVERB

You use **only** to emphasize that something is unimportant or small.

barely
*We had **barely** a teaspoonful of sugar left in the bowl.*

just
*"It's **just** a simple operation," the doctor said.*

merely
*"Julie is **merely** the office junior, but she tries to act like the boss," complained my cousin.*

simply
*It was **simply** a matter of snipping one of the wires to prevent the bomb from exploding.*

only (2) ADJECTIVE

If you talk about **only** one thing or person, you mean that there are no others.

single
*Mrs Cameron was the **single** person Lydia felt she could talk to.*

sole
*Robinson Crusoe thought he was the **sole** inhabitant of his island.*

solitary
*The prisoner was the **solitary** occupant of a whole row of cells.*

✔ If you are an **only child**, you have no brothers or sisters.

open (1) ADJECTIVE

Something that is **open** is not closed or fastened, allowing things to pass through.

ajar
*As the door was **ajar**, Hadiya peeped in.*

gaping
*The explosion left a **gaping** hole in the wall.*

unlocked
*"I've left the door **unlocked**," Mum shouted up to my bedroom window.*

yawning
*In front of the two hobbits lay a **yawning** chasm. How were they to cross it?*

open (2) VERB

When you **open** something, or when it **opens**, it is moved so that it is no longer closed.

unfasten
*Fiona **unfastened** the gate and the chickens rushed to meet her.*

unlock
*"**Unlock** this door and let me out!" the prison warder bawled.*

unwrap
*I went through to Mum and Dad's room to **unwrap** my presents.*

open (3) VERB

If something **opens**, or is opened, it starts or begins.

begin
*Each day business **begins** at the shop at nine o'clock.*

commence
*The chairman **commenced** the meeting by introducing his new assistant.*

get going
*My birthday party really **got going** when Mum brought the cake out.*

ANTONYM: finish

open (4) ADJECTIVE

Someone who is **open** is honest and not secretive.

candid
*"Please be **candid** in your replies," the judge asked the witness.*

frank

*"To be **frank**," Mum told Dad, "I'd rather go to the cinema than the theatre."*

honest

*Mrs Ghandi told us that it is always best to be **honest**.*

ANTONYM: close

opposite (1) ADJECTIVE

If things are **opposite**, they are completely different.

conflicting

*The journalists were receiving **conflicting** reports about how the talks were going.*

contrary

***Contrary** to what people thought, the old man was very generous to charity.*

contrasting

***Contrasting** with last year's disaster, the school play was a great success this year.*

opposing

*We were friends even though we had **opposing** points of view.*

ANTONYM: alike

opposite (2) NOUN

If people or things are **opposites**, they are completely different from each other.

contrary

*Aditi thought that she had done badly in the test, but she had, on the **contrary**, done well.*

converse

*Three times two is six, and the **converse** is also true.*

reverse

*If ever I ask my brother to do something, he always does the **reverse**.*

✔ If you say the opposite of what someone has said, you **contradict** them.

order (1) VERB

If you **order** someone to do something, you tell them firmly to do it.

command

*Lord Raglan **commanded** his light brigade to charge the Russian guns.*

direct

*The coach **directed** all the players to say nothing to the newspapers.*

instruct

*Mrs Caruso **instructed** us to walk along the cliff path in single file.*

order (2) VERB

When you **order** something, you ask for it to be brought or sent to you.

apply for

*My older brother has **applied for** his provisional driving licence.*

book

*Dad **booked** our train tickets in advance.*

request

*Mr Kwami **requested** some new equipment for the sports hall.*

order (3) NOUN

An **order** is a command given by someone in authority.

command

*For disobeying the **command** of his officer, the airman was dismissed.*

instruction

*The boss's **instructions** were to finish the job whatever the cost.*

ordinary ADJECTIVE

Something that is **ordinary** is not special or different in any way.

conventional

*Gran likes a **conventional** hairstyle.*

normal

*It is quite **normal** for people to have sleepless nights now and then.*

routine

*"Don't worry, madam," the police officer said. "It's just a **routine** enquiry."*

standard

*"At the cinema, even a **standard** size of popcorn would feed a regiment," laughed Dad.*

usual

*It seemed like a **usual** Saturday, but then something unexpected happened.*

ANTONYM: unusual or rare

A
B
C
D
E
F
G
H
I
J
K
L
M
N
O
P
Q
R
S
T
U
V
W
X
Y
Z

organize (1) VERB

If you **organize** something, you plan and arrange it.

arrange
*Mum **arranged** a surprise party for Dad's 40th birthday.*

coordinate
*Our class was asked to **coordinate** the preparation of the hall ready for speech day.*

direct
*Dad **directs** plays for the local drama group.*

manage
***Managing** a sports team is never an easy job.*

plan
*My sister and her fiancé **planned** their wedding reception in great detail.*

organize (2) VERB

If you **organize** a group of things, you arrange them in a sensible order.

arrange
*Dawn enjoyed **arranging** the pottery sheep in a different order.*

catalogue
*It took ages to **catalogue** all the books in the school library.*

classify
*Mrs Zubin asked us to **classify** the flowers according to colour.*

sort
*Before mail is delivered, it is **sorted** into areas, then towns, then streets.*

ANTONYM: jumble

other ADJECTIVE

Other people or things are different from those already mentioned.

additional
*The general called for **additional** troops to reinforce the lines.*

alternative
*"Is there an **alternative** date we could travel on?" Mum asked.*

further
*Mrs Given asked us if we had any **further** suggestions.*

outfit NOUN

An **outfit** is a set of clothes.

clothes
*Brad didn't really bother about what sort of **clothes** he wore.*

costume
*You should have seen my sister's fancy-dress **costume**!*

gear
*"If you're going sailing, don't forget your wet-weather **gear**," Mum called.*

kit
*I left my sports **kit** in the changing room.*

outing NOUN

An **outing** is a trip made for pleasure.

excursion
*The coach company runs **excursions** to all sorts of places.*

jaunt
*Dad fancied a **jaunt**, so off we all went to the seaside.*

trip
*Before we went on our class **trip**, we had lots of work to prepare for it.*

outside (1) NOUN

The **outside** of something is the part that surrounds or encloses the rest of it.

exterior
*The tatty **exterior** of the old hotel gave the wrong impression.*

face
*On the **face** of it, the problem looked simple.*

surface
*The outer **surface** of the rocket is designed to withstand terrific heat.*

ANTONYM: inside

outside (2) ADJECTIVE

Something that is **outside** is not inside.

exterior
*My brother was up a ladder finishing the **exterior** paintwork.*

external
***External** doors have to be thicker and sturdier than internal ones.*

outdoor
We had a scrumptious picnic before the **outdoor** *concert.*

outer
The castle's **outer** *wall had slits, through which arrows were fired.*

ANTONYM: inner or inside

over (1) ADJECTIVE
Something that is **over** is completely finished.

at an end
The term was **at an end**, *and the holidays stretched before us.*

complete
The work of restoring the old farmhouse is now **complete**.

concluded
With business **concluded**, *the two women were pleased to head home.*

finished
With his career **finished** *because of ill health, the politician retired to the country.*

over (2) PREPOSITION
Something that is **over**, is more than what is required.

above
The driver was stopped for travelling at a speed **above** *the speed limit.*

higher than
I was very pleased when I got a mark **higher than** *the one I had expected in the test.*

in excess of
The lottery winner received a sum **in excess of** *10 million pounds.*

ANTONYM: under

own ADJECTIVE
If something is your **own**, it belongs to you or is associated with you.

personal
My **personal** *opinion is that the film was dull.*

private
Behind the locked door was the duke's **private** *suite of rooms.*

A
B
C
D
E
F
G
H
I
J
K
L
M
N
O
P
Q
R
S
T
U
V
W
X
Y
Z

Pp

pad NOUN
A **pad** is a set of sheets of paper glued together at one end.

jotter
*I couldn't understand the notes I'd scribbled in my **jotter**.*

notebook
*Writing in his **notebook**, the policeman took down details from the witness.*

writing pad
*My **writing pad** has holes punched in it, so that pages can be filed.*

pain NOUN
Pain is a feeling of discomfort and hurt in your body, caused by an illness or injury.

ache
*The **ache** in Gran's leg improved overnight.*

discomfort
*Sitting in the same seat for hours often causes **discomfort**.*

soreness
*Marina had a lot of **soreness** in her legs when she finished the marathon.*

twinge
*A sudden **twinge** made me stop and hold my arm for a moment.*

✔ Words for severe pain include **agony**, **distress** and **suffering**.

painful (1) ADJECTIVE
Something that is **painful** causes physical pain.

aching
*I had an **aching** side from laughing so hard.*

agonizing
*Marlon said that when he fractured his knee the pain was **agonizing**.*

excruciating
*You could tell from Mum's face that the pain was **excruciating**.*

sore
*With a **sore** throat, Almira was in no condition to join the choir.*

tender
*My thumb was **tender** for days after I slammed it in the door.*

throbbing
*The pop star's ears were **throbbing** with the screams of the crowd.*

ANTONYM: painless or pain-free

painful (2) ADJECTIVE
Something that is **painful** causes emotional pain.

agonizing
*Dad had an **agonizing** wait to know if he'd got the job.*

distressing
*It must be **distressing** for the police to have to break bad news to people.*

upsetting
*The girl's spiteful remarks were deeply **upsetting** to her friends.*

paint VERB
If you **paint** a picture of someone or something, you make a picture of them using paint.

depict
*In The Fighting Temeraire, Turner **depicts** a heroic old ship being towed to the shipyard.*

portray
*I tried to **portray** Khalil's face, but his skin ended up tomato-coloured.*

pair NOUN
A **pair** is two things of the same type, often meant to be used together.

couple
*In the race, a **couple** of horses threw their riders.*

duo
*Comic-book characters Batman and Robin were known as "The Dynamic **Duo**".*

twosome
*I call my big sister and her friend "the gruesome **twosome**".*

pale ADJECTIVE
If someone or something is **pale**, they are not strong or bright in colour.

ashen
*I could tell something was terribly wrong by my mum's **ashen** face.*

colourless
*The sun had bleached the curtains until they were fairly **colourless**.*

faded
***Faded** from being sat on by a million people, the cinema seats were past their best.*

light
*The shirt was a **light** shade of blue.*

wan
*By the end of winter I always look a bit **wan**.*

panic (1) VERB
If you **panic**, you become so afraid or anxious that you cannot act sensibly.

become hysterical
*My aunt almost **became hysterical** when she lost her dog.*

go to pieces
*My cousin never **goes to pieces** in a crisis.*

lose your nerve
*The parachute jumper **lost his nerve** and stayed on board the plane.*

panic (2) NOUN
Panic is a sudden strong feeling of fear or anxiety.

alarm
*Filled with **alarm**, Keifer realized that he only had one way of escape.*

dismay
*With **dismay** Amitava saw the child run out into the road.*

fright
*When the lion sprang forward, the antelope scattered in **fright**.*

hysteria
***Hysteria** spread through the crowd and people started screaming and crying.*

terror
*The mountaineers were struck with **terror** as they saw the avalanche heading towards them.*

pant VERB
If you **pant**, you take short, quick breaths through your mouth.

gasp
*I was **gasping** by the end of the race.*

puff
*The large lady **puffed** up the hill, only to see the bus disappearing.*

wheeze
*With her asthma, Lydia used her inhaler to stop herself **wheezing**.*

parcel NOUN
A **parcel** is something wrapped up in paper.

package
*A white van delivered a mystery **package** addressed to my dad.*

packet
*At my party Mum brought out a huge **packet** for pass-the-parcel.*

part (1) NOUN
A **part** of something is a piece of it, and not all of it.

component
*There were several different **components** to the board game.*

element
*A big **element** of success in any sport is the will to win.*

fraction
*Kym won the egg and spoon race by a **fraction** of a second.*

fragment
*We kept finding **fragments** of glass for days after I'd dropped the bottle.*

portion
*"Just a small **portion** of pie for me, please," Kristin said.*

segment
*Oranges divide easily into **segments**.*

ANTONYM: whole

Part of	
…a book	chapter, passage, extract
…a journey	stage
…a meal	course
…a play	scene, act
…a poem	line, verse
…a song	verse, chorus

A
B
C
D
E
F
G
H
I
J
K
L
M
N
O
P
Q
R
S
T
U
V
W
X
Y
Z

part (2) NOUN
Part of a business or organization is a section of it.

branch
*My mum works in the local **branch** of a bank.*

department
*In any big store, my sister always heads for the toy **department**.*

division
*Dad's company is just one **division** of a huge corporation.*

section
*The **section** where Dad works deals with the staff wages.*

part (3) NOUN
A **part** of a place is an area or section of it.

area
*One **area** of the lawn was brown where Ian had sprinkled weedkiller.*

district
*Cities are divided up into many **districts**.*

region
*Brittany is a large **region** of western France.*

zone
*At an airport, there are clearly marked **zones** where planes park.*

part (4) NOUN
A **part** is one of the roles in a play or film.

character
*The main **character** in Shakespeare's play* Hamlet *is the Prince.*

role
*We thought that the actress was excellent in the **role** of the Princess.*

take part in VERB
If you **take part in** an activity, you do it together with other people.

be involved in
*My mum **is involved in** some charity work.*

join in
*It took some time for the shy boy to **join in** with the game.*

participate in
*Mrs Nemeth wants the school to **participate in** an area quiz.*

play a part in
*Through his alertness, Ricky **played a part in** saving the yachtsman's life.*

partly ADVERB
Partly can mean to some extent, but not completely.

partially
*From our seats the view of the stage was **partially** blocked by a pillar.*

somewhat
*We were **somewhat** surprised to find a stray dog on our doorstep.*

to some extent
*Although I didn't start it, **to some extent** the argument was my fault.*

up to a point
*"I agree with you **up to a point**," said Mr Blake, " but it's not as simple as that."*

ANTONYM: completely

party (1) NOUN
A **party** is a social occasion when people meet to enjoy themselves, often in order to celebrate something.

celebration
*The evening was a **celebration** of Gran and Grandad's silver wedding anniversary.*

get-together
*That night, Mum was going to a **get-together** with her office friends.*

reception
*It was a brilliant wedding **reception**, with mountains of tasty food.*

party (2) NOUN
A **party** is a group of people who are doing something together.

crew
*In a theatre, it is the stage **crew**'s job to move the scenery.*

gang
*Most of the original canals were hand-dug by **gangs** of workmen.*

squad
*Major Benjamin sent an explosives **squad** to blow up the bridge.*

team
*Working as a **team**, we soon solved the problem.*

pass (1) VERB
If you **pass** someone or something, you go past them without stopping or you exceed them.

exceed
*Dad was fined for **exceeding** the speed limit.*

go beyond
*The train **went beyond** the platform before it stopped, and had to reverse.*

overtake
*Did you see that driver **overtake** on a bend?*

surpass
*The quality of our work **surpassed** Mrs Mistry's expectations.*

pass (2) VERB
If you **pass** an examination, you are successful in it.

qualify
*After taking her final exams, my aunt **qualified** as a doctor.*

succeed
*After three attempts at the driving test, my brother **succeeded**.*

ANTONYM: fail

pass (3) VERB
If you **pass** something to someone, you give it to them.

convey
*Mr Djemba asked me to **convey** his thanks to my parents.*

give
*I paid the shopkeeper and she **gave** the bag of shopping to me.*

send
*The ice hockey goalkeeper **sent** the puck across to the winger.*

transfer
*Picking up the ball, the fielder **transferred** it to her right hand.*

transmit
*A spy was caught **transmitting** messages to the enemy.*

past (1) NOUN
The **past** is the period of time before the present.

days gone by
*In **days gone by**, cars had to have a man walking in front of them with a flag.*

former times
*Leslie's family were wealthy cotton manufacturers in **former times**.*

long ago
*The old men told stories of **long ago**.*

olden days OLD-FASHIONED
*In **olden days**, travel was either by horse or on foot.*

the old days
*Gran often tells me about **the old days**, when rock'n'roll first started.*

yesteryear OLD-FASHIONED
*Some people look back fondly on **yesteryear**.*

ANTONYM: future

past (2) ADJECTIVE
If you say someone is a **past** pupil, athlete and so on, you mean that they were once that.

ex-
*The soccer coach was an **ex**-miner.*

former
*As a **former** pupil of the school, my mum still knows some of the teachers.*

previous
*Apparently, the **previous** head teacher, Mrs Kirkland, was a curious character*

ANTONYM: current or present

pattern NOUN
A **pattern** is a design of shapes repeated at regular intervals.

decoration
*Round my story I drew a **decoration** in a border.*

design
*Wedgwood pottery has a distinctive blue and white **design**.*

motif
*My bedroom curtains have a rose **motif**.*

pay

pay (1) VERB

If you **pay**, you give someone money in exchange for something.

cough up INFORMAL

"Come on, **cough up!**" my brother told me after I lost the bet.

recompense

Dad **recompensed** Mr Ghosh for the window I had broken with my ball.

settle

Working overtime for some weeks, my cousin was able to **settle** his debts.

pay (2) VERB

If it **pays** to do something, it is to your advantage to do it.

be worthwhile

The effort you put into school now will **be worthwhile** in the future.

benefit

The tennis coaching really **benefited** Simon.

pay (3) NOUN

Someone's **pay** is the money they receive for working.

earnings

I've no idea what my parents' **earnings** are.

income

Mr Micawber wisely thought that one's **income** should be more than one's spending.

salary

A person's **salary** is paid monthly into their bank account.

wages

Wages are often paid weekly, and perhaps in cash.

peace NOUN

Peace is a state of undisturbed calm and quiet.

calm

When the last pupil departed, Mr Kiely felt an inner **calm** descend.

quiet

"While you're reading we'll have absolute **quiet**," Mrs Enckleman insisted.

silence

At the dead of night, there was **silence**.

stillness

City people either love or hate the **stillness** of the countryside.

tranquillity

The **tranquillity** of the hills was shattered by the roar of a jet fighter.

✔ If a country is at **peace**, it is not at war. Another word that sounds like peace is **piece**.

peaceful ADJECTIVE

Someone or something that is **peaceful** is quiet and calm.

placid

My sweet little sister is a very **placid** child.

restful

The ballet music from Swan Lake is very **restful**.

serene

The baby looked very **serene** asleep in his cot.

tranquil

With no wind, the lake was **tranquil**, reflecting the hills beyond.

undisturbed

My mum works night shifts and likes to be **undisturbed** during the day.

peculiar ADJECTIVE

Something **peculiar** is strange and unusual.

bizarre

The fire-eater on the unicycle made a **bizarre** spectacle.

extraordinary

It's **extraordinary** that some people don't realize how wonderful books are.

odd

"That's **odd**," Ted remarked. "There's someone in the derelict cottage."

weird

"It is **weird** to think that, two days from now, we will be on holiday," my best friend said.

peep VERB

If you **peep** at something, you have a quick, secretive look at it, or you look at it through a small opening.

peek

"This is my wedding dress, so no **peeking!**" my big sister said.

snatch a glimpse
*We managed to **snatch a glimpse** of the film star through the crowd.*

sneak a look
*Carmel **sneaked a look** through the window to catch a glimpse of her birthday cake.*

pen (1) NOUN
A **pen** is an instrument with a pointed end used for writing with ink.

✔ A **pen friend** is someone living in a different place or country whom you write to regularly, although you may never have met each other.

> **Some types of pen:**
> ballpoint pen   fountain pen
> Biro™   marker
> felt-tip pen   quill OLD-FASHIONED

pen (2) NOUN
A **pen** is a small, fenced area where farm animals are kept.

> **A pen for**
> ...pigs   **sty**
> ...sheep   **fold**
> ...cattle   **cattle pen, cowshed, byre**
> ...horses   **loose box, stable**
> ...hens   **coop**

people (1) PLURAL NOUN
People are human beings – men, women and children.

humans
Humans, unlike other creatures, walk upright on two legs.

mankind
Mankind is made up of many races.

people (2) NOUN
The **people** of a particular country or race are all the men, women and children of that country or race.

citizens
*In 1789, the **citizens** of Paris rose up against the king.*

inhabitants
*The **inhabitants** of Manchester are known as Mancunians.*

population
*By 2025, three-quarters of the world's **population** will live in cities.*

public
*This path is for the **public** to walk on.*

perfect ADJECTIVE
Something that is **perfect** is as good as it possibly can be.

faultless
*The ballerina gave a **faultless** dancing display.*

flawless
*I never know how solo musicians manage to give **flawless** performances.*

immaculate
*Dad looked **immaculate** as he prepared for my sister's wedding.*

impeccable
*The old duke had **impeccable** manners.*

ANTONYM: faulty or imperfect

perhaps ADVERB
You use **perhaps** when you are not sure if something is true or possible.

maybe
*"Hmmm, **maybe** I'll go," Mitchi said, "but **maybe** I won't."*

possibly
*It was **possibly** the best drink I had ever tasted.*

permission NOUN
If you have **permission** to do something, you are allowed to do it.

approval
*We asked for the head teacher's **approval** to have a class charity sale.*

authorization
*"No entry without **authorization**", the sign read.*

consent
*Mum and Dad gave their **consent** for me to go on the school trip.*

a
b
c
d
e
f
g
h
i
j
k
l
m
n
o
p
q
r
s
t
u
v
w
x
y
z

person NOUN

A **person** is a man, woman or child.

human

Before 1969, no **human** had stood on the moon.

human being

A **human being** is an amazingly complex and wonderful piece of machinery.

individual

"Which wretched **individual** did this?" Mr Wright thundered.

soul

Not a **soul** was on the beach.

personal ADJECTIVE

Something **personal** belongs or relates to a particular person.

individual

On the plane we were all given **individual** meals on trays.

private

Bhavin and I didn't dare go in the office marked "**Private**".

persuade VERB

If you **persuade** someone to do something, or **persuade** them that something is true, you get them to do or believe it by giving them good reasons.

cajole

My mother **cajoled** me into going shopping.

coax

The donkey took a lot of **coaxing** before it would shift.

convince

I was glad that Marjani **convinced** me to go to the cinema with her, as I enjoyed the film.

talk someone into

Chris **talked me into** playing cards.

phone VERB

See **telephone**

phoney or **phony** ADJECTIVE

Something that is **phoney** is false, not genuine and meant to trick.

bogus

The police warned people in the area to beware of **bogus** callers.

counterfeit

You could tell it was **counterfeit** money, as the ink rubbed off.

fake

I thought the whole programme was **fake**. No one would behave like that!

false

Great grandma puts her **false** teeth in a glass by her bed.

forged

The spy travelled the world with various **forged** passports.

imitation

The house was clad in **imitation** stone – it looked awful.

ANTONYM: authentic or real or genuine

pick (1) VERB

If you **pick** someone or something, you choose them.

choose

I **chose** a creamy chocolate with a swirly top.

decide on

Dad and Mum couldn't **decide on** where to go for our holidays.

nominate

Our class **nominated** Kemal as team captain.

opt for

My brother **opted for** History and French at secondary school.

select

When buying melons, it's important to **select** ripe ones.

vote for

Taylor was upset because only one or two of us **voted for** her.

pick (2) VERB

If you **pick** a flower or a fruit, you break it off from where it is growing.

gather

We **gathered** a lovely bunch of daffodils for our mother.

harvest

Before wheat can be **harvested**, it has to be a golden colour.

pluck
*Marylyn **plucked** an apple from the tree.*

pick on VERB
If you **pick on** someone, you treat them unkindly and unfairly.

bully
*Cattle in a herd will often **bully** a cow that is in some way weaker.*

tease
*When he annoys me, I **tease** my big brother about his messy hair.*

torment
*My brother gets his own back by **tormenting** me because I'm little.*

picture NOUN
A **picture** is a drawing, painting, photograph or television image of someone or something.

illustration
*Roald Dahl's books have lively **illustrations**.*

image
*Will had a mental **image** of his father as an Arctic explorer.*

sketch
*Some painters make a **sketch** before they start to paint.*

piece NOUN
A **piece** of something is a portion or part of it.

bit
*"Anybody got a **bit** of paper?" Martin asked from behind me.*

chunk
*The hungry traveller ripped a **chunk** of bread from the loaf.*

fragment
*When the microwave overheated, **fragments** of my pizza splattered everywhere.*

morsel
*"Not a **morsel** of food will I give you, boy!" boomed the workhouse supervisor.*

share
*Everyone in the family had a **share** of Mum's lottery win.*

✔ Another word that sounds like piece is **peace**.

See **part (1)**

pierce VERB
If a sharp object **pierces** something, it goes through it, making a hole.

bore
*Dad's drill **bored** smoothly through the wall and into the water pipe.*

penetrate
*As soon as the drill **penetrated** the pipe, water gushed everywhere.*

prick
*When nurses test your blood, they **prick** your thumb.*

puncture
*The piece of protruding metal **punctured** the tyre.*

stab
*The upturned drawing pin **stabbed** the sole of my foot when I trod on it.*

pile (1) NOUN
A **pile** is a quantity of things lying on top of one another.

heap
*All round the garden lay **heaps** of leaves that we'd raked up.*

mass
*In the angler's tin was a **mass** of wriggling maggots.*

mound
*In order to create the slide in the playground, a bulldozer piled up a **mound** of earth.*

mountain
*Within the shed was a huge **mountain** of turnips.*

stack
*The **stack** of baked-bean cans toppled noisily to the shop floor.*

pile (2) VERB
If you **pile** things somewhere, you put them on top of one another.

heap
*Gran would persist in **heaping** scrambled egg on my plate.*

stack
*After Dad had **stacked** the hay bales, we played commandoes on top of them.*

A
B
C
D
E
F
G
H
I
J
K
L
M
N
O
P
Q
R
S
T
U
V
W
X
Y
Z

pill NOUN

A **pill** is a small, round tablet of medicine that you swallow.

capsule
*I don't mind taking **capsules**, because they slip down easily.*

tablet
*"Take one **tablet** twice a day," the nurse said.*

pinch (1) VERB

If you **pinch** something, you squeeze it between your thumb and first finger.

nip
*Jana has the annoying habit of **nipping** me to get my attention.*

squeeze
*My brother is always **squeezing** his spots.*

tweak
*When my Dad's asleep, I **tweak** his beard.*

pinch (2) VERB INFORMAL

If someone **pinches** something, they steal it.

pilfer
***Pilfering** is a problem in some supermarkets.*

snatch
*Thieves **snatched** the lady's bag and ran off with it.*

steal
*"Who has **stolen** my golden coins?" boomed the distraught ogre.*

swipe INFORMAL
*"Okay, who has **swiped** my pencil?" I asked.*

walk off with
*My friend Leila had **walked off with** my pen.*

pitch NOUN

A **pitch** is an area of ground marked out for playing a game such as football or cricket.

ground
*When we arrived at the **ground**, the rain was teeming down.*

playing field
*The team ran onto the **playing field**.*

sports field
*Recently, the **sports field** has been extended.*

✔ Sports such as tennis and badminton are played on a **court**.

pity (1) NOUN

Pity is a feeling of sadness and concern for someone.

compassion
*The duke couldn't help feeling **compassion** for the penniless widow.*

concern
*The father's **concern** for his sick child showed in his face.*

sympathy
*Anyone who teaches my big sister has my utmost **sympathy**!*

pity (2) VERB

If you **pity** someone, you feel sorry for them.

feel sorry for
*Mum **felt sorry for** the poorly old gentleman and took him round some soup.*

sympathize with
*Grace **sympathized with** anyone who was out in the storm.*

place (1) NOUN

A **place** is a particular point, position, building or area.

location
*"Please give me your exact **location**," the radio operator said.*

position
*From our **position** in the circle, we had a great view of the stage.*

site
*"This field," the guide said, "was the **site** of a battle 600 years ago."*

spot
*We found a lovely **spot** by the river for our picnic.*

✔ If you talk about the place where you live, you could be talking about your **house**, **area**, **city**, **town**, **village** or **region**.

place (2) VERB

If you **place** something somewhere, you put it there.

deposit
*I **deposited** my book on Mrs Jalali's desk and went out to play.*

lay
*"I'll now call upon the mayoress to **lay** the first brick," the chairman said.*

position
*We **positioned** ourselves so that we could see the finish of the race.*

stand
*The painter **stood** his ladder against the wall and got into his overalls.*

station
*Guards were **stationed** every 10 metres along the route of the procession.*

✔ **Lay** and **lie** are often confused. Remember that you **lie** down and hens **lay** eggs.

See **leave (3)**

take place PHRASE
*When something **takes place**, it happens.*

come about
*"It all **came about** when I was in the air force," Gramps began.*

happen
*"At what time did the accident **happen**?" asked the nurse.*

occur
*Curiously, Shakespeare's death **occurred** on the same date as his birth.*

plain (1) ADJECTIVE
Something that is **plain** is very simple in style, with no pattern or decoration.

bare
*The room had **bare** wooden floors, but still felt cosy.*

basic
*Cadets wear a **basic** uniform with few badges.*

simple
*Monks and nuns wear very **simple** clothes, known as habits.*

ANTONYM: fancy or ornate

plain (2) ADJECTIVE
Something that is **plain**, is obvious or easy to understand.

apparent
*It was **apparent** that something was wrong with the plane's engine.*

clear
*The instructions on the box were very **clear**.*

distinct
*A **distinct** sound of voices travelled across the quiet lake.*

evident
*Looking at the time, it was **evident** that we were going to miss the bus.*

obvious
*The relief on the passengers' faces when the plane landed was **obvious** to see.*

unmistakable
*There was the **unmistakable** smell of baking in the air.*

ANTONYM: unclear

plan (1) NOUN
A **plan** is a method of achieving something that has been worked out beforehand.

plot
*The originators of the Gunpowder **Plot** planned to blow up Parliament.*

scheme
*Fortunately, the baddies' dastardly **scheme** failed.*

strategy
*The footballers' **strategy** had taken months to perfect.*

plan (2) VERB
If you **plan** something, you decide in detail what you are going to do.

arrange
*I helped Mum **arrange** my little brother's birthday party.*

devise
*The duke **devised** a cunning plan to escape from the castle dungeons.*

draft
*Mrs Schwarz always makes us **draft** our stories before we actually write them.*

prepare
*Because of the weather forecast, no one had **prepared** for rain.*

think up
*Dylan and I **thought up** an idea for a den.*

plan (3) VERB

If you **plan** to do something, you intend to do it.

aim

*My sister **aims** to join the navy.*

intend

*Meredith's brother **intends** to train as a nurse.*

mean

*Dad keeps asking me what I **mean** to do with my life.*

propose

*"So, how do you **propose** to pay for this new computer game you want?" asked Mum.*

planet NOUN

A **planet** is a large sphere in space that orbits a sun.

✔ **Earth** and **Mars** are both planets that revolve around our sun.

Something natural that orbits a planet or star is a **satellite**. The **moon** is a satellite of Earth.

> The main planets in our solar system are:
> Mercury (nearest the sun)
> Venus
> Earth
> Mars
> Jupiter
> Saturn
> Uranus
> Neptune
> Pluto (farthest from the sun)

play (1) VERB

When people **play**, they take part in games or use toys for fun.

amuse yourself

*Babies often **amuse themselves** with rattles and other noisy things.*

enjoy yourself

*Dad was quietly **enjoying himself** with my train set.*

entertain yourself

*We were told to **entertain ourselves** outside for a while.*

frolic OLD-FASHIONED

*The young children **frolicked** in the meadow.*

romp

*Gran said that in her young days, they used to **romp** around in the hay field.*

play (2) VERB

If you **play** someone at a game or sport, you compete against them.

challenge

*Our neighbouring school **challenged** us to a game of netball.*

compete against

*Our school will **compete against** Gorton in the quiz final.*

take on

*My brother and I **took on** Dad and Uncle Mansur at pool.*

play (3) VERB

If an actor **plays** a character in a play or film, they perform that role.

act the part of

*It was great! When we read it aloud, Euan had to **act the part of** Mrs Twit.*

play the role of

*The director was not sure who would **play the role of** the King.*

portray

*My sister **portrayed** Sleeping Beauty well.*

play (4) NOUN

A **play** is a story acted out in the theatre, on the radio or on television.

drama

*Most **dramas** from ancient Greece have a chorus of women in them.*

performance

*In all, the theatre company put on three **performances**, plus a dress rehearsal.*

show

*The end-of-term **show** was a great success.*

✔ Types of plays include **comedy**, **farce**, **musical**, **pantomime**, **revue** and **tragedy**.

player NOUN

A **player** is someone who plays a game or sport.

competitor

*It is important to be a keen **competitor** if you want to win at sports.*

contestant
*"Bring the next **contestants** in, please!" called the game-show host.*

participant
*Grandad was no longer a **participant** in cricket, but enjoyed watching it.*

playful ADJECTIVE
A person or animal who is **playful** is friendly and light-hearted.

frisky
*Our cat was very **frisky** when we first had her.*

lively
*Mr Hislop is a **lively** teacher, and we've always learnt a lot by the end of his lessons.*

mischievous
*My **mischievous** sister is always playing tricks on me.*

ANTONYM: serious

pleasant (1) ADJECTIVE
If a person is **pleasant**, they are nice and their company is enjoyable.

amiable
*Fortunately, Mum thinks most of my friends are very **amiable**.*

charming
*The landlord was **charming** – always well-mannered and very humorous.*

cheerful
*You could guarantee that the lady in the corner shop would be **cheerful**.*

friendly
*"A **friendly** smile goes a long way," my granny says.*

likeable
*I find Mrs Walker more **likeable** than our previous teacher.*

pleasant (2) ADJECTIVE
If an event is **pleasant**, it is enjoyable.

delightful
*"It is **delightful** to meet you," Mum said as our new neighbours walked in.*

enjoyable
*Bhupendra and I had an **enjoyable** time skimming stones over the water.*

lovely
*The weather was **lovely**: plenty of sun and a gentle breeze.*

ANTONYM: unpleasant

please VERB
If something **pleases** you, it makes you feel happy and satisfied.

amuse
*"Something obviously **amuses** you," said Mr Murray, somewhat sneeringly.*

delight
*The firework display **delighted** the crowds.*

entertain
*The puppet show **entertained** dozens of children for an hour.*

give pleasure to
*Concerts **give pleasure to** many people.*

satisfy
*The inspector was **satisfied** by what she saw in our school.*

ANTONYM: displease or annoy or upset

pleased ADJECTIVE
If you are **pleased** with something, it makes you feel happy and satisfied.

contented
*Even though it was a few years old, John was very **contented** with his car.*

delighted
*Dad wrote to say how **delighted** he was with the new conservatory.*

glad
*We were very **glad** to get home after our long journey.*

over the moon INFORMAL
*"I'm **over the moon** with our win," the coach purred.*

satisfied
*My brother is never **satisfied**, whatever he is given for his birthday.*

thrilled
*The millionaire summoned the chef to say how **thrilled** he was with the meal.*

ANTONYM: dissatisfied

pleasure NOUN

Pleasure is a feeling of happiness, satisfaction or enjoyment.

amusement

*TV provides **amusement**, but it's no substitute for getting out and doing things yourself.*

delight

*To her **delight**, Nimah passed the piano exam.*

enjoyment

*It's amazing what **enjoyment** you can get from just throwing a ball about.*

happiness

*Many people find **happiness** in helping others.*

satisfaction

*Mum gained great **satisfaction** from the quilt she made.*

plenty NOUN

If you have **plenty** of something, you have more than enough for your needs.

a great deal

*Mrs Suleiman needs **a great deal** of patience to teach our class!*

an abundance

*Deserts have **an abundance** of sand but a shortage of water.*

masses INFORMAL

*It was a brilliant tea, with **masses** of cakes.*

plot (1) NOUN

A **plot** is a secret plan made by a group of people.

conspiracy

*Several plotters joined the **conspiracy** to overthrow the king.*

plan

*The **plan** was to pretend we were going out, then sneak back for the surprise party.*

scheme

*The traitors' **scheme** failed and they all had to flee the country.*

plot (2) NOUN

The **plot** of a film, novel or play is the story.

narrative

*The **narrative** of the book was rather complicated but very exciting.*

story line

*For a soap opera, one team decides the **story line**, while another team writes the script.*

plot (3) VERB

If people **plot** to do something, they plan it secretly.

conspire

*Three of us **conspired** to have a midnight feast, but it would take a lot of planning if we were to pull it off.*

plan

*Sauron **planned** to take possession of the all-important ring.*

scheme

*Flashman was always **scheming** to make life hard for others.*

plug VERB

If you **plug** a hole, you block it with something.

block

*Fallen leaves **blocked** the drain cover and prevented the rain from draining away.*

seal

*Mum used some white gooey stuff to **seal** the gap round the bath.*

stop up

*Beavers **stop up** whole rivers by building dams made of trees.*

poem NOUN

A **poem** is a piece of writing, usually arranged in short rhythmic lines, with words chosen for their sound or impact.

Some types of poem:

acrostic poem	nonsense poem
ballad	nursery rhyme
cinquain	ode
haiku	sonnet
limerick	tanka

point (1) NOUN

A **point** is the thin, sharp end of something such as a needle or knife.

prong

*I accidentally jabbed myself with the **prong** of my fork.*

spike
As bills are paid, the restaurant manager puts them on a spike.

tip
The tip of the cardinal's sword grazed the musketeer's cheek.

point (2) NOUN
A **point** is the purpose or the most important part of something.

aim
The aim of the lesson was to improve our handwriting.

goal
The goal of the jumble sale was to raise money for charity.

object
I couldn't quite see the object of the game until I had read the instructions.

purpose
"What's the purpose of that twiddly bit?" I enquired of the salesperson.

point (3) NOUN
A **point** is a particular time.

instant
At that instant, Ron disappeared through the apparently solid wall.

moment
We had reached the moment when the winner would be announced.

point (4) VERB
If you **point** at or to something, you hold out your finger towards it to show where it is.

draw attention to
Grandpa drew attention to a hawk hovering nearby.

indicate
The sign indicated to the right for the city centre and left for other directions.

poisonous ADJECTIVE
A **poisonous** substance will harm or kill you if you swallow it or absorb it.

toxic
The sign warned that the tanker's cargo was highly toxic.

venomous
The cobra is a particularly venomous snake.

ANTONYM: harmless or nontoxic

poke VERB
If you **poke** someone or something, you give them a push with your finger or a sharp object.

dig
I had to dig Zaid gently in the ribs to keep him awake through the film.

elbow
Kylie elbowed me, so I elbowed her back.

jab
"If you jab me with that pencil again …", I warned Dean.

nudge
I nudged my pal to warn him that Mrs Hussein was watching.

prod
As I tried to sleep, my kid sister kept prodding me.

police officer NOUN
A **police officer** is a member of the police force.

> Types of police officer:
> constable   inspector
> detective   sergeant

polite ADJECTIVE
Someone who is **polite** has good manners and is not rude to other people.

courteous
The hotel manager welcomed the guests in a courteous manner.

respectful
It's important to be respectful to older people.

well-behaved
All the children were well-behaved when they met the queen.

well-mannered
Well-mannered people remember to say "please" and "thank you".

ANTONYM: impolite or rude

a b c d e f g h i j k l m n o **p** q r s t u v w x y z

pollute

pollute VERB

If something **pollutes** water, air or land, it makes it dirty and dangerous to use or live in.

contaminate

*Farm fertilizers and pesticides sometimes **contaminate** streams.*

foul

*The school had a problem with dogs **fouling** the sports field.*

poison

*Industrial smoke from factories and power plants **poisons** the atmosphere.*

poor (1) ADJECTIVE

Someone who is **poor** has very little money.

badly off

*My parents were quite **badly off** when they were first married.*

broke

*"I'm **broke**," the gambler confessed.*

penniless

*The **penniless** orphan wandered the streets of the city.*

poverty-stricken

*In Victorian times, a lot of families were **poverty-stricken**.*

✔ If someone owes a lot of money they are **in debt**.
If someone cannot pay their debts they are **bankrupt**.

ANTONYM: rich or wealthy

poor (2) ADJECTIVE

Something that is **poor** is of a low quality or standard.

inferior

*Built of **inferior** materials, the flats eventually started to crumble.*

mediocre

*"This is a **mediocre** effort," Mrs Cole warned.*

shoddy

*The factory manager warned that he would not tolerate **shoddy** workmanship.*

unsatisfactory

*"Your potion is distinctly **unsatisfactory**," complained the wizard.*

poor (3) ADJECTIVE

A **poor** person is deserving of pity or unlucky.

miserable

*Thoroughly **miserable**, Ellie and Nadine sat on the steps and wept.*

pathetic

*Begging on the street, the woman and her dog made a **pathetic** sight.*

unfortunate

*The **unfortunate** child had lost both his parents in an accident.*

wretched

*Mr Bumble's workhouse was full of **wretched** children slaving their lives away.*

poorly ADJECTIVE

If you are **poorly**, you feel ill.

off colour

*"I'm feeling a little **off colour**," Mum confided.*

out of sorts INFORMAL

*Linda felt **out of sorts**, and asked if she could stay at home.*

under the weather INFORMAL

*By the end of the day, Miss Taylor really looked **under the weather**.*

See **ill**

popular ADJECTIVE

Someone or something that is **popular** is liked or approved of by a lot of people.

fashionable

*The south of France is very **fashionable** for holidays.*

favourite

*The Caribbean is a **favourite** part of the world for ship cruises.*

in demand

*My brother's band was **in demand** for dances and parties.*

trendy

*They turned the local bank into a **trendy** wine bar.*

well-liked

*Bhoomi's report said she was **well-liked** by others in the class.*

ANTONYM: unpopular

port NOUN

A **port** is a town or area that has a harbour or docks.

docks

*All along the **docks** were huge cranes for shifting containers.*

harbour

*Round the **harbour**, fishermen in oilskins were unloading small boats.*

*See **harbour***

posh ADJECTIVE INFORMAL

Something that is **posh** is smart, fashionable and expensive.

exclusive

*The **exclusive** hotel had a new health spa.*

grand

*The duchess lived in a very **grand** house.*

high-class

*The **high-class** restaurant served wonderful food at astronomical prices.*

luxurious

*Zoë was thrilled with the **luxurious** four-poster bed in her room.*

swanky INFORMAL

*The footballer bought his wife a **swanky** car for her birthday.*

position (1) NOUN

A **position** is the place where someone or something is.

location

*Using the map's grid, you can plot the exact **location** of almost anything.*

site

*"This is the exact **site** of the ancient burial chamber," explained the tour guide.*

whereabouts

*It was quite tricky for the divers to find the **whereabouts** of the old shipwreck.*

position (2) NOUN

When someone or something is in a particular **position**, they are sitting or lying in that way.

posture

*Working at a computer, it's important to have the right **posture**.*

stance

*Maurice has a good batting **stance**.*

position (3) NOUN

The **position** that you are in is the situation that you are in.

circumstances

*Having won the lottery, our neighbour's **circumstances** changed for the better.*

situation

*The soldier was in a serious **situation**.*

possible (1) ADJECTIVE

If something is **possible**, it can be done.

feasible

*"Is it **feasible** to put a window here?" Mum asked the architect.*

practicable

*"It wouldn't be **practicable** to cross the Channel in this weather," the ferry captain announced.*

ANTONYM: impossible

possible (2) ADJECTIVE

If something is **possible**, it can happen.

conceivable

*"It's **conceivable** that the town could flood," the mayor said.*

imaginable

*"For me, the best place **imaginable** to go on holiday is Skegness," Gran told us.*

ANTONYM: impossible

pour (1) VERB

If something **pours** somewhere, it flows there quickly and in large quantities.

cascade

*During the downpour, water **cascaded** from overflowing gutters.*

flow

*The dam is designed so that surplus water **flows** over the top.*

gush

*Water from the broken pipe **gushed** upwards into the street.*

stream

*People **streamed** through the gates and out into the street.*

a b c d e f g h i j k l m n o **p** q r s t u v w x y z

pour (2) VERB

If it is **pouring** with rain, it is raining very heavily.

bucket down INFORMAL
*"Don't go out yet, it's **bucketing down**," my gran warned.*

pelt
*Rain was **pelting** down, so I sheltered in a doorway.*

raining cats and dogs INFORMAL
*We were going to go to the park, but then it started **raining cats and dogs**.*

power (1) NOUN

Power is control over people and events.

authority
*In our school, the head teacher has the most **authority**.*

command
*During the revolution, the army generals seized **command**.*

control
*Dictators are people who have absolute **control** over their country.*

domination
*Goldfinger was intent on world **domination**.*

influence
*The judge was a woman of great **influence**, which she used wisely.*

rule
*In 1645, the **rule** of the English king was broken by Parliament.*

power (2) NOUN

Power is a physical strength.

energy
*Mr Chakrabarty seems to have boundless **energy**.*

force
*Using all her **force**, the woman pushed the broken-down car off the road.*

might
*The wizard's army attacked the fortress with all their **might**.*

strength
*Wrestlers need great **strength** to hurl each other around.*

power (3) NOUN

Your **power** to do something is your ability to do it.

ability
*Mrs Finch reckoned Daksha had the **ability** to be a writer.*

capability
*The submarines had the **capability** to launch missiles.*

potential
*You could see that the young actress had the **potential** to be a star.*

powerful (1) ADJECTIVE

Someone or something that is **powerful** has a lot of strength.

mighty
*The weightlifter flexed his **mighty** muscles.*

robust
*Fortunately, the castle gate was **robust** enough to withstand the ram.*

strong
*The boxer was as **strong** as an ox.*

sturdy
*The camera was mounted on a **sturdy** tripod.*

ANTONYM: puny or weak

powerful (2) ADJECTIVE

Someone or something **powerful** has control or influence over others.

commanding
*Our team was in a **commanding** position at half-time.*

dominant
*The lead singer was the **dominant** member of the pop group.*

influential
*My uncle is an **influential** businessman.*

ANTONYM: powerless

practice NOUN

Practice is regular training or exercise that you do to improve your skill at something.

drill
*Every term the whole school goes through the fire **drill**.*

exercise
*The army **exercise** involved tanks, helicopters and landing craft.*

preparation
*My sister had to do a lot of **preparation** for her part in the play.*

rehearsal
*Doing lots of **rehearsal** can be tough, but the result is worthwhile.*

training
*When they join up, soldiers have to undergo rifle **training**.*

✔ The noun **practice** ends in *ice*.

practise VERB
If you **practise** something, you do it regularly in order to do it better.

go over
*Mrs Murray made us **go over** what we would do if a fire broke out.*

go through
*We **went through** how to line up and file out into the yard in case of fire.*

rehearse
*After **rehearsing** for two hours, we felt more confident.*

train
*The team **trains** hard all week, but rests before a match.*

✔ The verb **practise** ends in *ise*.

praise (1) VERB
If you **praise** someone, you say good things about them, or tell them they have done well.

applaud
*The press **applauded** the passer-by who had dived into the river to save the child.*

compliment
*It was nice of Grandad to **compliment** me on my table manners.*

congratulate
*Mr Silvester **congratulated** Rio on his painting.*

pay tribute to
*At the funeral, a friend **paid tribute to** Grandma's kindness.*

praise (2) NOUN
Praise is what you say or write when you praise someone or something.

compliment
*The head teacher paid me a **compliment** about my work.*

congratulations
*Ratty offered **congratulations** to Toad on his new car.*

tribute
*The number of people at her leaving party was a **tribute** to how much Mrs Ahmed was liked.*

precious (1) ADJECTIVE
Something that is **precious** is important to you and should be looked after or used carefully.

cherished
*"Be careful. That clock is a **cherished** item!" Mum warned.*

treasured
*For many years, the desk had been a **treasured** possession in our family.*

precious (2) ADJECTIVE
Something **precious** is valuable.

priceless
*The jewels were **priceless**, so the duchess only wore them on special occasions.*

valuable
*"Any painting by that artist is now very **valuable**," said the gallery owner.*

*See **expensive***

predict VERB
If you **predict** something, you say what you think will happen in the future.

forecast
*The weather person on the TV **forecasts** a showery day.*

foresee
*Before I'd even lifted the tray, Mum **foresaw** what would happen.*

foretell
*"I'm convinced that some gifted people can **foretell** the future," said Auntie Clare.*

prophesy
*The wizard **prophesied** that a new king would come to the throne.*

prefer VERB

If you **prefer** one thing to another, you like it better than the other thing.

favour

*I **favour** going on holiday to Spain, but Dad wants to go to the Lake District.*

go for

*"Will you **go for** a cola or a lemonade?" Dad asked.*

incline towards

*I would **incline towards** going for a bike ride rather than watching TV.*

prepare VERB

If you **prepare** something, or **prepare** for something, you get it ready or get ready for it.

arrange

*My auntie had **arranged** the party for Saturday afternoon.*

make arrangements

*"Can I rely on you to **make arrangements** for the music?" Sophie asked me.*

organize

*Mum **organized** everything for choir practice in the evening.*

pave the way

*The generals hoped the air strikes would **pave the way** for the land attack.*

present (1) SAID "PREZ-ENT" NOUN

A **present** is something that you give to someone for them to keep.

donation

*The school received a generous **donation** from a former pupil.*

gift

*As a special **gift**, Mum bought Dad a mountain bike.*

offering

*At the temple altar, the Inca priest raised an **offering** to the gods.*

present (2) SAID "PREZ-ENT" ADJECTIVE

If someone is **present** at a place or an event, they are there.

at hand

*Fortunately, a doctor was **at hand** when the lady collapsed.*

in attendance

*Queen Victoria's doctors were **in attendance** at her deathbed.*

on hand

*First-aiders were **on hand** at the festival in case of emergency.*

ANTONYM: absent

present (3) SAID "PRI-ZENT" VERB

If you **present** someone with something, or if you present it to them, you formally give it to them.

bestow

*The king **bestowed** a great honour on the town.*

donate

*It was good of the group to **donate** their fee to the charity.*

grant

*Smiling secretly, the genie offered to **grant** Aladdin three wishes.*

present (4) SAID "PRI-ZENT" VERB

If someone **presents** a show, they put it on.

perform

*Our class **performed** a play for the parents.*

put on

*The orchestra **puts on** an outdoor concert here each summer.*

stage

*London hopes to **stage** the Olympic Games.*

press VERB

If you **press** something, you push or hold it firmly against something else.

compress

*Recycled cardboard is shredded, soaked and **compressed**.*

crush

*Grapes are **crushed** to make grape juice and wine.*

squash

*"If I were an ant, I'd always be afraid of getting **squashed**," said my funny little sister.*

squeeze

*Auntie Betty **squeezed** me so hard I thought I would burst!*

pretend VERB

If you **pretend** that something is the case, you try to make people believe that it is true when it is not.

act as if
When the ball sailed through the window, I **acted as if** nothing had happened.

feign
Graham **feigned** not to have seen the sign: "Do not eat in corridors".

make believe
When I was small, I used to **make believe** my bed was a flying carpet.

✔ To pretend that you are someone else is to **impersonate** them.
To pretend that you are doing an action is to **simulate** it.

pretty (1) ADJECTIVE

If someone or something is **pretty**, they are attractive and pleasant to look at.

attractive
My sister thinks the boy next door is really **attractive**.

beautiful
The ballerina looked **beautiful** in her tutu.

bonny
My little cousin may be a **bonny** baby, but she certainly makes a noise!

good-looking
"If my sister is **good-looking**, I'm a teapot!" said my horrid brother.

lovely
The view from the balcony was **lovely**.

ANTONYM: ugly

pretty (2) ADVERB INFORMAL

Pretty can mean quite or rather.

fairly
Mr Bissu said it was a **fairly** good effort, but that I could improve.

moderately
Lisa was **moderately** happy with her work.

rather
I was **rather** disappointed with my mark in the spelling test.

reasonably
Mum said the hotel bed was **reasonably** comfortable.

somewhat
Frodo was **somewhat** surprised to see Gandalf appear from nowhere.

prevent VERB

If you **prevent** something, you stop it happening.

avert
The Railway Children **averted** a disaster by stopping the train.

block
The government **blocked** the proposal to raise taxes.

foil
"Thanks to a tip-off, police today **foiled** an armed robbery," said the newsreader.

hinder
My baby brother does his best to **hinder** me when I'm working.

impede
Fallen rocks are **impeding** the progress of the rescue workers.

thwart
The plotters were **thwarted** in their attempt to blow up Parliament.

ANTONYM: encourage

previous ADJECTIVE

A **previous** time or thing is one that occurred before the present one.

earlier
The artist's **earlier** work includes some impressive still-life paintings.

former
Dad's car had two **former** owners, but seemed to be in good condition.

past
The school invited all its **past** teachers to the opening ceremony.

preceding
Our family had been away the **preceding** summer.

ANTONYM: following or subsequent

a b c d e f g h i j k l m n o **p** q r s t u v w x y z

price NOUN

A **price** is the amount of money that you pay to buy something.

charge

"That's the standard **charge** for a car service, sir," the garage man said.

cost

"There is a small **cost** for entry to the castle grounds," the tour guide said.

expense

Dad felt that the trip to Disneyland was worth the **expense**.

rate

The **rate** for a haircut has gone up recently.

✔ The price you pay for a journey on a bus, taxi, train or plane is the **fare**.

The price you pay to send a letter or parcel is the **postage**.

The price you pay to use a private road or bridge is a **toll**.

The price you pay to join a club or organization is the membership **fee**.

prick VERB

If you **prick** something, you stick a sharp object into it.

jab

I **jabbed** my thumb on a pair of compasses.

pierce

Although the point had **pierced** my skin, very little blood came out.

puncture

The dagger **punctured** the knight's chain mail but only scratched his chest.

stab

Mum **stabbed** her finger on a thorn when she was pruning the rose bush.

prickly ADJECTIVE

Something that is **prickly** has many sharp, fine points.

sharp

Roses are noted for their lovely smell and their **sharp** thorns.

spiky

Horse chestnuts hide conkers inside **spiky** casings.

spiny

Porcupines are **spiny** creatures with huge pointed quills.

thorny

Inevitably, the ball rolled into the heart of the **thorny** bush.

priest NOUN

A **priest** is someone whose job it is to perform religious ceremonies.

Some types of priest:	
Army or forces	**padre**
Baptist	**pastor**
Buddhist	**lama**
Church of England	**vicar**, **clergyman**, **rector**, **curate**
Hindu	**guru**
Jewish	**rabbi**
Methodist	**minister**
Muslim	**imam**
Roman Catholic	**priest**

prison NOUN

A **prison** is a building where people who have broken the law are locked up as a punishment.

detention centre

The accused woman was sent to a **detention centre** before her trial.

dungeons OLD-FASHIONED

"My **dungeons** await you," said the wicked baron to his enemy.

jail

My mum teaches pottery to the inmates of a local **jail**.

penitentiary AMERICAN

Kimble was a fugitive from the state **penitentiary**.

prisoner NOUN

A **prisoner** is someone who is kept in prison or held in captivity.

captive

In a daring raid, the platoon of brave soldiers released all the **captives**.

convict

Convicts are usually required to do some sort of work in jail.

hostage

*"Bank robbers snatched three **hostages** in an armed raid today," read the newspaper article.*

✔ Someone who is captured by an enemy in a time of war is a **prisoner of war**.

private (1) ADJECTIVE

Something that is **private** is for the use of only one person or group of people, rather than for the general public.

exclusive

*"On this liner, the Royal Suite has its own **exclusive** sun deck," Mum read from the brochure.*

personal

*A letter marked "**personal**" should only be opened by the person to whom it is addressed.*

ANTONYM: public

private (2) ADJECTIVE

Something that is **private** is meant to be kept secret.

confidential

*As it was **confidential** that Mum was expecting a baby, I told no one.*

secret

*Moneypenny told Bond that the information was **secret**, for his ears only.*

ANTONYM: in public

prize NOUN

A **prize** is a reward given to the winner of a competition or game.

award

*Dad's firm received an **award** for the quality of its cheese.*

honour

*"I'm very proud to accept this **honour**," the moist-eyed actress said as she was handed the statuette.*

trophy

*The champion had tears in his eyes as he held the **trophy** aloft.*

✔ The top-money prize in a lottery is known as the **jackpot**.
The money prize that someone wins can be called their **winnings**.

probable ADJECTIVE

Something that is **probable** is likely to happen or likely to be true.

expected

*As trouble was **expected**, there were more police than usual on duty.*

likely

*"It's **likely** we'll have showers today," the weatherman said.*

on the cards INFORMAL

*Gamblers always kid themselves that a big win is **on the cards**.*

✔ When something is so likely it is almost certain, it is **inevitable**.

ANTONYM: improbable

probably ADVERB

If something will **probably** happen, it is likely but not certain to happen.

almost certainly

*Mrs Macumba told the driver we would **almost certainly** need a brief stop.*

doubtless

*"**Doubtless** you've heard today's big news," Mum said.*

in all probability

*United will win the league, **in all probability**.*

presumably

*"You would **presumably** like the box wrapped?" the saleswoman enquired.*

problem (1) NOUN

A **problem** is an unsatisfactory situation that causes difficulties.

complication

*In theory, the operation was simple, but there were **complications**.*

dilemma

*It was a real **dilemma**: to catch the train or wait for my friends.*

headache

*The non-arrival of the new desks was just one of Mrs Carragher's **headaches**.*

snag

*Building work was going well, until the plumbers hit a **snag**.*

a b c d e f g h i j k l m n o **p** q r s t u v w x y z

problem (2) NOUN

A **problem** is a puzzle or question that you solve using logical thought or mathematics.

brain-teaser
*Mrs Southgate enjoyed setting us **brain-teasers** on Friday afternoons.*

puzzle
*Which way out of the maze, that was the **puzzle**!*

question
*There was the serious **question** of whether the school could raise enough money.*

ANTONYM: answer or solution

produce (1) VERB

If someone or something **produces** something, they make it.

construct
*The factory **constructs** aeroplanes.*

create
*TV writers have **created** a new series about a cook who loves gardening.*

manufacture
*Mum's firm **manufactures** garden furniture.*

produce (2) VERB

If someone or something **produces** something, they cause it to happen.

bring about
*Flaws in the plane's wing **brought about** the air crash.*

cause
*Our new car **caused** much excitement in my family.*

give rise to
*High summer temperatures **give rise to** many bush fires.*

result in
*The hot weather **resulted in** a huge demand for soft drinks.*

programme NOUN

A **programme** is something that is broadcast on television or radio.

broadcast
*The **broadcast** went out three days after it was recorded.*

production
*The **production** was directed by Hamish Haddock.*

show
*Kayleigh's favourite television programmes are quiz **shows**.*

progress (1) SAID "PROH-GRESS" NOUN

Progress is the process of gradually improving or getting near to achieving something.

development
*"There has been considerable **development** in Ben's writing," said Mr Flannagan.*

improvement
*My report said I had shown steady **improvement** during the year.*

✔ Sudden, significant progress is a **breakthrough**.

progress (2) SAID "PRO-GRESS" VERB

If you **progress**, you become more advanced or skilful at something.

advance
*Techniques in medicine have **advanced** greatly in the last 20 years.*

improve
*My gran's condition was **improving**, the nurse said.*

make headway
*After weeks of rehearsal, our show was **making headway**.*

prohibit VERB

If someone **prohibits** something, they forbid it or make it illegal.

ban
*Smoking is **banned** in most public buildings.*

forbid
*Running in corridors is **forbidden** at school.*

make illegal
*Using mobile phones while driving has been **made illegal**.*

outlaw
*Cigarette advertising is gradually being **outlawed**.*

✔ You prohibit a person *from* doing something.

ANTONYM: allow

A B C D E F G H I J K L M N O P Q R S T U V W X Y Z

project NOUN
A **project** is a carefully planned task that requires a lot of time or effort.

assignment
*Qadira handed her **assignment** in just before the deadline.*

scheme
*China has completed a **scheme** to build a massive reservoir.*

task
*"Ladies and gentlemen, the **task** before us is a hard one," the chairman said.*

promise (1) VERB
If you **promise** to do something, you say that you will definitely do it.

assure
*Ethan **assured** his boss that he would carry out the mission successfully.*

give your word
*"I **give my word** that I will return," the explorer exclaimed.*

guarantee
*"Do you **guarantee** that this bridge is safe to cross?" asked the tank driver.*

pledge
*The businessman **pledged** to give his staff a pay rise.*

swear
*The clerk asked the witness to **swear** that her evidence would be the truth.*

vow
*Sir Lancelot **vowed** that he would serve King Arthur faithfully.*

promise (2) NOUN
A **promise** is a statement made by someone that they will definitely do something.

assurance
*I gave Dad my **assurance** that I would be home on time.*

guarantee
*"I give you my **guarantee** that I'll do better next time," I told Mum.*

pledge
*The gambler signed a **pledge** that he would never bet again.*

vow
*Rebecca made a **vow** that, one day, she would live in that very house.*

proper ADJECTIVE
If you do something in the **proper** way, you do it correctly.

appropriate
*Quiet speaking is **appropriate** in libraries.*

correct
*Giving an elderly person your seat is the **correct** thing to do.*

fitting
*After the meal, at a **fitting** moment, Mum made her speech.*

suitable
*Carina hoped that her dress was **suitable** for the occasion.*

ANTONYM: improper or unsuitable

property NOUN
A person's **property** is something, or all the things, that belong to them.

belongings
*The guard reminded us to take all our **belongings** when we got off the train.*

possessions
*All Oliver's **possessions** in the world could be tied up in a handkerchief.*

protect VERB
If you **protect** someone or something, you prevent them from being harmed.

defend
*It is a bodyguard's job to **defend** their client.*

guard
*In banks, a glass screen is there to **guard** against robberies.*

safeguard
*The miser **safeguarded** his money by putting it under his bed.*

shelter
*The old log cabin **sheltered** us from the downpour.*

shield
*A line of police **shielded** the politician from the protesters.*

protection

protection NOUN

Protection is something that protects you from being harmed.

armour
Police in dangerous situations have to wear body armour.

defence
Ordinary glass is no defence against bullets.

safeguard
Fitting a decent alarm is one safeguard against burglary.

security
The old people's home offered comfort and security.

shield
Knights of old went into battle with a sword and shield.

protest (1) SAID "PRO-**TEST**" VERB

If you **protest**, you say or do something to show that you strongly disapprove of something.

argue
The unions were arguing for better pay.

complain
Jivin's mother complained that he had been bullied.

demonstrate
A huge crowd demonstrated in the streets against the new tax.

disagree
Dad disagrees with lots of government policies.

object
When the chairlady wanted to end the meeting, my Mum stood up and objected.

oppose
About half the people in town opposed the new bypass.

protest (2) SAID "**PRO**-TEST" NOUN

A **protest** is a demonstration or statement to show that you strongly disapprove of something.

complaint
There were several complaints about what the mayor had said.

demonstration
The demonstration was large but the crowd remained peaceful.

outcry
A public outcry resulted when plans for the new road were published.

proud ADJECTIVE

If you are **proud** of something, you feel satisfaction and pleasure because of something you own or have achieved.

gratified
The actor was gratified by the applause.

honoured
"I feel honoured to work with such a respected scientist," said the assistant.

pleased
My big sister was pleased with the results she had achieved.

ANTONYM: ashamed

prove VERB

If you **prove** that something is true, you show by means of argument or evidence that it is definitely true.

confirm
Police confirmed that the stolen goods had been recovered.

demonstrate
This experiment demonstrates that flames need oxygen to burn.

establish
Eventually, Mrs Bridge established that there was no missing purse.

show
Jonathan showed that he wasn't afraid of heights by diving off the high board.

verify
In court, the witness was asked to verify the statement he had made earlier.

provide VERB

If you **provide** someone with something, you give it to them or make it available to them.

contribute
Governments agreed to contribute food and equipment to the earthquake victims.

equip
The millionaire equipped himself with all the latest gadgets.

supply
*That firm **supplied** all the expedition's tents and ropes.*

pull VERB
If you **pull** something, you get hold of it and move it towards you with force.

drag
*The fisherman **dragged** his boat into the water.*

haul
*The two red-faced tug-of-war teams dug in with their heels and **hauled** on the rope.*

heave
***Heaving** for all they were worth, the sailors raised the anchor.*

tug
*When the diver **tugged** on her line, the surface crew brought her up.*

pull delicately:
pick
*After being sat upon by our dog Tess, I had to **pick** her hairs off my coat.*

pluck
*You can strum a guitar or **pluck** strings individually.*

pull out:
extract
*Using tweezers, Mum **extracted** the splinter from my thumb.*

remove
*Very delicately, the vet **removed** the marble that our cat had swallowed.*

withdraw
*The nurse **withdrew** the needle so gently after my injection that I didn't even feel it.*

pull suddenly:
jerk
*When you tow a car, the rope often **jerks**, which can snap it.*

wrench
*Desperate to escape, the trapped man **wrenched** the door off its hinges.*

yank
*Gaman **yanked** the door handle, which then dropped off.*

pull out VERB
If you **pull out** of an arrangement, you decide not to do it.

quit
*When she was caught cheating, the woman had to **quit** the game show.*

withdraw from
*Owing to sickness, our team **withdrew from** the league.*

punch VERB
If you **punch** someone or something, you hit them hard with your fist.

jab
*My brother **jabbed** me playfully in the arm to get my attention.*

pummel
*The boxer **pummelled** the punchbag nonstop for five minutes.*

strike
*The angry man **struck** the table in frustration.*

thump
*The little bully who **thumped** my brother landed himself in detention for the rest of the week.*

punish VERB
To **punish** someone means to make them suffer for doing wrong.

discipline
*The coach resolved to **discipline** anyone who was late for practice.*

penalize
*Our fullback was **penalized** for bringing down an attacker.*

sentence
*The young offender was **sentenced** to one year's community service.*

punishment NOUN
Punishment is the action taken to make someone suffer for doing wrong.

penalty
*The **penalty** for walking on the grass is a £20 fine.*

sentence
*There are different **sentences** given for different crimes.*

a
b
c
d
e
f
g
h
i
j
k
l
m
n
o
p
q
r
s
t
u
v
w
x
y
z

A
B
C
D
E
F
G
H
I
J
K
L
M
N
O
P
Q
R
S
T
U
V
W
X
Y
Z

pupil NOUN

The **pupils** at a school are the children who attend it.

schoolboy

*Shakespeare wrote about the **schoolboy** going reluctantly to school.*

schoolgirl

*When Mum was a **schoolgirl**, she used to carry her satchel on her back.*

student

*My big brother is a **student** at the local further education college.*

pure (1) ADJECTIVE

Something that is **pure** is not mixed with anything else.

natural

*"Our cereal contains only **natural** ingredients", the packet boasted.*

wholesome

*Eating **wholesome** food is the first step to being healthy.*

ANTONYM: impure

pure (2) ADJECTIVE

Something that is **pure** is clean and free from harmful substances.

germ-free

*Hospitals try to keep their wards as **germ-free** as possible.*

unpolluted

*Country air is **unpolluted** compared with city air.*

ANTONYM: impure

pure (3) ADJECTIVE

Something that is **pure** is complete and total.

absolute

*Mum said her stay at the health farm was **absolute** bliss.*

complete

*They said my story was **complete** fiction, but it actually happened!*

total

*From start to finish, for me the film was **total** enjoyment.*

utter

*"You're talking **utter** nonsense," my brother laughed.*

purpose (1) NOUN

The **purpose** of something is the reason for it.

function

*The **function** of the decimal point is to separate whole numbers from fractions.*

object

*"The **object** of this lesson is to learn more about the environment," Miss O'Sullivan told the class.*

point

*I don't really get the **point** of horse riding. All I do is fall off.*

reason

*"What's the **reason** for that dial?" I asked my grandad.*

purpose (2) NOUN

Your **purpose** is the thing that you want to achieve.

aim

*My **aim** is to collect stamps from every country in Europe.*

intention

*When he stormed into my bedroom, I could tell that my brother's **intention** was not peaceful.*

object

*"The **object** of the game is to make the most money," explained Deepak.*

point

*"What was the **point** of saying that?" I asked Mandy.*

on purpose PHRASE

If you do something **on purpose**, you do it deliberately.

deliberately

*"You did that **deliberately**!" my brother shouted.*

intentionally

*I didn't **intentionally** trip him – it really was an accident.*

ANTONYM: unintentionally

push (1) VERB

If you **push** someone or something, you use force to move them away from you.

drive
*The farmer **drove** the fence posts into the ground with a huge mallet.*

force
*The attackers tried to **force** the gate inward with their ram.*

ram
*Once more the huge tree trunk **rammed** the wooden entrance.*

shove
*The defenders managed to **shove** the gate back into place.*

thrust
*The cowboy **thrust** open the saloon doors and strode in.*

ANTONYM: pull

push (2) VERB

If you **push** someone, you use force to move them out of the way.

elbow
*The bully tried to **elbow** me out of the way.*

jostle
*The people in the crowd were all **jostling** to move forward.*

put VERB

If you **put** something somewhere, you move it into that position.

deposit
*"Please **deposit** your keys on the desk when you leave the hotel," said the receptionist.*

lay
*"**Lay** your gun down, and come out with your hands up!" the sheriff shouted.*

place
*Mum **placed** the box carefully on the table. What on earth was in it?*

rest
*I lay back and **rested** my legs on the stool.*

stand
*"Make sure you **stand** that ladder firmly in place," Grandad advised.*

put off (1) VERB

If something **puts** you **off**, it stops you from concentrating on what you are doing.

distract
*I find that the radio **distracts** me from writing.*

faze
*However hard I try to distract her, nothing **fazes** my sister when she's concentrating.*

throw
*The tennis champion wasn't **thrown** by booing from some spectators.*

unsettle
***Unsettled** by problems at home, the actress gave a poor performance.*

put off (2) PHRASE

If you **put off** doing something, you delay it.

defer
*"I propose," said the mayor, "that we **defer** our decision until next week."*

delay
*We had to **delay** our holiday because of strikes at the airport.*

postpone
*The match was **postponed** due to bad weather.*

put off (3) VERB

If something **puts** you **off** something else, it causes you to stop being interested in or enjoying it.

deter
*A few falls didn't **deter** Kate from wanting to ride a horse.*

discourage
*I was **discouraged** by my poor mark in the maths test.*

put out VERB

If you **put out** a fire or flame, you stop it from burning.

extinguish
*Instead of **extinguishing** the flames, the wind fanned them to a new fury.*

snuff out
*With a pinch of her wetted fingers, Gran **snuffed out** the candle.*

a
b
c
d
e
f
g
h
i
j
k
l
m
n
o
p
q
r
s
t
u
v
w
x
y
z

A
B
C
D
E
F
G
H
I
J
K
L
M
N
O
P
Q
R
S
T
U
V
W
X
Y
Z

put up (1) VERB

If you **put up** something, you build or erect it.

assemble

*The model I tried to **assemble** turned out a gluey monstrosity.*

construct

*Dad **constructed** a swing for us in the yard.*

erect

*Builders need permission to **erect** scaffolding near a road.*

pitch

*The flood made us regret **pitching** our tent near the stream.*

ANTONYM: dismantle or pull down

put up (2) VERB

If someone **puts up** prices, they raise them.

increase

*The government intends to **increase** taxes.*

raise

*As from next month, train fares will be **raised** by three per cent.*

ANTONYM: reduce

put up with PHRASE

If you **put up with** something, you let it happen without complaining.

bear

*Even the tough explorer found the bitter cold hard to **bear**.*

endure

*The shipwrecked sailors **endured** weeks in an open boat.*

stand

*"I can't **stand** that din any more," Dad shouted upstairs.*

tolerate

*Mrs O'Shea refused to **tolerate** bad behaviour of any kind.*

puzzle VERB

If something **puzzles** you, it confuses you and you do not understand it.

baffle

*Completely **baffled** by the maze, I was forced to look at the plan in my pocket.*

bewilder

*Gary was **bewildered** by the complicated instructions for putting up the shelves.*

confuse

*"Don't let maths **confuse** you," said Mr Najeev. "It's simple really."*

mystify

*Having seen the whole film, I was still **mystified** at the end.*

perplex

*The explorers were **perplexed**. Surely they had been at this spot before!*

Qq

quantity NOUN
A **quantity** is an amount that you can measure or count.

amount
*The recipe said to add a small **amount** of salt – just a pinch.*

number
*A sizeable **number** of people wanted to go on the trip.*

> **Other nouns related to quantity:**
> a **quantity** of
>
> | | |
> |---|---|
> | ...drink | measure |
> | ...food | portion |
> | ...land | expanse |
> | ...money | sum |
> | ...sand | volume |
> | ...timber | length |
> | ...water | volume |

quarrel (1) NOUN
A **quarrel** is an angry argument.

argument
*My brother and I had an **argument** over who would use the computer.*

difference of opinion
*Mrs Hardy and Miss Mellberg had a **difference of opinion** about homework.*

disagreement
*There was a **disagreement** between Mum and Dad about our holiday destination.*

dispute
*The workers had a **dispute** with management about the length of tea breaks.*

feud
*The Campbells and the MacDonalds had a long-running and bloody **feud**.*

fight
*Kiesha and I made up after we'd had a **fight**.*

row SOUNDS LIKE "COW"
*Heidi had a **row** with her parents about the state of her room.*

quarrel (2) VERB
If people **quarrel**, they have an angry argument.

argue
*I didn't like to **argue**, but I'm sure what Mr Barry said was wrong.*

bicker
*My sister and brother spent the whole journey **bickering**.*

disagree
*Ratty and Badger **disagreed** about how to deal with Mr Toad.*

fall out
*Jamal and I **fell out** over who won the game.*

fight
*I hardly ever **fight** with my brothers and sisters, and when I do we soon make up.*

squabble
*"Stop **squabbling**, you two!" Dad shouted up the stairs.*

question (1) NOUN
A **question** is a sentence that asks for information.

enquiry
*Dad went to the town hall with an **enquiry** about local taxes.*

query
*"Before you start the test, have you any **queries**?" Mrs Unsworth asked.*

ANTONYM: answer

question (2) VERB
If you **question** someone, you ask them questions.

cross-examine
*The counsel for the prosecution **cross-examined** the defence witness.*

interrogate
*The spy was taken away to be **interrogated** by secret agents.*

query
*Mrs Kenna **queried** my use of the word "nice" when other words would have been better.*

quiz INFORMAL
*Mum **quizzed** my big sister to find out why she was so late back.*

a b c d e f g h i j k l m n o p **q** r s t u v w x y z

quick (1) ADJECTIVE

If you are **quick**, you move or do things with great speed.

brisk

*Dad and I took the dogs for a **brisk** walk.*

fast

*My grandad is a very **fast** runner.*

hasty

*Katie had a habit of being too **hasty** to judge other people.*

hurried

*After a **hurried** sandwich, Mr Henshaw dashed off to an afternoon meeting.*

rapid

*A **rapid** tyre change meant that the driver was still in the lead when he left the pits.*

speedy

*E-mails are a **speedy** way of sending messages.*

swift

*The actor had a **swift** costume change at the end of the first scene.*

ANTONYM: slow

quick (2) ADJECTIVE

Someone who is **quick** is intelligent and able to understand things easily.

alert

*The advertisement wanted an **alert**, lively office junior.*

bright

*A **bright** officer on the beat spotted the burglars behaving suspiciously.*

intelligent

*Khaled's report said that he was an **intelligent** boy who worked hard.*

quick-witted

*The **quick-witted** girl grabbed the dog and pulled it to safety.*

sharp

*Some **sharp** work by the wicketkeeper dismissed the batsman.*

smart

*"It was **smart** of you to come up with an idea like that," Mum said.*

ANTONYM: slow

quickly ADVERB

Something that happens **quickly** happens with great speed.

fast

*My Uncle Ted drives very **fast**.*

hastily

*As her Dad walked in, Nadine **hastily** switched the video game off and turned to her homework.*

hurriedly

***Hurriedly** throwing a few things in an overnight bag, Dad rushed Mum to hospital because the baby was coming.*

rapidly

*The courier dashed **rapidly** through the door with a message from HQ.*

speedily

*"I want this article written **speedily**," the editor told the reporter.*

swiftly

*After his mistakes, the tennis umpire was **swiftly** replaced by someone else.*

ANTONYM: slowly

quiet (1) ADJECTIVE

If someone or something is **quiet**, they are not making much noise, or they are not making any noise at all.

hushed

*Speaking in a **hushed** voice, the guide told us about the cathedral.*

silent

*When the director called "Action", everyone except the actors had to be **silent**.*

soundless

*With a **soundless** movement, Bond sprang from behind the door.*

ANTONYM: loud or noisy

quiet (2) ADJECTIVE

A **quiet** place, time or situation is calm and peaceful.

calm

*The **calm** evening with the light sea breeze was a great change from the storm of the night before.*

peaceful
*Scotland's highland scenery is **peaceful** as well as beautiful.*

serene
*She relaxed in the beautiful **serene** park.*

tranquil
*The shore of the lake was a **tranquil** setting for the wedding.*

quiet (3) ADJECTIVE
A **quiet** person is shy and does not usually say much.

reserved
*The artist was a **reserved** man who kept himself to himself.*

retiring
*Being a **retiring** sort of person, Miss McCall wanted no fuss on her birthday.*

shy
*From being very **shy**, my brother has suddenly become noisy and confident.*

ANTONYM: loud or outgoing

quiet (4) NOUN
Quiet can mean silence or lack of noise.

peace
*Mum says she loves the **peace** and quiet after we've gone to bed.*

silence
*As the last child departed, **silence** fell on the school corridors.*

stillness
*The **stillness** of the summer night was soothing.*

tranquillity
*The memorial garden was a haven of **tranquillity** in a busy city.*

quit VERB
If you **quit** something, you leave it or stop doing it.

leave
Barry finally left the army after 25 years' service.

resign
*Dad **resigned** from the police force to become a private detective.*

step down
*After a string of poor results, the coach decided to **step down**.*

quite (1) ADVERB
Quite can mean fairly but not very.

fairly
*I was **fairly** happy with my test results, but aimed to do better next time.*

moderately
*"Tomorrow will be **moderately** warm," the weatherman said confidently.*

rather
*Mum was **rather** disappointed not to be elected as a councillor.*

somewhat
*Johnathan was **somewhat** pleased that the parachute jump was postponed.*

quite (2) ADVERB
Quite can mean completely.

absolutely
*Dad was **absolutely** adamant that we needed to turn left.*

entirely
*I was **entirely** taken aback by my sister's decision to join the navy.*

fully
*"I am **fully** confident that my decision is correct," my friend said pompously.*

perfectly
*"I am **perfectly** sure you'll manage while I'm away," said Mum's boss.*

totally
*Bhoomi had not **totally** recovered from her cold when she came back to school.*

wholly
*Frodo decided he had been **wholly** mistaken in undertaking such a perilous journey.*

a
b
c
d
e
f
g
h
i
j
k
l
m
n
o
p
q
r
s
t
u
v
w
x
y
z

Rr

A
B
C
D
E
F
G
H
I
J
K
L
M
N
O
P
Q
R
S
T
U
V
W
X
Y
Z

race (1) NOUN

A **race** is a competition to see who is fastest at something.

competition
*Brandon and I had a **competition** to see who could be first in the playground.*

contest
*Our town holds a famous pie-eating **contest** each year.*

dash
*Grandad used to run in the 100-yard **dash** when he was a boy.*

race (2) VERB

If you **race** somewhere, you go there as quickly as possible.

dash
*Paul **dashed** out of the room laughing.*

fly
*"I must **fly**," said Kit, "or I'll miss my train."*

hurry
*"We'll have to **hurry** Dad, or the shops will be shut!" Jenny said.*

run
*Alison started to **run** as she saw the bus coming round the corner.*

speed
*The car came **speeding** round the corner with a police car behind it.*

tear
*The door flew open and Wendy **tore** into the house and up the stairs.*

rage NOUN

A **rage** is a strong, uncontrollable anger.

anger
*Consumed with **anger**, the evil wizard sent thunderbolts from the heights of his tower.*

fit of temper
*In a **fit of temper**, my sister threw my socks out of the window.*

fury
*Jason stomped off in a **fury** when I told him I'd lost his CD.*

tantrum
*Mum say that when I was two I used to have **tantrums** all the time.*

ragged ADJECTIVE

If fabric is **ragged**, it is torn or frayed, with rough edges.

frayed
*My baby brother drags his blanket everywhere, so now it's all **frayed** around the edges.*

shabby
*"You must get a new tracksuit," Mum told Dad. "That one's starting to look **shabby**."*

tattered
*My rag doll is very **tattered** these days, because I used to take her everywhere.*

threadbare
*Despite his wealth, a **threadbare** suit was all the miser ever wore.*

worn-out
*The long-distance walker abandoned yet another **worn-out** pair of shoes.*

raid (1) NOUN

A **raid** is a sudden, surprise attack.

attack
*The **attack** on the US battleships was sudden and unexpected.*

break-in
*Police thought the **break-in** had occurred between one o'clock and two o'clock in the morning.*

invasion
*The D-Day **invasion** of 1944 was the world's biggest-ever amphibious landing.*

raid (2) VERB

When people **raid** a place, they enter it by force in order to attack it or to look for something or someone.

attack
*Howling with rage, Boadicea's fierce army **attacked** the Roman citadel.*

invade
*In 1066, the Normans **invaded** the shores of Britain.*

plunder
*Having **plundered** the town, the Vikings returned to their longboats.*

rain (1) NOUN

Rain is water falling from the clouds in small drops.

cloudburst
*We were in the lead, but a **cloudburst** put an end to the match.*

deluge
*The **deluge** left the field several centimetres deep in water.*

downpour
*After the **downpour**, the sky cleared and the sun came out.*

rainfall
*Mountainous areas attract the highest level of **rainfall**.*

✔ Steady, fine rain is **drizzle**.
Rain that frequently starts and stops is **showers**.

rain (2) VERB

When it **rains**, small drops of water fall from clouds in the sky.

rain heavily
bucket down INFORMAL
*It **bucketed down**, and rain poured from overflowing gutters.*

pelt
*Typical! I hadn't brought a coat so it **pelted** with rain.*

pour
*For the entire day of our outing, it **poured** down.*

rain cats and dogs INFORMAL
*We had to stay in at playtime because it was **raining cats and dogs**.*

teem
*In tropical climates, it **teems** with rain on many days during the rainy season.*

rain lightly
drizzle
*As we left the house it started to **drizzle**.*

spit
*As it was only **spitting**, I decided to go out but took an umbrella with me.*

range NOUN

A **range** is a selection or choice of different things of the same kind.

assortment
*On the sweet trolley was an **assortment** of delicious desserts.*

selection
*For her prize, Mum could choose from a **selection** of perfumes.*

variety
*You can buy an amazing **variety** of trainers.*

rapid ADJECTIVE

Something that is **rapid** is happening or moving very quickly.

brisk
*Mr Goma set off at a **brisk** trot.*

hasty
*After using the phoney credit card, the fraudsters made a **hasty** exit.*

hurried
*Because of an early bedtime, my homework was rather **hurried**.*

speedy
*In our card, we wished Mrs Keown a **speedy** recovery from the flu.*

swift
*The alert girl's **swift** action saved the day.*

ANTONYM: slow

rare ADJECTIVE

Something that is **rare** is not common or does not often happen.

scarce
*"Oak carving like this is **scarce** these days," said the expert.*

uncommon
*The young Wolfgang Mozart had an **uncommon** gift for music.*

unique
*"This style of painting is quite **unique**," said the curator of the art gallery.*

unusual
*It was **unusual** to hear a cuckoo so early in the year.*

✔ Note that **unique** can only be used to describe something if there is only one of its kind.

ANTONYM: common

a b c d e f g h i j k l m n o p q **r** s t u v w x y z

rather (1) ADVERB

Rather can mean fairly or to a certain extent.

fairly

*Our car is **fairly** old, but Dad says that it still goes well.*

moderately

*Mrs Bernard said she was **moderately** pleased with our test results.*

quite

*"I'm **quite** surprised to see you here," Auntie Madge said.*

relatively

*It was **relatively** early when we got home, so we had time to play before tea.*

somewhat

*I was excited, but **somewhat** alarmed, to be doing a bungee jump.*

slightly

*We were **slightly** late, but hoped we wouldn't be in too much trouble.*

to a certain extent

***To a certain extent**, I was pleased to be going back to school.*

rather (2) ADVERB

If you would **rather** do one thing than another, you would prefer to do it.

preferably

*Mum said she would **preferably** have had a Chinese meal.*

sooner

*"Personally, I would **sooner** eat Greek food," said my sister.*

raw (1) ADJECTIVE

Raw food is uncooked.

fresh

*Sushi is a small piece of **fresh** fish within a rice surround.*

uncooked

***Uncooked** or partly cooked meat can cause stomach upsets.*

ANTONYM: cooked

---

raw (2) ADJECTIVE

A **raw** substance is in its natural state, before being processed.

basic

*In aluminium manufacture, the **basic** material used is bauxite.*

natural

*Our central heating and hot water are heated by **natural** gas.*

unprocessed

***Unprocessed** wool is greasy with lanoline and needs to be cleaned.*

ray NOUN

A **ray** is a beam of light.

beam

*Every few seconds, the **beam** from the lighthouse swept round the bay.*

shaft

*Deep within the cave, Frodo saw a **shaft** of sunlight ahead.*

stream

*A **stream** of light shone down between the clouds.*

reach (1) VERB

When you **reach** a place, you arrive there.

arrive at

***Arriving at** America in 1620, the Pilgrim Fathers set up their own colony.*

get to

*The mountaineers planted their flag in the snow when they **got to** the summit.*

make

*The first transatlantic flight only just **made** the coast of Ireland.*

reach (2) VERB

When something **reaches** somewhere, it extends as far as that place or point.

climb to

*The road **climbed to** the top of the hill and then snaked down the other side.*

extend

*By 1870 the railway **extended** as far as the USA's west coast.*

stretch to

*The desert **stretched to** the horizon.*

touch

*The suburbs of the city now **touched** the foot of the mountain.*

reach (3) VERB

When you **reach** your goal, you achieve it.

achieve

*The rower was the first to **achieve** five Olympic golds in different years.*

attain

*My brother **attained** the highest maths mark in the school's history.*

read (1) VERB

When you **read** something that is written, you look at it and understand or say aloud the words that are there.

dip into

*Bonnie liked to browse through the library, **dipping into** several books.*

pore over

*Engineers **pored over** the plans, trying to find where the fault might lie.*

scan

*Dad **scanned** the job adverts in the newspaper.*

skim through

*With reference books, you often have to **skim through** an entry to make sure it's useful.*

study

*I sat at my desk **studying** my school report in cheerful disbelief.*

read (2) VERB

If you can **read** someone's mind or moods, you can judge what they are feeling or thinking.

comprehend

*Her expression was difficult to **comprehend**.*

decipher

*Kim could not **decipher** from Mr Abdul's expression whether she had done well in the test.*

interpret

*I **interpreted** Mum's cross look to mean that I was late.*

ready (1) ADJECTIVE

If something or someone is **ready**, they are prepared for doing something.

all set

*The family was **all set** to go on holiday when Mum had her accident.*

geared up INFORMAL

*We were all **geared up** for the school trip.*

prepared

*Having our waterproofs with us, we were **prepared** for rain.*

ANTONYM: unprepared

ready (2) ADJECTIVE

If someone is **ready**, they are willing to do something.

eager

*The young soldiers were **eager** to go on exercise, the older ones less so.*

glad

*"If you need assistance, I'll be **glad** to help," our neighbour said.*

keen

***Keen** to do well, the student studied day and night for the exam.*

willing

*My sisters were **willing** to do any job that needed doing.*

real (1) ADJECTIVE

Something that is **real** is genuine and not artificial.

authentic

*Most of the autographs were **authentic**, but one or two were fake.*

genuine

*"That chair is a **genuine** Chippendale," the expert exclaimed.*

ANTONYM: artificial or fake

real (2) ADJECTIVE

Something that is **real** is actually true and not imagined.

actual

*"This is the **actual** throne on which King Arthur sat," said the guide.*

genuine

*The millionaire's wish to help save the rainforests was **genuine**.*

true

*"Is this a **true** record of what you said?" the magistrate asked the woman standing in the witness box.*

ANTONYM: imagined or insincere

A
B
C
D
E
F
G
H
I
J
K
L
M
N
O
P
Q
R
S
T
U
V
W
X
Y
Z

realize VERB
If you **realize** something, you become aware of it or understand it.

appreciate
*The twins did not **appreciate** the danger they were in.*

become aware
*Dad slowly **became aware** that the crocodile was looking at him.*

grasp
*At first I didn't **grasp** what was happening.*

recognize
*It is important to **recognize** the importance of regular exercise.*

understand
*"You must **understand** how important maths is," the head teacher said.*

really (1) ADVERB
You use **really** when you are talking of the true facts about something.

actually
*"To think we are **actually** flying to Australia!" I marvelled.*

honestly
*"I **honestly** don't know what to say," Mrs Neill sighed.*

in fact
*Grandad looked well enough, but **in fact** he was quite poorly.*

truly
*We had a **truly** wonderful day on the island.*

really (2) ADVERB
You use **really** to emphasize a point.

absolutely
*My sister is **absolutely** terrified of spiders.*

extremely
*"I'm **extremely** sorry, but we have sold out," the shopkeeper said.*

reason NOUN
A **reason** is the fact that explains why something happens.

cause
*Months after the disaster, scientists were no nearer to finding the **cause**.*

excuse
*Miss Gresko pointed out that there was no **excuse** for disobedience.*

explanation
*"Is there an **explanation** for this?" the sergeant asked, picking up the dirty boots.*

justification
*The worker could see no **justification** for his sacking.*

motive
*Holmes was puzzled about the suspect's **motive** for committing murder.*

reasonable (1) ADJECTIVE
Someone or something that is **reasonable** is fair and sensible.

fair
*Mrs Rufus is always **fair** when she marks our homework and tests.*

sensible
*A meeting seemed the only **sensible** way to deal with the issue.*

ANTONYM: unreasonable

reasonable (2) ADJECTIVE
A **reasonable** price is fair and not too high.

fair
*Dad thought that the dealer was asking a **fair** price for the old car.*

inexpensive
*Charity shops are an **inexpensive** source of clothes and books.*

moderate
*The developer bought the house at a **moderate** price, and sold it for a fortune.*

ANTONYM: expensive

receive (1) VERB
When you **receive** something, you get it after someone has given or sent it to you.

accept
*The show's producer **accepted** the award on behalf of all the cast.*

collect
*Mum **collected** a free gift with her first order from the catalogue.*

obtain
*For his curiosity, the elephant's child **obtained** a longer trunk.*

receive (2) VERB
To **receive** something can mean to have it happen to you.

suffer
*Gran began to **suffer** unpleasant headaches.*

sustain
*In the accident, my sister **sustained** a fractured arm.*

undergo
*The ex-soccer star had to **undergo** a liver transplant.*

recent ADJECTIVE
A **recent** event is something that happened a short time ago.

current
***Current** affairs are the events which are happening in today's world.*

fresh
*The reporter had just received **fresh** information about the kidnap.*

latest
*Where my dad works, they have all the **latest** computer gadgets.*

new
*The head teacher sent a letter to parents explaining some **new** school rules.*

up-to-date
*The internet can be a good source of **up-to-date** information.*

ANTONYM: old

record (1) SAID "**REK**-ORD" NOUN
A **record** is a written account of something.

diary
*I started my **diary** on New Year's Day, but gave up after the 4th of January.*

file
*In the past, **files** were kept in cabinets. Now more and more are stored on computer.*

log
*The captain kept a **log** of his voyage to the outer galaxies.*

minutes
*"Who'll take the **minutes** of our meeting?" the chairperson asked.*

register
Names of pupils and details of attendance are kept in a register.

record (2) SAID "RI-**KORD**" VERB
If you **record** information, you write it down so that it can be referred to later.

document
*The events were **documented** in the local newspapers.*

log
*Captain Picard **logged** the explosion of a distant planet.*

note
*"**Note** the main points of the story now and write it up in full for homework," Mr Bailey said.*

register
*When you arrive at a hotel, you have to **register** your name.*

recover VERB
When you **recover**, you get better after being ill.

convalesce
*Grandma is still **convalescing** in hospital after her operation.*

get better
*It took me a couple of weeks to **get better** after having my tonsils out.*

get well
*When Mrs Buckle was ill we sent her a card saying "**Get well** soon!"*

improve
*According to the nurse, Grandad was **improving** slowly.*

pull through
*In spite of his grave injuries, the motorcyclist **pulled through**.*

recuperate
*After operations, patients go back to the ward to **recuperate**.*

revive
***Reviving** after her faint, the old lady sat and sipped water.*

a
b
c
d
e
f
g
h
i
j
k
l
m
n
o
p
q
r
s
t
u
v
w
x
y
z

recycle VERB

When you **recycle** something, you use it again for a different purpose.

reclaim

Materials such as paper, card and metal can be reclaimed for reuse.

reprocess

Nuclear waste is reprocessed to extract usable substances.

reuse

"Not enough of what we throw away is reused in other forms," said Mum.

salvage

Many things that we take to dumps are salvaged and resold.

reduce VERB

If you **reduce** something, you make it smaller in size or amount.

cut

The politician promised that his party would cut taxes if they won the election.

decrease

In built-up areas, a driver's speed should decrease considerably.

lessen

A healthy diet lessens the risks of disease.

lower

Air conditioning lowers the temperature in hot interiors.

ANTONYM: increase

refuse VERB

If you **refuse** something, you say no to it, or decide firmly that you will not do it or do not accept it.

decline

My dad declined the offer of a job in the USA.

reject

Haughtily, the princess rejected Sir Mordred's proposal of marriage.

turn down

The player turned down the chance of a move to Italy.

ANTONYM: accept

regular (1) ADJECTIVE

Regular events happen at equal or frequent intervals.

constant

The constant throb of the ship's engines lulled me to sleep.

even

When doctors take your pulse, they hope to hear an even beat.

rhythmic

The wind kept up a rhythmic flapping of the flags.

steady

In any band, the drummer's job is to maintain a steady rhythm.

regular (2) ADJECTIVE

Something that is **regular** is usual or normal.

customary

Our neighbour was going out for his customary evening walk.

everyday

Helicopters were an everyday sight over our valley.

habitual

"You are a habitual thief and liar," the judge told the defendant.

normal

It was normal for us to visit Aunt Emma each spring.

usual

It is usual for my sister and brother to argue at least once a day.

ANTONYM: abnormal or irregular

relation NOUN

Your **relations** are the people who are related to you, such as aunts, uncles and grandparents.

kin

"Most of our kin come originally from Ireland," said the American visitor.

kinsman or kinswoman

The wicked prince killed his kinsmen in order to become king.

relative

Amrit had many relatives in India.

relax VERB

When you **relax**, you become calm and less worried or tense.

laze
*We spent the holiday **lazing** on the beach.*

rest
*The doctor advised Faizah to **rest** as much as possible after the operation.*

take it easy
*"Now just **take it easy**," the police officer advised the angry young man.*

unwind
*Dad always goes for a swim when he wants to **unwind**.*

release (1) VERB

If you **release** someone or something, you set them free.

discharge
*Having been found not guilty, the prisoner was **discharged**.*

free
*Sir Galahad rode up to the tower, determined to **free** the imprisoned damsel.*

liberate
*The rebels hoped to **liberate** their country from the evil dictator's rule.*

*See **rescue***

release (2) VERB

If you **release** something, you unfasten it.

loose
*Sadira **loosed** her horse into the paddock after she'd groomed him.*

undo
*With some effort, the prisoner managed to **undo** his ropes.*

unfasten
*Ron struggled to **unfasten** the rusty bolt that was keeping the door shut.*

reliable ADJECTIVE

Reliable people and things can be trusted and depended upon.

dependable
*It had been a **dependable** old car, and Mum was sorry to sell it.*

faithful
*Wooster's **faithful** butler, Jeeves, was always around to sort things out.*

responsible
*Mrs Konchevsky said she needed a **responsible** person to run an errand.*

trustworthy
*It is important that a best friend is **trustworthy**.*

ANTONYM: unreliable

rely VERB

If you **rely** on someone or something, you trust and depend on them.

bank on
*I was **banking on** my brother to give me a hand with the washing-up.*

count on
*"Can I **count on** your vote?" the councillor asked Mum.*

depend on
*Many people in the world **depend on** electricity in their life and work.*

have confidence in
*Miss Powell said she **had confidence in** me to captain the team well.*

trust
*I **trusted** my sister with the chocolate, and look what happened!*

remain (1) VERB

If you **remain** in a particular place, you stay there.

linger
*Several people **lingered** outside school, chatting while they waited to be collected.*

stay behind
*Mr Stubbs told us to **stay behind** after the rest of the class had gone.*

stay put INFORMAL
*When the car broke down, Dad told us to **stay put** while he went for help.*

wait
*"**Wait** here until I come back," William told his brother George.*

ANTONYM: leave

A B C D E F G H I J K L M N O P Q R S T U V W X Y Z

remain (2) VERB

If you **remain**, you continue to exist.

continue
*"The annual school race, which we founded, **continued** for many years," said Mr Smith.*

endure
*Strange traditions **endure** almost everywhere in the world.*

persist
*Despite treatment, Orlando's nasty rash **persisted**.*

survive
*After the fire, little of the thatched cottage **survived**.*

✔ The **remains** of something are the parts that are left after most of it has been destroyed or used.

remember VERB

If you **remember** someone or something from the past, you still have an idea of them and you are able to think about them.

call to mind
*"You might **call to mind** the last time we had this discussion," Dad said when I asked about an increase in my pocket money.*

recall
*Most people can **recall** their first day at school.*

recollect
*Dad **recollected** that he had cried for his mum when he started school.*

ANTONYM: forget

remind VERB

If someone **reminds** you of something, they help you remember it.

bring to mind
*Mum said that my accident **brought to mind** a time when she had fallen off her bike.*

jog your memory
*"If I forget to repay you, just **jog my memory**," I said to Rosa.*

refresh your memory
*Mr Alpay asked me to **refresh his memory** about last year's sports day.*

remove VERB

If you **remove** something, you take it away.

clear away
*"Please will you **clear away** the tea things?" Mum asked.*

delete
*If you write on a PC or a word processor, it's easy to **delete** mistakes.*

detach
*The engine was **detached** from the train carriages in the sidings.*

eliminate
*In each round of a knockout competition, the losers are **eliminated**.*

erase
*Once I'd finished the neat version of my composition, I **erased** my pencil notes.*

repair VERB

If you **repair** something that is damaged, you mend it.

fix
*Dad took my watch to the jewellers to get it **fixed**.*

overhaul
*Before it could work again, the locomotive needed to be completely **overhauled**.*

renovate
*Dan specializes in **renovating** old houses.*

service
*Most cars and machines need to be **serviced** regularly.*

ANTONYM: damage

repay VERB

To **repay** someone is to give back money that is owed.

compensate
*The builders had to **compensate** Mr Watson for the damage to his garden.*

pay back
*"I can lend you the money if you can **pay me back** by the end of the week," said Jelani.*

recompense
*"I'd like to **recompense** you for all your help," the neighbour said.*

refund

If a product is of poor quality, shops have to refund your money.

settle up

"I'll just settle up the bill and then we'll go," Dad said as we packed our bags at the hotel.

repeat VERB

If you repeat something, you say, write or do it again.

redo

My brother had to redo his exams as he failed the first time.

reiterate

Mr Hussein yet again reiterated what he'd told us a thousand times before.

retell

We asked Gran to retell the story of getting her first bicycle.

replace VERB

If someone or something replaces someone or something else, they take their place.

substitute

When she wasn't looking, we substituted water for Mum's wine.

succeed

The prince succeeded his mother on the throne when she died.

take over from

Last term Mrs Mill took over from Mr Weir as head teacher.

take the place of

In Grandad's view, nothing can take the place of old steam trains.

reply (1) VERB

If you reply to something, you say or write something as an answer to it.

acknowledge

The prime minister acknowledged my letter, but 1 received no further reply.

answer

When I rang Marshall's house, his dad answered.

respond

It was a great service, but the opposing tennis player responded with an even faster return.

retort

When I asked her what she was doing, my sister retorted, "Mind your own business!"

reply (2) NOUN

A reply is what you say or write when you answer someone.

acknowledgment

The council sent no acknowledgment to the letter I had written.

answer

The traveller knocked at the door, but received no answer.

response

We had a huge response to our appeal for old stamps.

retort

I was only asking the time, but I received a rude retort.

report (1) NOUN

A report is an account of an event or situation.

account

Dad wasn't convinced by my account of how the window got broken.

description

Charles Dickens wrote superb descriptions of his characters.

record

Police have to keep a record of every interview they conduct.

statement

Witnesses are required to make a statement of what they saw.

report (2) VERB

If you report that something has happened, you inform someone about it.

recount

We had to recount in our own words the story of Wilbur the pig.

relate

On her return, Ulima related the whole saga of being in the film.

state

The insurance form asks you to state what happened.

A
B
C
D
E
F
G
H
I
J
K
L
M
N
O
P
Q
R
S
T
U
V
W
X
Y
Z

represent (1) VERB
If a picture or writing **represents** something, it is intended to show or describe that thing in a particular way.

depict
*My painting **depicted** a spider halfway up a bottle.*

illustrate
*When I'd finished my account, Miss Johanssen asked me to **illustrate** it.*

portray
*The film **portrays** Robin Hood as being a cheerful, heroic type.*

represent (2) VERB
If a sign or symbol **represents** something, it is accepted as meaning that thing.

mean
*The = sign **means** that one thing is equal to another.*

stand for
*The initials UN **stand for** United Nations.*

symbolize
*In badges and logos, a dove is often used to **symbolize** peace.*

rescue (1) VERB
If you **rescue** someone, you save them from a dangerous or unpleasant situation.

free
*The gallant knight **freed** the fair maiden from her captivity.*

liberate
*In a daring raid, the police managed to **liberate** the hostages.*

release
*At last, the driver was **released** from the wreckage of her car.*

save
*A passer-by dived into the sea and **saved** the drowning child.*

rescue (2) VERB
If you **rescue** something, you save it from being lost or destroyed.

recover
*Gold bullion was **recovered** from the wreck of the sunken galleon.*

retrieve
*Investigators managed to **retrieve** the stolen paintings.*

salvage
*Little could be **salvaged** from the blaze.*

resign VERB
If you **resign** from your job, you give it up.

hand in your notice
*As she wanted to set up her own business, Mum **handed in her notice**.*

quit
*"Then I **quit**!" shouted the footballer, and stormed out of the dressing room.*

step down
*Due to illness, the manager had to **step down**.*

✔ If a king or queen resigns, they are said to **abdicate**.

respect (1) VERB
If you **respect** someone, you admire and like them.

admire
*I **admire** people who can keep calm whatever the circumstances.*

honour
*At a special dinner, the city **honoured** its former mayor.*

value
*Teachers **value** children who are well-behaved and hard-working.*

respect (2) NOUN
Respect is a feeling of admiration for someone's good qualities or achievements.

admiration
*The world had great **admiration** for the African statesman.*

esteem
*The captain had the **esteem** of all the members of his crew.*

responsible (1) ADJECTIVE
A **responsible** person is sensible, trustworthy and reliable.

conscientious
*Waseem's report said he was a **conscientious** worker.*

mature
*Shania was a **mature** girl who was obviously going to do well.*

reliable
*The advert asked for a **reliable** delivery person.*

sensible
*You can always rely on my sister to be **sensible** in a crisis.*

trustworthy
*"I need someone **trustworthy** to take this note to the office for me," said Miss Quentin.*

ANTONYM: irresponsible

responsible (2) ADJECTIVE
If you are **responsible** for something, you are the cause of it.

at fault
*It was difficult to tell if anyone was **at fault** for the accident.*

to blame
*I confessed that I was **to blame** for the mess in the kitchen.*

*See **guilty***

rest (1) VERB
If you **rest**, you take a break from what you are doing and relax for a while.

laze
*After all our hard work in the morning, we **lazed** about in the afternoon.*

lounge
*Mum **lounged** on the sofa after work.*

pause
*The secretary **paused** to have a sip of tea.*

relax
*Dad loves to read the paper while **relaxing** in a bath.*

take a breather INFORMAL
*"Why not **take a breather**?" the foreman suggested to his workmen.*

rest (2) NOUN
If you have a **rest**, you do not do anything active for a while.

break
*"Take a **break**," Mum said. "You've earned it."*

nap
*Gramps often has a **nap** in the afternoon.*

relaxation
*After the battle, troops were sent away for rest and **relaxation**.*

snooze INFORMAL
*Great Grandma likes a **snooze** in her chair at any time of day.*

rest (3) NOUN
The **rest** of something is all the parts that are left or have not been mentioned.

balance
*"You can pay a deposit on the bike now and the **balance** later," said the salesman.*

remainder
*When we'd all had a slice of cake, the **remainder** was kept for later.*

restless ADJECTIVE
If you are **restless**, you find it hard to stay still or relaxed because you are bored or impatient.

fidgety
*My little brother gets **fidgety** if he has to sit still for a while.*

jumpy
*As the time for his exam results approached, Zack became very **jumpy**.*

on edge
*Before the game, the whole team was **on edge**.*

unsettled
*Knowing that we were going to the airport in the afternoon, I was **unsettled** all morning.*

ANTONYM: relaxed

result NOUN
The **result** of an action or situation is what happens because of it.

consequence
*Anya's pony was lame, and as a **consequence** had to miss the show.*

effect
*Harry's potion had an instant **effect** on the frog.*

outcome
*All the reporters awaited the **outcome** of the court case.*

return

A B C D E F G H I J K L M N O P Q R S T U V W X Y Z

return (1) VERB

If you **return** to a place, you go back there.

come back

*My sister enjoys university, but loves **coming back** home.*

reappear

*Seconds after leaving, Mum **reappeared**, having forgotten her keys.*

revisit

*Gran looked forward to **revisiting** her birthplace.*

return (2) VERB

If you **return** something to someone, you give it back to them.

hand back

*After checking my pass, the driver **handed** it **back**.*

refund

*As the new computer was faulty, the store **refunded** Jackson's money.*

restore

*The clock was **restored** to its rightful owner.*

ANTONYM: take

revenge NOUN

Revenge is the act of hurting someone who has hurt you.

retaliation

*My sister kept annoying me so, in **retaliation**, I booby-trapped her bed.*

vengeance

*Sauron sought **vengeance** on those who dared to invade Mordor.*

revolting ADJECTIVE

Something that is **revolting** is horrible and disgusting.

disgusting

*"What a **disgusting** taste!" was all my brother could say about the pie I'd cooked.*

horrible

*Mum said it was **horrible** even to think about the state of my room.*

loathsome

*The **loathsome** creature slimed its way up from the depths.*

nauseating

***Nauseating** things make you feel sick.*

repulsive

*Little Nell could not stand Quilp's **repulsive** appearance.*

reward NOUN

A **reward** is something you are given because you have done something good.

bonus

*If Mum's firm has done well, all the employees get a **bonus** at Christmas.*

honour

*For her part in the game, Gina had the **honour** of carrying the trophy.*

prize

*My sister's **prize** was a visit to a television studio to watch a programme being made.*

repayment

*The medal was some **repayment** for all the time and effort the athlete had put in.*

rich ADJECTIVE

Someone who is **rich** has a lot of money or possessions.

affluent

*Mr Higgins lives in a very **affluent** part of town.*

loaded SLANG

*"My Uncle Abdul is **loaded**," boasted Sabirah.*

prosperous

***Prosperous** people tend to live in large houses.*

wealthy

*My uncle became **wealthy** after inventing a folding go-kart.*

well-off

*"**Well-off** people often worry too much about money," observed Grandma.*

rid VERB

To **rid** a place of something unpleasant means to succeed in removing it.

clear

*We **cleared** the cellar of all the flood water.*

free

*Spraying with vile-smelling chemicals **freed** the house of woodworm.*

get rid of PHRASE

If you **get rid of** something you do not want, you remove it or destroy it.

delete

*It's a simple matter to **delete** any section if you write using a PC.*

dispose of

*"How can I **dispose of** the evidence?" the criminal pondered.*

dump

*"It's terrible the way people **dump** rubbish in the countryside," Mrs Cookson complained.*

ride NOUN

A **ride** is a journey on a horse or bicycle or in a vehicle.

drive

*Grandad took us for a **drive** in the country.*

jaunt

*Our **jaunt** into the city centre was great fun.*

journey

*Simon packed a book to read during the coach **journey**.*

trip

*For our prize, we won a **trip** on a real steam train.*

ridiculous ADJECTIVE

Someone or something that is **ridiculous** is very foolish.

absurd

*It's **absurd** to suggest that cars would run more smoothly on square wheels.*

foolish

*"What a **foolish** suggestion!" was Rhys's opinion of my cunning plan.*

ludicrous

*It was **ludicrous** to doubt Lilly's honesty.*

preposterous

*The idea of motorcars would have seemed **preposterous** in Saxon times.*

ANTONYM: sensible

right (1) ADJECTIVE

If something is **right**, it is correct.

accurate

*Weather forecasts are not always **accurate**.*

correct

*"That is the **correct** answer," said the quiz show host.*

true

*"Are these minutes a **true** record of the meeting?" the chairman asked.*

ANTONYM: incorrect or wrong

right (2) ADJECTIVE

The **right** decision, action or person is the best or most suitable one.

appropriate

*Lightweight clothes are more **appropriate** for summer than winter.*

fitting

*As she had helped cook it, it was only **fitting** that Zaria should get a share of the cake.*

proper

*Grandad showed me the **proper** way to saw wood.*

suitable

*Legolas waited for a **suitable** time to depart.*

right (3) ADVERB

You can use **right** to emphasize the exact time or position of something.

exactly

*Luckily, the taxi arrived **exactly** on time, at eight o'clock.*

precisely

*The parachutist landed **precisely** on the mark.*

ring VERB

When a telephone or bell **rings**, it makes a clear, loud sound.

chime

*The clock on the mantelpiece **chimes** rather musically.*

clang

*On old fire engines, firefighters would **clang** the bell by hand.*

peal

*The bells **pealed** to mark the beginning of the new year.*

toll

*A single bell **tolled** solemnly as the funeral procession passed by.*

A
B
C
D
E
F
G
H
I
J
K
L
M
N
O
P
Q
R
S
T
U
V
W
X
Y
Z

riot (1) NOUN

When there is a **riot**, a crowd of people behave violently in a public place.

commotion
*You could hear the **commotion** from round the corner.*

disturbance
*Police arrested those who had caused the **disturbance**.*

uproar
*One controversial speaker caused **uproar** in the meeting.*

riot (2) VERB

When people **riot**, they behave violently in a public place.

rampage
*Rioters **rampaged** through the streets, breaking windows and shouting.*

revolt
*Asked to pay crippling taxes, the poor peasants **revolted** against the king.*

run wild
*After the match, the supporters of the losing team **ran wild** in the streets.*

rip VERB

If you **rip** something, you tear it.

split
*When the man bent down, his trousers **split**!*

tear
*In fury, Mrs Carr **tore** the comic up.*

rise (1) VERB

If something **rises**, it moves upwards.

ascend
*Over the intercom, the pilot told us we were **ascending** to 30 000 feet.*

climb
*The aeroplane grew smaller as it **climbed**.*

go up
*The hot-air balloon **went up** into the air.*

mount
*As the money came in, the piles of banknotes **mounted**.*

ANTONYM: descend

rise (2) VERB

If prices **rise**, things get more expensive.

go up
*"The cost of houses has **gone up** enormously," the estate agent said.*

increase
*"The cost of postage has **increased** again," moaned Mum.*

ANTONYM: fall

risk NOUN

Someone or something that is a **risk** is likely to cause harm or have bad results.

danger
*People who drive fast are a **danger** to others.*

gamble
*Taking a **gamble**, the racing driver decided not to stop for new tyres.*

hazard
*That frayed electrical wire is a real **hazard**.*

road NOUN

A **road** is a long stretch of hard ground built between two places so that people can travel along it easily.

✔ A road with the same entrance and exit is called a **dead end** or **cul-de-sac**.

Types of main road:
autobahn (Germany)
autoroute (France)
motorway, dual carriageway (Britain)
expressway, freeway, highway (USA)
autopista (Spain)
freeway, highway (Australia)
freeway (South Africa)
state highway, regional highway, expressway, motorway (New Zealand)

Types of town road:

avenue	crescent
boulevard	place
close	street

Types of country road:

drive	minor road
lane	track

roar VERB

If something **roars**, it makes a very loud noise.

bellow

The buffalo **bellowed** in anger as the hunters approached cautiously.

howl

When the moon is full, you can hear the husky dogs **howl** in the icy wastes.

thunder

"Do as I say, boy!" **thundered** Squeers at Nicholas Nickleby.

rob VERB

If someone **robs** a person or place, they steal money or property from them.

burgle

While Mum's friends were away, their house was **burgled**.

defraud

The clerk tried to **defraud** his employers.

loot

Marauding Vikings **looted** the treasures of the monasteries.

steal from

The robbers had an elaborate plan to disable the burglar alarm and **steal from** the jewellery shop.

swindle

Two employees were sacked for **swindling** money from the company.

✔ Someone who robs a person or place is a **burglar**, **robber** or **thief**.

robbery NOUN

Robbery is the action of robbing a person or place.

burglary

Burglary involves breaking into someone else's property.

theft

"**Theft** is a nasty crime. I bet thieves wouldn't like having things stolen!" said Granny.

rock VERB

When something **rocks**, or you **rock** it, it moves regularly backwards and forwards or from side to side.

sway

We started **swaying** to the beat of the music.

swing

The pendulum of a clock **swings** to and fro.

rogue NOUN

A **rogue** is a dishonest or mischievous person.

rascal

Long John Silver was more of a **rascal** than a thoroughly evil pirate.

scoundrel

"You **scoundrel**, sir!" bellowed the mayor. "You'll pay for this!"

villain

A black-hearted **villain**, Sykes had few friends in the world.

room (1) NOUN

If there is **room** for something, there is enough space for it.

elbow room

"Push up," said Jay. "I need some **elbow room**."

space

"If you arrive early, there'll be plenty of **space** to sit," advised the ticket seller.

room (2) NOUN

A **room** is a separate section in a building, divided from other rooms by walls.

Different rooms in a house:

bathroom	hallway
bedroom	kitchen
cloakroom	living room
conservatory	lounge
dining room	lobby
en suite bathroom	study

A room

...at the top of a house – **attic** or **loft**

...at the bottom of a house – **cellar** or **basement**

...where several people sleep in a boarding school or hostel – **dormitory**

...where patients sleep in a hospital – **ward**

...where patients are operated on in a hospital – **operating theatre**

...where scientists work – **laboratory**

---

rot VERB

When food, wood or other substances **rot**, or when something rots them, they decay and fall apart.

biodegrade
*Most plastics will not **biodegrade**, which makes them a threat to the environment.*

decay
*When they die, plants and animals **decay**.*

decompose
*The fallen autumn leaves were **decomposing** on the forest floor.*

rotten ADJECTIVE

Something that is **rotten** has decayed.

decayed
*Compost heaps contain **decayed** and decaying plants.*

mouldy
*After being left out for two weeks, the cheese had gone **mouldy**.*

perished
*During the transport strike, tons of vegetables **perished** in their sacks.*

ANTONYM: fresh

rough (1) ADJECTIVE

A **rough** surface is uneven and not smooth.

bumpy
*The rickety bicycle rattled over the **bumpy** cobbled street.*

irregular
*An **irregular** surface is useless for bowling.*

jagged
*Iris trod on the **jagged** edge of a broken bottle and badly cut her foot.*

rocky
*The **rocky** ground was not ideal for pitching our tent.*

stony
*Our car bumped and bounced along the winding **stony** track.*

uneven
*Amir tripped up on the **uneven** footpath.*

ANTONYM: soft or smooth

rough (2) ADJECTIVE

Something that is **rough** is coarse and hairy.

bristly
*Cutthroat Jake's pirate beard was **bristly** and grizzled.*

bushy
*The old major had a big, **bushy** moustache.*

coarse
*My brother's extreme haircut felt **coarse** when I touched it.*

ANTONYM: smooth

rough (3) ADJECTIVE

If a sea is **rough**, the wind and waves are high.

choppy
*Our boat bounced around in the **choppy** water.*

raging
***Raging** seas smashed into the old pier.*

stormy
***Stormy** weather was forecast.*

turbulent
*The wind howled over the **turbulent** sea.*

wild
*It was a **wild** night, and not a night to be out on the sea.*

ANTONYM: calm

rough (4) ADJECTIVE

Someone who is **rough** treats someone in a harsh or violent way.

brutal
*Prison guards were **brutal** in their punishment of the captive.*

harsh
*Boxers often have to take **harsh** treatment in the ring.*

tough
*Life in the jungle is often **tough**.*

ANTONYM: gentle or sympathetic

rough (5) ADJECTIVE

Someone who is **rough** has manners that are rude and insensitive.

blunt
*Arthur was known for his **blunt** speaking.*

rude

*The neighbour was known as a **rude**, unpleasant woman.*

ANTONYM: courteous

rough (6) ADJECTIVE

Rough can mean approximate.

approximate

*"Give me the **approximate** time when you'll finish," Mum said.*

vague

*Bhavesh had a **vague** idea of what Mrs Cunningham wanted.*

ANTONYM: exact or precise

rough (7) ADJECTIVE

A **rough** voice is harsh.

gruff

*A **gruff** voice answered the telephone.*

rasping

*Quilp's **rasping** voice ran through the courtyard.*

ANTONYM: soothing or soft

rough (8) ADJECTIVE

A **rough** sketch is very basic.

crude

*From a **crude** sketch on an envelope came an award-winning car.*

rough-and-ready

*"This is a **rough-and-ready** plan, but it will do," the builder said.*

ANTONYM: detailed or precise

roughly ADVERB

Roughly can mean almost or approximately.

about

*"We'll need **about** 20 sausages and ten bread rolls for the barbecue," Mum told Dad.*

approximately

*"At **approximately** three o'clock, the parade will be in the town centre," the announcement read.*

around

***Around** 300 people came to the wedding.*

ANTONYM: precisely

round ADJECTIVE

Something **round** is shaped like a ball or a circle.

circular

*The round peg goes in the **circular** hole.*

rounded

*The **rounded** nib of the pen helped it to glide smoothly over the page.*

spherical

*Our planet is roughly **spherical** in shape.*

round up VERB

If you **round up** people or animals, you gather them together.

assemble

*Mrs Sneddon **assembled** us all in the playground to see the eclipse.*

collect

*Dad sent me round to the neighbours to **collect** my brother and sister for tea.*

gather

*For shearing, Farmer Gabriel **gathered** his sheep in one large pen.*

herd

*At milking time, cows are **herded** into the farmyard.*

muster

*"In the event of an emergency," the captain announced, "please **muster** on the foredeck."*

row (1) RHYMES WITH "COW" NOUN

A **row** can be an argument.

argument

*Leah could hear a terrific **argument** going on next door.*

disagreement

*Just occasionally, my best friend and I have a real **disagreement**, but we always make up.*

dispute

*A **dispute** about pay caused the workforce to go on strike.*

quarrel

*The two brothers had a **quarrel** about who should inherit the farm.*

squabble

***Squabbles** are always breaking out between my two brothers.*

a
b
c
d
e
f
g
h
i
j
k
l
m
n
o
p
q
r
s
t
u
v
w
x
y
z

A
B
C
D
E
F
G
H
I
J
K
L
M
N
O
P
Q
R
S
T
U
V
W
X
Y
Z

row (2) RHYMES WITH "COW" NOUN
A **row** can be a lot of noise.

cacophony
The school band was tuning up – what a ***cacophony****!*

din
*Above the **din**, I heard Mrs Ahmed open the classroom door.*

racket
*"What on earth is this **racket** all about?" shouted Mrs Jensen as she came in.*

row (3) RHYMES WITH "SNOW" NOUN
A **row** is several objects or people in a line.

file
*We had to walk in single **file** to the main hall for assembly.*

line
*Several **lines** of cars waited for the ferry.*

queue
*For once, the dinner **queue** was not too long.*

series
*Strip cartoons are formed from a **series** of pictures and captions.*

rub out VERB
If you **rub** something **out**, you delete it.

delete
*With one keystroke, Dad managed to **delete** all his evening's work.*

erase
*If you work in pencil, it's easy to **erase** what you've done.*

remove
*Mr Rafferty suggested that I **remove** "nice" and substitute "pleasant".*

rubbish (1) NOUN
Rubbish is unwanted things or waste material.

garbage
Garbage lay piled up in and around the bin.

junk
*Dad suggested I help him sort out any **junk** in the garage.*

litter
*"It's amazing how casual some people are about dropping **litter**," observed Haresh.*

refuse
*"I hate it when public **refuse** bins are left to overflow," said Gran.*

scrap
*In the iron foundry, any **scrap** is put back into the furnace.*

trash AMERICAN
*Americans call their waste material "**trash**".*

waste
*In the western world, human **waste** goes into the sewers and on for treatment.*

rubbish (2) NOUN
If you talk **rubbish**, you say something foolish.

bunkum INFORMAL
*Dad thought the man was talking **bunkum**.*

drivel
*That book was such **drivel** that I only read one chapter of it.*

hot air INFORMAL
*Everyone knew that Jim was talking **hot air**.*

nonsense
*"It's utter **nonsense** to believe the world is flat!" I told my little brother.*

piffle INFORMAL
*"Don't talk **piffle**, Jeeves!" Wooster exclaimed peevishly.*

twaddle INFORMAL
*Mr Carp told Billy he was talking **twaddle**.*

rude ADJECTIVE
Someone who is **rude** is not polite.

abusive
*The player was sent off for being **abusive** to the referee.*

bad-mannered
*It is **bad-mannered** to interrupt people who are talking.*

cheeky
*My brother can be very **cheeky** sometimes.*

ill-mannered
*The **ill-mannered** boy never said "please" or "thank you".*

insolent
*Teachers in our school won't stand for pupils who are **insolent** to them.*

insulting

*If you don't reply to an invitation, it is **insulting** to the host.*

offensive

*Keisha thought that Pauline's remark was **offensive**.*

ANTONYM: polite or courteous or well-mannered

ruin VERB

*If you **ruin** something, you destroy or spoil it completely.*

destroy

*Wartime air raids had **destroyed** the city centre.*

devastate

*The hurricane **devastated** a vast swathe of the coastline.*

spoil

*Adara **spoilt** her book by scribbling on the cover.*

wreck

*"Don't **wreck** your exam chances by staying up late," Dad advised.*

*See **damage***

ruins PLURAL NOUN

Ruins *are what is left after something has been severely damaged.*

debris

*After the explosion, a huge amount of **debris** remained to be cleared.*

wreckage

***Wreckage** from the aircraft was strewn across the hillside.*

rule VERB

*When someone **rules** a country or a group of people, they govern it and are in charge of its affairs.*

control

*Mrs Samuels **controls** our class very firmly.*

govern

*Usually, the party with the most votes is the one that **governs** the country.*

lead

*Some countries are **led** by a prime minister, others by a president.*

reign

*Queen Victoria **reigned** over Britain for most of the 19th century.*

ruler NOUN

*A **ruler** is a person who rules a country.*

> **Types of ruler:**
>
> | | |
> |---|---|
> | emperor | president |
> | head of state | prince |
> | king | queen |
> | maharajah | sheikh |
> | monarch | sovereign |

run (1) VERB

*When you **run**, you move quickly, with both feet leaving the ground at each stride.*

jog

*My grandad still goes out **jogging** each day.*

trot

*My brother **trotted** downstairs to answer the door.*

run fast:

dart

*When the vet had finished, our dog Jim **darted** for the door.*

dash

*Craig must have been crazy to **dash** across the road like that.*

gallop

*The winning horse **galloped** over the finishing line to a loud cheer from the crowd.*

sprint

*On the last lap, Tyrone **sprinted** for the finish.*

tear

*Although my sister **tore** down the road, her friend had disappeared.*

run clumsily:

career

*Out of control, the horse and cart **careered** down the hill.*

lollop INFORMAL

*Our dog Wuffles came **lolloping** up to greet me.*

lumber

*The great carthorse **lumbered** down the road pulling the wagon.*

run (2) VERB

If you **run** an activity or a place, such as a school or a shop, you are in charge of it.

administer
*Mum **administers** a team of salespeople.*

be in charge of
*My dad **is in charge of** the store's kitchenware department.*

control
*A lady at a desk **controls** the lighting for the show.*

direct
*As the incident was serious, the chief of police **directed** the rescue.*

manage
*When I grow up, I want to **manage** a factory.*

run (3) VERB

When a machine **runs**, it is operating.

function
*The ancient laptop **functioned** well for the thesaurus writer.*

operate
*Our washing machine **operates** easily if you know which button to press.*

work
*"I can use a computer," said Dad, "but I'll never understand how one **works**!"*

run (4) VERB

If a liquid, river or road **runs** somewhere, it flows there or takes that particular course.

flow
*The waterfall **flowed** noisily over the cliff.*

gush
*Boiling water **gushed** from Dad's leaking car radiator.*

pour
*As the cyclists climbed the hill, you could see the sweat **pouring** off them.*

stream
*The river **streamed** over the border into the next country.*

trickle
*The stream **trickled** gently over the rocks.*

runny ADJECTIVE

Something that is **runny** is flowing or moving like liquid.

liquid
*The **liquid** chocolate is then poured into moulds to make chocolate Easter bunnies.*

watery
*"This gravy's very **watery**," the diner grumbled.*

ANTONYM: solid

rush VERB

If you **rush** somewhere, or if you are rushed there, you go there quickly.

dash
*I **dashed** to the post office to try and catch the last post.*

hasten
*Sir Bedivere **hastened** to the side of the dying King Arthur.*

hurry
*"We'll have to **hurry** or we'll miss the train," Mum said.*

scurry
*Our hamster Harold **scurried** round and round in his wheel.*

speed
*The police car **sped** towards the scene of the accident.*

See **run (1)**

Ss

sack VERB

If someone is **sacked**, they are dismissed from their job by their employer.

discharge

The private was **discharged** from the army for dishonest behaviour.

dismiss

A postman or woman might be **dismissed** if they fail to deliver their letters.

fire

Dad had to **fire** one of his staff the other day.

ANTONYM: employ

sad (1) ADJECTIVE

If you are **sad**, you feel unhappy.

dejected

Gollum sat, **dejected**, in the dark of his cave.

depressed

My friend Althea was **depressed** about moving away.

despondent

Having failed to find a job, Jeremy was becoming **despondent**.

distressed

The **distressed** lady stared at her smashed car through tear-filled eyes.

down

I felt very **down** about going back to school.

downcast

Georgia was **downcast** after failing her exam.

down-in-the-dumps

"You look **down-in-the-dumps**," Dad said. "What's the matter?"

glum

Abdel's **glum** face told me immediately what his exam result was.

low

Mum was a bit **low** when Dad had to go away on business for a few weeks.

melancholy

Melancholy for his lost love, the knight loitered by the lake, alone and pale.

miserable

I was **miserable** when I broke my arm.

tearful

There were many **tearful** faces at Mrs Kahn's leaving party.

unhappy

The soccer player was **unhappy** with the way he had played.

upset

Mum was very **upset** about the broken vase.

ANTONYM: happy

sad (2) ADJECTIVE

If something is **sad**, it makes you feel unhappy or upset.

depressing

I found the film very **depressing**.

heart-rending

It was **heart-rending** to think that many of those children were orphans.

moving

In a **moving** scene, the old man embraced his long-lost son.

ANTONYM: happy

sadness NOUN

Sadness is a feeling of unhappiness.

dejection

Her exam results filled Marcia with **dejection**.

despair

Losing his family brought Mr Cort to the brink of **despair**.

grief

The **grief** shone in Lyra's eyes as she parted from Will for the last time.

misery

Deena was a picture of **misery** as she sat in the corner.

sorrow

For months after the plane crash, the town was a place of **sorrow**.

unhappiness

An air of **unhappiness** filled the old house.

ANTONYM: happiness

safe

A B C D E F G H I J K L M N O P Q R **S** T U V W X Y Z

safe (1) ADJECTIVE
If you are **safe**, you are not in any danger.

in safe hands
We knew that Hammy, our hamster, was **in safe hands** *when we left him with our gran.*

out of danger
We were relieved, after her operation, to hear Gran was **out of danger**.

safe and sound
"The missing walkers have been found **safe and sound**," *the journalist reported.*

safe (2) ADJECTIVE
Something that is **safe** does not cause harm or danger.

harmless
The weedkiller is supposed to be **harmless** *to animals.*

nontoxic
Toys for young children must be made of **nontoxic** *materials.*

uncontaminated
Despite the chemical leak, the river nearby remained **uncontaminated**.

wholesome
"This food is **wholesome** *and very good for you," said Mum.*

✔ A safe vehicle is **roadworthy**.
A safe boat or ship is **seaworthy**.

ANTONYM: dangerous

safety NOUN
Safety is the state of being safe or protected.

protection
For **protection** *from fairy spells, Tamara and Kylie had to wear mirrored sunglasses.*

refuge
The hostel was a place of **refuge** *for people in danger.*

security
For his **security**, *the prisoner was ushered through the crowd by armed guards.*

shelter
The two hobbits sought **shelter** *in a vast cave in the side of the mountain.*

same (1) ADJECTIVE
If two things are the **same**, they are like one another.

alike
The twins were **alike** *in several ways.*

identical
"That's weird! We've got an **identical** *vase at home," Lexi said.*

matching
"A **matching** *pair of candlesticks – what am I bid?" the auctioneer began.*

similar
Although **similar** *in looks, Michaela and her sister have very different characters.*

uniform
"Each can of beans needs to be of **uniform** *flavour and quality," explained the factory manager.*

ANTONYM: different

same (2) ADJECTIVE
If something stays the **same**, it is not different from what it was.

consistent
The umpire was **consistent**: *each player received the same treatment.*

unaltered
Despite her illness, Nora's sense of humour remained **unaltered**.

unchanged
After all those years, the house looked **unchanged**.

unvarying
With **unvarying** *accuracy, the snooker player potted every ball.*

✔ Words that mean the same as each other are **synonyms**.

ANTONYM: inconsistent or varying

save (1) VERB
If you **save** someone or something, you rescue them or help to keep them safe.

come to the rescue
Fortunately, my sister **came to the rescue** *and gave me a lift.*

preserve
*Chris **preserved** leaves by pressing them in blotting paper.*

rescue
*A helicopter **rescued** the injured crewman, taking him to hospital.*

safeguard
*Insurance **safeguards** you if things get lost or damaged.*

salvage
*The tug **salvaged** the abandoned tanker.*

See **protect**

save (2) VERB
If you **save** something, you keep it so that you can use it later.

hoard
*Fagin carefully **hoarded** the stolen goods.*

put by
*"We've got a little money **put by** for a rainy day," Gran told Mum.*

reserve
*Navdip **reserved** a few sandwiches, in case there were any latecomers to the party.*

salt away
*No one knew that the old lady had **salted away** so much money.*

ANTONYM: spend or use

save (3) VERB
If you **save** time, money or effort, you stop it from being wasted.

cut back
*Looking right at me, Dad said we needed to **cut back** on our phone bill.*

economize
*It was difficult for the pop star to **economize**, having once been so rich.*

ANTONYM: waste

say (1) VERB
If you **say** something, you speak words.

say a lot:
babble
*Little George sat in his pushchair, **babbling** away to himself.*

burble
*As Grandad snoozed, Old Chalkie **burbled** on about his childhood.*

chatter
*Lila, who sits on our table, never stops **chattering**.*

prattle
*I do wish James would stop **prattling** about nothing.*

say angrily:
snap
*"Just do as I say!" my mother **snapped** at my brother and me.*

snarl
*The gangster **snarled**, "You're in for a bit of bother now, matey!"*

say hesitantly:
stammer
*The little girl **stammered** that she h-h-hadn't d-d-done it.*

stutter
*"W-would you l-like a cup of tea?" the office junior **stuttered** to his boss.*

say loudly:
bawl
*Our neighbour is always **bawling** at his children.*

bellow
*"And don't you dare come back!" the farmer **bellowed** at the poachers.*

call out
*"Is there anyone home?" Mum **called out** as she came through the door.*

cry
*"Hello!" **cried** Aunty Ruby across the shop. "Fancy seeing you here!"*

exclaim
*"Well, I'll be blowed!" **exclaimed** the man in the blazer.*

shout
*A **shout** went up from the crowd when the ball went into the net.*

yell
*Milly hopped round the yard, **yelling** that she'd been stung.*

say miserably:
groan
*"Not Monday again!" my sister **groaned**, as I bounced onto her bed.*

moan
*The injured navigator **moaned** then slipped into unconsciousness.*

whine
*My kid brother is always **whining** that I never play with him.*

say quickly:
gabble
*"There's no need to **gabble**, Angela," Miss Macken said. "Start again slowly."*

jabber
*The parrot **jabbered** away in its cage, quite happy with its own company.*

say quietly:
mumble
*"I'm sorry, miss," Elliot **mumbled**.*

murmur
*There was a **murmuring** from the crowd, and a woman was pushed forward.*

mutter
*Harry could hear Ron **muttering** a spell under his breath.*

whimper
*Tearful and bedraggled, the child **whimpered** that he was lost.*

whisper
*"It's a secret. Can I **whisper**?" Anita asked.*

say slowly:
drawl
*"Y'all are welcome," old Grandpa Walton **drawled** from his rocking chair.*

drone
*Mrs Blake over the road always **drones** on and on about her garden!*

say suddenly:
blurt out
*Neha **blurted out** that she was going to be sick.*

butt in
*"Please don't **butt in**, Harry," Mrs Dursley said.*

interject
*"That's not true!" **interjected** Susi.*

interrupt
*"I wish you wouldn't keep **interrupting**, Nadine," Ellie said.*

say strongly or formally:
announce
*Last night my brother **announced** he was joining the navy.*

declare
*The president **declared** that anyone who disagreed was a traitor.*

pronounce
*"I now **pronounce** you husband and wife" are the key words of a church wedding service.*

state
*The freed defendant **stated** that he was delighted with the verdict.*

say (2) VERB
If you **say** something, you make a remark about something.

mention
*"Did I **mention** that I've been invited to a party on Saturday?" asked Zahin.*

put in
*"Or we could stay near a golf course," **put in** my father, brightly.*

remark
*My mum **remarked** on how many birds were in the garden.*

say (3) VERB
If you **say** what you mean, you express what you are thinking.

communicate
*"I'd like you to try to **communicate** your opinions in your homework," said Mrs Moss.*

express
*Dumbledore **expressed** his views firmly.*

put into words
*Padma found it hard to **put into words** what she was feeling.*

saying NOUN
A **saying** is a well-known sentence or phrase that tells you something about life.

expression
*"The show must go on" is an **expression** that is familiar to many people.*

motto

*"Dare to be wise" is the **motto** of our school.*

proverb

*Grandad's favourite **proverb** is "A stitch in time saves nine".*

quotation

*My mum was always coming out with **quotations** from Shakespeare.*

scarce ADJECTIVE

If something is **scarce**, there is not very much of it.

few and far between

*On the island, filling stations were **few and far between**.*

in short supply

*During winter, good weather for photography is **in short supply**.*

rare

*Golden eagles are mountain birds **rare** in European lands.*

ANTONYM: plentiful

scare VERB

If something **scares** you, it frightens you.

alarm

*"Don't be **alarmed**," the nurse said. "You'll only feel a little prick."*

frighten

*We keep our dogs on a lead so that they do not **frighten** sheep.*

give someone a fright

*I really **gave my sister a fright** with that gorilla mask!*

put the wind up INFORMAL

*Zoltan **put the wind up** me when he pretended to be a ghost.*

shock

*The spate of murders **shocked** the whole city and made people afraid to go out at night.*

startle

*My mum was **startled** when the seagull suddenly swooped on her sandwich.*

terrify

*In wartime, people must be **terrified** when the air-raid sirens sound.*

scary ADJECTIVE INFORMAL

If something is **scary** it is frightening.

alarming

*We found the sudden blast of the foghorn truly **alarming**.*

bloodcurdling

*From another flat in the block came a **bloodcurdling** scream.*

frightening

*The programme was too **frightening** to watch.*

spine-chilling

*Harry goes through many **spine-chilling** tussles with the forces of evil.*

terrifying

*Hanging onto the rope was a **terrifying** ordeal for the fallen climber.*

score NOUN

A **score** is the number of goals, runs or points obtained by the two opponents in a game.

marks

*Mrs Ferguson gave me full **marks** for my maths test.*

result

*"Did you hear the **result** of the big game?" Bruce asked me.*

tally

*The German had notched up an impressive **tally** of grand prix wins.*

total

*After she had marked my answers, Liz told me my **total**.*

scrape VERB

If something **scrapes** something else, it rubs against it harshly.

grate

*As the old car trundled along, its broken exhaust **grated** on the road surface.*

graze

*Iman **grazed** her knee on a wall when she fell off her bike.*

rasp

*Metal **rasped** on metal as Dad filed away at my bike frame.*

scratch

*The cat **scratched** on the door to be let in.*

A
B
C
D
E
F
G
H
I
J
K
L
M
N
O
P
Q
R
S
T
U
V
W
X
Y
Z

scream (1) VERB

If you **scream**, you shout or cry in a loud, high-pitched voice.

bawl

*That spoilt toddler really **bawled** when she was refused sweets!*

cry

*"Death to the enemy!" the warrior chief **cried**, as he plunged into battle.*

shriek

*You should have heard my sister **shriek** when she saw the toy mouse.*

squeal

*Marsha **squealed** with delight when she saw her birthday present.*

scream (2) NOUN

A **scream** is a loud, high-pitched cry.

cry

*Searching for the lost child, police heard a sudden **cry** from the woods.*

shriek

*The zombie let out a **shriek** and began to crumple – daylight had dawned.*

squeal

*The **squeals** of the hungry piglets could be heard all around the farmyard.*

scruffy ADJECTIVE

Someone or something **scruffy** is dirty and untidy.

bedraggled

*Wuffles, our dog, was a **bedraggled** heap when our neighbour found him.*

ragged

*My football kit was looking pretty **ragged**.*

shabby

*You could tell from her **shabby** coat that times were not too good for the ex-actress.*

tattered

***Tattered** and blackened, the cartoon cat emerged from the explosion.*

tatty

*"That exercise book is too **tatty** for me to mark," Mr Singh said in disgust.*

ANTONYM: smart

search (1) VERB

If you **search** for something, you look for it very thoroughly.

comb

*Police **combed** the area for the missing twins and eventually found them safe and well.*

hunt

*I **hunted** everywhere for my pencil, and eventually found it in my pencil case!*

look high and low

*Long John Silver **looked high and low**, but couldn't find the hidden treasure.*

ransack

*Thieves **ransacked** the flat and stole several items of jewellery.*

rummage through

*The investigator **rummaged through** the bin, but found no useful evidence.*

scour

*"I've hidden some sweets," Mum said. "I suggest you **scour** the yard."*

✔ To search for gold or other valuable minerals is to **prospect**.

search (2) NOUN

A **search** is an attempt to find something.

hunt

*Detectives are continuing the **hunt** for the killer.*

quest

*The pirate's lifelong **quest** for treasure ended in heartbreak.*

✔ A **search party** is a group of people who search for a missing person.

seaside NOUN

The **seaside** is a place by the sea, especially where people go on holiday.

beach

*At Mediterranean resorts, the **beaches** are often swarming with people.*

coast

*On the **coast**, the weather was superb, while inland it was cloudy.*

coastline

*"This stretch of **coastline** is the habitat of many wading birds," Uncle Colin told me.*

seashore

*Dad and I wandered along the **seashore** looking for driftwood.*

Words from a seaside port:

docks	lifeboat station
ferry	lighthouse
harbour	quay
jetty	warehouse

Words from a seaside resort:

amusements	hotel
beach	pier
bed and breakfast	promenade
guesthouse	souvenir shop

Words from the natural seaside:

cliffs	sand
driftwood	sand dunes
estuary	seashore
mud flats	seaweed
pebble	shingle

second NOUN

A **second** is one of the 60 parts that a minute is divided into.

flash

*In a **flash**, Wuffles our dog had gobbled the meat I had dropped.*

instant

*For an **instant**, Sam thought the dressing gown on the door was a ghost.*

jiffy INFORMAL

*"I'll be back in a **jiffy**," Colleen promised.*

moment

*The **moment** Mum's back was turned, my sister was pulling faces.*

twinkling of an eye

*Ratty, in the **twinkling of an eye**, had the kettle boiling.*

secret ADJECTIVE

Something that is **secret** is known to only a small number of people and hidden from everyone else.

classified

*"That information is **classified**," M said. "I couldn't possibly reveal it."*

confidential

*Anything you say to your doctor is **confidential**.*

hush-hush INFORMAL

*The scientists were working on a very **hush-hush** project.*

private

*Some court hearings are kept **private**, without any press there.*

top-secret

*Moneypenny handed Bond a file marked "**Top-Secret**".*

see (1) VERB

If you **see** something, you look at it or notice it with your eyes.

behold OLD-FASHIONED

*Ever since Reinhold first **beheld** Everest, he wanted to climb it.*

clap eyes on INFORMAL

*"I hadn't **clapped eyes on** old Porky for years," Grandpa chortled.*

glimpse

*Fiona managed to **glimpse** the film star through the crowds.*

notice

*Ken **noticed** that one of his tyres was flat.*

observe

*The nurse **observed** a change in my grandad's condition.*

perceive

*"I **perceive**," Holmes said, "that you have recently bought new boots."*

sight

*From the east, the lookout **sighted** smoke on the horizon.*

spot

*It wasn't hard to **spot** that Mum was expecting a baby.*

watch

*From her window, Alisha was able to **watch** the whole of the carnival.*

witness

*The passer-by claimed to have **witnessed** three men running from the bank.*

See **look**

A
B
C
D
E
F
G
H
I
J
K
L
M
N
O
P
Q
R
S
T
U
V
W
X
Y
Z

see (2) VERB
If you **see** something, you understand it or realize what it means.

appreciate
"It is difficult to **appreciate** the size of the blue whale," said the naturalist.

comprehend
"You do not seem to **comprehend** the seriousness of the offence," said the judge.

follow
It was quite hard to **follow** from the instructions how to put the shelves together.

get INFORMAL
"I just don't **get** how to do long division," moaned Bharat.

grasp
After she had explained several times, I finally **grasped** what Daphne was saying.

realize
The twins **realized** that they would need help.

understand
At last, Steve **understood** what had happened.

see (3) VERB
If you go to **see** someone, you visit them.

call on
I often **call on** my grandma on the way home from school.

look up INFORMAL
When Dad went to London on business he **looked up** an old school friend.

visit
"I've really enjoyed **visiting** you all," said Auntie Megan.

see (4) VERB
If you **see** to something, you make sure that it is done.

attend to
Legolas **attended to** the horses, while Frodo saw to the baggage.

be responsible for
In our school, Mr Brockbank **is responsible for** music and drama.

look after
"Can you **look after** the washing-up while I tidy round?" Mum asked.

organize
Kevin and his team **organized** the church fête.

sort out
With her courteous, calm approach, Myra was good at **sorting out** angry customers.

seem VERB
If something **seems** to be the case, it appears to be the case, or you think it is the case.

appear
"It **appears** that we've run out of honey," Dad remarked at breakfast.

give the impression of
At first Mrs Facey **gave the impression of** being a real dragon, but she's really quite nice.

look
"The game **looks** easy, but wait till you try it!" said Holden.

seldom ADVERB
Something that **seldom** happens, does not happen very often.

hardly ever
Dad **hardly ever** loses his temper.

not often
I'm **not often** late for school because Mum makes sure I leave home on time.

only once in a while
Only once in a while does my sister become a real nuisance.

rarely
"**Rarely** has anyone got such high marks," Miss Benjamin said, beaming.

ANTONYM: often

selfish ADJECTIVE
If you are **selfish**, you care only about yourself, and not about other people.

egotistical
Film stars are notorious for being demanding and **egotistical**.

greedy
It was pretty **greedy** of Salimah to hog all the meringues.

self-centred
Self-centred people generally like to talk about themselves.

sell VERB

Someone who **sells** things, deals in a particular type of goods to earn money.

deal in

*Jon **dealt in** antique furniture and knows a great deal about the trade.*

peddle

*The old lady scratched a living by **peddling** clothes pegs door-to-door.*

retail

*A nearby filling station wants to **retail** alcohol, but the council won't allow it.*

trade in

*Steptoe's Market **trades in** all sorts of second-hand odds and ends.*

send VERB

When you **send** something to someone, you arrange for it to be delivered to them.

dispatch

*"Yes, sir, we **dispatched** your order this morning," came the reply.*

mail

*My auntie in America said she had **mailed** my birthday card.*

post

*School reports are **posted** to our parents at the end of each term.*

sense (1) NOUN

Sense is the ability to think and behave sensibly.

common sense

*Rimon had the **common sense** to tell Mrs Milner what he had seen.*

intelligence

*My brother does such silly things, I sometimes wonder about his level of **intelligence**!*

reason

*The customer almost lost her temper, but finally saw **reason**.*

wisdom

*Aslan was a creature of great knowledge and **wisdom**.*

wit

*Thank goodness Francis had the **wit** to phone for an ambulance!*

sense (2) NOUN

A **sense** of a word is one of its meanings.

connotation

*Even simple words sometimes have more than one **connotation**.*

meaning

*I asked Mr Hammond which **meaning** of the word "sink" he meant.*

sensible ADJECTIVE

If a person or idea is **sensible**, they show good sense and judgment.

practical

*It wouldn't really be **practical** to run a restaurant on Mount Everest.*

prudent

*Mrs Svensson praised us for being **prudent** when we crossed the road.*

rational

*The paramedic was able to remain calm and **rational** in an emergency.*

realistic

*"It is not **realistic** to expect to win every game," Mrs Fern told the team.*

wise

*The **wise** old wizard was always willing to advise others.*

ANTONYM: foolish or impractical

separate (1) SAID "SEP-AR-UT" ADJECTIVE

If something is **separate** from something else, the two things are not connected.

apart

*The new pupil stood slightly **apart** from the others.*

detached

***Detached** houses are not joined to others.*

individual

*I love the **individual** chocolate desserts Mum sometimes buys us as a treat.*

isolated

*Our holiday cottage was **isolated** – not another soul for miles!*

ANTONYM: connected or together

*See **alone***

a
b
c
d
e
f
g
h
i
j
k
l
m
n
o
p
q
r
s
t
u
v
w
x
y
z

separate (2) SAID "SEP-AR-ATE" VERB
If you **separate** people or things, you cause them to be apart from each other.

detach
*The courageous railwayman managed to **detach** the blazing wagon from the rest of the train.*

disconnect
*Our television would not work as the aerial had been **disconnected**.*

divide
*A curtain **divided** the kitchen area from the rest of the bedsit.*

part
*Dad **parted** the fighting dogs with a bucket of cold water.*

split
*"Why not **split** the chocolate and each have some?" Mum suggested.*

ANTONYM: join

series NOUN
A **series** is a number of things coming one after the other.

sequence
*The author had written a **sequence** of detective novels.*

string
*For five years, United had a **string** of soccer successes.*

succession
*We'd waited for ages, then a **succession** of buses came at once.*

serious (1) ADJECTIVE
A **serious** problem or situation is very bad and worrying.

critical
*The car engine was in a **critical** state: any longer without oil would have finished it.*

grave
*A sombre announcement came from the palace: the king's condition was **grave**, and people should prepare for the worst.*

severe
*X-rays showed that Ken had a **severe** fracture of the ankle.*

serious (2) ADJECTIVE
Serious matters are important and should be thought about carefully.

important
*Even Bilbo felt the wizard's request was too **important** to turn down.*

significant
*Oxygen made a **significant** difference to Hillary's chances of reaching the summit.*

weighty
*"This is a **weighty** matter," said the prime minister, "and is not to be ignored."*

serious (3) ADJECTIVE
If you are **serious** about something, you really mean it.

committed
*"You have to be **committed** to the game if you want to stay in the team," the coach said.*

determined
*Nisha was quite **determined** when it came to her career.*

sincere
*The millionaire's offer sounded too generous, but he was **sincere** about it.*

serious (4) ADJECTIVE
People who are **serious** are thoughtful, quiet and do not laugh much.

grave
*Our **grave** Uncle Arthur was quiet over lunch.*

solemn
*Usually **solemn**, Laith roared with laughter at Petra's joke.*

stern
*Although Mrs Jansen is a **stern** teacher, I enjoy her lessons.*

serve (1) VERB
When someone **serves** customers in a shop, bar or restaurant, they help them and supply them with what they want.

assist
*"May I **assist** you?" said the lady in the cosmetics department.*

attend to
*Naturally enough, the staff **attended to** the people at the front of the queue first.*

wait on
*We were **waited on** by my sister's friend.*

serve (2) VERB
If you **serve** food or drink to people, you give it to them.

distribute
*The kind women **distributed** food to the earthquake victims.*

dole out
*As the prisoners queued, food was **doled out** into their bowls.*

*See **provide***

set (1) NOUN
A **set** is a group of things that go together.

batch
*I burnt the first **batch** of scones, but the second set were delicious.*

collection
*Carter has a superb **collection** of stamps.*

group
*Mrs Crouch hung the paintings in a **group** on the art room wall.*

✔ Two things that make a set are called a **pair**.

set (2) VERB
If you **set** something, you decide on it.

decide on
*Mum and Dad **decided on** 9.30 as our starting time.*

determine
*It was **determined** that 007 would be the agent's number.*

establish
*Manchester was **established** as the company's headquarters.*

fix
*Qasim and I **fixed** a time to meet up.*

set (3) VERB
To **set** can mean to become firm or hard.

harden
*The cat ran over the cement before it had **hardened**.*

solidify
*The sour milk had **solidified** in a rather unpleasant manner.*

set off or **set out** VERB
If you **set off** or **set out** on a journey, you start it.

depart
*Frodo and his companion **departed** before anyone else was awake.*

leave
*We **left** for our holidays before I had really woken up.*

shake VERB
If something **shakes**, it moves from side to side or up and down with small, quick movements.

jolt
*Along the bumpy roads the old jalopy **jolted**.*

quiver
*When Wuffles our dog saw the rabbit, he started **quivering** with excitement.*

shiver
*Such was the cold that the explorers **shivered** constantly.*

shudder
*When it struck the iceberg, the whole vessel **shuddered**.*

tremble
*Mr Brownlow found the orphan on his doorstep, **trembling** with cold.*

vibrate
*On the cobbled French roads, the whole vehicle **vibrated**.*

shape NOUN
The **shape** of someone or something is the form or pattern of their outline.

build
*From his shadow, it looked like the man had a burly **build**.*

figure
*My mum's **figure** is good for her age.*

form
*The mythological centaur took the **form** of a horse with the head of a man.*

outline
*The designer sketched the **outline** of the car.*

silhouette
*The police officer could clearly see the attacker's **silhouette** on the blind.*

share (1) VERB

If two people **share** something, they both use it, do it or have it.

distribute
*After our service, the harvest produce was **distributed** among old people of the area.*

divide
*We **divided** the rest of the cake between us.*

go halves INFORMAL
*My brother and I **went halves** on the cost of the bike.*

split
*The four of us **split** the sweets between us.*

share (2) NOUN

A **share** of something is a portion of it.

portion
*I asked for a small **portion** of pie.*

quota
*Each state school receives its **quota** of the country's education money.*

ration
*During wartime, food **rations** were very restricted.*

sharp (1) ADJECTIVE

A **sharp** object has an edge or point that is good for cutting or piercing things.

jagged
***Jagged** rocks tore a hole in the ship's hull.*

pointed
*All that the peasant had with which to defend himself was a **pointed** stick.*

razor-sharp
*"Be careful," warned Dad. "That is a **razor-sharp** knife."*

ANTONYM: blunt

sharp (2) ADJECTIVE

Someone who is **sharp** can pick up ideas very quickly.

alert
*The **alert** watchman noticed flames coming from the warehouse.*

astute
*"It was **astute** of you to see that the swimmer was in trouble," the manager told the lifeguard.*

observant
*The wanted man was spotted by an **observant** police officer.*

perceptive
*"Michael is a very **perceptive** young man and will go far," said Professor Peabody.*

quick-witted
*A **quick-witted** guard punctured the getaway car's tyres.*

ANTONYM: slow

sharp (3) ADJECTIVE

A **sharp** pain is strong and sudden.

acute
*Grandad complained of an **acute** pain in his stomach.*

intense
*That first night, Crusoe had an **intense** feeling of loneliness.*

sharp (4) ADJECTIVE

A **sharp** picture is well-defined and not blurred.

clear
*After the rain, the view of the distant hills was beautifully **clear**.*

distinct
*Dad fiddled with the focus on the projector until the picture was **distinct**.*

well-defined
*The security camera produced **well-defined** pictures of the bank robber.*

ANTONYM: blurred

shelter (1) VERB

To **shelter** someone or something means to protect them from bad weather or danger.

protect
*A tree may not **protect** you from a lightning strike in a storm.*

safeguard
*The knight promised the king that he would **safeguard** the princess from danger.*

shield
*The bus shelter **shielded** us from the worst of the rain.*

shelter (2) NOUN
If a place gives **shelter**, it protects you from bad weather or danger.

haven
*A country cottage was the pop star's **haven** from all the publicity.*

protection
*Although small, the umbrella offered some **protection** from the rain.*

refuge
*The hobbits sought **refuge** in a cave until the Black Riders had passed.*

sanctuary
*In medieval times, churches offered **sanctuary** to outlaws on the run.*

shine (1) VERB
When something **shines**, it is bright because it gives out or reflects light.

gleam
*Gran's polished brass **gleamed** on the sideboard.*

glint
*Excalibur, the enchanted sword, **glinted** above the lake.*

glisten
*Snow lay everywhere, and the treetops **glistened**.*

glitter
*I made a birthday card for Mum and covered it with little bits of something that **glittered**.*

shimmer
*We watched the ferry set sail across the sea, which was **shimmering** in the sunlight.*

sparkle
*The duchess's diamond **sparkled** in the candlelight.*

✔ Something that shines in the dark is **luminous**.

shine (2) NOUN
If something has a **shine**, its surface shines.

gloss
*You varnish something to put a **gloss** on it.*

radiance
*A coal fire on a winter's night gives out a lovely **radiance**.*

sheen
*Kalila brushed her pony until its coat had a **sheen**.*

shiny ADJECTIVE
Shiny things are bright and look as if they have been polished.

gleaming
*After I'd finished, Mum's car was **gleaming**.*

glistening
***Glistening** icicles dangled from frozen roofs.*

glossy
*I like to brush our dog until her coat is **glossy**.*

sleek
*My uncle drew up in a **sleek** new sports car.*

ANTONYM: dull

ship NOUN
A **ship** is a large boat that carries passengers or cargo.

boat
***Boats** range in size from tiny dinghies to supertankers.*

craft
*The estuary was crammed with **craft**.*

vessel
*Before that fateful day, everyone thought the Titanic was an unsinkable **vessel**.*

shiver VERB
When you **shiver**, you tremble slightly because you are cold or scared.

quake
*Our poor dog **quakes** with fear whenever there's a thunderstorm.*

quiver
*The bomb-disposal expert's hand **quivered** for a moment as he went to cut the wire.*

shake
*Jake sat **shaking** in front of the fire until his cold, wet clothes had dried off.*

shudder
*As we sat at the bus stop in the snow, I started **shuddering** with the cold.*

tremble
*Bonnie **trembled** at the thought of the test coming up.*

a b c d e f g h i j k l m n o p q r **s** t u v w x y z

shocking ADJECTIVE

Something **shocking** upsets you because it is unpleasant and unexpected.

appalling

"I think it's **appalling** that they want to demolish that lovely building!" Mum exclaimed.

dreadful

When the climber fell so far it was a **dreadful** experience, but she came out of it unscathed.

horrifying

It was **horrifying** to think how close we came to having an accident.

outrageous

The major considered it **outrageous** not to wear a tie at dinner.

shoot VERB

To **shoot** can mean to fire a gun.

discharge

The first mate **discharged** his musket, killing one of the pirates.

fire

"Starboard guns – **fire!**" bellowed the captain.

open fire

As the battleship swung round, its huge guns **opened fire**.

shop NOUN

A **shop** is a place where things are sold.

✔ A shopping centre, if it is pedestrianized (no cars allowed), is called a **mall** or a **precinct**.

Some types of shops:

boutique	hypermarket
cash-and-carry	newsagent
corner shop	supermarket
department store	superstore

shopping NOUN

Your **shopping** is the goods you have bought in a shop.

goods

The notice read, "Customers may collect large **goods** from the rear of the store".

purchases

People put their **purchases** in baskets or trolleys when they go round supermarkets.

short (1) ADJECTIVE

Something **short** does not last very long.

brief

After a **brief** pause to clear her throat, Mrs McQueen began to speak.

fleeting

The birdwatcher caught a **fleeting** glimpse of the eagle.

momentary

At the end of the concert there was a **momentary** silence, followed by applause.

short-lived

The singer's success was **short-lived** – after one hit he faded from the limelight.

short-term

String provided a **short-term** solution for our car's dangling exhaust pipe.

temporary

There was a **temporary** delay while the train driver ate his sandwiches.

ANTONYM: long

short (2) ADJECTIVE

Someone or something **short** is small in height, length or distance.

dumpy

The seven dwarves were **dumpy** characters who sang a lot.

little

A **little** distance ahead the road divided and we weren't sure which way to go.

low

There was a **low** outbuilding round the back of the house.

small

"It's only a **small** hill – you will all get up it," Mr Barraclough encouraged everyone.

squat

The cottage we stayed in on holiday was a **squat** little place with windows in the roof.

wee SCOTTISH

At the foot of the mountain, beside the loch, stood a **wee** house.

ANTONYM: tall or long

short (3) ADJECTIVE

If something is in **short** supply, you do not have enough of it.

limited
*In the drifting boat, water was **limited** and had to be rationed.*

scarce
*During the drought, food was very **scarce** and people became hungry.*

ANTONYM: abundant

short (4) ADJECTIVE

A **short** piece of writing is not very long.

brief
*"Write a **brief** description of your house," Mr Coopland told us.*

concise
*Entries in a dictionary should be **concise** and not too long-winded.*

succinct
*Mum wrote a **succinct** letter to the council about parking on our street.*

ANTONYM: lengthy

shortage NOUN

If there is a **shortage** of something, there is not enough of it.

deficiency
*A **deficiency** of vitamin C gave 18th-century sailors a disease called scurvy.*

lack
*Owing to a **lack** of support, the show has been cancelled.*

scarcity
*The **scarcity** of houses led to a rise in price.*

shortfall
*There is a 5000-person **shortfall** in recruitment for the army.*

✔ A shortage of food is a **famine**.
A shortage of water is a **drought**.

shot (1) NOUN

A **shot** is the sound of a gun being fired.

blast
*One **blast** of the colonel's shotgun scared the tiger away.*

report
*The **report** of a gun was heard deep in the jungle.*

shot (2) NOUN INFORMAL

If you have a **shot** at doing something, you try to do it.

attempt
*Before 1953, there were many unsuccessful **attempts** to climb Everest.*

crack INFORMAL
*"I'll have a **crack** at the mission, sir!" the lieutenant said.*

effort
*The old golfer resolved to have one last **effort** for the title.*

try
*"I'm going to have a **try** at the painting competition," I told Mum and Dad.*

shout (1) VERB

If you **shout** something, you say it very loudly.

bawl
*The sergeant major **bawled** at everyone, including his wife.*

bellow
*"Help!" **bellowed** Bilbo. "I'm trapped!"*

call
*I could hear someone **calling** my name but I couldn't see anyone.*

yell
*As a toddler, I used to **yell** every time I had my hair cut.*

ANTONYM: whisper

shout (2) VERB

If you **shout** at someone, you speak angrily to them.

rant
*Pacing up and down, the corporal **ranted** at his platoon.*

rave
*The old castaway hopped up and down, **raving** and tearing his hair.*

roar
*From the other side of the field, we could hear Mr Philpot **roaring** in anger.*

a
b
c
d
e
f
g
h
i
j
k
l
m
n
o
p
q
r
s
t
u
v
w
x
y
z

show

A
B
C
D
E
F
G
H
I
J
K
L
M
N
O
P
Q
R
S
T
U
V
W
X
Y
Z

show (1) VERB
If you **show** someone how to do something, you demonstrate it to them.

demonstrate
*"Allow me to **demonstrate**, madam," said the salesman.*

instruct
*Mr Klein **instructed** us on how to give first aid.*

teach
*Miranda's friend **taught** her how to ride.*

show (2) VERB
If you **show** something, you let someone see it.

display
*Our school's sports trophies are **displayed** in a cabinet.*

exhibit
*Mrs Sherringham arranged for us to **exhibit** our art in the local town hall.*

present
*In court, one lawyer **presents** the case for the prosecution, another for the defence.*

show (3) VERB
If you **show** something to someone, you prove it.

demonstrate
*Brunel **demonstrated** the power of the screw propeller.*

prove
*"This display will **prove** my amazing powers!" announced the magician.*

show (4) VERB
If a picture **shows** someone or something, it represents or depicts them.

depict
*The Mona Lisa **depicts** a young lady with a curious smile.*

illustrate
*I drew a diagram to **illustrate** the water cycle.*

portray
*Painters like Monet **portrayed** everything in terms of colour and light.*

represent
*In Van Gogh's picture, the orange circle **represents** the rising moon.*

show (5) VERB
If you **show** someone to a room or seat, you lead them there.

direct
*"Please could you **direct** me to the airport," the tourist asked.*

escort
*At the theatre, an usher **escorted** us to our seats.*

guide
*An elderly lady **guided** us round the museum.*

show (6) NOUN
A **show** is a display or exhibition.

display
*Our year group put on a gymnastics **display**.*

exhibition
*I decided to enter some of my photographs in the **exhibition**.*

presentation
*Our class **presentation** of the term's work was a great success.*

show (7) NOUN
A **show** is a form of entertainment at the theatre or on television.

concert
*Everyone enjoyed the **concert** given by the school orchestra.*

presentation
*Before the film started, there were trailers for future **presentations**.*

production
*For our Christmas **production**, we are going to do Oliver.*

show off VERB INFORMAL
If someone is **showing off**, they are trying to impress people.

boast
*Quasim **boasted** about his new trainers.*

brag
*Verrucca kept **bragging** that her parents were wealthy.*

crow
*If someone wins at sport, they do not need to **crow** about it.*

flaunt
*Our next-door neighbour is very wealthy, but doesn't like to **flaunt** it.*

gloat
*Dursley was always **gloating** about Harry's situation.*

swagger
*My cousin **swaggered** around in his new soccer kit.*

shrink VERB
If something **shrinks**, it becomes smaller.

contract
*When you cook spinach, it **contracts** to half the size.*

diminish
*With each step we took, the distance between us and home **diminished**.*

dwindle
*As the days passed, the shipwreck survivors' supplies gradually **dwindled**.*

shrivel
*When grapes are dried, they **shrivel** to become currants and raisins.*

wither
*Without water, the plant had **withered** and died.*

ANTONYM: grow

shut VERB
If you **shut** something, you close it.

close
*Mum asked me to **close** the drawer before someone banged into it.*

fasten
*"**Fasten** the gate so the dogs don't escape," my sister called.*

lock
***Locked** out of her house, Sonya sat on the steps and waited for her mum to get home.*

push to
*"Please **push** the door **to** on your way out," Mrs Dharawal requested.*

seal
*I **sealed** my sandwich box firmly, to make sure the sandwiches stayed fresh.*

ANTONYM: open

shut up VERB INFORMAL
If you tell someone to **shut up**, you want them to stop talking.

hush
*"**Hush**, I thought I heard a noise," Nadine said urgently.*

keep quiet
*"Please **keep quiet** in the library", the notice read.*

pipe down INFORMAL
*I wish my little brother would **pipe down** sometimes. He's always talking!*

shy ADJECTIVE
A **shy** person is quiet and uncomfortable in the company of other people.

bashful
*With her head down and a **bashful** expression, my little sister began to sing her song.*

reserved
*The new girl was quite **reserved**, so everyone tried to make her feel welcome.*

self-conscious
*"I'm not normally **self-conscious**, but I hate wearing fancy dress," said Chane.*

timid
*"Excuse me, but am I in the right room?" the **timid** newcomer enquired.*

ANTONYM: confident

sick (1) ADJECTIVE
If you are **sick**, you are ill.

in poor health
*Grandad had been **in poor health** for some time, but is now on the road to recovery.*

poorly
*As Petra felt **poorly**, she asked to go home early.*

under the weather INFORMAL
*"I'm sorry to hear your mum's **under the weather**," Mrs Roberts said.*

unwell
*Because the opera singer felt **unwell**, his part was taken by an understudy.*

ANTONYM: well

sick (2) ADJECTIVE

If you feel **sick**, you feel as if you are going to vomit.

ill

*After my third slice of cake I started to feel **ill**, so I declined a fourth.*

nauseous

*The smell coming from the factory was enough to make anyone feel **nauseous**.*

queasy

*"Please can I sit in the front. I always feel **queasy** when I sit in the back," complained my sister.*

sick of ADJECTIVE

If you are **sick of** doing something, you think you have been doing it for too long.

bored with

*After a few minutes, I become **bored with** computer games.*

fed up with

***Fed up with** the constant thud of music, Dad finally came and asked us to turn it down.*

tired of

*Duncan was **tired of** his sister bossing him around.*

side (1) NOUN

The **sides** of something are its different surfaces or edges.

Other nouns related to side:
The **side** of…

…an army	**flank**
…a dice	**face**
…a page	**margin**
…a river	**bank, shore**
…a road	**curb, verge**
…a table	**edge**

side (2) NOUN

The two **sides** in a war, argument, game or relationship are the two people or groups involved.

camp

*"You cannot switch **camps** halfway through," Miss Parvinder warned before the debate.*

faction

*There was much disagreement between different **factions** in the government.*

party

*Dad supports a different political **party** from Mum.*

team

*My favourite soccer **team** comes from Manchester, but it's not United!*

sign (1) NOUN

A **sign** is a board or notice with words, a picture or a symbol on it, giving information or a warning.

notice

*The estate agent came round and put up a "For Sale" **notice** outside our house.*

placard

*The protesters marched through the streets with their **placards** held high.*

poster

*For our class show, we made a **poster** for the school board.*

sign (2) NOUN

A **sign** is a mark or other piece of evidence that tells you something.

clue

*Police brought in dogs to hunt for **clues** about the crime.*

hint

*The pains in his chest were a **hint** that Gramps should take it easy.*

indication

*A red traffic light is an **indication** that drivers should stop.*

warning

*There had been no **warning** that the earthquake was going to hit the town.*

sign (3) NOUN

A **sign** is a mark or symbol that always has a particular meaning.

emblem

*Certain **emblems** are used to hallmark silver.*

symbol

*The cross is an important **symbol** of Christianity.*

signal (1) NOUN

A **signal** is a gesture, sound or action that is meant to give a message to someone.

gesture
With a sweeping **gesture**, the conductor thanked the orchestra.

indication
Mrs Scowcroft's pointing finger was an **indication** that I was in big trouble.

sign
Some people think that seeing a magpie is a **sign** of bad luck.

✔ The hand signals that deaf people use to communicate with are called **sign language**.

> **Some things that give signals:**
>
> | | |
> |---|---|
> | alarm | hooter |
> | beacon | lighthouse |
> | bell | road sign |
> | buoy | siren |
> | flag | smoke |
> | flare | traffic light |
> | foghorn | whistle |

signal (2) VERB

If you **signal**, you make a gesture, sound or action that is meant to give a message to someone.

gesticulate
The policeman **gesticulated** angrily at the driver to stop.

gesture
Mrs Ameobi silently **gestured** to us to listen carefully.

motion
Dad **motioned** for me to come towards him quietly, so as not to disturb the baby.

wave
My idiotic friend Byron kept **waving** to people he didn't know.

silence NOUN

When there is **silence**, there is no sound.

hush
As the eclipse's shadow moved across the sun, a **hush** fell on the land.

peace
The **peace** of the hillside was shattered by the deafening noise of a jet fighter.

quiet
City people are often disturbed by the **quiet** of the countryside.

stillness
Somewhere in the **stillness** of the ancient monastery, a low bell began to toll.

silent (1) ADJECTIVE

If a place is **silent**, there is no sound.

hushed
The lights went down and the theatre was **hushed**, waiting for the show to begin.

quiet
"A **quiet** atmosphere is essential when you're trying to write," Mrs Angel insisted.

soundless
The night was **soundless**: the sheep lay asleep and the stars shone brightly.

still
Apart from the soft burble of the stream, all in the valley was **still**.

ANTONYM: noisy

silent (2) ADJECTIVE

If you are **silent**, you are not saying anything.

dumb
Struck **dumb** with surprise, Charlie watched the ground disappear beneath him.

lost for words
For once, Mrs St John was **lost for words** at her leaving party.

mute
The audience was **mute** with admiration after the marvellous performance by the singer.

noiseless
With **noiseless** steps, Barney crept to the edge of the dump.

speechless
Dad was **speechless** with rage at the sight of his wrecked greenhouse.

tongue-tied
When it came to present the bouquet, my sister was **tongue-tied**.

silly (1) ADJECTIVE
Something that is **silly** is foolish.

absurd
*"Humans on Mars! Don't be **absurd**," Grandad muttered.*

daft
*When my brother won the raffle, he just stood there with a **daft** grin on his face.*

idiotic
*Although Tyree's idea was an **idiotic** one, I went along with it.*

ridiculous
*My uncle tells **ridiculous** tales about kippers swimming and haggis flying.*

ANTONYM: sensible

silly (2) ADJECTIVE
Someone who is **silly** is childish.

daft
*Although it is **daft** to laugh when others are being serious, I sometimes can't help it!*

immature
*"I want no more **immature** behaviour in this classroom!" exclaimed Mr Ince.*

irresponsible
*"Playing with matches is an **irresponsible** thing to do," Mum told me severely.*

ANTONYM: sensible

simple ADJECTIVE
Something that is **simple** is easy to understand or do.

clear
*The instructions were **clear**, but somehow we still messed it up!*

elementary
*Sherlock Holmes believed that detective work was **elementary** for anybody.*

straightforward
*Fortunately, Gran's operation was a **straightforward** one.*

uncomplicated
*Boiling is an **uncomplicated** way to cook an egg.*

understandable
*It was an **understandable** mistake for anyone to make.*

ANTONYM: complicated

single ADJECTIVE
A **single** thing is only one and not more.

individual
*In the cloakroom we each have **individual** pegs.*

separate
*On holiday, we all had **separate** rooms.*

sole
*My brother's **sole** reason for being nice to me was to borrow my bike.*

solitary
*I couldn't find a **solitary** book on the subject that we'd been told to read about.*

✔ If there is only a single one of something in the world, it is **unique**.

ANTONYM: multiple

sit VERB
When you **sit**, you rest your bottom on something such as a chair or the floor.

be seated
*"Please **be seated**," Ratty said to Mole.*

perch
*There were no chairs left, so I **perched** on the radiator.*

settle
*Grandad **settled** in an armchair, and promptly fell asleep.*

ANTONYM: stand

situation (1) NOUN
A **situation** is what is happening in a particular place at a particular time.

case
*Dale was usually at home but, in this **case**, was nowhere to be found.*

circumstances
*The running track was wet, so in the **circumstances** my time was a good one.*

plight
*With sharks all around, the swimmer found himself in a terrible **plight**.*

position
*The prime minister said that the current economic **position** was a good one.*

state of affairs
*"I'm afraid this **state of affairs** will not do," our head teacher warned us.*

situation (2) NOUN
The **situation** of a town or a building is its surroundings and its position.

location
*The **location** of the ranch was outside town.*

setting
*What a **setting** for a picnic: white sand, turquoise sea and waving palm trees!*

site
*Being close to the railway station, the **site** for the new hotel was ideal.*

size (1) NOUN
The **size** of something is how big it is.

dimensions
*We had to know the fridge's **dimensions** to see if it would fit our kitchen.*

proportions
*In the tropics, plants grow to huge **proportions**.*

size (2) NOUN
The **size** of something can mean the fact that it is very large.

immensity
*As the mountaineers looked up at Everest, they realized the **immensity** of the task.*

magnitude
*Believe it or not, most stars have a far greater **magnitude** than our sun.*

vastness
*Crusoe marvelled at the **vastness** of the ocean around his island.*

skill NOUN
Skill is the knowledge and ability that enable you to do something well.

expertise
*When I was doing my homework, Mum's **expertise** with a computer came in useful.*

knack
*There's a **knack** to blowing bubbles with gum.*

proficiency
*After three years of classes, my auntie had acquired some **proficiency** at painting.*

talent
*Sabra had a **talent** for acting, but was she tough enough to make it a career?*

technique
*Driving a racing car requires a different **technique** from driving a normal car.*

skin (1) NOUN
Skin is the natural covering of a person or animal.

coat
*Before the cat show, we brushed Tibbles' **coat** to make her shiny.*

hide
*The **hides** of cattle are tanned to make leather.*

skin (2) NOUN
Skin is the outer covering of a fruit or vegetable.

peel
*Orange **peel** is not always easy to remove.*

rind
*Mum added finely chopped lemon **rind** to the cake mixture.*

sleep (1) VERB
When you **sleep**, you close your eyes and your whole body rests.

doze
*Despite our music, Great Grandma **dozed** in her rocking chair.*

kip INFORMAL
*When we were on holiday we all **kipped** after lunch as it was too hot to play outside.*

slumber
*Goldilocks still **slumbered** as the bears approached their house.*

snooze
*The pier was full of people **snoozing** in deckchairs.*

take a nap
*"If you're tired, **take a nap**," my mum suggested.*

✔ Animals that **hibernate** spend the winter in a state like a deep sleep.

sleep

sleep (2) NOUN

A **sleep** is when you close your eyes and your whole body rests.

doze
*"I think I'll have a **doze**," Grandad said, from the depths of his armchair.*

kip INFORMAL
*"If you want a **kip**, that's okay by me," my sister said.*

nap
*Sneezewort was taking a **nap** when the doorbell rang.*

rest
*Before he set out, Mole felt a short **rest** was called for.*

siesta
*Because of the heat, many Mediterranean people have an afternoon **siesta**.*

slumber
*The prince awoke from his **slumber** to find a frog on his pillow.*

snooze
*It was amazing that the driver could have a **snooze** just before the race.*

sleepy ADJECTIVE

If you are **sleepy**, you are tired and feel like sleeping.

drowsy
*Before operations, they often give you a tablet to make you feel **drowsy**.*

tired
*After playing out for three hours, I felt **tired**.*

ANTONYM: wide-awake

slide VERB

When something **slides**, it moves smoothly over or against something else.

glide
*Good skaters **glide** gracefully over the ice.*

skid
*To prevent **skidding** on icy roads, the council spreads salt and grit on them.*

skim
*The stone I threw **skimmed** gracefully across the water.*

slip
*The toddler's feet **slipped** from under him and he fell on his bottom.*

slither
*The colourful rock snake **slithered** slowly over the ground.*

slight ADJECTIVE

Something that is **slight** is small in amount or degree.

insignificant
*"Don't trouble me with **insignificant** details," the prime minister snapped.*

minor
*Mr Iversen's arthritis was only a **minor** inconvenience for him on the walk.*

small
*Just a **small** amount of some spices can make a big difference to the flavour of a dish.*

trivial
*It didn't seem worth bothering Dad with such a **trivial** matter.*

slim ADJECTIVE

A **slim** person has very little fat.

slender
*One sister was **slender**, the other quite plump.*

trim
*After some weeks at her keep-fit class, Mum was looking **trim**.*

slip (1) VERB

If you **slip**, you accidentally lose your balance.

lose your footing
*Having **lost his footing**, the climber dangled from his rope.*

skate
*On the wet floor, my feet **skated** from under me and I landed on my behind.*

skid
*As Kaila came running round the corner she **skidded** on the grass.*

slide
*When the snow hardened, we could **slide** in the playground.*

slither
*We **slithered** our way down the muddy slope.*

slip (2) VERB
If you **slip** somewhere, you go there quickly and quietly.

sneak
*Mr Toad **sneaked** out of jail, dressed as a washerwoman.*

steal
*At the dead of night, Ron and Hermione **stole** down the stairs.*

tiptoe
*Mum spotted me **tiptoeing** into the kitchen.*

sloppy (1) ADJECTIVE
Sloppy work is careless or badly done.

messy
*Mr Carr knew Martin's essay would be **messy**.*

slapdash
*"This is **slapdash** stuff, Zara!" Mrs Kureshi barked. "Do it again."*

slipshod
*I was in such a hurry that my maths homework was pretty **slipshod**.*

untidy
*Mum despaired about my brother's **untidy** appearance.*

ANTONYM: careful

sloppy (2) ADJECTIVE
Someone or something that is **sloppy** is sentimental.

romantic
*For Dad, the bunch of flowers was quite a **romantic** gesture.*

slushy INFORMAL
*"I hate those **slushy** films with people kissing in them," Ben said.*

slow ADJECTIVE
Someone or something that is **slow** is moving, happening or doing something with very little speed.

leisurely
*We had a **leisurely** day by the sea, sometimes swimming, sometimes just lazing.*

ponderous
*The weightlifter's movements were like an elephant's: heavy and **ponderous**.*

sluggish
*My brother is **sluggish** when it comes to getting ready in the morning.*

unhurried
*Moving at her own **unhurried** pace, the waitress laid the tables.*

ANTONYM: fast

slow down VERB
If something **slows down**, or something slows it down, it moves or happens more slowly.

decelerate
*The jet ski **decelerated** and gently swished up onto the beach.*

reduce speed
*Police warn motorists to **reduce speed** in foggy conditions.*

ANTONYM: accelerate

slowly ADVERB
If something happens **slowly**, it happens with very little speed.

at a snail's pace
*Either side of the roadworks, traffic moved **at a snail's pace**.*

by degrees
***By degrees**, the huge bridge girder was shifted into place.*

gradually
*Despite his lead, the runner realized that the pack was **gradually** gaining.*

unhurriedly
***Unhurriedly**, Mum unbolted the punctured wheel, carefully putting the nuts aside.*

ANTONYM: rapidly

smack VERB
If you **smack** someone, you hit them with your open hand.

slap
*My brother had a red cheek where his girlfriend **slapped** him.*

spank
*In the olden days, **spanking** children was common.*

A B C D E F G H I J K L M N O P Q R **S** T U V W X Y Z

small (1) ADJECTIVE
Something **small** is not large in size.

little
*"We're organizing a **little** party for Granny and Grandpa," Mum announced.*

miniature
*Down at the park, there is a **miniature** railway which you can ride on.*

undersized
*The runt of a litter of pigs is the one that is **undersized**.*

✔ Something that is very small is **microscopic**, **minute** or **tiny**.

ANTONYM: big or large

small (2) ADJECTIVE
A **small** person is not large in size or height.

diminutive
*The giant failed to see the **diminutive** figure of Jack below his knees.*

petite
*Our neighbour is a **petite** woman – at 11 I'm as tall as she is.*

slight
*In spite of her **slight** build, the gymnast was very strong.*

ANTONYM: big or tall

small (3) ADJECTIVE
Something **small** is not large in amount.

meagre
*Copperfield struggled to live on his **meagre** allowance.*

negligible
*In the desert, the annual rainfall is **negligible**.*

paltry
*"Sir, you insult me with such a **paltry** sum of money!" Mr Bumble snorted.*

ANTONYM: plentiful

small (4) ADJECTIVE
Something **small** is not large in importance.

insignificant
*"It's too **insignificant** an issue to argue about," said my friend.*

petty
*"Don't worry me with **petty** matters," my dad said huffily.*

trifling
*To the millionaire, a thousand dollars is a **trifling** sum.*

unimportant
*Tabloid newspapers often put **unimportant** stories on the front cover.*

ANTONYM: important or large

smart (1) ADJECTIVE
A **smart** person is clean and neatly dressed.

elegant
*Dad looked **elegant** in his dinner suit, dress shirt and bow tie.*

neat
*With the kitchen scissors, my sister helped to make my hair **neat**.*

stylish
*Mr Nemeth was wearing a **stylish** new suit.*

ANTONYM: scruffy

smart (2) ADJECTIVE
A **smart** person is clever.

bright
*Katie was **bright** and hoped to go to university.*

quick-witted
*"You have to be **quick-witted** to appear on quiz shows," observed Grandpa.*

sharp
*A **sharp** lookout spotted the lifeboat.*

smash (1) VERB
If you **smash** something, you break it into a lot of pieces by hitting it or dropping it.

demolish
*Out of control, the truck **demolished** a garage and came to rest in a garden.*

destroy
*Our roof was **destroyed** when the oak tree blew down.*

shatter
*A loose stone flew up and **shattered** our car windscreen.*

smash (2) VERB

To **smash** against something means to hit it with great force.

collide
In the storm, the ferry collided with the pier.

hammer
The crane swung round and its great iron ball hammered into the building's wall.

ram
Propelled by the might of 20 Romans, the huge pole rammed into the city gates.

smell (1) NOUN

A pleasant **smell** is a nice odour or scent.

aroma
The aroma of roasting coffee beans drifted into the street.

fragrance
"Why not try our new fragrance?" urged the perfume saleswoman.

perfume
Scented candles give off a pleasant perfume.

scent
In the rose garden, the scent was almost overpowering.

smell (2) NOUN

An unpleasant **smell** is an odour or scent that is not nice.

odour
My brother's trainers give off a dreadful odour, particularly when he's been running.

pong BRITISH AND AUSTRALIAN INFORMAL
Our dog, Wuffles, gives off quite a pong when he gets wet.

reek
The reek of cigarette smoke filled the small café we stopped at.

stench
The stench of the flooded sewers was overpowering.

stink
Rotten eggs create a powerful stink.

whiff
There was a real whiff of gas somewhere outside our house.

smell (3) VERB

If you **smell** something, you notice it with your nose.

scent
The dogs scented a deer nearby and started to bark and strain on their leads.

sniff
Dad strode out of the hotel door to sniff the seaside air.

smell (4) VERB

If someone or something **smells** in an unpleasant way, they do not smell very nice.

reek
My sister reeked of Mum's perfume – she'd put on far too much.

stink
Our car stank of petrol after Dad had overfilled the tank.

smelly ADJECTIVE

Someone or something **smelly** has a strong and unpleasant smell.

evil-smelling
The witch moved towards the children, holding an evil-smelling potion.

foul-smelling
Many sewers are less foul-smelling than you would think.

stinking
I tipped the stinking leftovers of the cauliflower-cheese into the bin outside.

smile VERB

When you **smile**, the corners of your mouth move outwards and slightly upwards, because you are pleased or amused.

beam
Mr Linderoth beamed and presented Ganesh with the trophy.

grin
Rudy grinned as he thought of the trick he had played on Melvin.

smirk
"There's nothing to smirk about, Laurel," snapped Mrs Dublin.

ANTONYM: frown

a
b
c
d
e
f
g
h
i
j
k
l
m
n
o
p
q
r
s
t
u
v
w
x
y
z

smooth

smooth (1) ADJECTIVE
A **smooth** surface has no roughness and no holes in it.

even
*When I had rubbed the surface down, it was **even** enough to paint.*

glassy
*The **glassy** lake reflected the mountains that surrounded it.*

polished
*The **polished** pebbles had been worn down by the sea.*

ANTONYM: rough

smooth (2) ADJECTIVE
Smooth hair or fabric is soft to the touch.

glossy
*Mum's hair always looks very **glossy** when she's been to the hairdresser.*

silky
*After our dog Tess had been in the sea, her coat felt **silky**.*

sleek
*The owner stroked the **sleek** neck of the winning racehorse.*

velvety
*I ran my hand across the **velvety** material.*

*See **shiny***

snack NOUN
A **snack** is a small, quick meal.

bite
*Gran suggested we had a **bite** before our journey.*

nibbles INFORMAL
*Although there was no sit-down meal, **nibbles** were provided.*

refreshments
*At the fête, **refreshments** included hot dogs and burgers.*

sneak VERB
If you **sneak** somewhere, you go there quietly, trying not to be seen or heard.

creep
*Hermione **crept** into the cellar, her heart pounding.*

slink
*The puppy **slunk** out of the room, knowing he'd been naughty to chew the leg of the chair.*

slip
*Dressed in black from head to toe, the spy **slipped** past the watchman.*

steal
*Gollum tried to **steal** away from the cave, but he was spotted.*

tiptoe
*As his father snored, Aldo **tiptoed** silently past the door.*

sneaky ADJECTIVE
Someone who is **sneaky** is dishonest or deceitful.

crafty
*My Uncle Fred is a very **crafty** card player.*

deceitful
*Verrucca was a **deceitful** girl who was always telling lies.*

devious
*Kameko was upset by Tamara's **devious** plot to keep the party secret from her.*

dishonest
*Only a **dishonest** person would not hand in a purse they found.*

sly
*The **sly** old witch offered the princess a poisonous apple.*

soft (1) ADJECTIVE
If something is **soft**, it is not hard, stiff or firm.

pulpy
*Although the mango was **pulpy**, it was still fit to eat.*

spongy
*The ball wouldn't bounce on the wet, **spongy** earth of the lawn.*

squashy
*To be at their best, melons should not be too **squashy**.*

supple
*The expensive shoes were made from lovely **supple** leather.*

ANTONYM: hard or firm

soft (2) ADJECTIVE

If fabric or hair is **soft**, it is nice to touch.

downy
Wuffles, our dog, loves to slide underneath my ***downy*** *duvet.*

fleecy
My waterproof jacket has a ***fleecy*** *lining to zip in for cold weather.*

furry
I love hugging Mum when she's wearing her ***furry*** *sweater.*

silky
Show dogs receive hours of brushing on their ***silky*** *coats.*

velvety
The tissues were supposed to feel ***velvety****, but they didn't to me.*

ANTONYM: coarse

soft (3) ADJECTIVE

If a breeze is **soft**, it is gentle.

gentle
What had been merely a ***gentle*** *breeze turned into a strong wind.*

light
A ***light*** *wind billowed the sails and set Columbus on his way.*

soft (4) ADJECTIVE

If lighting is **soft**, it is dim.

dim
In the ***dim*** *light of the vault, Ron made out two piercing eyes.*

subdued
A dimmer switch allows you to adjust your lights from bright to ***subdued****.*

ANTONYM: bright

soft (5) ADJECTIVE

If a sound is **soft**, it is quiet and gentle.

faint
From our cottage, we could hear the ***faint*** *wash of the sea on the shore.*

gentle
From my bedroom I could hear Mum's ***gentle*** *singing in the baby's room.*

muted
The ***muted*** *sound of conversation came from beyond the heavy oak door.*

soothing
Soon the hypnotist's ***soothing*** *voice had Kieron in a trance.*

whispering
The children could hear ***whispering*** *voices coming from behind the closed door.*

ANTONYM: loud or harsh

soldier NOUN

A **soldier** is a person in an army.

> A new soldier is a **recruit**.
> A general word for soldiers is **troops**.
> Soldiers who fight on foot are **infantry**.
> Soldiers who fight in tanks (or who used to fight on horses) are **cavalry**.
> Soldiers who specialize in firing big guns are **artillery**.
> A soldier on guard is a **sentry**.
> The type of soldiers who are based on ships are called **marines**.
> A soldier who will fight for any country in return for money is a **mercenary**.

solve VERB

If you **solve** a problem or a question, you find a solution or answer to it.

answer
I sometimes have trouble ***answering*** *the clues in crosswords.*

crack
Through luck, hard work and sheer brilliance, the Enigma code was ***cracked****.*

decipher
Deciphering *ancient writing on cave walls was Claudia's speciality.*

explain
The puzzle of the statue's missing jewel was hard to ***explain****.*

get to the bottom of
At last we ***got to the bottom of*** *the mystery.*

work out
Jiro struggled to ***work out*** *where his error was.*

a b c d e f g h i j k l m n o p q r **s** t u v w x y z

some ADJECTIVE
You use **some** to refer to a quantity or number when you are not stating the exact quantity or number.

a few
*"Why don't you invite **a few** friends?"* Mum suggested.

a number of
*A **number of** tourists got off the bus.*

a quantity of
*Police announced that **a quantity of** diamonds had gone missing.*

one or two
*The charity had expected **one or two** volunteers, but was flooded with offers.*

sometimes ADVERB
Something that happens **sometimes**, happens occasionally, rather than always or never.

at times
*At **times**, our dad can get rather irritable.*

every now and then
*Mrs Saha takes us for a class walk **every now and then**.*

from time to time
*From **time to time**, we see old Mr Ormerod totter down to the shops.*

now and then
*Now **and then**, you'll hear a cuckoo.*

once in a while
*Once **in a while**, Mole would long for his cosy home.*

ANTONYM: always or never

soon ADVERB
If something is going to happen **soon**, it will happen in a very short time.

before long
*When I woke it was bright but, **before long**, the rain had started.*

in a little while
*I kept prodding away at the hole, and **in a little while** I could see daylight.*

presently
*Baldmoney wandered through the trees, **presently** coming to a clearing.*

shortly
*"Another programme will follow **shortly**,"* the radio announcer informed us.

ANTONYM: later

sore ADJECTIVE
If part of your body is **sore**, it causes you pain and is uncomfortable.

inflamed
*Dad's **inflamed** knee meant no squash for him.*

painful
*My toe was really **painful** where my clumsy brother had stood on it.*

raw
*Where her boots had rubbed, Meredith's foot was **raw**.*

tender
*Weeks after the kettle accident, Lamar's hand was still **tender**.*

sorry (1) ADJECTIVE
If you are **sorry** about something you have done, you feel sadness or regret because of it.

apologetic
*"It's no use being **apologetic** unless you regret what you've done,"* said Mr Frost.

ashamed
*Euan was **ashamed** at having stolen the ruler.*

remorseful
*Tyla was genuinely **remorseful**.*

repentant
*From Hassan's mournful face, his teacher could tell he was truly **repentant**.*

ANTONYM: unashamed

sorry (2) ADJECTIVE
If you are **sorry** for someone else, you feel sympathy towards them.

compassionate
*When Gran died, everybody at Mum's work was **compassionate**.*

sympathetic
*Mr Forlan was **sympathetic** when I explained my difficulty.*

ANTONYM: unsympathetic

sort (1) VERB

If you **sort** things, you arrange them into different groups.

categorize
*Movies are **categorized** according to their suitability for different ages.*

classify
*Mattie **classified** her fossil finds according to geological period.*

grade
*Gravel is **graded** by size as it falls through a series of metal meshes.*

organize
*Mr Morrison told the captains to **organize** us into teams.*

put in order
*Before delivering them, Akil had to **put** the newspapers **in order**.*

sort (2) NOUN

Different **sorts** of something are different types of it.

category
*Books are divided into two main **categories**: fiction and non-fiction.*

class
*Wuffles our dog was entered in the "Happiest Dog in Show" **class**.*

group
*Weathermen classify clouds into several different **groups**.*

kind
*It was hard to tell what **kind** of plane it was from so far away.*

type
*My big sister said the film star wasn't her **type** of actor.*

Other nouns related to sort:

∧ **sort** of

…animal	**species**
…book or film	**genre**
…car	**make**
…dog	**breed**
…people	**race**
…plant	**variety**

---

sort out VERB

If you **sort out** a problem or misunderstanding, you find a solution to it.

clear up
*With a simple explanation, Mrs Earnshaw **cleared up** our misunderstanding.*

deal with
*Dad **dealt with** all the arrangements for the family holiday.*

solve
*Mum **solved** the problem of how to fit all the suitcases into the car.*

sour ADJECTIVE

If something is **sour**, it has a sharp, acid taste like lemons or vinegar.

acidic
*I don't like the taste of fresh grapefruit – it's too **acidic** for me.*

bitter
***Bitter** medicines often have sweetener added to them.*

sharp
*Lemons taste too **sharp** for most people to eat them whole.*

tart
*The lemon cake was quite **tart**.*

vinegary
*"That salad dressing is too **vinegary** for me," complained Granny.*

✔ When milk turns sour it **curdles**.

space (1) NOUN

Space is the area that is empty or available in a place, building or container.

capacity
*The adverts boasted about the **capacity** of the people carrier.*

elbow room
*At the wedding reception, there was little **elbow room** at the tables.*

room
*As there wasn't enough **room** in the flat, we moved to a house.*

volume
*Most of the box's **volume** was taken up by polystyrene packaging.*

space

space (2) NOUN

Space is the area beyond the earth's atmosphere surrounding the stars and planets.

> **Words related to space:**
>
> asteroid   meteorite
> astronaut   moon
> black hole   orbit
> blast off   planet
> capsule   rocket
> comet   satellite
> control centre   space shuttle
> flight path   space station
> landing   splashdown
> launch pad   star
> meteor   touchdown

space (3) NOUN

A **space** is a gap between two things.

blank
*"If you're not sure of the answer, leave a **blank**," said Mr Kelly.*

gap
*Through the **gap** between the door and its frame wafted the smell of fresh bread.*

opening
*The cat squeezed through the tiny **opening** between the fence posts.*

spare ADJECTIVE

Something that is **spare** is extra, or kept to be used when it is needed.

extra
*Kemal said he could work a few **extra** hours.*

free
*I chipped in that I had some **free** time on Tuesday afternoon.*

surplus
*Dad told us to work off our **surplus** energy by chopping firewood.*

speak VERB

When you **speak** to someone, you use your voice to say words.

communicate
*The factory was so noisy, it was hard for the workers to **communicate** with each other.*

express
*The head teacher **expressed** her thanks to the parents for their support.*

say
*"Once we enter the woods, you must not **say** a word," warned Gandalf.*

talk
*"Doesn't that Venusian **talk** with a strange voice?" Jane muttered.*

utter
*"Don't **utter** a word once we get inside," warned the captain.*

special ADJECTIVE

Someone or something **special** is different from other people or things, often in a way that makes them more important or better than others.

exceptional
*I overheard Mr Lescott say that Hiroshi has an **exceptional** talent.*

important
*"Don't hang up. This is **important**!" urged the reporter.*

momentous
*The queen's visit was a **momentous** occasion for the school.*

out of the ordinary
*"It's **out of the ordinary** to see otters here," the wildlife expert said.*

unique
*The salesman said it was a **unique** opportunity to buy at that price.*

ANTONYM: ordinary

speed (1) NOUN

Speed is the rate at which something moves or happens.

haste
*In her **haste** to catch the bus, my sister forgot her sports kit.*

pace
*Poor old Dad couldn't keep up with the **pace** of our volleyball game.*

rapidity
*I noticed the tide coming in with alarming **rapidity**.*

rate
*Cars come off the production line at a **rate** of dozens per day.*

swiftness
*We were impressed by the **swiftness** of the postal service.*

velocity
*A bullet reaches a **velocity** of around 1000 miles per hour.*

*See **hurry***

speed (2)   VERB
If you **speed** somewhere, you move or travel there quickly.

go like the wind
*When we found the injured climber, Mick **went like the wind** to get help.*

race
*The huge wave **raced** towards the shore with enormous speed.*

tear
*The greyhound **tore** round the racetrack after the rabbit.*

zoom   INFORMAL
*As soon as the traffic lights turned green, the motorbike **zoomed** off.*

*See **hurry***

spend (1)   VERB
When you **spend** money, you buy things with it.

fork out
*The celebrity **forked out** a fortune on designer clothes and shoes.*

pay out
*I **paid out** quite a lot for my new bike, but it was worth it.*

splash out
*With my birthday money, I **splashed out** on an expensive computer game.*

✔ If you spend money wastefully, you **fritter it away** or **squander it.**

spend (2)   VERB
If you **spend** time or energy, you use it.

devote
*After Grandad retired, he **devoted** all his energy to gardening.*

pass
*Waiting for the ferry, we **passed** our time playing a silly game called "Bunnies".*

while away
*The old woman **whiled away** the winter hours spinning wool.*

ANTONYM: waste

spin   VERB
If someone or something **spins**, it turns quickly around a central point.

pirouette
*As the ballerina **pirouetted**, the music whirled and soared.*

revolve
*The water flowed down the chute and the ancient mill wheel began to **revolve**.*

rotate
*A car's wheels **rotate** extremely fast.*

twist
*I **twisted** round to see who was kicking me.*

whirl
*As we **whirled** round, the rest of the fair became a blur of lights and jangly music.*

spite   NOUN
Spite is the desire to deliberately hurt or upset somebody.

bitterness
*Full of **bitterness**, Miss Prinn plotted to kill the man who had left her at the altar.*

hate
*The prisoner was full of **hate** for his jailers.*

ill-feeling
*You could tell there was **ill-feeling** between the two brothers.*

in spite of   PHRASE
In spite of is used to begin a statement that makes the rest of what you are saying seem surprising.

despite
*Our school fête was a great success **despite** the appalling weather.*

regardless of
***Regardless** of the danger, the medic crawled out to rescue the wounded soldier.*

split VERB

If something **splits**, or if you **split** it, it divides into two or more parts.

come apart

"The handle s-s-sort of **c-c-came apart** in my hand," I stammered.

crack

The road ahead was flooded because a water pipe had **cracked**.

separate

The two halves of the egg **separated**, and the runny liquid slid into the pan.

splinter

As the vessel struck, the timber pier **splintered**.

tear

You could see the agony on her face when the sprinter **tore** a muscle.

split up VERB

If a couple **split up**, they begin to live apart.

break up

Katie was more than upset that her parents had **broken up**.

part

My brother and his girlfriend **parted** after only going out for three weeks.

separate

After **separating** for some months, the couple were reunited.

✔ If a married couple split up permanently and legally, they get a **divorce**.

spoil (1) VERB

To **spoil** something means to damage it or stop it being successful or satisfactory.

damage

Centuries of wind and weather had **damaged** the cathedral stonework.

deface

My friend **defaced** the poster by giving the woman a moustache.

destroy

The protester toppled the statue in an attempt to **destroy** it.

harm

"I will see that you come to no **harm**," promised the princess's fairy godmother.

mess up

"It would really **mess** things **up** if I failed my exams," said my worried brother.

ruin

Dad **ruined** Mum's white shirt by putting it in the wash with my red sweater.

wreck

My painting was completely **wrecked** when I knocked over the water jar.

spoil (2) VERB

To **spoil** children means to give them everything they want, making them selfish.

cosset

I enjoy going to stay with Grandma and Grandpa, as they **cosset** me.

mollycoddle

Our neighbours **mollycoddled** their son Timmy and now he's a total pain.

pamper

The **pampered** poodle had a bow in its hair and was carried everywhere.

overindulge

"You must not **overindulge** your cat with chocolates," the vet warned Mrs Peacock. "It's not healthy."

ANTONYM: deprive

spooky ADJECTIVE

Something that is **spooky** is frightening and creepy.

bloodcurdling

All at once, a **bloodcurdling** scream rent the cold night air.

eerie

From deep within the cave came an **eerie** howling noise.

ghostly

Along the battlements walked the **ghostly** shape of a Viking warrior.

mysterious

A murder had been committed, but where was the body? Highly **mysterious**!

spine-chilling

In a **spine-chilling** moment, a hand shot towards my face out of the darkness.

sport NOUN

Sport is games and other enjoyable activities that need physical effort and skill.

> **Some different sports:**
>
> aerobics   horse riding
> athletics   jogging
> badminton kayaking
> baseball   lacrosse
> basketball mountaineering
> canoeing   netball
> cricket   rock climbing
> cross-country running rugby
> diving   swimming
> football   tennis
> hockey   volleyball

spot (1) NOUN

A **spot** is a small, round coloured area on a surface.

blemish

*My lovely cousin hasn't got a single **blemish** on her smooth skin.*

blotch

*Mrs Naylor was less than pleased with the ink **blotch** on my maths work.*

mark

*Because there was a **mark** on one of them, Mum bought the shoes cheaply.*

smudge

*"What's that **smudge** on your exercise book?" I asked Dirran.*

speck

*There was a **speck** of mud on the carpet after I'd walked through with dirty shoes.*

spot (2) NOUN

A **spot** is a particular place.

location

*"The exact **location** where the stars are getting married is a secret," said the reporter.*

position

*The **position** for the foundation stone was right by the hospital entrance.*

site

*Mountains would make an impractical **site** for an airport.*

spot (3) VERB

If you **spot** something, you suddenly see it.

catch sight of

*On holiday, we **caught site of** three dolphins.*

notice

*"Did you **notice** what she was wearing?" my sister enquired.*

observe

*From her hideout, the police officer **observed** the suspect leaving home.*

spray (1) VERB

If you **spray** a liquid over something, you cover it with drops of the liquid.

shower

*Sally **showered** me with fizzy lemonade.*

splash

*As the car drove past, it **splashed** a pedestrian with muddy water.*

sprinkle

*Uncle Leo has bought a device that **sprinkles** the lawn with water every few hours.*

squirt

*I took revenge by **squirting** my sister with the hose pipe.*

spray (2) NOUN

Spray is many small drops of liquid splashed or forced into the air.

fountain

*When the water main burst, a **fountain** shot into the air.*

mist

*At Niagara, the falling water creates a constant **mist** below.*

shower

*The sprinkler came on and sent a **shower** of water over the lawn.*

spread VERB

If you **spread** a substance on a surface, you put a thin layer of it on the surface.

daub

*Many old houses were built by **daubing** clay and muck over interwoven wood.*

smear

*My baby brother **smeared** chocolate all over his face.*

sprinkle VERB

If you **sprinkle** a liquid or powder over something, you scatter it over it.

pepper

*To scare the rustlers, the rancher **peppered** the air with shotgun pellets.*

shower

*The winning driver **showered** the two runners-up with champagne.*

splash

*When you are hot, **splashing** cold water on your face can help to cool you down.*

spray

*"If you **spray** me with that hose, I will find a way to get you back," my brother warned.*

squash VERB

If you **squash** something, you press it so that it becomes flat or loses its shape.

compress

*At the landfill site, huge bulldozers **compressed** the waste in the hole.*

crush

*I saw a programme where an old car was **crushed** into a tiny cube.*

flatten

*The best way to **flatten** cans for recycling is to take both ends off.*

trample

*In some places, grapes are still **trampled** under foot to get the juice out.*

squeeze VERB

If you **squeeze** something somewhere, you force it into a small space.

cram

*Eight of us were **crammed** into one go-kart as it roared down the hill.*

jam

*Harshita couldn't **jam** any more clothes into her suitcase.*

pack

*They had tried to **pack** more people into the hall than there was room for.*

squash

*On the plane, I was **squashed** between a huge couple from Texas.*

stuff

*Store detectives caught the man trying to **stuff** the CD in his pocket.*

wedge

*Dad managed to **wedge** a piece of wood under the table leg to make it steady.*

squirt VERB

If a liquid **squirts**, or you **squirt** it, it comes out of a narrow opening in a thin, fast stream.

gush

*Water **gushed** from the burst pipe.*

spurt

*Oil came **spurting** out of the oil well.*

See **spray**

stagger VERB

If someone **staggers**, they walk unsteadily because they are ill or drunk.

lurch

*The monster **lurched** forward, then fell.*

reel

*The man **reeled** a little as he walked out of the bar with his friends.*

totter

*When Tristan broke his leg, he had to **totter** round on crutches for weeks.*

stand VERB

If you cannot **stand** someone or something, you do not like them at all.

endure

*Dad told Steph he couldn't **endure** the music any longer.*

suffer

*Mum is not one to **suffer** fools gladly.*

tolerate

*"I cannot **tolerate** sloppy work," a red-faced Mrs Taggart shouted.*

stand for VERB

If something **stands for** something, it represents or means that.

represent

*On maps, a cross **represents** a church.*

symbolize

*The star of David is an emblem which **symbolizes** Judaism.*

star NOUN

A **star** is a famous actor, sports player or musician.

celebrity
"Minor **celebrities** are always trying to be seen on television," observed Craig.

personality
Many show-business **personalities** raise money for charities.

stare VERB

If you **stare**, you look at something for a long time.

gawp
Passers-by stopped to **gawp** at the amazing display in the shop window.

gaze
I **gazed** at Mum's trendy new hairstyle.

ogle
"What are you **ogling** at?" my brother asked.

See **watch**

start (1) VERB

If you **start** something, or something **starts**, you begin it or it begins.

commence
Commencing at nine o'clock, school lasts until late afternoon.

get going
The workers **got going** with the new road.

get under way
No sooner had the match **got under way**, than a player was injured.

> To **start**
> ...a computer is to **boot up**.
> ...a motorbike is to **kick-start** it.
> ...again is to **resume** or **restart**.

ANTONYM: finish

start (2) VERB

If you **start** a new business or other venture, you create it.

create
From a small record shop, the couple **created** a huge music empire.

found
"This company was **founded** by Joshua Fothergill in 1879," said the guide proudly.

initiate
The airline **initiated** a new service flying to New Zealand.

launch
"The Fizzo Company is due to **launch** a new soft drink," the spokeswoman said.

start (3) NOUN

The **start** of something is the point or time at which it begins.

beginning
A sore throat is often the **beginning** of a cold, in my experience.

birth
Blues music had its **birth** in the ill-treatment of slaves in the southern USA.

dawn
The **dawn** of the motor car era was at the end of the 19th century.

outset
From the **outset**, you could see that Goran was going to be a great tennis player.

stay VERB

If you **stay** in one place, you do not move away from it.

hang around INFORMAL
The postman **hung around** for a minute or two, but no one answered the door.

linger
Unwilling to go away, the dog **lingered**, waiting for his owner.

loiter
"Get to class and stop **loitering** in the playground," Mr Foxe told the stragglers.

remain
After the meeting ended, we **remained** behind to help put the chairs away.

settle
In the 18th and 19th centuries, many immigrants **settled** in America.

wait
"**Wait** there until I come back," Dad said to us as he dashed off.

a b c d e f g h i j k l m n o p q r **s** t u v w x y z

steady ADJECTIVE

Something that is **steady** is firm and not moving about.

firm
*"In tennis it's important to have a **firm** grip on your racket," the coach explained.*

secure
*Dad made sure that the ladder was **secure** before he climbed up to the window.*

stable
*Tightrope walkers carry a huge pole to help keep them **stable**.*

ANTONYM: unsteady

steal VERB

If someone **steals** something, they take it without permission and without meaning to return it.

nick INFORMAL
*"Don't **nick** my biscuits while I'm out of the room," I warned Dilip.*

pinch
*The naughty boys **pinched** some apples from Mr MacDonald's tree.*

swipe
*Someone **swiped** Jay's coat, which he'd left hanging in the cloakroom.*

walk off with
*Someone had **walked off with** my ruler.*

Words for stealing:
Stealing

...by assault	**mugging**
...during a riot	**looting**
...from a home	**burglary, housebreaking**
...from a shop	**shoplifting**
...from coaches	**highway robbery**
	OLD-FASHIONED
...from company money	**embezzlement, fraud**
...from ships	**piracy**
...game	**poaching**
...small items	**pilfering**
...someone's writing	**plagiarism**

steep ADJECTIVE

A **steep** slope rises sharply and is difficult to go up.

precipitous
*From the crag high above, a **precipitous** slope stretched down to the lake.*

sheer
*Below the climber was a **sheer** drop of a thousand metres.*

vertical
*Part of the theme-park ride was a **vertical** drop into total darkness.*

ANTONYM: gradual

step (1) NOUN

A **step** is the movement of lifting your foot and putting it down again when you are walking, running or dancing.

footstep
*Mr Parnaby's **footsteps** echoed on the tiled floor of the corridor.*

pace
*Nervously, the volunteer took a **pace** forward from the line.*

stride
*We had to measure how many giant **strides** it took us to cross the field.*

step (2) NOUN

A **step** is one of a series of actions that you take in order to achieve something.

move
*"Working hard at school is the best **move** that anyone can make," advised the pop star.*

phase
*"In summer, the final **phase** of our building work will begin," the head teacher announced.*

stage
*"The next **stage** will be to transfer pupils into the new classrooms," Mr Knight continued.*

stick (1) VERB

If you **stick** one thing to another, you attach it with glue or tape.

cement
*Plastic pipes are often **cemented** together with a special adhesive.*

fasten
*The secretary **fastened** the cheque to the letter before putting it in the envelope.*

glue
*My silly sister managed to **glue** her book to the desk.*

paste
*"Now **paste** your labels inside your books," Miss Sinclair instructed.*

tape
*I **taped** a small first-aid kit to the frame of my bike.*

stick (2) VERB
If something **sticks** to something else, it becomes fixed to it.

adhere
*Static electricity can make bits of paper **adhere** to your clothing.*

cling
*"The transparent film **clings** to the dish you wrap it round," Mum explained.*

stick (3) VERB
If you **stick** a long or pointed object into something, you push it in.

poke
*The inquisitive child **poked** her finger into the jelly.*

stab
***Stabbed** in the stomach with a dagger, the bandit reeled then fell.*

thrust
*The karate teacher **thrust** his hand forward with a loud shout.*

stick out VERB
If something **sticks out**, it projects from something else.

jut out
*Medieval houses **jutted out** over narrow streets.*

project
*The jib of the crane **projected** over the building site.*

protrude
*My cousin has an upper lip which **protrudes** over her lower lip.*

stick up for VERB INFORMAL
If you **stick up for** someone or something, you support or defend them.

side with
*Just for a change, I **sided with** my brother in this argument.*

stand up for
*It is important to **stand up for** what you believe in.*

sticky ADJECTIVE
If something is **sticky**, it is covered with a substance that can stick to other things.

adhesive
*"Attach the cardboard with **adhesive** tape," the television presenter explained.*

glutinous
*What should have been a trifle had turned into a **glutinous** mess.*

gooey INFORMAL
*Meringues are **gooey** to start with, crisp when baked.*

tacky
*"Don't touch that paint! It's still **tacky**," the decorator shouted.*

stiff ADJECTIVE
Something that is **stiff** is firm and not easily bent.

firm
*As the sand seemed **firm**, we decided we could safely walk on it.*

hard
*The concrete had set rock **hard**.*

inflexible
*Poles used in the pole vault event were once **inflexible**.*

rigid
*Once we'd got the framework **rigid**, we could put the rest of the tent up.*

solid
*The pond had turned to **solid** ice overnight.*

taut
*The fisherman pulled his rod up until the line was **taut** with the weight of the fish.*

ANTONYM: flexible

a
b
c
d
e
f
g
h
i
j
k
l
m
n
o
p
q
r
s
t
u
v
w
x
y
z

still ADJECTIVE

If someone or something is **still**, they stay in the same position without moving.

calm
*The sea was totally **calm**, with hardly a ripple.*

inert
*The sleeping baby lay **inert** in her cot.*

motionless
***Motionless** in the water, the Marie Celeste showed no sign of life.*

stationary
*My dodgem was **stationary** when my brother's bumper car crashed into it from behind.*

stop (1) VERB

If you **stop** doing something, you no longer do it.

call it a day INFORMAL
*It was late and, after writing for some hours, John decided to **call it a day**.*

cease
*Suddenly all the soldiers **ceased** firing. The war was over.*

desist
*"These interruptions must **desist**," said pompous Mr Quilley.*

finish
*"Are you never going to **finish** in there?" Mum called through the bathroom door.*

halt
*"Squad, **halt**!" the sergeant major bellowed.*

leave off
*Each morning the long-distance walker would begin exactly where she had **left off**.*

quit
*To stay healthy, my big sister decided to **quit** smoking.*

stop for a while:
break
*The film crew and cast **broke** for lunch.*

pause
*After **pausing** to take a swig of water, Mrs Scholes continued.*

stop gradually:
peter out
*The flow of sand in the hourglass **petered out**, and the time was up.*

run down
*Much to our relief, the wind-up musical box began to **run down**.*

stop suddenly:
break off
*The star **broke off** the interview to take a phone call.*

cut short
*Play in the tennis was **cut short** owing to a downpour.*

interrupt
*A sudden flash of lightning **interrupted** my thoughts.*

stop (2) VERB

If you **stop** someone from doing something, you prevent them from doing it.

hinder
*Protesters did their best to **hinder** the new road development.*

obstruct
*Crowds **obstructed** the workers' buses by standing in the road.*

prevent
*By sitting in the trees, people **prevented** them from being cut down.*

restrain
*Police were called in to **restrain** the campaigners.*

stop (3) VERB

If something **stops**, it comes to an end.

cease
*After three days the rain finally **ceased**.*

conclude
*Shows often **conclude** with all the actors taking a bow.*

end
*The concert **ended** with a firework show.*

finish
*Our school day **finishes** at around four o'clock.*

store (1) NOUN

A **store** is a supply of something that is kept until it is needed.

hoard
*No one knew about Gollum's secret **hoard** of shiny rings.*

reserve
*The government keeps a **reserve** of fuel for emergency situations.*

stock
*Unfortunately, the shop's **stock** of washing powder had run out.*

supply
***Supplies** of grain were running low.*

store (2) VERB
When you **store** something somewhere, you keep it there until it is needed.

hoard
*Ebenezer **hoarded** his money as a squirrel hoards nuts.*

stash
*The burglar **stashed** the stolen jewels under a floorboard until he could sell them.*

stock
*Mum and Dad's shop **stocks** all sorts of paint.*

stockpile
*During the fuel crisis, the government **stockpiled** coal.*

✔ Food for a home is stored in a **larder** or **pantry**.
Goods are stored in a **warehouse** or **depot**.
Grain is stored in a **granary**.
Valuables are stored in a **safe**, **strongroom** or **bank vault**.

storm NOUN
A **storm** is a period of bad weather, when there is heavy rain, a strong wind, and often thunder and lightning.

Different kinds of storm:

A rainstorm:
cloudburst	downpour
deluge	thunderstorm

A snowstorm:
blizzard	whiteout

A windstorm:
cyclone	tornado
gale	twister
hurricane	typhoon

stormy ADJECTIVE
If the weather is **stormy**, storms are happening.

raging
*Down its slipway, the lifeboat plunged into the **raging** sea.*

squally
*It was a **squally** shower, here one minute and gone the next.*

tempestuous
*The cave provided the travellers with some shelter from the **tempestuous** night.*

turbulent
*The weather was **turbulent**, with gusts of wind reaching 90 miles an hour.*

wild
*A **wild**, wet wind blew off the moor, rattling the windows of the old stone farmhouse.*

story NOUN
A **story** is a telling of events, real or imaginary, spoken or written.

account
*Gasping for breath, the rescued seaman gave an **account** of what had happened.*

anecdote
*Mrs Giggs was always telling us **anecdotes** from her early life.*

chronicle OLD-FASHIONED
*Monks laboured for many years to write a **chronicle** of their times.*

legend
*Ulysses and Theseus were figures in ancient Greek **legend**.*

narrative
*The fast-moving **narrative** of the book kept me gripped for hours.*

novel
*My brother and I prefer reading **novels** to watching television.*

tale
*The Suitcase Kid is a **tale** about a child whose parents have divorced.*

yarn
*Uncle Tim is good at telling **yarns**.*

✔ The general name for imaginary stories is **fiction**.

strange (1) ADJECTIVE
Someone or something **strange** is unusual or unexpected.

curious
*How **curious** – a light in the abandoned mill in the middle of the night!*

extraordinary
*The northern lights are an **extraordinary** and beautiful phenomenon.*

odd
*Beachcombers find many **odd** things along the shoreline.*

peculiar
*I had a **peculiar** feeling that someone was watching me.*

unusual
*Although one often hears a cuckoo, it's **unusual** to see them.*

weird
*The children felt there was something **weird** about Madam Doubtfire.*

ANTONYM: normal or ordinary

strange (2) ADJECTIVE
Something **strange** cannot be explained.

baffling
*Even for Sherlock Holmes it was a particularly **baffling** case.*

inexplicable
*For some **inexplicable** reason, my dad was standing on his head.*

mysterious
*A **mysterious** newcomer rode into the frontier town of Cactus Creek.*

stranger NOUN
A **stranger** is someone you have never met before.

alien
*When the family first moved abroad they felt like **aliens**, but they soon settled down.*

foreigner
*Some countries are more welcoming to **foreigners** than others.*

newcomer
*The **newcomers** received a friendly reception in the town.*

outsider
*I hated being made to feel like an **outsider**.*

stream (1) NOUN
A **stream** is a small river.

brook
*A **brook** flowed through the village.*

creek
*At low tide, the **creek** turned into a trickle.*

stream (2) NOUN
A **stream** is a steady flow of something.

current
*"Be careful of the strong **current** in the estuary," the canoeing instructor warned.*

jet
*As the pump started, a **jet** of water shot out of the hose.*

surge
*The dam broke, sending a huge **surge** of water down the valley.*

torrent
*When our bath overflowed, a **torrent** of water ran down the stairs.*

strength NOUN
Strength is how strong or powerful someone or something is.

brawn
*The muscleman's impressive **brawn** made him a huge hit in martial-arts films.*

might
*The rugby team's combined **might** made them formidable opponents.*

power
*Hydraulic machines like diggers have tremendous **power**.*

stamina
*Marathon runners need lots of **stamina**.*

ANTONYM: weakness

stress NOUN
Stress is worry and nervous tension.

pressure
*Dad was feeling the **pressure** of his work.*

strain
*It was quite a **strain** for Mum to look after Grandad when he was ill.*

worry
*The **worry** of losing her job gave Athena sleepless nights.*

stretch VERB
If you **stretch** something soft or elastic, you pull it to make it longer or bigger.

extend
*The fireman **extended** the hose by pulling it off the reel.*

lengthen
*Angela **lengthened** the dough with a rolling pin.*

strict ADJECTIVE
Someone who is **strict** controls other people very firmly.

firm
*Mr Meaks is a **firm** teacher but is always fair.*

harsh
***Harsh** punishment awaited anyone who disagreed with the emperor.*

severe
*For misbehaving, Kuldeep got a very **severe** warning from Mrs Greer.*

stern
*The warder's **stern** look was enough to scare even the toughest prisoner.*

ANTONYM: lenient

strong (1) ADJECTIVE
Someone who is **strong** has a lot of physical power.

brawny
*My sister's boyfriend is **brawny** but not brainy.*

muscular
*With training, the puny weakling was transformed into a **muscular** hulk.*

powerful
*It took a **powerful** punch to floor the heavyweight champion.*

sturdy
***Sturdy** volunteers helped lift the boxes of supplies into the trucks.*

ANTONYM: weak

strong (2) ADJECTIVE
Strong objects are able to withstand rough treatment, and are not easily damaged.

durable
*Most plastic objects are fairly **durable**.*

hard-wearing
***Hard-wearing** boots are essential for hiking.*

heavy-duty
*The farmer had a **heavy-duty** coat for going out into the fields in winter.*

robust
*Children's toys have to be **robust** to survive.*

sturdy
*Dad built us a **sturdy** table for the patio.*

tough
*"Your school shoes need to be **tough** for all the wear they get," said Mum.*

ANTONYM: fragile

strong (3) ADJECTIVE
Strong feelings are great or intense.

deep
*Dad's cousin Colin has a **deep** love of wildlife.*

fervent
*Malik is a **fervent** supporter of the Rangers.*

intense
*Mrs Murphy has an **intense** dislike for careless work.*

stubborn ADJECTIVE
Someone who is **stubborn** is determined not to change the way they think or how they do things.

determined
*My brother is a **determined** character. He doesn't often change his mind.*

obstinate
*Always **obstinate**, Violet Elizabeth threatened to scream if she didn't get her way.*

persistent
*Keith was very **persistent** about wanting to do ballet.*

pig-headed
***Pig-headed** people will never admit that they're wrong.*

ANTONYM: weak

A
B
C
D
E
F
G
H
I
J
K
L
M
N
O
P
Q
R
S
T
U
V
W
X
Y
Z

stuck-up ADJECTIVE INFORMAL

A **stuck-up** person is proud and conceited.

arrogant

*An **arrogant** person thinks they can do better than everybody else.*

conceited

***Conceited** people think they are very special, when they often aren't at all.*

pompous

*The **pompous** man insisted on being given a front-row seat.*

snobbish

*"Mrs Lampard is rather **snobbish** and unfriendly," Mum told Grandma.*

snooty INFORMAL

*Martha gave me a **snooty** look and waltzed off with her nose in the air.*

ANTONYM: humble

stuff (1) NOUN

You can refer to a group of things as **stuff**.

belongings

*"Fetch your **belongings** and go upstairs," Mum ordered.*

bits and pieces

*The **bits and pieces** from my model were spread over the table.*

equipment

*Divers have to check their **equipment** very carefully before they go in the water.*

gear

*All the sports **gear** at our school goes in a special shed.*

paraphernalia

*It's amazing the amount of **paraphernalia** kayakers need.*

stuff (2) VERB

If you **stuff** something somewhere, you push it there quickly and carelessly.

cram

*Azalea **crammed** her mouth full of strawberries.*

force

*Dad **forced** his shoes into the trunk, then sat on the lid.*

jam

*I **jammed** my feet into the shoes, but they were definitely too small.*

stupid ADJECTIVE

Someone or something that is **stupid** is not sensible or wise.

daft

*My **daft** brother is always getting into trouble.*

foolish

*Gramps said he'd done many **foolish** things as a young man.*

idiotic

*"That's an **idiotic** idea," Claire said rather scathingly to Andy.*

ignorant

*An **ignorant** woman barged past me in the queue for the cinema.*

irresponsible

*It's **irresponsible** to wander off without telling your parents.*

silly

*"What a **silly** thing to do," I thought to myself.*

ANTONYM: sensible or wise

subject NOUN

The **subject** of a book, programme or conversation is the thing or person it is about.

issue

*"Don't change the subject. The **issue** we're discussing is your homework," Mum said.*

matter

*"We will discuss the **matter** at the next staff meeting," the head teacher told Mr Benn.*

question

*The **question** our class had to debate was: "Should we have homework at the weekend?"*

topic

*The importance of multiplication tables is a **topic** often mentioned in classrooms.*

successful ADJECTIVE

If you are **successful** in something, you achieve what you want to do.

prosperous

*After early setbacks, Madhur was now a **prosperous** banker.*

suitable

triumphant
Triumphant after his victories, Caesar waved to the cheering Roman crowds.

victorious
Despite being victorious yet again, Nelson was mortally wounded.

ANTONYM: unsuccessful

sudden ADJECTIVE
Something that is **sudden** happens quickly and unexpectedly.

abrupt
When his cheating was exposed, the card player made an abrupt departure.

hasty
"It's foolish to make hasty decisions, if you have time to think," advised Mrs Duff.

unexpected
The unexpected arrival of the pop star caused a great commotion.

suddenly ADVERB
Something that happens **suddenly** happens quickly and unexpectedly.

on the spur of the moment
On the spur of the moment, Mum decided to take us to the seaside.

out of the blue INFORMAL
The lottery win came out of the blue.

without warning
Without warning, lightning struck the roof.

suggest VERB
When you **suggest** something, you offer it as an idea.

advise
The hairdresser advised Mum on what style would suit her.

make a suggestion
"If I might make a suggestion ...," Mr Faisal put in.

propose
Dad proposed that we went camping for our holidays.

recommend
"Many machine manufacturers recommend Whizzo soap powder", said the advert.

suit VERB
If an arrangement **suits** you, it is convenient and suitable for you.

be acceptable to
Miss Davies hoped the camp arrangements were acceptable to all parents.

be convenient
"Would the 20th be convenient for our next meeting?" the chairwoman asked.

please
"We aim to please our customers," the shop manager beamed.

satisfy
Dad wasn't sure if the dinner he'd cooked would satisfy all the family.

suitable (1) ADJECTIVE
If something is **suitable**, it is right or acceptable for a certain occasion, time or place.

appropriate
We were expected to wear appropriate clothes for a formal occasion.

apt
As the pilot was buried, it was apt that a plane should fly overhead.

fitting
The parade was not a fitting moment for the soldier to do a headstand.

proper
"Make sure you put proper shoes on," Mum shouted up.

ANTONYM: inappropriate

suitable (2) ADJECTIVE
If something is **suitable**, it is right or acceptable for a certain person.

acceptable
Mum and Dad hoped their offer for the house would be acceptable.

convenient
"Would Friday be convenient for delivery?" the furniture man enquired.

satisfactory
We hoped to find a satisfactory spot for a picnic.

ANTONYM: unsuitable

sunny ADJECTIVE

When it is **sunny**, the sun is shining.

bright

*Out to sea, the sky was **bright** and blue, but inland it was cloudy and dark.*

clear

*After the shower, it was so **clear** you could see for miles.*

fine

*Although **fine** weather was forecast, it rained heavily all day.*

summery

*The arrival of the swallows accompanied the **summery** weather.*

sunlit

*From the island beach, I gazed at **sunlit** cliffs across the water.*

ANTONYM: cloudy or overcast

sunset NOUN

Sunset is the time when the sun goes down.

dusk

*As **dusk** crept over the city, lights began to twinkle in the darkness.*

nightfall

***Nightfall** came and the birds fell silent in the great wood.*

sundown

*With **sundown** came the fort's final bugle call of the day.*

twilight

*At **twilight**, the bats begin to flutter in the gathering darkness.*

support (1) VERB

If something **supports** an object, it is underneath it and holding it up.

prop up

*To **prop** it **up**, scaffolding surrounded the leaning tower.*

reinforce

*Metal bars are used to **reinforce** the concrete in buildings.*

strengthen

*Steel girders are often used to help to **strengthen** skyscrapers.*

support (2) VERB

If you **support** someone, you give them money, help or encouragement.

assist

*Volunteers went along to **assist** the caterers supplying food and drink at the end of the marathon.*

back

*Our mayor **backed** the club's plan for a new sports field.*

encourage

*"Please come along to the match to **encourage** our cricket team," the head teacher said in assembly.*

stand by

*When the bullies tried to fight Kirk, several of us **stood by** him.*

stick up for INFORMAL

*"I'll **stick up for** you if you ask Dad for a raise in our pocket money," my little brother told me.*

suppose VERB

If you **suppose** that something is so, you think that it is likely.

assume

*Holmes **assumed** that Watson would accompany him to Baskerville Hall.*

expect

*Everyone **expected** our assembly to be good, and it was.*

imagine

*"I **imagine** you get very hot in here," Mum said to the checkout lady.*

presume

*Mr Higgins **presumed** that Winnie was ill, but I knew she wasn't.*

sure (1) ADJECTIVE

If you are **sure** about something, you know you are right.

certain

*"Are you **certain** this is the way?" Dad asked, doubtfully.*

confident

*Lyra was **confident** she could find an answer to the mystery.*

convinced

*Mrs Dyer was **convinced** that Jonah was telling the truth.*

positive

*"I am **positive** I left it here somewhere," muttered the professor.*

ANTONYM: unsure

sure (2) ADJECTIVE

If something is **sure** to happen, it will definitely happen.

bound

*"I said you were **bound** to break it," Mum muttered angrily.*

certain

*According to the trainer, the horse was **certain** to win.*

guaranteed

*"I tell you," said Kapil, "United are **guaranteed** to win the cup."*

ANTONYM: doubtful

surprise (1) NOUN

Surprise is the feeling caused when something unexpected happens.

alarm

*My brother called out in **alarm** during the night, but it was just a dream.*

amazement

*You could see the **amazement** on people's faces as the clown popped up out of the cake.*

astonishment

*Vernon's high marks filled him with **astonishment**.*

dismay

*To their **dismay**, the children saw their ball go flying over the wall.*

incredulity

*The audience watched the magician's trick with **incredulity**.*

shock

*It was a great **shock** to discover that our rabbit was going to have babies.*

wonder

*The crowds gazed in **wonder** as the magnificent fireworks exploded overhead.*

surprise (2) NOUN

A **surprise** is an unexpected event.

blow

*It was a big **blow** to Felicity when she failed her exams.*

bolt from the blue

*Leon's shock news was a **bolt from the blue**.*

bombshell INFORMAL

*The president's resignation came as a **bombshell** to the world.*

revelation

*What a **revelation** – a teacher who was a wrestler in his spare time!*

shock

*The singer got quite a **shock** when she was told that she had won the competition.*

surprise (3) VERB

If something **surprises** you, it gives you a feeling of surprise.

alarm

*Our dog, Tess, was **alarmed** by the thunder and lightning.*

amaze

*The shy new girl **amazed** us by singing so beautifully.*

astonish

*Jaidev **astonished** his team-mates by scoring six times.*

astound

*Everyone was **astounded** at the tightrope walker's skill.*

leave open-mouthed

*The sheer rudeness of the waitress **left** us **open-mouthed**.*

shock

*The death of Gran's friend **shocked** her deeply.*

stagger

*"I'm **staggered** to hear how badly we've done in the cricket," Dad complained.*

startle

*The deer was **startled** by the sound of voices and bounded into the woods.*

stun

*Shakira was **stunned** to hear that she'd been picked for the team.*

a b c d e f g h i j k l m n o p q r **s** t u v w x y z

A B C D E F G H I J K L M N O P Q R **S** **T U V W X Y Z**

surprise (4) VERB
If you **surprise** someone, they see you suddenly and unexpectedly.

burst in on
Police **burst in on** the thieves just as they had opened the safe.

catch off guard
Mum and I were **caught off guard** by the tide coming in so quickly.

catch red-handed
"If we lie in wait, we'll **catch** them **red-handed**," said the sergeant.

catch unawares
Dad **caught** me **unawares** with his camera as I was pulling a face.

surprised ADJECTIVE
If you are **surprised**, you have a feeling of surprise.

amazed
I was truly **amazed** that the magician managed to escape.

astonished
I was **astonished** to discover that the lovely actress was 70 years old.

astounded
Everyone was **astounded** by the result at the end of the competition.

open-mouthed
We were **open-mouthed** with amazement as the gymnast flew through the air.

taken aback
Julianne was **taken aback** to meet her teacher on the beach.

thunderstruck
To win a holiday in South America! Anika was totally **thunderstruck**.

suspicious (1) ADJECTIVE
If you are **suspicious** of someone, you do not trust them.

doubtful
Dad was **doubtful** about the second-hand car salesman.

sceptical
We were all highly **sceptical** of the salesman's glib talk.

suspicious (2) ADJECTIVE
If something is **suspicious**, it causes suspicion.

doubtful
There was something **doubtful** about the woman's appearance.

dubious
The low price of the Swiss watch made it highly **dubious**.

fishy INFORMAL
"There's something **fishy** about that van," the inspector said.

shady INFORMAL
With his moustache, trilby hat and turned-up collar, the man looked a **shady** customer.

swap or swop RHYMES WITH "STOP" VERB
If you **swap** one thing for another, you replace the first thing with the second.

exchange
The tourists **exchanged** the rest of their dollars for euros.

replace
Mum said it was time to **replace** our fridge with a newer one.

substitute
For security, a decoy van was **substituted** for the one carrying the gold.

switch
Police foiled the swindlers by **switching** the real notes for fake ones.

trade
Crafty Elian offered to **trade** his computer game for two of mine.

swindle NOUN
A **swindle** is a trick in which someone is cheated out of money or property.

fraud
Several people were jailed for their part in the insurance **fraud**.

racket
"I'm sure that market trader is involved in some sort of **racket**," thought the constable.

rip-off
"That ghost train was a real **rip-off**," Adrienne said in disgust.

scam INFORMAL

*The con men's **scam** was to trick people into buying useless watches.*

switch VERB

If you **switch** one thing for another, you replace the first thing with the second.

replace

*The magician **replaced** his wand with a bunch of flowers.*

substitute

*To thwart thieves, the duchess **substituted** fake jewels for the real ones.*

swap INFORMAL

*Nasir wanted to **swap** his bike for my computer.*

swop VERB

*See **swap***

sword NOUN

A **sword** is a weapon consisting of a very long blade with a short handle.

> **Different types of sword:**
> **cutlass**: broad, curved sword used by pirates
> **rapier**: thin sword used for fencing
> **sabre**: narrow, curved sword used in battle
> **samurai sword**: a sword used by Japanese warriors

swot VERB INFORMAL

If you **swot**, you study or revise very hard.

revise

*My big brother sat in the garden, **revising** for his exams.*

study

*If you want to pass exams, you have to **study**.*

A B C D E F G H I J K L M N O P Q R S T U V W X Y Z

Tt

take (1) VERB
If you **take** someone or something to a place, you get them there.

carry
We **carried** the heavy rock to the far corner of the garden.

convey
Mrs Merson asked me to **convey** her thanks to my mother for her help.

transport
The huge bear **transported** Lyra faster than she could ever have run.

take (2) VERB
If you **take** someone to a place, you lead them there.

escort
Warders **escorted** the prisoner back to her cell.

guide
The curator **guided** us round the museum.

lead
The trail of paw prints **led** us to the badger's sett in the woods.

usher
The cinema attendant **ushered** us to our seats.

take (3) VERB
When you **take** one number from another, you subtract it.

deduct
The shop owner **deducted** some money from my pay for the sandwich I had for lunch.

remove
Miss Singh asked us to **remove** ten apples and count how many were left.

subtract
Lesley **subtracted** four from ten and managed to get seven!

take (4) VERB
You can use **take** to mean need or require.

call for
"This mission **calls for** agents with courage," they were warned.

demand
Most exams **demand** a great deal of effort.

need
The welding job **needed** total concentration.

require
My cut **required** five stitches.

talk (1) VERB
When you **talk**, you say things to someone.

chat
Mum was **chatting** on the phone for hours!

chatter
Mr Mustaffa told us to stop **chattering** and start working.

gossip
Our neighbours **gossip** away over the wall.

hold a conversation
It's hard to **hold a conversation** when my brother plays his loud music.

speak
"Can you **speak** clearly, please," Dad shouted into his mobile.

See **say**

talk (2) NOUN
A **talk** is a conversation, discussion or speech.

address
The prime minister gave an **address** to a roomful of business people.

chat
"Let's have a **chat** about it tomorrow," Mum suggested.

conversation
The twins held a secret **conversation** behind the shed.

debate
Our class took part in a **debate** on school uniforms.

discussion
After a **discussion**, we were asked to write our ideas down.

lecture
The scientist gave a **lecture** on astrophysics.

speech
As chairman of the PTA, Dad was asked to give a **speech**.

talkative ADJECTIVE

If you are **talkative**, you talk a lot.

chatty

Our new neighbour seemed very chatty.

communicative

The shy newcomer was not very communicative.

long-winded

My uncle is rather long-winded in the stories he tells.

tall ADJECTIVE

If someone or something is **tall**, they are more than average height.

gangly

The gangly giraffe could reach leaves high on the tree.

lanky

Lanky people have a better chance at basketball.

soaring

Soaring mountains towered in front of us.

towering

Towering skyscrapers dominated the New York skyline.

ANTONYM: short

tangle (1) NOUN

A **tangle** is a mass of things that are twisted together and difficult to separate.

confusion

I finally found the right cable in the confusion of wires.

jumble

The towels had been left in a jumble on the changing-room floor.

knot

In the charmer's basket was a knot of writhing snakes.

muddle

The skipping-ropes are always in a muddle.

tangle (2) VERB

If you **tangle** something, you twist it into knots.

entangle

Why is it that phone wires always entangle themselves?

knot

After so long lost in the jungle, Karen's hair had knotted and become greasy.

twist

Somehow the cables had twisted together and Dad couldn't find the ends.

ANTONYM: untangle

tap VERB

If you **tap** something, you hit it lightly and quickly.

drum

Heavy rain drummed on the greenhouse roof.

knock

Who was knocking at the door so late at night?

rap

Mrs Pennant rapped on the desk to get our attention.

strike

The giant hammer struck the bell and the sound boomed out over the city.

target NOUN

A **target** is a result that you are trying to achieve.

aim

Their aim was to raise £1000 for charity.

ambition

Adhira's ambition is to become a florist.

goal

My brother's goal is to join the air force.

objective

The objective of the meeting was to choose a new class president.

taste (1) VERB

If you **taste** food or drink, you have a small amount to see what it is like.

nibble

I couldn't resist a nibble of the cake, even though Mum said I had to wait till tea time.

sample

In the supermarket, Mum and I had a sample of some cheese before we bought it.

sip

I sipped the ginger beer, but it tasted strong.

taste (2) NOUN

The **taste** of something is its flavour.

✔ If something has no strong taste, it is **bland** or **plain**.

> **The way some things taste:**
> candyfloss tastes — **sugary**
> chilli tastes — **hot, fiery**
> curry tastes — **hot, spicy**
> honey tastes — **sweet, syrupy**
> ice cream tastes — **sweet, creamy**
> lemons taste — **acidic, sharp, sour**
> oranges taste — **tangy**
> sausages taste — **meaty**
> strong coffee tastes — **bitter**

tasty ADJECTIVE

Something that is **tasty** has a pleasant flavour.

appetizing
*The school cook had laid on a really **appetizing** spread.*

delectable
*"That meal was **delectable**," I told Gran.*

delicious
*Instead of the usual bland taste, the burger was really **delicious**.*

mouthwatering
*On the buffet table were all sorts of **mouthwatering** treats.*

scrumptious INFORMAL
*My sister and I reckon that olives are **scrumptious**.*

ANTONYM: tasteless

tatty ADJECTIVE INFORMAL

Something that is **tatty** is worn out or untidy and rather dirty.

bedraggled
*After being lost for two days, our dog Wuffles returned in a **bedraggled** state.*

frayed
*Old Mr Stuart's collar and cuffs were **frayed** and greasy.*

shabby
*Dad said the house is starting to look **shabby** and needs a lick of paint.*

threadbare
*The hall carpet was **threadbare** due to so many people walking up and down it.*

worn out
Worn out through continuous wear, the farmer's jacket was fit only for the fire.

✔ The formal word for tatty is **tattered**.

ANTONYM: smart

teach VERB

If someone **teaches** you, they help you learn about something or show you how to do it.

coach
*Our neighbour **coaches** my soccer team on a Wednesday evening.*

educate
*A school's job is to **educate** its pupils.*

instruct
*The sergeant **instructed** the squad in how to use a rifle.*

train
*Mrs Hadji **trained** the team for the area athletics competition.*

teacher NOUN

A **teacher** is someone who teaches at a school or college.

coach
*A sports **coach** has to know how to get the best out of his or her team.*

instructor
*The driving **instructor** was very patient.*

professor
*University **professors** do research and writing as well as teaching.*

schoolteacher
*My uncle is a **schoolteacher** in Canada.*

tutor
*A **tutor** is sometimes a person who teaches people individually at home.*

team NOUN

A **team** is a group of people who play together against another group in a sport or game.

line-up INFORMAL
*With their new players, the Reds had a powerful **line-up**.*

outfit INFORMAL

"I'll turn that bunch of scruffs into the finest **outfit** *in the area," barked the PE teacher.*

side

Our **side** *was bound to win after all the training we'd had.*

squad

My older brother is a prop in the school rugby **squad**.

tear (1) RHYMES WITH "HAIR" VERB

If you **tear** something, you damage it by pulling so that a hole or rip appears in it.

ladder

Mum caught her tights on a nail and **laddered** *them.*

rip

Trying to climb an oak tree, I **ripped** *my jeans.*

shred

In the office there is a machine that **shreds** *documents into tiny strips.*

split

Our large uncle managed to **split** *his trousers when he bent down.*

tear (2) RHYMES WITH "HAIR" VERB

To **tear** can mean to go somewhere in a hurry.

charge

Joel **charged** *through the door after his brother.*

dart

Ingrid **darted** *across the deserted street.*

fly

I love **flying** *down the hill on my bike.*

race

We always **race** *home from school so that we don't miss our favourite TV programme.*

shoot

The leading runner **shot** *over the finishing line well ahead of the others.*

speed

The roadrunner beeped and then **sped** *past the coyote.*

zoom

With a screech of tyres the racing cars **zoomed** *over the starting line.*

tease VERB

If somebody **teases** you, they deliberately make fun of you or embarrass you.

mock

We secretly **mocked** *the teacher for his strange voice.*

poke fun at

We can **poke fun at** *my dad without him minding too much.*

ridicule

Kitty was asking to be **ridiculed** *by always arriving so late.*

taunt

The bully **taunted** *the small boy until he burst into tears.*

torment

My sister's friends delight in **tormenting** *me.*

telephone VERB

If you **telephone** someone, you speak to them using a telephone.

call

The advert invited you to **call** *the firm for a free sample.*

phone

Mum **phoned** *us when she arrived at the airport.*

ring

Mumtaz left a message asking me to **ring** *him when I got home.*

See **contact**

tell (1) VERB

If you **tell** something to someone, you let them know about it.

communicate

Through the window, Jude tried to **communicate** *his news using sign language.*

inform

If a pupil is ill, the parents have to **inform** *the school immediately.*

notify

When her purse was stolen, Mum had to **notify** *the police.*

point out

Mr Delap **pointed out** *that we were only a week away from our tests.*

A
B
C
D
E
F
G
H
I
J
K
L
M
N
O
P
Q
R
S
T
U
V
W
X
Y
Z

tell (2) VERB
If you **tell** someone something loudly or officially, you announce it.

announce
Announcing her retirement, the player said she would miss tennis.

proclaim
The emperor proclaimed the betrothal of his daughter.

tell (3) VERB
If you **tell** someone something that they didn't know, you reveal it to them.

confess
Finally, the suspect confessed that she had committed the crime.

reveal
The daily tabloid revealed that the star had had a face-lift.

tell (4) VERB
If you **tell** someone to do something, you order them to do it.

command
Iorek commanded his bears to advance on the fortress.

direct
The fire officer directed workers to leave the building.

instruct
Passengers were instructed to go on deck and wait by the lifeboats.

order
"I'm ordering you to do that now!" yelled the sergeant.

tell (5) VERB
If you **tell** something like a story or report, you narrate it.

narrate
The story we read for homework was narrated in the first person.

recount
An old sailor recounted his adventures in the navy.

relate
When she got home, Cristabel related all that she had seen.

report
Lookouts reported that they had seen smoke on the horizon.

tell (6) VERB
If you **tell** things apart, you judge one thing from another.

differentiate
Janet found it difficult to differentiate between plants and weeds.

distinguish
Even tiny babies can distinguish their mother from other people.

tell off VERB
If you **tell** someone **off**, you speak to them strongly because they have done something wrong.

lecture
Mum lectured me about coming in late again on a school night.

reprimand
My brother was reprimanded for forgetting his sports kit.

scold
Granny used to be scolded for not learning her multiplication tables.

temper NOUN
A **temper** is an angry mood.

fury
In her fury, the witch snapped her broomstick.

rage
The emperor's rage knew no limits, and often resulted in trouble.

tantrum
The crowd booed when the tennis star threw a tantrum.

lose your temper PHRASE
If you **lose your temper**, you become angry.

throw a tantrum
Have you ever seen a toddler throw a tantrum? What a sound!

throw a wobbly INFORMAL
I couldn't see why Dad threw a wobbly. It was an old clock, after all.

ANTONYM: keep calm

tempt VERB

If you **tempt** someone, you try to persuade them to do something by offering them something they want.

entice

*The wolf-grandmother **enticed** the children into the cottage.*

lure

*We tried to **lure** the fox by leaving meat near the chicken run.*

persuade

*Mum **persuaded** us to go shoe shopping.*

ANTONYM: discourage

tempting ADJECTIVE

If something is **tempting**, it is attractive and difficult to resist.

enticing

*The buffet included an **enticing** array of cakes and biscuits.*

inviting

*On a hot summer's day, the sea is particularly **inviting**.*

ANTONYM: uninviting

terrible (1) ADJECTIVE

Something that is **terrible** is serious and unpleasant.

awful

*Most people make **awful** mistakes at one time or another.*

frightful

*It was a **frightful** accident for us to witness.*

horrific

*The crash scene made a **horrific** sight.*

shocking

*The player was sent off for a **shocking** tackle.*

terrible (2) ADJECTIVE

Something that is **terrible** is of very bad or of poor quality.

appalling

*"This is **appalling** work," Mrs Berger barked. "Do it again!"*

awful

*My maths homework was **awful**.*

dreadful

*I had never seen such a **dreadful** movie!*

terrific ADJECTIVE

Something that is **terrific** is very pleasing or impressive.

excellent

*Our family had an **excellent** holiday in Austria.*

fantastic

*"What a **fantastic** goal!" the commentator screamed.*

magnificent

*The **magnificent** portrait seemed almost to look at you.*

marvellous

*From our block, there is a **marvellous** view over the city.*

superb

*My grandad complimented the chef on a **superb** meal.*

test (1) VERB

When you **test** something, you try it to find out what it is, what condition it is in, or how well it works.

analyze

*To find the cause of the disease, scientists **analyzed** the food we had eaten.*

check

*Men in special suits **checked** the building for contamination.*

evaluate

*Dad was given a brand-new car to **evaluate** and report on.*

test (2) VERB

To **test** someone means to ask questions to find out how much they know.

assess

*To **assess** our knowledge, Mrs Holland gave us a barrage of questions.*

evaluate

*"I'm now going to **evaluate** how much you've learnt in this lesson," she said.*

examine

*The class was **examined** on the term's work in maths.*

a b c d e f g h i j k l m n o p q r s **t** u v w x y z

test (3) NOUN

A **test** is a deliberate action or experiment to find out whether something works or how well it works.

analysis

An **analysis** of the water detected traces of pollution.

check

Dad's car went in for a safety **check**.

evaluation

We have to do an **evaluation** of a book we've read.

experiment

Scientists conducted an **experiment** with mice in a maze.

inspection

Every school has to have an **inspection** every now and then.

theft NOUN

Theft is the crime of stealing.

burglary

Burglary involves entering someone else's premises.

robbery

After the **robbery**, the getaway car wouldn't start.

shoplifting

The amount of **shoplifting** in the store had gone down since the security guard had started.

thick ADJECTIVE

Something **thick** has a large distance between its two sides.

broad

A weightlifter's shoulders are usually **broad**.

bulky

The courier delivered a **bulky** package.

chunky

Dad cut me off a **chunky** slice of bread.

ANTONYM: thin

thief NOUN

A **thief** is a person who steals.

burglar

The **burglar** fell while climbing down the drainpipe.

mugger

Police are clamping down on **muggers** in the city streets.

pickpocket

The Artful Dodger was Fagin's chief **pickpocket**.

robber

A band of **robbers** terrorized the western town.

shoplifter

Stores warn **shoplifters** that they will be taken to court.

thin (1) ADJECTIVE

Something that is **thin** is much narrower than it is long.

narrow

We squeezed through the **narrow** gap in the fence.

slender

Willow trees have **slender** branches that droop down in a very attractive way.

slim

The joke book was a **slim** volume.

thin (2) ADJECTIVE

A **thin** person or animal has very little fat on their body.

bony

The starving animal was **bony** and in very poor condition.

gaunt

My sister looked **gaunt** when she got home from her trip.

skinny

People said the tennis player was **skinny**, but she seemed fit enough.

undernourished

Sadly, there are far too many **undernourished** people in the world.

ANTONYM: fat

thin (3) ADJECTIVE

Thin fabric is made from fine materials.

delicate

Ancient fabrics are very **delicate** and tend to crumble when handled roughly.

fine
*The curtains were made of a **fine** net.*

flimsy
*Abbie's skirt was so **flimsy** it blew up in the wind.*

ANTONYM: thick

thin (4) ADJECTIVE
Thin liquids contain a lot of water and flow easily.

diluted
*On rough walls it's a good idea to start with **diluted** paint.*

runny
*I like my egg yolk **runny**, not hard.*

watery
*The hostages were given **watery** soup and a piece of bread.*

ANTONYM: thick

thing NOUN
A **thing** is an object, rather than a plant, animal or person.

article
*In the game you had to guess the **article** from its description.*

item
*"I have several **items** of lost property here," our form teacher announced.*

object
*Madeleine found some strange **objects** in the box from the attic.*

things PLURAL NOUN
Things are your clothes and possessions.

belongings
*On camp, Mrs Butt told me to tidy my **belongings**.*

gear
*We had to carry some of the **gear**.*

paraphernalia
*A parent delivered all the heavy **paraphernalia**.*

possessions
*She was in the USA, but Nancy's **possessions** were being shipped to China.*

stuff
*We'd forgotten about lots of the **stuff** we'd stored in the loft.*

think (1) VERB
When you **think** about ideas or problems, you use your mind to sort them out.

consider
*"Have you ever **considered** being a nurse?" Mrs Kemp asked me.*

contemplate
*Mum needed somewhere quiet in order to **contemplate**.*

ponder
*Will **pondered** for a while, then decided on his course of action.*

reflect
*I was **reflecting** whether to walk to school or catch a bus.*

think (2) VERB
If you **think** something, you believe it is true.

accept
*Mrs Johnson **accepted** that Tania was telling her the truth.*

believe
*Keon **believed** that he could pass his exams.*

reckon
*The spy **reckoned** someone was tailing him.*

think up VERB
If you **think** something **up**, you invent it.

create
*Between them, the two women **created** a range of comic characters.*

invent
*Two Hungarian brothers called Biro **invented** the ballpoint pen.*

thirsty ADJECTIVE
If you are **thirsty**, you feel as if you need to drink something.

dehydrated
*If it's hot and you've a headache, you're probably **dehydrated**.*

parched
*In the blazing heat of the desert, the cowboy was really **parched**.*

a
b
c
d
e
f
g
h
i
j
k
l
m
n
o
p
q
r
s
t
u
v
w
x
y
z

thought (1) NOUN
A **thought** is an idea or opinion.

concept
*The **concept** of the jet engine was completely new in 1930.*

idea
*"What a clever **idea**!" Mr Prutton exclaimed when I made my suggestion.*

notion
*I had a **notion** that the car in front would turn left.*

opinion
*Grandad was never shy about sharing his **opinions**.*

view
*Mrs Fortune asked me for my **view** on the story.*

thought (2) NOUN
Thought is the activity of thinking.

consideration
*"It sounds like a great idea. I'll give it my **consideration**," said Svetlana's boss.*

contemplation
*Mr Finnegan stared out of the window for ages, lost in **contemplation**.*

meditation
*Silent **meditation** helps people to relax.*

reflection
*After some **reflection**, I've changed my mind about what to do.*

thoughtful (1) ADJECTIVE
A **thoughtful** person thinks of what other people want or need and tries to be kind to them.

caring
*Most nurses are very **caring** people who take pleasure in helping others.*

considerate
*It was **considerate** of the gentleman to hold the door open for me.*

kind
*Mum told me that my present was a **kind** gesture.*

ANTONYM: thoughtless

thoughtful (2) ADJECTIVE
If you are **thoughtful**, you are quiet and serious, because you are thinking of something.

lost in thought
*As he sat on the swings, Wesley was **lost in thought**.*

pensive
*"You look **pensive**," Gran said. "What's the matter?"*

threaten VERB
If you **threaten** someone, you tell them you intend to harm them in some way.

bully
*A boy in Class 6 tried to **bully** me into giving him sweets.*

intimidate
*Because of her size, the girl reckoned she could **intimidate** me.*

menace
*The secret police **menaced** people they thought might be traitors.*

thrill NOUN
A **thrill** is a sudden feeling of great excitement, pleasure or fear.

buzz INFORMAL
*Dad said he received a real **buzz** from his flying lessons.*

kick INFORMAL
*Dennis got a **kick** out of playing jokes on people.*

pleasure
*Listening to beautiful music provides a simple **pleasure**.*

throw VERB
When you **throw** something, you let it go with a quick movement of your arm, so that it moves through the air.

chuck INFORMAL
*My mate Robbie **chucked** my sweater over the railings.*

fling
*Lateefa **flung** her bread roll at me, and that was the start of the food fight.*

heave
*The shot-putter **heaved** the iron ball as far as she could.*

hurl
*Javelins are the spears that athletes **hurl** as far as they can.*

sling
*Samuel took off his jacket and **slung** it onto the back seat of the car.*

toss
*The kilted Scotsman **tossed** the huge pole up and over the fence.*

throw away VERB
If you **throw away** something that you do not want, you get rid of it, usually by putting it in the rubbish bin.

discard
*"Don't **discard** your drinks cans – recycle them!" read the sign.*

dispose of
*The criminal's problem was how to **dispose of** the evidence.*

dump
*"Why do some people **dump** rubbish in the countryside?" asked Mum crossly.*

jettison
*To avoid landing in the sea, the balloonist had to **jettison** everything except the fuel.*

thump VERB
If you **thump** someone or something, you hit them hard with your fist.

clout INFORMAL
*Billy Carter often got **clouted** by his bullying brother.*

pound
*The boxer **pounded** the punchbag as if he meant business.*

punch
***Punched** by the lurking baddie, Bond lay dazed on the ground.*

wallop
*Grandad says he often used to get **walloped** at school.*

tidy (1) ADJECTIVE
Something that is **tidy** is neat and arranged in an orderly way.

neat
*A **neat** row of cottages lined the street.*

shipshape INFORMAL
*Mr Barmby told us he wanted our dormitory **shipshape**.*

spick-and-span INFORMAL
*Everything was **spick-and-span** for the sergeant's inspection.*

tidy (2) VERB
If you **tidy** a place, you make it neat by putting things in their proper place.

clear up
*We were ordered to **clear up** the mess we'd made in the kitchen.*

put in order
*Once things were **put in order**, we could go out to play.*

spruce up
*Dad decided to **spruce up** the garage, and tried to rope me in to help.*

tie VERB
If you **tie** one thing to another, you fasten it using cord of some kind.

attach
*The tiny terrier was **attached** to the post by a piece of string.*

bind
*As the bat handle was cracked, Nasser **bound** it with tape.*

knot
*There are various ways to **knot** a tie, but I can never remember any of them.*

secure
*Moira **secured** her bike to the lamppost with a chain and lock.*

✔ If you tie up a boat, you **moor** it.
If you tie up a horse, you **tether** it.

tight (1) ADJECTIVE
If clothes are **tight**, they fit you very closely.

close-fitting
*Even my sister looked smart in her **close-fitting** suit.*

snug
*My new jeans were a **snug** fit, but not easy to put on.*

ANTONYM: loose

a b c d e f g h i j k l m n o p q r s **t** u v w x y z

tight (2) ADJECTIVE

If a space is **tight**, there is little spare space.

confined
*A dungeon cell is usually a very **confined** space.*

constricted
*Because of a parked van, access to the street was **constricted**.*

cramped
*The cabin was **cramped**, with bunks, a washbasin and little else.*

restricted
*Space on deck was **restricted** as more tourists poured onto the boat.*

ANTONYM: spacious

tight (3) ADJECTIVE

If you hold **tight**, you hold on very firmly.

firm
*"Make sure you have a **firm** grasp of the rail when the ride starts," the man advised.*

secure
*The policeman had the thief in a **secure** grip.*

taut
*As soon as the towrope was **taut**, the car lurched forward.*

tilt VERB

If you **tilt** an object, or if it **tilts**, it is moved so that one end or side is higher than the other.

incline
*No sooner had we stood the tall clock up, than it started to **incline** forwards.*

lean
*The old tower in Pisa has gradually **leant** more and more over the years.*

list
*The stricken liner was **listing** heavily in the water.*

slant
*The roof **slanted** at 45 degrees.*

slope
*Our street **sloped** down to the river.*

tip
*Amisha pushed off with her feet and **tipped** the seesaw so that she was up in the air.*

time (1) NOUN

Time is a particular period in history.

age
*The 19th century was the **age** of steam power.*

days
*Gran remembers the **days** of steam trains.*

era
*The **era** of the great ocean liners ended as jet airliners entered service.*

period
*The **period** after the Second World War saw great shortages in Europe.*

time (2) NOUN

A **time** is a particular point when something happens.

moment
*This was the **moment** when Tim could have won the game.*

occasion
*For many people, weddings are big **occasions**.*

point
*At that **point**, the angry lady got up and walked out of the meeting.*

stage
*The next **stage** of the project was for the roof to be put on.*

Units of time:
second
minute   (60 seconds)
hour   (60 minutes)
day   (24 hours)
week   (7 days)
fortnight   (2 weeks)
month   (28, 29, 30 or 31 days)
year   (365 days, or 366 days in a leap year)

a.m. (Latin: *ante meridiem*) is **morning**
p.m. (Latin: *post meridiem*) is **afternoon**

12 noon is **midday**
10 years is a **decade**
100 years is a **century**
1000 years is a **millennium**

time (3) NOUN

A **time** is a particular period when something happens.

period
*During the holiday **period**, Dion helped his mother in the shop.*

season
*Autumn is the **season** for apple picking.*

spell
*Granny had a **spell** in hospital recently.*

stretch
*Dad thought a **stretch** of grounding was a suitable punishment for me.*

term
*The gangster was sent down for a long **term** in jail.*

while
*Fraser decided to go out for a short **while**.*

tiny ADJECTIVE

Something **tiny** is extremely small.

microscopic
*I got a **microscopic** bit of sand in my eye, but it really hurt!*

miniature
*These days, **miniature** cameras can produce high-quality pictures.*

minute
*The cameras hidden in cricket stumps are **minute**.*

ANTONYM: huge

tired (1) ADJECTIVE

If you are **tired**, you have less energy or enthusiasm than normal.

drained
*After her day's work, Mum looked **drained**.*

exhausted
*Frodo felt **exhausted** and looked around for somewhere to rest.*

weakened
***Weakened** by fever, the explorer remained in the hut.*

weary
*The **weary** hare lay down under a tree*

worn out
*By the end of term, poor Mrs Etherington was **worn out**.*

ANTONYM: energetic

tired (2) ADJECTIVE

If you are **tired**, you feel as if you want to sleep.

drowsy
*Still **drowsy**, Dimitri rose and blundered to the bathroom.*

sleepy
*Grandad often feels **sleepy** after lunch and dozes off in his armchair.*

ANTONYM: wide-awake

together (1) ADVERB

If people do something **together**, they do it with each other.

collectively
***Collectively**, schools in our area raised enough money to train a guide dog.*

hand in hand
*The owl and the pussycat danced **hand in hand** by the edge of the sand.*

jointly
*Our new library was funded **jointly** by the school and the PTA.*

shoulder to shoulder
***Shoulder to shoulder**, the soldiers fought off the attacking hordes.*

side by side
*The whole class worked **side by side** to dig the garden.*

together (2) ADVERB

If things happen **together**, they happen at the same time.

all at once
*I waited for an hour, then three buses came **all at once**.*

in unison
*When the head teacher came into the room, we all stood up **in unison**.*

simultaneously
*Guns fired a salute. **Simultaneously**, the fly-past jets roared overhead.*

a
b
c
d
e
f
g
h
i
j
k
l
m
n
o
p
q
r
s
t
u
v
w
x
y
z

tool NOUN

A **tool** is any hand-held piece of equipment that you use to help you do a particular kind of work.

implement

Garden implements include spades and forks.

instrument

A barometer is an instrument for measuring air pressure.

utensil

Dad likes to have all the correct kitchen utensils when he's cooking.

Some tools for do-it-yourself (DIY) work:

chisel	pliers
clamp	saw
drill	screwdriver
file	spanner
hammer	spirit level
plane	vice

Some garden tools:

chainsaw	secateurs
fork	shears
hoe	shovel
lawn mower	spade
pickaxe	strimmer
rake	trowel

Some decorating tools:

paintbrush	roller tray
pastebrush	scissors
pasting table	stepladder
roller	wallpaper brush

Some tools for bike or car repair:

foot pump	spanner
jack	tyre lever
pliers	wheel brace
socket set	wrench

---

top (1) NOUN

The **top** is the highest point, part or surface of something.

crest

Surfers aim to ride in on the crest of a wave.

height

At the height of her fame, the singer decided to retire.

peak

Athletes try to stay in the peak of condition.

summit

On the mountain summit, the climbers gazed around them in wonder.

ANTONYM: bottom

---

top (2) ADJECTIVE

The **top** of somewhere or something is the chief person or thing of a particular type.

foremost

Dr Zenden is the foremost cancer specialist.

greatest

Pele was perhaps the world's greatest soccer player.

leading

"We are the leading supplier of double-glazed windows", boasted the advert.

total ADJECTIVE

Total can mean complete.

absolute

I felt an absolute idiot in fancy dress.

complete

Reports came in that the mission had been a complete success.

out-and-out

There was no doubt that Goldfinger was an out-and-out villain.

sheer

Sheer determination got the runner to the finishing line in first place.

thorough

My baby brother can be a thorough nuisance at times.

utter

"Don't talk such utter nonsense," Mum said.

touch VERB

If you **touch** something, you put your fingers or hand on it.

feel

In the dark, I felt something rough and hard at eyelevel.

finger

The jeweller fingered the ring, all the while staring at it.

handle
The vet **handled** the poorly kitten very gently.

✔ If you get **in touch** with somebody, you contact them by e-mailing, faxing, telephoning, text messaging, visiting or writing to them.

tough (1) ADJECTIVE
Something that is **tough** is strong and difficult to break or damage.

durable
We have a set of **durable** plates for picnics.

hard-wearing
Road surfaces need to be **hard-wearing**.

resilient
The **resilient** little car lasted another year.

robust
It's a good job my baby sister's toys are **robust**, as she's not very gentle with them!

sturdy
The tree house was **sturdy** enough to hold four of us at once.

tough (2) ADJECTIVE
Food that is **tough** is difficult to cut and chew.

chewy
The meat was so **chewy** I had to leave it.

gristly
Occasionally, sausages can be **gristly** and hard to chew.

leathery
I struggled with a **leathery** piece of liver.

ANTONYM: tender

tough (3) ADJECTIVE
A **tough** task or way of life is difficult or full of hardship.

arduous
The climbing party faced an **arduous** trek through the foothills.

demanding
Marathon races are very **demanding**, physically and mentally.

gruelling
New recruits endured a **gruelling** month of exercise and discipline.

ANTONYM: easy

tragedy NOUN
A **tragedy** is a very sad or disastrous event or situation, especially one in which people are killed.

calamity
What a **calamity**! The falling chandelier smashed the wedding cake.

catastrophe
The earthquake was the third **catastrophe** to strike the country that year.

disaster
Disaster struck when the road bridge collapsed during rush hour.

misfortune
Losing your passport when on holiday is a serious **misfortune**.

train (1) VERB
If you **train**, you prepare for a sports match or race by doing exercises.

exercise
Most professional athletes **exercise** daily.

practise
The swimming team **practises** three mornings a week before school.

work out
My brother **works out** in the gym through the week and plays rugby at the weekend.

train (2) VERB
If you **train** someone, you help them prepare for a sports match or race.

coach
Mr Boateng **coached** the school soccer team.

drill
The soldiers were **drilled** until they could have paraded in their sleep.

instruct
Emma **instructs** trainee nurses.

traitor NOUN
A **traitor** is someone who betrays their country or the group that they belong to.

spy
The two **spies** were jailed for selling secrets.

turncoat
Striking workers threw eggs at the **turncoat** who went back to work.

a b c d e f g h i j k l m n o p q r s t u v w x y z

trap

A B C D E F G H I J K L M N O P Q R S **T** U V W X Y Z

trap VERB
If you **trap** someone or something, you catch them using a trap.

capture
Bandits **captured** the stagecoach in the canyon.

corner
With dogs one side and men on the other, the fox was **cornered**.

ensnare
Ensnared in barbed wire, the prisoner was forced to surrender.

travel VERB
If you **travel**, you go from one place to another.

journey
The messenger **journeyed** through the night.

voyage
In 1492, Columbus **voyaged** to the New World.

✔ When birds travel to follow the seasons they **migrate**.

Some ways that people travel:

by air	**fly**
by bicycle	**bike, cycle, pedal**
by getting lifts	**hitchhike, thumb**
by road	**drive, motor**
by ship	**cruise, sail, voyage**

Vehicles in which people travel:

air travel	aeroplane, airship, helicopter, plane (general word: aircraft)
rail travel	metro, monorail, subway, train, tram, tube, underground
road travel	bus, car, coach, minibus, taxi (general word: vehicle)
water travel	barge, boat, ferry, liner, narrowboat, ship (general word: vessel)

---

treasure VERB
If you **treasure** something, you look after it carefully because it is important to you.

cherish
The previous owners had **cherished** the house.

prize
The painting was one that the gallery's curator **prized** most.

value
Melinda really **values** her friendship with Hadia.

treat VERB
If you **treat** someone or something in a particular way, you behave that way towards them.

deal with
I admired the way my mum **dealt with** awkward customers.

handle
My brother Mark always knows how to **handle** difficult people.

tree NOUN
A **tree** is a large plant with a hard trunk, branches and leaves.

Coniferous trees, or **conifers**, have needles and cones.
Evergreen trees stay green all year round.
Deciduous trees lose their leaves in winter.
Young trees are called **saplings**.
Small trees are **bushes** or **shrubs**.

Some types of coniferous tree:

cedar	juniper	redwood
fir	pine	yew

Some types of deciduous tree:

ash	hazel	sweet chestnut
beech	horse chestnut	teak
birch	maple	walnut
elm	oak	willow
eucalyptus	poplar	

Some fruit trees:

apple	guava	peach
avocado	mango	pear
cherry	orange	plum

---

tremble VERB
If you **tremble**, you shake slightly, usually because you are frightened or cold.

quake
Millie was **quaking** when she went in to see the head teacher.

quiver
*The poor wet dog **quivered** under the table.*

shiver
*It's strange how you **shiver** when you go from cold air to warm air.*

tremendous (1) ADJECTIVE
Something that is **tremendous** is large or impressive.

almighty
*Suddenly, there was an **almighty** explosion.*

colossal
*A **colossal** iceberg loomed out of the mist ahead of the ship.*

enormous
*Then, with an **enormous** crunch, the two ships collided.*

huge
*One ship had a **huge** mass of tangled metal where its bow should have been.*

terrific
*There was a **terrific** gash in the side of the other ship.*

tremendous (2) ADJECTIVE
Something **tremendous** is very good or pleasing.

excellent
*The Shakespeare play we saw was **excellent**.*

great
*I thought the actor playing Hamlet was **great**.*

marvellous
*The rest of the cast were **marvellous** too.*

sensational
*The author's books have been a **sensational** success.*

wonderful
*It's **wonderful** to think of so many children enjoying books.*

trick (1) VERB
If someone **tricks** you, they deceive you.

bamboozle
*The quickness of the magician's fingers **bamboozled** me.*

con INFORMAL
*Gran was **conned** by two men pretending to be from the electricity company.*

deceive
*The shot **deceived** the goalkeeper by dipping in the air.*

dupe
*The trickster tried to **dupe** the tourist into buying Tower Bridge.*

fool
*"You certainly had me **fooled**!" I said to Skye as she took the wig off.*

trick (2) NOUN
A **trick** is an action done to deceive someone.

con INFORMAL
*The holiday villas in Spain turned out to be a total **con**.*

deception
*We were all taken in by the talented magician's cunning **deception**.*

hoax
*My sister made a **hoax** phone call pretending to be my teacher.*

practical joke
*My **practical joke** backfired when I got covered in flour myself.*

prank
*Gran says that she was always playing **pranks** as a child.*

trickle VERB
When a liquid **trickles** somewhere, it flows slowly in a thin stream.

dribble
*Water only **dribbled** from the tap. Where was the burst pipe?*

drip
*"What's that **dripping** from the fridge?" Mum asked.*

leak
*Water had **leaked** into all the cupboards below the sink.*

ooze
*Something slimy and smelly was **oozing** from the tank.*

seep
*Over the years, rain had **seeped** in through the roof.*

ANTONYM: gush

A
B
C
D
E
F
G
H
I
J
K
L
M
N
O
P
Q
R
S
T
U
V
W
X
Y
Z

tricky ADJECTIVE

Someone or something **tricky** is difficult to do or deal with.

awkward

*It was an **awkward** situation – to risk trouble or keep quiet?*

complicated

*I don't reckon Maths is as **complicated** as people sometimes think.*

delicate

***Delicate** matters need to be handled tactfully.*

difficult

*Raymond found the exam question very **difficult** to answer.*

trip (1) NOUN

A **trip** is a journey made to a place.

excursion

*Two coaches arrived to take us on the **excursion**.*

jaunt

*Mum and I went on a shopping **jaunt** to spend my birthday money.*

journey

*By train, the **journey** was relaxing and speedy.*

outing

*This year our class **outing** was to the seaside, where there was also a funfair.*

visit

*Before the **visit**, we did research on medieval castles.*

voyage

*In 1912, the Titanic sank on her maiden **voyage**.*

trip (2) VERB

If you **trip**, or **trip over**, you catch your foot on something and fall over.

lose your footing

*The sailor **lost his footing** as he was climbing the mast, and fell into the sea.*

stumble

*Gran **stumbled** over a lump of stone in the path.*

*See **fall***

trouble (1) NOUN

Trouble is a difficulty or problem.

bother

*"Changing goods is no **bother**, madam," the shopkeeper insisted.*

difficulty

*Swimming out to sea, Zeke soon got into **difficulty**.*

dire straits

*We were in **dire straits** when the car broke down in the middle of nowhere.*

hot water INFORMAL

*"You'll get into **hot water**, my young lady," Gran warned.*

misfortune

*It was Benjie's **misfortune** to run into his teacher when he was supposed to be ill.*

problem

*Mum had no **problem** in changing the car tyre.*

trouble (2) NOUN

If there is **trouble**, people are arguing or fighting.

commotion

*"What's all the **commotion**?" snapped Mrs Charlton, entering the room.*

disturbance

*Some **disturbance** outside the bar caused the police to arrive.*

unrest

*Before the revolution, there had been **unrest** in the capital for some time.*

trouble (3) VERB

If you **trouble** someone, you worry or bother them.

disturb

*Grandad didn't like being **disturbed** during his nap.*

inconvenience

*My brother didn't want to **inconvenience** Dad, but he did need a lift.*

pester

*"Stop **pestering** me!" I snapped. "The answer's still 'no'."*

*See **annoy***

trouble (4) VERB

If something **troubles** you, it worries or bothers you.

concern
The doctor was **concerned** about Grandad's health.

distress
We were all **distressed** to hear of our neighbour's accident.

upset
It **upsets** me to think of the time our dog had to be put down.

worry
"Try not to let the exam **worry** you," my auntie said.

true (1) ADJECTIVE

A **true** story or statement is based on facts and is not invented.

accurate
The notes were an **accurate** record of the conversation.

correct
"Is it **correct** that some people eat snails?" I asked.

factual
"What I need is **factual** writing, not a story," Miss Wilcox emphasized.

ANTONYM: false

true (2) ADJECTIVE

If something is **true**, it is real and genuine.

authentic
To think Dad owned an **authentic** vintage car!

genuine
The signature was definitely **genuine**, and not a forgery.

real
The jewels were not fake but **real**.

ANTONYM: fake

trust VERB

If you **trust** someone, you believe they are honest and reliable, and will treat you fairly.

believe in
I **believed in** what Ganesh was telling me.

depend on
You can always **depend on** Linda to help you.

have faith in
With our big match coming up, Miss Clemence **had faith in** us to win.

put your trust in
The hobbits were forced to **put their trust in** the wizard.

rely on
"Can I **rely on** you to keep a secret?" Ian asked.

ANTONYM: distrust

try (1) VERB

If you **try** to do something, you make an effort to do it.

attempt
The athlete **attempted** a jump higher than she'd ever achieved before.

do your best
Mrs Tessem said she was relying on us to **do our best** in the test.

endeavour
"You must **endeavour** to be honest at all times," Grandad advised.

have a go INFORMAL
Bilbo had never ridden before, but he was willing to **have a go**.

strive
By frantic baling, the crew **strove** to keep the boat afloat.

try (2) VERB

If you **try** something, you use it, taste it or experiment with it to see how good or suitable it is.

evaluate
Mum was sent a sample of a new perfume to **evaluate**.

put to the test
Sir Lancelot **put** the sword **to the test** in battle.

sample
While it was still hot, I **sampled** the cake that Dad had baked.

test
Having **tested** the van, the mechanic was satisfied.

try

try (3) NOUN

A **try** is an attempt to do something.

attempt

*Before success in 1953, many **attempts** had been made to climb Everest.*

bash INFORMAL

*"Go on! Have a **bash** at the rope slide," my brother urged.*

effort

*With his final **effort**, the jumper managed to clear the bar.*

shot INFORMAL

*Dad had another **shot** at starting the car.*

turn VERB

When you **turn**, you move so that you are facing or going in a different direction.

pivot

__Pivoting__ on his left leg, Frank blasted the ball with his right.

revolve

*The head teacher **revolved** in his swivel chair to see who had come in.*

rotate

*Our door key **rotates** clockwise to open, anticlockwise to lock.*

spin

__Spinning__ round, Yardan caught us creeping up on him.

swivel

*Mrs Gupta **swivelled** her chair round to face the class.*

twirl

*The dancers **twirled** in a blaze of colour.*

twist

__Twisting__ this way and that, Della managed to avoid the obstacles.

whirl

*"For the falcon to swoop, you **whirl** the meat around your head," demonstrated the keeper.*

turn down VERB

If you **turn down** an offer or request, you refuse or reject it.

decline

*Sadly, I had to **decline** Fola's party invitation.*

refuse

*The council **refused** an application to build a factory by the river.*

reject

*When he applied for art college, my brother was **rejected**.*

ANTONYM: accept

turn into VERB

When something **turns into** something else, it becomes something different.

be transformed into

*Through cleaning, our car **was transformed into** a respectable vehicle.*

become

*With a puff of the lamp, Aladdin **became** a wealthy nobleman.*

convert into

*A futon **converts** from a sofa **into** a bed.*

metamorphose into

*Caterpillars **metamorphose into** butterflies.*

mutate into

*Sometimes I wish my brother would **mutate into** a nicer creature!*

turn over VERB

If you **turn** something **over**, or it **turns over**, it moves so that the top part faces downwards.

capsize

*As the wind caught the dinghy, it **capsized**.*

flip over

*The magician **flipped over** a card, then another and another.*

overturn

*When cars skid badly, they sometimes **overturn**.*

turn up VERB

If someone or something **turns up**, they arrive or appear somewhere.

appear

*Just as we'd given her up, Samirah **appeared**, out of breath.*

arrive

*We **arrived** just in time for the show.*

attend

*My parents like to **attend** school meetings if they can.*

show up
*"Trust Brad to **show up** late," someone whispered in my ear.*

twist (1) VERB
When you **twist** something, you turn the two ends in opposite directions.

coil
***Coiling** itself round the pole, the snake made for the hole in the ceiling.*

wind
*"By **winding** the thread round, it becomes far stronger," Granny explained.*

twist (2) VERB
If you **twist** something, you move or bend it into a strange shape.

bend
*As part of her act, the woman used to **bend** iron bars.*

buckle
*Under the impact of collision, the front of the truck **buckled**.*

distort
*The heat of the furnace **distorts** the shape of the glass.*

mangle
*It's a miracle the girl escaped from the **mangled** wreckage.*

warp
*All Dad's old vinyl records **warped** in the sun.*

twist (3) VERB
If you **twist** part of your body, you injure it by turning it too sharply or in an odd direction.

sprain
*Bindiya **sprained** her ankle when she fell, playing tennis.*

wrench
*Dad was in pain after he **wrenched** his knee.*

type NOUN
If something is the same **type** as something else, they belong to the same group and have many things in common.

category
*I would put our head teacher in the "strict" **category**.*

class
*The "Pacific" was an old **class** of steam locomotive.*

kind
*A jackal is a **kind** of wild dog that can be found in Africa.*

sort
*Zina is the **sort** of person you like as soon as you meet her.*

variety
*Of the many **varieties** of roses, Mum likes climbers best.*

Type of	
...animal	breed, species
...book or film	genre
...car	make
...clothes	style
...people	race
...plant	variety

typical ADJECTIVE
Something that is **typical** of a person or animal is usual and what is to be expected of them.

average
*We are just an **average** family in an **average** house on an **average** street.*

characteristic
***Characteristic** of Mr Hendrie was a tendency to crack jokes.*

normal
*A **normal** day in our house might seem pretty crazy to you!*

standard
*To obtain a passport, you have to follow the **standard** procedure.*

usual
*It was **usual** for our neighbour to leave at around eight o'clock.*

a b c d e f g h i j k l m n o p q r s **t** u v w x y z

A
B
C
D
E
F
G
H
I
J
K
L
M
N
O
P
Q
R
S
T
U
V
W
X
Y
Z

Uu

ugly ADJECTIVE

Someone or something that is **ugly** is very unattractive or unpleasant.

hideous

*The monster had a **hideous** face, misshapen and warty.*

repulsive

*With such a **repulsive** appearance, the creature was bound to scare people.*

unattractive

*Everyone else disagreed, but Dad thought the pop star was **unattractive**.*

unsightly

*That disused shop is an **unsightly** feature of the high street.*

ANTONYM: beautiful

---

unbelievable (1) ADJECTIVE

Something that is **unbelievable** is so unlikely that it is hard to believe.

far-fetched

*Sam is always telling **far-fetched** stories.*

implausible

*Hadira's excuse was completely **implausible**.*

preposterous

*"What you say is absolutely **preposterous**!" spluttered the professor.*

unbelievable (2) ADJECTIVE

Something that is **unbelievable** is very surprising or wonderful.

astonishing

*The sunset over the bay made an **astonishing** sight.*

incredible

*With an **incredible** effort, the lifeboat man plucked the sailor from the sea.*

uncertain ADJECTIVE

If you are **uncertain** about something, you are not sure about it.

doubtful

*"It is **doubtful** whether we'll be able to go to the party," Mum said.*

dubious

*We were a bit **dubious** about the idea at first, but it turned out well.*

hesitant

*I was **hesitant** about going in the water because I am not a strong swimmer.*

undecided

*Ghita was **undecided** about her future plans.*

unsure

*Mrs Coulter was **unsure** where Lyra had gone.*

uncomfortable ADJECTIVE

If you feel **uncomfortable** in a situation, you feel worried or nervous.

awkward

*Dressed in a chicken costume, Seamus felt **awkward**.*

embarrassed

*I felt totally **embarrassed** when Mum started loudly talking about me.*

ill at ease

*You could see by Anthony's fidgeting that he was **ill at ease**.*

uneasy

***Uneasy** because of the silence, Petra watched and waited.*

ANTONYM: relaxed

---

unconscious ADJECTIVE

If someone is **unconscious**, they are unable to see, feel or hear anything that is going on.

in a coma

*After the accident, the teenager remained **in a coma** for several weeks.*

knocked out

*A jab of anaesthetic, and Wuffles our dog was soon **knocked out** for his operation.*

out cold INFORMAL

*When the ball hit her on the head, Trisha was **out cold** for some minutes.*

stunned

*Louis was momentarily **stunned**, having hit his head on the beam.*

✔ If you are made unconscious for an operation, you are **anaesthetized**.

ANTONYM: conscious

uncover VERB

If you **uncover** something, you take the cover off it.

expose
*Lisa lifted the stone to **expose** a huge insect habitat.*

reveal
*Two days' digging **revealed** a superb Roman mosaic.*

unveil
*The duchess pulled the cord to **unveil** the new statue.*

unwrap
*"Aren't you going to **unwrap** your present?" Dad enquired.*

ANTONYM: cover

under PREPOSITION

If something is **under** something else, it is below or beneath it.

below
***Below** the surface of the water swam many brightly coloured fish.*

beneath
***Beneath** the trees, the daffodils bloomed.*

underneath
*Dad ran a garage business **underneath** some railway arches.*

understand VERB

If you **understand** what someone says or what you read, you know what it means.

appreciate
*Poor Gran was too ill to **appreciate** what was going on.*

follow
*"I don't **follow**," said Dad, looking mystified.*

grasp
*I found the idea of decimals quite easy to **grasp**.*

realize
*"Did you **realize** that you were speaking to the new head teacher?" Crispin asked.*

take in
*It was a while before Femi could **take in** what was happening.*

undo VERB

If you **undo** something like a knot, you loosen or unfasten it.

unbutton
*To listen to my breathing, the doctor asked me to **unbutton** my shirt.*

unfasten
*No sooner had I **unfastened** her collar, than Wuffles our dog ran off.*

untie
*Damini eventually **untied** the knot.*

unzip
*We **unzipped** the tent and pulled back the flap to reveal a beautiful morning.*

See **open**

unfair ADJECTIVE

Something that is **unfair** does not seem right, reasonable or fair.

biased
*Viewers phoned in to complain that the programme was **biased**.*

prejudiced
*Some people are **prejudiced** when they discuss anybody who is different.*

unjust
*The verdict was **unjust**: an innocent woman was going to jail.*

ANTONYM: fair

unhappy ADJECTIVE

An **unhappy** person is sad and miserable.

depressed
*Niles was quite **depressed** when he didn't get a part in the play.*

down
*My sister was **down** about her exam results.*

gloomy
*The outlook for any country in the grip of a dictator is **gloomy**.*

miserable
*In the pouring rain, we had a thoroughly **miserable** day out.*

sad
*I felt **sad** to leave our little house.*

ANTONYM: happy

a
b
c
d
e
f
g
h
i
j
k
l
m
n
o
p
q
r
s
t
u
v
w
x
y
z

unkind ADJECTIVE

Someone who is **unkind** is unpleasant and rather cruel.

cruel
It was **cruel** of the owner to keep the dog tied up outside all day.

harsh
People in Victorian times were generally more **harsh** when dealing out punishment.

malicious
Some **malicious** person had started spreading some very nasty rumours.

mean
It was **mean** of Madison to say those things.

nasty
The **nasty** little girl kicked and scratched.

spiteful
My sister is sometimes **spiteful** to me when I annoy her.

unpleasant
Mrs Rae was rather **unpleasant** in a couple of her comments in my report.

unsympathetic
Mr Bumble was **unsympathetic** to Oliver's request for more food.

unknown (1) ADJECTIVE

If someone or something is **unknown**, they are not familiar or famous.

humble
The actor had started out as a **humble** waiter and was now world-famous.

obscure
My brother went to see some **obscure** pop group in concert.

unfamiliar
There were several **unfamiliar** names on the list of people attending the premiere.

unsung
There are many **unsung** heroes in our history.

unknown (2) ADJECTIVE

If someone's name or identity is **unknown**, people do not know who they are.

anonymous
A large sum of money was given by an **anonymous** donor.

nameless
"Someone, who shall be **nameless**, has broken a window," Mrs Sherwood said.

unidentified
An **unidentified** witness claims to have seen what happened at the scene of the accident.

unnamed
"Reports say that a man, as yet **unnamed**, was shot dead early today," said the newsreader.

unlucky ADJECTIVE

If you are **unlucky**, you are unfortunate and have bad luck.

hapless
Watched by the hawk, the **hapless** vole came out into the sunshine.

ill-fated
Through the night, the **ill-fated** vessel steamed towards the iceberg.

jinxed
Playing City, United seemed to be **jinxed**, as they always lost.

luckless
The **luckless** skier once more picked herself up from the snow.

unfortunate
Kardai had an **unfortunate** accident, coming off his bike.

wretched
Wretched beggars stretched out their arms to plead for food.

unnecessary ADJECTIVE

Something that is **unnecessary** is not necessary.

needless
The jockey was fined for **needless** use of the whip during the race.

nonessential
The members of the expedition were told to leave behind **nonessential** items.

superfluous
"We can do without your **superfluous** comments," Mrs Malik said acidly.

uncalled-for
The waiter's rudeness was **uncalled-for**.

ANTONYM: necessary

unpleasant (1) ADJECTIVE

An **unpleasant** person is unfriendly or rude.

disagreeable

Justin may be clever, but he's quite a **disagreeable** *man.*

horrid

*She was a **horrid** person, who never said a kind word to anyone.*

nasty

***Nasty** comments like that are totally unnecessary and harmful.*

obnoxious

*"What an **obnoxious** bloke he is," my sister remarked.*

See **bad-tempered**

unpleasant (2) ADJECTIVE

Something **unpleasant** is not enjoyable and may make you uncomfortable or upset.

disagreeable

I found the roller-coaster ride an altogether **disagreeable** *experience.*

horrible

*"Some tourist resorts are **horrible** places," commented Gran.*

repulsive

*The evil old miser leered at us in a **repulsive** manner.*

revolting

*"I can't eat this stuff – it's **revolting**!" I protested.*

unsuccessful ADJECTIVE

If you are **unsuccessful**, you do not succeed in what you are trying to do.

fruitless

*Our search proved **fruitless**. Tibbles was nowhere to be found.*

futile

*Mum made a **futile** attempt to find her missing ring in the dark.*

vain

*Paramedics made a **vain** attempt to save the old lady's life.*

ANTONYM: successful

unsuitable ADJECTIVE

Things that are **unsuitable** are not right or suitable for a particular purpose.

inappropriate

Young children often come out with **inappropriate** *comments.*

out of place

*Tim's unkind words were **out of place** at a wedding.*

unsuited

***Unsuited** to life behind a desk, my big brother joined the air force.*

wrong

*The purple curtains looked **wrong** in a green room.*

ANTONYM: suitable

untidy (1) ADJECTIVE

If a place is **untidy**, it is not tidy.

chaotic

*Mum said my bedroom was **chaotic**.*

cluttered

*Kyle's bedroom is more **cluttered** than mine.*

higgledy-piggledy INFORMAL

Everything in Karen's room is completely **higgledy-piggledy**.

jumbled

*When my sister borrows my tapes and CDs, she always leaves them **jumbled**.*

messy

*My brother's room is always **messy**.*

untidy (2) ADJECTIVE

If a person's work is **untidy**, it is not neat and well-arranged.

careless

*"This work is **careless**. Do it again," Miss Pearson ordered.*

messy

*Due to a leaking biro, Gary's work was **messy**.*

slipshod

***Slipshod** presentation is something Mr Stone won't tolerate.*

slovenly

*"**Slovenly** work will get lower marks than tidy work," said Mrs Cameron.*

A
B
C
D
E
F
G
H
I
J
K
L
M
N
O
P
Q
R
S
T
U
V
W
X
Y
Z

untidy (3) ADJECTIVE

If a person looks **untidy**, they do not look smart.

bedraggled
*Rehan looked **bedraggled** after walking ten miles in the rain.*

scruffy
*Dad always complains that my brother looks **scruffy**.*

unkempt
***Unkempt** hair needs washing and combing.*

untrue ADJECTIVE

Something that is **untrue** is not true.

false
*The suspect's alibi proved to be **false**.*

inaccurate
*Daniel gave an **inaccurate** version of what had happened.*

incorrect
*It is **incorrect** to say that the moon is made of blue cheese.*

misleading
*Tabloid newspapers sometimes give **misleading** information.*

wrong
*"I'm afraid what you say is **wrong**," Mrs Mohanty said.*

unusual ADJECTIVE

Something that is **unusual** is not usual and does not happen very often.

abnormal
*A lorry with an **abnormal** load needed a police escort.*

exceptional
*With **exceptional** skill, the skier negotiated the slalom at top speed.*

extraordinary
*How **extraordinary** it is to hear birds sing in the dead of night.*

freak
*A **freak** whirlwind destroyed our barn.*

odd
*It was **odd** to encounter a friend so far away from home.*

rare
*"First editions of Shakespeare plays are very **rare** indeed," said the bookseller.*

remarkable
*The New York skyline is a **remarkable** sight.*

strange
*Camels are **strange** in being able to survive for long periods without water.*

upset (1) ADJECTIVE

If someone is **upset**, they are unhappy and disappointed.

disappointed
*Dev was **disappointed** with his exam results.*

dismayed
*We were **dismayed** to find that the train had gone a minute before.*

distressed
*The little boy was **distressed** that he had lost his mother.*

saddened
*Our family was **saddened** by the death of our neighbour.*

tearful
*Will bid a **tearful** farewell to the girl he had grown so fond of.*

upset (2) VERB

If someone or something **upsets** you, it makes you feel worried or unhappy.

bother
*It took more than a few flies to **bother** Diane.*

dismay
*Mum **dismayed** us when she cut our pocket money.*

distress
*"You mustn't **distress** yourself," I said to the worried old lady.*

faze
*Thunder, jet planes, fireworks – nothing **fazed** our dog Wuffles.*

hurt
*Aba was **hurt** to think she had not been invited to the party.*

trouble
*My Gran was **troubled** by a pain in her back.*

worry
*The delay didn't **worry** the pilot, but the lack of fuel did.*

upside down ADJECTIVE
If something is **upside down**, it is the wrong way up.

inverted
*Sauce bottles are often left **inverted** to get all the sauce out.*

on its head
*The situation was turned **on its head** when the other team scored twice.*

topsy-turvy
*The house was all **topsy-turvy**, with the bedrooms downstairs and the kitchen upstairs.*

use (1) SAID **"YOOZ"** VERB
If you **use** something, you do something with it that helps you to do a job or sort out a problem.

apply
*Doctor Foster **applied** his scientific knowledge to build a rocket.*

employ
*The tennis player had to **employ** all her shots to win the match.*

make use of
*We **made use of** scrap parts to build ourselves a go-kart.*

operate
*The disabled lady **operated** her wheelchair with two fingers.*

utilize
*My dad says it is possible to **utilize** a tin can to mend a car exhaust pipe.*

✔ To use a sword or an axe is to **wield** it.

use (2) SAID **"YOOSS"** NOUN
A **use** is the purpose or value of something.

point
*I couldn't see the **point** of our homework.*

purpose
*The **purpose** of seat belts is to stop you hitting the windscreen or the seat in front in a crash.*

value
*"I cannot see the **value** of a video mobile phone," complained Grandad.*

useful ADJECTIVE
If something is **useful**, you can use it to help you in some way.

beneficial
*Just a little extra teaching proved very **beneficial** for Jo's maths.*

effective
*Tapes and CDs can be very **effective** in learning a foreign language.*

helpful
*We hope this thesaurus proves **helpful** to young writers!*

valuable
*Dad said I had given him **valuable** assistance when he was fixing the car.*

worthwhile
*"Go to an orchestral concert. You'll find it a **worthwhile** experience," advised Mr Kinsella.*

ANTONYM: useless

useless (1) ADJECTIVE
Something that is **useless** is no good for anything.

ineffective
*The tiny hammer was completely **ineffective**.*

of no use
*Wet suits are **of no use** in the desert.*

unusable
*My mobile phone was **unusable** after I'd dropped it in the bath.*

useless (2) ADJECTIVE
If a course of action is **useless**, it will not achieve what is wanted.

futile
*It is **futile** to take a television into the jungle, as there won't be anywhere to plug it in.*

hopeless
*For Scott, it was a **hopeless** situation: the food was gone and the blizzard still raged.*

impractical
*A camera tripod is **impractical** when you are following animals on the move.*

pointless
*Mum said it was **pointless** to take my best clothes to camp.*

usual ADJECTIVE

Something that is **usual** is expected and happens often.

everyday

*Arguments are an **everyday** occurrence in some households.*

normal

*It was **normal** for Mrs Quashie to walk her dogs twice a day.*

regular

*The fisherman took a **regular** trip to check his lobster pots.*

usually ADVERB

If something **usually** happens, it is expected and happens often.

as a rule

As a rule, old Mrs Grant doesn't go out of doors much.

normally

*Mum **normally** makes my breakfast, but at weekends I make my own.*

traditionally

***Traditionally**, there is a carnival in September.*

Vv

valuable ADJECTIVE
Something that is **valuable** is of great worth or very important.

costly
*Diamonds are more **costly** than pearls.*

expensive
*Millionaires tend to travel in **expensive** cars.*

precious
*The ring may have been powerful, but to Gollum it was **precious**.*

priceless
*"Our gallery is full of **priceless** works," the curator told us.*

treasured
*Great Gran's chair is a **treasured** possession in our family.*

✔ **Invaluable** means very valuable. It is not the opposite of valuable.

ANTONYM: worthless

value NOUN
Value is the importance or usefulness of something.

advantage
*Nailah could see the future **advantage** of working hard at school.*

benefit
*Mrs Oakley's help with my maths was of great **benefit**.*

merit
*The **merits** of sport are that it's enjoyable, keeps you fit and keeps you busy.*

usefulness
*There is no doubting the **usefulness** of computers.*

vanish VERB
If something **vanishes**, it disappears or does not exist any more.

disappear
*In a puff of smoke, the magician **disappeared**.*

evaporate
*When water boils, it **evaporates** into the air.*

fade
*As the sun **faded** from sight, lights twinkled in the harbour town.*

ANTONYM: appear

various ADJECTIVE
Various can be used to mean several different types of something.

assorted
*I love those tins of **assorted** biscuits.*

miscellaneous
*The magazine included articles on **miscellaneous** topics.*

vegetable NOUN
Vegetables are plants, or parts of plants, that can be eaten.

Some vegetables:	
artichoke	lettuce
asparagus	mushrooms
aubergine	onion
broccoli	parsnip
Brussels sprout	peas
cabbage	potatoes
carrots	spinach
cauliflower	swede
celery	sweet corn
courgette	sweet potato
cucumber	turnip
leek	yam

vehicle NOUN
A **vehicle** is a machine, often with an engine, used for moving people or goods from one place to another.

Some types of vehicle:	
ambulance	pick-up
bus	police car
cab	removal van
car	tanker
caravan	taxi
coach	tram
lorry	transporter
minibus	truck
minicab	van

a
b
c
d
e
f
g
h
i
j
k
l
m
n
o
p
q
r
s
t
u
v
w
x
y
z

A
B
C
D
E
F
G
H
I
J
K
L
M
N
O
P
Q
R
S
T
U
V
W
X
Y
Z

very ADVERB
Very is used before words to emphasize them.

absolutely
*Mrs Chakrabarti said she was **absolutely** delighted with my work.*

enormously
*My baby brother was **enormously** proud to be the team's mascot.*

exceedingly
*After the storm, I was **exceedingly** glad to get back home.*

extremely
*Mum was **extremely** cross with me for disobeying her.*

greatly
*Beethoven's music is **greatly** loved by many.*

highly
*A soldier's boots must be **highly** polished.*

most
*"We were **most** grateful for your help," the letter read.*

really
*Moley was **really** impressed by the river, and by the Water Rat.*

terribly INFORMAL
*"May I say how **terribly** honoured I am," began the prince.*

terrifically
*Drag racers are **terrifically** powerful cars.*

truly
*The fireworks display was **truly** magnificent.*

vicious (1) ADJECTIVE
If an action is **vicious**, it is cruel and violent.

barbaric
*The police said the man had suffered a **barbaric** attack.*

brutal
*The army launched a **brutal** attack on the enemy.*

cruel
*Rassendyll would always remember the **cruel** look in the jailer's eye.*

savage
*The lion launched a **savage** attack and brought the wildebeest down.*

violent
*Gangsters use **violent** methods to get what they want.*

vicious (2) ADJECTIVE
If what someone says is **vicious**, it is cruel and spiteful.

cruel
*His father's **cruel** words stayed with Timon for a lifetime.*

malicious
*Some people enjoy sharing **malicious** gossip.*

spiteful
*We all have to learn how to cope with **spiteful** remarks.*

view (1) NOUN
A **view** is everything you can see from a particular place.

outlook
*Grandad's bungalow had a lovely **outlook** over the sea.*

panorama
*From the top of the hill, a wonderful **panorama** stretched away before us.*

scene
*Our classroom was a very busy **scene**.*

view (2) NOUN
A **view** is a belief or opinion.

belief
*"It's my **belief** that big corporations have too much power," said the protester.*

opinion
*Jim and I had differing **opinions** on school.*

point of view
*From my **point of view**, school was not always fun, but very necessary.*

viewpoint
*Jim's **viewpoint** is that school was great fun, in spite of all the lessons.*

violence NOUN
Violence is behaviour that is intended to hurt or kill.

bloodshed
***Bloodshed** was common in the realm of the evil emperor.*

brutality

*"This was a crime of enormous **brutality**," the police spokesman said.*

brute force

*Guards used **brute force** to break down the door.*

savagery

*The **savagery** of the massacre was beyond all description.*

terrorism

*Sadly, some people resort to **terrorism** to try to get their way.*

violent (1) ADJECTIVE

Someone who is **violent** behaves in a way that is intended to hurt or kill.

bloodthirsty

***Bloodthirsty** Vikings roared through the village waving axes and flaming torches.*

brutal

*The **brutal** murderer was arrested by a team of undercover police officers.*

murderous

*With a **murderous** look in his eye, the pirate leapt aboard.*

vicious

***Vicious** criminals tend to be jailed for a long time.*

ANTONYM: gentle

violent (2) ADJECTIVE

A **violent** force is very strong and does harm or damage.

devastating

*The **devastating** power of the tornado swept away all in its path.*

powerful

*Each **powerful** blow of the battering ram set the gate shivering.*

raging

*The small boat was tossed hither and thither in the **raging** sea.*

wild

*"February is a time of **wild** weather in these parts," the farmer told us.*

visit VERB

If you **visit** someone, you go to see them and spend time with them.

call on

*Gran **called on** Mum to say hello and see how we all were.*

drop in on INFORMAL

*"Do **drop in on** me when you're passing," the old lady said.*

look up INFORMAL

*When we took a trip to London we **looked up** some old friends.*

pay a visit to

*We **paid a visit to** the Houses of Parliament.*

a
b
c
d
e
f
g
h
i
j
k
l
m
n
o
p
q
r
s
t
u
v
w
x
y
z

Ww

wait (1) VERB

If you **wait**, you spend time in a place or situation, usually doing little or nothing, before something happens.

hang around INFORMAL

*We had to **hang around** for ages at the bus stop before the bus came.*

hold on INFORMAL

*"Would you **hold on**, please," the voice on the phone said.*

linger

*After class, Chipo **lingered** outside to talk to Miss Pennington.*

pause

*We **paused** in our walk to get our breath back.*

remain

*The doctor has said that Grandpa will have to **remain** in hospital for the time being.*

stay

*Dad told us to **stay** where we were while he bought the tickets.*

wait (2) NOUN

A **wait** is a period of time before something happens.

delay

*A voice from the loudspeaker apologized for the **delay** in the train's arrival.*

hold-up

*Apparently, the **hold-up** at the crossroads was caused by faulty traffic lights.*

interval

*After a brief **interval**, the orchestra was ready and the conductor came on stage.*

pause

*There was a **pause** when the cricket match stopped because of the rain.*

wake VERB

When you **wake**, or something **wakes** you, you become conscious again after being asleep.

awake

*The campers **awoke** to find a goat nibbling their tent.*

awaken

*The sound of thunder **awakened** the dog, which started barking.*

come to

*When Marisa **came to**, all the others had got up and gone.*

rouse

*The farmer was **roused** at dawn by the crowing of the cockerel.*

stir

*It was early and few people were **stirring**.*

walk VERB

When you **walk**, you move along by putting one foot in front of the other on the ground.

go on foot

*It was only a short distance to the park, so we **went on foot**.*

walk slowly:
amble

*We **ambled** along the shore, looking for shells and driftwood.*

saunter

*After a hearty breakfast, Wooster **sauntered** out to buy a newspaper.*

stroll

*Couples **strolled** along the seafront in the sunshine.*

walk steadily:
march

*King Harold and his men **marched** rapidly towards Hastings.*

pace

*I was **pacing** up and down, waiting for the postman to arrive.*

plod

*All day we **plodded** through field after field.*

tramp

*Having **tramped** ten miles or so, we stopped to pitch camp.*

trek

*Scott and his men were forced to **trek** across the polar ice.*

troop

*After the game, the players **trooped** into the changing room.*

warn

trudge
*Joely **trudged** along, trying not to think of her blisters.*

walk purposefully:
stride
*Mr Radebe **strode** into the room and slammed the door.*

wander VERB
If you **wander** in a place, you walk around in a casual way.

drift
*A group of my sister's friends **drifted** into an amusement arcade.*

meander
*We **meandered** here and there along the beach, picking up pebbles.*

mooch
*My brother **mooched** off to be by himself.*

ramble
*We **rambled** through the woods, looking for edible mushrooms to pick.*

roam
*My parents had **roamed** all over the fair trying to find us.*

stroll
*After lunch the family **strolled** down by the river.*

want VERB
If you **want** something, you feel that you would like to have it or do it.

crave
*With all this loud music, Dad **craved** a bit of peace and quiet.*

desire
*"What do you **desire**, O Master?" the Genie of the Lamp enquired.*

fancy
*"I **fancy** a burger with plenty of sauce," my brother fantasized.*

hanker after
*On a Friday night, Dad always **hankers after** an Indian takeaway for dinner.*

long for
*During the long, cold winter Amanda **longed for** the warmth of summer.*

wish for
*Abha dearly **wished for** someone to play with.*

war NOUN
War is a period of fighting between countries or states, where weapons are used and many people may be killed.

battle
*The famous 1066 **battle** was fought several miles away from Hastings.*

combat
*Troops go into **combat** to defend their country.*

conflict
*The **conflict** between the two sides lasted for several years.*

fighting
*The **fighting** ceased when the armistice was signed.*

warfare
*Warfare** is a very unpleasant business.*

ANTONYM: peace

warm ADJECTIVE
Something that is **warm** has some heat, but not enough to be hot.

lukewarm
*"Waiter, this tea is **lukewarm**!" the customer complained.*

tepid
*As the washer had been on, my bath water was only **tepid**.*

ANTONYM: cool

warn VERB
If you **warn** someone, you tell them that they may be in danger or trouble.

alert
*Michael, having seen the stricken yacht, managed to **alert** the coastguard.*

forewarn
*The witches **forewarned** the king of his downfall.*

raise the alarm
*When she saw smoke pouring from the window, Raziya **raised the alarm**.*

*See **advise***

335

A
B
C
D
E
F
G
H
I
J
K
L
M
N
O
P
Q
R
S
T
U
V
W
X
Y
Z

warning NOUN
A **warning** is something done to warn somebody of a possible danger or problem.

alarm
*As soon as the **alarm** went, firefighters were dashing for their machines.*

alert
*Notice of the **alert** went out, and maximum security was introduced.*

caution
*Police issued a **caution** to my brother for riding his bike dangerously.*

notice
*All the houses in the neighbourhood were given **notice** about the new road.*

premonition
*Fiona had a **premonition** that something bad was going to happen.*

*See **sign***

wash VERB
If you **wash** something, you clean it with water and soap.

bathe
*When I grazed my knee, Dad **bathed** it and put a dressing on.*

cleanse
*Mum **cleansed** the kitchen floor with disinfectant.*

✔ If you wash your hair, you **shampoo** it.
If you wash clothes, you **launder** them.

waste (1) VERB
If you **waste** time, money or energy, you use too much of it on something that is not important or you do not need.

blow INFORMAL
*Having won all that money, the gambler **blew** it on more gambling.*

fritter away
*It's a shame to see people **fritter away** their money on nothing.*

squander
*United **squandered** all their chances to win.*

throw away
*"This is your big chance," Mum said. "Don't **throw** it **away**."*

waste (2) NOUN
Waste is rubbish or other material that is no longer wanted, or that is left over.

garbage
*The **garbage** from the restaurant goes into big bins round the back.*

leftovers
*We feed any **leftovers** to our pigs, Hoggy and Snuffler.*

remnants
*Achal and I managed to scoff the **remnants** of the adults' party food.*

rubbish
*"Make sure you pick up all your **rubbish**," said Mr Brahmin after our class picnic.*

scrap
*Much **scrap**, whether it's paper, plastic or metal, can be recycled.*

sewage
*In cities, **sewage** has to travel a long way through sewers before it can be treated.*

trash AMERICAN
*Our **trash** is collected weekly, and it is my job to put the bin out every Wednesday.*

watch VERB
If you **watch** something, you look at it for some time and pay attention to what is happening.

concentrate on
*Mrs Richards told us to **concentrate on** the board.*

gaze at
*My sister spends hours **gazing at** herself in the mirror.*

observe
*The ornithologist sat quietly in the hide to **observe** the birds on the lake.*

pay attention
*"Now **pay attention**, you men!" the major rapped.*

stare at
*The outlaw and the sheriff **stared at** each other across the dusty street.*

view
*"You will be able to **view** the play very well from these seats," the usher told us.*

watch out VERB

If you **watch out** for something or someone, you keep alert to see if they are near you.

be on the alert

*It pays to **be on the alert** for any sign of danger.*

be on your guard

*"**Be on your guard**," the colonel warned. "There are enemy spies about."*

beware

*A sign said, "**Beware** of falling boulders". Were we supposed to catch them?*

keep your eyes open

*The captain told his crew to **keep their eyes open** for enemy submarines.*

look out

*Mrs O'Brien suggested we **look out** for deer.*

wave (1) VERB

If you **wave** your hand, you move it from side to side.

beckon

*Zaria **beckoned** me over to her house.*

gesture

*With a flapping movement, the policeman **gestured** for Dad to pull in.*

signal

*A crewman on the ferry **signalled** us to park where he indicated.*

wave (2) VERB

If you **wave** something, or if it **waves**, it moves from side to side.

brandish

*In triumph, the victorious soldier **brandished** the enemy flag.*

flap

*The flag was **flapping** in the wind.*

flourish

*The musketeer **flourished** his sword, then held it aloft.*

flutter

*At the marina, boat pennants on the masts **fluttered** in the wind.*

shake

*Granny took the tablecloth outside and **shook** it to get the crumbs off.*

way (1) NOUN

The **way** of doing something is how you do it.

approach

*I liked Mrs Melville's **approach** to school – very firm, but good fun too.*

manner

*My Gran has an odd **manner** of reading a book, very close to her face.*

means

*Hitchhiking is one **means** of getting from A to B very cheaply.*

method

*Mr Moahnty explained the **method** of doing the experiment.*

procedure

*There is a particular **procedure** for poaching eggs properly.*

technique

*The **technique** of shooting at soccer involves keeping your head down.*

way (2) NOUN

The **way** to a place is how you get there.

direction

*"Which **direction** is the town centre, please?" asked the visitor.*

journey

*The **journey** to Mordor was a long and dangerous one for a hobbit.*

route

*Our **route** took us through beautiful scenery.*

weak (1) ADJECTIVE

If someone is **weak**, they do not have much strength or energy.

delicate

*Mum said she was feeling rather **delicate** after her dose of flu.*

faint

*Kaila felt quite **faint** when she got to the end of her running race.*

feeble

*Grandad was very **feeble** when he came out of hospital.*

frail

***Frail** old people are at risk from broken bones if they fall.*

a
b
c
d
e
f
g
h
i
j
k
l
m
n
o
p
q
r
s
t
u
v
w
x
y
z

weak (2) ADJECTIVE

Something that is **weak** is likely to break or fail.

flimsy
The **flimsy** fence soon fell down.

fragile
Mum's china teapot was **fragile**, as I found out when I dropped it.

rickety
I sat down gently in the **rickety** old chair.

unsafe
I told Violet the bridge was **unsafe**, but she wouldn't listen.

weapon NOUN

A **weapon** is an object used to fight or kill people in a fight or war.

> **Some weapons:**
>
> | | | |
> |---|---|---|
> | bayonet | knife | revolver |
> | bow and arrow | machine gun | sabre |
> | bomb | mine | shotgun |
> | cannon | missile | spear |
> | dagger | pistol | sword |
> | grenade | rapier | tomahawk |
> | gun | rifle | torpedo |

weather NOUN

Weather is the conditions of sunshine, rain, wind or snow at a particular time in a particular place.

✔ The study of weather and climate is **meteorology**.

> **Cold weather words:**
>
> | | | |
> |---|---|---|
> | blizzard | hail | slush |
> | frost | sleet | snow |
>
> **Windy weather words:**
>
> | | |
> |---|---|
> | gale | tornado |
> | hurricane | typhoon |
>
> **Rainy weather words:**
>
> | | |
> |---|---|
> | deluge | drizzle |
> | downpour | shower |
>
> **Hot weather words:**
>
> | | |
> |---|---|
> | drought | humidity |
> | heatwave | sunshine |

weight NOUN

Weight is the heaviness of something.

burden
The **burden** of a head teacher's responsibility is considerable.

load
In a suspension bridge, the **load** is carried by the piers at either end.

pressure
To save his colleagues, the miner bore the **pressure** of the rock on his shoulders.

well (1) ADJECTIVE

If you are **well**, you are healthy.

able-bodied
Admiral Lord Nelson wanted **able-bodied** sailors for his navy.

fit
Mum and Dad have joined a gym to get **fit**.

healthy
"If you want to stay **healthy**, eat proper food and take exercise," advised the nurse.

in good health
Our neighbour was **in good health** for a lady of nearly 80.

ANTONYM: ill

get well VERB

If someone **gets well**, they recover after an illness.

convalesce
The wounded sailor was sent to **convalesce** at a special home.

recover
Children tend to **recover** from injury more quickly than adults.

well (2) ADVERB

If you do something **well**, you do it to a high standard.

admirably
Ulan coped **admirably** when his mum was poorly.

brilliantly
My eldest brother did **brilliantly** at university, and is now a scientist.

expertly
Expertly, the helmsman guided the ferry into its berth.

splendidly
*Mum and Dad said we acted **splendidly** in the school play.*

successfully
*The harvest **successfully** in, it was time to relax for Farmer Palfrey.*

superbly
*Dad played **superbly** to win the tennis shield.*

wonderfully
*The choir sang **wonderfully** in the concert.*

ANTONYM: badly

wet (1) ADJECTIVE

Something that is **wet** is covered or soaked with water or other liquid.

Slightly wet:
clammy
*My forehead was **clammy**. Had I got the fever?*

damp
*A **damp** cloth is very effective for dusting.*

moist
*Those little **moist** wipes in a packet are good for car journeys.*

Very wet:
drenched
*After two hours in the rain, everybody was **drenched**.*

dripping wet
*Running only a few metres in the storm left us **dripping wet**.*

saturated
*When something is **saturated**, it can hold no more liquid.*

soaked
*By the time the boat trip ended, we were **soaked**.*

soggy
*Although the pitch was **soggy**, the game went ahead.*

spongy
*On top of the moor, the ground was **spongy** and full of water.*

waterlogged
*As the pitch was **waterlogged**, there was no chance of playing.*

wringing wet INFORMAL
*All my clothes were **wringing wet** when I finally got in out of the rain.*

ANTONYM: dry

wet (2) VERB

If you **wet** something, you make it wet.

drench
*My rotten brother **drenched** us with the hose pipe.*

saturate
*Gran's trifle was **saturated** with sherry, so I only had a small helping.*

soak
*After a hike, it's great to **soak** your feet in warm water.*

✔ Different nouns for wetness include **condensation**, **dampness**, **liquid** or **moisture**.

whole ADJECTIVE

The **whole** of something is all of it.

complete
*The **Complete** Works of Shakespeare is a very large book indeed.*

entire
*On our holiday we spent the **entire** time down on the beach.*

full
*A guide gave us the **full** tour of the old house, telling us all about its history.*

unabbreviated
*The **unabbreviated** version of a word or phrase is written in full.*

wicked (1) ADJECTIVE

A **wicked** person is very bad.

cruel
*Several Roman emperors were **cruel** in their punishments.*

evil
*A pair of **evil** eyes peered out from the slit in the door.*

villainous
*The twins were **villainous** to the core.*

A B C D E F G H I J K L M N O P Q R S T U V **W** X Y Z

wicked (2) ADJECTIVE

A **wicked** deed is very bad.

devilish
With **devilish** cunning, Blofeld masterminded his scheme for world domination.

diabolical
In the Middle Ages some **diabolical** tortures were employed.

malicious
Someone had been making **malicious** phone calls.

vicious
With a **vicious** thrust of her sword, the pirate queen ran the captain through.

vile
Blackmail is a **vile** crime.

ANTONYM: good

wide ADJECTIVE

Something **wide** measures a large distance from one side to another.

broad
Paris is famous for its **broad** avenues.

extensive
We took our dog, Tess, for a walk along the **extensive** beach close to the cottage.

large
The **large** caravan took up more than one berth in the campsite.

wild (1) ADJECTIVE

Wild animals and plants live in natural surroundings and are not looked after by people.

undomesticated
"Animals in the reserve are completely **undomesticated**," the guide told us.

untamed
The **untamed** jungle is full of wildlife.

ANTONYM: tame

wild (2) ADJECTIVE

Wild land is natural and uncultivated.

uncultivated
Further up the slopes, fields give way to **uncultivated** moorland.

unspoilt
The **unspoilt** beaches of northern Scotland are wonderful.

ANTONYM: cultivated

wild (3) ADJECTIVE

Wild behaviour is excited and uncontrolled.

frantic
Keanu was going **frantic**, trying to attract my attention.

hysterical
The plane was going to crash, and some passengers were growing **hysterical**.

out of control
Completely **out of control**, the mob smashed windows and looted stores.

riotous
Fortunately, **riotous** behaviour is rare in most countries.

uncontrollable
My sister had an **uncontrollable** urge to start leaping and yelling.

wild (4) ADJECTIVE

Wild weather is stormy.

blustery
Blustery weather is not the best time to go for a sail.

howling
A **howling** gale swept in from the Atlantic Ocean.

raging
Raging seas lashed against the harbour wall.

violent
Violent squalls ripped through the shops along the seafront.

willing ADJECTIVE

If you are **willing**, you are glad and ready to do what is wanted or needed.

agreeable
Elina's mum was **agreeable** to my staying the night.

cooperative
Our neighbours were very **cooperative** about sharing the cost of mending the fence.

game
Jon is always **game** to go for a bike ride.

prepared
*When Gran was ill, many people were **prepared** to take her meals to her.*

ready
*Mrs Tarnat was **ready** to go through my work any time I asked her to.*

ANTONYM: unwilling

See **keen**

win (1) VERB
If you **win** a fight, game or argument, you defeat your opponent.

be victorious
*The Greeks **were victorious** over the Persians at the Battle of Marathon.*

succeed
*In conquering Britain, Claudius **succeeded** where Julius Caesar had failed.*

triumph
*City **triumphed** over United in the final.*

ANTONYM: lose

win (2) VERB
If you **win** something, you succeed in obtaining it.

accomplish
*Our team **accomplished** victory in the general-knowledge quiz.*

achieve
*Safiya **achieved** the highest marks in the test.*

attain
*Willem Jansz **attained** a place in history as the first European to see Australia.*

gain
*Mrs Bramble had **gained** a reputation as an excellent teacher.*

✔ To win several times in succession is to be on a **winning streak**.

ANTONYM: fail

win (3) NOUN
A **win** is a victory in a game or contest.

conquest
*The Norman **conquest** of England took place in 1066 and after.*

success
*The Rovers' **success** was down to the hard work they had put in.*

triumph
*The driver celebrated his **triumph** with champagne.*

victory
*Admiral Nelson died as news came of his **victory** at Trafalgar.*

ANTONYM: defeat

wind (1) RHYMES WITH "TINNED" NOUN
Wind is a current of air that moves across the land and sea.

a gentle wind:
breeze
*A slight **breeze** rippled the silvery surface of the great lake.*

draught
*"Please shut the door – there's a **draught**," my father said.*

a violent wind:
cyclone
*Everyone was being warned about the approaching **cyclone**.*

gale
*A **gale** roared down the valley, whipping the autumn leaves off the trees.*

hurricane
*When the **hurricane** struck, whole roofs danced crazily in the sky.*

tornado
*The grey coil snaked up to the dense black cloud – a **tornado** was coming!*

typhoon
*A **typhoon** scattered the junks in the Chinese harbour.*

a sudden, unexpected wind:
gust
*The sudden **gust** sent the kite soaring high up into the clear blue sky.*

squall
*No sooner had the **squall** shaken up the leaves, than it was over.*

a b c d e f g h i j k l m n o p q r s t u v **w** x y z

wind (2) RHYMES WITH "**MIND**" VERB
If something **winds**, it twists and turns.

coil
*Slowly, the snake **coiled** itself round the prey, and squeezed.*

loop
*The cowboy **looped** the lasso round the pommel of his saddle.*

roll
*The cashier **rolled** the wrapping paper into a tube to make it easier for me to carry.*

twist
*A clematis plant **twists** itself round other plants.*

turn
*The snake **turned** back on itself, making a loop.*

wind (3) RHYMES WITH "**MIND**" VERB
If a road or river **winds**, it is not straight, but twists and turns.

bend
*The road **bends** several times in the next few miles.*

curve
***Curving** their way down the valley, the railway lines gleamed in the sun.*

meander
*The river **meandered** towards the sea.*

snake
*A commuter train **snaked** round the bend towards the station.*

twist
*The river **twisted** through the bottom of the valley.*

zigzag
*From the top of the cliff, a path **zigzagged** its way down to the sea.*

windy SAID "WIN-DEE" ADJECTIVE
If it is **windy**, there is a lot of wind.

blowy
*It was **blowy**, and the dust swirled in the deserted streets.*

blustery
*In the estuary, sailing boats leant away from the **blustery** wind.*

breezy
*We had our picnic on the **breezy** cliff top overlooking the small harbour.*

squally
***Squally** showers blow up quickly, then die away again just as suddenly.*

windswept
*The **windswept** beach was deserted on a winter's afternoon.*

ANTONYM: calm

winner NOUN
A **winner** is someone who wins something.

champ INFORMAL
*No one could box more than three rounds with the **champ**.*

champion
*To become **champion**, drivers have to win more races than anyone else.*

conqueror
*On her way to the title, she was the **conqueror** of several former champions.*

victor
*The Duke of Wellington was the **victor** at the Battle of Waterloo.*

ANTONYM: loser

wise ADJECTIVE
Someone who is **wise** can use their experience and knowledge to make sensible decisions and judgments.

perceptive
*It was **perceptive** of Helena to notice that Nuri was upset.*

prudent
*Dan was very **prudent**, and saved up his pocket money to buy the game he wanted.*

sensible
*Mrs Nolan praised Faraji for making such a **sensible** decision.*

shrewd
*Dad is a **shrewd** man when it comes to buying antiques.*

ANTONYM: foolish

wish VERB

If you **wish** for something, you desire or want it.

crave
*Although my sister **craved** a chocolate, she was determined not to have any.*

hanker after
*My friend Abiba **hankered after** a wet suit.*

long for
*I **longed for** the school holidays to arrive.*

yearn for
*Grandad **yearned for** the long-lost wartime days to return.*

wobble VERB

If something **wobbles**, it shakes or moves from side to side because it is loose or unsteady.

quake
*The ground **quaked** as a tank rumbled past.*

rock
*Believe it or not, all tall buildings **rock** slightly in the wind.*

sway
*As the wind blew, the tall pine tree **swayed** gently.*

teeter
*Some ladies **teeter** along on high-heeled shoes.*

totter
*My baby sister **tottered**, bandy-legged, towards the door.*

wobbly ADJECTIVE

Something **wobbly** is shaking or moving from side to side because it is loose or unsteady.

rickety
*Our shed is so **rickety** we daren't even hammer nails in to mend it.*

unbalanced
*For a moment the yacht was **unbalanced**, and tipped alarmingly.*

unstable
*Made **unstable** by the inrush of water, the ferry turned on its side.*

unsteady
***Unsteady** on his feet, the old man grabbed a nearby rail.*

ANTONYM: steady

wonder VERB

If you **wonder** about something, you think about it and try to guess or understand more about it.

ask yourself
*I often **ask myself** who might be out there in space.*

ponder
*Habika sat in the yard and **pondered** what she should do.*

puzzle
*We **puzzled** over why Tommy should have gone home so suddenly.*

wonderful ADJECTIVE

Someone or something **wonderful** is marvellous or impressive.

amazing
*It's **amazing** that a tortoise can live for over 150 years.*

fantastic INFORMAL
*I'm told that the northern lights are a **fantastic** sight.*

impressive
*The Sydney Harbour Bridge is an **impressive** structure.*

incredible
*From our hotel there was an **incredible** view over the valley.*

magnificent
*From below, the white summit of Everest looked **magnificent** in the dawn.*

marvellous
*White-water rafting is a **marvellous** experience.*

phenomenal
*To win five Olympic gold medals is a **phenomenal** achievement.*

remarkable
*"It is quite **remarkable** what chimpanzees can do," said the zookeeper.*

sensational
*"That new musical is **sensational**," Mrs Gupta told Mum.*

terrific INFORMAL
*We had a **terrific** time at Haresh's party.*

word

word NOUN

A **word** is a single unit of language in speech or writing which has a meaning.

expression

"Damsel" and "maiden" are old-fashioned expressions for "girl".

term

The word "giddle-gaddle" is just one of the many terms for an alleyway.

> The words that describe a picture are known as the **caption**.
> The words that you use are expressed in your **language**.
> The words that you know form your **vocabulary**.
> The words of a book are known as the **text**.
> The words of a play come from a **script**.
> The words of a conversation are known as **dialogue**.
> The words of a film come from a **film script**.
> The words of a song are its **lyrics**.

work (1) VERB

When you **work**, you spend time and energy doing something useful.

labour

Malika and I laboured away, building our tree house.

slave

After we'd been slaving for two hours, mum brought us a drink out.

slog away INFORMAL

In the meantime, my sister was slogging away at her exam work.

sweat SLANG

A gang sweated and strained to raise the giant stone.

toil

Toiling in the sun makes you very thirsty.

✔ To work with someone is to **cooperate** or **collaborate** with them.

ANTONYM: relax

work (2) VERB

People who **work** have a job which they are paid to do.

be employed

Mum is employed at a firm of engineers.

earn a living

Grandad earns his living as a bricklayer.

ANTONYM: be unemployed

work (3) VERB

If something **works**, it does what it is supposed to do.

function

These days most new cars function smoothly and reliably.

operate

On many bikes, the gears operate from a switch on the handlebars.

work (4) NOUN

Work is the type of job someone has.

career

I am hoping for a career as a journalist.

employment

Dad's first employment was as a waiter.

job

"What job does your dad do?" Ted asked.

occupation

My cousin's previous occupation was as a police officer.

profession

Teaching can be a rewarding profession.

trade

The building trade is sometimes busy, sometimes slack.

work (5) NOUN

Work is tasks that have to be done.

assignment

The journalist's assignment took her overseas.

chore

We all have a different chore to do around the house each week.

duty

"It is the duty of the monitor to check that everyone is ready," said Mrs Harley.

task
*Dev was given the **task** of collecting in everyone's homework.*

yakka AUSTRALIA AND NEW ZEALAND INFORMAL
*A decade of hard **yakka** on the land made Gramps old before his time.*

✔ The work that you produce is your **output**, **production** or **performance**.

worker NOUN
A **worker** is someone who does a regular paid job.

craftsman
*The carpenter was a skilled **craftsman**.*

employee
*Dad's firm has 700 **employees** working there.*

labourer
*The **labourers** stopped for lunch at one o'clock.*

workman
*Several **workmen** came to install the heating system.*

✔ The workers of one organization can be called the **employees**, **staff** or the **workforce**.

work out PHRASE
If you **work out** an answer to a problem, you solve it.

calculate
*I **calculated** it would take someone 23 years to walk to the moon (if they could!).*

figure out
*Philip finally **figured out** the way to fit the car wheel.*

solve
*Gran and Dad used to enjoy **solving** crossword puzzles.*

world NOUN
The **world** is the planet we live on.

earth
*The **earth** is precious but, sadly, many humans do their best to spoil it.*

globe
*All over the **globe**, life can be found in every form imaginable.*

planet
*Our **planet** orbits the sun once every year.*

worn out (1) ADJECTIVE
Something that is **worn out** is damaged or worn so much that it is no longer useful.

decrepit
*We teased Mr Hogg about his **decrepit** car.*

run down
*Many of the warehouses along the canal are **run down**.*

useless
*Keisha threw away the **useless** biro.*

See **tatty**

worn out (2) ADJECTIVE
Someone who is **worn out** is extremely tired.

exhausted
*At the end of term, Mrs Hibbert looked **exhausted**.*

shattered INFORMAL
*After the long car journey, we were all **shattered**.*

tired out
***Tired out** after a day's digging, Gramps slumped in the chair.*

weary
*By the time the walkers reached the inn, they were certainly **weary**.*

worried ADJECTIVE
If you are **worried**, you are unhappy and anxious about a problem, or about something unpleasant that might happen.

anxious
*I told Mum not to be **anxious** when I was away at camp.*

concerned
*Everyone was **concerned** about the recent spate of burglaries.*

distressed
*Our dog Jim gets **distressed** when anyone lets off fireworks nearby.*

troubled
*The old couple were **troubled** by their lack of money for heating.*

uneasy
*Since the break-in next door, Mum felt **uneasy** about going on holiday.*

a b c d e f g h i j k l m n o p q r s t u v **w** x y z

worry (1) VERB

If you **worry**, you feel anxious about a problem, or about something unpleasant that might happen.

brood
*Isha refused to tell me why he was **brooding**.*

feel uneasy
*Gran **felt uneasy**, knowing that our family was away.*

fret
*"I do wish you wouldn't **fret** about something so trivial," Dad said.*

worry (2) VERB

If you **worry** someone with a problem, you disturb or bother them by telling them about it.

bother
*I didn't like to **bother** Richard, but I desperately needed a hand.*

harass
*The young reporter **harassed** her editor until she was given a better job.*

hassle INFORMAL
*"Don't **hassle** me," Dad said. "I'll mend your bike tomorrow."*

trouble
*Although she didn't want to **trouble** folk, Mrs Staunton really did need daily help.*

worry (3) NOUN

A **worry** is a person or thing that causes you to feel anxious or uneasy.

headache INFORMAL
*Finding supply teachers can be a real **headache** for schools.*

trouble
*Mum and her neighbours often share their **troubles** over a cup of coffee.*

worthwhile ADJECTIVE

If something is **worthwhile**, it is important enough to spend time or effort doing it.

beneficial
*Mountain air is very **beneficial** for people with lung problems.*

helpful
*Talib found extra tuition in literacy very **helpful**.*

useful
*The television programme gave **several** useful tips on decorating.*

valuable
*"Your help with my project has been very **valuable**," Mum told us.*

worth it
*Although very tiring, the trek up to the volcano was **worth it**.*

ANTONYM: worthless

wrap VERB

If you **wrap** something, you fold cloth or paper around it.

bundle
*Whittington **bundled** his few belongings together and set out for the city.*

cloak
*That summer's morning, the valley was **cloaked** in mist.*

enclose
*A card was **enclosed** in the package containing my birthday present.*

envelop
*The whole affair was **enveloped** in mystery.*

surround
*With luck, the computer would be safe, **surrounded** by soft packaging.*

wreck VERB

To **wreck** something means to break, destroy or spoil it completely.

demolish
*A runaway truck **demolished** a bus shelter and a lamppost.*

devastate
*In 1945 two Japanese cities were **devastated** by nuclear bombs.*

ruin
*"You've **ruined** my painting, you oaf!" cried the artist.*

write off INFORMAL
*My big brother managed to **write off** his car against a tree.*

ANTONYM: create

wrong

wriggle VERB

If a person or animal **wriggles**, they twist and turn their body in a lively and excited way.

squirm

*It was haircut time, and my baby brother **squirmed** in the chair.*

worm

*In Victorian times, boys had to **worm** their way up chimneys.*

writhe

*Clutching her swollen leg, the wildlife expert **writhed** in agony.*

write VERB

When you **write**, you use a pen or pencil to form letters, words or numbers on a surface.

> To write badly is to **scrawl** or **scribble**.
> To write letters to someone is to **correspond** with them.
> To write down what people are saying is to **scribe**, to **record** or to **take minutes**.
> To write or draw a rough version of something is to **draft** it.
> To write specially on a document or on a surface is to **inscribe** it.

writer NOUN

A **writer** is a person who writes as a job.

author

*My favourite **author** came to talk to us at school today.*

creator

*The **creator** of the character Fungus the Bogeyman is Raymond Briggs.*

> A person who writes about other people's lives is a **biographer**.
> A person who writes novels is a **novelist**.
> A person who writes for a newspaper is a **correspondent**, **journalist** or **reporter**.
> A person who writes plays is a **playwright** or **dramatist**.
> A person who writes poetry is a **poet**.
> A person who writes music is a **composer**.

wrong (1) ADJECTIVE

If something is **wrong**, it is not correct, accurate or truthful.

false

*The judge accused the witness of making a **false** statement.*

inaccurate

*Tabloid newspapers are famous for printing **inaccurate** reports.*

incorrect

*"That's an **incorrect** answer," the quiz-show host said pompously.*

mistaken

*I was **mistaken**: the book was written by Tolkien, not C.S. Lewis.*

untrue

*It's **untrue** to say that new ideas are always better than old ones.*

ANTONYM: accurate or correct or right

wrong (2) ADJECTIVE

If something is **wrong**, it is bad or immoral.

dishonest

*It is **dishonest** to tell lies or to twist the truth.*

illegal

*Dropping litter is **illegal** in most countries, and in any case it is a bad habit.*

immoral

*Many people think that testing cosmetics on animals is **immoral**.*

wrong (3) ADJECTIVE

If someone is **wrong**, they are mistaken or have wrongly judged.

at fault

*The truck driver was **at fault** for driving too fast.*

in error

*My calculation was **in error** by several thousand pounds.*

mistaken

*"I was **mistaken** about that man," my auntie said. "I thought he was that chap off the telly."*

to blame

*My sister felt she was **to blame** for the broken glasses.*

a b c d e f g h i j k l m n o p q r s t u v **w** x y z

347

A
B
C
D
E
F
G
H
I
J
K
L
M
N
O
P
Q
R
S
T
U
V
W
X
Y
Z

Yy

yell VERB
If you **yell**, you shout loudly, usually because you are angry, excited or in pain.

bawl
*My brother **bawled** up the stairs that dinner was ready.*

bellow
*The sergeant **bellowed** orders at the cadets.*

cry out
*I **cried out** in pain when I stubbed my toe.*

shout
*Zaki and Zina were **shouting** about whose turn it was to do the washing-up.*

yellow NOUN OR ADJECTIVE
Yellow is the colour of buttercups, egg yolks or lemons.

> **Shades of yellow:**
> amber
> canary yellow
> gold
> lemon
> mustard
> saffron

young ADJECTIVE
A **young** person, animal or plant has not lived very long and is not yet mature.

> **The names of some young animals:**
> A young
> ...**bird** is a **chick**
> ...**cat** is a **kitten**
> ...**cow** is a **calf**
> ...**deer** is a **faun**
> ...**dog** is a **puppy**
> ...**duck** is a **duckling**
> ...**goose** is a **gosling**
> ...**hare** is a **leveret**
> ...**horse** is a **foal**
> ...**kangaroo** is a **joey**
> ...**lion** or **tiger** or **bear** is a **cub**
> ...**pig** is a **piglet**
> ...**rabbit** is a **kitten**
> ...**sheep** is a **lamb**
> ...**swan** is a **cygnet**

yummy ADJECTIVE INFORMAL
Food that is **yummy** is tasty.

appetizing
*Unfortunately, many **appetizing** snack foods are not very healthy.*

delicious
*My friend advised me to try the ice cream. It was **delicious**!*

scrumptious INFORMAL
*"That was a **scrumptious** meal, thank you,"* Polly said to my mum.

tasty
*Our cat Tibbles finds mice very **tasty**.*

Zz

zoom VERB
Zoom can mean to move very quickly.

dart
*The driver did not see the girl **dart** out from behind a van.*

dash
*When we heard the helicopter, we **dashed** to the window.*

hare
*Wuffles, our dog, **hared** after the ball and ploughed into the sea.*

shoot
*Suddenly, a car **shot** out from the tunnel and skidded round the corner.*

Index

Aa

a few . . . . **some**
a good way . . . . **far**
a great deal . . . . **lot**
a great deal . . . . **plenty**
a great distance. . . . . . . **far**
a helping hand. . . . . . . **help**
a large quantity . . . . . . **lot**
a number of. . . . . **some**
a piece of cake . . . . **easy**
a quantity of . . . . **some**
a second time . . . . **again**
a vast number . . . . **lot**
abandon . . . . **call off**
abandon . . . . **cancel**
abandon . . . . **give up**
abandon . . . . **leave**
abandoned . . . . **disused**
abduct. . . . . **kidnap**
abhor . . . . **hate**
abide by . . . . **obey**
ability . . . . **power**
ablaze . . . . **fire**
able. . . . . **capable**
able-bodied. . . . . **well**
abnormal. . . . . **unusual**
abominable . . . . **horrible**
abort . . . . **cancel**
about. . . . . **around**
about. . . . . **roughly**
above . . . . **over**
abrupt . . . . **sudden**
absent. . . . . **away**
absolute . . . . **complete**
absolute . . . . **pure**
absolute . . . . **total**
absolutely . . . . **completely**

absolutely . . . . **definitely**
absolutely . . . . **quite**
absolutely . . . . **really**
absolutely . . . . **very**
absorbing . . . . **interesting**
absurd. . . . . **crazy**
absurd. . . . . **mad**
absurd. . . . . **ridiculous**
absurd. . . . . **silly**
abundant. . . . . **many**
abusive . . . . **rude**
abysmal. . . . . **bad**
abyss . . . . **hole**
accept. . . . . **believe**
accept. . . . . **receive**
accept. . . . . **think**
acceptable . . . . **all right**
acceptable . . . . **fine**
acceptable . . . . **okay** or **OK**
acceptable . . . . **suitable**
accessible . . . . **handy**
accident . . . . **chance**
accident . . . . **crash**
accident-prone . . . . . . **clumsy**
acclaimed . . . . **famous**
accommodate . . . . **contain**
accomplish . . . . **do**
accomplish . . . . **win**
accomplished . . . . **capable**
accomplished . . . . **experienced**
account. . . . . **description**
account. . . . . **report**
account. . . . . **story**
accumulate . . . . **build up**
accumulate . . . . **gather**
accurate . . . . **careful**
accurate . . . . **exact**
accurate . . . . **right**

accurate	**true**
accuse	**blame**
ache	**pain**
achieve	**do**
achieve	**gain**
achieve	**reach**
achieve	**win**
aching	**painful**
acidic	**sour**
acknowledge	**admit**
acknowledge	**reply**
acknowledgement	**answer**
acknowledgement	**reply**
acquire	**buy**
acquire the ability	**learn**
act	**action**
act	**behave**
act as if	**pretend**
act the part of	**play**
action	**battle**
active	**energetic**
active	**lively**
activity	**exercise**
activity	**action**
activity	**interest**
actual	**real**
actually	**really**
acute	**sharp**
adapt	**adjust**
add to	**increase**
add up	**count**
add up to	**make**
added	**more**
additional	**extra**
additional	**more**
additional	**other**
address	**talk**
adequate	**all right**
adequate	**enough**
adequate	**okay** or **OK**
adequately	**enough**
adhere	**stick**

adhesive	**sticky**
adjacent	**close**
adjacent	**near**
adjacent	**next**
adjacent to	**beside**
administer	**run**
admirably	**well**
admiration	**respect**
admire	**like**
admire	**respect**
admit	**confess**
adorable	**lovely**
adoration	**love**
adore	**love**
adorn	**decorate**
adult	**grown-up**
advance	**go**
advance	**improve**
advance	**move**
advance	**progress**
advanced	**model**
advantage	**value**
adventure	**experience**
adventurous	**daring**
adversary	**enemy**
advertisement	**notice**
advise	**suggest**
affair	**business**
affair	**matter**
affect	**infect**
affectionate	**fond**
affluent	**rich**
afresh	**again**
afterwards	**after**
afterwards	**next**
age	**time**
aged	**old**
aggravate	**annoy**
agitation	**fuss**
agonizing	**painful**
agreeable	**convenient**
agreeable	**willing**

agreement	**deal**	allowed	**able**
ahead of schedule	**early**	almighty	**tremendous**
ahead of time	**early**	almost	**most**
aid	**help**	almost	**nearly**
ailing	**ill**	almost certain	**probably**
ailment	**disease**	alongside	**beside**
ailment	**illness**	alter	**change**
aim	**mean**	alternative	**other**
aim	**plan**	alternatively	**instead**
aim	**point**	always	**forever**
aim	**purpose**	amass	**build up**
aim	**target**	amass	**gather**
air	**look**	amaze	**surprise**
ajar	**open**	amazed	**surprised**
alarm	**fear**	amazement	**surprise**
alarm	**fright**	amazing	**extraordinary**
alarm	**horror**	amazing	**marvellous**
alarm	**panic**	amazing	**wonderful**
alarm	**scare**	ambition	**dream**
alarm	**surprise**	ambition	**hope**
alarm	**warning**	ambition	**target**
alarmed	**afraid**	amble	**walk**
alarming	**scary**	amiable	**friendly**
alert	**careful**	amiable	**nice**
alert	**observant**	amiable	**pleasant**
alert	**quick**	amicable	**friendly**
alert	**sharp**	amid	**among or amongst**
alert	**warn**		
alert	**warning**	amidst	**among or amongst**
alien	**stranger**		
alight	**fire**	amount	**quantity**
alight	**burn**	amount to	**make**
alight	**get off**	ample	**enough**
alike	**like**	amuse	**please**
alike	**same**	amuse yourself	**play**
alive	**living**	amusement	**fun**
all at once	**together**	amusement	**game**
all over	**around**	amusement	**laughter**
all set	**ready**	amusement	**pleasure**
all told	**altogether**	amusing	**funny**
allege	**claim**	an abundance	**plenty**
allow	**let**	analysis	**examination**

Index

analysis

analysis . . . . **test**
analyze . . . . **examine**
analyze . . . . **test**
ancient . . . . **early**
ancient . . . . **old**
anecdote . . . . **story**
anger . . . . **rage**
annihilate . . . . **destroy**
annihilate . . . . **kill**
announce . . . . **say**
announce . . . . **tell**
annoy . . . . **bother**
annoyance . . . . **anger**
annoyance . . . . **nuisance**
annoyed . . . . **angry**
annoyed . . . . **cross**
anonymous . . . . **unknown**
answer back . . . . **answer**
answer . . . . **reply**
answer . . . . **solve**
anti . . . . **against**
anticipate . . . . **expect**
anticipate . . . . **hope**
anticipation . . . . **hope**
antidote . . . . **cure**
antiquated . . . . **old-fashioned**
antique . . . . **old**
anxiety . . . . **care**
anxious . . . . **afraid**
anxious . . . . **nervous**
anxious . . . . **worried**
apart from . . . . **besides**
apart from . . . . **except**
apart . . . . **separate**
apologetic . . . . **sorry**
apoplectic . . . . **angry**
appalling . . . . **awful**
appalling . . . . **bad**
appalling . . . . **horrible**
appalling . . . . **shocking**
appalling . . . . **terrible**
apparatus . . . . **equipment**

apparatus . . . . **machine**
apparent . . . . **clear**
apparent . . . . **obvious**
apparent . . . . **plain**
appeal . . . . **ask**
appealing . . . . **interesting**
appear . . . . **arrive**
appear . . . . **seem**
appear . . . . **turn up**
appearance . . . . **look**
appetizing . . . . **delicious**
appetizing . . . . **nice**
appetizing . . . . **tasty**
appetizing . . . . **yummy**
applaud . . . . **praise**
appliance . . . . **machine**
apply . . . . **ask**
apply . . . . **use**
apply for . . . . **order**
apply yourself to . . . . . . **concentrate**
appointment . . . . **meeting**
appreciate . . . . **like**
appreciate . . . . **realize**
appreciate . . . . **see**
appreciate . . . . **understand**
appreciative . . . . **grateful**
apprehensive . . . . **nervous**
approach . . . . **method**
approach . . . . **move**
approach . . . . **way**
approaching . . . . **near**
appropriate . . . . **convenient**
appropriate . . . . **fit**
appropriate . . . . **proper**
appropriate . . . . **right**
appropriate . . . . **suitable**
approval . . . . **permission**
approximate . . . . **rough**
approximately . . . . **about**
approximately . . . . **around**
approximately . . . . **roughly**
apt . . . . **suitable**

archaic	old	ashamed	guilty
arctic	freezing	ashamed	sorry
arctic	icy	ashen	pale
ardent	enthusiastic	ask someone round	ask
arduous	hard	ask yourself	wonder
arduous	tough	assassinate	murder
area	district	assassination	murder
area	neighbourhood	assault	attack
area	part	assault	invasion
argue	claim	assemble	build
argue	protest	assemble	collect
argue	quarrel	assemble	gather
argue with	disagree	assemble	make
argument	quarrel	assemble	put up
argument	row	assemble	round up
arid	dry	assembly	meeting
arise	happen	assert	argue
armour	protection	assess	check
aroma	smell	assess	judge
around	about	assess	mark
around	roughly	assess	measure
arrange	organize	assessment	check
arrange	plan	assessment	examination
arrange	prepare	assignment	job
arrangement	deal	assignment	project
array	collection	assignment	work
arrest	capture	assist	help
arrest	catch	assist	serve
arrive	come	assist	support
arrive	turn up	assistance	help
arrive at	reach	associate	connect
arrogant	bossy	association	club
arrogant	stuck-up	association	connection
article	thing	association	link
artificial	fake	assorted	different
artificial	false	assorted	mixed
as	because	assorted	various
as a rule	usually	assortment	mixture
as well	also	assortment	range
ascend	climb	assume	suppose
ascend	move	assure	promise
ascend	rise	astonish	surprise

Index

astonished

astonished. . . . . **surprised**
astonishing . . . . **amazing**
astonishing . . . . **incredible**
astonishing . . . . **unbelievable**
astonishment. . . . . . . **surprise**
astound. . . . . **surprise**
astounded. . . . . **surprised**
astounding . . . . **amazing**
astounding . . . . **fabulous**
astounding . . . . **incredible**
astute . . . . **sharp**
at a snail's pace. . . . . . **slowly**
at an end. . . . . **over**
at ease . . . . **comfortable**
at fault. . . . . **guilty**
at fault. . . . . **responsible**
at fault. . . . . **wrong**
at hand . . . . **present**
at large . . . . **free**
at no time . . . . **never**
at once . . . . **now**
at one time . . . . **once**
at the moment. . . . . . . **now**
at the same time . . . . . . **at once**
at times. . . . . **sometimes**
atrocious. . . . . **dreadful**
atrocious. . . . . **bad**
attach . . . . **connect**
attach . . . . **fasten**
attach . . . . **fix**
attach . . . . **join**
attach . . . . **link**
attach . . . . **tie**
attack . . . . **charge**
attack . . . . **invade**
attack . . . . **invasion**
attack . . . . **raid**
attain. . . . . **reach**
attain. . . . . **win**
attempt . . . . **go**
attempt . . . . **shot**
attempt . . . . **try**
attend . . . . **turn up**

attend to . . . . **deal with**
attend to . . . . **serve**
attend to . . . . **see**
attention . . . . **care**
attentive . . . . **careful**
attract . . . . **interest**
attractive . . . . **beautiful**
attractive . . . . **handsome**
attractive . . . . **lovely**
attractive . . . . **pretty**
audience . . . . **crowd**
authentic. . . . . **genuine**
authentic. . . . . **real**
authentic. . . . . **true**
author . . . . **writer**
authority . . . . **control**
authority . . . . **expert**
authority . . . . **power**
authorization . . . . **permission**
authorize . . . . **let**
automated. . . . . **automatic**
automobile . . . . **car**
available . . . . **able**
average. . . . . **common**
average. . . . . **all right**
average. . . . . **normal**
average. . . . . **typical**
avert . . . . **prevent**
avoid. . . . . **dodge**
avoid. . . . . **get out of**
avoid. . . . . **go round**
avoid. . . . . **miss**
awake . . . . **wake**
awaken . . . . **wake**
award . . . . **give**
award . . . . **prize**
awful. . . . . **dreadful**
awful. . . . . **horrible**
awful. . . . . **terrible**
awkward . . . . **clumsy**
awkward . . . . **difficult**
awkward . . . . **tricky**
awkward . . . . **uncomfortable**

Index

Bb

babble . . . . **noise**
babble . . . . **say**
back . . . . **move**
back . . . . **support**
backbreaking . . . . **difficult**
backbreaking . . . . **hard**
background . . . . **circumstances**
backside . . . . **bottom**
badger . . . . **nag**
badly off . . . . **poor**
badly behaved . . . . **naughty**
bad-mannered . . . . **rude**
bad-tempered . . . . **grumpy**
baffle . . . . **puzzle**
baffled . . . . **confused**
baffling . . . . **confusing**
baffling . . . . **mysterious**
baffling . . . . **strange**
baggage . . . . **luggage**
baggy . . . . **loose**
balance . . . . **rest**
balanced . . . . **equal**
balanced . . . . **even**
bamboozle . . . . **fool**
bamboozle . . . . **trick**
ban . . . . **forbid**
ban . . . . **prohibit**
band . . . . **gang**
banger . . . . **car**
bank . . . . **count**
bank on . . . . **depend**
bank on . . . . **expect**
bank on . . . . **rely**
banquet . . . . **eat**
baptise . . . . **name**
bar . . . . **block**
barbaric . . . . **vicious**
bare . . . . **empty**
bare . . . . **plain**
barely . . . . **hardly**

barely . . . . **only**
bargain . . . . **cheap**
barge in . . . . **interrupt**
barney . . . . **argument**
barren . . . . **bare**
barren . . . . **dry**
barricade . . . . **barrier**
barrier . . . . **block**
barrier . . . . **gate**
base . . . . **bottom**
bash . . . . **hit**
bash . . . . **try**
bashful . . . . **shy**
basic . . . . **plain**
basic . . . . **raw**
bass . . . . **deep**
batch . . . . **set**
bathe . . . . **wash**
baton . . . . **club**
batter . . . . **beat**
batter . . . . **hit**
battle . . . . **contest**
battle . . . . **fight**
battle . . . . **war**
bawl . . . . **cry**
bawl . . . . **say**
bawl . . . . **scream**
bawl . . . . **shout**
bawl . . . . **yell**
be acceptable to . . . . . . **suit**
be acquainted with . . . . **know**
be adequate . . . . **do**
be all ears . . . . **listen**
be aware . . . . **feel**
be aware of . . . . **know**
be based on . . . . **depend**
be bothered . . . . **mind**
be careful . . . . **beware**
be certain of . . . . **believe**
be compelled to . . . . . . **have**
be concerned . . . . **care**
be convenient . . . . **suit**

be defeated . . . . **lose**
be employed . . . . **work**
be engrossed in . . . . . . **concentrate**
be enough . . . . **do**
be equal to . . . . **equal**
be familiar with . . . . . . **know**
be fond of . . . . **like**
be forced to . . . . **have**
be in charge of . . . . . . **control**
be in charge of . . . . . . **manage**
be in charge of . . . . . . **run**
be in stitches . . . . **laugh**
be involved in . . . . **part**
be jealous . . . . **envy**
be keen on . . . . **like**
be offended . . . . **mind**
be on the alert . . . . **watch out**
be on your guard . . . . . . **watch out**
be partial to . . . . **like**
be responsible for . . . . **see**
be rude to . . . . **abuse**
be seated . . . . **sit**
be significant . . . . **matter**
be sore . . . . **ache**
be successful in . . . . . . **manage**
be sufficient . . . . **do**
be suspended . . . . **hang**
be transformed into . . . . **turn into**
be unsuccessful . . . . . . **fail**
be victorious . . . . **win**
be worthwhile . . . . **pay**
be worthy of . . . . **deserve**
beach . . . . **seaside**
bead . . . . **drop**
beam . . . . **ray**
beam . . . . **smile**
bear . . . . **endure**
bear . . . . **hold**
bear . . . . **put up with**
beast . . . . **animal**
beast . . . . **monster**
beat . . . . **defeat**

beating . . . . **defeat**
beautiful . . . . **lovely**
beautiful . . . . **nice**
beautiful . . . . **pretty**
beckon . . . . **wave**
become aware . . . . **find out**
become aware . . . . **realize**
become hysterical . . . . . **panic**
become . . . . **get**
become . . . . **go**
become . . . . **turn into**
bed . . . . **bottom**
bedraggled . . . . **scruffy**
bedraggled . . . . **tatty**
bedraggled . . . . **untidy**
before long . . . . **soon**
beg . . . . **ask**
begin . . . . **open**
beginning . . . . **start**
begrudge . . . . **envy**
behaviour . . . . **manners**
behind . . . . **after**
behind . . . . **bottom**
behold . . . . **see**
belief . . . . **view**
believe . . . . **expect**
believe . . . . **think**
believe in . . . . **trust**
bellow . . . . **cry**
bellow . . . . **roar**
bellow . . . . **say**
bellow . . . . **shout**
bellow . . . . **yell**
belongings . . . . **luggage**
belongings . . . . **property**
belongings . . . . **stuff**
belongings . . . . **things**
beloved . . . . **dear**
below . . . . **under**
bend . . . . **twist**
bend . . . . **wind**
beneath . . . . **below**

Index

beneath . . . . **under**
beneficial . . . . **healthy**
beneficial . . . . **helpful**
beneficial . . . . **useful**
beneficial . . . . **worthwhile**
benefit . . . . **pay**
benefit . . . . **value**
benevolent . . . . **generous**
bequeath . . . . **leave**
berserk . . . . **mad**
berth . . . . **land**
beseech . . . . **ask**
beside yourself with
  anger . . . . **angry**
beside yourself . . . . . . **furious**
besides . . . . **also**
besides . . . . **except**
best-loved . . . . **favourite**
bestow . . . . **present**
bet . . . . **gamble**
beware . . . . **watch out**
bewilder . . . . **muddle**
bewilder . . . . **puzzle**
bewildered . . . . **confused**
bewildered . . . . **dazed**
bewildering . . . . **confusing**
beyond . . . . **above**
beyond any doubt . . . . . **definitely**
beyond belief . . . . **incredible**
biased . . . . **unfair**
bicker . . . . **argue**
bicker . . . . **quarrel**
bid . . . . **ask**
big . . . . **large**
big-hearted . . . . **generous**
bind . . . . **tie**
biodegrade . . . . **decay**
biodegrade . . . . **rot**
birth . . . . **start**
bisect . . . . **cut**
bit . . . . **piece**
bite . . . . **snack**

biting . . . . **freezing**
bits and pieces . . . . . . **stuff**
bitter . . . . **freezing**
bitter . . . . **icy**
bitter . . . . **sour**
bitterness . . . . **spite**
bizarre . . . . **crazy**
bizarre . . . . **peculiar**
blameless . . . . **innocent**
blank . . . . **space**
blanket . . . . **layer**
blast . . . . **bang**
blast . . . . **explosion**
blast . . . . **shot**
blatant . . . . **obvious**
blaze . . . . **burn**
blaze . . . . **fire**
bleak . . . . **bare**
bleat . . . . **complain**
blemish . . . . **mark**
blemish . . . . **spot**
blend . . . . **mix**
blend . . . . **mixture**
blessing . . . . **luck**
block . . . . **jam**
block . . . . **plug**
block . . . . **prevent**
blockage . . . . **block**
bloke . . . . **man**
bloodcurdling . . . . **scary**
bloodcurdling . . . . **spooky**
bloodshed . . . . **violence**
bloodthirsty . . . . **violent**
blotch . . . . **mark**
blotch . . . . **spot**
blow . . . . **bang**
blow . . . . **surprise**
blow . . . . **waste**
blow your own trumpet . **boast**
blowy . . . . **windy**
blubber . . . . **cry**
bluff . . . . **lie**

blunder . . . . **mistake**
blundering . . . . **clumsy**
blunt . . . . **rough**
blurt out . . . . **say**
blustery . . . . **wild**
blustery . . . . **windy**
board . . . . **get on**
boast . . . . **show off**
boat . . . . **ship**
bob . . . . **bounce**
bob . . . . **float**
bob down . . . . **duck**
bogus . . . . **fake**
bogus . . . . **false**
bogus . . . . **phoney** or
phony
boisterous . . . . **noisy**
bold . . . . **brave**
bolt . . . . **escape**
bolt . . . . **fasten**
bolt . . . . **gobble**
bolt . . . . **lock**
bolt from the blue . . . . . **surprise**
bombshell . . . . **surprise**
bond . . . . **connection**
bonny . . . . **pretty**
bonus . . . . **reward**
bony . . . . **thin**
book . . . . **order**
boom . . . . **cry**
booming . . . . **loud**
booming . . . . **loud**
boost . . . . **encourage**
boost . . . . **increase**
bore . . . . **pierce**
bored with . . . . **sick of**
boring . . . . **dull**
boss . . . . **leader**
botch . . . . **mess up**
bother . . . . **annoy**
bother . . . . **care**
bother . . . . **disturb**

bother . . . . **fuss**
bother . . . . **nuisance**
bother . . . . **trouble**
bother . . . . **upset**
bother . . . . **worry**
bottleneck . . . . **jam**
bottom . . . . **base**
bottomless . . . . **deep**
bound . . . . **bounce**
bound . . . . **jump**
bound . . . . **sure**
boundary . . . . **end**
bout . . . . **contest**
bout . . . . **match**
brag . . . . **boast**
brag . . . . **show off**
brainchild . . . . **invention**
brain-teaser . . . . **problem**
brainwave . . . . **idea**
brainy . . . . **clever**
branch . . . . **part**
brand . . . . **kind**
brand . . . . **make**
brandish . . . . **wave**
brave . . . . **dare**
brave . . . . **daring**
brave . . . . **endure**
bravery . . . . **courage**
bravery . . . . **guts**
brawl . . . . **fight**
brawn . . . . **strength**
brawny . . . . **strong**
break . . . . **burst**
break . . . . **gap**
break . . . . **rest**
break . . . . **stop**
break free . . . . **escape**
break of day . . . . **dawn**
break off . . . . **stop**
break out . . . . **escape**
break up . . . . **split up**
break-in . . . . **raid**

Index

breakable	**fragile**
breakdown	**failure**
breakneck	**fast**
breather	**break**
breathtaking	**amazing**
breed	**kind**
breeze	**wind**
breezy	**windy**
brief	**short**
brief	**short**
bright	**brainy**
bright	**brilliant**
bright	**cheerful**
bright	**clear**
bright	**clever**
bright	**quick**
bright	**smart**
bright	**sunny**
brighten	**light**
brightness	**light**
brilliance	**light**
brilliant	**brainy**
brilliant	**bright**
brilliantly	**well**
brimming	**full**
bring about	**cause**
bring about	**make**
bring about	**produce**
bring off	**manage**
bring to a close	**finish**
bring to mind	**remind**
bring up	**mention**
brisk	**bright**
brisk	**quick**
brisk	**rapid**
bristly	**rough**
brittle	**breakable**
brittle	**fragile**
broad	**general**
broad	**thick**
broad	**wide**
broadcast	**programme**

broke	**poor**
brokenhearted	**miserable**
brood	**worry**
brook	**stream**
bruise	**hurt**
brutal	**rough**
brutal	**vicious**
brutal	**violent**
brutality	**violence**
brute	**monster**
brute force	**violence**
bubble	**boil**
bubbly	**fizzy**
bubbly	**lively**
bucket down	**pour**
bucket down	**rain**
buckle	**bend**
buckle	**fasten**
buckle	**twist**
buddy	**friend**
budge	**move**
bug	**infection**
build	**body**
build	**make**
build	**shape**
build up	**increase**
bulge	**bump**
bulky	**heavy**
bulky	**thick**
bully	**pick on**
bully	**threaten**
bump	**crash**
bump	**lump**
bump into	**meet**
bump off	**kill**
bump off	**murder**
bumpy	**rough**
bundle	**bunch**
bundle	**wrap**
bung up	**block**
bungle	**mess up**
bunkum	**rubbish**

Index

burble

burble . . . . **say**
burden . . . . **load**
burden . . . . **weight**
burglar . . . . **thief**
burglary . . . . **robbery**
burglary . . . . **theft**
burgle . . . . **rob**
burial ground . . . . **graveyard**
buried . . . . **hidden**
burrow . . . . **dig**
burst in on . . . . **surprise**
bush . . . . **country**
bushy . . . . **rough**
business . . . . **company**
business . . . . **firm**
business . . . . **matter**
bustling . . . . **busy**
bustling . . . . **lively**
butcher . . . . **kill**
butt in . . . . **interrupt**
butt in . . . . **say**
butterfingered . . . . **clumsy**
buttocks . . . . **bottom**
button . . . . **fasten**
buzz . . . . **thrill**
buzzing . . . . **lively**
by degrees . . . . **slowly**
by yourself . . . . **alone**

Cc

cabin . . . . **hut**
cacophony . . . . **noise**
cacophony . . . . **row**
cadaver . . . . **body**
cajole . . . . **persuade**
cake . . . . **lump**
calamity . . . . **disaster**
calamity . . . . **tragedy**
calculate . . . . **count**
calculate . . . . **measure**
calculate . . . . **work out**

calculated . . . . **deliberate**
call . . . . **cry**
call . . . . **name**
call . . . . **shout**
call . . . . **telephone**
call for . . . . **take**
call it a day . . . . **stop**
call off . . . . **cancel**
call on . . . . **see**
call on . . . . **visit**
call out . . . . **say**
call to mind . . . . **remember**
callous . . . . **cruel**
calm . . . . **cool**
calm . . . . **gentle**
calm . . . . **peace**
calm . . . . **quiet**
calm . . . . **still**
camp . . . . **side**
cancel . . . . **call off**
cancelled . . . . **off**
candid . . . . **open**
cantankerous . . . . **cross**
capability . . . . **power**
capable . . . . **able**
capable . . . . **good**
capacity . . . . **space**
caper . . . . **dance**
capsize . . . . **turn over**
capsule . . . . **pill**
captain . . . . **leader**
captivating . . . . **interesting**
captive . . . . **prisoner**
capture . . . . **catch**
capture . . . . **arrest**
capture . . . . **trap**
care for . . . . **look after**
career . . . . **job**
career . . . . **run**
career . . . . **work**
carefree . . . . **easy**
careful . . . . **cautious**

careless	**untidy**
caress	**feel**
cargo	**load**
caring	**kind**
caring	**thoughtful**
carry	**bring**
carry	**take**
carry on	**continue**
carry on	**cope**
carry on	**keep**
carry out	**do**
carry out	**keep**
carry weight	**count**
cascade	**pour**
case	**argument**
case	**situation**
cash	**money**
catalogue	**list**
catalogue	**organize**
catastrophe	**disaster**
catastrophe	**tragedy**
catch	**hear**
catch off guard	**surprise**
catch red handed	**surprise**
catch sight of	**spot**
catch unawares	**surprise**
categorize	**sort**
category	**class**
category	**group**
category	**sort**
category	**type**
cause	**make**
cause	**produce**
cause	**reason**
caution	**care**
caution	**warning**
cautious	**careful**
cave in	**collapse**
cavity	**hole**
cavort	**dance**
cease	**stop**
ceaseless	**continuous**
celebrated	**famous**
celebration	**party**
celebrity	**star**
cement	**stick**
cemetery	**graveyard**
central	**middle**
centre	**base**
centre	**middle**
ceremony	**event**
certain	**definite**
certain	**sure**
certainly	**course**
certainly	**definitely**
certainty	**fact**
chain	**line**
challenge	**dare**
challenge	**play**
challenging	**difficult**
champ	**bite**
champ	**winner**
champion	**winner**
championship	**competition**
chance	**gamble**
chance	**luck**
change	**adjust**
changeable	**moody**
chaos	**jumble**
chaos	**mess**
chaotic	**messy**
chaotic	**untidy**
chap	**man**
char	**burn**
character	**part**
characteristic	**typical**
charge	**attack**
charge	**blame**
charge	**cost**
charge	**price**
charge	**tear**
charitable	**generous**
charm	**beauty**
charming	**nice**

Index

charming	**pleasant**	chop	**cut**
chasm	**hole**	choppy	**rough**
chat	**conversation**	chore	**job**
chat	**talk**	chore	**work**
chat about	**discuss**	chortle	**laugh**
chatter	**noise**	christen	**call**
chatter	**say**	christen	**name**
chatter	**talk**	chronicle	**story**
chatty	**talkative**	chubby	**fat**
cheat	**fiddle**	chuck	**throw**
check	**examine**	chuckle	**laugh**
check	**test**	chunk	**bit**
checkup	**check**	chunk	**block**
checkup	**examination**	chunk	**lump**
cheeky	**rude**	chunk	**piece**
cheerful	**bright**	chunky	**thick**
cheerful	**happy**	circle	**go round**
cheerful	**pleasant**	circular	**round**
cheerfulness	**happiness**	circumstances	**position**
cheery	**cheerful**	circumstances	**situation**
cherish	**treasure**	citizen	**inhabitant**
cherished	**dear**	citizens	**people**
cherished	**precious**	claim	**argue**
chewy	**tough**	clamber up	**climb**
chief	**leader**	clammy	**damp**
chief	**main**	clammy	**wet**
chiefly	**mainly**	clang	**ring**
chilled to the bone	**freezing**	clap eyes on	**see**
chilly	**cool**	clarification	**explanation**
chime	**ring**	clarify	**explain**
chink	**gap**	clasp	**hold**
chip	**cut**	class	**group**
chip in	**interrupt**	class	**kind**
chirpy	**cheerful**	class	**sort**
chisel	**cut**	class	**type**
chock-a-block	**full**	classified	**secret**
choice	**decision**	classify	**organize**
choke	**block**	classify	**sort**
chomp	**bite**	cleanse	**wash**
chomp	**chew**	clear	**empty**
choose	**pick**	clear	**obvious**
choosy	**fussy**	clear	**plain**

clear	rid	cluttered	untidy
clear	sharp	coach	teach
clear	simple	coach	teacher
clear	sunny	coach	train
clear away	remove	coarse	foul
clear up	sort out	coarse	rough
clear up	tidy	coast	seaside
clever	brainy	coastline	seaside
clever	bright	coat	skin
clever	neat	coating	layer
climax	ending	coax	persuade
climb	move	coffee shop	café
climb	rise	coil	curl
climb to	reach	coil	twist
cling	stick	coil	wind
cling to	hold	coincidence	chance
clip	cut	collapse	crumble
clip	fasten	collapse	fall
cloak	wrap	collapse	flop
clod	lump	collect	build up
clog	jam	collect	fetch
clog up	block	collect	gather
close	end	collect	get
close	near	collect	keep
close	shut	collect	receive
close at hand	near	collect	round up
close-fitting	tight	collection	number
closing	last	collection	set
clothes	outfit	collectively	together
clothing	clothes	collide	crash
cloudburst	rain	collide	smash
cloudless	clear	collide with	bump
cloudy	dull	collision	accident
clout	hit	collision	crash
clout	thump	colossal	big
clue	sign	colossal	enormous
cluster	bunch	colossal	giant
cluster	collect	colossal	great
clutch	hold	colossal	huge
clutter	jumble	colossal	large
clutter	junk	colossal	massive
clutter	mess	colossal	tremendous

colossus

colossus	**giant**	commit to memory	**learn**
colourless	**pale**	commit yourself	**decide**
column	**line**	committed	**serious**
comb	**search**	common	**general**
combat	**war**	common	**natural**
combination	**mixture**	common	**normal**
combine	**add**	common sense	**sense**
combine	**join**	commotion	**fuss**
combine	**mix**	commotion	**noise**
come about	**place**	commotion	**riot**
come across	**find**	commotion	**trouble**
come across	**meet**	communicate	**say**
come apart	**split**	communicate	**speak**
come back	**return**	communicate	**tell**
come clean	**confess**	communicate with	**contact**
come into sight	**appear**	communicative	**talkative**
come into view	**appear**	community	**area**
come to blows	**fight**	community	**neighbourhood**
come to grief	**fail**	compact	**little**
come to the rescue	**save**	company	**business**
come to	**wake**	company	**firm**
come together	**gather**	comparable	**alike**
come up with	**invention**	comparable with	**like**
comfort	**luxury**	compassion	**pity**
comfortable	**cosy**	compassionate	**sorry**
comfortable	**easy**	compel	**force**
comfortably	**easily**	compel	**make**
comfy	**comfortable**	compensate	**repay**
comfy	**cosy**	compete against	**play**
comical	**funny**	competence	**ability**
command	**control**	competent	**capable**
command	**lead**	competent	**good**
command	**order**	competition	**contest**
command	**power**	competition	**event**
command	**tell**	competition	**game**
commander	**captain**	competition	**match**
commander	**leader**	competition	**race**
commanding	**powerful**	competitor	**player**
commence	**begin**	compilation	**collection**
commence	**open**	compile	**collect**
commence	**start**	complain	**moan**
comment on	**mention**	complain	**protest**

Index

364

complaint	disease	conceivable	possible
complaint	illness	conceive	idea
complaint	protest	conceive	invention
complete	do	concentrate on	watch
complete	fill in	concept	thought
complete	finish	concern	affect
complete	full	concern	bother
complete	over	concern	care
complete	pure	concern	disturb
complete	total	concern	interest
complete	whole	concern	pity
completely	absolutely	concern	trouble
completion	finish	concerned	worried
complex	complicated	concerning	about
complicated	hard	concert	show
complicated	tricky	concise	short
complication	difficulty	conclude	complete
complication	problem	conclude	end
compliment	praise	conclude	stop
complimentary	free	concluded	over
comply	follow	concluding	last
component	part	conclusion	decision
composed	calm	conclusion	end
compound	mixture	concoct	make up
comprehend	get	conditions	circumstances
comprehend	read	conduct	guide
comprehend	see	conduct	lead
comprehensive	full	conduct	manners
comprehensive	general	conference	meeting
compress	press	confess	admit
compress	squash	confess	tell
comprise	contain	confident	certain
comprise	include	confident	hopeful
computerized	automatic	confident	sure
con	cheat	confidential	private
con	trick	confidential	secret
con man	cheat	confined	tight
conceal	bury	confirm	prove
conceal	hide	conflict	fight
concealed	hidden	conflict	battle
concede	give in	conflict	war
conceited	stuck-up	conflicting	opposite

conform

conform	**follow**	constant	**regular**
confuse	**mix up**	constantly	**always**
confuse	**puzzle**	constricted	**tight**
confused	**dazed**	construct	**build**
confusion	**muddle**	construct	**make**
confusion	**tangle**	construct	**produce**
congratulate	**praise**	construct	**put up**
congratulations	**praise**	construction	**building**
congregate	**gather**	consume	**eat**
conjuring	**magic**	contain	**hold**
conk out	**break down**	contain	**include**
connect	**fasten**	contaminate	**infect**
connect	**fix**	contaminate	**pollute**
connect	**join**	contaminated	**dirty**
connect	**link**	contemplate	**think**
connection	**link**	contemplation	**thought**
connotation	**sense**	contend with	**cope with**
conquer	**beat**	content	**happy**
conquer	**defeat**	contented	**comfortable**
conqueror	**winner**	contented	**glad**
conquest	**defeat**	contented	**pleased**
conquest	**win**	contentment	**happiness**
conscientious	**hard-working**	contest	**competition**
conscientious	**responsible**	contest	**game**
conscious	**deliberate**	contest	**race**
consent	**permission**	contestant	**player**
consequence	**effect**	context	**circumstances**
consequence	**result**	continual	**endless**
consider	**think**	continually	**always**
considerable	**great**	continue	**carry on**
considerably	**far**	continue	**get on**
considerate	**good**	continue	**keep**
considerate	**thoughtful**	continue	**last**
consideration	**thought**	continue	**remain**
consignment	**load**	continuous	**endless**
consist of	**contain**	continuously	**always**
consistent	**same**	contract	**deal**
consistently	**always**	contract	**shrink**
conspiracy	**plot**	contradict	**disagree**
conspire	**plot**	contraption	**invention**
constant	**continuous**	contraption	**machine**
constant	**even**	contrary	**opposite**

contrast . . . . **difference**
contrasting . . . . **different**
contrasting . . . . **opposite**
contribute . . . . **give**
contribute . . . . **provide**
control . . . . **drive**
control . . . . **manage**
control . . . . **power**
control . . . . **rule**
control . . . . **run**
conundrum . . . . **mystery**
convalesce . . . . **recover**
convalesce . . . . **well**
convenient . . . . **handy**
convenient . . . . **suitable**
conventional . . . . **normal**
conventional . . . . **ordinary**
converse . . . . **opposite**
convert . . . . **change**
convert into . . . . **turn into**
convey . . . . **bring**
convey . . . . **carry**
convey . . . . **move**
convey . . . . **pass**
convey . . . . **take**
convict . . . . **prisoner**
convince . . . . **persuade**
convinced . . . . **certain**
convinced . . . . **sure**
cooperate with . . . . **help**
cooperation . . . . **help**
cooperative . . . . **helpful**
cooperative . . . . **willing**
coordinate . . . . **organize**
cope . . . . **get on**
cope . . . . **manage**
cope with . . . . **endure**
copy . . . . **fake**
core . . . . **centre**
core . . . . **middle**
corner . . . . **trap**
corporation . . . . **business**

corporation . . . . **company**
corpse . . . . **body**
correct . . . . **adjust**
correct . . . . **mark**
correct . . . . **proper**
correct . . . . **right**
correct . . . . **true**
correspond . . . . **fit**
correspond . . . . **match**
corrupt . . . . **bad**
corrupt . . . . **crooked**
corrupt . . . . **dishonest**
corruption . . . . **evil**
cosset . . . . **spoil**
cost . . . . **price**
costly . . . . **dear**
costly . . . . **expensive**
costly . . . . **valuable**
costume . . . . **clothes**
costume . . . . **outfit**
cosy . . . . **comfortable**
cough up . . . . **pay**
count . . . . **matter**
count on . . . . **depend**
count on . . . . **expect**
count on . . . . **hope**
count on . . . . **rely**
count up . . . . **add**
countenance . . . . **face**
counterfeit . . . . **copy**
counterfeit . . . . **fake**
counterfeit . . . . **phoney** or
                                  phony
countless . . . . **many**
country . . . . **land**
countryside . . . . **country**
couple . . . . **connect**
couple . . . . **join**
couple . . . . **link**
couple . . . . **pair**
courage . . . . **guts**
courageous . . . . **brave**

Index

courteous . . . . **polite**
cover. . . . . **bury**
covet. . . . . **envy**
crack. . . . . **break**
crack. . . . . **shot**
crack. . . . . **solve**
crack. . . . . **split**
craft . . . . **boat**
craft . . . . **ship**
craftsman . . . . **worker**
crafty. . . . . **sneaky**
cram . . . . **jam**
cram . . . . **squeeze**
cram . . . . **stuff**
crammed. . . . . **full**
cramped . . . . **tight**
cranny. . . . . **crack**
crash. . . . . **accident**
crater . . . . **hole**
crave. . . . . **want**
crave. . . . . **wish**
crawl. . . . . **move**
craze. . . . . **fashion**
crazy . . . . **idiotic**
crazy . . . . **mad**
crease up . . . . **laugh**
create . . . . **cause**
create . . . . **invention**
create . . . . **make**
create . . . . **make up**
create . . . . **produce**
create . . . . **start**
create . . . . **think up**
creation. . . . . **invention**
creator. . . . . **inventor**
creator. . . . . **writer**
creature. . . . . **animal**
creek. . . . . **stream**
creep. . . . . **move**
creep. . . . . **sneak**
crest . . . . **top**
crevice . . . . **crack**

crew . . . . **party**
criminal . . . . **crooked**
crippled. . . . . **lame**
crispy . . . . **crisp**
critical . . . . **desperate**
critical . . . . **serious**
croaky. . . . . **hoarse**
crook. . . . . **criminal**
crooked. . . . . **dishonest**
crop up . . . . **happen**
cross . . . . **angry**
cross . . . . **grumpy**
cross-examine. . . . . . . **question**
crotchety. . . . . **cross**
crotchety. . . . . **grumpy**
crouch. . . . . **bend**
crouch. . . . . **duck**
crow . . . . **boast**
crow . . . . **show off**
crowd . . . . **bunch**
crowd . . . . **gang**
crowd . . . . **number**
crucial . . . . **essential**
crucial . . . . **immediate**
crude. . . . . **dirty**
crude. . . . . **rough**
cruel . . . . **bad**
cruel . . . . **nasty**
cruel . . . . **unkind**
cruel . . . . **vicious**
cruel . . . . **wicked**
cruelty. . . . . **abuse**
crumple. . . . . **collapse**
crunch. . . . . **chew**
crunchy. . . . . **crisp**
crush. . . . . **press**
crush. . . . . **squash**
cry. . . . . **say**
cry. . . . . **scream**
cry out. . . . . **groan**
cry out. . . . . **yell**
cuddle. . . . . **hug**

Index

cull . . . . **kill**
culminate. . . . . **end**
culmination . . . . **ending**
cunning . . . . **crafty**
curiosity . . . . **interest**
curious . . . . **funny**
curious . . . . **mysterious**
curious . . . . **nosy**
curious . . . . **odd**
curious . . . . **strange**
curled . . . . **curly**
currency . . . . **money**
current. . . . . **flow**
current. . . . . **new**
current. . . . . **recent**
current. . . . . **stream**
curse. . . . . **abuse**
curve. . . . . **bend**
curve. . . . . **wind**
custom . . . . **habit**
customary . . . . **regular**
cut. . . . . **reduce**
cut back . . . . **save**
cut short . . . . **stop**
cyclone . . . . **wind**

Dd

daft . . . . **mad**
daft . . . . **silly**
daft . . . . **stupid**
dam up . . . . **block**
damage. . . . . **injure**
damage. . . . . **spoil**
damaging . . . . **bad**
damaging . . . . **harmful**
damp. . . . . **wet**
danger. . . . . **chance**
danger. . . . . **risk**
dangerous. . . . . **bad**
dangerous. . . . . **fierce**
dangerous. . . . . **harmful**

dangle. . . . . **droop**
dangle. . . . . **hang**
daring . . . . **brave**
daring . . . . **courage**
dart . . . . **move**
dart . . . . **nip**
dart . . . . **run**
dart . . . . **tear**
dart . . . . **zoom**
dash . . . . **drop**
dash . . . . **hurry**
dash . . . . **nip**
dash . . . . **race**
dash . . . . **run**
dash . . . . **rush**
dash . . . . **zoom**
dated. . . . . **old-fashioned**
daub . . . . **spread**
dawdle . . . . **hang about**
dawdle . . . . **lag**
dawn. . . . . **start**
daybreak . . . . **dawn**
daydream . . . . **dream**
days gone by. . . . . **past**
days . . . . **time**
dazed . . . . **dizzy**
dazzling. . . . . **bright**
dazzling. . . . . **brilliant**
dead to the world . . . . . **asleep**
deafening . . . . **loud**
deafening . . . . **noisy**
deal in . . . . **sell**
deal with . . . . **cope with**
deal with . . . . **sort out**
deal with . . . . **treat**
debatable . . . . **doubtful**
debate. . . . . **argue**
debate. . . . . **discuss**
debate. . . . . **talk**
debris . . . . **litter**
debris . . . . **ruin**
decay . . . . **crumble**

decay . . . . **rot**
decayed . . . . **rotten**
decaying . . . . **bad**
deceased . . . . **dead**
deceit . . . . **lie**
deceitful . . . . **dishonest**
deceitful . . . . **sneaky**
deceive . . . . **cheat**
deceive . . . . **fool**
deceive . . . . **trick**
decelerate . . . . **slow down**
decent . . . . **good**
deception . . . . **trick**
deceptive . . . . **false**
decide on . . . . **pick**
decide on . . . . **set**
decidedly . . . . **far**
decipher . . . . **read**
decipher . . . . **solve**
declare . . . . **claim**
declare . . . . **say**
decline . . . . **decrease**
decline . . . . **refuse**
decline . . . . **turn down**
decompose . . . . **crumble**
decompose . . . . **decay**
decompose . . . . **rot**
decoration . . . . **pattern**
decorative . . . . **fancy**
decrease . . . . **fall**
decrease . . . . **reduce**
decrepit . . . . **worn out**
dedication . . . . **determination**
deduct . . . . **take**
deed . . . . **action**
deep . . . . **strong**
deface . . . . **damage**
deface . . . . **spoil**
defeat . . . . **failure**
defect . . . . **fault**
defence . . . . **protection**
defenceless . . . . **helpless**

defend . . . . **protect**
defer . . . . **put off**
deficiency . . . . **shortage**
define . . . . **describe**
definite . . . . **clear**
definitely . . . . **certainly**
definitely . . . . **course**
definition . . . . **meaning**
defraud . . . . **rob**
defrost . . . . **melt**
defy . . . . **dare**
dehydrated . . . . **thirsty**
dejected . . . . **miserable**
dejected . . . . **sad**
dejection . . . . **sadness**
delay . . . . **hold up**
delay . . . . **put off**
delay . . . . **wait**
delayed . . . . **late**
delectable . . . . **delicious**
delectable . . . . **tasty**
delete . . . . **remove**
delete . . . . **rid**
delete . . . . **rub out**
deliberately . . . . **purpose**
delicate . . . . **awkward**
delicate . . . . **breakable**
delicate . . . . **fine**
delicate . . . . **fragile**
delicate . . . . **thin**
delicate . . . . **tricky**
delicate . . . . **weak**
delicious . . . . **nice**
delicious . . . . **tasty**
delicious . . . . **yummy**
delight . . . . **happiness**
delight . . . . **please**
delight . . . . **pleasure**
delight in . . . . **love**
delighted . . . . **happy**
delighted . . . . **glad**
delighted . . . . **pleased**

Index

delightful . . . . **beautiful**
delightful . . . . **good**
delightful . . . . **lovely**
delightful . . . . **nice**
delightful . . . . **pleasant**
delinquent . . . . **hooligan**
deluge . . . . **flood**
deluge . . . . **rain**
delve . . . . **dig**
demand . . . . **ask**
demand . . . . **need**
demand . . . . **take**
demanding . . . . **difficult**
demanding . . . . **tough**
demolish . . . . **destroy**
demolish . . . . **smash**
demolish . . . . **wreck**
demonstrate . . . . **display**
demonstrate . . . . **prove**
demonstrate . . . . **show**
demonstrated . . . . **protest**
demonstration . . . . **display**
demonstration . . . . **protest**
denote . . . . **mean**
depart . . . . **go**
depart . . . . **leave**
depart . . . . **set off** or
 set out
department . . . . **part**
depend . . . . **count**
depend on . . . . **rely**
depend on . . . . **trust**
dependable . . . . **faithful**
dependable . . . . **reliable**
depict . . . . **paint**
depict . . . . **represent**
depict . . . . **show**
deposit . . . . **keep**
deposit . . . . **leave**
deposit . . . . **place**
deposit . . . . **put**
depressed . . . . **miserable**

depressed . . . . **sad**
depressed . . . . **unhappy**
depressing . . . . **sad**
depths . . . . **bottom**
deputize . . . . **fill in**
derelict . . . . **disused**
descend . . . . **drop**
descend . . . . **move**
description . . . . **report**
desert . . . . **leave**
deserted . . . . **disused**
deserted . . . . **empty**
design . . . . **invention**
design . . . . **pattern**
designer . . . . **inventor**
desire . . . . **want**
desist . . . . **stop**
desolate . . . . **bare**
despair . . . . **sadness**
desperation . . . . **despair**
despise . . . . **hate**
despite . . . . **spite**
despondent . . . . **sad**
destiny . . . . **luck**
destroy . . . . **ruin**
destroy . . . . **smash**
destroy . . . . **spoil**
destruction . . . . **damage**
destructive . . . . **harmful**
detach . . . . **remove**
detach . . . . **separate**
detached . . . . **alone**
detached . . . . **separate**
detailed . . . . **exact**
detain . . . . **hold up**
detain . . . . **jail**
detect . . . . **notice**
detention centre . . . . . . **prison**
deter . . . . **put off**
determine . . . . **judge**
determine . . . . **set**
determined . . . . **serious**

Index

determined

determined . . . . **stubborn**
detest . . . . **dislike**
detest . . . . **hate**
detonate . . . . **go off**
detonate . . . . **let off**
detonation . . . . **explosion**
detrimental . . . . **harmful**
devastate . . . . **destroy**
devastate . . . . **ruin**
devastate . . . . **wreck**
devastating . . . . **violent**
develop . . . . **grow**
develop . . . . **grow up**
develop . . . . **improve**
development . . . . **increase**
development . . . . **progress**
devilish . . . . **wicked**
devious . . . . **sneaky**
devise . . . . **idea**
devise . . . . **invention**
devise . . . . **make up**
devise . . . . **plan**
devote . . . . **spend**
devoted . . . . **faithful**
devour . . . . **eat**
devour . . . . **gobble**
diabolical . . . . **wicked**
dialect . . . . **language**
dialogue . . . . **conversation**
diary . . . . **record**
diet . . . . **food**
differ . . . . **disagree**
difference . . . . **change**
difference of opinion . . . **argument**
difference of opinion . . . **quarrel**
differentiate . . . . **tell**
difficult . . . . **hard**
difficult . . . . **tricky**
difficulty . . . . **trouble**
dig . . . . **poke**
digit . . . . **number**
dilemma . . . . **difficulty**

dilemma . . . . **jam**
dilemma . . . . **mess**
dilemma . . . . **problem**
diligent . . . . **hard-working**
diluted . . . . **thin**
dim . . . . **dark**
dim . . . . **dumb**
dim . . . . **faint**
dim . . . . **soft**
dimensions . . . . **measurement**
dimensions . . . . **size**
diminish . . . . **decrease**
diminish . . . . **shrink**
diminutive . . . . **little**
diminutive . . . . **small**
dimwit . . . . **fool**
din . . . . **noise**
din . . . . **row**
dine . . . . **eat**
dingy . . . . **dark**
dip into . . . . **read**
dire straits . . . . **trouble**
direct . . . . **control**
direct . . . . **guide**
direct . . . . **manage**
direct . . . . **order**
direct . . . . **organize**
direct . . . . **run**
direct . . . . **show**
direct . . . . **tell**
direction . . . . **control**
direction . . . . **way**
directly . . . . **immediately**
director . . . . **leader**
dirty . . . . **mess up**
disabled . . . . **lame**
disadvantage . . . . **catch**
disagree . . . . **argue**
disagree . . . . **object**
disagree . . . . **protest**
disagree . . . . **quarrel**
disagreeable . . . . **unpleasant**

Index

372

disagreement.	**argument**	dismay	**horror**
disagreement.	**quarrel**	dismay	**panic**
disagreement.	**row**	dismay	**surprise**
disappear	**vanish**	dismay	**upset**
disappoint.	**let down**	dismayed.	**upset**
disappointed	**upset**	dismiss	**fire**
disapprove	**mind**	dismiss	**sack**
disapprove	**object**	dismount.	**get off**
disapprove of	**criticize**	disobedient	**bad**
disapprove of	**dislike**	disobedient	**naughty**
disaster	**failure**	dispatch	**kill**
disaster	**tragedy**	dispatch	**send**
discard	**throw away**	display.	**show**
discharge	**release**	displeased.	**angry**
discharge	**sack**	dispose of	**dump**
discharge	**shoot**	dispose of	**rid**
discipline.	**punish**	dispose of	**throw away**
discomfort.	**pain**	dispute	**disagree**
disconnect	**separate**	dispute	**argument**
discourage	**put off**	dispute	**quarrel**
discover	**find out**	dispute	**row**
discover	**find**	disrespectful	**bad-mannered**
discover	**hear**	disrespectful	**cheeky**
discover	**learn**	disrupt.	**interrupt**
discreet	**careful**	distance	**length**
discussion.	**conversation**	distant.	**faint**
discussion.	**talk**	distant.	**far**
disease	**bug**	distinct	**clear**
disease	**illness**	distinct	**different**
disease	**infection**	distinct	**plain**
disembark	**get off**	distinct	**sharp**
disgust	**horror**	distinction	**difference**
disgusting	**foul**	distinguish.	**tell**
disgusting	**nasty**	distinguished.	**important**
disgusting	**revolting**	distort	**twist**
dishonest	**crooked**	distract	**put off**
dishonest	**sneaky**	distress	**hurt**
dishonest	**wrong**	distress	**trouble**
disintegrate	**crumble**	distress	**upset**
disintegrate	**break up**	distress	**worried**
dismal	**dull**	distressed	**sad**
dismay	**fright**	distressed	**upset**

distressing . . . . **bad**
distressing . . . . **painful**
distribute . . . . **give out**
distribute . . . . **serve**
distribute . . . . **share**
district . . . . **area**
district . . . . **neighbourhood**
district . . . . **part**
distrust . . . . **doubt**
distrustful . . . . **doubtful**
disturb . . . . **bother**
disturb . . . . **trouble**
disturbance . . . . **riot**
disturbance . . . . **trouble**
dither . . . . **hesitate**
dive . . . . **move**
divide . . . . **cut**
divide . . . . **separate**
divide . . . . **share**
division . . . . **part**
dizzy . . . . **faint**
do an impression of . . . . **imitate**
do away with . . . . **kill**
do your best . . . . **try**
dock . . . . **land**
docks . . . . **port**
document . . . . **record**
dodge . . . . **avoid**
dodge . . . . **get out of**
dodge . . . . **go round**
dodge . . . . **miss**
doggedly . . . . **hard**
dole out . . . . **serve**
dominant . . . . **powerful**
domination . . . . **power**
domineering . . . . **bossy**
donate . . . . **give**
donate . . . . **present**
donation . . . . **present**
doodle . . . . **draw**
dosh . . . . **money**
dote on . . . . **love**

double-cross . . . . **cheat**
double-crosser . . . . . . **cheat**
doubtful . . . . **suspicious**
doubtful . . . . **uncertain**
doubtless . . . . **probably**
dough . . . . **money**
down . . . . **sad**
down . . . . **unhappy**
down in the mouth . . . . **moody**
down-in-the-dumps . . . . **sad**
downcast . . . . **sad**
downfall . . . . **defeat**
downy . . . . **soft**
doze . . . . **sleep**
drab . . . . **dull**
draft . . . . **plan**
drag . . . . **pull**
drain . . . . **empty**
drained . . . . **tired**
drama . . . . **play**
dramatic . . . . **exciting**
drastic . . . . **desperate**
draught . . . . **wind**
draw attention to . . . . . **point**
drawback . . . . **catch**
drawback . . . . **disadvantage**
drawl . . . . **say**
drawn-out . . . . **long**
dread . . . . **fear**
dread . . . . **horror**
dreadful . . . . **awful**
dreadful . . . . **bad**
dreadful . . . . **horrible**
dreadful . . . . **shocking**
dreadful . . . . **terrible**
dream . . . . **hope**
dream . . . . **imagine**
dream up . . . . **idea**
dream up . . . . **invention**
dream up . . . . **make up**
dreary . . . . **boring**
dreary . . . . **dull**

Index

drench. . . . . **wet**
drenched. . . . . **wet**
dress. . . . . **clothes**
dribble. . . . . **drip**
dribble. . . . . **trickle**
drift . . . . **float**
drift . . . . **wander**
drill . . . . **practice**
drill . . . . **train**
drip . . . . **drop**
drip . . . . **trickle**
dripping wet . . . . **wet**
drive . . . . **determination**
drive . . . . **energy**
drive . . . . **force**
drive . . . . **journey**
drive . . . . **push**
drive . . . . **ride**
drive someone up
  the wall . . . . **annoy**
drivel. . . . . **nonsense**
drivel. . . . . **rubbish**
drizzle . . . . **rain**
drizzly . . . . **damp**
drone. . . . . **say**
droop . . . . **flop**
droop . . . . **hang**
drop . . . . **fall**
drop in on . . . . **visit**
drop out of sight . . . . . **disappear**
droplet. . . . . **drop**
drowsy . . . . **sleepy**
drowsy . . . . **tired**
drum . . . . **tap**
dry land. . . . . **land**
dubious. . . . . **doubtful**
dubious. . . . . **suspicious**
dubious. . . . . **uncertain**
duck . . . . **bend**
duck out of . . . . **avoid**
dull . . . . **cloudy**
dull . . . . **faint**

dumb . . . . **silent**
dummy . . . . **model**
dump . . . . **rid**
dump . . . . **throw away**
dumpy. . . . . **short**
dungeons . . . . **prison**
duo . . . . **pair**
dupe . . . . **cheat**
dupe . . . . **trick**
duplicate . . . . **copy**
durable . . . . **strong**
durable . . . . **tough**
duration. . . . . **length**
dusk . . . . **dark**
dusk . . . . **evening**
dusk . . . . **sunset**
duty. . . . . **job**
duty. . . . . **work**
dwelling. . . . . **home**
dwelling. . . . . **house**
dwindle . . . . **decrease**
dwindle . . . . **die**
dwindle . . . . **shrink**

Ee

eager. . . . . **enthusiastic**
eager. . . . . **keen**
eager. . . . . **ready**
eagerness . . . . **excitement**
eagle-eyed . . . . **observant**
earlier . . . . **previous**
earliest . . . . **first**
earn. . . . . **deserve**
earn a living. . . . . **work**
earnings . . . . **pay**
ear-splitting . . . . **loud**
ear-splitting . . . . **noisy**
earth . . . . **ground**
earth . . . . **land**
earth . . . . **world**
easily broken. . . . . **breakable**

Index

eavesdrop	**listen**
eccentric	**odd**
economical	**cheap**
economize	**save**
ecstasy	**happiness**
ecstatic	**happy**
edge	**creep**
edge	**end**
edge	**move**
edgy	**nervous**
educate	**teach**
education	**knowledge**
eerie	**creepy**
eerie	**mysterious**
eerie	**spooky**
effect	**result**
effective	**useful**
effervescent	**fizzy**
efficient	**capable**
effort	**shot**
effort	**try**
effortless	**easy**
effortlessly	**easily**
egotistical	**selfish**
elaborate	**complicated**
elaborate	**fancy**
elbow	**poke**
elbow	**push**
elbow room	**room**
elbow room	**space**
elderly	**old**
elegance	**beauty**
elegant	**nice**
elegant	**smart**
element	**part**
elementary	**simple**
elevate	**lift**
eliminate	**remove**
elsewhere	**away**
elude	**avoid**
embark	**get on**
embark on	**begin**

embarrassed	**ashamed**
embarrassed	**uncomfortable**
embarrassing	**awkward**
embarrassment	**disgrace**
emblem	**sign**
embrace	**hug**
emerge	**appear**
eminent	**great**
eminent	**important**
emotion	**feeling**
emperor	**king**
employ	**use**
employed	**busy**
employee	**worker**
employer	**boss**
employment	**work**
empty	**hungry**
enchanting	**lovely**
enclose	**wrap**
encounter	**meet**
encourage	**support**
encouraging	**hopeful**
end	**back**
end	**complete**
end	**finish**
end	**stop**
endeavour	**try**
ending	**end**
endlessly	**always**
endure	**have**
endure	**last**
endure	**put up with**
endure	**remain**
endure	**stand**
energetic	**lively**
energy	**life**
energy	**power**
enhance	**increase**
enjoy	**like**
enjoy	**love**
enjoy yourself	**play**
enjoyable	**good**

enjoyable. . . . . **nice**
enjoyable. . . . . **pleasant**
enjoyment . . . . **fun**
enjoyment . . . . **pleasure**
enlarge . . . . **increase**
enlist . . . . **join**
enormous . . . . **big**
enormous . . . . **giant**
enormous . . . . **great**
enormous . . . . **huge**
enormous . . . . **large**
enormous . . . . **massive**
enormous . . . . **tremendous**
enormously . . . . **very**
enquire . . . . **ask**
enquiry . . . . **question**
enraged. . . . . **angry**
enraged. . . . . **furious**
enrol . . . . **join**
ensnare . . . . **catch**
ensnare . . . . **trap**
entail . . . . **involve**
entangle . . . . **tangle**
entertain yourself. . . . . . **play**
entertain . . . . **please**
entertaining . . . . **nice**
entertainment . . . . **fun**
enthralling . . . . **exciting**
enthralling . . . . **interesting**
enthusiasm . . . . **excitement**
enthusiast . . . . **fan**
enthusiastic. . . . . **excited**
enthusiastic. . . . . **keen**
enthusiastic. . . . . **mad**
entice . . . . **tempt**
enticing . . . . **tempting**
entire. . . . . **complete**
entire. . . . . **full**
entire. . . . . **whole**
entirely . . . . **completely**
entirely . . . . **quite**
entrance . . . . **gate**
entwine . . . . **curl**

envelop . . . . **wrap**
envious . . . . **jealous**
envisage . . . . **imagine**
episode . . . . **event**
equal. . . . . **even**
equip. . . . . **provide**
equipment . . . . **stuff**
equivalent . . . . **equal**
era. . . . . **time**
erase. . . . . **remove**
erase. . . . . **rub out**
erect . . . . **build**
erect . . . . **put up**
errand . . . . **job**
error . . . . **mistake**
escapade . . . . **adventure**
escape . . . . **avoid**
escape . . . . **get out of**
escort . . . . **lead**
escort . . . . **show**
escort . . . . **take**
essential . . . . **necessary**
establish . . . . **prove**
establish . . . . **set**
estate . . . . **land**
esteem . . . . **respect**
estimate . . . . **guess**
estimate . . . . **judge**
eternally . . . . **forever**
etiquette . . . . **manners**
evacuate . . . . **empty**
evade . . . . **avoid**
evade . . . . **dodge**
evade . . . . **miss**
evaluate. . . . . **judge**
evaluate. . . . . **test**
evaluate. . . . . **try**
evaluation . . . . **test**
evaporate . . . . **disappear**
evaporate . . . . **vanish**
even . . . . **flat**
even . . . . **level**

even

even	**regular**
even	**smooth**
event	**competition**
eventual	**future**
eventually	**last**
everlasting	**endless**
every now and then	**sometimes**
everyday	**common**
everyday	**regular**
everyday	**usual**
everything included	**altogether**
everywhere	**around**
evident	**clear**
evident	**obvious**
evident	**plain**
evil	**bad**
evil	**wicked**
evil-smelling	**smelly**
ex-	**old**
ex-	**past**
exact	**accurate**
exactly	**right**
exam	**examination**
examination	**check**
examine	**check**
examine	**look**
examine	**test**
excavate	**dig**
excavation	**hole**
exceed	**pass**
exceedingly	**very**
excellent	**fantastic**
excellent	**good**
excellent	**great**
excellent	**terrific**
excellent	**tremendous**
exceptional	**brilliant**
exceptional	**high**
exceptional	**special**
exceptional	**unusual**
excessive	**high**
exchange	**change**
exchange blows	**fight**
exchange views on	**discuss**
exchange	**swap** or **swop**
excitement	**enthusiasm**
exclaim	**say**
excluding	**except**
exclusive	**posh**
exclusive	**private**
excruciating	**painful**
excursion	**outing**
excursion	**trip**
excuse	**explanation**
excuse	**forgive**
excuse	**reason**
execute	**kill**
exercise	**drill**
exercise	**practice**
exercise	**train**
exertion	**exercise**
exhausted	**tired**
exhausted	**worn out**
exhausting	**hard**
exhibit	**display**
exhibit	**show**
exhibition	**display**
exhibition	**show**
exist	**live**
existence	**life**
existing	**living**
exit	**leave**
exorbitant	**expensive**
expand	**grow**
expanse	**area**
expect	**suppose**
expected	**likely**
expected	**probable**
expedition	**journey**
expense	**cost**
expense	**price**
expensive	**valuable**
experience	**endure**
experience	**feel**

Index

experience . . . . **have**
experienced . . . . **expert**
experiment . . . . **test**
expert . . . . **experienced**
expert . . . . **good**
expertise . . . . **experience**
expertise . . . . **skill**
expertly . . . . **well**
expire . . . . **die**
explain . . . . **describe**
explain . . . . **solve**
explanation . . . . **excuse**
explanation . . . . **meaning**
explanation . . . . **reason**
explode . . . . **burst**
explode . . . . **go off**
exploit . . . . **action**
exploit . . . . **adventure**
explore . . . . **investigate**
expose . . . . **uncover**
express . . . . **say**
express . . . . **speak**
expression . . . . **look**
expression . . . . **saying**
expression . . . . **word**
extend . . . . **hold out**
extend . . . . **increase**
extend . . . . **reach**
extend . . . . **stretch**
extended . . . . **long**
extensive . . . . **big**
extensive . . . . **long**
extensive . . . . **wide**
extent . . . . **area**
extent . . . . **length**
extent . . . . **measurement**
exterior . . . . **outside**
exterminate . . . . **kill**
external . . . . **outside**
extinct . . . . **dead**
extinguish . . . . **put out**
extra . . . . **luxury**

extra . . . . **more**
extra . . . . **spare**
extract . . . . **pull**
extraordinary . . . . **incredible**
extraordinary . . . . **peculiar**
extraordinary . . . . **strange**
extraordinary . . . . **unusual**
extreme . . . . **great**
extreme . . . . **high**
extremely . . . . **really**
extremely . . . . **very**

Ff

fabric . . . . **cloth**
face . . . . **outside**
faction . . . . **side**
factual . . . . **accurate**
factual . . . . **true**
fad . . . . **fashion**
fade . . . . **die**
fade . . . . **disappear**
fade . . . . **vanish**
faded . . . . **pale**
fail . . . . **break down**
fail . . . . **let down**
faint . . . . **collapse**
faint . . . . **dim**
faint . . . . **dizzy**
faint . . . . **soft**
faint . . . . **weak**
fair . . . . **all right**
fair . . . . **okay** or **OK**
fair . . . . **reasonable**
fairly . . . . **pretty**
fairly . . . . **quite**
fairly . . . . **rather**
faithful . . . . **reliable**
fake . . . . **false**
fake . . . . **phoney** or
phony
fall . . . . **move**

fall apart . . . . **break up**
fall out . . . . **argue**
fall out . . . . **quarrel**
fall through . . . . **fail**
false . . . . **fake**
false . . . . **phoney** or **phony**
false . . . . **untrue**
false . . . . **wrong**
falsehood . . . . **lie**
falter . . . . **hesitate**
famished . . . . **hungry**
fanatical . . . . **mad**
fancy . . . . **want**
fantastic . . . . **terrific**
fantastic . . . . **wonderful**
fantasy . . . . **dream**
far-fetched . . . . **unbelievable**
far-flung . . . . **far**
faraway . . . . **far**
fare . . . . **get on**
farewell . . . . **goodbye**
fascinate . . . . **interest**
fascinating . . . . **interesting**
fashionable . . . . **popular**
fast . . . . **instant**
fast . . . . **quick**
fast . . . . **quickly**
fast asleep . . . . **asleep**
fasten . . . . **connect**
fasten . . . . **fix**
fasten . . . . **link**
fasten . . . . **lock**
fasten . . . . **shut**
fasten . . . . **stick**
fated . . . . **luck**
faultless . . . . **perfect**
faulty . . . . **bad**
favour . . . . **prefer**
favoured . . . . **favourite**
favourite . . . . **popular**
faze . . . . **put off**

faze . . . . **upset**
fear . . . . **horror**
fearful . . . . **afraid**
fearful . . . . **awful**
fearless . . . . **brave**
fearless . . . . **daring**
fearsome . . . . **frightening**
feasible . . . . **possible**
feast . . . . **eat**
feast your eyes on . . . . . **look**
feat . . . . **adventure**
feat . . . . **action**
features . . . . **face**
fed up with . . . . **sick of**
feeble . . . . **weak**
feed . . . . **eat**
feel . . . . **believe**
feel . . . . **touch**
feel in your bones . . . . . **feel**
feel sorry for . . . . **pity**
feel uneasy . . . . **worry**
feign . . . . **fake**
feign . . . . **pretend**
fell . . . . **cut**
fellow . . . . **man**
ferocious . . . . **fierce**
ferret about . . . . **hunt**
fervent . . . . **strong**
festoon . . . . **decorate**
fetch . . . . **get**
feud . . . . **argument**
feud . . . . **quarrel**
few and far between . . . **scarce**
fib . . . . **lie**
fictitious . . . . **false**
fictitious . . . . **imaginary**
fidget . . . . **fiddle**
fidgety . . . . **restless**
fiend . . . . **fan**
fiend . . . . **monster**
fight . . . . **argument**
fight . . . . **quarrel**

Index

fighting	. . . .	**war**
figure	. . . .	**body**
figure	. . . .	**number**
figure	. . . .	**shape**
figure out	. . . .	**do**
figure out	. . . .	**work out**
file	. . . .	**line**
file	. . . .	**record**
file	. . . .	**row**
fill out	. . . .	**fill in**
film	. . . .	**layer**
filth	. . . .	**dirt**
filthy	. . . .	**dirty**
filthy	. . . .	**foul**
final	. . . .	**last**
finale	. . . .	**end**
finalize	. . . .	**complete**
finally	. . . .	**last**
find fault with	. . . .	**criticize**
find out	. . . .	**learn**
fine	. . . .	**nice**
fine	. . . .	**sunny**
fine	. . . .	**thin**
finest	. . . .	**best**
finger	. . . .	**feel**
finger	. . . .	**touch**
finish	. . . .	**complete**
finish	. . . .	**do**
finish	. . . .	**end**
finish	. . . .	**stop**
finished	. . . .	**over**
fire	. . . .	**sack**
fire	. . . .	**shoot**
firearms	. . . .	**gun**
firm	. . . .	**business**
firm	. . . .	**company**
firm	. . . .	**hard**
firm	. . . .	**steady**
firm	. . . .	**stiff**
firm	. . . .	**strict**
firm	. . . .	**tight**
first	. . . .	**early**
first-class	. . . .	**excellent**
first-rate	. . . .	**excellent**
fishy	. . . .	**suspicious**
fit	. . . .	**lively**
fit	. . . .	**well**
fit of temper	. . . .	**rage**
fitness	. . . .	**condition**
fitting	. . . .	**proper**
fitting	. . . .	**right**
fitting	. . . .	**suitable**
fix	. . . .	**arrange**
fix	. . . .	**fasten**
fix	. . . .	**mend**
fix	. . . .	**repair**
fix	. . . .	**set**
fix together	. . . .	**connect**
fix up	. . . .	**arrange**
fixed	. . . .	**firm**
fizz	. . . .	**bubbles**
flail	. . . .	**flap**
flame	. . . .	**burn**
flames	. . . .	**fire**
flap	. . . .	**wave**
flash	. . . .	**second**
flat	. . . .	**even**
flatten	. . . .	**squash**
flaunt	. . . .	**show off**
flaw	. . . .	**fault**
flawless	. . . .	**perfect**
flee	. . . .	**escape**
fleece	. . . .	**coat**
fleecy	. . . .	**soft**
fleeting	. . . .	**short**
flicker	. . . .	**burn**
flimsy	. . . .	**breakable**
flimsy	. . . .	**fragile**
flimsy	. . . .	**fine**
flimsy	. . . .	**thin**
flimsy	. . . .	**weak**
fling	. . . .	**throw**
flip over	. . . .	**turn over**
flit	. . . .	**fly**

Index

float

float . . . . **move**
flog . . . . **beat**
floor . . . . **bottom**
flop . . . . **droop**
flop . . . . **fail**
flourish . . . . **grow**
flourish . . . . **wave**
flow . . . . **pour**
flow . . . . **run**
fluid . . . . **liquid**
fluster . . . . **bother**
flutter . . . . **flap**
flutter . . . . **wave**
fly . . . . **race**
fly . . . . **tear**
foam . . . . **bubbles**
foaming . . . . **fizzy**
focus . . . . **centre**
focus . . . . **concentrate**
focus on . . . . **emphasize**
foe . . . . **enemy**
foil . . . . **prevent**
follow . . . . **chase**
follow . . . . **copy**
follow . . . . **get**
follow . . . . **obey**
follow . . . . **see**
follow . . . . **understand**
following . . . . **after**
following . . . . **next**
fondle . . . . **feel**
fondness . . . . **love**
fool . . . . **idiot**
fool . . . . **trick**
fool around . . . . **mess about** or **mess around**
foolish . . . . **idiotic**
foolish . . . . **ridiculous**
foolish . . . . **stupid**
foot . . . . **base**
foot . . . . **bottom**
footstep . . . . **step**

forbid . . . . **ban**
forbid . . . . **prohibit**
force . . . . **jam**
force . . . . **make**
force . . . . **power**
force . . . . **push**
force . . . . **stuff**
forecast . . . . **predict**
foreigner . . . . **stranger**
foremost . . . . **best**
foremost . . . . **main**
foremost . . . . **top**
foresee . . . . **predict**
foretell . . . . **predict**
forever . . . . **always**
forewarn . . . . **warn**
forge . . . . **copy**
forged . . . . **fake**
forged . . . . **false**
forged . . . . **phoney** or **phony**
forgery . . . . **copy**
forgery . . . . **fake**
forgive . . . . **let off**
fork out . . . . **spend**
forlorn . . . . **lonely**
form . . . . **body**
form . . . . **shape**
former times . . . . **past**
former . . . . **old**
former . . . . **past**
former . . . . **previous**
formerly . . . . **before**
formerly . . . . **once**
formidable . . . . **difficult**
fort . . . . **castle**
forthcoming . . . . **future**
forthcoming . . . . **near**
fortify . . . . **defend**
fortress . . . . **castle**
fortuitous . . . . **lucky**
fortunate . . . . **lucky**

fortune. . . . . **chance**
fortune. . . . . **luck**
foster. . . . . **encourage**
foul . . . . **dirty**
foul . . . . **disgusting**
foul . . . . **nasty**
foul . . . . **pollute**
foul-smelling . . . . **smelly**
found. . . . . **start**
foundation . . . . **base**
fountain . . . . **spray**
fraction . . . . **bit**
fraction . . . . **part**
fracture . . . . **break**
fragile . . . . **breakable**
fragile . . . . **weak**
fragment . . . . **bit**
fragment . . . . **part**
fragment . . . . **piece**
fragrance. . . . . **smell**
frail . . . . **weak**
frame of mind . . . . **mood**
frank . . . . **honest**
frank . . . . **open**
frantic . . . . **wild**
fraud . . . . **swindle**
frayed . . . . **ragged**
frayed . . . . **tatty**
freak . . . . **unusual**
free . . . . **able**
free . . . . **let out**
free . . . . **release**
free . . . . **rescue**
free . . . . **rid**
free . . . . **spare**
free of charge . . . . **free**
freezing . . . . **icy**
frequently . . . . **often**
fresh . . . . **cool**
fresh . . . . **new**
fresh . . . . **raw**
fresh . . . . **recent**

fret . . . . **worry**
friendless. . . . . **lonely**
friendly . . . . **pleasant**
fright . . . . **panic**
frighten . . . . **bully**
frighten . . . . **scare**
frightened . . . . **afraid**
frightening . . . . **scary**
frightful . . . . **awful**
frightful . . . . **dreadful**
frightful . . . . **terrible**
frisky. . . . . **playful**
fritter away . . . . **waste**
frizzy . . . . **curly**
frolic . . . . **play**
from time to time. . . . . . **occasionally**
from time to time. . . . . . **sometimes**
froth . . . . **bubbles**
frothy. . . . . **fizzy**
frozen . . . . **freezing**
frozen . . . . **icy**
fruitless . . . . **unsuccessful**
fulfil . . . . **keep**
full. . . . . **complete**
full. . . . . **whole**
fully . . . . **completely**
fully . . . . **quite**
fully-grown . . . . **grown-up**
fumble. . . . . **feel**
fuming. . . . . **angry**
function . . . . **behave**
function . . . . **event**
function . . . . **go**
function . . . . **job**
function . . . . **purpose**
function . . . . **run**
function . . . . **work**
fur . . . . **coat**
furious. . . . . **angry**
furious. . . . . **mad**
furry . . . . **soft**
further . . . . **encourage**

Index

further . . . . **extra**
further . . . . **more**
further . . . . **other**
furthermore . . . . **also**
fury . . . . **anger**
fury . . . . **rage**
fury . . . . **temper**
fusion . . . . **mixture**
fuss . . . . **complain**
futile . . . . **hopeless**
futile . . . . **unsuccessful**
futile . . . . **useless**

Gg

gabble . . . . **say**
gag . . . . **joke**
gain . . . . **win**
gale . . . . **wind**
gallop . . . . **run**
gamble . . . . **risk**
game . . . . **willing**
gang . . . . **bunch**
gang . . . . **party**
gangly . . . . **tall**
gap . . . . **hole**
gap . . . . **space**
gape . . . . **look**
gaping . . . . **open**
garbage . . . . **rubbish**
garbage . . . . **waste**
gargantuan . . . . **enormous**
gargantuan . . . . **massive**
garments . . . . **clothes**
gash . . . . **cut**
gasp . . . . **pant**
gasping . . . . **breathless**
gate . . . . **crowd**
gateway . . . . **gate**
gather . . . . **collect**
gather . . . . **learn**
gather . . . . **pick**

gather . . . . **round up**
gauge . . . . **measure**
gaunt . . . . **thin**
gawp . . . . **stare**
gaze . . . . **look**
gaze . . . . **stare**
gaze at . . . . **watch**
gear . . . . **clothes**
gear . . . . **equipment**
gear . . . . **kit**
gear . . . . **outfit**
gear . . . . **stuff**
gear . . . . **things**
geared up . . . . **ready**
generally . . . . **mainly**
generous . . . . **good**
gentle . . . . **soft**
gentleman . . . . **man**
genuine . . . . **actual**
genuine . . . . **real**
genuine . . . . **true**
germ . . . . **bug**
germ-free . . . . **pure**
germinate . . . . **grow**
gesticulate . . . . **signal**
gesture . . . . **signal**
gesture . . . . **wave**
get . . . . **see**
get better . . . . **recover**
get by . . . . **cope**
get by . . . . **manage**
get going . . . . **open**
get going . . . . **start**
get hold of . . . . **hold**
get in touch with . . . . . . **contact**
get on someone's
  nerves . . . . **annoy**
get out of . . . . **avoid**
get to the bottom of . . . **solve**
get to . . . . **reach**
get under way . . . . **start**
get well . . . . **recover**

get-together . . . . **meeting**
get-together . . . . **party**
get-up-and-go . . . . **energy**
get-up-and-go . . . . **life**
getting on . . . . **old**
ghastly . . . . **awful**
ghastly . . . . **dreadful**
ghostly . . . . **spooky**
giant . . . . **big**
giant . . . . **large**
giant . . . . **monster**
giddy . . . . **dizzy**
giddy . . . . **faint**
gift . . . . **ability**
gift . . . . **present**
gifted . . . . **brilliant**
gigantic . . . . **big**
gigantic . . . . **enormous**
gigantic . . . . **giant**
gigantic . . . . **great**
gigantic . . . . **huge**
gigantic . . . . **large**
giggle . . . . **laugh**
gist . . . . **meaning**
give . . . . **pass**
give an explanation of . . **explain**
give permission . . . . **let**
give pleasure to . . . . **please**
give rise to . . . . **produce**
give someone a fright . . **scare**
give someone their
   marching orders . . . . . **fire**
give the impression of . . **seem**
give up . . . . **leave**
give way . . . . **collapse**
give your word . . . . **promise**
glad . . . . **happy**
glad . . . . **pleased**
glad . . . . **ready**
glance . . . . **look**
glassy . . . . **smooth**
gleam . . . . **shine**

gleaming . . . . **bright**
gleaming . . . . **shiny**
glide . . . . **fly**
glide . . . . **move**
glide . . . . **slide**
glimpse . . . . **look**
glimpse . . . . **see**
glint . . . . **glitter**
glint . . . . **shine**
glisten . . . . **glitter**
glisten . . . . **shine**
glistening . . . . **bright**
glistening . . . . **shiny**
glitch . . . . **fault**
glitter . . . . **shine**
glittering . . . . **bright**
gloat . . . . **show off**
global . . . . **international**
globe . . . . **earth**
globe . . . . **world**
gloom . . . . **dark**
gloom . . . . **despair**
gloomy . . . . **cloudy**
gloomy . . . . **dark**
gloomy . . . . **dim**
gloomy . . . . **dull**
gloomy . . . . **unhappy**
glorious . . . . **magnificent**
gloss . . . . **shine**
glossy . . . . **shiny**
glossy . . . . **smooth**
glow . . . . **light**
glowing . . . . **bright**
glue . . . . **stick**
glum . . . . **sad**
glutinous . . . . **sticky**
gluttonous . . . . **greedy**
gnaw . . . . **bite**
gnaw . . . . **chew**
go beyond . . . . **pass**
go for . . . . **prefer**
go halves . . . . **share**

Index

go into hiding

go into hiding	**hide**
go like the wind	**speed**
go on foot	**walk**
go over	**practise**
go through	**practise**
go to pieces	**panic**
go up	**rise**
go with	**match**
go wrong	**break down**
goal	**aim**
goal	**point**
goal	**target**
gobble	**eat**
godsend	**luck**
goggle	**look**
good fortune	**luck**
good looks	**beauty**
good-looking	**handsome**
good-looking	**pretty**
good-natured	**friendly**
goodness	**kindness**
goods	**shopping**
gooey	**sticky**
gorge	**eat**
gorgeous	**beautiful**
gorgeous	**lovely**
gossip	**talk**
govern	**lead**
govern	**rule**
grade	**level**
grade	**sort**
gradually	**slowly**
grand	**great**
grand	**magnificent**
grand	**posh**
grant	**admit**
grant	**present**
grasp	**follow**
grasp	**get**
grasp	**learn**
grasp	**realize**
grasp	**see**
grasp	**understand**
grate	**scrape**
gratified	**proud**
grave	**bad**
grave	**desperate**
grave	**serious**
graze	**scrape**
great	**large**
great	**massive**
great	**tremendous**
greater than	**above**
greatest	**top**
greatly	**very**
greedy	**selfish**
green with envy	**envious**
green with envy	**jealous**
grief	**sadness**
grieve for	**miss**
grime	**dirt**
grimy	**dirty**
grin	**smile**
grip	**hold**
gripping	**interesting**
gristly	**tough**
groan	**moan**
groan	**say**
groove	**cut**
grope	**feel**
ground	**earth**
ground	**land**
ground	**pitch**
grounds	**argument**
grounds	**land**
group	**arrange**
group	**class**
group	**club**
group	**gang**
group	**set**
group	**sort**
grouse	**complain**
grow	**get**
grown-up	**adult**

Index

growth.	**gain**
growth.	**increase**
grubby.	**dirty**
gruelling	**tough**
gruesome	**awful**
gruff	**rough**
grumble.	**complain**
grumble.	**moan**
grumpy	**cross**
grumpy	**bad-tempered**
guarantee	**promise**
guaranteed	**definite**
guaranteed	**sure**
guard.	**defend**
guard.	**protect**
guard against	**beware**
guffaw.	**laugh**
guidance	**advice**
guide.	**lead**
guide.	**take**
guiltless.	**innocent**
guilty	**ashamed**
gulp.	**drink**
gulp.	**eat**
gulp.	**gobble**
gush	**pour**
gush	**run**
gush	**squirt**
gust.	**wind**
guts.	**courage**
guy	**man**
guzzle	**drink**
guzzle	**gobble**

Hh

habitual	**normal**
habitual	**regular**
hack	**cut**
hair-raising	**frightening**
half-baked.	**foolish**
halt	**interrupt**

halt	**stop**
halve	**cut**
hammer.	**smash**
hamper	**hinder**
hand	**give**
hand back	**return**
hand in hand	**together**
hand in your notice	**resign**
handicap	**disadvantage**
handle.	**deal with**
handle.	**drive**
handle.	**feel**
handle.	**touch**
handle.	**treat**
handy	**close**
handy	**convenient**
hang around	**stay**
hang around	**wait**
hanker after	**want**
hanker after	**wish**
hapless	**unlucky**
happen	**come about**
happen	**go on**
happen	**place**
happiness	**pleasure**
happy	**glad**
harass.	**annoy**
harass.	**worry**
harbour	**port**
hard.	**stiff**
hard at work	**busy**
hard luck.	**luck**
hard to handle.	**awkward**
hard to please	**fussy**
hard-hearted	**cruel**
hard-wearing.	**strong**
hard-wearing.	**tough**
harden.	**set**
hardly any	**few**
hardly ever	**seldom**
hare.	**zoom**
hare-brained	**foolish**

Index

hare-brained

hare-brained . . . . **idiotic**
harm . . . . **abuse**
harm . . . . **damage**
harm . . . . **hurt**
harm . . . . **injure**
harm . . . . **spoil**
harmed . . . . **hurt**
harmless . . . . **safe**
harrowing . . . . **awful**
harsh . . . . **rough**
harsh . . . . **strict**
harsh . . . . **unkind**
harvest . . . . **pick**
hassle . . . . **nag**
hassle . . . . **nuisance**
hassle . . . . **worry**
haste . . . . **hurry**
haste . . . . **speed**
hasten . . . . **hurry**
hasten . . . . **rush**
hastily . . . . **quickly**
hasty . . . . **quick**
hasty . . . . **rapid**
hasty . . . . **sudden**
hate . . . . **spite**
haul . . . . **drag**
haul . . . . **pull**
have a difference of
   opinion . . . . **argue**
have a go . . . . **try**
have a hunch . . . . **feel**
have a sensation of . . . . **feel**
have an argument . . . . **argue**
have an effect on . . . . . **affect**
have confidence in . . . . **rely**
have faith in . . . . **believe**
have faith in . . . . **trust**
have forty winks . . . . . **sleep**
have no time for . . . . . **dislike**
have the courage . . . . . **dare**
haven . . . . **shelter**
hazard . . . . **danger**

hazard . . . . **risk**
hazardous . . . . **dangerous**
hazy . . . . **faint**
hazy . . . . **foggy**
head . . . . **boss**
head . . . . **front**
head . . . . **lead**
head . . . . **leader**
head-to-head . . . . **contest**
head-to-head . . . . **match**
headache . . . . **problem**
headache . . . . **worry**
headquarters . . . . **base**
healed . . . . **better**
healthy . . . . **fit**
healthy . . . . **well**
heap . . . . **pile**
heaps . . . . **lot**
hear about . . . . **learn**
heart . . . . **centre**
heart . . . . **middle**
heart-rending . . . . **sad**
heartless . . . . **cruel**
heave . . . . **drag**
heave . . . . **pull**
heave . . . . **throw**
heavy-duty . . . . **strong**
hectic . . . . **busy**
hefty . . . . **heavy**
height . . . . **top**
helpful . . . . **convenient**
helpful . . . . **handy**
helpful . . . . **useful**
helpful . . . . **worthwhile**
herd . . . . **round up**
here and there . . . . **about**
here and there . . . . **around**
heroism . . . . **courage**
hesitant . . . . **doubtful**
hesitant . . . . **uncertain**
hidden . . . . **invisible**
hide . . . . **bury**

Index

hide. . . . . coat
hide. . . . . skin
hideous . . . . awful
hideous . . . . horrible
hideous . . . . ugly
higgledy-piggledy . . . . . untidy
high-class . . . . posh
high-pitched . . . . high
high-spirited . . . . lively
higher quality. . . . . better
higher than . . . . above
higher than . . . . over
highlight . . . . emphasize
highly . . . . very
hilarious. . . . . funny
hilarity . . . . laughter
hinder . . . . block
hinder . . . . delay
hinder . . . . hold up
hinder . . . . prevent
hinder . . . . stop
hinge on . . . . depend
hint . . . . sign
hitch . . . . difficulty
hither and thither . . . . . . about
hoard. . . . . gather
hoard. . . . . save
hoard. . . . . store
hoax . . . . trick
hobble. . . . . limp
hobbling . . . . lame
hobby . . . . interest
hoist . . . . lift
hold. . . . . argue
hold. . . . . contain
hold. . . . . keep
hold a conversation . . . . talk
hold back . . . . hinder
hold on . . . . wait
hold out. . . . . last
hold responsible . . . . . . blame
hold to ransom . . . . kidnap

hold up . . . . delay
hold up . . . . interrupt
hold-up . . . . delay
hold-up . . . . jam
hold-up . . . . wait
hollow . . . . hole
hollow out . . . . dig
home. . . . . house
homicide . . . . murder
honest. . . . . open
honestly . . . . really
honour. . . . . keep
honour. . . . . prize
honour. . . . . respect
honour. . . . . reward
honoured. . . . . proud
hoodwink . . . . fool
hop . . . . limp
hopeless . . . . desperate
hopeless . . . . impossible
hopeless . . . . useless
hopelessness . . . . despair
horizontal . . . . flat
horizontal . . . . level
horrendous . . . . awful
horrible . . . . awful
horrible . . . . mean
horrible . . . . nasty
horrible . . . . revolting
horrible . . . . unpleasant
horrid . . . . awful
horrid . . . . horrible
horrid . . . . unpleasant
horrific. . . . . awful
horrific. . . . . terrible
horrifying . . . . shocking
horror . . . . fright
host. . . . . number
hostage. . . . . prisoner
hot air . . . . rubbish
hot under the collar . . . . angry
hot water. . . . . trouble

Index

hound . . . . **chase**
hover . . . . **float**
however . . . . **but**
howl . . . . **cry**
howl . . . . **roar**
howling . . . . **wild**
HQ . . . . **base**
hub . . . . **centre**
hub . . . . **middle**
hubbub . . . . **noise**
huge . . . . **big**
huge . . . . **enormous**
huge . . . . **giant**
huge . . . . **large**
huge . . . . **massive**
huge . . . . **tremendous**
hullabaloo . . . . **noise**
human . . . . **person**
human being . . . . **person**
humane . . . . **kind**
humanity . . . . **kindness**
humans . . . . **people**
humble . . . . **unknown**
humid . . . . **damp**
humiliated . . . . **ashamed**
humiliation . . . . **disgrace**
humorous . . . . **funny**
hump . . . . **lump**
hunch . . . . **guess**
hunk . . . . **lump**
hunt . . . . **chase**
hunt . . . . **look**
hunt . . . . **search**
hurdle . . . . **jump**
hurl . . . . **throw**
hurricane . . . . **wind**
hurried . . . . **quick**
hurried . . . . **rapid**
hurriedly . . . . **quickly**
hurry . . . . **nip**
hurry . . . . **race**
hurry . . . . **rush**

hurt . . . . **ache**
hurt . . . . **upset**
hurtle . . . . **move**
hush . . . . **shut up**
hush . . . . **silence**
hushed . . . . **quiet**
hushed . . . . **silent**
hush-hush . . . . **secret**
husky . . . . **hoarse**
hysteria . . . . **panic**
hysterical . . . . **wild**

Ii

icy . . . . **freezing**
idea . . . . **feeling**
idea . . . . **hunch**
idea . . . . **thought**
identical . . . . **alike**
identical . . . . **same**
identical to . . . . **like**
idiot . . . . **fool**
idiotic . . . . **silly**
idiotic . . . . **stupid**
idle . . . . **lazy**
idolize . . . . **love**
ignite . . . . **fire**
ignite . . . . **let off**
ignite . . . . **light**
ignorant . . . . **stupid**
ill . . . . **sick**
ill at ease . . . . **uncomfortable**
ill-fated . . . . **unlucky**
ill-feeling . . . . **spite**
ill-mannered . . . . **rude**
ill-treat . . . . **abuse**
ill-treatment . . . . **abuse**
illegal . . . . **wrong**
illness . . . . **disease**
illuminate . . . . **light**
illustrate . . . . **represent**
illustrate . . . . **show**

Index

illustration . . . . example
illustration . . . . picture
image . . . . picture
imaginable . . . . possible
imagine . . . . dream
imagine . . . . suppose
imbecile . . . . idiot
imitate . . . . copy
imitation . . . . copy
imitation . . . . dummy
imitation . . . . fake
imitation . . . . model
imitation . . . . phoney or
                                phony
immaculate . . . . clean
immaculate . . . . perfect
immature . . . . childish
immature . . . . silly
immediate . . . . instant
immediately . . . . now
immediately . . . . once
immense . . . . big
immense . . . . huge
immense . . . . large
immense . . . . massive
immensity . . . . size
imminent . . . . near
immoral . . . . wrong
immunity . . . . defence
impact . . . . effect
impact . . . . force
impartial . . . . fair
impeccable . . . . perfect
impede . . . . block
impede . . . . prevent
impending . . . . future
imperative . . . . necessary
impersonate . . . . copy
impersonate . . . . imitate
impertinent . . . . cheeky
implausible . . . . unbelievable
implement . . . . tool

implore . . . . ask
important . . . . big
important . . . . great
important . . . . serious
important . . . . special
impractical . . . . useless
impression . . . . effect
impressive . . . . magnificent
impressive . . . . wonderful
imprison . . . . jail
improve . . . . progress
improve . . . . recover
improved . . . . better
improvement . . . . progress
impudent . . . . cheeky
in a coma . . . . unconscious
in a flash . . . . fast
in a flash . . . . moment
in a huff . . . . moody
in a jiffy . . . . moment
in a little while . . . . soon
in a trice . . . . moment
in addition . . . . also
in advance . . . . early
in all probability . . . . . . probably
in an instant . . . . moment
in attendance . . . . present
in demand . . . . popular
in error . . . . wrong
in excess off . . . . over
in fact . . . . really
in flames . . . . fire
in good condition . . . . . fit
in good condition . . . . . healthy
in good health . . . . well
in good shape . . . . fit
in good shape . . . . healthy
in good time . . . . early
in no time at all . . . . . . moment
in order . . . . okay or OK
in particular . . . . especially
in place . . . . instead

in poor health	**sick**	independently	**alone**
in safe hands	**safe**	indicate	**mean**
in short supply	**scarce**	indicate	**point**
in spite of	**despite**	indication	**sign**
in the middle of	**among** or **amongst**	indication	**signal**
in the past	**once**	indignant	**angry**
in the region of	**around**	indignation	**anger**
in total	**altogether**	indispensable	**essential**
in two minds	**doubtful**	indistinct	**dull**
in unison	**together**	indistinct	**faint**
in your birthday suit	**bare**	indistinguishable	**alike**
inaccurate	**careless**	individual	**person**
inaccurate	**untrue**	individual	**personal**
inaccurate	**wrong**	individual	**separate**
inappropriate	**unsuitable**	individual	**single**
incensed	**mad**	indoors	**inside**
incessant	**continuous**	indulgence	**luxury**
inch	**move**	industrious	**hard-working**
incident	**event**	industriously	**hard**
incident	**experience**	industry	**business**
incline	**tilt**	ineffective	**useless**
incline towards	**prefer**	inert	**still**
include	**add**	inevitable	**certain**
include	**contain**	inexpensive	**cheap**
income	**pay**	inexpensive	**reasonable**
incompetent	**hopeless**	inexplicable	**mysterious**
inconsiderate	**bad-mannered**	inexplicable	**strange**
inconvenience	**bother**	infant	**baby**
inconvenience	**disadvantage**	infant	**little**
inconvenience	**nuisance**	infantile	**childish**
inconvenience	**trouble**	infection	**bug**
incorporate	**include**	inferior	**bad**
incorrect	**untrue**	inferior	**poor**
incorrect	**wrong**	inferno	**fire**
increase	**gain**	infinite	**big**
increase	**put up**	inflamed	**sore**
increase	**rise**	inflexible	**stiff**
incredible	**marvellous**	influence	**affect**
incredible	**unbelievable**	influence	**effect**
incredible	**wonderful**	influence	**power**
incredulity	**surprise**	influential	**important**
		influential	**powerful**

inform	tell		instruct	order
infrequent	few		instruct	show
infuriated	angry		instruct	teach
infuriated	furious		instruct	tell
inhabit	live		instruct	train
inhabitants	people		instruction	order
inherent	natural		instructor	teacher
initiate	start		instrument	tool
injure	hurt		insult	abuse
injured	hurt		insulting	rude
inkling	hunch		insults	abuse
inkling	idea		intelligence	sense
innate	natural		intelligent	bright
inner	inside		intelligent	clever
inner	middle		intelligent	brainy
innocent	gullible		intelligent	quick
inquire	ask		intend	aim
inquiring	curious		intend	mean
inquisitive	curious		intend	plan
inquisitive	nosy		intense	deep
insane	crazy		intense	sharp
insane	mad		intense	strong
insignificant	slight		intent	determined
insignificant	small		intention	purpose
insist	claim		intentional	deliberate
insolent	rude		intentionally	purpose
inspect	check		intercontinental	international
inspect	examine		interest	enthusiasm
inspection	check		interested	curious
inspection	examination		interior	inside
inspection	test		interject	say
inspire	encourage		interminable	long
inspiring	exciting		internal	inside
instance	example		interpret	explain
instant	immediate		interpret	read
instant	moment		interpretation	explanation
instant	point		interrogate	ask
instant	second		interrogate	question
instantaneous	immediate		interrupt	disturb
instantly	immediately		interrupt	say
instantly	once		interrupt	stop
instinctive	natural		interval	break

Index

interval . . . . **wait**
intimidate . . . . **bully**
intimidate . . . . **threaten**
intrepid . . . . **brave**
intricate . . . . **complicated**
intrigue . . . . **interest**
introduction . . . . **beginning**
intrude . . . . **interrupt**
intrude on . . . . **disturb**
intruder . . . . **burglar**
inundate . . . . **flood**
invade . . . . **raid**
invariably . . . . **always**
invasion . . . . **attack**
invasion . . . . **raid**
invent . . . . **make up**
invent . . . . **think up**
inverted . . . . **upside down**
investigate . . . . **examine**
investigation . . . . **examination**
invite . . . . **ask**
inviting . . . . **tempting**
involve . . . . **affect**
involve . . . . **include**
involvement . . . . **interest**
irate . . . . **angry**
irate . . . . **mad**
irregular . . . . **rough**
irresponsible . . . . **silly**
irresponsible . . . . **stupid**
irritable . . . . **bad-tempered**
irritable . . . . **cross**
irritable . . . . **grumpy**
irritable . . . . **moody**
irritate . . . . **annoy**
irritated . . . . **angry**
irritation . . . . **anger**
isolated . . . . **alone**
isolated . . . . **lonely**
isolated . . . . **separate**
issue . . . . **business**
issue . . . . **give out**

issue . . . . **matter**
issue . . . . **subject**
item . . . . **thing**
itemize . . . . **list**

Jj

jab . . . . **poke**
jab . . . . **prick**
jab . . . . **punch**
jabber . . . . **say**
jagged . . . . **rough**
jagged . . . . **sharp**
jail . . . . **prison**
jam . . . . **squeeze**
jam . . . . **stuff**
jargon . . . . **language**
jaunt . . . . **outing**
jaunt . . . . **ride**
jaunt . . . . **trip**
jealous . . . . **envious**
jerk . . . . **pull**
jest . . . . **joke**
jet . . . . **stream**
jettison . . . . **dump**
jettison . . . . **throw away**
jiffy . . . . **second**
jinxed . . . . **unlucky**
jittery . . . . **nervous**
job . . . . **work**
jog . . . . **run**
jog your memory . . . . . **remind**
join . . . . **connect**
join . . . . **fasten**
join . . . . **link**
join in . . . . **part**
jointly . . . . **together**
jolly . . . . **bright**
jolly . . . . **cheerful**
jolly . . . . **happy**
jolt . . . . **shake**
jostle . . . . **push**

Index

jotter . . . . **pad**
journey . . . . **go**
journey . . . . **ride**
journey . . . . **travel**
journey . . . . **trip**
journey . . . . **way**
joy . . . . **happiness**
joyful . . . . **happy**
jubilant . . . . **happy**
jubilation . . . . **happiness**
judgement . . . . **decision**
jumble . . . . **junk**
jumble . . . . **mess up**
jumble . . . . **muddle**
jumble . . . . **tangle**
jumbled . . . . **untidy**
jumpy . . . . **nervous**
jumpy . . . . **restless**
junk . . . . **rubbish**
just . . . . **fair**
just . . . . **only**
just about . . . . **almost**
justification . . . . **excuse**
justification . . . . **reason**
justify . . . . **defend**
justify . . . . **deserve**
jut out . . . . **stick out**
juvenile . . . . **child**
juvenile . . . . **childish**

Kk

keel over . . . . **fall**
keen . . . . **enthusiastic**
keen . . . . **fierce**
keen . . . . **ready**
keep an eye on . . . . **mind**
keep fit . . . . **exercise**
keep on . . . . **continue**
keep on . . . . **get on**
keep quiet . . . . **shut up**
keep watch . . . . **guard**
keep your eyes open . . . **watch out**
key . . . . **essential**
kick . . . . **thrill**
kid . . . . **child**
kid . . . . **joke**
kidnap . . . . **capture**
killing . . . . **murder**
kin . . . . **relation**
kind . . . . **class**
kind . . . . **friendly**
kind . . . . **nice**
kind . . . . **sort**
kind . . . . **thoughtful**
kind . . . . **type**
kindle . . . . **fire**
kindle . . . . **light**
kindly . . . . **kind**
kingdom . . . . **country**
kinky . . . . **curly**
kinsman . . . . **relation**
kinswoman . . . . **relation**
kip . . . . **sleep**
kit . . . . **outfit**
knack . . . . **skill**
knock . . . . **bump**
knock . . . . **bang**
knock . . . . **tap**
knocked out . . . . **unconscious**
knot . . . . **tangle**
knot . . . . **tie**
knotty . . . . **difficult**
know how . . . . **experience**
knowledge . . . . **experience**
knowledgeable . . . . **expert**

Ll

laborious . . . . **difficult**
labour . . . . **work**
labourer . . . . **worker**
lace . . . . **fasten**
lack . . . . **shortage**

Index

lack of success

lack of success	**failure**
ladder	**tear**
laid back	**cool**
laid up	**ill**
land	**country**
land	**earth**
land	**ground**
lanky	**tall**
lap	**circle**
large	**wide**
largely	**mainly**
last-minute	**late**
latch	**lock**
late	**dead**
later than	**after**
latest	**new**
latest	**last**
latest	**recent**
launch	**start**
lay	**place**
lay	**put**
lay it on thick	**exaggerate**
laze	**relax**
laze	**rest**
lead	**front**
lead	**guide**
lead	**rule**
lead	**take**
lead to	**cause**
lead to	**go**
leader	**boss**
leading	**best**
leading	**top**
leak	**trickle**
lean	**tilt**
leap	**jump**
learn	**hear**
learner	**beginner**
learning	**knowledge**
least	**minimum**
leathery	**tough**
leave	**quit**
leave	**set off** or **set out**
leave in the lurch	**let down**
leave off	**stop**
leave open mouthed . . .	**surprise**
lecture	**speak**
lecture	**talk**
lecture	**tell off**
leftovers	**waste**
legend	**story**
leisurely	**easy**
leisurely	**slow**
lend a hand	**help**
lengthen	**stretch**
lengthy	**long**
lessen	**decrease**
lessen	**reduce**
lethal	**deadly**
level	**even**
level	**flat**
level-headed	**calm**
liable	**likely**
liberate	**free**
liberate	**let out**
liberate	**release**
liberate	**rescue**
liberated	**free**
lick	**beat**
lie low	**hide**
lifestyle	**life**
light	**fine**
light	**fire**
light	**pale**
light	**soft**
light-headed	**dazed**
light-headed	**dizzy**
light-headed	**faint**
light-hearted	**bright**
light-hearted	**cheerful**
like a shot	**fast**
likeable	**pleasant**
likelihood	**chance**

Index

likely	certain	lock	fasten
likely	probable	lock	shut
limit	end	lofty	high
limited	short	log	record
limping	lame	loiter	hang about
line	row	loiter	stay
line-up	team	lollop	run
linger	hang about	long ago	past
linger	lag	long for	want
linger	remain	long for	wish
linger	stay	long-established	old
linger	wait	long-standing	old
link	connect	long-winded	talkative
link	connection	look	seem
link	join	look after	care for
liquid	runny	look after	mind
list	tilt	look after	see
litter	rubbish	look forward to	hope
little	short	look high and low	hunt
little	small	look high and low	search
little by little	gradually	look out	beware
lively	bright	look out	watch out
lively	busy	look up	see
lively	energetic	look up	visit
lively	playful	lookout	guard
livid	angry	loom	appear
livid	furious	loop	wind
livid	mad	loose	release
load	fill	loot	rob
load	weight	lose your footing	slip
loaded	full	lose your footing	trip
loaded	rich	lose your nerve	panic
loathe	dislike	lost for words	silent
loathe	hate	lost in thought	thoughtful
loathsome	disgusting	loud	noisy
loathsome	revolting	lounge	lie
locality	district	lounge	rest
locality	neighbourhood	lout	hooligan
location	place	love	like
location	position	lovellness	beauty
location	situation	lovely	beautiful
location	spot	lovely	nice

Index

lovely. . . . . **pleasant**
lovely. . . . . **pretty**
loving . . . . **fond**
low . . . . **deep**
low . . . . **sad**
low . . . . **short**
lower. . . . . **reduce**
lowest . . . . **least**
lowest . . . . **minimum**
loyal . . . . **faithful**
luck. . . . . **chance**
luckless. . . . . **unlucky**
lucky break . . . . **luck**
ludicrous . . . . **mad**
ludicrous . . . . **ridiculous**
lug. . . . . **carry**
lug. . . . . **drag**
lukewarm. . . . . **warm**
lumber. . . . . **move**
lumber. . . . . **run**
lumbering . . . . **clumsy**
lump . . . . **block**
lump . . . . **bump**
lunge. . . . . **move**
lurch . . . . **move**
lurch . . . . **stagger**
lure . . . . **tempt**
luxurious . . . . **posh**

Mm

magnificent . . . . **great**
magnificent . . . . **terrific**
magnificent . . . . **wonderful**
magnitude. . . . . **size**
mail. . . . . **send**
maintain . . . . **argue**
maintain . . . . **claim**
major. . . . . **main**
make. . . . . **reach**
make a decision . . . . . . **decide**
make a difference . . . . . **count**

make a difference . . . . . **matter**
make a getaway . . . . . . **escape**
make a hash of . . . . **mess up**
make a suggestion . . . . **suggest**
make arrangements. . . . **prepare**
make believe . . . . **pretend**
make clear. . . . . **explain**
make contact . . . . **contact**
make enquiries . . . . . . **investigate**
make headway . . . . . . **progress**
make illegal . . . . **ban**
make illegal . . . . **prohibit**
make progress. . . . . . . **improve**
make up your mind . . . . **decide**
make use of . . . . **use**
make your escape. . . . . **escape**
malicious. . . . . **mean**
malicious. . . . . **nasty**
malicious. . . . . **unkind**
malicious. . . . . **vicious**
malicious. . . . . **wicked**
mammoth . . . . **big**
man. . . . . **adult**
manage. . . . . **control**
manage. . . . . **cope**
manage. . . . . **get on**
manage. . . . . **lead**
manage. . . . . **organize**
manage. . . . . **run**
manager . . . . **boss**
mangle . . . . **twist**
mankind . . . . **man**
mankind . . . . **people**
manner . . . . **way**
manufacture . . . . **make**
manufacture . . . . **produce**
march . . . . **walk**
mark . . . . **spot**
marks . . . . **score**
marsh . . . . **bog**
marvellous. . . . . **fabulous**
marvellous. . . . . **incredible**

Index

marvellous. . . . . **terrific**
marvellous. . . . . **tremendous**
marvellous. . . . . **wonderful**
mask. . . . . **hide**
mass. . . . . **amount**
mass. . . . . **crowd**
mass. . . . . **pile**
massacre. . . . . **kill**
masses . . . . **lot**
masses . . . . **plenty**
massive. . . . . **big**
massive. . . . . **enormous**
massive. . . . . **giant**
massive. . . . . **huge**
massive. . . . . **large**
master. . . . . **captain**
master. . . . . **learn**
match . . . . **contest**
match . . . . **equal**
match . . . . **fit**
match . . . . **game**
matching. . . . . **same**
mate . . . . **friend**
material. . . . . **cloth**
materialize. . . . . **come**
maths . . . . **mathematics**
matter . . . . **business**
matter . . . . **count**
matter . . . . **subject**
mature. . . . . **grow up**
mature. . . . . **grown-up**
mature. . . . . **responsible**
maul . . . . **feel**
maybe. . . . . **perhaps**
meadow . . . . **field**
meagre . . . . **small**
mean. . . . . **aim**
mean. . . . . **involve**
mean. . . . . **nasty**
mean. . . . . **plan**
mean. . . . . **represent**
mean. . . . . **unkind**

meander . . . . **wander**
meander . . . . **wind**
meaning . . . . **sense**
means. . . . . **way**
measly. . . . . **small**
meddle . . . . **interfere**
meddle . . . . **mess**
meddlesome . . . . **nosy**
medicine . . . . **cure**
mediocre. . . . . **poor**
meditation . . . . **thought**
melancholy . . . . **miserable**
melancholy . . . . **sad**
melt away . . . . **disappear**
memorize . . . . **learn**
menace . . . . **danger**
menace . . . . **threaten**
menacing . . . . **frightening**
mend. . . . . **fix**
mention. . . . . **say**
merciful . . . . **good**
merciless. . . . . **cruel**
merely. . . . . **only**
merge . . . . **join**
merit . . . . **deserve**
merit . . . . **value**
merry. . . . . **cheerful**
merry. . . . . **happy**
mess . . . . **muddle**
mess up . . . . **muddle**
mess up . . . . **spoil**
messy . . . . **sloppy**
messy . . . . **untidy**
metamorphose . . . . **turn into**
metamorphosis . . . . **change**
method . . . . **way**
meticulous. . . . . **careful**
microscopic. . . . . **minute**
microscopic. . . . . **tiny**
middle. . . . . **centre**
might. . . . . **strength**
might. . . . . **power**

Index

mighty

mighty	**big**		misty	**foggy**
mighty	**powerful**		misunderstanding	**muddle**
mild	**gentle**		misuse	**abuse**
miles	**far**		mix-up	**muddle**
mimic	**imitate**		moan	**complain**
mind	**care**		moan	**groan**
mingle	**mix**		moan	**grumble**
mini	**little**		moan	**say**
miniature	**small**		mob	**crowd**
miniature	**tiny**		mock	**fun**
minimum	**least**		mock	**tease**
miniscule	**minute**		model	**dummy**
minor	**slight**		model	**make**
minute	**tiny**		moderate	**reasonable**
minutes	**record**		moderately	**fairly**
miraculous	**marvellous**		moderately	**pretty**
miscellaneous	**mixed**		moderately	**quite**
miscellaneous	**various**		moderately	**rather**
mischievous	**bad**		modern	**new**
mischievous	**naughty**		modify	**adjust**
mischievous	**playful**		moist	**damp**
miserable	**poor**		moist	**wet**
miserable	**sad**		mollycoddle	**spoil**
miserable	**unhappy**		moment	**point**
miserly	**mean**		moment	**second**
misery	**sadness**		moment	**time**
misfortune	**luck**		momentary	**short**
misfortune	**tragedy**		momentous	**big**
misfortune	**trouble**		momentous	**special**
mishap	**accident**		monarch	**king**
mislaid	**lost**		monotonous	**boring**
mislay	**lose**		monster	**giant**
misleading	**untrue**		mooch	**wander**
misplace	**lose**		moody	**bad-tempered**
misplaced	**lost**		moonlit	**clear**
missing	**lost**		morass	**bog**
mission	**expedition**		more or less	**about**
mission	**job**		more suitable	**better**
mist	**fog**		moreover	**also**
mist	**spray**		moron	**fool**
mistaken	**wrong**		morsel	**bit**
mistreat	**abuse**		morsel	**piece**

mortal . . . . **deadly**
most recent . . . . **last**
most . . . . **very**
mostly . . . . **mainly**
motif . . . . **pattern**
motion . . . . **action**
motion . . . . **signal**
motionless . . . . **still**
motivate . . . . **encourage**
motive . . . . **reason**
motor car . . . . **car**
motto . . . . **saying**
mouldy . . . . **rotten**
mound . . . . **heap**
mound . . . . **pile**
mount . . . . **get on**
mount . . . . **mountain**
mount . . . . **rise**
mountain . . . . **heap**
mountainous . . . . **big**
mourn . . . . **miss**
mouthwatering . . . . . . **tasty**
move . . . . **action**
move house . . . . **move**
move . . . . **step**
moving . . . . **sad**
mow . . . . **cut**
much . . . . **far**
muck . . . . **dirt**
muck . . . . **mud**
muck about . . . . **mess about** or **mess around**
mucky . . . . **dirty**
mucky . . . . **messy**
muddle . . . . **jumble**
muddle . . . . **mess up**
muddle . . . . **mix up**
muddle . . . . **tangle**
muddled . . . . **confused**
muddled . . . . **messy**
muddy . . . . **cloudy**
muffled . . . . **dull**

muffled . . . . **faint**
muffled . . . . **low**
mug . . . . **attack**
mugger . . . . **thief**
muggy . . . . **damp**
multitude . . . . **crowd**
mumble . . . . **mutter**
mumble . . . . **say**
munch . . . . **chew**
murder . . . . **kill**
murderous . . . . **violent**
murk . . . . **dark**
murk . . . . **fog**
murky . . . . **cloudy**
murky . . . . **dark**
murky . . . . **foggy**
murmur . . . . **mutter**
murmur . . . . **say**
muscular . . . . **strong**
muster . . . . **round up**
mutate . . . . **change**
mutate . . . . **turn into**
mute . . . . **silent**
muted . . . . **low**
muted . . . . **soft**
mutinous . . . . **disobedient**
mutter . . . . **say**
mysterious . . . . **creepy**
mysterious . . . . **funny**
mysterious . . . . **spooky**
mysterious . . . . **strange**
mystify . . . . **puzzle**
mystifying . . . . **mysterious**
mythological . . . . **imaginary**

Nn

nab . . . . **capture**
nail . . . . **fasten**
naïve . . . . **gullible**
naked . . . . **bare**
name . . . . **call**

nameless

nameless . . . . **unknown**
nap . . . . **rest**
nap . . . . **sleep**
narrate . . . . **tell**
narrative . . . . **plot**
narrative . . . . **story**
narrow . . . . **thin**
nasty . . . . **evil**
nasty . . . . **horrible**
nasty . . . . **mean**
nasty . . . . **unkind**
nasty . . . . **unpleasant**
nation . . . . **country**
nation . . . . **land**
native . . . . **inhabitant**
natural . . . . **pure**
natural . . . . **raw**
nature . . . . **character**
naughty . . . . **bad**
nauseating . . . . **revolting**
nauseous . . . . **sick**
near . . . . **move**
nearby . . . . **close**
nearby . . . . **handy**
nearby . . . . **near**
nearly . . . . **almost**
neat . . . . **smart**
neat . . . . **tidy**
necessitate . . . . **involve**
need . . . . **take**
needle . . . . **annoy**
needless . . . . **unnecessary**
negligible . . . . **small**
neighbourhood . . . . **area**
neighbourhood . . . . **district**
neighbouring . . . . **close**
neighbouring . . . . **near**
neighbouring . . . . **next**
nerve . . . . **guts**
nervous . . . . **afraid**
nevertheless . . . . **but**
new . . . . **recent**

newborn child . . . . **baby**
newcomer . . . . **stranger**
next to . . . . **beside**
nibble . . . . **bite**
nibble . . . . **eat**
nibble . . . . **taste**
nibbles . . . . **snack**
nick . . . . **arrest**
nick . . . . **cut**
nick . . . . **jail**
nick . . . . **steal**
nifty . . . . **neat**
nigh . . . . **near**
nightfall . . . . **evening**
nightfall . . . . **sunset**
nincompoop . . . . **idiot**
nip . . . . **pinch**
nipper . . . . **child**
nippy . . . . **cool**
no trouble . . . . **easy**
noiseless . . . . **silent**
noisy . . . . **loud**
nominate . . . . **pick**
none . . . . **nothing**
nonessential . . . . **unnecessary**
nonsense . . . . **rubbish**
nonstop . . . . **continuous**
nontoxic . . . . **safe**
normal . . . . **common**
normal . . . . **natural**
normal . . . . **ordinary**
normal . . . . **regular**
normal . . . . **typical**
normal . . . . **usual**
normally . . . . **usually**
nose . . . . **move**
nosy . . . . **curious**
not able to bear . . . . **dislike**
not guilty . . . . **innocent**
not often . . . . **seldom**
not quite . . . . **almost**
note . . . . **record**

Index

notebook	**pad**	obnoxious	**unpleasant**
notice	**see**	obscene	**foul**
notice	**sign**	obscenities	**abuse**
notice	**spot**	obscure	**unknown**
notice	**warning**	observant	**sharp**
notify	**tell**	observe	**follow**
notion	**idea**	observe	**look**
notion	**thought**	observe	**notice**
nought	**nothing**	observe	**see**
nourishment	**food**	observe	**spot**
novel	**story**	observe	**watch**
novice	**beginner**	obsolete	**old-fashioned**
now and then	**occasionally**	obstacle	**difficulty**
now and then	**sometimes**	obstacle	**barrier**
nowadays	**now**	obstacle	**block**
nude	**bare**	obstinate	**stubborn**
nudge	**poke**	obstruct	**block**
nugget	**lump**	obstruct	**hinder**
nuisance	**bother**	obstruct	**stop**
number	**quantity**	obstruction	**barrier**
numeracy	**mathematics**	obstruction	**block**
numeral	**number**	obtain	**buy**
numerous	**many**	obtain	**receive**
nurse	**care for**	obvious	**clear**
nutrition	**food**	obvious	**plain**
nutritious	**healthy**	occasion	**event**
		occasion	**time**
		occupation	**job**
Oo		occupation	**work**
		occupied	**busy**
obey	**follow**	occupier	**inhabitant**
object	**aim**	occupy	**invade**
object	**mind**	occupy	**live**
object	**point**	occur	**come about**
object	**protest**	occur	**go on**
object	**purpose**	occur	**happen**
object	**thing**	occur	**place**
object to	**disagree**	occurrence	**event**
objective	**aim**	odd	**funny**
objective	**target**	odd	**peculiar**
oblige	**make**	odd	**strange**
obliging	**helpful**	odd	**unusual**
obnoxious	**disgusting**		

odour . . . . **smell**
of no use. . . . . **useless**
off colour. . . . . **poorly**
offended . . . . **hurt**
offender. . . . . **criminal**
offensive . . . . **foul**
offensive . . . . **invasion**
offensive . . . . **nasty**
offensive . . . . **rude**
offer . . . . **hold out**
offering . . . . **present**
ogle. . . . . **stare**
ogre. . . . . **giant**
ogre. . . . . **monster**
olden days. . . . . **past**
oldest . . . . **first**
omit. . . . . **forget**
on all sides of . . . . **around**
on edge. . . . . **restless**
on every side of. . . . . . . **around**
on hand. . . . . **present**
on holiday . . . . **away**
on its head . . . . **upside down**
on no account . . . . **nervous**
on the cards . . . . **probable**
on the house . . . . **free**
on the other hand . . . . **but**
on the point of. . . . . . . **about to**
on the spur of the
  moment. . . . . **suddenly**
on the whole . . . . **mainly**
on top of . . . . **above**
on-the-spot . . . . **instant**
once in a while . . . . **sometimes**
once in a while . . . . **occasionally**
once more. . . . . **again**
one or two. . . . . **some**
one-time . . . . **old**
only just. . . . . **hardly**
only once in a while. . . . **seldom**
ooze . . . . **trickle**
opaque . . . . **cloudy**

open fire . . . . **shoot**
open-mouthed. . . . . . . **surprised**
opening. . . . . **beginning**
opening. . . . . **gap**
opening. . . . . **hole**
opening. . . . . **space**
operate . . . . **behave**
operate . . . . **go**
operate . . . . **run**
operate . . . . **use**
operate . . . . **work**
opinion . . . . **thought**
opinion . . . . **view**
opponent. . . . . **enemy**
oppose . . . . **disagree**
oppose . . . . **object**
oppose . . . . **protest**
opposed . . . . **different**
opposed to . . . . **against**
opposing. . . . . **opposite**
opposition . . . . **enemy**
opt for. . . . . **choose**
opt for. . . . . **pick**
optimistic . . . . **hopeful**
option . . . . **choice**
orbit . . . . **circle**
ordeal . . . . **experience**
order . . . . **condition**
order . . . . **force**
order . . . . **make**
order . . . . **tell**
orderly. . . . . **neat**
ordinary. . . . . **common**
ordinary. . . . . **natural**
organic . . . . **natural**
organization. . . . . **business**
organize . . . . **arrange**
organize . . . . **prepare**
organize . . . . **see**
organize . . . . **sort**
origin. . . . . **beginning**
origin. . . . . **cause**

original	first	over	above
original	genuine	over the moon	pleased
original	old	overbearing	bossy
originator	inventor	overcast	cloudy
ornate	fancy	overcast	dull
other than	besides	overcome	defeat
ought to	have	overdo	exaggerate
out cold	unconscious	overdue	late
out of breath	breathless	overeat	eat
out of control	wild	overemphasize	exaggerate
out of danger	safe	overhaul	repair
out of place	unsuitable	overhear	hear
out of sight	hidden	overindulge	spoil
out of sight	invisible	overlook	forget
out of sorts	poorly	overpower	defeat
out of the blue	suddenly	overpriced	expensive
out of the ordinary	special	overstate	exaggerate
out of the question	impossible	overtake	pass
out of your mind	mad	overturn	turn over
out-and-out	total	overweight	fat
out-of-this-world	fantastic	owing to	because
outback	country	own	have
outcome	effect	own up	admit
outcome	result	own up	confess
outcry	protest		
outdated	old-fashioned		
outdoor	outside		
outer	outside		

Index

Pp

pace	speed
pace	step
pace	walk
pack	fill
pack	jam
pack	squeeze
package	parcel
packed	full
packet	parcel
paddock	field
padlock	fasten
padlock	lock
painful	sore
painstaking	careful
pal	friend

outfit	team
outing	trip
outlaw	forbid
outlaw	prohibit
outline	shape
outlook	view
outraged	angry
outrageous	crazy
outrageous	shocking
outset	start
outsider	stranger
outstanding	best
outstanding	excellent
outstanding	great

pale. . . . . **faint**
paltry. . . . . **small**
pamper . . . . **spoil**
panic. . . . . **fear**
panic. . . . . **fright**
panorama . . . . **view**
parade. . . . . **display**
paraphernalia . . . . **equipment**
paraphernalia . . . . **stuff**
paraphernalia . . . . **things**
parched. . . . . **dry**
parched. . . . . **thirsty**
pardon. . . . . **forgive**
pardon. . . . . **let off**
part . . . . **bit**
part . . . . **separate**
part . . . . **split up**
partially . . . . **partly**
participant . . . . **player**
participate in . . . . **part**
particular. . . . . **fussy**
particularly. . . . . **especially**
party . . . . **bunch**
party . . . . **side**
pass . . . . **give**
pass . . . . **spend**
pass away . . . . **die**
pass out . . . . **collapse**
pass through . . . . **go**
passable . . . . **all right**
passable . . . . **okay** or **OK**
passion . . . . **enthusiasm**
passion . . . . **excitement**
passion . . . . **feeling**
passionate. . . . . **enthusiastic**
passionate. . . . . **mad**
past. . . . . **previous**
past their prime . . . . **old**
paste. . . . . **stick**
pastime . . . . **game**
pastime . . . . **interest**
pasting . . . . **defeat**

pasture . . . . **field**
patch. . . . . **area**
patch. . . . . **mend**
path. . . . . **course**
pathetic. . . . . **hopeless**
pathetic. . . . . **poor**
pause . . . . **break**
pause . . . . **delay**
pause . . . . **hesitate**
pause . . . . **rest**
pause . . . . **stop**
pause . . . . **wait**
pave the way. . . . . **prepare**
paw. . . . . **feel**
pay a visit to . . . . **visit**
pay attention . . . . **concentrate**
pay attention . . . . **watch**
pay back . . . . **repay**
pay for. . . . . **buy**
pay out . . . . **spend**
pay tribute to. . . . . **praise**
peace . . . . **quiet**
peace . . . . **silence**
peaceful . . . . **calm**
peaceful . . . . **quiet**
peace-loving . . . . **gentle**
peak . . . . **mountain**
peak . . . . **top**
peal. . . . . **ring**
peck . . . . **eat**
peculiar. . . . . **funny**
peculiar. . . . . **odd**
peculiar. . . . . **strange**
peddle. . . . . **sell**
peek . . . . **peep**
peel. . . . . **skin**
peep . . . . **look**
peer. . . . . **look**
pelt . . . . **pour**
pelt . . . . **rain**
penalize. . . . . **punish**
penalty . . . . **punishment**

penetrate . . . . **go through**
penetrate . . . . **pierce**
penitentiary . . . . **jail**
penitentiary . . . . **prison**
penniless . . . . **poor**
penny-pinching . . . . **mean**
pensive . . . . **thoughtful**
pepper . . . . **sprinkle**
perceive . . . . **notice**
perceive . . . . **see**
perceptive . . . . **observant**
perceptive . . . . **sharp**
perceptive . . . . **wise**
perch . . . . **sit**
perfectly . . . . **quite**
perforation . . . . **hole**
perform . . . . **do**
perform . . . . **present**
performance . . . . **play**
perhaps . . . . **maybe**
peril . . . . **danger**
perilous . . . . **dangerous**
period . . . . **time**
periodically . . . . **occasionally**
perish . . . . **decay**
perish . . . . **die**
perished . . . . **rotten**
perishing . . . . **freezing**
permit . . . . **let**
perpetual . . . . **endless**
perpetually . . . . **always**
perplex . . . . **muddle**
perplex . . . . **puzzle**
perplexed . . . . **confused**
perplexing . . . . **confusing**
perplexing . . . . **hard**
perseverance . . . . **determination**
persevere . . . . **carry on**
persevere . . . . **continue**
persevere . . . . **get on**
persist . . . . **carry on**
persist . . . . **continue**

persist . . . . **keep**
persist . . . . **remain**
persistent . . . . **determined**
persistent . . . . **stubborn**
personal . . . . **own**
personal . . . . **private**
personality . . . . **character**
personality . . . . **star**
persuade . . . . **tempt**
pester . . . . **nag**
pester . . . . **trouble**
peter out . . . . **die**
peter out . . . . **stop**
petite . . . . **small**
petrified . . . . **afraid**
petrify . . . . **frighten**
petty . . . . **small**
phantom . . . . **ghost**
phase . . . . **step**
phenomenal . . . . **fabulous**
phenomenal . . . . **marvellous**
phenomenal . . . . **wonderful**
phone . . . . **call**
phone . . . . **telephone**
phoney . . . . **fake**
phrasing . . . . **language**
physically fit . . . . **healthy**
physique . . . . **body**
pick . . . . **choose**
pick . . . . **pull**
pick up . . . . **learn**
pickpocket . . . . **thief**
picture . . . . **imagine**
piece . . . . **bit**
pierce . . . . **go through**
pierce . . . . **prick**
piercing . . . . **high**
piercing . . . . **loud**
piercing . . . . **noisy**
piffle . . . . **rubbish**
piggish . . . . **greedy**
pig-headed . . . . **stubborn**

pigsty . . . . **mess**
pile . . . . **heap**
pile-up. . . . . **crash**
pilfer . . . . **pinch**
pilot. . . . . **captain**
pin. . . . . **fasten**
pinch. . . . . **steal**
pine for . . . . **miss**
pioneer . . . . **inventor**
pipe down . . . . **shut up**
piping . . . . **high**
pirouette . . . . **spin**
pit . . . . **hole**
pitch . . . . **ground**
pitch . . . . **put up**
pivot . . . . **turn**
placard . . . . **sign**
place. . . . . **arrange**
place. . . . . **leave**
place. . . . . **put**
placid . . . . **peaceful**
plain . . . . **clear**
plain . . . . **natural**
plain . . . . **obvious**
plainly . . . . **definitely**
plan. . . . . **aim**
plan. . . . . **arrange**
plan. . . . . **mean**
plan. . . . . **organize**
plan. . . . . **plot**
planet . . . . **earth**
planet . . . . **world**
play a part in . . . . **part**
play around . . . . **mess about** or
                              mess around
play the role of . . . . **play**
playing field. . . . . **pitch**
plead. . . . . **ask**
pleasant . . . . **good**
pleasant . . . . **lovely**
pleasant . . . . **nice**
please. . . . . **suit**

pleased . . . . **glad**
pleased . . . . **happy**
pleased . . . . **proud**
pleasing. . . . . **nice**
pleasure . . . . **fun**
pleasure . . . . **happiness**
pleasure . . . . **thrill**
pledge. . . . . **promise**
plight. . . . . **difficulty**
plight. . . . . **situation**
plod. . . . . **walk**
plop. . . . . **drip**
plot . . . . **area**
plot . . . . **plan**
plough into . . . . **crash**
pluck. . . . . **grab**
pluck. . . . . **pick**
pluck. . . . . **pull**
plummet . . . . **dive**
plummet . . . . **drop**
plump . . . . **fat**
plunder . . . . **raid**
plunge. . . . . **dive**
plunge. . . . . **drop**
podgy . . . . **fat**
point of view . . . . **view**
point out . . . . **mention**
point out . . . . **tell**
point . . . . **purpose**
point . . . . **time**
point . . . . **use**
pointed . . . . **sharp**
pointless . . . . **hopeless**
pointless . . . . **useless**
poison. . . . . **pollute**
poke . . . . **stick**
poke fun at . . . . **fun**
poke fun at . . . . **tease**
poke your nose in . . . . **interfere**
polished . . . . **smooth**
polluted. . . . . **dirty**
pompous. . . . . **stuck-up**

Index

ponder	. . . .	**think**
ponder	. . . .	**wonder**
ponderous	. . . .	**slow**
pong	. . . .	**smell**
poorly	. . . .	**ill**
poorly	. . . .	**sick**
population	. . . .	**people**
pore over	. . . .	**read**
portion	. . . .	**part**
portion	. . . .	**share**
portray	. . . .	**paint**
portray	. . . .	**play**
portray	. . . .	**represent**
portray	. . . .	**show**
position	. . . .	**arrange**
position	. . . .	**place**
position	. . . .	**situation**
position	. . . .	**spot**
positive	. . . .	**certain**
positive	. . . .	**definite**
positive	. . . .	**sure**
possess	. . . .	**have**
possessions	. . . .	**belongings**
possessions	. . . .	**property**
possessions	. . . .	**things**
possibility	. . . .	**chance**
possibly	. . . .	**maybe**
possibly	. . . .	**perhaps**
post	. . . .	**send**
poster	. . . .	**notice**
poster	. . . .	**sign**
posterior	. . . .	**bottom**
postpone	. . . .	**call off**
postpone	. . . .	**put off**
postponed	. . . .	**off**
postponement	. . . .	**delay**
posture	. . . .	**position**
potential	. . . .	**power**
pothole	. . . .	**hole**
pounce	. . . .	**dive**
pounce	. . . .	**jump**
pound	. . . .	**beat**
pound	. . . .	**hit**
pound	. . . .	**knock**
pound	. . . .	**thump**
pour	. . . .	**flow**
pour	. . . .	**rain**
pour	. . . .	**run**
pour out	. . . .	**empty**
pouring	. . . .	**heavy**
poverty-stricken	. . . . . .	**poor**
power	. . . .	**control**
power	. . . .	**force**
power	. . . .	**strength**
powerful	. . . .	**important**
powerful	. . . .	**strong**
powerful	. . . .	**violent**
powerless	. . . .	**helpless**
practicable	. . . .	**possible**
practical	. . . .	**handy**
practical	. . . .	**sensible**
practical joke	. . . .	**trick**
practically	. . . .	**almost**
practically	. . . .	**nearly**
practice	. . . .	**experience**
practise	. . . .	**train**
practised	. . . .	**experienced**
prank	. . . .	**trick**
prattle	. . . .	**say**
preceding	. . . .	**previous**
precious	. . . .	**valuable**
precipitous	. . . .	**steep**
precise	. . . .	**accurate**
precise	. . . .	**careful**
precise	. . . .	**exact**
precisely	. . . .	**right**
predicament	. . . .	**mess**
predict	. . . .	**expect**
preferable	. . . .	**better**
preferably	. . . .	**rather**
preference	. . . .	**choice**
preferred	. . . .	**favourite**
prejudiced	. . . .	**unfair**
premonition	. . . .	**warning**

preparation . . . . **practice**
prepare . . . . **arrange**
prepare . . . . **plan**
prepared . . . . **ready**
prepared . . . . **willing**
preposterous . . . . **mad**
preposterous . . . . **ridiculous**
preposterous . . . . **unbelievable**
present . . . . **give**
present . . . . **show**
presentation . . . . **display**
presentation . . . . **show**
presently . . . . **soon**
preserve . . . . **save**
pressure . . . . **stress**
pressure . . . . **weight**
presumably . . . . **probably**
presume . . . . **believe**
presume . . . . **suppose**
pretend . . . . **fake**
pretty . . . . **beautiful**
pretty . . . . **lovely**
prevent . . . . **block**
prevent . . . . **hinder**
prevent . . . . **stop**
previous . . . . **old**
previous . . . . **past**
previously . . . . **before**
price . . . . **cost**
priceless . . . . **precious**
priceless . . . . **valuable**
pricey . . . . **dear**
prick . . . . **pierce**
primitive . . . . **early**
primitive . . . . **old**
principal . . . . **main**
prison . . . . **jail**
private . . . . **own**
private . . . . **personal**
private . . . . **secret**
prize . . . . **reward**
prize . . . . **treasure**

probability . . . . **chance**
probable . . . . **likely**
probe . . . . **investigate**
problem . . . . **fault**
problem . . . . **trouble**
procedure . . . . **drill**
procedure . . . . **method**
procedure . . . . **way**
proceed . . . . **carry on**
proceed . . . . **move**
proclaim . . . . **tell**
prod . . . . **poke**
produce . . . . **cause**
produce . . . . **make**
production . . . . **programme**
production . . . . **show**
profession . . . . **job**
profession . . . . **work**
professional . . . . **expert**
professor . . . . **teacher**
proficiency . . . . **skill**
proficient . . . . **expert**
profile . . . . **description**
profound . . . . **deep**
progress . . . . **move**
prohibit . . . . **ban**
prohibit . . . . **forbid**
project . . . . **stick out**
prolonged . . . . **long**
promising . . . . **hopeful**
promote . . . . **encourage**
prompt . . . . **immediate**
prompt . . . . **instant**
promptly . . . . **immediately**
prong . . . . **point**
pronounce . . . . **say**
prop up . . . . **support**
proper . . . . **right**
proper . . . . **suitable**
property . . . . **belongings**
property . . . . **house**
property . . . . **land**

prophesy	**predict**
proportions	**size**
proposal	**idea**
propose	**aim**
propose	**plan**
propose	**suggest**
prosperous	**rich**
prosperous	**successful**
protect	**defend**
protect	**guard**
protect	**look after**
protect	**shelter**
protection	**defence**
protection	**safety**
protection	**shelter**
protest	**object**
protrude	**stick out**
prove	**show**
proverb	**saying**
provoke	**annoy**
provoke	**make**
prowl	**move**
prudent	**sensible**
prudent	**wise**
prune	**cut**
pry	**interfere**
public	**people**
puff	**pant**
puffed out	**breathless**
puffing and panting	**breathless**
pull the trigger	**fire**
pull through	**recover**
pulpy	**soft**
pummel	**punch**
pun	**joke**
punch	**hit**
punch	**thump**
puncture	**go through**
puncture	**hole**
puncture	**pierce**
puncture	**prick**
purchase	**buy**

purchases	**shopping**
purpose	**aim**
purpose	**point**
purpose	**use**
pursue	**chase**
pursue	**follow**
pursue	**hunt**
pursuit	**interest**
push to	**shut**
put by	**save**
put down	**kill**
put in order	**sort**
put in order	**tidy**
put in	**say**
put into words	**say**
put on show	**display**
put on	**present**
put the case	**argue**
put the wind up	**scare**
put to death	**kill**
put to the test	**try**
put your trust in	**trust**
puzzle	**mystery**
puzzle	**problem**
puzzle	**wonder**
puzzled	**confused**
puzzling	**confusing**
puzzling	**difficult**
puzzling	**funny**
puzzling	**hard**

Qq

quagmire	**bog**
quake	**shiver**
quake	**tremble**
quake	**wobble**
qualify	**pass**
quandary	**jam**
quantity	**amount**
quantity	**number**
quarrel	**argument**

Index

quarrel

quarrel . . . . **fall out**
quarrel . . . . **argue**
quarrel . . . . **row**
quarrelsome . . . . **bad-tempered**
queasy . . . . **sick**
queer . . . . **odd**
query . . . . **doubt**
query . . . . **ask**
query . . . . **question**
quest . . . . **search**
question . . . . **doubt**
question . . . . **ask**
question . . . . **problem**
question . . . . **subject**
questionable . . . . **doubtful**
queue . . . . **jam**
queue . . . . **line**
queue . . . . **row**
quickly . . . . **fast**
quick-witted . . . . **bright**
quick-witted . . . . **quick**
quick-witted . . . . **sharp**
quick-witted . . . . **smart**
quiet . . . . **calm**
quiet . . . . **low**
quiet . . . . **peace**
quiet . . . . **silence**
quiet . . . . **silent**
quieten . . . . **calm down**
quit . . . . **give up**
quit . . . . **leave**
quit . . . . **pull out**
quit . . . . **resign**
quit . . . . **stop**
quite . . . . **fairly**
quite . . . . **rather**
quiver . . . . **shake**
quiver . . . . **shiver**
quiver . . . . **tremble**
quiz . . . . **ask**
quiz . . . . **question**
quota . . . . **share**
quotation . . . . **saying**

Rr

rabble . . . . **crowd**
race . . . . **move**
race . . . . **speed**
race . . . . **tear**
racket . . . . **noise**
racket . . . . **row**
racket . . . . **swindle**
radiance . . . . **light**
radiance . . . . **shine**
rage . . . . **anger**
rage . . . . **temper**
ragged . . . . **scruffy**
raging . . . . **rough**
raging . . . . **stormy**
raging . . . . **violent**
raging . . . . **wild**
raid . . . . **attack**
raid . . . . **invasion**
rain cats and dogs . . . . . **rain**
rainfall . . . . **rain**
raining cats and dogs . . **pour**
raise . . . . **lift**
raise . . . . **put up**
raise the alarm . . . . **warn**
ram . . . . **jam**
ram . . . . **push**
ram . . . . **smash**
ramble . . . . **wander**
rampage . . . . **charge**
rampage . . . . **riot**
rank . . . . **line**
ransack . . . . **search**
rant . . . . **shout**
rap . . . . **knock**
rap . . . . **tap**
rapid . . . . **fast**
rapid . . . . **quick**
rapidity . . . . **speed**
rapidly . . . . **fast**
rapidly . . . . **quickly**

Index

rare	few	reasonable	cheap
rare	scarce	reasonably	fairly
rare	unusual	reasonably	pretty
rarely	seldom	rebellion	mutiny
rascal	rogue	rebellious	disobedient
rasp	scrape	recall	remember
rasping	hoarse	receive the news	hear
rasping	rough	recent	new
rate	price	receptacle	container
rate	speed	reception	party
rather	fairly	reckon	guess
rather	pretty	reckon	think
rather	quite	reckon up	count
ration	share	reclaim	recycle
rational	sensible	recline	lie
rave	shout	recognize	realize
ravenous	hungry	recollect	remember
raw	icy	recommend	advise
raw	sore	recommend	suggest
razor-sharp	sharp	recommendation	advice
reach	go	recompense	pay
reach a decision	decide	recompense	repay
reaction	answer	reconnoitre	explore
ready	willing	record	list
ready to	about to	record	report
real	actual	recount	report
real	true	recount	tell
realistic	sensible	recover	rescue
reality	fact	recover	well
realize	find out	recovered	better
realize	see	recuperate	recover
realize	understand	redo	repeat
really	very	reduce	decrease
reappear	return	reduce speed	slow down
rear	back	reduction	fall
rear end	bottom	reek	smell
reason	argue	reel	stagger
reason	argument	refer to	mention
reason	excuse	reflect	think
reason	explanation	refresh your memory	remind
reason	purpose	refreshing	cool
reason	sense	refreshments	snack

refuge

refuge	**safety**	relaxing	**comfortable**
refuge	**shelter**	release	**free**
refund	**repay**	release	**let out**
refund	**return**	release	**rescue**
refuse	**litter**	released	**free**
refuse	**rubbish**	relentless	**fierce**
refuse	**turn down**	reliable	**responsible**
regarding	**about**	relish	**love**
regardless of	**despite**	relocate	**move**
regardless of	**spite**	rely	**count**
region	**district**	rely on	**depend**
region	**area**	rely on	**expect**
region	**part**	rely on	**trust**
register	**list**	remain	**hang about**
register	**record**	remain	**last**
register	**record**	remain	**stay**
regular	**even**	remain	**wait**
regular	**normal**	remainder	**rest**
regular	**usual**	remains	**body**
regularly	**always**	remark	**say**
regularly	**often**	remarkable	**extraordinary**
rehearsal	**practice**	remarkable	**unusual**
rehearse	**practise**	remarkable	**wonderful**
reign	**rule**	remedy	**cure**
reinforce	**support**	remnants	**waste**
reiterate	**repeat**	remorseful	**sorry**
reject	**refuse**	remote	**far**
reject	**turn down**	remote	**lonely**
relate	**connect**	remove	**pull**
relate	**describe**	remove	**rub out**
relate	**report**	remove	**take**
relate	**tell**	rendezvous	**meeting**
relationship	**connection**	renovate	**mend**
relationship	**link**	renovate	**repair**
relative	**relation**	renowned	**famous**
relatively	**rather**	repair	**fix**
relax	**rest**	repair	**mend**
relaxation	**rest**	repayment	**reward**
relaxed	**calm**	repeatedly	**always**
relaxed	**comfortable**	repeatedly	**often**
relaxed	**cool**	repentant	**guilty**
relaxed	**easy**	repentant	**sorry**

replace . . . . **change**
replace . . . . **fill in**
replace . . . . **swap** or **swop**
replace . . . . **switch**
replenish . . . . **fill**
replica . . . . **copy**
replica . . . . **model**
replicate . . . . **copy**
reply . . . . **answer**
report . . . . **describe**
report . . . . **description**
report . . . . **shot**
report . . . . **tell**
represent . . . . **show**
represent . . . . **stand for**
reprieve . . . . **let off**
reprimand . . . . **tell off**
reprocess . . . . **recycle**
reproduction . . . . **copy**
reproduction . . . . **fake**
repulsive . . . . **foul**
repulsive . . . . **revolting**
repulsive . . . . **ugly**
repulsive . . . . **unpleasant**
request . . . . **ask**
request . . . . **order**
require . . . . **involve**
require . . . . **need**
require . . . . **take**
required . . . . **necessary**
rescue . . . . **save**
research . . . . **investigate**
resent . . . . **envy**
resent . . . . **mind**
resentful . . . . **envious**
resentful . . . . **jealous**
reserve . . . . **save**
reserve . . . . **store**
reserved . . . . **quiet**
reserved . . . . **shy**
reside in . . . . **live**
residence . . . . **home**

residence . . . . **house**
resident . . . . **inhabitant**
resign . . . . **quit**
resign from . . . . **give up**
resilient . . . . **tough**
resistance . . . . **defence**
respectful . . . . **polite**
respond . . . . **answer**
respond . . . . **reply**
response . . . . **answer**
response . . . . **reply**
responsibility . . . . **job**
responsible . . . . **guilty**
responsible . . . . **reliable**
rest . . . . **break**
rest . . . . **put**
rest . . . . **relax**
rest . . . . **sleep**
restful . . . . **comfortable**
restful . . . . **peaceful**
restore . . . . **return**
restrain . . . . **stop**
restricted . . . . **tight**
result . . . . **effect**
result . . . . **score**
result in . . . . **produce**
retail . . . . **sell**
retain . . . . **keep**
retaliation . . . . **revenge**
retell . . . . **repeat**
retiring . . . . **quiet**
retort . . . . **answer**
retort . . . . **reply**
retrace your steps . . . . . **go back**
retreat . . . . **go back**
retreat . . . . **move**
retrieve . . . . **fetch**
retrieve . . . . **get**
retrieve . . . . **rescue**
return . . . . **answer**
return . . . . **go back**
reuse . . . . **recycle**

Index

reveal	**tell**
reveal	**uncover**
revelation	**surprise**
reverse	**back**
reverse	**move**
reverse	**opposite**
revise	**swot**
revisit	**return**
revive	**recover**
revolt	**mutiny**
revolt	**riot**
revolting	**disgusting**
revolting	**foul**
revolting	**unpleasant**
revolution	**mutiny**
revolve	**go round**
revolve	**spin**
revolve	**turn**
rhythmic	**regular**
richness	**luxury**
rickety	**weak**
rickety	**wobbly**
ricochet	**bounce**
riddle	**mystery**
ridicule	**fun**
ridicule	**tease**
ridiculous	**crazy**
ridiculous	**foolish**
ridiculous	**mad**
ridiculous	**silly**
right away	**once**
right away	**immediately**
right	**fair**
rigid	**firm**
rigid	**hard**
rigid	**stiff**
rind	**skin**
ring	**call**
ring	**telephone**
ringleader	**leader**
riotous	**wild**
rip	**tear**
rip off	**cheat**
rip-off	**swindle**
ripple	**flow**
rise	**gain**
rise	**increase**
risk	**danger**
risk	**dare**
risk	**gamble**
risky	**dangerous**
rival	**enemy**
rivet	**fasten**
riveting	**interesting**
roam	**wander**
roar	**shout**
roar of laughter	**laugh**
robber	**burglar**
robber	**thief**
robbery	**theft**
robotic	**automatic**
robust	**powerful**
robust	**strong**
robust	**tough**
rock	**wobble**
rocky	**rough**
role	**job**
role	**part**
roll	**wind**
romantic	**sloppy**
romp	**play**
room	**space**
roomy	**big**
rot	**decay**
rot	**nonsense**
rotate	**go round**
rotate	**spin**
rotate	**turn**
rotten	**bad**
rotund	**fat**
rough	**bumpy**
rough-and-ready	**rough**
roughly	**about**
roughly	**around**

round off . . . . **complete**
rounded . . . . **round**
rouse . . . . **wake**
rout . . . . **defeat**
route . . . . **course**
route . . . . **way**
routine . . . . **habit**
routine . . . . **ordinary**
row . . . . **argument**
row . . . . **argue**
row . . . . **line**
row . . . . **noise**
row . . . . **quarrel**
rowdy . . . . **noisy**
rubbish . . . . **litter**
rubbish . . . . **nonsense**
rubbish . . . . **waste**
rude . . . . **bad-mannered**
rude . . . . **cheeky**
rude . . . . **dirty**
rude . . . . **foul**
rude . . . . **nasty**
rude . . . . **rough**
ruin . . . . **destroy**
ruin . . . . **spoil**
ruin . . . . **wreck**
rule . . . . **lead**
rule . . . . **power**
rummage through . . . . . **search**
run . . . . **manage**
run . . . . **race**
run down . . . . **stop**
run down . . . . **worn out**
run rings round . . . . **beat**
run wild . . . . **charge**
run wild . . . . **riot**
runny . . . . **thin**
rupture . . . . **burst**
rush . . . . **charge**
rush . . . . **hurry**
rush . . . . **nip**
ruthless . . . . **cruel**

Ss

sack . . . . **fire**
sad . . . . **unhappy**
saddened . . . . **upset**
safe . . . . **all right**
safe and sound . . . . . . **safe**
safeguard . . . . **defence**
safeguard . . . . **defend**
safeguard . . . . **protect**
safeguard . . . . **protection**
safeguard . . . . **save**
safeguard . . . . **shelter**
sag . . . . **droop**
sag . . . . **flop**
salary . . . . **pay**
salt away . . . . **save**
salvage . . . . **recycle**
salvage . . . . **rescue**
salvage . . . . **save**
sample . . . . **example**
sample . . . . **taste**
sample . . . . **try**
sanctuary . . . . **shelter**
sands . . . . **beach**
satisfaction . . . . **happiness**
satisfaction . . . . **pleasure**
satisfactory . . . . **all right**
satisfactory . . . . **fine**
satisfactory . . . . **okay or OK**
satisfactory . . . . **suitable**
satisfied . . . . **happy**
satisfied . . . . **pleased**
satisfy . . . . **please**
satisfy . . . . **suit**
satisfying . . . . **nice**
saturate . . . . **wet**
saturated . . . . **wet**
saunter . . . . **walk**
savage . . . . **fierce**
savage . . . . **vicious**
savagery . . . . **violence**

Index

save

save . . . . **rescue**
say . . . . **speak**
scale . . . . **climb**
scam . . . . **swindle**
scan . . . . **look**
scan . . . . **read**
scarce . . . . **rare**
scarce . . . . **short**
scarcely . . . . **hardly**
scarcity . . . . **shortage**
scare . . . . **frighten**
scared . . . . **afraid**
scatter . . . . **sprinkle**
scene . . . . **view**
scenic . . . . **nice**
scent . . . . **smell**
sceptical . . . . **doubtful**
sceptical . . . . **suspicious**
scheme . . . . **plan**
scheme . . . . **plot**
scheme . . . . **project**
scholarship . . . . **knowledge**
schoolboy . . . . **pupil**
schoolgirl . . . . **pupil**
schoolteacher . . . . **teacher**
scoff . . . . **eat**
scold . . . . **tell off**
scoop out . . . . **dig**
scorch . . . . **burn**
scoundrel . . . . **rogue**
scour . . . . **hunt**
scour . . . . **search**
scout . . . . **explore**
scrap . . . . **bit**
scrap . . . . **cancel**
scrap . . . . **fight**
scrap . . . . **junk**
scrap . . . . **rubbish**
scrap . . . . **waste**
scratch . . . . **scrape**
screw . . . . **fasten**
scrounge . . . . **ask**

scruffy . . . . **untidy**
scrumptious . . . . **delicious**
scrumptious . . . . **nice**
scrumptious . . . . **tasty**
scrumptious . . . . **yummy**
scrutinize . . . . **examine**
scrutinize . . . . **look**
scuffle . . . . **fight**
scurry . . . . **hurry**
scurry . . . . **rush**
seal . . . . **close**
seal . . . . **plug**
seal . . . . **shut**
seam . . . . **layer**
search . . . . **explore**
search . . . . **hunt**
search . . . . **look**
seashore . . . . **beach**
seaside . . . . **beach**
season . . . . **time**
secluded . . . . **lonely**
second . . . . **moment**
secret . . . . **private**
secrete . . . . **bury**
secrete . . . . **hide**
secreted . . . . **hidden**
section . . . . **part**
secure . . . . **close**
secure . . . . **fasten**
secure . . . . **firm**
secure . . . . **fix**
secure . . . . **lock**
secure . . . . **steady**
secure . . . . **tie**
secure . . . . **tight**
security . . . . **protection**
security . . . . **safety**
see to . . . . **deal with**
see-through . . . . **clear**
seek . . . . **look**
seep . . . . **trickle**
seething . . . . **angry**

segment	**part**
segregate	**divide**
seize	**grab**
seize	**invade**
seize	**kidnap**
seize up	**break down**
select	**choose**
select	**pick**
selection	**choice**
selection	**range**
self-centred	**selfish**
self-conscious	**shy**
self-propelling	**automatic**
selfish	**greedy**
send	**pass**
sensational	**amazing**
sensational	**fantastic**
sensational	**incredible**
sensational	**tremendous**
sensational	**wonderful**
sense	**feel**
sense	**meaning**
senseless	**idiotic**
sensible	**careful**
sensible	**responsible**
sensible	**wise**
sentence	**punish**
sentence	**punishment**
sentry	**guard**
separate	**divide**
separate	**single**
separate	**split up**
separated	**split**
separately	**alone**
sequence	**series**
serene	**peaceful**
serene	**quiet**
series	**list**
series	**row**
serious	**bad**
serious	**big**
serious	**immediate**

service	**repair**
set	**class**
set	**group**
set	**harden**
set ablaze	**fire**
set about	**begin**
set free	**free**
set light to	**light**
set off	**go**
set your sights on	**aim**
setback	**delay**
setting	**situation**
settle	**arrange**
settle	**pay**
settle	**sit**
settle	**stay**
settle up	**repay**
severe	**serious**
severe	**strict**
sewage	**waste**
shabby	**ragged**
shabby	**scruffy**
shabby	**tatty**
shack	**hut**
shadow	**follow**
shadowy	**dark**
shadowy	**dim**
shady	**crooked**
shady	**suspicious**
shaft	**hole**
shaft	**ray**
shake	**shiver**
shake	**wave**
shambles	**mess**
shame	**disgrace**
shape	**condition**
share	**piece**
sharp	**prickly**
sharp	**quick**
sharp	**smart**
sharp	**sour**
sharply	**hard**

shatter	**break**		shore	**beach**
shatter	**smash**		short-lived	**short**
shattered	**worn out**		short-term	**short**
shave	**cut**		shortfall	**shortage**
shed	**hut**		shortly	**soon**
shed tears	**cry**		shot	**go**
sheen	**shine**		shot	**try**
sheer	**complete**		should	**have**
sheer	**steep**		shoulder-to-shoulder	**together**
sheer	**total**		shout	**cry**
sheet	**layer**		shout	**say**
shelter	**protect**		shout	**yell**
shelter	**safety**		shove	**push**
shield	**guard**		show	**play**
shield	**protect**		show	**programme**
shield	**protection**		show	**prove**
shield	**shelter**		show off	**boast**
shift	**move**		show someone the door	**fire**
shimmer	**glitter**		show up	**arrive**
shimmer	**shine**		show up	**come**
shimmering	**bright**		show up	**turn up**
shining	**bright**		shower	**spray**
ship	**boat**		shower	**sprinkle**
shipshape	**neat**		shred	**tear**
shipshape	**tidy**		shrewd	**wise**
shirk	**away**		shriek	**cry**
shiver	**shake**		shriek	**scream**
shiver	**tremble**		shriek of laughter	**laugh**
shock	**scare**		shrill	**high**
shock	**surprise**		shrivel	**burn**
shocked	**dazed**		shrivel	**shrink**
shocking	**awful**		shudder	**shake**
shocking	**dreadful**		shudder	**shiver**
shocking	**terrible**		shuffle	**jumble**
shoddy	**bad**		shuffle	**limp**
shoddy	**poor**		shun	**avoid**
shoot	**fire**		shut	**close**
shoot	**move**		shy	**quiet**
shoot	**tear**		sick	**ill**
shoot	**zoom**		sickening	**disgusting**
shoplifter	**thief**		sickening	**nasty**
shoplifting	**theft**		sickness	**disease**

Index

sickness	illness
side	team
side by side	together
side with	stick up for
sidestep	dodge
siesta	sleep
sigh	groan
sigh	moan
sight	see
sign	signal
sign up for	join
signal	wave
significance	meaning
significant	big
significant	immediate
significant	serious
signify	mean
silence	peace
silence	quiet
silent	quiet
silhouette	shape
silky	smooth
silky	soft
silly	foolish
silly	stupid
similar	alike
similar	same
similar to	like
simple	easy
simple	plain
simply	easily
simply	only
simulate	fake
simultaneously	once
simultaneously	together
since	because
sincere	genuine
sincere	honest
sincere	serious
singe	burn
single	only
single out	choose
single-minded	determined
sinister	creepy
sip	drink
sip	taste
site	place
site	position
site	situation
site	spot
situation	circumstances
situation	matter
situation	position
sizable	big
size	area
size	measurement
skate	move
skate	slip
sketch	draw
sketch	picture
skid	slide
skid	slip
skilful	capable
skilful	experienced
skilful	good
skilful	neat
skill	ability
skilled	expert
skim	slide
skim through	read
skinny	thin
skipper	captain
skirmish	fight
slab	lump
slack	lazy
slack	loose
slant	tilt
slap	hit
slap	smack
slapdash	careless
slapdash	sloppy
slash	cut
slaughter	kill
slaughter	murder

slave . . . . **work**
slay . . . . **kill**
slay . . . . **murder**
sleek . . . . **shiny**
sleek . . . . **smooth**
sleepy . . . . **tired**
slender . . . . **narrow**
slender . . . . **slim**
slender . . . . **thin**
slide . . . . **slip**
slight . . . . **small**
slightly . . . . **rather**
slim . . . . **narrow**
slim . . . . **thin**
slime . . . . **mud**
sling . . . . **throw**
slink . . . . **creep**
slink . . . . **move**
slink . . . . **sneak**
slip . . . . **mistake**
slip . . . . **slide**
slip . . . . **sneak**
slipshod . . . . **careless**
slipshod . . . . **sloppy**
slipshod . . . . **untidy**
slit . . . . **cut**
slither . . . . **slide**
slither . . . . **slip**
slog away . . . . **work**
slope . . . . **tilt**
sloppy . . . . **careless**
sloppy . . . . **loose**
slovenly . . . . **untidy**
slow . . . . **dumb**
slow down . . . . **delay**
slowly . . . . **gradually**
sludge . . . . **mud**
sluggish . . . . **slow**
slumber . . . . **sleep**
slump . . . . **flop**
slushy . . . . **sloppy**
sly . . . . **crafty**

sly . . . . **sneaky**
smack . . . . **hit**
small . . . . **short**
small . . . . **slight**
smallest . . . . **minimum**
smart . . . . **ache**
smart . . . . **brainy**
smart . . . . **bright**
smart . . . . **clever**
smart . . . . **neat**
smart . . . . **quick**
smash . . . . **break**
smash . . . . **crash**
smear . . . . **mark**
smear . . . . **spread**
smirk . . . . **smile**
smooth . . . . **even**
smooth . . . . **flat**
smooth . . . . **level**
smoulder . . . . **burn**
smudge . . . . **mark**
smudge . . . . **spot**
snack bar . . . . **café**
snag . . . . **catch**
snag . . . . **difficulty**
snag . . . . **disadvantage**
snag . . . . **problem**
snake . . . . **wind**
snap . . . . **break**
snap . . . . **say**
snappy . . . . **cross**
snarl . . . . **say**
snatch a glimpse . . . . . . **peep**
snatch . . . . **grab**
snatch . . . . **kidnap**
snatch . . . . **pinch**
sneak . . . . **creep**
sneak . . . . **slip**
sneak a look . . . . **peep**
sniff . . . . **smell**
snigger . . . . **laugh**
snip . . . . **cut**

Index

snivel. . . . . **cry**
snobbish . . . . **stuck-up**
snoop . . . . **investigate**
snooty. . . . . **stuck-up**
snooze . . . . **rest**
snooze . . . . **sleep**
snuff out . . . . **put out**
snug . . . . **cosy**
snug . . . . **tight**
so long . . . . **grab**
soak . . . . **wet**
soaked . . . . **wet**
soar. . . . . **fly**
soar. . . . . **move**
soaring . . . . **high**
soaring . . . . **tall**
sob . . . . **cry**
society . . . . **club**
soft . . . . **low**
soggy . . . . **wet**
soil . . . . **earth**
soil . . . . **ground**
soiled . . . . **dirty**
solder . . . . **fasten**
sole. . . . . **only**
sole. . . . . **single**
solemn . . . . **serious**
solid . . . . **firm**
solid . . . . **hard**
solid . . . . **stiff**
solidify. . . . . **harden**
solidify. . . . . **set**
solitary . . . . **alone**
solitary . . . . **lonely**
solitary . . . . **only**
solitary . . . . **single**
solo. . . . . **alone**
solution . . . . **liquid**
solve . . . . **do**
solve . . . . **sort out**
solve . . . . **work out**
somewhat . . . . **fairly**

somewhat . . . . **partly**
somewhat . . . . **pretty**
somewhat . . . . **quite**
somewhat . . . . **rather**
sooner. . . . . **rather**
sooner than . . . . **before**
soothe. . . . . **calm down**
soothing . . . . **soft**
sorcery . . . . **magic**
sore. . . . . **painful**
soreness . . . . **pain**
sorrow. . . . . **sadness**
sorry . . . . **ashamed**
sorry . . . . **guilty**
sort . . . . **class**
sort . . . . **organize**
sort . . . . **type**
sort out . . . . **deal with**
sort out . . . . **see**
soul. . . . . **person**
sound asleep. . . . . **asleep**
soundless . . . . **quiet**
soundless . . . . **silent**
sour. . . . . **bitter**
source . . . . **cause**
sovereign. . . . . **king**
space . . . . **gap**
space . . . . **room**
spacious . . . . **big**
span . . . . **length**
spank . . . . **smack**
sparkle . . . . **shine**
sparkling . . . . **brilliant**
sparkling . . . . **fizzy**
speak . . . . **talk**
speak up for . . . . **defend**
specialist. . . . . **expert**
species . . . . **kind**
specific . . . . **exact**
specifically . . . . **especially**
specimen. . . . . **example**
speck . . . . **spot**

Index

spectacular

spectacular . . . . **great**
spectators . . . . **crowd**
spectre . . . . **ghost**
speech . . . . **talk**
speechless . . . . **silent**
speed . . . . **move**
speed . . . . **race**
speed . . . . **rush**
speed . . . . **tear**
speedily . . . . **fast**
speedily . . . . **quickly**
speedy . . . . **fast**
speedy . . . . **quick**
speedy . . . . **rapid**
spell . . . . **time**
spellbinding . . . . **interesting**
spherical . . . . **round**
spick-and-span . . . . . . **neat**
spick-and-span . . . . . . **tidy**
spike . . . . **point**
spiky . . . . **prickly**
spin . . . . **turn**
spine-chilling . . . . **scary**
spine-chilling . . . . **spooky**
spiny . . . . **prickly**
spiral . . . . **curl**
spirit . . . . **ghost**
spirit . . . . **life**
spit . . . . **rain**
spiteful . . . . **mean**
spiteful . . . . **nasty**
spiteful . . . . **unkind**
spiteful . . . . **vicious**
splash . . . . **drip**
splash . . . . **spray**
splash . . . . **sprinkle**
splash out . . . . **spend**
splendid . . . . **good**
splendid . . . . **magnificent**
splendidly . . . . **well**
splendour . . . . **beauty**
splendour . . . . **luxury**

splinter . . . . **break**
splinter . . . . **split**
split . . . . **burst**
split . . . . **divide**
split . . . . **hole**
split . . . . **rip**
split . . . . **separate**
split . . . . **share**
split . . . . **tear**
split second . . . . **moment**
split your sides . . . . **laugh**
spoil . . . . **damage**
spoil . . . . **mess up**
spoil . . . . **ruin**
spongy . . . . **soft**
spooky . . . . **creepy**
sport . . . . **game**
sports field . . . . **pitch**
spot . . . . **mark**
spot . . . . **notice**
spot . . . . **place**
spot . . . . **see**
spot-on . . . . **accurate**
spotless . . . . **clean**
sprain . . . . **twist**
sprawl . . . . **lie**
spray . . . . **sprinkle**
spread . . . . **grow**
sprightly . . . . **lively**
spring . . . . **jump**
sprinkle . . . . **spray**
sprint . . . . **run**
sprout . . . . **grow**
spruce up . . . . **tidy**
spurt . . . . **squirt**
spy . . . . **traitor**
squabble . . . . **argue**
squabble . . . . **argument**
squabble . . . . **fall out**
squabble . . . . **quarrel**
squabble . . . . **row**
squad . . . . **party**

Index

squad	team
squall	wind
squally	stormy
squally	windy
squander	waste
squash	press
squash	squeeze
squashy	soft
squat	crouch
squat	short
squeal	scream
squeeze	hug
squeeze	pinch
squeeze	press
squirm	fidget
squirm	wriggle
squirt	spray
stab	go
stab	pierce
stab	prick
stab	stick
stable	firm
stable	steady
stack	heap
stack	pile
stacks	lot
stadium	ground
stage	present
stage	step
stage	time
stagger	surprise
staggering	amazing
stained	dirty
stalk	follow
stalk	hunt
stamina	energy
stamina	strength
stammer	say
stance	position
stand	endure
stand	place
stand	put
stand	put up with
stand by	support
stand for	represent
stand in	fill in
stand up for	stick up for
standard	common
standard	level
standard	ordinary
standard	typical
staple	fasten
stare	look
stare at	watch
starlit	clear
start	begin
startle	scare
startle	surprise
starving	hungry
stash	store
state	condition
state	country
state	report
state	say
state of affairs	situation
state-of-the-art	model
statement	report
station	place
stationary	still
staunch	faithful
stay	wait
stay behind	remain
stay put	remain
steady	even
steady	regular
steal	move
steal	pinch
steal	slip
steal	sneak
steam	boil
steer	guide
steer	lead
steer clear of	avoid
stench	smell

Index

step by step

step by step . . . . **gradually**
step down . . . . **quit**
step down . . . . **resign**
step on it . . . . **hurry**
stern . . . . **serious**
stern . . . . **strict**
stick up for . . . . **defend**
stick up for . . . . **support**
stick your neck out . . . . **gamble**
stiff . . . . **hard**
stiffen . . . . **harden**
still . . . . **calm**
still . . . . **silent**
stillness . . . . **peace**
stillness . . . . **quiet**
stillness . . . . **silence**
stingy . . . . **mean**
stink . . . . **smell**
stinking . . . . **smelly**
stir . . . . **move**
stir . . . . **wake**
stirring . . . . **exciting**
stock . . . . **keep**
stock . . . . **store**
stockpile . . . . **store**
stony . . . . **rough**
stoop . . . . **bend**
stoop . . . . **crouch**
stoop . . . . **duck**
stop by . . . . **visit**
stop up . . . . **plug**
store . . . . **keep**
storm . . . . **attack**
storm . . . . **charge**
stormy . . . . **rough**
story line . . . . **plot**
stout . . . . **fat**
stow away . . . . **hide**
straggle . . . . **lag**
straight away . . . . **immediately**
straight away . . . . **now**
straightforward . . . . **simple**

strain . . . . **stress**
strange . . . . **crazy**
strange . . . . **unusual**
strategy . . . . **plan**
stream . . . . **class**
stream . . . . **flow**
stream . . . . **pour**
stream . . . . **ray**
stream . . . . **run**
strength . . . . **force**
strength . . . . **power**
strengthen . . . . **support**
strenuous . . . . **difficult**
strenuous . . . . **hard**
stress . . . . **emphasize**
stretch . . . . **area**
stretch . . . . **time**
stretch to . . . . **reach**
stride . . . . **step**
stride . . . . **walk**
strike . . . . **attack**
strike . . . . **beat**
strike . . . . **bump**
strike . . . . **punch**
strike . . . . **tap**
string . . . . **series**
strive . . . . **try**
stroke . . . . **feel**
stroke of bad luck . . . . . **luck**
stroke of luck . . . . **chance**
stroke of luck . . . . **luck**
stroll . . . . **walk**
stroll . . . . **wander**
strong . . . . **deep**
strong . . . . **fierce**
strong . . . . **powerful**
stronghold . . . . **castle**
structure . . . . **building**
struggle . . . . **fight**
struggle . . . . **battle**
stubborn . . . . **awkward**
student . . . . **pupil**

Index

study	**examination**
study	**examine**
study	**look**
study	**read**
study	**swot**
stuff	**belongings**
stuff	**fill**
stuff	**jam**
stuff	**squeeze**
stuff	**things**
stumble upon	**find**
stumble	**trip**
stun	**surprise**
stunned	**dazed**
stunned	**unconscious**
stunning	**beautiful**
stunning	**nice**
sturdy	**powerful**
sturdy	**strong**
sturdy	**tough**
stutter	**say**
style	**fashion**
style	**language**
stylish	**smart**
subdued	**faint**
subdued	**low**
subdued	**soft**
subject	**matter**
submerge	**flood**
submit	**give in**
subsequent	**future**
subsequent	**next**
subsequently	**after**
subsequently	**next**
substitute	**change**
substitute	**fill in**
substitute	**replace**
substitute	**swap** or **swop**
substitute	**switch**
subtract	**take**
succeed	**pass**
succeed	**replace**
succeed	**win**
succeed in	**manage**
success	**win**
successfully	**well**
succession	**series**
succinct	**short**
suds	**bubbles**
suffer	**endure**
suffer	**receive**
suffer	**stand**
suffer defeat	**lose**
sufficient	**enough**
sufficiently	**enough**
suggest	**advise**
suggest	**idea**
suggestion	**advice**
suggestion	**idea**
suit	**fit**
suitable	**convenient**
suitable	**fine**
suitable	**fit**
suitable	**proper**
suitable	**right**
sulky	**bad-tempered**
sulky	**grumpy**
sulky	**moody**
sullen	**bad-tempered**
sullen	**moody**
sum	**amount**
summery	**sunny**
summit	**top**
summon	**ask**
sundown	**sunset**
sunlit	**sunny**
sunrise	**dawn**
sunset	**evening**
superb	**excellent**
superb	**fabulous**
superb	**fantastic**
superb	**great**
superb	**terrific**
superbly	**well**

Index

superfluous	**unnecessary**
superior	**better**
supervise	**lead**
supervisor	**boss**
supple	**soft**
supplementary	**extra**
supply	**give**
supply	**give out**
supply	**provide**
supply	**store**
support	**defend**
support	**encourage**
support	**hold**
supporter	**fan**
supportive	**helpful**
suppose	**believe**
suppose	**guess**
supreme	**best**
sure	**certain**
sure	**definite**
surface	**outside**
surge	**flow**
surge	**stream**
surpass	**pass**
surplus	**spare**
surprising	**extraordinary**
surrender	**give in**
surrender	**give up**
surround	**wrap**
surrounded by	**among** or **amongst**
survey	**examination**
survey	**explore**
survey	**look**
survey	**measure**
survive	**cope**
survive	**last**
survive	**live**
survive	**remain**
surviving	**living**
suspect	**doubt**
suspect	**feel**
suspect	**guess**
suspicion	**doubt**
suspicion	**feeling**
suspicion	**idea**
suspicious	**doubtful**
sustain	**receive**
swagger	**show off**
swamp	**flood**
swamp	**bog**
swanky	**posh**
swap	**change**
swap	**switch**
swarm	**crowd**
sway	**rock**
sway	**wobble**
swear at	**abuse**
swear words	**abuse**
sweat	**work**
sweep	**flow**
swell	**grow**
swelling	**bump**
swelling	**lump**
swerve round	**dodge**
swift	**fast**
swift	**quick**
swift	**rapid**
swiftly	**fast**
swiftly	**quickly**
swiftness	**speed**
swig	**drink**
swindle	**cheat**
swindle	**fiddle**
swindle	**rob**
swindler	**cheat**
swing	**hang**
swing	**rock**
swipe	**pinch**
swipe	**steal**
switch	**swap** or **swop**
swivel	**turn**
swoop	**dive**
swoop	**move**

symbol . . . . **sign**
symbolize . . . . **represent**
symbolize . . . . **stand for**
sympathetic. . . . . **kind**
sympathetic. . . . . **sorry**
sympathize with. . . . . . **pity**
sympathy . . . . **kindness**
sympathy . . . . **pity**

Tt

tablet. . . . . **pill**
tackle . . . . **do**
tackle . . . . **equipment**
tacky. . . . . **sticky**
tactful . . . . **careful**
tail. . . . . **follow**
tailback . . . . **jam**
take a breather . . . . **rest**
take a chance . . . . **gamble**
take a look around. . . . . **explore**
take a nap. . . . . **sleep**
take captive. . . . . **capture**
take care of . . . . **deal with**
take care of . . . . **mind**
take cover . . . . **hide**
take in . . . . **fool**
take in . . . . **understand**
take it easy . . . . **relax**
take on . . . . **play**
take over from . . . . **replace**
take place . . . . **come about**
take place . . . . **go on**
take place . . . . **happen**
take someone into
  custody. . . . . **arrest**
take someone's life . . . . **kill**
take the place of . . . . . . **replace**
taken aback. . . . . **surprised**
talc . . . . **story**
talent. . . . . **ability**
talent. . . . . **skill**

talented . . . . **brilliant**
talk . . . . **speak**
talk someone into . . . . . **persuade**
tall. . . . . **high**
tally . . . . **score**
tamper. . . . . **interfere**
tamper. . . . . **mess**
tangle . . . . **jumble**
tangle . . . . **muddle**
tantrum . . . . **rage**
tantrum . . . . **temper**
tap . . . . **knock**
tape. . . . . **stick**
target. . . . . **aim**
tart . . . . **bitter**
tart . . . . **sour**
task. . . . . **job**
task. . . . . **project**
task. . . . . **work**
taste . . . . **drop**
taste . . . . **eat**
tasty . . . . **delicious**
tasty . . . . **yummy**
tattered . . . . **ragged**
tattered . . . . **scruffy**
tatty. . . . . **scruffy**
taunt . . . . **tease**
taut . . . . **stiff**
taut . . . . **tight**
teach. . . . . **show**
team . . . . **party**
team . . . . **side**
tear . . . . **hole**
tear . . . . **race**
tear . . . . **rip**
tear . . . . **run**
tear . . . . **speed**
tear . . . . **split**
tearful . . . . **sad**
tearful . . . . **upset**
tease . . . . **fun**
tease . . . . **joke**

Index

tease

tease	**pick**
teashop	**café**
technique	**method**
technique	**skill**
technique	**way**
tedious	**boring**
tedious	**dull**
teem	**rain**
teeter	**wobble**
telephone	**call**
temper	**anger**
temper	**mood**
temperament	**character**
temperamental	**moody**
tempestuous	**stormy**
temporary	**short**
tenant	**inhabitant**
tend	**care for**
tend	**guard**
tend	**look after**
tender	**fond**
tender	**painful**
tender	**gentle**
tender	**sore**
tepid	**warm**
term	**length**
term	**name**
term	**time**
term	**word**
terminate	**end**
termination	**finish**
terrible	**awful**
terrible	**bad**
terrible	**dreadful**
terrible	**horrible**
terribly	**very**
terrific	**marvellous**
terrific	**tremendous**
terrific	**wonderful**
terrifically	**very**
terrified	**afraid**
terrify	**frighten**
terrify	**scare**
terrifying	**frightening**
terrifying	**scary**
terror	**fright**
terror	**fear**
terror	**horror**
terror	**panic**
terrorism	**violence**
terrorize	**frighten**
terrorize	**bully**
test	**check**
test	**examination**
test	**try**
textiles	**cloth**
thankful	**grateful**
thanks to	**because**
thaw	**melt**
the good old days	**past**
the human race	**man**
the latest	**model**
the majority of	**most**
theft	**robbery**
these days	**now**
thief	**burglar**
thin	**narrow**
think up	**plan**
this minute	**once**
thorny	**prickly**
thorough	**careful**
thorough	**complete**
thorough	**good**
thorough	**total**
thoroughly	**absolutely**
though	**although**
thoughtful	**good**
thoughtful	**kind**
thrash	**beat**
threadbare	**ragged**
threadbare	**tatty**
threat	**danger**
threaten	**bully**
thrill	**excitement**

thrilled	excited	tired	sleepy
thrilled	pleased	tired of	sick of
thrilling	exciting	tired out	worn out
throaty	hoarse	tiring	hard
throb	ache	title	name
throbbing	painful	titter	laugh
throw	put off	to a certain extent	rather
throw a tantrum	temper	to blame	guilty
throw a wobbly	temper	to blame	responsible
throw away	dump	to blame	wrong
throw away	waste	to some extent	partly
thrust	push	toddler	baby
thrust	stick	toil	work
thud	bang	tolerate	put up with
thud	bump	tolerate	stand
thump	bump	toll	ring
thump	hit	tongue	language
thump	punch	tongue-tied	silent
thunder	roar	too	also
thunderous	noisy	tools	equipment
thunderstruck	surprised	tools	kit
thwart	block	top-secret	secret
thwart	prevent	top-up	fill
tide	flow	topic	matter
tidy	neat	topic	subject
tie	fasten	topple	fall
tied	even	topsy-turvy	upside down
tight fisted	mean	torment	pick on
tight spot	jam	torment	tease
time after time	always	tornado	wind
time after time	often	torrent	flood
timid	afraid	torrent	stream
timid	shy	torrential	heavy
tinker	mess	toss	throw
tiny	little	tot	baby
tiny	minute	tot up	add
tip	advice	tot up	count
tip	point	total	add
tip	tilt	total	amount
tiptoe	creep	total	make
tiptoe	slip	total	pure
tiptoe	sneak	total	score

Index

431

totally

totally . . . . **completely**	tranquil . . . . **quiet**
totally . . . . **absolutely**	tranquillity . . . . **peace**
totally . . . . **quite**	tranquillity . . . . **quiet**
totter . . . . **stagger**	transfer . . . . **move**
totter . . . . **wobble**	transfer . . . . **pass**
touch . . . . **feel**	transform . . . . **change**
touch . . . . **reach**	transformation . . . . **change**
touch down . . . . **land**	translucent . . . . **clear**
tough . . . . **hard**	transmit . . . . **pass**
tough . . . . **rough**	transparent . . . . **clear**
tough . . . . **strong**	transport . . . . **bring**
tournament . . . . **competition**	transport . . . . **carry**
tournament . . . . **contest**	transport . . . . **fetch**
towering . . . . **high**	transport . . . . **move**
towering . . . . **tall**	transport . . . . **take**
toxic . . . . **poisonous**	trap . . . . **catch**
trace . . . . **draw**	trash . . . . **rubbish**
track . . . . **chase**	trash . . . . **waste**
track . . . . **course**	travel . . . . **go**
track . . . . **follow**	treacherous . . . . **dangerous**
track down . . . . **find**	treasured . . . . **dear**
trade . . . . **change**	treasured . . . . **precious**
trade . . . . **business**	treasured . . . . **valuable**
trade . . . . **job**	treat . . . . **luxury**
trade . . . . **swap** or **swop**	treatment . . . . **cure**
trade . . . . **work**	treeless . . . . **bare**
trade in . . . . **sell**	trek . . . . **expedition**
traditional . . . . **old**	trek . . . . **journey**
traditional . . . . **old-fashioned**	trek . . . . **walk**
traditionally . . . . **usually**	tremble . . . . **shake**
tragedy . . . . **disaster**	tremble . . . . **shiver**
trail . . . . **lag**	trend . . . . **fashion**
train . . . . **exercise**	trendy . . . . **popular**
train . . . . **practise**	tribute . . . . **praise**
train . . . . **teach**	trick . . . . **cheat**
training . . . . **exercise**	trick . . . . **fool**
training . . . . **practice**	trickle . . . . **drip**
trajectory . . . . **course**	trickle . . . . **run**
tramp . . . . **walk**	tricky . . . . **awkward**
trample . . . . **squash**	tricky . . . . **difficult**
tranquil . . . . **calm**	trifling . . . . **small**
tranquil . . . . **peaceful**	trim . . . . **cut**

Index

trim . . . . **decorate**
trim . . . . **slim**
trip . . . . **outing**
trip . . . . **ride**
triumph . . . . **win**
triumphant . . . . **successful**
trivial . . . . **slight**
troop . . . . **walk**
trophy . . . . **prize**
trot . . . . **run**
trouble . . . . **bother**
trouble . . . . **disturb**
trouble . . . . **upset**
trouble . . . . **worry**
troubled . . . . **worried**
troublesome . . . . **awkward**
troublesome . . . . **difficult**
troublesome . . . . **naughty**
trouncing . . . . **defeat**
trudge . . . . **walk**
true . . . . **accurate**
true . . . . **actual**
true . . . . **exact**
true . . . . **genuine**
true . . . . **real**
true . . . . **right**
truly . . . . **really**
truly . . . . **very**
truncheon . . . . **club**
trundle . . . . **move**
trust . . . . **believe**
trust . . . . **count**
trust . . . . **depend**
trust . . . . **hope**
trust . . . . **rely**
trusting . . . . **gullible**
trustworthy . . . . **honest**
trustworthy . . . . **reliable**
trustworthy . . . . **responsible**
truth . . . . **fact**
truthful . . . . **honest**
try . . . . **go**

try . . . . **shot**
trying . . . . **difficult**
tug . . . . **pull**
tumble . . . . **fall**
tune . . . . **adjust**
turbulent . . . . **rough**
turbulent . . . . **stormy**
turn . . . . **get**
turn . . . . **go**
turn . . . . **wind**
turn down . . . . **refuse**
turn loose . . . . **free**
turn up . . . . **arrive**
turn up . . . . **come**
turncoat . . . . **traitor**
tussle . . . . **fight**
tutor . . . . **teacher**
tutor group . . . . **class**
twaddle . . . . **nonsense**
twaddle . . . . **rubbish**
tweak . . . . **adjust**
tweak . . . . **pinch**
twiddle . . . . **fiddle**
twilight . . . . **evening**
twilight . . . . **sunset**
twinge . . . . **pain**
twinkling . . . . **bright**
twinkling of an eye . . . . . **second**
twirl . . . . **turn**
twist . . . . **curl**
twist . . . . **bend**
twist . . . . **spin**
twist . . . . **tangle**
twist . . . . **turn**
twist . . . . **wind**
twist . . . . **wriggle**
twit . . . . **idiot**
twitch . . . . **fidget**
twosome . . . . **pair**
type . . . . **class**
type . . . . **kind**
type . . . . **sort**

Index

typhoon . . . . **wind**
typical . . . . **normal**

Uu

umpteen . . . . **many**
unaltered . . . . **same**
unattractive . . . . **ugly**
unavoidable . . . . **certain**
unbalanced . . . . **wobbly**
unbelievable . . . . **incredible**
unbiased . . . . **fair**
unbroken . . . . **continuous**
unbutton . . . . **undo**
uncalled-for . . . . **unnecessary**
uncertain . . . . **doubtful**
uncertainty . . . . **doubt**
unchanging . . . . **same**
uncomfortable . . . . **awkward**
uncommon . . . . **rare**
uncomplicated . . . . **simple**
uncontaminated . . . . . . **safe**
uncontrollable . . . . **wild**
unconventional . . . . **odd**
uncooked . . . . **raw**
uncooperative . . . . **difficult**
uncooperative . . . . **awkward**
uncoordinated . . . . **clumsy**
uncultivated . . . . **wild**
undecided . . . . **uncertain**
under no circumstances **nervous**
under . . . . **below**
under the weather . . . . . **poorly**
under the weather . . . . . **sick**
undergo . . . . **endure**
undergo . . . . **have**
undergo . . . . **receive**
underneath . . . . **below**
underneath . . . . **under**
undernourished . . . . . . **thin**
undersized . . . . **small**
understand . . . . **follow**

understand . . . . **get**
understand . . . . **know**
understand . . . . **learn**
understand . . . . **realize**
understand . . . . **see**
understandable . . . . . . **simple**
understanding . . . . **experience**
understanding . . . . **kind**
understanding . . . . **kindness**
understanding . . . . **knowledge**
undisturbed . . . . **peaceful**
undo . . . . **release**
undomesticated . . . . . . **wild**
undoubtedly . . . . **certainly**
undoubtedly . . . . **course**
undressed . . . . **bare**
unearth . . . . **find**
uneasy . . . . **uncomfortable**
uneasy . . . . **worried**
uneven . . . . **bumpy**
uneven . . . . **rough**
unexpected . . . . **accidental**
unexpected . . . . **sudden**
unfamiliar . . . . **unknown**
unfashionable . . . . **old-fashioned**
unfasten . . . . **open**
unfasten . . . . **release**
unfasten . . . . **undo**
unflappable . . . . **calm**
unfortunate . . . . **poor**
unfortunate . . . . **unlucky**
unfurnished . . . . **empty**
unhappiness . . . . **sadness**
unhappy . . . . **sad**
unharmed . . . . **all right**
unheard-of . . . . **extraordinary**
unhurried . . . . **slow**
unhurriedly . . . . **slowly**
unhurt . . . . **all right**
unidentified . . . . **unknown**
uniform . . . . **same**
unimportant . . . . **small**

uninhabited . . . . **empty**
uninjured . . . . **all right**
unintelligent . . . . **dumb**
unintentional . . . . **accidental**
uninteresting . . . . **dull**
uninterrupted . . . . **continuous**
unique . . . . **extraordinary**
unique . . . . **rare**
unique . . . . **special**
unite . . . . **connect**
unite . . . . **join**
universal . . . . **general**
universal . . . . **international**
unjust . . . . **unfair**
unkempt . . . . **untidy**
unkind . . . . **nasty**
unload . . . . **empty**
unlock . . . . **open**
unlocked . . . . **open**
unmistakable . . . . **plain**
unnamed . . . . **unknown**
unoccupied . . . . **empty**
unplanned . . . . **accidental**
unpleasant . . . . **awful**
unpleasant . . . . **foul**
unpleasant . . . . **nasty**
unpleasant . . . . **unkind**
unpolluted . . . . **pure**
unpredictable . . . . **moody**
unprocessed . . . . **raw**
unprotected . . . . **helpless**
unquestionably . . . . **definitely**
unreal . . . . **imaginary**
unrest . . . . **trouble**
unsafe . . . . **dangerous**
unsafe . . . . **weak**
unsatisfactory . . . . **bad**
unsatisfactory . . . . **poor**
unsecured . . . . **loose**
unseen . . . . **invisible**
unselfish . . . . **generous**
unsettle . . . . **disturb**

unsettle . . . . **put off**
unsettled . . . . **restless**
unsightly . . . . **ugly**
unspoiled . . . . **wild**
unstable . . . . **wobbly**
unsteady . . . . **faint**
unsteady . . . . **wobbly**
unsuited . . . . **unsuitable**
unsung . . . . **unknown**
unsure . . . . **doubtful**
unsure . . . . **uncertain**
unsuspecting . . . . **gullible**
unsympathetic . . . . **unkind**
untamed . . . . **wild**
untidy . . . . **messy**
untidy . . . . **sloppy**
untie . . . . **undo**
untrue . . . . **false**
untrue . . . . **wrong**
unusable . . . . **useless**
unused . . . . **new**
unusual . . . . **extraordinary**
unusual . . . . **rare**
unusual . . . . **strange**
unvarying . . . . **same**
unveil . . . . **uncover**
unwell . . . . **ill**
unwell . . . . **sick**
unwind . . . . **relax**
unwise . . . . **foolish**
unworkable . . . . **impossible**
unwrap . . . . **open**
unwrap . . . . **uncover**
unwrap . . . . **undo**
unzip . . . . **undo**
up in arms . . . . **furious**
up to a point . . . . **partly**
up-to-date . . . . **model**
up-to-date . . . . **new**
up-to-date . . . . **recent**
upgrade . . . . **improve**
uprising . . . . **mutiny**

Index

uproar . . . . **noise**
uproar . . . . **riot**
upset . . . . **hurt**
upset . . . . **sad**
upset . . . . **trouble**
upsetting . . . . **painful**
urge . . . . **advice**
urge . . . . **encourage**
urgent . . . . **immediate**
useful . . . . **convenient**
useful . . . . **good**
useful . . . . **helpful**
useful . . . . **worthwhile**
usefulness . . . . **value**
useless . . . . **hopeless**
useless . . . . **worn out**
user-friendly . . . . **handy**
usher . . . . **take**
usual . . . . **common**
usual . . . . **normal**
usual . . . . **ordinary**
usual . . . . **regular**
usual . . . . **typical**
usually . . . . **mainly**
utensil . . . . **tool**
utilize . . . . **use**
utter . . . . **complete**
utter . . . . **pure**
utter . . . . **speak**
utter . . . . **total**
utterly . . . . **absolutely**
utterly . . . . **completely**

Vv

vacant . . . . **empty**
vague . . . . **dim**
vague . . . . **rough**
vain . . . . **hopeless**
vain . . . . **unsuccessful**
valuable . . . . **precious**
valuable . . . . **useful**

valuable . . . . **worthwhile**
value . . . . **respect**
value . . . . **treasure**
value . . . . **use**
vandal . . . . **hooligan**
vandalism . . . . **damage**
vandalize . . . . **damage**
vanish . . . . **disappear**
variation . . . . **difference**
varied . . . . **different**
variety . . . . **choice**
variety . . . . **kind**
variety . . . . **make**
variety . . . . **mixture**
variety . . . . **range**
variety . . . . **type**
various . . . . **mixed**
vast . . . . **big**
vast . . . . **enormous**
vast . . . . **great**
vast . . . . **huge**
vast . . . . **large**
vast . . . . **massive**
vastness . . . . **size**
vault . . . . **jump**
velocity . . . . **speed**
velvety . . . . **smooth**
velvety . . . . **soft**
vengeance . . . . **revenge**
venomous . . . . **poisonous**
venture . . . . **adventure**
venture . . . . **dare**
verdict . . . . **decision**
verify . . . . **prove**
versus . . . . **against**
vertical . . . . **steep**
very . . . . **actual**
vessel . . . . **boat**
vessel . . . . **container**
vessel . . . . **ship**
veteran . . . . **old**
veto . . . . **forbid**

Index

vibrate . . . . **shake**
vicinity . . . . **neighbourhood**
vicious . . . . **cruel**
vicious . . . . **evil**
vicious . . . . **violent**
vicious . . . . **wicked**
victor . . . . **winner**
victorious . . . . **successful**
victory . . . . **win**
view . . . . **look**
view . . . . **thought**
view . . . . **watch**
viewpoint . . . . **view**
vigorous . . . . **energetic**
vigorous . . . . **lively**
vigorously . . . . **hard**
vigour . . . . **energy**
vile . . . . **disgusting**
vile . . . . **evil**
vile . . . . **nasty**
vile . . . . **wicked**
villain . . . . **criminal**
villain . . . . **rogue**
villainous . . . . **evil**
villainous . . . . **wicked**
vinegary . . . . **sour**
vintage . . . . **old**
violent . . . . **vicious**
violent . . . . **wild**
virtually . . . . **almost**
virtually . . . . **nearly**
virus . . . . **bug**
virus . . . . **infection**
visit . . . . **see**
visit . . . . **trip**
visualise . . . . **imagine**
vital . . . . **essential**
vital . . . . **important**
vital . . . . **necessary**
vitality . . . . **energy**
vitality . . . . **life**
vivid . . . . **bright**

volume . . . . **amount**
volume . . . . **space**
voracious . . . . **greedy**
vote for . . . . **pick**
vow . . . . **promise**
voyage . . . . **journey**
voyage . . . . **travel**
voyage . . . . **trip**
vulgar . . . . **dirty**
vulgar . . . . **foul**
vulnerable . . . . **helpless**

Ww

wages . . . . **pay**
wait . . . . **delay**
wait . . . . **remain**
wait . . . . **stay**
wait on . . . . **serve**
walk off with . . . . **steal**
walk off with . . . . **pinch**
wallop . . . . **beat**
wallop . . . . **hit**
wallop . . . . **thump**
wan . . . . **pale**
war . . . . **fight**
warden . . . . **guard**
warfare . . . . **war**
warm-hearted . . . . **kind**
warning . . . . **sign**
warp . . . . **bend**
warp . . . . **twist**
wary . . . . **careful**
wary . . . . **cautious**
washout . . . . **failure**
waste . . . . **litter**
waste . . . . **rubbish**
watch . . . . **see**
watch out . . . . **beware**
water's edge . . . . **beach**
waterlogged . . . . **wet**
watery . . . . **runny**

Index

437

watery	**thin**	whine	**moan**
wave	**flap**	whine	**say**
wave	**signal**	whinge	**complain**
wavy	**curly**	whinge	**grumble**
way	**course**	whinge	**moan**
way	**method**	whirl	**spin**
way of life	**life**	whirl	**turn**
weak	**helpless**	whisper	**say**
weakened	**tired**	whispering	**soft**
wealthy	**rich**	whole	**complete**
weary	**tired**	whole	**full**
weary	**worn out**	wholehearted	**enthusiastic**
wedge	**jam**	wholesome	**healthy**
wedge	**squeeze**	wholesome	**natural**
wee	**short**	wholesome	**pure**
weep	**cry**	wholesome	**safe**
weigh up	**judge**	wholly	**quite**
weight	**load**	whopper	**lie**
weighty	**heavy**	whopping	**massive**
weighty	**serious**	wicked	**bad**
weird	**funny**	wicked	**evil**
weird	**peculiar**	wickedness	**evil**
weird	**strange**	widespread	**general**
welcoming	**friendly**	wild	**excited**
weld	**fasten**	wild	**rough**
well-behaved	**polite**	wild	**stormy**
well-defined	**sharp**	wild	**violent**
well-known	**famous**	wilds	**country**
well-liked	**popular**	will	**determination**
well-mannered	**polite**	willing	**keen**
well-matched	**even**	willing	**ready**
well-off	**rich**	wilt	**droop**
were beaten	**lose**	wily	**crafty**
whack	**hit**	wind	**curl**
wheeze	**pant**	wind	**twist**
wheezing	**breathless**	windswept	**windy**
whereabouts	**position**	wipe the floor with	**beat**
while	**although**	wisdom	**knowledge**
while	**time**	wisdom	**sense**
while away	**spend**	wise	**sensible**
whimper	**say**	wisecrack	**joke**
whine	**grumble**	wish for	**want**

wit . . . . **sense**
witchcraft . . . . **magic**
with all your might . . . . . **hard**
with ease . . . . **easily**
with the exception of . . . **except**
withdraw . . . . **leave**
withdraw . . . . **move**
withdraw . . . . **pull**
withdraw from . . . . **pull out**
wither . . . . **shrink**
within . . . . **inside**
within easy reach . . . . . **near**
without a stitch on . . . . . **bare**
without difficulty . . . . . **easily**
without doubt . . . . **certainly**
without hesitation . . . . **once**
without warning . . . . . . **suddenly**
witness . . . . **see**
witty . . . . **funny**
wizard . . . . **expert**
wizardry . . . . **magic**
wobbly . . . . **loose**
wolf . . . . **gobble**
woman . . . . **adult**
wonder . . . . **surprise**
wonderful . . . . **fabulous**
wonderful . . . . **great**
wonderful . . . . **tremendous**
wonderfully . . . . **well**
wording . . . . **language**
work . . . . **behave**
work . . . . **go**
work . . . . **run**
work out . . . . **do**
work out . . . . **solve**
work out . . . . **train**
worked up . . . . **excited**
working . . . . **busy**
workman . . . . **worker**
world . . . . **earth**
worldwide . . . . **international**

worm . . . . **wriggle**
worn out . . . . **tired**
worn-out . . . . **ragged**
worried . . . . **nervous**
worry . . . . **bother**
worry . . . . **care**
worry . . . . **disturb**
worry . . . . **stress**
worry . . . . **trouble**
worry . . . . **upset**
worth it . . . . **worthwhile**
worthwhile . . . . **useful**
worthy . . . . **fit**
wound . . . . **hurt**
wound . . . . **injure**
wounded . . . . **hurt**
wrap up . . . . **complete**
wrath . . . . **anger**
wreck . . . . **destroy**
wreck . . . . **ruin**
wreck . . . . **spoil**
wreckage . . . . **ruin**
wrench . . . . **pull**
wrench . . . . **twist**
wrestle . . . . **fight**
wretched . . . . **miserable**
wretched . . . . **poor**
wretched . . . . **unlucky**
wriggle . . . . **fidget**
wringing wet . . . . **wet**
write off . . . . **wreck**
writhe . . . . **wriggle**
writing pad . . . . **pad**
wrong . . . . **false**
wrong . . . . **unsuitable**
wrong . . . . **untrue**
wrongdoing . . . . **evil**

Yy

yakka . . . . **work**
yank . . . . **pull**

yarn

yarn. . . . . story
yawning. . . . . deep
yawning. . . . . open
yearn for . . . . wish
yell . . . . cry
yell . . . . say
yell . . . . shout
yesteryear . . . . past
yet. . . . . but
yob . . . . hooligan
young . . . . little
youngster . . . . child

Zz

zany . . . . odd
zeal . . . . enthusiasm
zero. . . . . nothing
zigzag . . . . wind
zip. . . . . fasten
zone . . . . area
zone . . . . part
zoom. . . . . move
zoom. . . . . speed
zoom. . . . . tear

Index